MW01639572

A Wealth of Thought

Franz Boas on Native American Art

A Wealth of Thought

Franz Boas on Native American Art

Edited by Aldona Jonaitis

University of Washington Press
Seattle and London

Douglas & McIntyre
Vancouver/Toronto

95 96 97 98 5 4 3 2 1
Printed in the United States of America
Design by Corinna Campbell
Composition by Wilsted & Taylor

University of Washington Press
PO Box 50096, Seattle, WA 98145

Library of Congress Cataloging-in-Publication Data
A wealth of thought : Franz Boas on Native American art / edited by Aldona Jonaitis.
p. cm.
Includes bibliographical references (p.) and index.
ISBN 0-295-97325-0 (cloth). — ISBN 0-295-97384-6 (pbk.)
1. Indian art—Northwest Coast of North America. 2. Indian art. 3. Art, Primitive.
I. Boas, Franz, 1858–1942. II. Jonaitis, Aldona, 1948– .
E78.N78W43 1994
704′.03979—dc20 94-15180
CIP

Published simultaneously in Canada by Douglas & McIntyre, 1615 Venables Street, Vancouver, British Columbia V5L 2H1

Canadian Cataloguing in Publication Data
Boas, Franz, 1858–1942
A wealth of thought
Includes bibliographical references.
ISBN 1-55054-180-3
1. Indian art—Northwest coast of North America. 2. Art, Primitive—Northwest coast of North America. I. Jonaitis, Aldona, 1948– . II. Title.
E78.N78B62 1994 709′.01′109795 C94-910583-X

The paper used in this publication meets the minimum requirements of American National Standard for Information Sciences—Permanence of Paper for Printed Library Materials, ANSI Z39.48-1984.

"My fancy was first struck by the flight of imagination exhibited in the works of art of the British Columbians. . . . I divined what a wealth of thought lay hidden behind the grotesque masks and the elaborately decorated utensils of these tribes."

—*Franz Boas,* The Kwakiutl of Vancouver Island

Contents

Preface

Welcome!

Greetings! O people of all tribes.

Our thanks that we have come together in this great house.

Our thanks that we have come to view the regalia of our predecessors, the works of our past chiefs.

And, so we have come here to gather, O people of all tribes.

So that we can come to look.

You are proud, O chief—you are proud of the treasures of your ancestors, of those things that we have come to see in this great house.

I have said it!

I have said it, O chiefs.

Why should we not be proud of these things for they have been saved so that we can see them.

That is it!

That is it! O people of all tribes.

—Speech in Kwakwala by Adam Dick, translated by Bobby Joseph, a recording of which welcomed visitors to the American Museum of Natural History's exhibition "Chiefly Feasts: The Enduring Kwakiutl Potlatch."

In October 1991 a new exhibit opened at the American Museum of Natural History. "Chiefly Feasts: The Enduring Kwakiutl Potlatch" featured the artworks that George Hunt had collected for Franz Boas at the turn of the century. At the opening, two great-grandsons of George Hunt, Bill Cranmer and Tony Hunt, stood before a crowd of hundreds of staff and visitors and proudly voiced the sentiments expressed earlier by Adam Dick in his welcoming speech.

This opening ceremony was by any definition an historic moment. More than forty Kwakwaka'wakw from Vancouver Island had traveled to New York City to validate an exhibition celebrating their ongoing artistic and ceremonial traditions.[1] A leitmotif of the event was the tremendous service Boas had performed for the Kwakwaka'wakw people by recording and publishing their histories and preserving for all the artistic treasures on display at the American Museum. Descendants of Boas

1. The people whom Boas called the Kwakiutl today prefer the term Kwakwaka'wakw, which means "speakers of Kwakwala." In this essay I use the preferred term.

spoke warmly of their continued relationships with the Kwakwaka'wakw whose culture had dazzled their distinguished ancestor and continues to dazzle later generations.

I sat listening to the speeches, wondering what Boas would have thought had he been present. As his letters reveal clearly, he had a great love for these people whose culture he feared was about to disappear. He was especially fond of George Hunt, a gentle, quiet man whose brilliance has never been adequately acknowledged.[2] Here, in the museum where Boas had worked for ten years trying to record for posterity the complex nature of Kwakwaka'wakw culture, were descendants of his Native friends, as well as two people he had known personally, Agnes Hunt Cranmer and William Hunt, who praised his efforts and honored his legacy. A man of immense social conscience and personal integrity, Boas had produced a vast body of scholarship informed by a commitment to prove the equality of all human beings and to encourage respect for and understanding of different traditions. Had his ghost been present in the museum's Hall of Ocean Life where the opening ceremony was taking place, he would, I think, have been pleased. The people of New York City finally had the opportunity to observe the truth of his premise that all cultures and their material manifestations are worthy of admiration and esteem.

My first encounter with Boas came when I was in graduate school in the 1970s and read his lengthy—seemingly endless—descriptions of Kwakwaka'wakw art and culture. For someone intent on obtaining the truth about a topic, Boas was, frankly, frustrating. He provided abundant information, but never seemed to tie it up with a conceptualizing ribbon into a neat package that would enable me to understand the baroque art of the Kwakwaka'wakw. Moreover, his book *Primitive Art* (1927) seemed to me obscure, tedious, and of limited usefulness for my academic investigations.

Later, while researching a book on the American Museum of Natural History's Northwest Coast Indian art collection (Jonaitis 1988a), I read his correspondences with George Hunt, John Swanton, and others and discovered behind all the scholarship a passionate, sympathetic, very real man. These letters and the wealth of materials on the Kwakwaka'wakw that Boas and Hunt left in the American Museum's archives then became the source for documenting the artworks exhibited in "Chiefly Feasts."[3] My earlier frustration over Boas's unwillingness to theorize and draw conclusions had turned to admiration for his devotion to meticulous docu-

2. The Kwakwaka'wakw elders who remember George Hunt describe him as distinguished and quiet; his brilliance is evident in his meticulous scholarship and thoughtful correspondences.

3. My two research assistants, Stacy A. Marcus and Judith Ostrowitz, did most of the archival work on these artifacts. They were assisted at different times by Peter Macnair, Gloria Cranmer Webster, and Wayne Suttles.

mentation of the Kwakwaka'wakw, for his untiring activities aimed at collecting Kwakwaka'wakw art and artifacts, and for the social commitment that informed all of his anthropological endeavors.

This is a timely moment to evaluate Boas's contributions to "primitive art," for many of the points he makes correspond to concepts put forth by the so-called "new art historians" who reject the hegemony of western art styles, the isolation of art history from economic and social history, and the hierarchical and elitist divisions between high and popular art.[4] As will become clear in this book, Boas's writings on art reveal that such concepts are not new: for one who believed in the equality of all human cultures, art could not be considered inferior or superior. Moreover, his conviction that a group's art style arose in part as a result of its cultural conditions and history contradicts the notion of an art existing in isolation from social and economic factors. And, by treating all art, by women and by men, as of equal significance, he effectively thwarts any concept of "high" art.[5]

Decolonization and the efforts of Native people around the globe to control their historical representation and cultural property have inspired a rethinking of the anthropologist's role.[6] Contemporary critical theorists tend to reject classics and canons, which they view as embodiments of entrenched, male, Euro-American power and thus impediments to the liberation of previously stifled voices. To make room for these new voices, it is often necessary to dethrone old authorities. It would be easy to consider Boas, often called the "father of American anthropology," as a prime candidate for such dismissal. Indeed, some of what he wrote deserves critical analysis; however, a careful reading of his work on Native American art suggests that we take a more nuanced view. I propose that in the writings included in this volume, premised as they are on a resistance to premature theoretical closure and an egalitarian ideology, Boas created the space that Native people could ultimately occupy to assert their own voice.

It is appropriate to reassess Boas's writings from the perspective we have gained as a result of the current crisis in representation and the reconsideration of the nature of art history and anthropology. Indeed, my own reading of his work has changed over the past several years from the moment I embarked on collecting his articles on art history for republication.[7]

4. Ruth Phillips (1989) has recently elegantly demonstrated the new art history's applicability to her study of Huron art. For more on new trends in art history, see Baxandall 1974, Belting 1987, Preziosi 1989, Hiller 1991, Berger 1992, and Phillips 1992.

5. For several interesting essays on new perspectives on "primitive art," see Hiller 1991.

6. See the following for useful discussions of recent trends in anthropology: Ames 1992, Atkinson 1990, Clifford 1987 and 1988, Clifford and Marcus 1986, Geertz 1988, Kuper 1988, Marcus and Fisher 1986, Manganaro 1990, Maranhao 1990, Sanjek 1990, and Rosaldo 1989.

7. Through this review, I hope to contribute to the ongoing reassessment of the positive contributions anthropology and anthropological art history can make. Some scholars writing in *Recapturing An-*

This book has had a long history. In 1985 Janet Catherine Berlo invited me to participate in a College Art Association panel in Los Angeles on "Reevaluating Our Predecessors: Ethnographic Art Historians Look Back," intended to assess, with an historical perspective, the contributions of some of the early interpreters of Native art. Later on that year, I was on another panel chaired by Berlo, "Native American Art History: Reassessing the Early Years," held at the Native American Art Studies Association meeting in Ann Arbor, Michigan. I spoke at both meetings on the political dimensions of Franz Boas's art history.[8] I found his art history so interesting that I decided to edit a book of his essays.

Preparing the exhibit for "Chiefly Feasts" consumed much of the next several years and I had to put the Boas project aside. Finally, in 1992, the quincentennial of Columbus's "discovery" of America and a year profoundly meaningful for Native Americans as the country reevaluated its history in light of their seminal role, I returned to it. The heightened consciousness of the historical relationships between Natives and non-Natives so prevalent that year motivated me to think more critically about how Boas represented Indian art. Insights derived from recent scholarship contributed additional dimensions.[9] When I reread these articles in preparation

---

thropology: Working in the Present (Fox 1991) suggest means by which anthropology can usefully contribute to knowledge, while discarding elements no longer acceptable. Joan Vincent (1991:47) suggests that an historical analysis of early anthropologists like Boas, which connects their work to their social and political period, "advances an assessment of the critically distinctive, but many-layered relationship between anthropology and colonialism." She urges in particular revitalizing the "classics" of ethnography by careful scrutiny of the texts in this kind of historical and contextualizing fashion. Michel-Rolph Trouillot (1991:39) suggests that anthropologists reassess the value of past ethnographic research and writing, "with a fair tally of the knowledge anthropologists have produced in the past, sometimes in spite of themselves." In this book, I attempt to respond to these challenges. In the first essay, I review the development of Boas's art history ideas and position them in their historical moment; in the concluding article, I demonstrate the profound impact Boas has had on twentieth-century studies of Northwest Coast art.

8. Berlo then edited a collection of papers from these two sessions, which became the book *The Early Years of Native American Art History: The Politics of Scholarship and Collecting*, published by the University of Washington Press in 1992.

9. For some of the recent works on postmodernist theory, see Alexander and Seidman 1990, Jencks 1991 and 1992, Kroker 1992, MacCannell 1992, West 1989, Harvey 1989, and especially Jameson 1991. For some discussions of postmodernism and Native cultures, see Todd 1992 and Townsend-Gault 1992.

In an essay in the amusingly titled book *Zeitgeist in Babel*, Charles Jencks (1991:19–20) tabulates a series of concepts that embody the differences between modernism and postmodernism. Thus, in contrast to the holistic nature of modernist writings, postmodernist ones are piecemeal; the straightforward is contrasted to the hybrid, simplicity to complexity, purist to eclectic, and harmonious integration to collage and collision. In a radio interview with Gayatry Chakravorty Spivak, moderator Geoffrey Hawthorn reflects upon the situation: ". . . these are confusing times, in which older universal traditions and certainties seemed, even though recently to be quite solid and reliable, no longer to offer the same security. . . . We can never connect, we can certainly never know that we connect with the things that there are in the world. . . . All we can know is what we say about the world—our talk, our sentences, our discourse, our texts" (Spivak 1990:17). Ames (1992:14) suggests a more moderate position: "The two

for their publication, it became clear that many resonated with contemporary critical thought and the continued vitality of Kwakwaka'wakw artistic and cultural traditions.

I have framed this collection of articles, written between 1889 and 1916, with an introduction discussing the development of Boas's art history ideas and a postscript. The introduction connects the essays reprinted here to portions of his classic *Primitive Art* and positions them in their historical moment. Because every later scholar of Northwest Coast art is, in one way or another, indebted to Boas, in my concluding essay I demonstrate the profound impact he has had on twentieth-century studies of Northwest Coast art. The relevance of his writings still today and the respect with which he is viewed by modern-day Kwakwaka'wakw demonstrate that his work complements the new voices of liberty. I think he would have recognized and delighted in those voices, loud and clear, at the opening of "Chiefly Feasts."

In editing this volume, one of the most difficult problems the publisher and I encountered was how to handle the orthography of Boas's early writings. The articles reprinted here contain numerous words from native languages, particularly Kwakwala, the language of the Kwakwaka'wakw. Because over time Boas changed his orthography, we initially thought it would be useful to transcribe Native terms into a common orthography such as that developed by the U'Mista Cultural Centre in Alert Bay, British Columbia. The difficulty of accomplishing this and its potential for confusion convinced us to take a different approach. In order to be faithful to the original texts, we have published Native words just as they appeared in Boas's text.

The figures have been renumbered for this volume, and in one case—"Primitive Art," chapter 8—the illustrations have been dropped to avoid duplication with other articles. Corrections or other alterations to achieve consistency in style are minor in nature and were kept to a minimum. I have omitted some of the italic type used for proper names in the original articles and have provided an occasional emendation to the text in brackets.

A very important book on Boas came out after my essays were in production and I would like to bring it to the reader's attention. *Franz Boas, Ethnologe-Anthropologe-Sprachwissenschaftler: Ein Wegereiter der modernen Wissenschaft vom Menschen* [Franz Boas, ethnographer-anthropologist-linguist: a pioneer of the modern science of man] (1992) catalogues an exhibition on Boas at the Berlin State Library from December 17, 1992, to March 6, 1993. It contains essays by Michael Durr, Erich Kas-

extremes are to be avoided: the imperialist assumption that the scholar . . . has a natural or automatic right to intrude upon the histories and cultures of others 'in the interests of science and knowledge'; and the nihilistic postmodernist claim that all knowledge is relative, all voices are equal."

ten, and Egon Renner on Boas's anthropology, ethnographic methodology, and role in the development of American anthropology. Of particular interest to the present study is Erich Kasten's "Masken, Mythen, und Indianer: Franz Boas's Ethnographie und Museumsmethode" [Masks, myths, and Indians: Franz Boas's ethnography and museology] (pp. 79–102). The exhibition included letters, photographs, publications by Boas and his students, and artifacts Boas acquired from the Inuit and Kwakwaka'wakw, as well as contemporary Northwest Coast art.

ACKNOWLEDGMENTS

I would like to thank several colleagues who willingly read this manuscript and made excellent and valuable suggestions for improving it. First, I express my deep appreciation for the time and energy my two art historical colleagues and close friends Janet Catherine Berlo and Ruth B. Phillips devoted to these pages. Bill Holm and Wayne Suttles also read the manuscript and made extremely useful comments. In addition, I wish to thank other colleagues who read all or parts of the work: Michael Ames, Douglas Cole, Stanley Freed, Ira Jacknis, Arnold Krupat, Herman Lebovics, and Esther Pasztory.

Jay Powell offered useful advice on the orthography, and Wayne Suttles gave me a great deal of help in trying to adhere as closely as possible to Boas's original spelling, while correcting obvious typographic errors.

Several individuals assisted in reproducing the illustrations for the book, and I thank them for their good work: Craig Cheset, Betty Derasmo, Dennis Finnan, and Joel Pollick. I would also like to express my appreciation to Geralyn Abinader for her help in coordinating this project. And, as always, let me thank my good friends and esteemed colleagues at the University of Washington Press.

A Wealth of Thought

Franz Boas on Native American Art

Introduction: The Development of Franz Boas's Theories on Primitive Art

ALDONA JONAITIS

In 1885 the young Franz Boas assisted Adolph Bastian in preparing an exceptional array of British Columbian art, recently collected by Adrian Jacobsen, for the new North American exhibit at the Royal Ethnographic Museum in Berlin (Cole 1985:58–67). Soon after, when a troupe of Bella Coolas visited Berlin in January 1886, Boas had the opportunity to meet several Northwest Coast Indians and see them dancing in masquerade, wearing Chilkat blankets, and creating rhythmic music with carved rattles (Cole 1982).[1] In an article published in the *Berliner Tageblatt*, Boas wrote about the elegant art of the Bella Coolas: "Here we behold with amazement a wonderful technique in the use of carver's knife and paintbrush and a finely developed artistic sense. . . . Wonderously beautiful are some of the carved house posts which are erected by this tribe and which represent the family tree; no less notable are the beautifully carved stone implements, axes, hammers, bowls and the like. The repeated motif of all decorations on these objects, as also on the clothing, is a stylized eye" (translated in Cole 1982:119, 122).

Later that year, Boas made the long trip to the North Pacific region to gain first-hand experience among these Indians whose art fascinated him so, and began a life-long attachment to the natives of British Columbia.[2] Boas treated art as an element of culture in his monographs on the Kwakiutl, "The Social Organization and the Secret Societies of the Kwakiutl Indians" (1897b) and "The Kwakiutl of Vancouver Island" (1909). The 1897 monograph is particularly important in this context, as it offers extensive detailed information on the ceremonial context of much Kwakiutl art.

In addition to including art in these rather comprehensive studies, Boas wrote several essays that addressed issues of style and symbolism. His earliest art historical articles dealt solely with art of the Northwest Coast Indians, while his later ones included art of other Native American peoples. His culminating art historical statement, *Primitive Art* (1927), added examples from Asia, the Pacific, Africa, and Siberia. Boas's art historical literature has profound historical value since it embodies a major change in primitive art theory from the evolutionism that dominated the

1. Also see Haberland 1988 for an interesting discussion of the Bella Coola in Germany in 1885–86.

2. On the anthropology and career of Franz Boas, see especially Cole 1985, Rohner 1969, Stocking 1968 and 1974, Jacknis 1984 and 1985, Lesser 1981, and Krupat 1990.

nineteenth century to a twentieth-century form of relativism, usually referred to as historical particularism.[3] As such, Boas's art history is of a piece with his social anthropology; as George Marcus and Michael Fischer state in *Anthropology as Cultural Critique*: "Boas used ethnography to debate residual issues derived from the framework of nineteenth-century evolutionary thought and to challenge racist views of human behavior, then ascendant" (1986:130). Boas's art history was part of his broader scientific agenda that included not simply discrediting evolutionism but offering alternate explanations if possible. In terms of art, Boas was ultimately to stress the roles that culture, history, and the artist's psychology and creative processes play in the development of an art style.

NINETEENTH-CENTURY EVOLUTIONIST ANTHROPOLOGY

To understand fully the significance of Boas's art historical analyses, it is necessary to summarize the prevailing evolutionist anthropological theories he challenged.[4] By the end of the nineteenth century, social evolutionism had thoroughly permeated the study of anthropology, and the notion of "survival of the fittest" appeared in diverse texts, serving to explain many cultural phenomena, including art.[5] Briefly, the several versions of the theory agreed that humankind had evolved from lower primates in a series of phases which progressed from simple to more complex forms, culminating in the Caucasian race, the highest and to that point the most perfect product—the "fittest"—of the sequence. A corollary proposition held that as culture followed biology, the most primitive societies were the simplest, while the more highly evolved western cultures were the most sophisticated and complex.[6]

In their cultural studies, evolutionist anthropologists applied what is called the "comparative method," which equated prehistoric groups with living primitive societies. In its most simplified version, this history of human development suggested an analogy between the growth of an individual human and the development of society, with primitive society being equivalent to a child, and civilized culture being like an adult. As they progressed toward civilized perfection, following a course strictly governed by universal rules, all ethnic groups passed through the same stages. As a result, even groups geographically distant from one another shared similar manifestations in areas as diverse as social structure, technology, and art style.

3. I use the term "primitive art" here to cover the material Boas dealt with in his book.

4. For an intriguing study of the British evolutionists, see Stocking 1987.

5. Ernst Grosse even argued that art played a role in social survival: ". . . art is no idle play, but an indispensable social function, one of the most efficient weapons in the struggle for existence" (1897:312).

6. The biological model informed the work of some of the most important early cultural evolutionists such as Herbert Spencer, Lewis Henry Morgan, and Edward B. Tylor. (See Haller 1971, Stocking 1987, and Kuper 1991 for more on this.)

At the heart of this theory was the concept of independent invention, which hypothesized that all peoples at the same level of cultural development tend to invent the same artifacts and ways of living (Stocking 1968:112 ff.).

It is important to point out that not all nineteenth-century anthropology was based on totally erroneous theories, and that some evolutionist concepts remain in the corpus of anthropological thinking. For example, the practice of interpreting archaeological evidence by making analogies with ethnographic groups is still being done, under the ethnoarchaeological approach. Moreover, social evolutionism as an interpretive tool is still being used, particularly by Marxist anthropologists. The two fundamental differences between what was promoted by the nineteenth-century anthropologists and what is now understood by contemporary cultural evolutionists are that (1) no one seriously argues that all groups pass through the same series of stages, and (2) no one claims that any group is culturally superior to any other on the basis of its evolutionary position.

During the period we are discussing, however, anthropological evolutionism carried with it a predisposition to racialist explanation. Indeed, as Marvin Harris (1968:130) states, "no major figure in the social sciences between 1860 and 1890 escaped the influence of evolutionary racism." Either implicitly or explicitly, this theory suggested that one group, the whites, had evolved the farthest and thus was mentally, biologically, and morally superior to all others. Some anthropologists of this era believed that because of the nature of the evolutionary process, the "primitive," darker-skinned people would never reach the apex of creation occupied by whites. Even if they did improve their social, economic, political, and artistic condition, these people would never be able to "catch up" to the whites, who would continue to forge ahead with their more sophisticated technologies and ever greater intellectual and scientific achievements.[7]

One significant manifestation of their purported inferiority was the mental ability of darker-skinned peoples. Herbert Spencer (1896), who claimed that primitive man's mental processes were reflexive responses to natural stimuli, concluded that only in whites had highly developed thought processes capable of abstraction evolved. E. B. Tylor (1871), a major Victorian evolutionist who did make useful

7. Lewis Henry Morgan (1877), for example, believed that despite each advance primitive peoples might make, the more advanced groups would forever be outdistancing them. W J McGee (1903 speech, quoted in Haller 1971:107) described how the lower races could not "keep up" with the more advanced, and thus were "the mental and moral beggars of the community who may not be trusted on horseback but only in the rear seat of the wagon." And Edward B. Tylor (1881:74) stated, "History points [up] the great lesson that some races have marched on in civilization while others have stood still or fallen back, and we should partly look for an explanation of this in differences of intellectual and moral powers between such tribes as the native Americans and Africans, and the Old World nations who overmatch and subdue them."

contributions to anthropological theories, especially in the field of religion, insisted that unlike the modern European adult who had a large and sophisticated brain, the primitive was like a child with a less developed brain and lesser mental capacities.

Contemporary physical anthropology supported the correlative notion that development of cranial capacity corresponded with the progressive stages of human development. W J McGee, of the Bureau of American Ethnology and first president of the American Anthropological Association, firmly believed that brain sizes corresponded closely with culture grade, and that as a group evolved, the average brain size of its members became larger since more advanced stages of development demanded more complex neural activities (McGee 1897, 1899). Consistent with these notions is McGee's assertion that "the savage stands strikingly close to sub-human species in every aspect of mental as well as bodily habits and bodily structure" (McGee 1901:13).[8]

Sometimes the evolutionists used the supposed inferiority of nonwhites as scientific justification for a form of segregation. Daniel Brinton, eminent University of Pennsylvania professor of anthropology and president of the American Association for the Advancement of Science, was particularly concerned about the disastrous consequences of racial mixtures. In his book *Races and Peoples* (1890), Brinton took a hard line against marriages between members of different races, arguing that racial mixtures led to sterility, short lives, and feeble constitutions (pp. 284–87). He then insisted that racial purity must be maintained and interracial marriages discouraged.

Franz Boas, a German Jew from a politically liberal family, found the tenets of social evolutionism abhorrent.[9] He rejected the concept that race and culture could be integrated into a single evolutionary sequence that followed strict rules, just as he rejected the racism that the evolutionist theories justified and validated. His antievolutionism and antiracism began early in his career when, on his first field trip in 1883 among the Canadian Inuit, he recognized how racial prejudice blinded whites from correctly assessing the intrinsic values of other races. In a letter sent from the field, he wrote: "I often ask myself what advantages our 'good society' possesses over that of the 'savages,' and find the more I see of their customs that we have no right to look down on them" (translated in Cole 1983:33).

Then, in 1894, on the basis of further experiences with the Kwakiutl, Boas became more outspoken in his beliefs about the sophistication of primitive mentality, and attacked Spencer's generalizations on primitive mentality. In an address to the American Association for the Advancement of Science, Boas argued against traditional racial assumptions which linked racial differences to hierarchies of race and

8. The inferiority of the nonwhite races supported by social evolutionism provided a useful justification for imperialism. See Manganaro 1990:28; Stocking 1991:4.

9. For more on Franz Boas and politics, see Stocking 1979.

culture. He insisted that historical factors contributed to the development of all cultures, that standards for evaluating achievements of different peoples are relative, and that mental differences that appear to be racial in origin can be explained on the basis of different traditions (Boas 1894; see also Stocking 1968:215 ff.).[10]

NINETEENTH-CENTURY EVOLUTIONIST ART HISTORY

If cultures evolved from lower ones to higher ones, so, the argument went, did art styles. At the end of the nineteenth century, many of those who wrote on primitive art assumed that all art styles underwent some sort of evolutionary process not unlike the biological and cultural processes undergone by their creators.[11] Artworks of primitive peoples represented examples of early phases of that process, in contrast to the advanced type of art made by civilized peoples. The implication, of course, was that the art of civilized peoples was superior in all ways to that of the "savages."[12] Although these evolutionists could reach no consensus on what kind of art was associated with which period, many agreed that art evolved in a unilinear progression. For some this progression was purely formal, while others associated the evolution of formal elements with a group's progress through cultural stages.[13]

One of the earliest and most outspoken proponents of the "improvement" of art through evolutionary processes was the sociologist Herbert Spencer (1857), who wrote that the evolution of art fit into a cosmic process of evolution of mind, society, and civilization. Like plants, animals, and socioeconomic structures, art evolved from simplicity to complexity, and from homogeneity to heterogeneity. In Spencer's vastly oversimplified scheme, the earliest art was an integration of architecture, painting, and sculpture in service of a theocratic government. During the course of evolution, these art forms became distinct, just as their subject matters gradually differentiated the sacred and the secular.

Most European art historians accepted the general notion of evolution in art, but, failing to agree on how that evolution proceeded, adhered to one of two evolutionist schools, technical/materialism or realist/degenerationism. For the most part, these analysts focused on two-dimensional art rather than sculpture, presum-

10. See Suttles and Jonaitis (1990:74–77) for a summary of Boas's contributions to Northwest Coast anthropology.

11. See Goldwater (1986:15–50) for an excellent summary of early attitudes to primitive art.

12. The relative value of "primitive art" as compared to the art of more developed cultures is still, surprisingly, not universally accepted. When I was in graduate school in the 1970s, Douglas Fraser would describe his colleagues' disdain for this type of art. Even today, members of an art history department at a major university have questioned the "maturity" of Native American art history.

13. Just as evolution continues to serve a useful purpose in anthropological theory (see pp. 4–5), it also remains a viable concept for some art historical analyses. See especially Munro 1963 for a sophisticated treatment of evolution in art.

ably because they believed it was in decoration that the origins of art could be found (Goldwater 1986:21). Gottfried Semper's highly influential *Der Stil in den technischen und tektonischen Künsten* (1861–63) claimed that art originated as imitation of techniques of architecture. Thus, the oldest forms are abstract and geometric; artists gradually assigned meaning to those designs that developed over time into identifiable images. In contrast, Alfred Haddon (1895) was of the opinion that the earliest artworks were realistic; these gradually "degenerated" into geometric designs. Henry Balfour (1893), Hjalmar Stolpe (1892), Karl von den Steinen (1894), and others believed that the earliest type of art was naturalistic, followed by increasing stylization of form.[14] An interesting version of this realist/degenerationist school was found in the writings of Ernst Grosse (1897), a German ethnologist and sociologist who argued that groups at the same socioeconomic level of development produced similar art styles. According to Grosse, the simplest hunters and gatherers, whose livelihoods depended on great skill in observation and manual dexterity, produced relatively realistic art, whereas the later agriculturalists and herdsmen, who did not need such acute senses and skills, lost the ability to create realistic art.

In the United States, Frederic Ward Putnam (1886) was one of the few members of the realist/degenerationist school. In contrast, William H. Holmes of the Bureau of American Ethnology supported the technical/materialist theory of art history, arguing that technique and materials were sources of decorative forms, and that the earliest art was a geometric imitation of techniques like basketry (Holmes 1888, 1890, 1903). Holmes theorized further that such geometric art gave way to nonideographic art, which in turn gave way to delineative art, in an evolutionist sequence governed by strict laws. Every art style in existence either had gone through this sequence to its end or (like the art of primitive peoples) had stopped at some earlier stage. A partial explanation for this retarded artistic development could have been that the primitive artist, living a limited and difficult existence at the mercy of an uncontrollable environment, was rarely capable of creativity, aesthetic pleasure, or imaginative exercises (see Thoresen 1977:109–11; Hinsley 1981:103–5). John Wesley Powell, also of the Bureau of American Ethnology, described a rigid developmental sequence of art history connecting stages of style development to Lewis Henry Morgan's phases of social development: in the savage stage the artist uses outlining, in the barbaric stage he invents relief, in the kingly stage he develops perspective, and in civilized culture he advances to the chiaroscuro technique (Powell 1899:732).

14. However, Boas (1908b:321) notes that in 1905, von den Steinen had begun to emphasize technical considerations in art. Moreover, Stolpe and von den Steinen had differing opinions about the nature of these progressions from naturalism to stylization. See Goldwater (1986:22–30) for a discussion of the theoretical nuances of these and other early students of primitive art.

The strength of the bias for unilineal evolutionism sometimes prevented scholars from understanding certain data that contradicted these explanations. An interesting example of this is the article published in the *1880–1881 Annual Report of the Bureau of American Ethnology* by Henry Henshaw (1883), "Animal Carvings from Mounds of the Mississippi Valley." In this analysis of archaeological animal carvings, Henshaw noted that some contemporaneous pieces were conventionalized and others were naturalistic—something that, in theory, should not happen if these stylistic modes followed an evolutionary development. Nonetheless, Henshaw held that "at least as far as the North American Indians are concerned, . . . the road to conventionalism has always led through imitation" (1883:165–66). Despite evidence that two distinct and supposedly chronologically separate styles coexisted, on the strength of the evolutionist paradigm, Henshaw continued to support the notion that one preceded the other. It was Boas who used the numerous examples of similar styles coexisting to disprove the evolutionary theories of the development of primitive art.

During the first several decades of the twentieth century, other approaches to primitive art were subject to Boas's scrutiny. One of these concerned what Boas believed to be a far too one-sided evaluation of the expressive nature of art. As early as 1894, Ernst Grosse wrote that the fundamental purpose of art was to express ideas. Others who privileged the expressive or communicative nature of art included Yrjö Hirn (1900), Max Verworn (1920), and Richard Thurnwald (1926). For Wilhelm Wundt (1919), art stood in the center of a continuum between myth and language. For Boas, a scholar unwilling to accept any simple explanations of phenomena, particularly those that could not be proved, to ascribe to the origin of art its communicative aspects ignored the equally significant formal or nonexpressive qualities. Equally unacceptable to Boas was the theory put forth by Ernst Vatter (1926), who promoted the idea of an anonymous primitive artist completely lacking in individualism and creativity. To deny primitive artists their personal identity was equivalent to denying them humanity; while these artists functioned within cultural systems that influenced the kind of art they produced, they were by no means slavish copyists of predetermined forms.

FRANZ BOAS ON PRIMITIVE ART

Born and educated in Germany, Franz Boas was familiar with both European and American art historical and anthropological literature. In order to contradict the evolutionist ideas held by many of his contemporaries as absolute truths, Boas emphasized the variety of history; the profound influence of diffusion; the formal, symbolic, and stylistic variations found in various groups, and sometimes within the same group; and ultimately the role of imagination and creativity on the part of the artist.[15] Where the evolutionists claimed a rigid sequence of art forms, Boas described specific cases in which those sequences did not apply. Where any writer imposed a simplifying or universalizing theory, Boas demonstrated how the complexity of the artistic process, exemplified by data he and his colleagues had obtained, disproved that theory. In reading through Boas's works on art, it becomes clear that he intentionally and systematically disputed these evolutionist concepts, and each discussion of form, style, and meaning was meant to disprove a previously accepted idea about art. As he did this, he continually suggested different ways to interpret art and understand the artistic process. His motivation to dispute evolutionism resulted in numerous new approaches to art history.

The articles included in this volume, written over several decades starting in the late 1880s, reveal Boas's intellectual development as an art historian. Initially tentative in his opposition to art historical evolutionism, Boas became increasingly assertive as he matured intellectually. The subjects of his first analyses of art were the paintings and carvings of the Northwest Coast Indians. His earliest writings, done between 1888 and 1895, are largely descriptive, as this was the period during which he was familiarizing himself with Northwest Coast art. As his knowledge of this exceptional regional style deepened, it became clear to him that Northwest Coast art presented interesting artistic problems that could not be solved by then prevalent theories, so between 1896 and 1900, Boas systematically analyzed Northwest Coast art to demonstrate the inadequacies of evolutionist interpretations. His writings on art become very confident after 1900, as, with new information provided by colleagues and students, he went beyond the Northwest Coast to include other Native American artworks in his analyses and in his direct attacks on the evolutionists. It was at this point that he began to investigate the influence of psychology on art. Boas ultimately consolidated these endeavors in his book-length study *Primitive Art*, published in 1927.[16]

The Earliest Writings, 1888–95 Most of Boas's earliest writings on art were descriptions of the artistic elements of Northwest Coast Indian culture, many based on his fieldwork during which he showed consultants photographs and drawings of artworks in museum collections and asked them to interpret their iconography and explain their use (Boas 1890a:7, 12).[17] For example, one of the products of his 1886 trip to

15. Thoresen (1977) correctly points out the significance of the writings of other turn-of-the-century anthropologists, especially Kroeber (1900a, 1901) and Wissler (1904), as manifestations of this shift away from evolutionism. Although both Kroeber and Wissler studied with and were enormously influenced by Boas, each apparently provided him with interesting material and ideas in return. See also Jacknis 1992 for a useful and subtle discussion of this.

16. See Jacknis 1992 for a similar discussion of the development of Boas's art theory.

17. See Jacknis 1984 for more on Boas's use of photographs in the field.

northern Vancouver Island was "The Houses of the Kwakiutl Indians, British Columbia" (1888b), in which he described the structure, design, and interior decoration of Kwakiutl architecture and explained the connections between carvings found in these houses and family legends.[18] In the 1890 and 1891 reports to meetings of the British Association for the Advancement of Science, Boas described Salish house posts, Nootka carving and painting, and Kwakiutl and Bella Coola masquerades (1890b, 1891a). In these descriptive writings, he approached artworks as components of a larger cultural picture.[19]

During this period, Boas was beginning to speculate on the history of artistic forms, hypothesizing on the origins of a type of art among one of the Northwest Coast groups and then reconstructing its diffusion to other groups. In a report to the New York Academy of Sciences in 1889, Boas commented that "certain designs originated among the Kwakiutl, but reached their highest stage of development among the Haidas" (Boas 1889:116).[20] In "The Development of Culture in Northwest America" (1888a), Boas continued along this path, suggesting that the Kwakiutl invented not only winter dances but also the totem pole:[21]

I am inclined to believe that another custom of the North West Americans besides their dances originated among the Kwakiutl. I mean the use of heraldic columns. This view may seem unjustified, considering the fact that such columns are made nowhere with greater care than in the northern regions, among the Tsimshian and Haida, and farther north and south they are less frequent and less elaborately carved. The Haida, however, frequently took up foreign ideas with great energy, and developed them independently. . . . It appears that the tribe has a remarkable faculty of adaptation (1888a:195).

He goes on to explain that it is only among the Kwakiutl that mythological tales refer frequently to totem poles, thus apparently justifying his assertion that the Kwa-

18. Virtually all this material reappeared in his monograph *The Social Organization and the Secret Societies of the Kwakiutl Indians* (1897b:366–91).

19. In this essay I use Boas's names for the Kwakiutl and Nootka which were in use at the time he wrote. Today these people prefer being called Kwakwaka'wakw and Nuu-chah-nulth, respectively.

20. The actual origin of totem poles is obscure, although they definitely date to precontact times. Early descriptions of interior posts were frequent in the writings of the first explorers and traders in the region, but the only records of large exterior freestanding poles were from the Haida village of Dadans on the Queen Charlottes and the Tlingit village at Yakutat Bay. None was described among any other group. Within a short period of time, however, poles became common among other coastal groups, probably because of both the availability of metal tools and the intertribal contacts that resulted from the fur trade (Cole and Darling 1990:132).

21. The "winter dances" referred to here are the Red Cedar Bark or Tseka ceremonies of the Kwakiutl, which took place over several weeks at the end of the nineteenth century and included masquerades, dancing, and feasting. See Holm 1990a, Suttles 1991.

kiutl originated the art form.[22] Then, observing some similarities between Eskimo and Tlingit masks, both of which have small carved faces attached to the larger face of the mask itself, he proposed "that a mutual influence existed here" (1888a:196). In "The Use of Masks and Head-ornaments on the Northwest Coast of America" (1890a), Boas reiterated his theory of the innovativeness of the Kwakiutl, whom he credited with inventing the masks worn during winter ceremonies. He also commented that groups borrow ideas and copy artistic forms which "strike their fancy"; examples of this are the Tsimshian raven rattle among the Kwakiutl, the Chilkat blanket among groups as far south as Comox, and the Tsimshian ermine headdress among people as distant as Victoria (Boas 1890a:8). Boas was to become increasingly interested in reconstructing the origin and distribution among ethnic groups of artistic styles and motifs. This would later become a particularly useful means of discrediting evolutionist art history.

Boas on Northwest Coast Art Style, 1896–1900 In 1896, as he intensified his studies of style and symbolism, Boas began to tackle the complexities of the artistic process. In his two-page "Decorative Art of the Indians of the North Pacific Coast," published in *Science* (1896), Boas challenged the notion that all Northwest Coast art was totemic by identifying certain objects whose animal form did not derive from social meaning. Although a large proportion of Northwest Coast animal images depict crests associated with family histories, Boas noted that some animal representations on hunting implements and food bowls related to certain natural attributes of the animals themselves. Granting that totemism was a significant incentive in the development of Northwest Coast art, he suggests that once the use of conventionalized animal imagery to decorate objects had been established, artists began applying similar designs to objects unrelated to totemism. Thus a halibut club assumed the shape of the sea lion or killer whale because these are successful fishers, while the grease dish represented a blubber-rich seal. Disputing restrictive and limiting unicausal theories, Boas asserted that his analysis of animal imagery in Northwest Coast art was "one of the numerous ethnological phenomena which, although apparently simple, cannot be explained psychologically from a single cause but are due to several factors" (1896:102–3).[23]

In 1897, Boas wrote his most elaborate and important work on art thus far, "The Decorative Art of the Indians of the North Pacific Coast," published in the *Bulletin*

22. Note that Boas later modifies his position on the centrality of the Kwakiutl in Northwest Coast art history and credits the northern groups with much artistic innovation. See below, pp. 27–28.

23. Boas repeated these points in his 1899 "Summary of the Work of the Committee in British Columbia," written for the British Association for the Advancement of Science. See Stocking 1974:102–5 for Boas's brief summary about Northwest Coast art.

of the American Museum of Natural History.[24] This was to become his first systematic argument against an evolutionary explanation of the development of conventionalized imagery. In his introductory comments, Boas seemed to accept as true in some instances the realist/degenerationist theory of Frederic Ward Putnam:[25]

It has been shown that the motives of the decorative art of many peoples developed largely from representations of animals. In course of time, forms that were originally realistic became more and more sketchy, and more and more distorted. Details, even large portions, of the subject so represented, were omitted, until finally the design attained a purely geometric character (1897a:123).

Boas then pointed out that this did not occur in one region, the Northwest Coast:

The decorative art of the Indians of the North Pacific Coast agrees with this oft-observed phenomenon in that its subjects are almost exclusively animals. It differs from other arts in that the process of conventionalizing has not led to the development of geometric designs, but that the parts of the animal body may still be recognized as such (1897a:123).

The Northwest Coast artist adhered to an iconographic canon that determined certain identifying characteristics of animals, such as the beaver's large incisors and crosshatched tail, the killer whale's large dorsal fin, and the eagle's large, downward-curving beak.[26] According to Boas, the artistic requirement that any animal image had to include all identifying elements of the animal led to highly conventionalized depictions when that animal decorated certain surfaces. On a three-dimensional sculpture, the artist could represent his subject, with all its characteristic features, in a fully naturalistic fashion (and the Northwest Coast artist was capable of very naturalistic representations); this became more problematic when he was presented with a two-dimensional surface. Sometimes that artist needed to abstract and distort the animal-subject in order to make it fit on the surface being decorated. Often, when a three-dimensional animal was depicted on a two-dimensional surface, the artist resorted to what is termed "split representation," in which the animal's body is split down the middle, flattened out, and shown in both profiles connected at the center. Sometimes, it was not possible for the artist to portray every feature of the

24. The guidebook to the hall (Boas 1900a) briefly mentions several of Boas's principal points about Northwest Coast style.

25. It is perhaps relevant that Putnam, Boas's mentor and supporter, was on staff at the American Museum of Natural History and instrumental in Boas's being hired there in 1895 (see Jonaitis 1988a:135).

26. Although Edmund Carpenter (1975:16) asserts that it was George Emmons who informed Boas about the identification of Northwest Coast animal images, Frederica de Laguna (1991:200) comments that while Boas and Emmons may have discussed this topic, Emmons's manuscript on Tlingit art (1991:200–209) is evidently influenced by Boas.

entire animal, so he resorted to representing its characteristic motifs, in which case the rendering became truly symbolic. Here on the Northwest Coast, therefore, the relative realism or abstraction of an image depended on the shape of the surface upon which the artist depicted different animals and their culturally dictated identifying characteristics.

Boas once again discussed this relationship between animal imagery and the shape of the surface on which it appeared in his "Facial Paintings of the Indians of Northern British Columbia," published in 1898 as part of volume 1 of the Jesup Expedition Publications.[27] Repeating the introductory comments of his 1897 monograph, Boas began his text by accepting the realist/degenerationist theory that among "most primitive people we find a tendency to the development of geometric designs." He then asserted that this did not occur in Northwest Coast art (1898b:13). To test his theory that in this region the form of the object being decorated with all the necessary animal symbols influenced the relative naturalism of the representation, Boas analyzed the painting applied to the most complex possible surface, the human face. After describing a wide range of Northwest Coast facial paintings, Boas concluded that geometric designs in these paintings did not necessarily evolve from naturalistic ones but were artistic responses to the problems posed by the shape of the face.

To investigate this question, Boas collected face paintings from Charles Edenshaw, "one of the most famous artists" of the Haida, and arranged them in a sequence from the most realistic to the most abstract. As it turned out, the fullest and most realistic representations appeared on the faces of the highest-ranking people, while those of lower rank had more conventionalized face paintings. In some cases, the facial features became part of the design, while in others, they were ignored, with the face serving as a flat surface. While sometimes the depicted animal was readily identified, it could be so abstract that identification was virtually impossible without an explanation by the informant. In this study, Boas noted the appearance of what he claims to be unique in the Northwest Coast: animal symbols in the form of pure geometric designs. Some of these abstract motifs, moreover, could represent different animals, requiring identification by the owner of the image. Boas would periodically return to the point that at times iconographic identification could be

27. The Jesup North Pacific Expedition, 1897–1902, was sponsored by the American Museum of Natural History and organized by Boas (see Jonaitis 1988a:154–213). The aim of this expedition was to study the ethnological relations between the peoples of the Northwest Coast of America and northeastern Siberia (Boas 1898a). The American Museum of Natural History subsidized a monograph series, the *Publications of the Jesup North Pacific Expedition*, which included several volumes on art. Those publications are part of a larger Museum monograph series, *American Museum of Natural History Memoirs*. The same volume, therefore, has two different volume numbers, that for the Jesup *Publications* and that for the *Memoirs*; this has created some confusion.

obscure; this supported his recurrent theme that uncomplicated answers to questions of meaning simply did not exist.

In his concluding comments, Boas (1898b:24) asserts that "the collection is of theoretical interest mainly because it shows that the difficulty of adapting the subject of decoration to the decorative field has been a most powerful element in substituting geometrical forms for less conventional designs, and in showing a series of important transitional forms." It should be pointed out that this case is less convincing than that presented the year before in "The Decorative Art of the Indians of the North Pacific Coast." The variety of imagery on these facial paintings suggests less that the artist was trying to solve formal problems (as he seems to have been doing in the split representation) and more that he could choose from a range of styles depending upon factors that at least in some cases had to do with the rank of the individual being painted (as he himself noted early in the essay). Although he would repeat the idea that a primitive artist at times freely chose from a range of artistic possibilities when socially dictated conventions did not completely restrict his choice, Boas did not return in later publications to this topic of facial paintings.

In addition to questioning the relationship between naturalistic and stylized images, Boas studied the relationship between art style and linguistic families. In British Columbia, the Coast Salish have a distinctly different art style from their linguistic relatives, the Salish-speaking Thompson people of the interior of the province. During the Jesup North Pacific Expedition, Boas had a British Columbia resident, James Teit, collect examples of Thompson Indian art. The pieces Teit collected resembled Plains Indian art far more than they did Northwest Coast art. In his contribution to Teit's monograph in the Jesup series on the Thompson Indians, Boas (1900b) compared Coast and Interior Salish art, pointing to the absence of plastic art among the latter, so different from the highly three-dimensional art of the Northwest Coast. Unlike the Northwest Coast artists, Thompson painters decorated their implements with designs not prompted by the shape of the surface. The iconography of the two types of artworks created by linguistically related peoples differed as well. Unlike the universally understood imagery of most Northwest Coast representations (although, of course, not all, as he demonstrated in the facial painting article), Thompson decorative designs, often abstract and ambiguous, could be interpreted differently and sometimes apparently arbitrarily by different people. Designs on implements, which related to their use, differed from those on ceremonial pieces, which depicted owners' dreams. These comparisons implicitly demonstrated the inadequacy of any theory positing a direct connection between language and art style. In his "Conclusion" to the Thompson monograph, Boas attempted to reconstruct the history of Salish speakers, some of whom he suggested had migrated to the Northwest Coast where they borrowed certain art forms from their neighbors, others of whom lived on the plateau and were influenced by Plains Indians.[28]

Boas on Native American Art, from 1901 By the first decade of the twentieth century, Boas had at his disposal more materials with which he could dispute grand universalizing theories. These included Northwest Coast materials acquired during the Jesup Expedition by Teit, Livingston Farrand (1900), and John Swanton (1905); Siberian pieces collected during that same fieldwork by Berthold Laufer (1902), Waldemar Jochelson (1908, 1926), and Waldemar Bogoras (1904) in Siberia; northern Mexican art by Carl Lumholtz (1904); and Plains and California art described by Boas's students, including A. L. Kroeber (1900a, 1901), Clark Wissler (1904), and Roland B. Dixon (1902). Confident in his grasp of the Northwest Coast, Boas could now expand beyond that culture area in his efforts to dismantle the false grand narrative of evolutionism. He also turned greater attention to the creative process, and to the psychological and cultural factors that influenced art production. His articles published between 1901 and 1916 thus represent his mature statements on art history as well as his final contributions to that discipline prior to the publication of *Primitive Art* in 1927.

In 1903, Boas expanded his study of primitive art beyond the Northwest Coast in "The Decorative Art of the North American Indians," published in *Popular Science Monthly*.[29] In this essay that analyzes the significance of a culture in determining meaning in art, Boas proposed history as a substitute for evolutionism. He begins by dismissing the realist/degenerationism of Haddon (1895) and then appears to accept the theory of Semper (1861–63), Cushing (1886), and Holmes (1888, 1890) that the origin of decorative forms can probably be found in technique. In particular, he favors the work of Schurtz (1900) and Hamlin (1898) who note that once a design is created, the group using it on its art "read in" meaning appropriate to their culture. In this case Boas tacitly positions himself in opposition to the number of scholars like Grosse (1897) and Hirn (1900) for whom the expressive and communicative aspects of art are primary. He qualifies this by adding that this origin has little relevance to the meaning ascribed to the image by the people who use it for decorative purposes.

28. In this essay, Boas described the Salish as being a "receptive race, quick to adopt foreign modes of thought" (1900b:390), perhaps due to "a low stage of development of their early culture, or to social conditions unfavorable to the continued growth of their own culture" (1900b:387). The first explanation sounds rather evolutionist, whereas the second is far more in keeping with his concept of cultural receptivity. See Suttles 1987 for more on the question of the position of the Salish in the Northwest Coast; and Suttles 1990 for recent studies on the Salish.

29. Boas chose this piece, as well as his Alaskan needlecase essay (1908b) and "Representative Art of Primitive Peoples" (1916), to include in *Race, Language and Culture* (1940); this would suggest that he too felt that these three essays represented his most significant statements on art historical issues.

Then, directing his words to those who preferred evolutionist to historical explanations, Boas asserted that if one group's art style really arose in isolation from another group's, as a result of either a technical/materialist or a realist/degenerationist process, the art of each group would be different. On the Plains, where art produced by many different ethnic groups is remarkably uniform, this was clearly not the case. According to Boas, history, not evolution, explained the presence of certain images in art. As an example of the diffusion of a motif, Boas charted the appearance of a rather complex geometric design found both on ancient Pueblo art and among many different Plains people. This motif, Boas proposed, originated on Pueblo pottery and spread northwards. Interestingly, what the image meant to various Plains groups differed considerably. Stressing the significance of culture in these historical processes, Boas explained that when new motifs enter into the artistic vocabulary of a people, they ascribe meaning to them appropriate to their values and world view.

In this same article, Boas notes the coexistence of realistic and geometric imagery on the Plains, where relatively realistic designs often decorated sacred, ceremonial objects while more geometric images appeared on secular pieces used every day. He ascribed to this the culturally determined differences in the purpose of the art: "In ceremonial objects the ideas represented are more important than the decorative effect, and it is intelligible that the resistance to conventionalism may be strong" (although he acknowledged that in other cases, the need for secrecy may result in obscure representations) (1903:485).

In addition to becoming both more assertive and more universal in his objections to evolutionist art history, Boas became more sensitive to the subtleties and complexities of the artistic process.

We conclude from all this that the explanation of designs is secondary almost throughout and due to a late association of ideas and forms, and that as a rule a gradual transition from realistic motives to geometric forms did not take place. The two groups of phenomena—interpretation and style—appear to be independent. . . . the history of the artistic development of a people, and the style that they have developed at any given time, predetermine the method by which they express their ideas in decorative art; and . . . the type of ideas that a people is accustomed to express by means of decorative art predetermines the explanation that will be given to a new design. . . . The idea which a design expresses at the present time is not necessarily a clew to its history. It seems probable that idea and style exist independently, and influence each other constantly (1903:497).

Whereas a style can result from historical factors in which imagery and design diffuse into a group from the outside, the meaning the accepting culture ascribes to the new style must resonate with the concepts that constitute that group's culture. Thus, a people's culture, which influences everything they do or say, affects their art as well. In this essay, Boas noted the occurrence of an artistic phenomenon both in the primitive and civilized worlds, a theme to which he returned several times in subsequent essays. He gave the following example. As is the case in the Plains where conventionalized and stylized images appear simultaneously, in modern architecture, domestic stained glass tends to be geometric, while in churches it is usually representational; wallpaper in the home tends to be abstract, whereas wallpaper in public settings has more symbolic representations.

After this 1903 article, Boas continued analyzing Native American art, posing questions on style, symbolism, and history, trying to test prevalent art historical theories. In a guide booklet to the American Museum of Natural History's exhibitions of primitive art (1904), Boas took the opportunity to communicate his ideas on art and culture to the public by leading the visitor through displays of Northwest Coast, Plains, Eastern Woodlands, California, and Mexican Indians. Here he repeated his point that certain groups borrowed motifs from others and, in the process, ascribed different, culturally specific meanings to the same artistic image.

In 1907 Boas made substantial contributions to George T. Emmons's Chilkat blanket monograph in the Jesup series. Most bibliographies list "The Chilkat Blanket," volume three of the *Publications of the Jesup North Pacific Expedition*, as being written by George T. Emmons; some but not all give the complete title of the volume, "The Chilkat Blanket; with Notes on the Blanket Designs by Franz Boas." In this monograph, Emmons wrote twenty-one pages, mostly on techniques and usage of these textiles (Emmons 1907:329–50), while Boas analyzed their imagery in his forty-nine-page "Notes on the Blanket Designs" (Boas 1907:351–400). Boas used these highly abstract textiles to compare and contrast imagery and meaning, once again concluding that form and meaning are not always connected, and that culturally imposed rules limit the freedom with which an artist can represent a particular image. Although in 1897 Boas had carefully listed the identifying features of Northwest Coast imagery, here he pointed out that sometimes the nature of the abstraction characteristic of Chilkat blankets obscures those features so thoroughly that even the Natives themselves disagree on what they represent.

The basic composition of most Chilkat blankets is tripartite, with the central field being the largest. That central field contains the principal representation of the animal or animals depicted, while the two symmetrical flanking fields illustrate the sides and back of the central animal (split down the middle), its den, or smaller animals. Boas compared this composition to that on boxes and dancing aprons. One interesting phenomenon Boas noted is that Emmons and Swanton interpreted the same blanket in very different ways; this, he suggests, is because "no fixed time of conventionalization exists" (1907:386–87) within the parameters of this particular kind of art. Because the weaver must depict the subject matter in a consistent fashion determined by the culturally imposed formal rules of Chilkat blanket manufacture, regardless of the animal intended to be represented, images sometimes become extremely abstract. Not only are the principal subjects of these blankets sometimes difficult to identify definitely, some of the decorative elements on them are obscure. The various abstract motifs found on these textiles fluctuate in meaning; the so-called red-winged flicker motif, for example—which never depicts any part of a bird—sometimes represents bones and limbs, and sometimes is simply a formal, meaningless element in a design. Boas also makes a brief excursion into the history of the Chilkat blanket, noting two older blankets unlike the others under discussion. These (numbers 35 and 36a) could have been the original type that the Chilkat Tlingit altered when they acquired this kind of textile from the Tsimshian. He then briefly mentioned a few modern blankets but dismissed them with the comment that in them, "the old conventionalism is breaking down entirely" (1907:391). This is an example of Boas's bias that history worth recording and analyzing occurred before the influences of white culture brought about a disassembling of Native culture.

In 1908, Boas published a brief survey of "Clubs Made of Bone of Whale" from Washington and British Columbia (1908a), turning his attention to the art of the Nootka.[30] In that same year he published what is arguably his most important art historical article, "Decorative Designs of Alaskan Needlecases: A Study in the History of Conventional Designs, Based on Materials in the U.S. National Museum" (Boas: 1908b).[31] This essay on Eskimo art is an elegant refutation of both the realist/degenerationists and the technical/materialists, as well as a major statement of the significance of artistic creativity. He begins by contrasting the realist/degenerationists to the technical/materialists, but now notes that there is a third distinctive theory of the development of decorative forms—promoted by Boas, his student Alfred

30. Boas did not deal with the Nootka (or the Salish for that matter) very thoroughly in his art historical writings. In the concluding essay to this volume, I suggest some possible reasons for this that fit into his theoretical interests (see below, p. 314). Another reason, however, less closely tied to his scholarship, could be practical. While conducting research on the Nootka whalers' washing shrine, Richard Inglis and I (see Jonaitis and Inglis 1992) found a 1902 letter that Boas had sent to Hunt in which he said that the Kwakiutl collections were complete and now it was time to start working on the Nootka. Presumably Boas realized that to accomplish his goals to reconstruct Northwest Coast art history, he needed more abundant materials from the west coast of Vancouver Island than the American Museum of Natural History had. Perhaps because Hunt spent a very long time purchasing the whalers' shrine (Cole 1985; Jonaitis 1988a:182–83), he had little time to collect anything else from the area. Unfortunately, Boas left the American Museum in 1905 and thus could not realize his goals of acquiring more Nootka materials that would have enriched the collections upon which he based his scholarship.

31. Fox (1991:100–101) discusses this article in the context of Boasian culture history.

Kroeber (1901), and Clark Wissler (1904)[32]—in which interpretation and style are independent.[33]

The form of the needlecase itself is ancient, Boas argued, and contains various parts which "excite the imagination of the artist." The geometric decorative field develops, according to the nature of Eskimo art, into animals or parts of animals (1908b:337). After presenting an exhaustive and extremely detailed analysis of the wide variety of Alaskan needlecases, which range in style from realistic to conventional, Boas made the bold statement that no proof exists that the decorative designs on these cases evolved either from realistic motifs (his "motives") or from influence of technique; instead, "the only satisfactory explanation lies in the assumption that the multifarious forms are due to the play of the imagination with a fixed old conventional form, the origin of which remains entirely obscure" (p. 337).

Boas asserted that one could easily arrange these objects in a series, placing the naturalistic pieces at one end and the stylized ones at the other end, and then interpret the series as progressing either from naturalistic to stylized or from stylized to naturalistic.[34] Neither one nor the other of these series provided any proof of historical sequence, and thus could not be accepted as a verifiable reconstruction of the art historical process. Classification does not imply a genetic series. There exists simultaneously within the human mind a tendency toward abstraction and a tendency toward realism, with each manifesting itself in different ways. Repeating a point made earlier in "Decorative Art," Boas also commented that the diversity of explanations of the same motif implies that once a group borrows a form, they interpret it according to their cultural values.

The role of the artist's psychology in art creation became a central focus in this essay. Boas pointed out that while the primitive artist worked within a cultural system that posed certain restrictions on what he could and could not do, the artist could, within those limits, be creative. This he had already demonstrated in terms of the Chilkat blanket, where regardless of the animal depicted, the artist was constrained by one of two fundamental compositions within which the animal had to be fitted. The Eskimo, Boas argued, tended to decorate their carving with zoomorphic imagery; thus, the knob on a needlecase became a perfect field for transformation into a seal head. While tradition and convention imposed some restrictions on the artist decorating the needlecase with seal imagery, he could draw on both his

32. Wissler briefly studied with Boas. See Freed and Freed 1983.

33. See Boas's "Decorative Art of the North American Indians" (1903). This point is in keeping with semiotic theory of Saussure (1964), who points to the arbitrary connections between the signifier and the signified in linguistics.

34. In his essay on Sioux decorative art, Clark Wissler made the following not dissimilar point, "The assumption that the law of growth in decorative art is from the representative to the conventional reduces the problem to one of analysis. It is conceivable, however, that the same result could be reached in the reverse order; viz., by synthesis" (1904:232).

imagination and his creativity in his carving. Boas proposed that a significant factor in the creation of new art forms was the sheer enjoyment felt by the artist while producing art: "one of the most important sources in the development of primitive decorative art is analogous to the pleasure that is given the achievements of the virtuoso" (p. 340). Indeed, Boas suggested that certain stylistic variations might have been the result of an artist's imaginative play, which functions in the context of the traditional constraints that determine artistic conventions.

Once again insisting on the complexity of the question of decorative art, Boas asserted that its development "can not be simply interpreted by the assumption of a general tendency toward conventionalism or by the theory of an evolution of technical motives into realistic motives by a process of reading in, but that a considerable number of other psychic processes must be taken into consideration if we desire to obtain a clear insight into the history of art" (p. 341). So convinced was Boas about the significance of such mental processes that he encouraged several of his students, including Ruth Bunzel, to pursue studies along these lines. He himself organized a project with James Teit, H. K. Haeberlin, and Helen Roberts, who investigated the "attitude of the individual artist toward his work" among the Interior Salish of British Columbia (Haeberlin et al. 1928:131). The resulting monograph, "Coiled Basketry in British Columbia and Surrounding Region," for which Boas wrote a two-page introduction and a short conclusion, came out one year after *Primitive Art* (Jacknis 1992).

In his 1916 article, "Representative Art of Primitive Peoples," Boas described the intimate relationship between an artist's technical skill and the aesthetic effect of his art. Reiterating points made in the Alaskan needlecase article, he suggested that an artist's enjoyment of the creative process and technical experiments could lead to new artistic designs, and that representational decorative art and geometrical decorative art were two different types of artistic activity, neither of which could be proved to be older than the other. Boas then addressed a problem posed earlier in his 1897 monograph on Northwest Coast art—the rendering of a three-dimensional object on a two-dimensional surface—but with a considerably different objective, for here he compared perspective in European and nonwestern art.

According to Boas, the primitive artist attempts to represent all or most of the features essential for the recognition of a subject, whereas the European artist uses a perspective technique to show the object as it appears at any given moment. Although accepting this essential difference between most European and primitive art, Boas identifies a variety of European artworks that depict their subjects in a fashion that Boas feels is similar to that of primitive art. Narrative painting, such as a depiction of Adam and Eve in the Garden of Eden followed by the Expulsion, does not illustrate a single moment in time, but instead shows a sequence of events. Dutch painting details with great clarity every element within a broad visual range, instead of blurring all but a small portion of the field of vision, as is the case when one actually observes a scene. Boas described how most artists depict objects with what he refers to as their "permanent" colors (i.e., a flesh-colored face, a red rose); this convention, so much a part of western art tradition, makes it difficult for viewers to understand paintings by modern artists who attempted to render passing color effects, such as a face made green by a tree's shadow or made red by the reflection of a red wall or curtain.

Boas concluded this short essay with the brief but significant statement that the "absence of realistic forms in the representative art of primitive tribes is not due to lack of skill" (p. 23), citing the example of the Northwest Coast artist who can at will create exceptionally naturalistic sculptures. Instead, he proposed, one "must rather seek for the condition of their art in the depth of the feeling which demands the representation of the permanent characteristics of the object in the representative design" (p. 23). Thus art styles of a primitive society and a literate one were different not because the primitive artist was inferior or was unable to create a naturalistic representation, but because of the constraints imposed by each culture to create a certain kind of art.

PRIMITIVE ART (1927)

In the 1920s, the Oslo Institute for Comparative Research in Human Culture invited Boas, who was by that time the most distinguished anthropologist in the United States, to present a series of lectures on primitive art. Here was an opportunity for Boas to consolidate the ideas he had been developing since Northwest Coast art first captured his fancy and present them in a unified form, first in these lectures and then in the Oslo Institute's 1927 publication *Primitive Art* (Herskovits 1953:97).[35]

Primitive Art is far more than the compilation of Boas's various antievolutionist critiques, for in it he offers a general perspective on the problems of primitive art, a sensitive appreciation of the creative process, and a more mature statement of his aesthetic ideas. He also expands his range of examples to include not only Native America, but Africa, the Pacific, and Siberia as well. In the preface, Boas presents his objective: "to determine the dynamic conditions under which art styles grow up" (p. 7). He then describes the universality of the aesthetic experience and the twofold source of artistic effect—form and meaning—neither of which can be proved to be older than the other. He stresses the importance of "highly developed and perfectly controlled technique" that becomes the fixed form which determines the measure of aesthetic excellence; "without a formal basis the will to create something

35. Harvard University Press issued an American edition of the Oslo work in 1928; in 1955, Dover reprinted the book.

that appeals to the sense of beauty can hardly exist" (pp. 11–12). The body of the text consists of individual chapters on formal elements, representational art, symbolism, style, Northwest Coast art, and the nonvisual arts. The various points he makes derive in large measure from his previous writings, which in several cases he elaborates and focuses more sharply. Drawing together his ideas on art, Boas discusses the complexity of the artistic process in a relatively coherent fashion. That coherence, I must stress, is indeed relative; because of his unwillingness to come to premature theoretical closure, his definitive statements concerning art are not as frequent as his discussions of its complexities. As I pointed out in my introductory essay, this now can be evaluated as a positive rather than negative feature of the book.

The chapter "Graphic and Plastic Arts: The Formal Element in Art" examines the great significance of technical virtuosity in the creation of art. Indicating that in many cases the aesthetic appeal of primitive art lies in its formal qualities rather than in its iconographic significance or emotional expressions, Boas highlights the mechanical skills and the technical virtuosity of primitive artists, which, as he pointed out in his Alaskan needlecase piece, provide the creator with pleasure. Here Boas does identify certain features that appear to be universal in art: symmetry, a kind of rhythmic repetition that could be the result of the physical actions of the artist creating the work, and emphasis on form, meaning that the artist uses decoration to emphasize the form of the object being decorated. Not all art, he asserts, especially decorative art, conveys meaning or emotion; even art that does represent something includes a formal element "directly due to the impression derived by form" (p. 63).

In the section "Representative Art" (which I will term representational), Boas discusses content that provides an artwork with emotional value quite distinct from its formal aesthetic effect. According to Boas, meaning alone does not make a representation an artwork, for, to create art, the artist must be a technical master; crudely drawn images such as Plains pictographs are not art but simply depictions of animals, humans, and tents. He then identifies two modes in which representational art can depict its subject in three dimensions: one, by depicting its outline simply and forcefully, perhaps filling that outline with decorative elements; the other, giving all the components of the figure with little concern for the whole (p. 69). This leads to a discussion of two dimensional images, those that depict all the characteristics of the subject and those that depict only those parts that are seen at any one moment. Here are the two basic means by which the primitive artist portrays reality: symbolic drawing and its opposite, perspective drawing, neither of which can be proved older than the other and each of which sometimes contains elements of the other. Repeating examples he had used in his 1916 essay of narrative paintings that represent a span of time and the Dutch still lifes with their unnatural clarity of each individual element, Boas demonstrates that not all western art slavishly follows the principles of perspective. He identifies examples of perspective drawing in Eskimo engravings, Bushman rock paintings, and paleolithic cave paintings to show that this representational technique is not the final product of an evolutionary process, but is instead the manifestation of one of several possible visual renderings.

Boas then turns to the relationship between stylized or symbolic art and realistic art (p. 80). Instead of accepting a developmental scheme from abstraction to naturalism, or vice versa, Boas suggests that stylistic differences can derive from the presence or absence of certain technical constraints. He argues that in some cases technique has greater significance than the representation itself, producing a more stylized art in which formal elements become more meaningful and imbued with more emotional value (p. 82). Where, in contrast, the artist's creativity is not restricted by culturally determined requirements to use a particular technique for all his artworks, a more naturalistic art might develop. In addition, since carving and sculpture are relatively less limiting and restricting techniques than graphic representation, the three-dimensional work of a people is sometimes more naturalistic than their two-dimensional art, as is the case on the Northwest Coast (p. 85).

Boas's next topic is "Symbolism," the study of those artistic elements that at first might seem abstract and without meaning but which have considerable significance to the people upon whose art they appear. Here he draws on the work of his students Kroeber, Dixon, Wissler, St. Clair, and Bunzel, and repeats the notion of historical influences discussed in his 1903 "The Decorative Art of the North American Indians," as well as the conclusions from his Chilkat blanket work, in order to analyze the meaning of geometric or seemingly nonobjective art. Some cultures assign to certain designs a profound meaning universally understood, while other cultures offer extremely divergent explanations of similar or identical images. Sometimes, two or more different cultures interpret identical images quite differently. Moving from inconsistent explanations of abstract images to the impossibility of reconstructing a verifiable sequence, Boas insists that some art can develop from realistic to stylized, and other art from stylized to naturalistic. Without historical proof of such a development, a sequence can be interpreted either way. The only method to reconstruct the development of an art style is by the geographic method, which analyzes the distribution of art styles and their variations in an area. If the same form with the same interpretation occurs over a large area, with those in the center being realistic and those in the outlying regions being stylized, then it can be assumed that the development progressed from realistic to conventionalized. If, in contrast, the realistic and conventional forms with inconsistent meanings are distributed randomly throughout the area, then either a conventional form became assigned a representational meaning or a realistic form became unrecognizable and stylized. Somewhat modifying his analysis of Alaskan needlecases (1908b), Boas suggests that due to the widespread distribution and great frequency of geometric designs, "the earliest form is geometric," but that "the habit of carving animal forms has induced the artist to produce the variants described here" (p. 126). In his conclusion to this chapter, Boas describes how among those peoples whose art "wavers between the symbolic and representative modes of delineation, opportunity arises for the occurrence of realistic and abbreviated forms, side by side" (p. 143).

In his fourth chapter, "Style," Boas identifies that which determines the formal treatment of both symbols and geometric motifs, and asks how deeply one can understand "the historical and psychological conditions under which art styles grow up and flourish" (p. 144). Boas demonstrates how the profound conservatism of a people, their resistance to change, ensures the art style's relative permanence and stability over time. So strong is adherence to tradition that style can restrict the inventiveness of a potentially original artist (pp. 156, 158). This conservatism can result in the application of a style that originated in one medium to another medium, as for example in the case of a pot imitating basketry. The technician, a weaver, for example, can play with technique and thus "discover" simple ornamental decorations. In this chapter, Boas brings the reader's attention to the creativity of women artists and the influences they may have, as basketmakers and weavers, on the development of their group's art style: "the most highly developed art is liable to impose its style upon other industries, and that mat weaving and basketry have been particularly influential in developing new forms and powerful in imposing them upon other fields" (p. 182). This brief statement about female creativity hints at Boas's acceptance of the equality of male and female art, and goes along with his supporting the research by women like his students Ruth Bunzel (1929) and Gladys Reichard (1934, 1936, 1939a, 1939b), and Kroeber's student Lila O'Neale (1932) who studied the creativity of potters and weavers (Berlo 1992).

In this chapter, Boas directs his attention to the artist, granting him his deserved status; "only in the case of slovenly work have we referred to the artisan" (p. 155). Raising a point made earlier in his Alaskan needlecase article (1908b), Boas suggests that one of the most important means of understanding art is to penetrate the "attitudes and actions of the artist." Acknowledging the difficulty of this, Boas goes on to insist that the primitive artist, even the individual bound to a particular traditional style, has within himself "creative genius" (p. 156). It is worth pointing out that in these pages, Boas uses the male pronoun, even when he is referring to female artists. We must assume that his language does not imply the superiority of male over female artists, but, instead, is in keeping with the literary conventions of the day.

Why do so many stylistic variations on simple techniques exist? There is no simple answer to this question, for the psychological and historical components of art history are so complex as to render impossible any satisfactory explanation of the origin of a style. All that can be done is "to unravel some of the threads that are woven into the present fabric and determine some of the lines of behavior that may help us to realize what is happening in the minds of the people" (p. 155). To understand the art style of a group, it is necessary to compare it with that of contiguous areas, for no art style can be fully understood as the result of an internal development within a culture, nor as only an expression of the group's "cultural life." Rather, historical influences and diffusion of technical processes, formal elements and systems of arrangements of motifs contribute to the art style of any one group (p. 176). The chapters on formal art, representational art, symbolism, and style together cover the various elements in this immensely complex process of artistic development.

After dealing with general concepts touching primitive art, Boas applies his general principles to the art of a specific geographic area, the Northwest Coast. This, the longest chapter of the book, is a revised version of his 1897 monograph, with considerable new information and analysis, much of it drawn from his other Northwest Coast publications discussed in this essay. Boas begins by identifying two very different styles of art found among the North Pacific people: the symbolic and referential art made by men and the formal and nonobjective art made by women. In this chapter, he devotes a fair amount of space to the women's art of basketry and mat weaving (pp. 289–94). In his introduction to men's art, he repeats the points he made in 1897, that representational art comes in both naturalistic and conventionalized modes, and the form of the decorated object plays a major role in determining the manner by which one of these symbols is represented, as in the simultaneous image. Drawing on his analysis of the Chilkat blanket (1907), he points out how conventional composition of the artwork determines placement of design (p. 257), and explains that symbols of animals are usually understood by the entire group but are sometimes unique and understood only by the artwork's owner (pp. 212–16). He also comments that sometimes artists display considerable freedom in their creation of animal images, diverging from rigid norms.[36]

In "The Social Organization and the Secret Societies of the Kwakiutl Indians," Boas analyzed the representational art of the Northwest Coast, but dealt little with the formal treatment of the decorative field in that art. Although in his earlier work Boas had suggested that the "eye" design signified a joint mark and was thus consistently meaningful (1897a:175), here he says the motif is sometimes simply a decorative element. Then he proceeds to enumerate those seemingly completely abstract, geometric elements of Northwest Coast art such as chevrons and zigzags,

36. Swanton's monograph on the Haida (1905:147–54) quotes Boas at length on notes taken in 1897 from Charles Edenshaw regarding a set of gambling sticks. In *Primitive Art*, Boas gives only a short paragraph to this material (1927:212), although he does reproduce the gambling sticks (figs. 200, 201).

as well as the various curvilinear motifs we now call constricted eyelids, ovoids, U forms, and the like, pointing out that some of these are decorative fillers devoid of meaning, while others have deep significance for the artist and his audience (pp. 251–57).[37] That some fully abstract designs have symbolic significance and others are purely decorative contradict neat and simplistic schemes on the relationships of imagery and meaning.

Boas also points out that although Northwest Coast art is primarily representational (with the exception of women's art), geometric elements are not entirely absent, because short parallel lines, cross-hatchings, and circle-and-line patterns appear on some artworks. This brings him to several conclusions: that geometric design "may be recognized even in this highly developed symbolic art," that some motifs have no meaning at all but are used for "purely ornamental purposes," and that the exuberant and baroque symbolic style was developed only relatively recently, pushing out these geometric designs that were probably more widely used in the past (p. 279). With this, Boas begins his proposed reconstruction of Northwest Coast art history.

Although in much of Boas's art history he does not venture too deeply into the broader sociological significance of art, he does touch upon the relationship between Northwest Coast art and social structure. Refining a point he made in 1896, Boas points to the overwhelming importance these Indians ascribe to display of rank, especially by means of artistic renderings of totemic emblems. This, he suggests, demonstrates a dialectical relationship between the development of the use of totemic emblems to symbolize social standing and the development of an exuberant artistic spirit in the region. Totemism provided the incentive for artistic development of a symbolic style which gradually subsumed the earlier, more geometric style by introducing greater numbers of animals and limiting the geometric designs. However, he also suggests that the importance of artistic representation in this culture doubtless stimulated and enhanced the social significance of heraldry (pp. 280–81).

As early as 1888 in "The Development of Culture in Northwest America," and one year later in "Tattooing of the Haida," Boas had attempted to reconstruct the history of the development of a regional style, such as the supposed Kwakiutl origin of the totem pole. Now in 1927 he is suggesting that the center of the Northwest Coast symbolic decorative style, which will be referred to here, following Holm's terminology, as the formline style, originated in northern British Columbia and southeastern Alaska. By comparing the art of the Kwakiutl, Nootka, and northern Northwest Coast Indians with that of the Coast Salish, Interior Salish, and the Eskimo, pointing out similarities and differences, Boas presented a historical recon-

37. It was Bill Holm (1965) who first named these stylistic elements. See below, pp. 309–11.

struction of Northwest Coast style, based on his theory that the geometric style is older and that the formline style developed in response to social factors. The people of Vancouver Island, he proposed, maintain the older geometric style in their trays, boxes, and baskets. Illustrating a series of Nootka clubs made of whalebone described in his 1908 essay, Boas pointed to the "fixed art style" characteristic of the more ancient Northwest Coast regional style also found among the Salish (1927: 283–86). During the nineteenth century, the Indians of northern British Columbia and southeastern Alaska invented a more complex formline style. As a result, among the Tsimshian, Haida, and Tlingit one finds far less use of geometrical ornamentation than among the Nootka and the Coast Salish, and far richer ornamentation with motifs such as the eye design, double curve, and slit design. All the tribes have vestiges of the antique style in the women's arts of basketry and matting.

Between those northern Northwest Coast groups and the southern Vancouver Island and mainland British Columbian peoples are the Kwakiutl, who use a version of the formline style for heraldic purposes, but use geometric ornamentation for objects of everyday use. Boas asserts that the formline art was indeed a recent introduction to the Kwakiutl, for old informants claim that before 1860 the houses and their decorations resembled those of the Coast Salish (p. 289). Boas characterizes Kwakiutl art as having "distortions in painting [that] are, if anything, more daring than those of the Haida," but little of the interlocking of animal images typical of the northern region (p. 288).

To complete his historical survey, Boas compares Northwest Coast art with the art of the neighboring peoples. Wood carving from the Columbia River area and northern California, although different in style, displays similarities in terms of woodworking techniques, while north of the Tlingit, among the Alaskan Eskimo, an abundance of masks suggests a Northwest Coast influence. But that influence is reciprocal, for the Tlingit may have adopted from the Eskimo the idea of attaching little animals to the features of the mask (p. 295). Then, drawing on his collaborative work with James Teit (1900b), Boas points out the dissimilarity between coastal art and that of the Interior Salish, which has much closer affinities with Plains Indian art.

After an interesting excursion into the topic of literature, music, and dance, Boas concludes *Primitive Art* with a summary of its major points.[38] He reiterates his premise that art arises from both technical endeavors and from expressive needs, but actually does favor the former. Since certain elements—symmetry, rhythm, and emphasis on form—are practically universal, they can be assumed to be most ancient,

38. By including these other arts in his book, Boas foreshadows the later interest of African art historians such as Roy Sieber and Robert Farris Thompson in performance art. I am indebted to Janet Berlo for this observation.

most fundamental. But other than those antique foundations, it is simply not possible to assume any kind of universal causation of artistic development; the pattern of artistic expression, the type of geometric motifs, the treatment of the decorative field, and the degree of realism in any art style cannot be attributed to strict, unilinear processes. Moreover, even within the art of a single culture, uniform style is not always the rule. Those who excel in technical activities become the community's artists, whether they are men or women; in those situations where both men and women produce different things, two distinct art styles can emerge, as is the case on the Northwest Coast. Once again, however, Boas points to the fertility of female activities as inspirations for art styles: "It is . . . more frequent that the style of the dominant industry may be imposed upon work made by other processes. Weaving in coarse material seemed to be a most fertile source of patterns that art imitated in paintings, carvings, and pottery" (p. 355).

Boas asserts that "the pattern of artistic expression that emerges from a long, cumulative process determined by a multiplicity of causes fashions the form of the art work" (p. 354), thus one cannot conclude anything on a grand and abstract scale. His detailed analysis of actual case studies of particular art styles, his focus on the creative process, and his privileging of history all support his rejection of unprovable theories. In *Primitive Art*, Boas systematically rejects such theories by demonstrating cases in which they do not apply, and proposes a variety of different explanations for the invention and dissemination of artistic images including both cultural conservatism and creativity. In his Northwest Coast chapter, Boas offers an alternative approach to the study of art, by first identifying the principles of representation and then suggesting a historical reconstruction of the art style, drawing on the art of neighboring peoples. This last point is worth stressing. Many twentieth-century scholars of Native art believed that without support from written documents, it was impossible to reconstruct a history without access to "permanent" artworks made of stone or metal. Since so much of primitive art is made of wood and natural materials that decompose over time, many art historians felt bound to an ahistoric analysis of nineteenth-century objects. By using Boas's historical approach, art historians could include greater time depth in their studies.[39]

Characterizing Boas's contributions to art historical scholarship is no easy task, as he premised his studies on the tremendous complexity of the artistic process that makes simple explanations impossible. In his efforts to avoid imposing predetermined unicausal factors in the creation of art styles while consciously purging Native art history of a racist bias, Boas produced a rich body of literature which, as the concluding chapter of this book will demonstrate, profoundly influenced much twentieth-century work on Native art.

39. I have included a brief summary of Boas's principal ideas about art at the end of this essay.

THE SOCIAL CONTEXT OF BOAS'S ART HISTORY

Boas was not a scholar who merely challenged a point of view with which he disagreed. Although his social activism is best known from the period after he left the American Museum and settled into the Anthropology Department at Columbia University, Boas seems early in his life to have had strong social sentiments. Thus one can argue that his treatment of primitive art, in addition to being an interesting analysis of that subject and an attack on what Boas felt to be a wrong-headed theory, was a challenge to a mode of thought which at the end of the nineteenth century had destructive social consequences.[40]

To understand the broader ramifications of Boas's theories on art it is necessary to review the social implications of the evolutionist's theories. There was a tendency then, as there is today, to believe that science is objective, rational, and unconnected to social considerations. In fact, science has never been value-free. At the turn of the century, the writings of Brinton, McGee, and others provided "scientific" justification for the increasingly racist attitudes of the native-born American white population.[41] For example, they supported, with "facts," attitudes which held that Native Americans and other people of color were, simply, genetically inferior to whites. Although the Indian stood somewhat higher in the evolutionary ladder than blacks, many whites believed that his wild natural instincts would get the better of him and he would soon vanish from the earth, unable to evolve further and live in civilization. Although at this time there were some who thought well of the Indians, the general white assessment of their character was not favorable.

Dislike and distrust of Indians was mild compared with the increasingly virulent attitudes toward and outrageous treatment of American blacks. Here, too, evolutionist theories justified such treatment. Since these freed slaves and their descendants, like their Native American counterparts, were seen to occupy a lower rung on the evolutionary ladder, it was not necessary to treat them in a civilized manner. Racist attitudes often greeted the new European immigrants as well (Gossett 1972:292–93). During the 1890s, Jews and southern Europeans entered the United States in great numbers, encountering here hostility on the part of native-born citizens who feared that alien "races" were weakening American blood (Higham 1963:94, 110). Late nineteenth-century white supremacy received a major boost during the Spanish-American War when this country finally established an empire

40. In his book on anthropology and social theory, Robert Ulin (1984:2) states how Boas's opposition to "unilineal evolutionism within anthropological theory was paralleled by his opposition to racism and other social inequities within American society."

41. For a fascinating account of how international expositions reinforced a racial hierarchy with scientific credibility, see Rydell (1984).

over "colored" people. This was the climate in which Franz Boas worked out his ideas on art—as well as many of his thoughts on culture.

The prevailing American racialist thinking became increasingly blatant as science and racism allied themselves ever more tightly during the first decades of the twentieth century. The president of the American Museum of Natural History from 1908 to 1932, Henry Fairfield Osborn, a distinguished paleontologist, was a firm believer in the connection between race and social standing, and became an enthusiastic supporter of eugenics, the pseudoscience based on the assumption that the human race could be improved through selective breeding.

Osborn's close friend was Madison Grant, who bemoaned the negative influence on white Anglo-Saxon society of immigrants, especially the Jews. Advancing his own reading of Mendelian genetics, Grant asserted that "the cross between the three European races and a Jew is a Jew" (quoted in Higham 1963:156). Grant, president of the New York Zoological Society, in 1906 caged a Pigmy black in the primate house, presumably as an illustration of a Negro-ape on the evolutionary scale (Horowitz 1975:450). Then, in 1916, Grant published the immensely popular *The Passing of the Great Race*, which described this country's dismal fate: becoming overrun by immigrants of inferior eastern and central European races. Grant praised the tremendous virtues of "Nordic blood," and feared its assimilation by intermixture with blood of inferior races: "It must be borne in mind that the specializations which characterized the higher races are of relatively recent development, are highly unstable and when mixed with generalized or primitive characters tend to disappear. Whether we like to admit it or not, the result of the mixture of two races, in the long run, gives us race reverting to the more ancient, generalized, and lower type" (Grant 1916:17). To prevent such racial suicide, Grand proposed several remedies, including passage of expanded laws against miscegenation, sterilization of persons with "deficiencies," encouragement of greater reproduction of the fit, and "a complete change in our political structure . . . superseding our present reliance on the influence of education by a readjustment based on racial values" (Grant 1916:60).

Osborn, Grant, and others reflected the growing racism which was to become truly destructive after World War I. During the late teens and twenties, the Ku Klux Klan became powerful in both the South and the North, anti-Catholicism and anti-Semitism ran rampant, universities imposed quotas limiting the number of Jewish students, psychologists developed intelligence testing which "proved" the mental inferiority of nonwhites, and Congress passed several bills restricting immigration in order to curb the masses of darker-skinned southern and eastern European "races" flooding into the United States.

Throughout all this, Franz Boas kept challenging the scientific basis of racist theories and presenting new information to resist such ideas. Thus, the 1927 publication of *Primitive Art* was not merely an intellectual exercise meant to argue against esoteric evolutionistic art history. It also embodied an antiracist statement. By the 1920s, Boas's ideas had been disseminated in a university context, and thus were generally accepted by the profession of anthropology (in part because so many university anthropologists had been trained by Boas).[42] Yet the racist attitudes that anthropologists had managed largely to eliminate from their profession still prevailed among the American public. *Primitive Art* actually came out during some of the darkest years in the history of American race prejudice.[43] All the manifestations in American society of racialist thinking and policy that had early been reinforced by science were still prevalent, even if anthropology itself no longer supported them.

By bringing attention to the similarities among the different peoples of the world, *Primitive Art* provided data on western and nonwestern perspective techniques to support assertions of racial equality. Boas noted that a symbolic reading of an abstract motif is not limited to primitive societies, for even in our own civilization, form and color can possess a significance unrelated to the actual shape and hue. As examples, he used national flags, the Nazi swastika, and the Star of David as images that can produce extremely deep emotions by virtue of their symbolic significance rather than their subject matter (pp. 100–102). Then, after describing how members of the same ethnic group can interpret the same motif differently, Boas pointed out that to a Canadian the maple leaf can communicate patriotic feeling quite different from the response of a person who reads that leaf as symbolic of the autumn season. The crescent can symbolize to some a beautiful summer night, to others the Turkish nation; or it can simply be perceived as an elegant form (pp. 105–6). Moreover, primitive cultures are not the only ones with conservative tastes; Boas identified those manifestations of conservatism in our own culture such as localized food preferences, and male versus female attire (pp. 148–50). With such allusions to cross-cultural traits, Boas saw art as a means of forming connections among peoples rather than increasing their distance.

Boas used the preface and conclusion of *Primitive Art* to attack the core doctrine of evolutionism and the theory of ethnic inequality deducible from it. In his preface he began with the two premises that underpin his book: the identical mental processes of all humans, and the historical causation of all cultural phenomena.[44] He then asserted that "the mental processes of man are the same everywhere, regardless of race and culture, and regardless of the apparent absurdity of beliefs and customs.

42. Some of the better known of these are A. L. Kroeber, Ruth Benedict, Robert Lowie, and Margaret Mead.

43. As George Stocking has pointed out (1968:270–308, 1985:114–15), there was a brief reaction in the anthropological establishment against the antievolutionism of Boas and his students at the end of World War I. This reaction was, of course, ultimately unsuccessful.

44. This is not dissimilar to some of Tylor's ideas. See Lowie 1937.

Some theorists assume a mental equipment of primitive man distinct from that of civilized man. I have never seen a person in primitive life to whom this theory would apply" (p. 1). On the next page, Boas alludes to his own experiences with non-western cultures:

Anyone who has lived with primitive tribes, who has shared their joys and sorrows, their privations and their luxuries, who sees them not solely as subjects of study to be examined like a cell under the microscope, but feeling and thinking human beings, will agree that there is no such thing as a "primitive mind," a "magical" or "prelogical" way of thinking, but that each individual in "primitive" society is a man, a woman, a child of the same kind, of the same way of thinking, feeling and acting as man, woman, or child in our own society (p. 2).

At the end of his book, Boas extended that judgment to the highest manifestation of the human spirit. Drawing from his arguments for the complexity of the mind of primitive man as well as for the multidimensional psychological nature of the creative and aesthetic process, he asserted that primitive man has as much capability for aesthetic appreciation as civilized man. The only difference is the relative lack of a fixed style and greater artistic opportunities in western art: "I believe we may safely say that in the narrow field of art that is characteristic of each people the enjoyment of beauty is quite the same as among ourselves. . . . It is the quality [i.e., the broader scope] of the experience, not a difference in mental makeup that determines the difference between modern and primitive art production and art appreciation" (p. 356). With these words on art, Boas aligned himself with those intellectuals and scholars—many of them anthropologists like himself—increasingly drawn to ideas of social equality and the universality of our humanity. His ideas, along with those of other liberal and leftist intellectuals, would become more widely accepted as the spirit of the New Deal took hold of the United States in the 1930s.[45]

Franz Boas's research on the history of art—and I stress the word history here—began as part of his multiple-pronged attack on evolutionism. A fundamental assumption of evolutionism was that single answers to questions could be found, that a kind of universal law governed the understanding of nature and culture. Recently, such grand universalizing discourses have been discredited as significant manifestations of elitism and social, racial, and ethnic hierarchies. Particularly troublesome is the fact that these texts, written by omniscient experts who remain outside and above their product, create a timeless discourse that purports to represent authenticity and truth.[46] Although he did not use the jargon in vogue today, Boas would

45. However, as Torgovnick (1990:249) points out, Boas's progressive, egalitarian ideas need repeating in today's world.

46. See, for example, Foucault 1972 and Lyotard 1984.

have agreed with the critique of evolutionism as a metanarrative that disempowers Native people.

In keeping with the efforts of many modern scholars to question the validity of cherished truths, some writers have scrutinized the concept of "culture." Culture—meaning that which is learned within a particular community or society—was Boas's alternative to evolutionary theories to which so many late nineteenth-century anthropologists adhered. Finding unacceptable the racial foundations of evolutionism, Boas explained differences between western and nonwestern peoples as manifestations of different, yet equal, cultures, thus using anthropology to promote the concept of human equality. Moreover, for Boas, one of the most compelling deficiencies of evolutionism from a methodological perspective was its tendency to create laws prior to actually analyzing the data those laws purportedly explained; he objected strenuously to using formulae to interpret a priori ethnographic material. Boas, for both scientific and ethical reasons, rejected the imposition in anthropological research of what we in the late twentieth century would label an evolutionist grand narrative.

As is sometimes the case in the history of ideas, a liberating theory in one moment can have elements that at a later moment prove to be less liberating. Valuable as a challenge to the racism of nineteenth-century evolutionism, culture today is one of the grand universalizing definitions of humanity that some scholars have been dismantling. James Clifford was one of the first in recent years to draw attention to the fact that the concept of a unified culture is anachronistic in a multi-cultural world (1988:95).[47] Clifford points in particular to collecting artifacts as one manifestation of the search for "wholeness, continuity and essence" (1988:233).[48] The supposedly coherent, unified, static, and essentially ahistoric features that have characterized discourses on Native cultures distinguish them from the diversified, dynamic, and historical features of Euro-American societies.[49]

It must be stressed that the current criticisms of "culture" are far more applicable

47. Several Northwest Coast ethnographers, including Margaret Blackman, Frederica de Laguna, Philip Drucker, Wilson Duff, Michael Kew, and Wayne Suttles, have produced works that acknowledge acculturation and its consequences.

48. In an especially assertive critique, Virginia Dominguez (1992) insists that any discourse on culture is elitist, even when what is being described as culture is populist. As Dominguez states (pp. 34–35), "It is tempting to read the use of 'culture' to refer to nonelite circles or to large, diverse communities as an adaptation of a populist, anthropological sense of culture. But the fact is that in these situations 'cultures' are being evaluated and placed on some hierarchical scale of comparative value with an objectified European culture sitting pretty at the top. This is the elite European/Eurocentric sense of culture masking itself as populist."

49. Lila Abu-Lughod (1991) accepts the premise that the notion of culture carries with it a vehicle for separating different peoples and thus maintaining a state of hierarchy and proposes that anthropologists "pursue, without exaggerated hopes for the power of their texts to change the world, a variety of strategies for writing *against* culture" (pp. 137–38).

to the theories of the British structural/functionalists than to Boasian historical particularism. For Richard G. Fox (1991:100–104), an adequate assessment of Boas requires understanding his concepts both of culture and of culture history; elements of the latter concept provide some responses to contemporary criticisms of the former.[50] Culture history postulates that cultures are assemblages of traits, some of which were invented locally, others obtained by diffusion from elsewhere. Being the products of history, cultures are not necessarily integrated totalities; indeed, it would be erroneous to assume a priori that any cultural elements within a group are necessarily related without careful scrutiny of the data. Boasian culture history, in keeping with Boas's critique of evolutionism, eschewed the imposition of any theoretical framework on any body of data, and appears to be quite far removed from any kind of grand universalizing discourse.

Indeed, Boas's concept of culture, especially as it relates to art history, can result in liberation rather than disempowerment. One significant feature of this is the openness with which Boas's notion of culture allows for inconsistencies that ultimately allow room for multiple voices. In an ironic twist to the postmodernist attacks on the grand narrative of culture, some have criticized Boas for the apparent randomness of the information given in his publications, which prevents the reader from obtaining a unified picture of any one culture.[51] Arnold Krupat (1990, 1992) reads Boas from the perspective of the late nineteenth-century turning away in philosophy and science from absolute certainty to relativity and suggests that Boas also appears to have had, at some level, "a commitment to sustaining contradiction" (Krupat 1992:90). While Krupat expresses uncertainty as to whether Boas worked in this fashion to forestall a premature synthesis or to prevent any synthesis, he does point out that in the 1932 presidential address to the American Association for the Advancement of Science, published later as the first essay on "culture" in *Race, Language and Culture* (1940), Boas explicitly asserts that laws governing culture cannot be found. And, while Boas most often was interested in the coherent and orderly phenomena of culture, he did on occasion display a fascination with chaos, "an old-fashioned variant of postmodern free play" (Krupat 1990:144).[52]

Although Krupat, appropriately, warns against reading Boas as a precursor to postmodernism, some current intellectual trends illuminate features of Boas's art history that might in the past have been bypassed. Reading and rereading the essays

50. Fox (1991:100–101) briefly discusses Boas's art history, noting that Kroeber and Radin both thought Boas did not do enough actual history of art.

51. It is, for example, bewildering to read all of Boas's Kwakiutl materials, which offer vast amounts of information about myth, art, religion, social organization, and technology, without presenting a neatly packaged representation of Kwakiutl "culture" that can be understood as a unified whole. See also White 1963, 1966 and Goldman 1975:vii–xi.

52. In "Irony in Anthropology: The Work of Franz Boas," Krupat's principal focus is "the trope identified by the West for the expression of skepticism as a response to uncertainty" (1990:135).

reprinted in this book as well as *Primitive Art* (1927) makes it very clear that we are not dealing with a grand narrative; indeed, a major motivation in Boas's art history is to reject the false premises of evolutionism and to promote the complexities of historical and psychological processes. Boas warned against too rigid an interpretation of art as solely the product of culture that ignores the influence of history:

It has often been observed that cultural traits are exceedingly tenacious and that features of hoary antiquity survive until the present day. This has led to the impression that primitive culture is almost stable and has remained what it is for many centuries. This does not correspond to the facts. Wherever we have detailed information we see forms of objects and customs in constant flux, sometimes stable for a period, then undergoing rapid changes. Through this process elements that at one time belonged together as cultural units are torn apart. Some survive, others die, and so far as objective traits are concerned, the cultural form may become a kaleidoscopic picture of miscellaneous traits that, however, are remodelled according to the changing spiritual background that pervades the culture and transforms the mosaic into an organic whole (Boas 1927:6–7).

Although Boas ends this quote with a reference to the totality of a culture, he does give it history. At a moment in time, the elements that constitute culture might fit together nicely, but historical changes can disrupt that fit. And, in what could be considered an almost contradictory refinement to his representation of the "organic whole," later in *Primitive Art*, Boas both warns against "treating tribes too much as standardized units," pointing to the individualism inherent in both primitive and western societies (1927:84–85), and stresses that under no circumstances are "primitive forms . . . absolutely stable" (1927:150). With these words, Boas set the stage for subsequent scholars who would address the histories of continuity and change in Native American art.

A Brief Summary of Boas's Art History

A. Formal considerations
   1. Certain universals do exist: symmetry, rhythmic repetition, emphasis on form.
   2. Technique plays a major role in the development of an art style.
   3. Relative naturalism or stylization of art results from a variety of factors both technical and cultural.

B. Iconographic considerations
   1. Meaning in art is culturally determined.
   2. Groups assign meaning to images from outside groups appropriate to their culture.
   3. Meaning is sometimes universal within a group, sometimes individual.

C. Historical considerations
   1. Designs originate among one group and diffuse elsewhere.
   2. Groups borrow images appropriate to their needs.
   3. To reconstruct art history, the distribution of style and meaning—*which are independent of one another*—must be analyzed.

D. Psychological considerations
   1. Pleasure in the act of technical virtuosity is an important element in the creation of art.
   2. Conservatism and cultural conventions impose restrictions over artistic creativity and innovation.
   3. Within cultural restrictions, creativity and originality are evident among all artists.

1. Tattooing of the Haida

This brief note on Boas's presentation to the New York Academy of Sciences on Haida tattooing includes an early statement by Boas on his belief that the Kwakiutl originated some motifs which the Haida developed to the highest stage.

Stated Meeting.

The President, Dr. Newberry, in the chair.

Thirty-five persons present.

Dr. Franz Boas exhibited a number of photographs of tattooed Indians from the Queen Charlotte Islands, B.C. This people, the Haida, are the only ones in the habit of tattooing their whole bodies—wrists, arms, breast, back, legs, and feet—the designs being conventional representations of animals, the "crest" of the person on whom they are tattooed. The tattooing is done by puncture and by rubbing soot into the wounds. The patterns are exactly analogous to the paintings and carvings of those people. Tattooing is not unknown to the neighboring tribes, but chiefly confined to marks on the wrists and eventually on the ankles. Such designs are found, for instance, among the Tsimshian. Tattooing on the arm and breast is also found among the Nutkas [Nuu-chah-nulth] of the west coast of Vancouver Island, but in this case it is connected with religious practices, not with the social organization—the totems of the people—as it is among the Haidas. A photograph of a Nutka was exhibited, showing a human figure on the breast. The same individual had long, parallel cuts running from the collarbone down to the belly, and from the shoulders all along the arms. These wounds are inflicted at the initiation of the young man into a secret society and are called "Tlo-koala," a word borrowed from the Kwakiutl language.

Besides these photographs of tattooed men, others illustrating a few types of Indians were shown, and attention was called to the broadness of their faces, the light color of their skins, and the shortness of their heads. Deformed heads are found only as far north as Milbank Sound and Gardner Channel. A few photographs of excessively deformed heads from the north point of Vancouver Island showed the effects of bandaging, which results in a great elongation of the occipital part of the head.

Replying to a question of the chairman, Dr. Boas stated that the style of art of the northern Tlingit, the Haida, Kwakiutl, Nutka, and Salish can be easily distinguished. He believes that certain designs originated among the Kwakiutl, but

Reprinted from *Transactions*, New York Academy of Sciences, pp. 115–16, 1889.

reached their highest stage of development among the Haidas. The Salish have some peculiarities not shared by any of the other tribes.

The President referred to his own observations on the carvings among some twenty tribes of that region, and to the artistic skill displayed by those along the coast, whose work bears a decided resemblance to that of the races of Central America—possibly indicating a genetic relationship—and contrasts strongly with the inferior skill in carving shown by the inland tribes of our Northwestern territory.

2. The Use of Masks and Head Ornaments on the Northwest Coast of America

Boas first briefly discusses the difficulty of obtaining information on the meaning of Northwest Coast art. Then he categorizes three types of masks: the helmets found in the north (among the Tlingit), masks attached to housefronts and totem poles, and dancing masks. Two classes of dancing masks of the Bella Coola and the Kwakiutl are those worn at potlatches and those worn during the winter ceremonials. The remainder of the essay is a description of the winter ceremonies of the Kwakiutl with references to some of the paraphernalia worn by participants.

This essay represents a preview of Boas's 1897 "Social Organization and the Secret Societies of the Kwakiutl Indians" and his 1898 "Mythology of the Bella Coola Indians." In those later publications, he used somewhat different linguistic notations from those he uses here.

Our museums contain large collections of masks from the Northwest Coast of America, but it is only occasionally that the descriptions and catalogues give information as to their use and meaning. On my first visit to British Columbia, in 1886, I paid special attention to this subject. A considerable collection of drawings and photographs of masks, which I carried with me, did not help me materially in my investigations. I frequently showed the drawings to Indians whom I expected to be conversant with everything referring to this subject, but it was only in rare cases that they recognized the masks and were able to give any information as to their use and meaning. Very soon I arrived at the conclusion that, except in a few instances, the masks were no conventional types representing certain ideas known to the whole people, but were either inventions of the individuals who used them, or that the knowledge of their meaning was confined to a limited number of persons. The former hypothesis did not seem probable, as the same types of masks are found in numerous specimens and in collections made at different times and by different persons. Among the types which are comparatively frequently found, I mention the Tsonō'k˙oa[1] of the Kwakiutl, . . . the crane, eagle, and raven.

Further inquiries showed that the probability of ascertaining the meaning of a mask increased when the particular village was visited in which the specimen was

Reprinted from *Internationales Archiv für Ethnographie*, vol. 3, pp. 7–15, 1890.

1. *k˙* a guttural *k*, almost *kr*. *q* the German ch in Bach. *sl* an exploded *l*. [Boas's 1890 transcriptions were not always accurate. By 1898 he had improved and had adopted different values for some symbols (Suttles, pers. com.)—Ed.]

collected. It was thus that I ascertained the meaning of the double mask figured in Woldt's "Cpt. Jacobsen's Reise an der Nordwestküste Amerikas" [Jacobsen 1884:129]. The outer face represents a deer; the inner, a human face. It refers to the tradition of the origin of the deer, which originally was a man, but was transformed, on account of his intention to kill the son of the deity, into its present shape. At last I found that the use of masks is closely connected with two institutions of these tribes—with their clans or gentes, and with their secret societies. The latter class of masks is confined to the Kwakiutl, Nutka, and Tsimshian, and I believe that they originated with the first-named people. The meaning of each mask is not known outside the gens or society to which it belongs. [Boas uses "gens" or "clan" here for what he later calls "numaym" (see Suttles 1991).]

This fact makes the study one of great difficulty. It is only by chance that a specimen belonging to one of our collections can be identified, as only in rare exceptions the place where it was purchased is clearly stated. The majority of specimens are purchased in Victoria, where they are collected by traders, who, of course, keep no record of their origin.

Besides this, the Indians are in the habit of trading masks, and copying certain models which strike their fancy from neighboring tribes. The meaning of these specimens is, of course, not known to the people who use it, and it is necessary to study first the source from which such carvings were derived. Thus the beautiful raven rattles of the Tsimshian are frequently imitated by the Kwakiutl, and the beautifully woven Chilcat blankets are used as far south as Comox. The carved headdresses of the Tsimshian, the Amhalai't (used in dances), with their attachment of ermine skins, are even used by the natives of Victoria.

My inquiries cover the whole coast of British Columbia. In the extreme northern part of this region a peculiar kind of mask, which has been so well described by Krause [1885], is used as a helmet. I do not think that this custom extends very far south. Setting this aside, we may distinguish two kinds of masks: dancing masks and masks attached to housefronts and heraldic columns.

The latter are especially used by tribes of Kwakiutl lineage and by the Bilqula [Bella Coola]. All masks of this kind are clan masks, having reference to the crest of the house owner or post owner. They are generally made of cedarwood and from three to five feet high. One of the most beautiful specimens I have seen is a mask of the sun, forming the top of an heraldic column in Alert Bay, Vancouver Island. It belongs to the chief of the gens Sī'sentlē of the Nimkish tribe. The latter is the second in rank among the tribes of the Kwakiutl group, which form one of the subdivisions of the linguistic stock of the same name. The clan claims to be descended from the sun, who assumed the shape of a bird, and came down from heaven. He was transformed into a man, and settled in the territory of the Nimkish tribe. The name of this mask is Tlēselak˙ umtl (sun mask, from *tlē'sela*, sun; *ik˙ umtl*, mask). It has a bird's face, and is surrounded by rays. Certain clans of the Bilqula have the mythical Masmasalā'niq, covered by an immense hat, on the tops of their housefronts; but the use of masks for this purpose is, on the whole, not very extensive.

In order to understand their meaning and use, it is necessary to investigate very thoroughly the social organization of each tribe, and to study these masks in connection with the carvings represented on the posts and beams of the houses and with the paintings found on the housefronts. Thus the Kwakiutl proper are the highest in rank among the group to which the Nimkish belong. They are divided into four groups, which rank as follows: first, the Kue'tela; next the K''o'moyue or Kue'qa (the latter being their war name); then the Lo'kuilila; and finally the Walaskwakiutl. Each of these is divided into a number of clans, some of which, however, belong to two or three of these divisions. I shall mention here the divisions of the Kue'tela only, again arranged according to rank, and shall add their principal carvings.

1. The noblest clan is that of Matakila. Their chief wears a mask representing the gull, and they use also masks of animals representing the food of the gull. Their beams are not carved.

2. Kwokwa'k˙um. The posts supporting the beams of the house represent the grizzly bear, on top of which a crane is sitting. Their mask represents the crane.

3. Gye'qsem. Their post represents a crane standing on a man's head.

4. La'alaqs'end'aio, who are the servants of the Kwokwa'k˙um. Their post is a killer (*Delphinus orca*) with a man's body.

5. Si'sintlē (the same clan as that of the Nimkish). Their carving is the sun. Besides this, they use a dog's mask, representing the dog which accompanied the sun when he was transformed into a man, the Tsonō'k˙oa, and several other carvings.

Each clan has a number of secondary carvings which have reference to the traditions relating the adventures of its ancestor.

As will be seen from this list, the emblems are also used as dancing masks. The use of masks for this purpose is spread all over the coast, being found among the Tlingit as well as among the tribes near Victoria; but among the latter very few types of masks are used, and it is the privilege of certain tribes and clans to wear them. . . . a number of these masks are illustrated. Before discussing their meaning, I have to say a few words as to the use of dancing masks.

We may distinguish two classes of dancing masks—those peculiar to the several clans and those belonging to secret societies.

The former are of two different kinds—masks used at the potlatch (the festival at which property is given away), and masks used for the mimical performances in winter, when dances representing the traditions of the clans are acted. Masks must not be used in summer and during daylight, except the potlatch masks. The latter are worn by chiefs in the dance opening this festival. After the guests have arrived, the chief who gives the festival opens the ceremonies by a long dance, in which he wears the principal mask of his gens. Thus the chief of the gens Sī'sintlē of the Kwakiutl uses the sun or the Tsonō'k˙oa. . . . Other masks of this kind represent the ancestor of the clan. Thus I found a mask representing Nomas (= the old one [fig. 1]), the brother of the raven, used by the chief of a clan of the Tlauitsis, of which he is the ancestor. A few gentes do not always use masks at such occasions, but have large posts representing the ancestor, which are hollowed out from behind. The mouth of such a post forms a speaking tube, through which the chief addresses the assembly, thus acting the part of his ancestor.

By far the most interesting masks are those used in the winter dances. The Kwakiutl and all the neighboring tribes which belong to the same ethnological group have two different kinds of winter dances—one called Yā'wiqa by the Kwakiutl, Nō'ntlem by the Tlatlasik˙oala, Tlōola'qa by the Wik'ē'nok, and Sisau'kh by the Bilqula; the other called Tsā'ek˙a, Tsē'tsa'ek˙a, or Tlōk˙oa'la, and Kū'siut by the same separate tribes. The former dance takes place during the month of November among the southern tribes, early in October among the Bilqula. The latter is danced from December to February by the Kwakiutl, and from November to January by the Bilqula.

The masks [illustrated] are used in the dance Sisau'kh of the Bilqula. Figs. 2 and 3 represent the mythical K˙ōmō'k˙oa and his wife. K˙ōmō'k˙oa is a sea monster, the father and master of the seals, who takes those who have capsized in their canoes to the bottom of the sea. This being plays a very important part in the legends of many clans, marrying a daughter of the ancestor, or lending him his powerful help. I believe these legends originally belonged to the Kwakiutl, and have been borrowed by the Bilqula. The name K˙ōmō'k˙oa is undoubtedly of Kwakiutl origin; it has also been borrowed by the Çatlō'ltq [Comox tribe], the southern neighbors of the Kwakiutl. The masks are used in several mimical performances.

Figs. 4 and 5 belong together. They belong to a clan in whose history K˙ōmō'k˙oa plays an important part. K˙ōmō'k˙oa had married a girl, and the adventures of their son are acted in the dance. The young man (Fig. 4) calls the eagle (Fig. 5) and asks him to carry him all over the world. The eagle complies with his requests, and on returning the young man tells his experiences, how he had visited all countries and peoples and found them not to be real men, but half human, half animal. This latter idea is widely spread among the inhabitants of the Northwest Coast.

The next figure (6) is the mythical Masmasalā'niq. . . . The special mask represented here is used in a dance in which Masmasalā'niq appears in his house, at the entrance of which stands his messenger, Atlqulā'tenum, who calls, and announces the arrival of the various dancers, the Thunderbird, the Snēnē'ik˙ (the Tsōnōk˙'oa of the Bilqula), and others. Unfortunately I was unable to obtain this mask. It represents a human face, covered with parallel stripes which run from the upper left

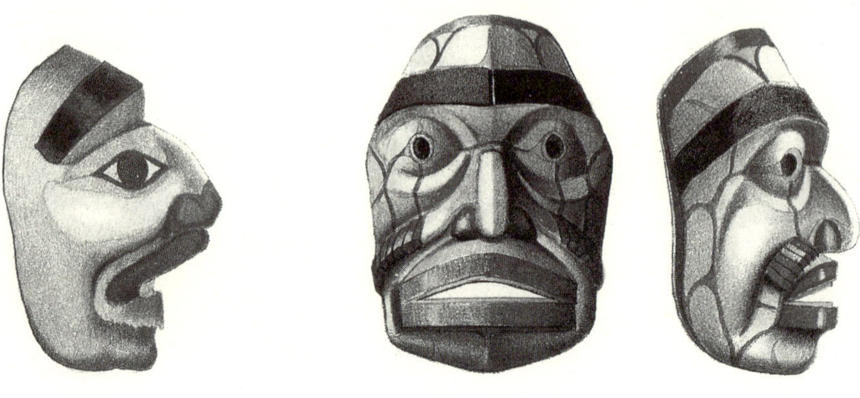

FIG. 1. Kwakiutl mask representing brother of the raven

FIG. 2. Bella Coola mask of sea monster

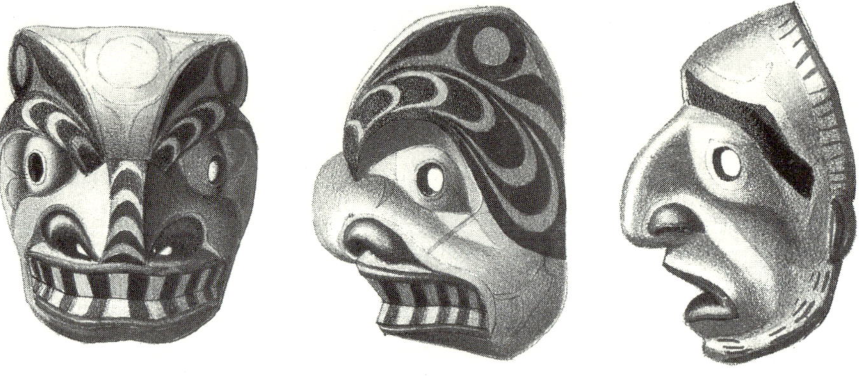

FIG. 3. Bella Coola mask of wife of sea monster

FIG. 4. Bella Coola mask of young man

side to the lower right side of the face, and are alternately red and blue. He carries a baton painted in the same way.

Fig. 7 is probably not used in the Sis'au'kh, but belongs to the potlatch. It is a head ornament in the shape of the killer (*Delphinus orca*). Only the head, the tail, and the fins are represented. I was told that the idea of the headdress is to represent this whale as a canoe, the red horns being the paddles. Although this idea corresponds to some extent to the myths of the neighboring tribes, I doubt the correctness of this explanation. The horns, it will be seen, form a crown similar to the crowns of copper horns and mountain-goat horns used by the Tsimshian and Haida; and I believe our specimen is an imitation of the latter.

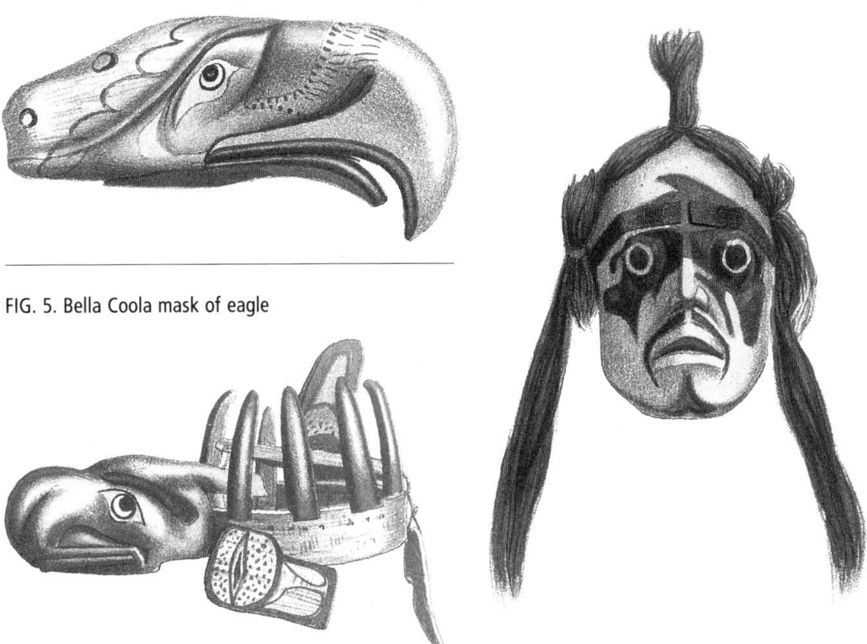

FIG. 5. Bella Coola mask of eagle

FIG. 7. Bella Coola headdress in shape of killer whale

FIG. 6. Bella Coola mask of mythic being

Although the last three figures are rather poor specimens of carving and painting, they nevertheless command considerable interest. The round mask (Fig. 8) represents the spirit Anulikū'ts'ai, and is used in the dance opening the Sisau'kh. Three spirits—Atlmoktoai'ts, Nōnōsēkne'n, and Anulikū'ts'ai—are said to live in the woods. Through their help men acquire the art of dancing, and whosoever wishes to become a good dancer invokes Atlmoktoai'ts to help him. It is said that they live in a subterranean lodge dug out by Nonosekne'n. From February until October they stay in this house, but then they leave it and approach the villages. As soon as they, and more especially Anulikū'ts'ai, appear, the dance Sisau'kh begins. Their appearance is the subject of the first mimical performance of the dancing season. A man wearing his mask waits outside the houses, and asks everybody whom he encounters why he does not dance, and through his presence instigates him to dress up and make his appearance at the great dance which is celebrated at night.

Fig. 9 represents the half moon. The mask is used in a dance together with the new and full moons. The mask is worn by a woman, and the being she represents is named Aiahilako.

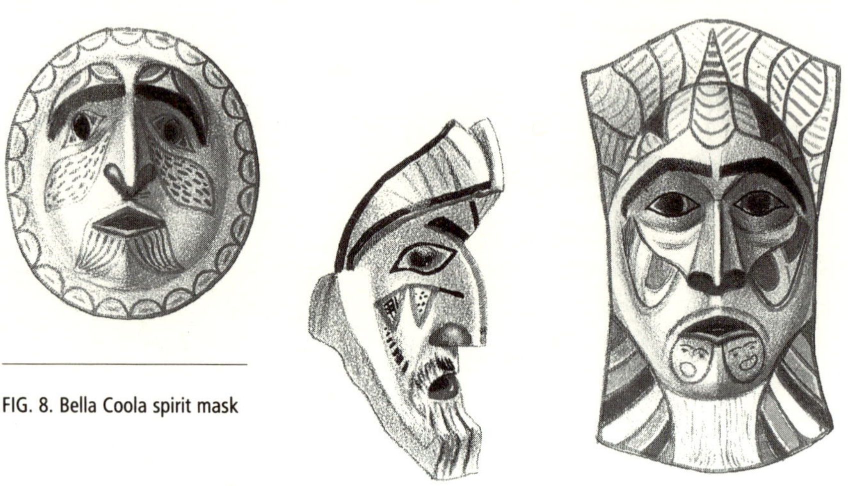

FIG. 8. Bella Coola spirit mask

FIG. 9. Bella Coola half-moon mask

FIG. 10. Bella Coola mask in shape of a copper

Fig. 10 has the shape of the well-known copper plates which are so highly valued on the Northwest Coast. Its name is Tlā'lia (copper plate). The legend to which this mask refers says that a man went into a distant country to search for a wife. At last he met Tlā'lia, the mistress of the copper plates. He married her, and it was thus that they first came to be known to the Bilqula.

I said above that this dance of the Bilqula corresponds to the Nō'ntlem of the Tlatlasik' oala. The double mask figured on page 129 of Woldt's book [Jacobsen 1884] belongs to this dance. In the village Qumta'spē, which is commonly called and spelled Newetti by English traders, I collected a whole set of such masks, representing the "feast of the raven." This collection has been deposited in the Royal Ethnological Museum at Berlin. The central figure is the raven, to whose face two movable wings are attached. The other figures represent animals which took part in the feast. The first part of the dance represents the raven catching the salmon, which is later on fried. The animals are invited to partake in the meal, and the events of this feast are represented in the dance. It was on that occasion that they received their present form, while before they had been half-human beings.

At the end of the Nō'ntlem season the Tsa'eka begins. During this season the whole tribe is divided into a number of groups, which form secret societies. Among the Kwakiutl I observed seven groups, the principal of which is called the Me'emk˙oat. To this group belong the Ha'mats'a, the crane, the Ha maa, grizzly bear, and the Nū'tlematl. The first, second, and third of these are the "man-eaters." The other groups are the following:

2. K·ōk·oski'mo, who are formed by the old men.
3. Māa'mq'enok· (the killers), who are formed by the young men.
4. Mō'smōs (the dams), the married women.
5. K·ā'kiao (the partridges), the unmarried girls.
6. Hē'melk· (those who eat continually), the old chiefs.
7. K·ēki'qalak· (the jackdaw), the children.

Every one of these groups has its separate feast, in which no member of another group is allowed to partake; but before beginning their feast they must send a dish of food to the Hāmats'a. At the opening of the feast the chief of the group—for instance, of the K·ā'kiao—will say, "The partridges always have something nice to eat," and then all peep like partridges. All these groups try to offend the Mē'emk· oat, and every one of these has some particular object by which he is offended. The grizzly bear must not be shown any red color, his preference being black. The Nū'tlematl and crane do not like to hear a nose mentioned, as theirs are very long. Sometimes the former try to induce men to mention their noses, and then they burn and smash whatever they can lay their hands on. For example: a Nū'tlematl blackens his nose. Then the people will say, "Oh, your head is black!" but if somebody should happen to say, "What is the matter with your nose?" he would take offense. Sometimes they cut off the "noses" of canoes because of their name. The Nū'tlematl must be as filthy as possible.

Sometimes a chief will give a feast to which he invites all these groups. Then nobody is allowed to eat before the Hā'mats'a has had his share and if he should decline to accept the food offered to him, the feast must not take place. After he has once bitten men, he is not allowed to take part in feasts.

The chief's wife must make a brief speech before the meal is served. She has to say, "I thank you for coming. Be merry and eat and drink." If she should make a mistake by deviating from the formula, she has to give another feast.

The first of these classes, the Me'emk·oat, are a real nest of secret societies. I failed to gain a full understanding of this subject, which offers one of the most interesting but at the same time most difficult problems of Northwest American ethnology. I am particularly in doubt as to in how far the secret societies are independent of the clans. It seems to me, from what I was able to learn, that the crests of the clans and the insignia of the secret societies are acquired in the same way. They are obtained by marriage. If a man wants to obtain a certain carving or the membership of a secret society, he must marry the daughter of a man who is in possession of this carving or is a member of the secret society; but this can be done only by consent of the whole tribe, who must declare the candidate worthy of becoming a member of this society or of acquiring that crest. In the same way the chieftaincy of one of these societies devolves upon the husband of the chief's daughter. If the chief of a certain clan or of a secret society has no daughter, a sham marriage is celebrated between the chief's son and the future chief. But in some instances, the daughter or son succeeds immediately the father.

The ceremonies are as follows. When it has been decided that a man is worthy of acquiring a crest, he sends messengers to his intended wife's father to ask his permission to marry the girl. If the father consents, he demands fifty blankets, or more, according to his rank, to be paid at once, and double the amount to be paid three months later. After these two payments have been made, the young man is allowed to live with his wife in his parents-in-law's house. There he must live three months, and, after having paid a hundred blankets more, is allowed to take his wife to his home. Sometimes the girl's father receives as much as five hundred blankets in the course of time.

When the young man comes to live in his father-in-law's house, the latter returns the fifty blankets which formed the first installment of the payment for the girl. At this time the young man gives a feast (without giving away blankets), and on this occasion the old man states at what time he intends to return the rest of the payment. During this feast the young man rises, and in a long speech asks his wife's father to give him his crest (carvings) and name. The father must comply with this request, and announces when he is going to transfer his rank and dignity. This is done at a great festival. I am not quite sure whether the whole tribe, or the clan alone, takes part in it. The father-in-law takes his copper and formally makes it over, together with his name and carving, to the young man who presents the guests with blankets.

These facts are derived from information which I obtained in Oumta'spē (Newetti), Fort Rupert, and Alert Bay, and from a thorough study of the traditions of these tribes, in which the membership of secret societies and carvings are always obtained by marriage. Notwithstanding this, the man who is thus entitled to become a member of the secret society must be initiated.

The members of these societies, when performing their dances, are characterized by headdresses and certain styles of painting, some of which are represented in Figures 11–20, as I found them used by the Tlatlasik˙oa'la.

The most important among them is the Hā'mats'a [derived from *ham*, "to eat"]. I have described his initiation in the first number of the "Journal of American Folk-Lore" [Boas 1888c:58], and shall confine myself here to a brief description of his attire. The new Hā'mats'a dances four nights—twice with rings of hemlock branches, twice with rings of cedar bark which has been dyed red. Strips of cedar bark are tied into his hair, which is covered with eagle down. His face is painted black. He wears three neck rings [head rings] of cedar bark arranged as shown in Figs. 11–13, and each of a separate design. Strips of cedar bark are tied around his wrists and ankles. He dances in a squatting position, his arms extended to one side,

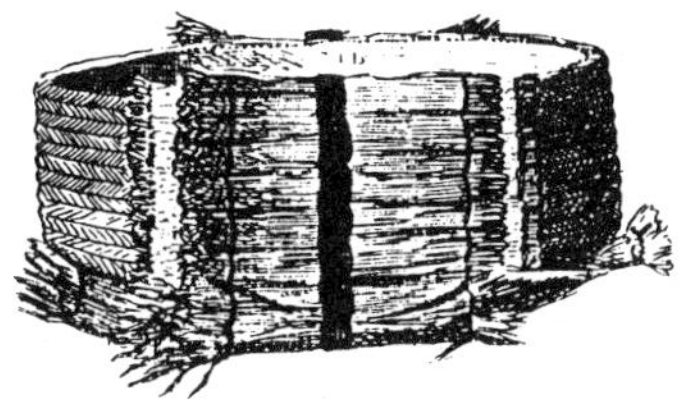

FIG. 11. Kwakiutl head ring for Hā'mats'a

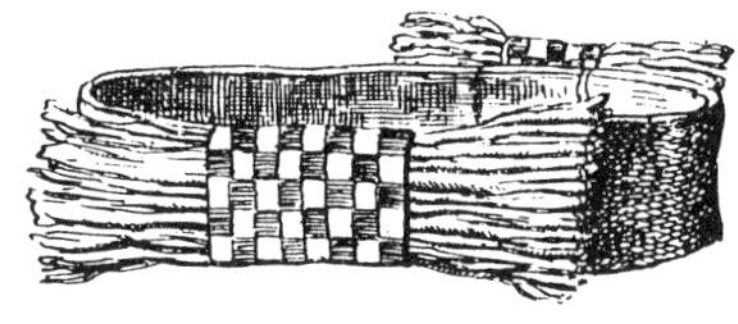

FIG. 12. Kwakiutl head ring for Hā'mats'a

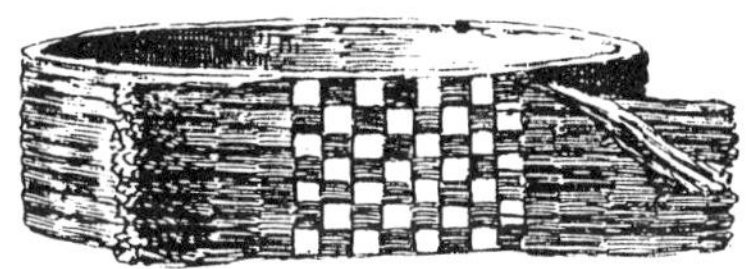

FIG. 13. Kwakiutl head ring for Hā'mats'a

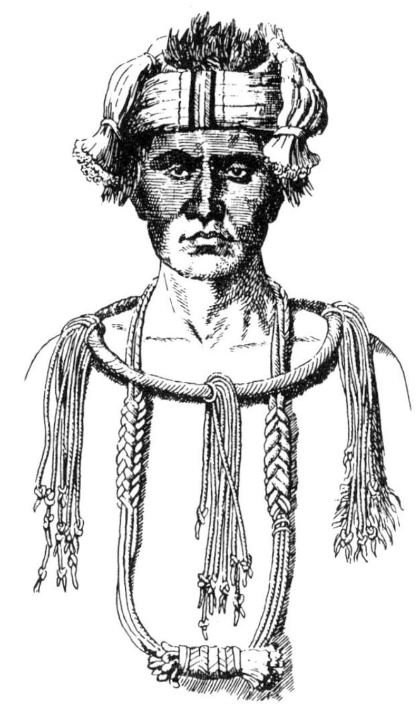

FIG. 14. Kwakiutl attire for Mā'mak'ʼa

as though he were carrying a corpse. His hands are trembling continually. First he extends his arms to the left, then he jumps to the right, at the same time moving his arms to the right. His eyes are staring, and his lips protruding voluptuously. The new Ha'mats'a is not allowed to have intercourse with anybody, but must stay for a whole year in his rooms. He must not work until the end of the following dancing season. The Hā'mats'a must use a kettle, dish, and spoon of their own for four months after the dancing season is at an end; then these are thrown away, and they are allowed to eat with the rest of the tribe. During the time of the winter dance, a pole called *ha'mspiq* is erected in the house where the Hā'mats'a lives. It is wound with red cedar bark, and made so that it can be made to turn round. Over the entrance of the house a ring of red cedar bark is fastened, to warn off those who do not belong to the secret society. The same is done by the other secret societies, each using its peculiar ornament.

Another society is called Mā'mak'ʼa. The initiation of a new member is exactly like that of the Hā'mats'a. The man or woman who is to become Mā'mak·'a disappears in the woods, and stays for several months with Mā'mak·'a, the spirit of this group, who gives him a magic staff and a small mask. The staff is made of a wooden tube and a stick that fits into it, the whole being covered with cloth. In dancing, the Mā'mak·'a carries this staff between the palms of his hands, which he presses against each other, moving his arms at the same time up and down like a swimmer. Then he opens his hands, separating the palms, and the stick is seen to grow and to decrease in size. When it is time for the new Mā'mak·'a to return from the woods, the inhabitants of the village go to search for him. They sit down in a square somewhere in the woods, and sing four new songs. Then the new Mā'mak·'a appears, adorned with hemlock branches. While the Hā'mats'a is given ten companions, the Mā'mak·'a has none. The same night he dances for the first time. If he does not like one of the songs, he shakes his staff, and immediately the spectators cover their heads with their blankets. Then he whirls his staff, which strikes one of the spectators, who at once begins to bleed profusely. Then Mā'mak·'a is reconciled by a new song, and he pulls out his staff from the stricken man's body. He must pay the latter two blankets for this performance, which, of course, is agreed upon beforehand. The attire of the Mā'mak·'a is shown in Fig. 14. His face is painted black, except the chin and the upper lip.

The Olala (Fig. 15) is another member of this group. The braid on the right side of his head is made of red cedar bark. He also wears a neck ring, and strips of bark tied around his wrists and ankles. This figure is particularly remarkable, as the Tsimshian designate by this name the Hā'mats'a. Undoubtedly the Olala was acquired by them through intermarriage with the Hēiltsuk (erroneously called Bella Bella). They call the Olala also Wihalai't (= the great dance).

The Lâ lenoq represents the ghost. He wears black eagle feathers (Fig. 16) in a ring of white cedar bark, to which fringes are attached which cover his face. He wears shirt and blanket, and a plain neck ring made of red cedar bark, . . . without any attachments. He carries a rattle (Fig. 17), which represents an eagle and is about a foot long. He does not dance, but lies down, only shaking his rattle.

The Sī'lic (Fig. 18) when dancing carries a long tube of softened kelp, closed at one side by a piece of wood, in his mouth. Suddenly he begins to blow it up, and the tube begins to grow out of his mouth, representing a snake.

The Ts'ē'k·ois (Fig. 19) carries a great number of small whistles imitating the voices of birds. The Tlē'qalaq is represented in Fig. 20. He wears a raven headdress, and his genius is the spirit Wi'nalakilis. The latter lives on the sea, continually traveling in a boat. If a man happens to see him, he falls sick. Wā'tanum, another figure of these dances, wears a beard of red cedar bark, rising from the middle part of his forehead. His face is painted all black.

All these figures belong to the Mē'emk·oat, every one representing a class pro-

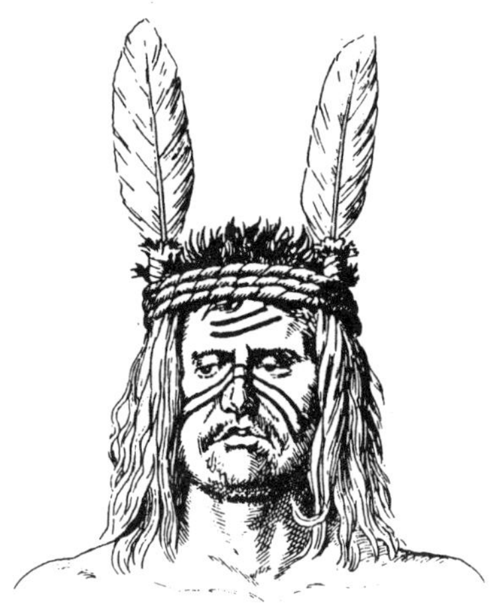

FIG. 15. Kwakiutl attire for Olala

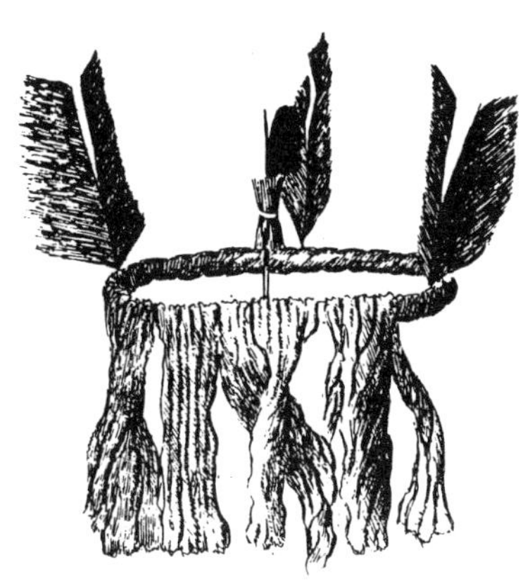

FIG. 16. Kwakiutl attire for ghost dancer

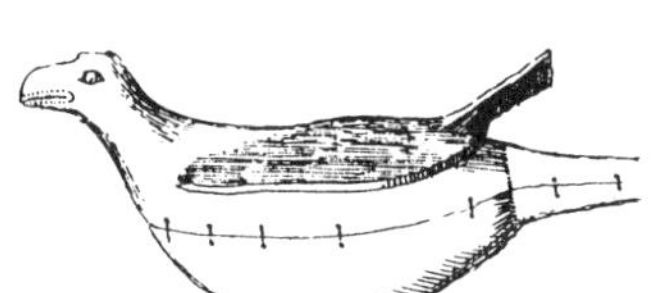

FIG. 17. Kwakiutl ghost dancer rattle

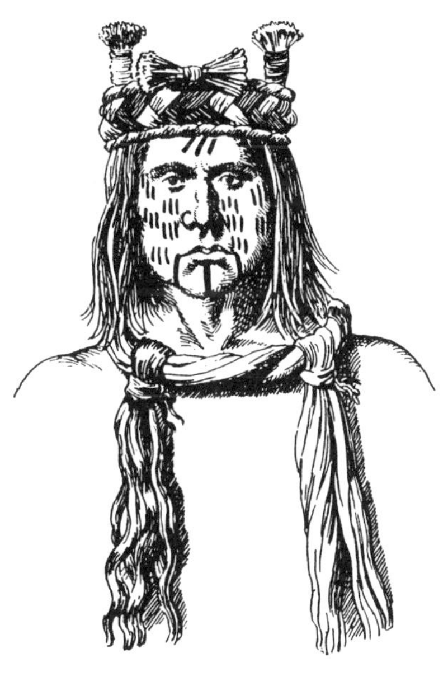

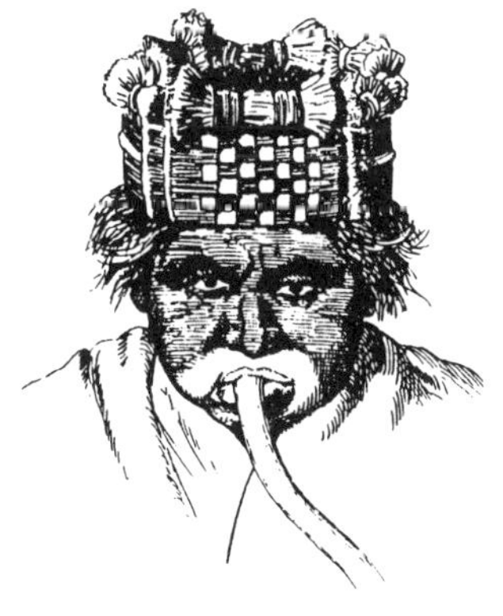

FIG. 18. Kwakiutl attire for Sī'lic

FIG. 19. Kwakiutl attire for Ts'ē'k'ois

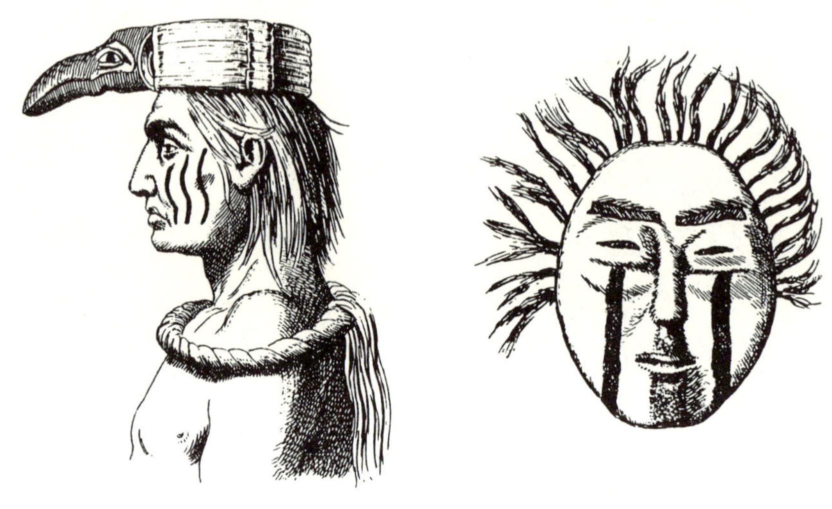

FIG. 20. Kwakiutl attire for Tlē'qalaq

FIG. 21. Kwakiutl Nō'ntlemkyila mask

tected by a certain spirit. As the meaning of these dances is kept secret by the societies, it is extremely difficult to obtain any information as to their significance. Each figure has a song peculiar to itself; but these songs, of which I obtained a considerable number, do not convey any information, as they are nothing but boastful announcements of the power and renown of each figure.

I indicated above that each of these figures has a peculiar way of dancing. A description of one of these dances may be of interest. Unfortunately I did not see it myself, but the information was obtained from a native whom I have reason to consider trustworthy. He said:

"During the dance Tsā'ek˙a whistles Ts'ē'koityala, which makes those who hear its sound happy, and Tliqiqs are frequently used. When the dance Tō'quit is to be performed, these whistles are heard in the woods and in the dancing house. A curtain is put up near the fire, separating a small room from the main hall, and in the evening all assemble to witness the dance. Several dancers hide behind the curtain, while others beat time with heavy sticks on the roof and on the walls of the house. During this time the whistles are silent; but as soon as the men on the roof stop beating time, the whistles are heard again. Now the audience begin beating time with sticks, at the same time singing, 'A! Ai! ai! ai! aia aia!' the tone being drawn down from a high key, down through an octave. Then four women make their appearance, their hair combed so as to entirely hide their faces. They go around the fire, and disappear behind the curtain. After four songs are sung, the chief declares that they have disappeared in the woods.

"The following day everybody—men, women, and children—is invited by one man or another, and they dance with masks. The next morning all go into the woods to look for the four women. They sing four new songs, and then the women make their appearance. They have become the Mā'mak''a, Kō'minok's, Hā'mats'a, and Tō'quit. The latter moves only very little when dancing. She holds her elbows pressed firmly against her sides. The palms of her hands are turned upward, and she moves them a little upward and downward. She sings, 'Ya, ya, ya!' and wears a necklet of hemlock branches. The four women next go home, accompanied by the crowd. When Tō'quit enters the house, the audience beat time with a rapid movement. She begins to dance; and when, after a short time, she cries, 'Whip, whip, whip' the people stop singing and beating time. Four times she runs tripping around the fire, forward and backward, holding her hands as described above. Then she turns around, and moves her arms in the same way as Mā'mak''a (see p. 50). Three times she opens her hands, trying to obtain her whistle from her spirit, but she does not succeed until the fourth time. She whirls the whistle against the people, who immediately stoop and cover their heads with their blankets, continuing to beat time. After a short time they uncover their faces to see what Tō'quit has been doing. It is supposed that meanwhile her genius is with her, and as a sign of his presence she holds a huge fish in her hands. She then takes up a knife and cuts it in two. Immediately it is transformed into Ci'tlem, the chief of the double-headed snakes. It grows rapidly in length, moves along the floor, climbs the posts of the house, and finally disappears on the beams.

"Now the audience begin once more to beat time, covering their faces. On looking up, they see Nō'ntlemkyila by the side of the Tō'quit, dancing and whistling. Suddenly a gull alights on his head, and soon rises again, carrying his head."

A few specimens of the Nō'ntlemkyila are in the collection at Berlin, and one more I have seen in Washington. It is a small wooden figure, rudely carved, with moveable arms and legs. The figure is perfectly flat, being shown only in front view. The head is a flat disk (fig. 21), fastened by means of a pin to the body. The eyes are narrow, and two broad lines made of mica run vertically downward below the eyes. The hair is made of bushels of human hair. Numerous mechanical devices of this kind, moved by invisible strings, are used in the winter dances.

The winter dance is concluded by the Tsā'ek'amtl (= Tsā'ek'amask). This concluding ceremony I found in use as well among the Wik'ē'nok' as among the Tlatlasik'oala and Kwakiutl. The first call it Ha'stemitl; the last Haialikyauae. When the time of this dance approaches, the Wik'ē'nok' erect a large scaffold in the middle part of the rear wall of the house, on which Ha'stemitl is danced by a chief's daughter. The scaffold is built by four chiefs. Its posts are tied together with red and white cedar bark. A shaman stands in the door of the house, his duty being to announce the arrival of the dancer. Another sits in the left rear corner on the platform of the house, playing the drum. Two more stand to the right and left of the scaffold, and move their hands slowly toward the dancer. When the dancer enters the house, the spectators must cover their heads with their blankets. Whoever does not obey this law must pay her a certain number of blankets. The spectators sit in the front part of the house, and accompany her dance with songs and beating time. The scaffold is destroyed after Ha'stemitl has danced four nights. This is the end of the winter dances; and neither the Hā'mats'a nor the Nū'tlematl, the Mā'mak''a, nor any of the other figures are allowed to continue their practices, their privileges only reviving at the beginning of the following dancing season.

3. The Decorative Art of the Indians of the North Pacific Coast

Boas points out that although many images in the art of the Northwest Coast Indians do represent totems, some depict animals selected for reasons other than totemic meaning. Sometimes the animal depicted is obviously associated with the use of the object upon which its image appears, and sometimes there is a functional connection that is indirect or symbolic. The actual shape of the object may also have suggested an animal image to the artist. Boas is in this piece intent upon conveying the point that a single explanation for animal imagery, in this case totemism, is inadequate, for the Northwest Coast artist was motivated by several factors.

It is well known that the native tribes of the North Pacific coast of America ornament their implements with conventionalized representations of animals. The tribes of this region are divided in clans which have animal totems, and it is generally assumed that the carvings represent the totem of the owner of the implement. This view is apparently sustained by the extensive use of the totem as a crest. It is represented on "totem poles" or heraldic columns, on the fronts of houses, on canoes, on the handles of spoons, and on a variety of objects.

It can be shown, however, that by no means all the carvings made by the natives of this region have this meaning. A collection of data made in a number of museums show that certain objects are preferably ornamented with representations of certain animals, and in many cases an intimate connection exists between the use to which the object is put and its design.

This is very evident in the case of the fish club, which is used for dispatching halibut and other fish before they are hauled into the canoe. Almost all the clubs that I have seen represent the sea lion or the killer whale, the two sea animals which are most feared by the Indians, and which kill those animals that are to be killed by means of the club. The idea of giving the club the design of the sea lion or killer whale is therefore rather to give it a form appropriate to its function and perhaps secondarily to give it by means of its form great efficiency. This view is corroborated by the following incident which occurs in several tales: A person throws his fish club overboard and it swims away and kills seals and other sea animals, cuts the ice and performs other feats taking the shape of a sea lion or of a killer whale. Here also belongs the belief recorded by Alexander Mackenzie [1891:51]: "The Haida firmly

Reprinted from *Science*, vol. 4, pp. 101–3, 1896.

believe, if overtaken by night at sea and reduced to sleep in their canoes, that by allowing such a club to float beside the canoe attached to a line it has the property of scaring away whales and other monsters of the deep which might otherwise harm them."

Here is another instance in which I find a close relation between the function of the object and its design. Small grease dishes have almost invariably the shape of the seal or sometimes that of the sea lion, that is, of those animals which furnish a vast amount of blubber. Grease of sea animals is considered as the sign of wealth. In many tales abundance of food is described by saying that the sea near the houses was covered with the grease of seal, sea lion, and whales. Thus the form of the seal seems to symbolize affluence.

Other grease dishes and food dishes have the form of canoes, and here I believe a similar idea has given rise to the form. The canoe symbolizes that a canoe load of food is presented to the guests, and that this view is probably correct is indicated by the fact that in his speeches the host often refers to the canoe filled with food which he gives to his guests. The canoe form is often modified, and a whole series of types can be established forming the transition between canoe dishes and ordinary trays. Dishes of this sort always bear a conventionalized face at each short end, while the middle part is not decorated. This is analogous to the style of the decoration of the canoe. The design represents almost always the hawk. I am not certain what has given origin to the prevalence of this design. On the whole the decoration of the canoe is totemistic. It may be that it is only the peculiar manner in which the beak of the hawk is represented which has given rise to the prevalence of this decoration. The upper jaw of the hawk is always shown so that its point reaches the lower jaw and turns back into the mouth. When painted or carved in front view the beak is indicated by a narrow wedge-shaped strip in the middle of the face, the point of which touches the lower margin of the chin. The sharp bow and stern of a canoe with a profile of a face on each side, when represented on a level or slightly rounded surface, would assume the same shape. Therefore, it may be that originally the middle line was not the beak of the hawk, but the foreshortened bow or stern of the canoe. This decoration is so uniform that the explanation given here seems to me very probable.

On halibut hooks we find very often decorations representing the squid. The reason for selecting this motive must be looked for in the fact that the squid is used for baiting the hooks.

I am not quite certain if the decoration of armor and weapons is totemistic or symbolic. Remarkably many helmets represent the sea lion, many daggers the bear, eagle, wolf, and raven, while I have not seen one that represents the killer whale, although it is one of the ornaments that are most frequently shown on totemistic designs.

I presume this phenomenon may be accounted for by a consideration of the ease with which the conventionalized forms lend themselves to decorating certain parts of implements. It is difficult to imagine how the killer whale should be represented on the handle of a dagger without impairing its usefulness. On the other hand, the long thin handles of ladles made of the horn of the big-horn sheep generally terminate with the head of a raven or of a crane, the beak being the end of the handle. This form was evidently suggested by the slender tip of the horn, which is easily carved in this shape. The same seems to be true in the cases of lances or knives, the blades of which are represented as the long protruding tongues of animals, but it may be that in this case there is a complex action of a belief in the supernatural power of the tongue and in the suggestions which the decorator received from the shape of the object he desired to decorate.

To sum up, it seems that there are a great number of cases of decoration which cannot be considered totemistic, but which are either symbolic or suggested by the shape of the object to be decorated. It seems likely that totemism was the most powerful incentive in developing the art of the natives of the North Pacific coast; but the desire to decorate in certain conventional forms once established, these forms were applied in cases in which there was no reason and no intention of using the totemistic mark. The thoughts of the artist were influenced by considerations foreign to the idea of totemism. This is one of the numerous ethnological phenomena which, although apparently simple, cannot be explained psychologically from a single cause but are due to several factors.

4. The Decorative Art of the Indians of the North Pacific Coast

This is a detailed analysis of Northwest Coast art style, based on what Boas hypothesizes is the artist's need both to depict an identifiable animal and to adjust its shape to the form of the object or surface on which it appears. After presenting the identifying characteristics of the various animals that constitute the subject matter of Northwest Coast art, Boas illustrates how the process of representing these animals on the different types of artworks can result in considerable distortion and abstraction.

It has been shown that the motives of the decorative art of many peoples developed largely from representations of animals. In course of time, forms that were originally realistic became more and more sketchy, and more and more distorted. Details, even large portions, of the subject so represented, were omitted, until finally the design attained a purely geometric character.

The decorative art of the Indians of the North Pacific coast agrees with this oft-observed phenomenon in that its subjects are almost exclusively animals. It differs from other arts in that the process of conventionalizing has not led to the development of geometric designs, but that the parts of the animal body may still be recognized as such. The body of the animal, however, undergoes very fundamental changes in the arrangement and size of its parts. In the following paper I shall describe the characteristics of these changes, and discuss the mental attitude of the artist which led to their development.

In treating this subject, we must bear in mind that almost all the plastic art of the Indians of the North Pacific coast is decorative art. While some primitive people—for instance, the Eskimo—produce carvings which serve no practical ends, but are purely works of art, all the works of the Indian artists of the region which we are considering serve at the same time a useful end; that is to say, the form of the object is given, and the subject to be represented is more or less subordinate to the object on which it is shown. Only in the cases of single totemic figures is the artist free to mold his subject without regard to such considerations; but, owing to the large size of such figures, he is limited by the cylindrical form of the trunk of the tree from which he carves his figures. We may therefore say that the native artist is

Reprinted from the *Bulletin of the American Museum of Natural History*, vol. 9, pp. 123–76, 1897. Except where noted otherwise, all specimens illustrated in this volume are from the collection of the American Museum of Natural History.—Ed.

in almost all his works limited by the shape of the object on which he represents his subject.

The plastic arts of the Indians are carving and painting, in which latter we may include tattooing and weaving. Carving is done mostly in wood, but also in stone and horn. It is either in the round, in bas-relief, or, although more rarely, in high relief. There is no art of pottery.

The artists have acquired a high technique, which proves that realistic representations of animals are not beyond their powers. The following are a few exquisite examples of realistic carvings. The helmet (Fig. 1) is decorated with the head of an old man affected with partial paralysis. Undoubtedly this specimen must be considered a portrait head. Nose, eyes, mouth, and the general expression, are highly characteristic. The mask (Fig. 2) represents a dying warrior. The artist has represented faithfully the wide lower jaw, the pentagonal face, and the strong nose of the Indian. The relaxing muscles of the mouth and tongue, the drooping eyelids, and the motionless eyeballs, mark the agonies of death. The conception is so realistic that the mask creates a ghastly impression. Fig. 3 represents a dancing hat decorated with the design of a seal. Fig. 4 is a small float representing a swimming puffin. Fig. 5 is a rattle in the form of a swimming goose. The characteristic bend of its neck and the characteristic color of head and neck are very true to nature.

In these cases the artist has rendered the form of his model faithfully. The object on which the representation of his model was placed allowed him the use of the figure without any alteration. This is not often the case. Generally the object to be decorated has a certain given form to which the decoration must be subordinated, and the artist is confronted with the problem of how to adjust his subject to the form of the object to be decorated.

Before attempting an explanation of the method adopted by the artist in the solution of this problem, we must treat another aspect of our subject. We must premise that in consequence of the adaptation of the form to the decorative field, the native artist cannot attempt a realistic representation of his subject, but is often compelled to indicate only its main characteristics. In consequence of the distortion of the animal body, due to its adaptation to various surfaces, it would be all but impossible to recognize what animal is meant, if the artist did not emphasize what he considers the characteristic features of animals. These are so essential to his mind that he considers no representation adequate in which they are missing. In many cases they become the symbols of the animal. We find, therefore, that each animal is characterized by certain symbols, and great latitude is allowed in the treatment of all features other than symbols.

I will illustrate this feature of the art of the Indians of the North Pacific coast by means of a number of characteristic examples.

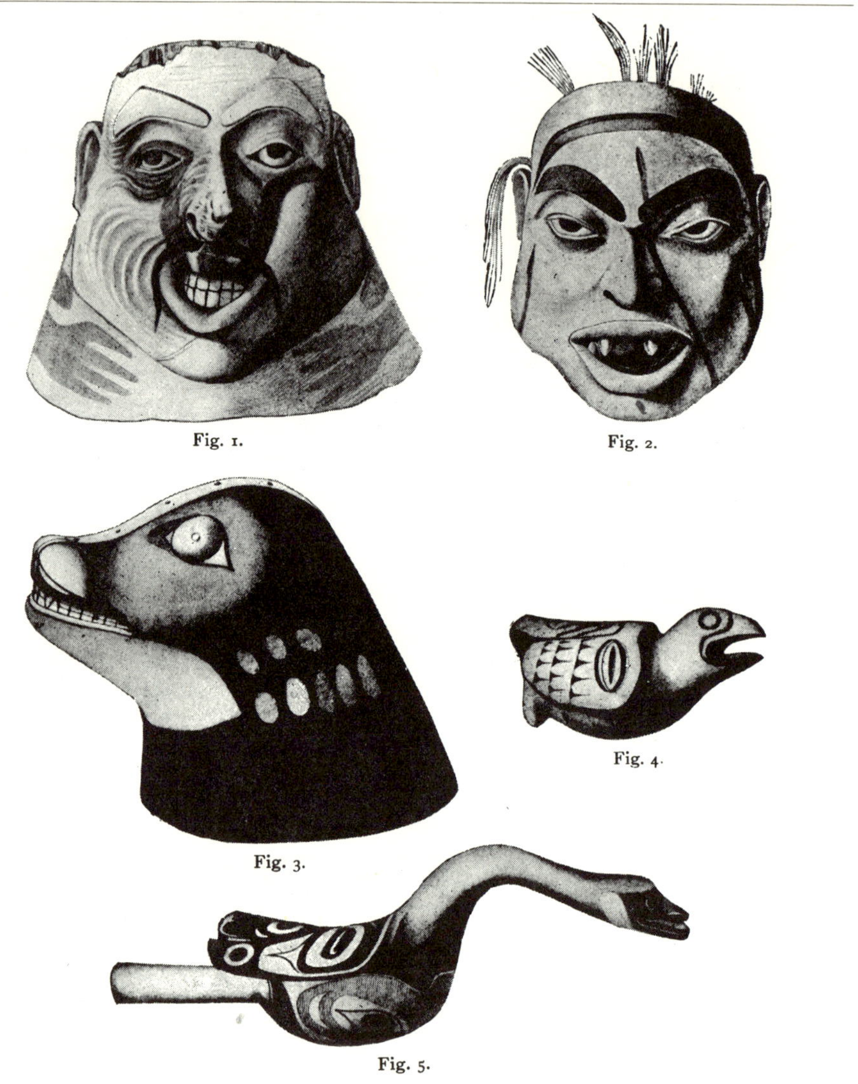

FIG. 1 (E/3453). Helmet with carving representing a paralytic man. Tribe, Tlingit. Height, 21.5 cm; width, 28 cm; depth, 28 cm.

FIG. 2 (E/2501). Mask representing a dying warrior. Tribe, Tlingit. Height, 24 cm; width, 19 cm; depth, 11 cm.

FIG. 3 (E/434). Dancing hat representing a seal. Tribe, Tlingit. Height, 21 cm; width, 24 cm; depth, 23 cm.

FIG. 4 (E/1001). Small float representing a swimming puffin. Tribe, Tlingit. Length, 6 cm.

FIG. 5 (16/300). Rattle representing a goose. Tribe, Haida. Length, 30 cm.

Fig. 6 is a figure from a totem pole, which represents the beaver. It will be noticed that the face is treated somewhat like a human face, particularly the region around eyes and nose. The position of the ears, however, indicates that the artist intended to represent an animal head, not a human head. While the human ear is represented, in its characteristic form, on a level with the eye (Figs. 26 and 28), animal ears are indicated over the forehead; that is to say, approximately in the position in which they appear in a front view of the animal. Their characteristic shape may be seen in Figs. 6 and 7, and in many others. While the ears characterize the head as that of an animal, the two large incisors serve to identify the rodent par excellence—the beaver. The tail of the animal is turned up in front of its body. It is ornamented by cross-hatching, which is intended to represent the scales on the beaver's tail. In its forepaws it holds a stick. The large incisors, the tail with cross-hatching, and the stick, are symbols of the beaver, and each of these is a sufficient characteristic of the animal.

Fig. 7 is another representation of a beaver from a totem pole. It resembles Fig. 6 in all details, except that the stick its missing. The beaver is simply holding its forepaws raised nearly to its chin. There are other carvings in which the beaver is shown with four or five toes, but the symbols described here never vary.

In Fig. 8, which is the handle of a spoon, we find only the first of the symbols of the beaver represented, namely, its incisors. Only the head and the forepaws of the animal are shown; and in its mouth are indicated an upper and a lower pair of incisors, all the other teeth being omitted. There is nothing except the teeth to indicate that the artist intended to represent the beaver.

Fig. 9 is the front of a dancing headdress, which is attached to a framework made of whalebone, and set on top with bristles of the sea lion. To the back is attached a long train of ermine skins. The outer side of the carved front is set with abalone shells. The squatting figure which occupies the center of the front represents the beaver. The same symbols which were mentioned before will be recognized here. The face is human; but the ears, which rise over the eyebrows, indicate that an animal is meant. Two large pairs of incisors occupy the center of the open mouth. The tail is turned up in front of the body, and appears between the two hind legs, indicated by cross-hatching. The forepaws are raised to the height of the mouth, but they do not hold a stick. It will be noticed that on the chest of the beaver another head is represented, over which a number of small rings stretch toward the chin of the beaver. Two feet, which belong to this animal, extend from the corners of its mouth toward the haunches of the beaver. This animal represents the dragonfly, which is symbolized by a large head and a slender segmented body. In many representations of the dragonfly there are two pairs of wings attached to the head. The face of this animal resembles also a human face; but the two ears, which rise over the eyebrows, indicate that an animal is meant. Combinations of two animals

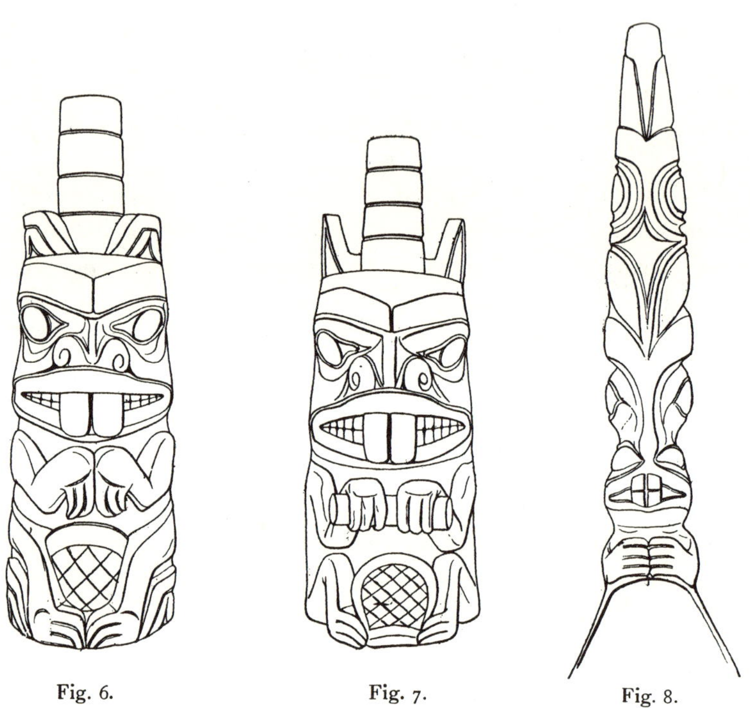

FIG. 6 (16/556). Lowest figure from model of a totem pole, carved in slate, representing a beaver. Tribe, Haida. Height, 22.5 cm.

FIG. 7 (16/551). Lowest figure from model of a totem pole, carved in slate, representing a beaver. Tribe, Haida. Height, 19 cm.

FIG. 8 (19/1129). Handle of a spoon made of mountain-goat horn, design representing a beaver. Tribe, Tlingit. Length of handle, 8 cm.

of this sort are found very frequently, a smaller figure of one animal being represented on the chest of a larger carving. Examples of this kind will be seen in Figs. 13 and 17.

Fig. 10 is a halibut hook, the point of which is carved with a design of the sculpin. The symbols of the fish are fins and tail. Those of this species of fish are two spines rising over its mouth, and joined dorsal fins. In this figure the sculpin is represented swallowing a fish, the tail of which protrudes from its mouth. The two

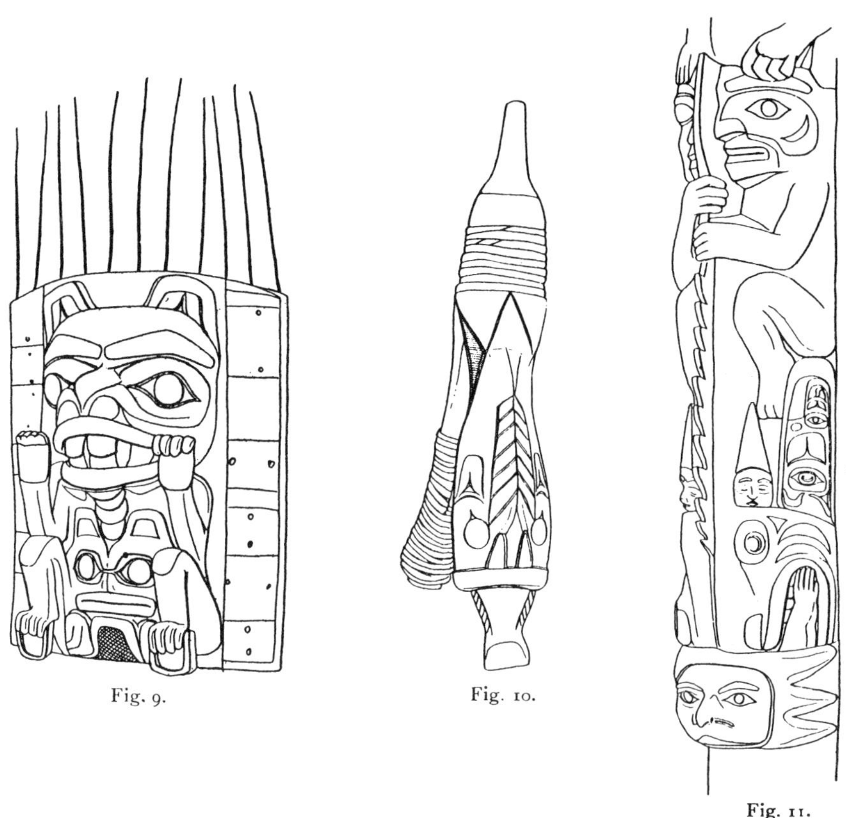

FIG. 9 (16/245). Headdress representing a beaver. The dragonfly is shown on the chest of the beaver. Tribe, Haida. Height, 18 cm.

FIG. 10 (E/1251). Halibut hook with design representing a sculpin swallowing a fish. Tribe, Tlingit. Length of point, 26.5 cm.

FIG. 11 (16/567). Part of a totem pole with design representing a sculpin. Tribe, Tsimshian. Height from base to tip of tail, 220 cm.

spines appear immediately over the lips, their points being between the two eyes, which are represented by two circles with small projections. The two pectoral fins are indicated in bas-relief over the eyes. The joined dorsal fins extend from the eyes upward toward the narrowest part of the body. The tail of the animal extends toward the place where point and shank of the hook are bound together by means of a strip of spruce root.

The same animal is represented in a slightly different way in Fig. 11, which rep-

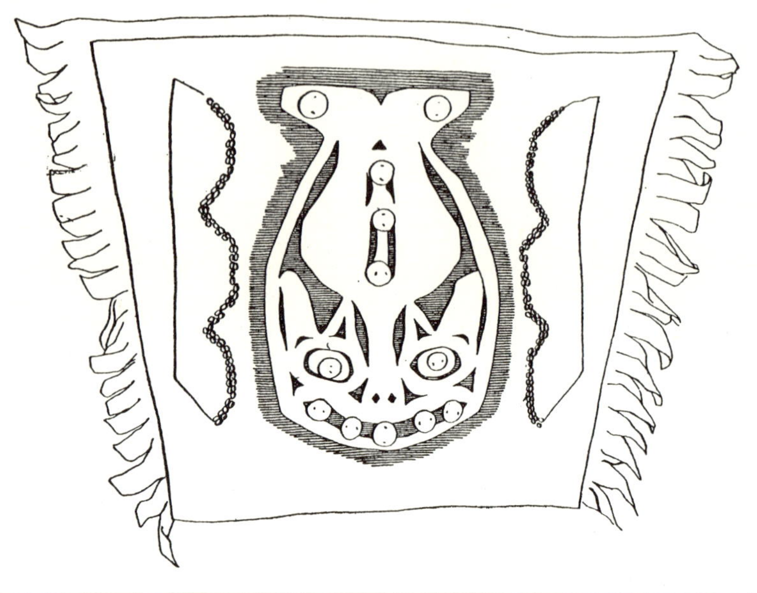

FIG. 12 (16/328). Woollen legging with an appliqué design representing a sculpin. Tribe, Haida. Length, 28.5 cm; greatest width, 31 cm, 38 cm with fringes.

resents the lower portion of a totem pole. The lowest figure is probably the sun, or perhaps a starfish. Its arms extend upward, and are being bitten by a sculpin, which later is shown with its head downward, its back forward, and its tail extending upward. The head will be easily recognized. Two crescent-shaped ornaments above the corners of the mouth represent the gills of the fish. Above these are seen the pectoral fins. On the level of the pectoral fins toward the middle appear the symbols of the sculpin, namely, the two spines, the lower portions of which are decorated with small human faces. The eye is represented under the spine. The dorsal fin commences at the height of the eyes, and finally merges into the tail. The tail end of the fish is clasped by a human figure, which appears cut in two by the fish tail. This carving is also characterized by two symbols—the two spines and the joined dorsal fins.

Fig. 12 represents a legging made of blue cloth with a red cloth appliqué of the figure of a sculpin. The sides of the legging are trimmed with leather fringes. The general shape of the fish will be easily recognized. Its teeth are represented by buttons of abalone shells, which are sewed on the cloth. The eyes and the dorsal fin are indicated in the same manner. Two small triangles cut out to the right and left of the mouth represent the gills. Immediately over the eyes, and extending toward the middle of the back, we find the two spines, indicated by two slender triangular pieces of red cloth cut out in their middle part. The pectoral fins are indicated by two broader pieces of red cloth extending from the eyes outward and upward toward the margin of the body of the fish. The dorsal fin is indicated by the long slits along the back of the animal. In this case the species is best characterized by the two spines which appear over the eyes.

In Figs. 13–16 I give a selection of carvings representing the hawk. The hawk is symbolized by an enormous hooked beak, which is curved backward so that its slender point touches the chin. In many cases the face of the bird is represented as that of a human being. In this case the nose is given the shape of the symbol of the hawk. It is extended in the form of a beak, and drawn back into the mouth, or merged into the face below the lower lip.

Fig. 13 is the front of a headdress, which is used like the one described before (Fig. 9). The upper, larger face is that of the hawk. The face is human; but the ears, which rise over the eyebrows, indicate that an animal is meant. The body of the animal is exceedingly small, and is hidden behind the smaller, lower face. Its outlines are seen under this face, in the middle of the lower edge of the carving. It is not quite certain whether the two wings, which are grasped by the arms, are those of the hawk, or whether they belong to the face which is carved on the body of the bird. It will be noticed that over the arm, which is grasping the wing, another wing is carved. Possibly this carving is intended to represent the wing of the hawk, while the central raised wing is that of the being holding the two central wings.

Fig. 14 is the handle of a spoon, on which is represented the head of a hawk, symbolized by its beak. The top of the spoon represents a man who is holding a small animal with a segmented body, which may represent the dragonfly, although the head seems rather smaller than we are accustomed to see in representations of the dragonfly.

In Figs. 15 and 16 the same symbols of the hawk will be recognized.

Fig. 17, the front of a headdress representing the eagle, is very similar to the preceding series; but it differs from these carvings in that the beak of the bird is not turned back so as to touch the face, but ends in a sharp point extending downward. The wings of the eagle are shown extending from the margin of its body inward. The feet are seen at the sides of the lower margin of the carving, under the wings. On the body of the eagle a rather realistic carving of a frog is shown. The characteristic difference between the eagle and the hawk will also be noticed in the painting on a drum (Fig. 63), in which also the beak ends in a sharp point directed downward, and not turned back toward the face.

Figs. 18 and 19 are representations of the killer whale. In the rattle (Fig. 18) the form of the whale will be easily recognized. Its tail is bent downward. The large head, one of the characteristic features of the whale, is much more pronounced in

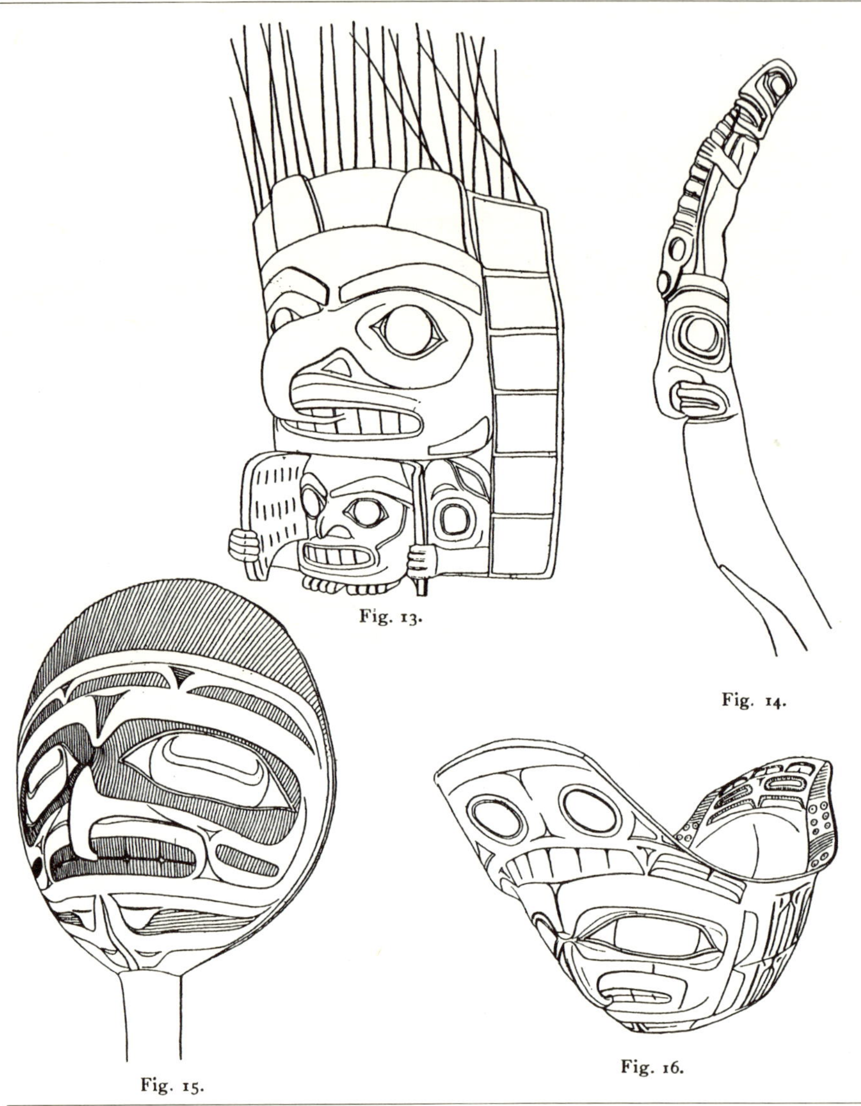

FIG. 13 (16/252). Headdress representing a hawk. Tribe, Tsimshian. Height, 20.5 cm; width, 18.5 cm.

FIG. 14 (16/105). Handle of a spoon made of mountain-goat horn; lowest figure represents a hawk; upper figure represents a man holding a dragonfly. Tribe, probably Tsimshian. Length of carved part of handle, 10 cm.

FIG. 15 (E/1371). Rattle with design of a hawk. Tribe, Tlingit. Height without handle, 17 cm.

FIG. 16 (19/696). Dish made of mountain-sheep horn. Tribe, Tlingit. Greatest length, 26 cm.

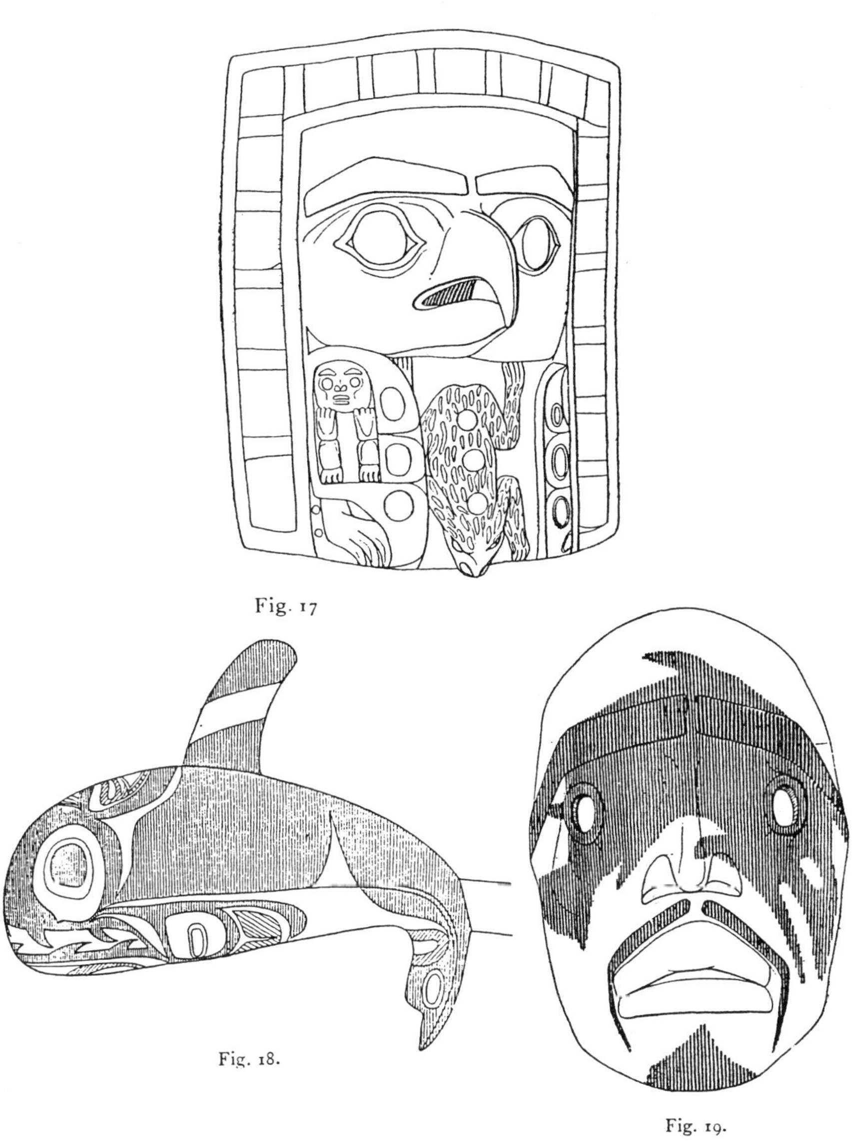

FIG. 17 (16/249). Headdress representing an eagle bearing a frog on its chest. Tribe, Tsimshian. Height, 19 cm; width, 15 cm.

FIG. 18 (16/304). Rattle representing a killer whale. Tribe, Haida or Tsimshian. Length, 25 cm.

FIG. 19 (16/773). Mask with painting representing a killer whale. Tribe, Bella Coola. Height, 28 cm; width, 20 cm; depth, 15 cm.

this than in the next figure. The eye appears on the front part of the rattle. Under the eye we see the large mouth, which is set with a number of curved spines. They are intended to represent the teeth. Immediately behind the mouth, on the lower part of the carving, we find the flippers. The painted ornament, which has the form of a small face, in front of the huge dorsal fin, is intended to represent the blowhole. We find in this specimen a fuller series of the symbols of the whale (namely, a large head, a mouth set with teeth, the blowhole, and a dorsal fin) than in the next specimen (Fig. 19).

In Fig. 19 the whale is painted on a mask so that the head is placed on the left cheek of the face. The back extends over the forehead, and the tail is on the right cheek. The whole animal is given the form of a fish whose tail and pectoral fin, or rather flipper, are essential characteristics. The specific characteristic, or the symbol, of the killer whale is its large dorsal fin, which rises over the eyebrows. The eye of the animal is indicated by a white spot. Its mouth is open, and is also left uncolored.

The following series (Figs. 20–23) are representations of the shark. Whenever the whole body of this animal is represented, it is characterized by a heterocerc tail, a large mouth, the corners of which are drawn downward, a series of curved lines on each cheek which represent the gills, and a high tapering forehead, which is often decorated with two circles and a series of curved lines similar to those found on the cheeks.

In Fig. 20 we see the upper part of a totem pole, on which a shark is represented devouring a halibut. The head has the characteristic symbols, to which are added here the numerous sharp teeth which are found often, but not regularly, as symbols of the shark. The greater part of the body has been omitted by the artist, since the animal is sufficiently identified by the symbols found on the head; but under the chin will be noticed the two pectoral fins which identify it as a fish.

Fig. 21 is the handle of a copper dagger on which the mouth with depressed corners, the curved lines on the cheeks, and the ornament rising over the forehead characterize the shark.

Fig. 22 is a small pipe on which the entire shark is represented. The square end at the right-hand side is the face of the animal, which is shown in front view in the smaller figure. Eyes and mouth are inlaid with abalone shell. On account of the narrowness of the face, the three curved lines generally found on the cheeks are placed under the mouth. The forehead has the characteristic height and tapering shape described before. The opposite end of the pipe shows the heterocerc tail turned upward. On the sides are carved the pectoral fins, which extend over about one-half of the whole length of the sides of the pipe.

Fig. 23 is a copy of a tattooing on the back of a Haida woman. Here we have

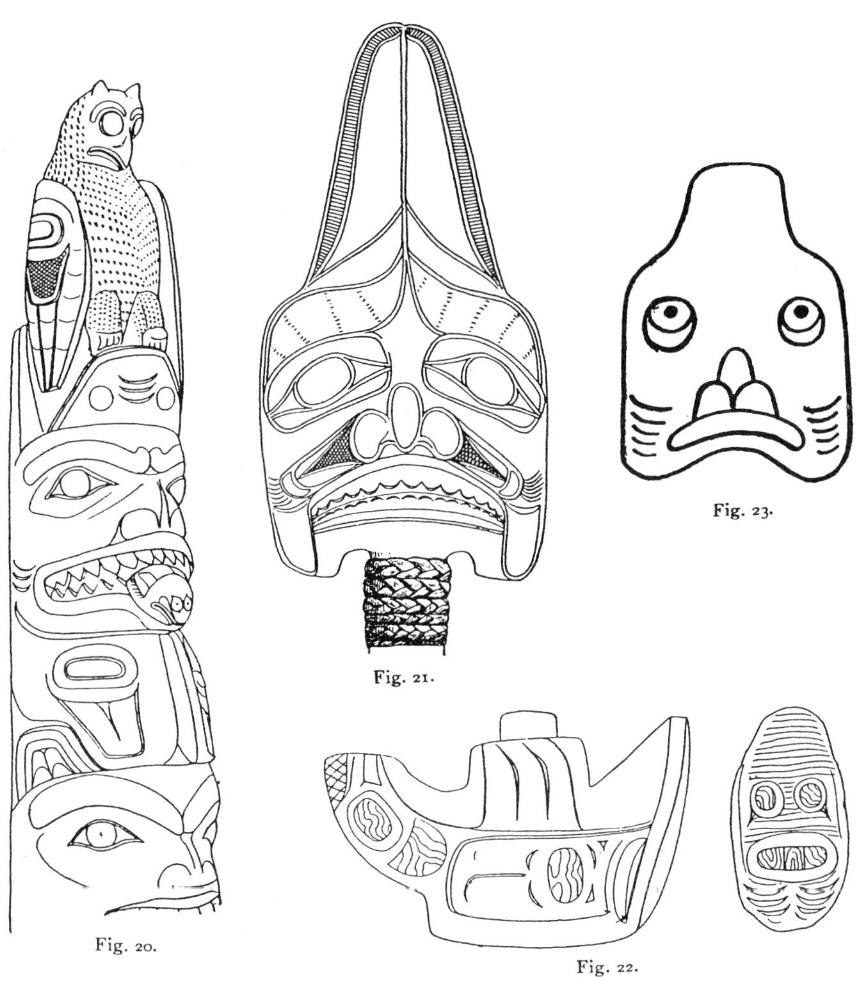

Fig. 20. Fig. 21. Fig. 22. Fig. 23.

FIG. 20 (16/1161). Part of model of a totem pole carved in slate with design representing a shark surmounted by an eagle. Tribe, Haida. Length of shark figure, 13.5 cm; width, 6.5 cm.

FIG. 21 (E/2037). Handle of a dagger representing the head of a shark. Tribe, Tlingit. Length of handle, 15 cm; width, 7.5 cm.

FIG. 22 (19/98). Wooden pipe, representing a shark. Tribe, Tlingit. Length, 10 cm; height, 6 cm; depth, 3 cm.

FIG. 23. Tattooing representing a shark. Tribe, Haida. (From a photograph.)

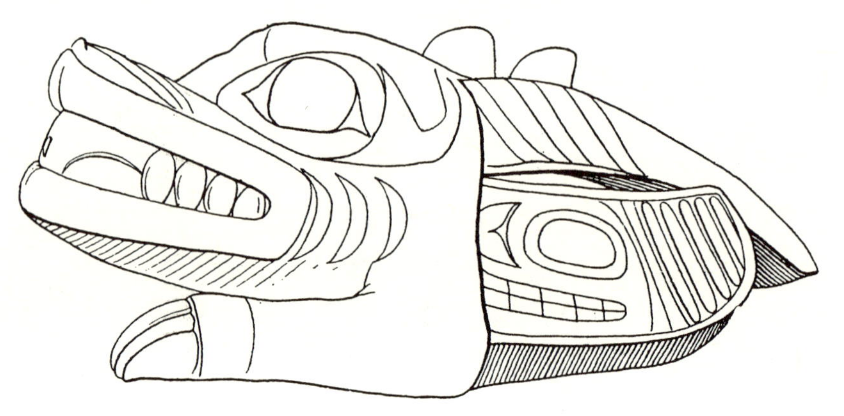

FIG. 24 (19/377). Wood carving representing a fabulous monster with a bear's head and paws, and the body of a killer whale. Tribe, Tlingit. Length, 33.5 cm; width, 23.5 cm; height, 13 cm.

only the outline of the head of a shark, again characterized by a peculiarly high forehead, the depressed corners of the mouth, and curved lines on each cheek.

Fig. 24 represents a fabulous sea monster with the head and forelegs of a bear and the body of a killer whale, but with two or three dorsal fins. Flippers are attached to the forelegs. The head of the specimen shows one of the most characteristic symbols of the bear, namely, the wide mouth set with teeth, the tongue protruding. The large paws are a second symbol of the bear. The sea monster is also symbolized by the three crescents which are shown behind the corner of the mouth. These are intended to represent gills. We shall find a series of representations of this fabulous monster later on (Figs. 73, 75, 76, and 77).

Let us briefly recapitulate what we have thus far tried to show. Animals are characterized by their symbols, and the following series of symbols has been described in the preceding remarks:

1. Of the *beaver*: large incisors, scaly tail, and a stick held in the forepaws.

2. Of the *sculpin*: two spines rising over the mouth, and a continuous dorsal fin.

3. Of the *hawk*: large curved beak, the point of which is turned backward so that it touches the face.

4. Of the *eagle*: large curved beak, the point of which is turned downward.

5. Of the *killer whale*: large head, large mouth set with teeth, blowhole, and large dorsal fin.

6. Of the *shark*: an elongated rounded cone rising over the forehead, mouth with depressed corners, a series of curved lines on the cheeks, two circles and curved lines

on the ornament rising over the forehead, round eyes, numerous sharp teeth, and heterocerc tail.

7. Of the *bear*: large paws, and large mouth set with teeth, with protruding tongue.

8. Of the *sea monster*: bear's head, bear's paws with flippers attached, and gills and body of the killer whale, with several dorsal fins.

9. Of the *dragonfly*: large head, segmented, slender body, and wings.

So far I have considered the symbols only in connection with their use in representing various animals. It now becomes necessary to inquire in what manner they are used to identify the animals. We have seen that in a number of the preceding cases entire animals were represented, and that they were identified by means of these symbols. When we investigate this subject more closely, we find that the artist is allowed wide latitude in the selection of the form of the animal. Whatever the form may be, as long as the recognized symbols are present, the identity of the animal is established. We have mentioned before that the symbols are often applied to human faces, while the body of the figure has the characteristics of the animal.

We find this principle applied in Fig. 25, which represents a totem pole. Three animals are shown in this carving. Each of these has a human face, to which are added the symbols that characterize the animal. In the top figure the ears indicate that the head represents that of an animal; while the arms, to which the flippers are attached, indicate that the sea monster (see Fig. 24) is meant. The next figure below represents the shark. It has a human face, and it seems that originally a large lip with a labret was attached to it, which, however, was lost before the specimen came into possession of the Museum. This would indicate that a female shark is represented. Its symbols in this case are the peculiar high ornament which rises over its forehead, and the fins, which are placed under the chin. The face of the lowest figure resembles the faces of the two upper figures very closely. Its body, which is shown under the face, makes it clear that the artist intended to represent a fish; and the two large spines which rise over the eyebrows specify that the figure represents a sculpin.

While in these cases the entire animals have been represented, in others only parts of animals are shown in conventional forms which combine elements of the human form with those of the animal. In other cases the symbols are applied to a purely human face.

Fig. 26 is a human face with human ears. Only the nose indicates that the mask is not intended to represent a human being. It is strongly curved, and drawn back into the mouth, thus symbolizing that the mask is intended to represent the hawk.

In Fig. 27 we see the face of a woman with a moderately large labret. The ears, as explained before, are those of an animal. The nose, which has been lost, had undoubtedly the form of a bird's beak. Thus the face was characterized as that of a

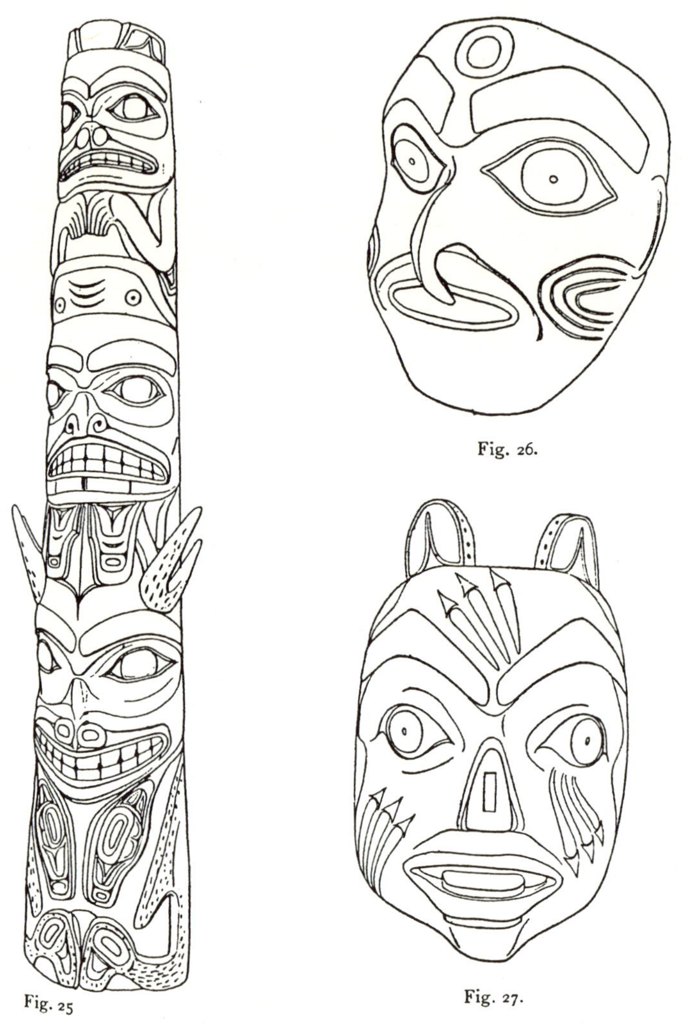

FIG. 25 (16/550). Model of a totem pole with three figures representing, from below upward, a sculpin, dogfish, and sea monster. Tribe, Haida. Height, 47.5 cm.

FIG. 26 (E/1591). Mask representing a hawk. Tribe, Tlingit. Height, 21.5 cm; width, 17.5 cm; depth, 10 cm.

FIG. 27 (E/337). Mask with painting symbolizing the red-winged flicker. Tribe, Tlingit. Height (excluding ears), 25 cm; width, 20 cm; depth, 11 cm.

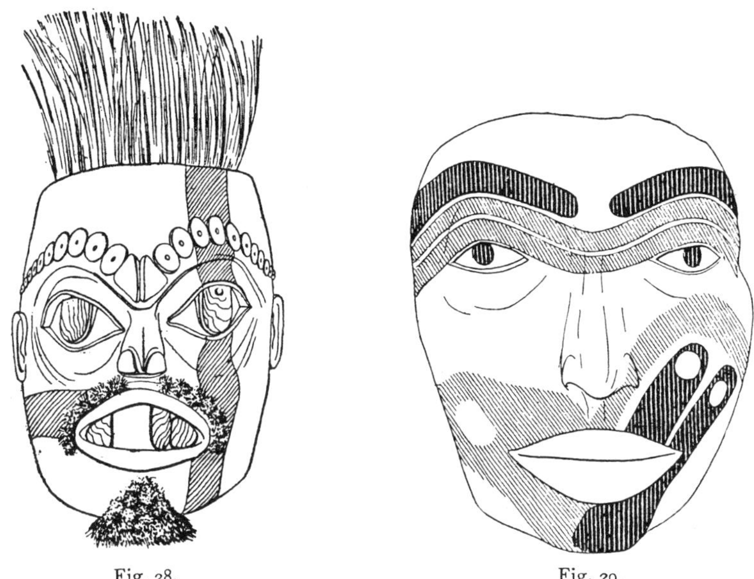

FIG. 28 (19/920). Small mask with eyebrows, symbolizing the squid. Tribe, Tlingit. Height (excluding hair), 11 cm; width, 9.5 cm; depth, 5.5 cm.

FIG. 29 (E/1629). Mask with painting symbolizing the killer whale. Tribe, Tlingit. Height, 18 cm; width, 15 cm; depth, 8 cm.

bird. It was specified partly by the form of the beak, but principally by the ornaments painted in red and black on cheeks and forehead. These represent the feathers of the red-winged flicker.

Fig. 28 is a small carved mask which was worn in front of a headband of swan's down. It represents a human face. In place of the eyebrows we find two rows of circles, which represent the sucking cups of the squid. By means of this symbol the face is recognized as that of the squid.

In the same manner the mask (Fig. 29) is identified as the killer whale by the two black ornaments painted on the left cheek and extending down to the chin. They represent the dorsal fin of the killer whale.

These symbols are also used as facial paintings by dancers, who are thus recognized as personifying the animal in question, or as belonging to the social group presided over by the animal. At social or religious festivals ceremonies are performed which are in most cases dramatizations of myths, in which the dancer represents either the animal, or the spirit that appeared to his ancestor. In many of the composite masks used on such occasions, the ancestor himself is represented by a small figure placed on the mask, thus indicating that he was carried away by the animal which the dancer personifies. In other festivals, legends are dramatized which refer to the events that took place "before the animals took off their blankets"; that is, at the time when there was no clear distinction between men and animals. In these ceremonies the dancers appear with paintings or other decoration symbolizing the animals. To this class belongs the ornament (Fig. 30) which represents the dorsal fin of a killer whale, and which is worn attached to the back part of the blanket. These ornaments and paintings are found most extensively among the Kwakiutl tribes.

It appears, therefore, that as, first of all, the artist tried to characterize the animals he intended to represent by emphasizing their most prominent characteristics, these gradually became symbols which were recognized even when not attached to the animal form, and which took the place of representations of the entire animal.

Having thus become acquainted with a few of the symbols of animals, we will next investigate in what manner the native artist adapted the animal form to the object he intended to decorate. First of all, we will direct our attention to a series of specimens which show that the native artist endeavors, whenever possible, to represent the whole animal on the object that he desires to decorate.

Fig. 31 is a club used for killing seals and halibut before they are landed in the canoe. The carving represents the killer whale. If the principal symbol of the killer whale, its dorsal fin, were placed in an upright position on the club, the implement would assume an exceedingly awkward shape. On the other hand, the artist could not omit the dorsal fin, since it is the most important symbol of the animal. Therefore he has bent it downward along the side of the body, so that it covers the flipper. The tail of the whale would have interfered with the handle, and for this reason it has been turned forward over the back of the whale, so as to be in close contact with the body.

The distortion of the body has been carried still further in Fig. 32, which is the handle of a spoon, and represents the same animal. The large head of the whale, to which the flippers are attached, will be easily recognized near the bowl of the spoon. The body has been twisted backward so that the tail almost touches the mouth. The carving is only on the back of the spoon, and the two projections just below the mouth will be recognized as the two tips of the whale's tail, which has been split along its lower side and then distended along the back of the spoon. The dorsal fin has thus been brought into a position so as to extend along the handle of the spoon. It is seen projecting upward from the head of the whale, between the legs of the man who forms the tip of the handle.

Fig. 33 is a small totem pole representing the shark. The tip of its tail forms the top of the pole, while the face is placed at its lower end. Since most of the symbols

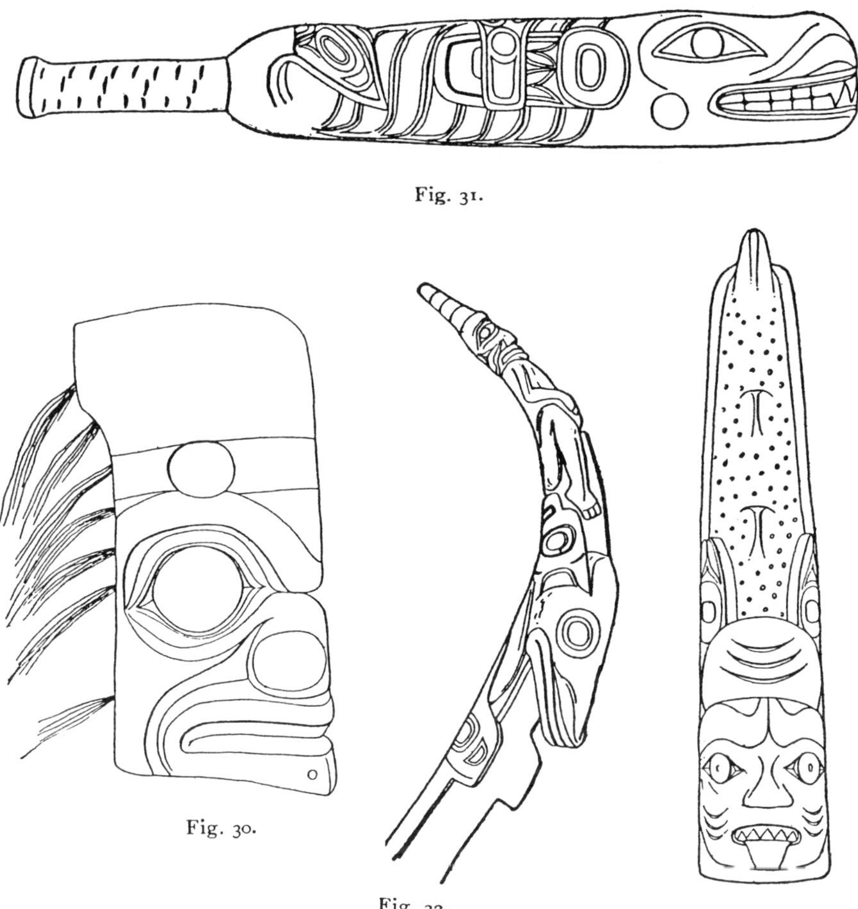

FIG. 30 (E/923). Wood carving representing the dorsal fin of the killer whale. Tribe, Tlingit. Height, 25 cm; thickness, 3 cm.

FIG. 31 (E/242). Fish club carved to represent the killer whale. Tribe, Tlingit. Total length, 49 cm; height, 8 cm; thickness, 5 cm.

FIG. 32 (16/113). Handle of horn spoon with design representing a killer whale. Tribe, probably Tsimshian. Length of handle, 15 cm.

FIG. 33 (16/1167). Model of a totem pole representing a shark. Tribe, Haida. Height, 27 cm; width, 5 cm; depth, 4 cm.

of the shark are found on its face, it was necessary to bring the face into such a position as to be seen in front view, but the artist also desired to show the back of the fish. For this reason the head has been twisted around entirely, so that it appears in front view over the back of the fish. In order that the flippers, an important symbol of the fish, might be made visible, they have been pushed backward far beyond the place to which they properly belong.

The speaker's staff (Fig. 34), which also represents the shark, has been distorted in the same manner; but here the head has been turned round entirely, so that it faces the back of the fish. The pectoral fins are shown below the chin.

In Fig. 35, which is a berry spoon representing a shark, the lower jaw of the animal has been entirely omitted. The flat bowl of the spoon is formed by the palate of the fish, while its back is the lower side of the spoon.

The changes of position and of the relative sizes of parts of the body, which result from such adaptations to the form of the object to be decorated, are still more far-reaching in the following specimens.

Fig. 36 is a shark represented on the top of a totem pole. The head of the animal is shown in the form of a human face with the characteristic symbols. Under the chin are two flippers. The body must be considered turned upward; but it has been shortened so much that only the tail remains, which rises immediately above the face.

In Fig. 37 (a wooden dancing hat) the symbols of the killer whale are attached to its head. Since the whole body was omitted in this case, it was necessary to remove the symbols from the back to the head. We see the dorsal fin rising over the eyes, the flippers attached to the head behind the eyebrows.

In Fig. 38, which represents a halibut hook carved with a design of the beaver, we find that the two incisors, the symbols of the beaver, have been moved over to the right side of the animal which is represented on the point of the hook. While in reality only one of the incisors would be visible in this view, the artist, in order to be certain that his idea would be understood, moved the two incisors so as to make both visible. We find that in all these cases the artist has taken great liberty with the form of the animal body, and has treated it so that the symbols become clearly visible. On the whole, we may say that the artist endeavors to represent the whole animal. When this is not possible, all its essential parts are shown. The insignificant ones are often omitted.

We have now to treat a series of peculiar phenomena which result from the endeavor on the part of the artist to adjust the animal that he desires to represent to the decorative field in such a manner as to preserve as far as possible the whole animal, and bring out its symbols most clearly.

Fig. 39 is the top view of a wooden hat on which is carved the figure of a sculpin. The animal is shown in top view, as though it were lying with its lower side on the

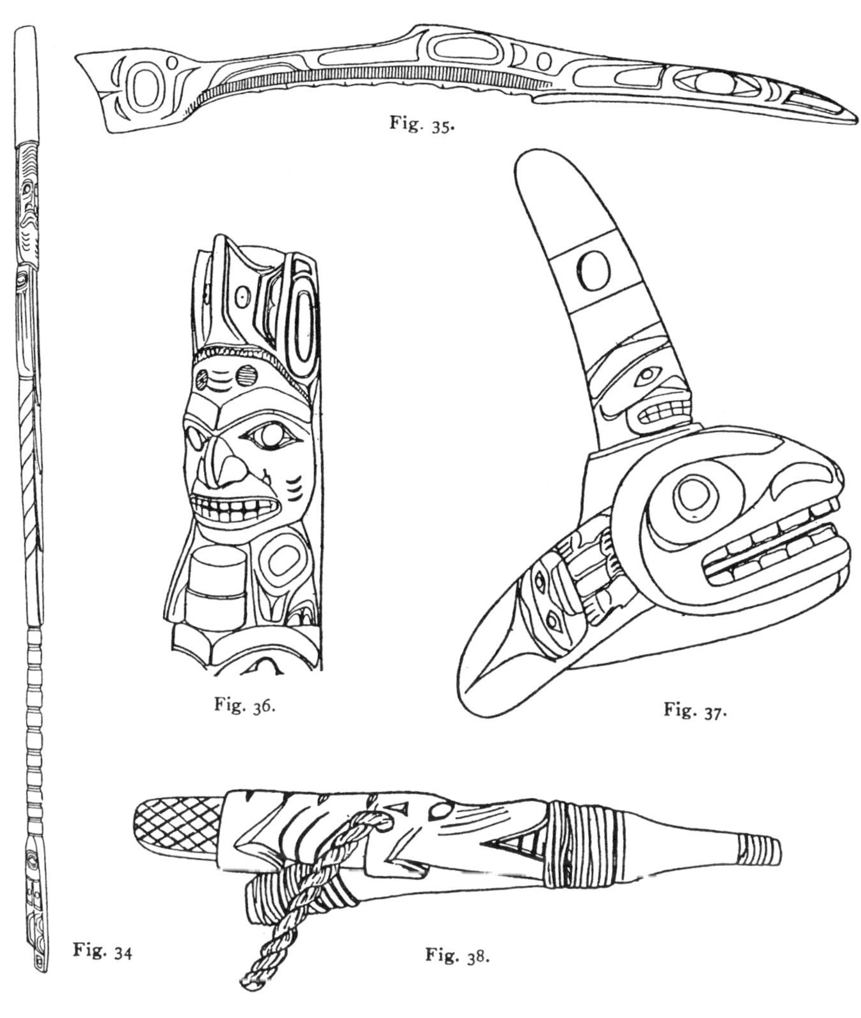

FIG. 34 (19/790). Speaker's staff representing a shark. Tribe, Tlingit. Length, 184 cm.

FIG. 35 (E/2502). Berry spoon representing a shark. Tribe, Tsimshian. Length, 36 cm; width, 4.5 cm.

FIG. 36 (16/1154). Part of a totem pole representing a shark. Tribe, Haida. Height of shark carving, 20 cm; width, 8.5 cm; depth, 7.5 cm.

FIG. 37 (16/580). Dancing hat representing a killer whale. Tribe, Tsimshian. Total height, 50 cm; width, 28 cm; depth, 30.5 cm.

FIG. 38 (19/1152). Halibut hook with design representing a beaver. Tribe, Tlingit. Length of point, 32.5 cm.

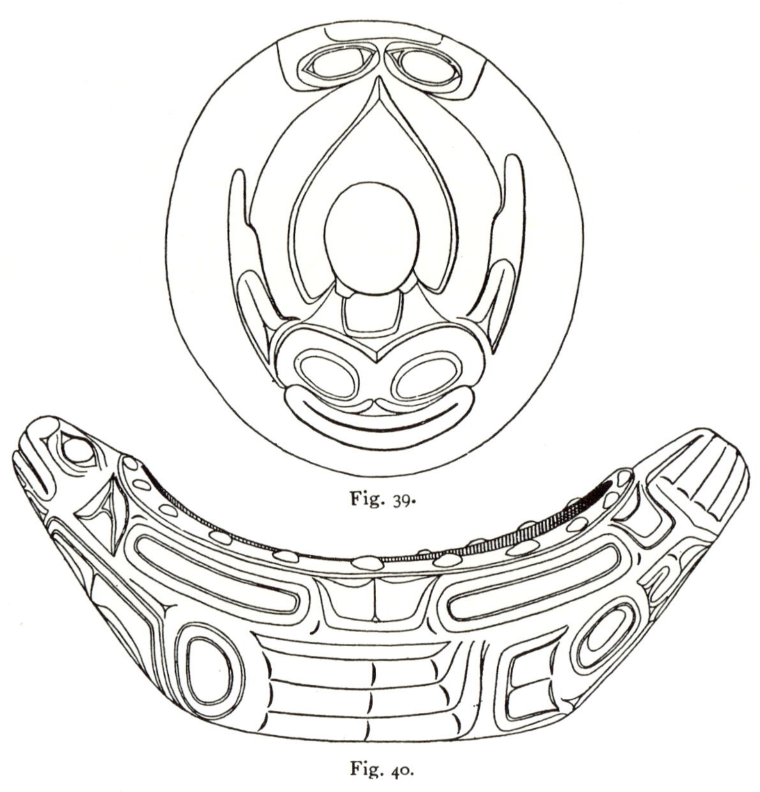

Fig. 39.

Fig. 40.

FIG. 39 (16/282). Dancing hat with design representing a sculpin. Tribe, Haida or Tsimshian. Height, 14 cm; width, 36 cm; depth, 40 cm.

FIG. 40 (E/1365). Grease dish in the shape of a seal. Tribe, Tlingit. Length, 41.5 cm; width, 21 cm; depth in center, 9.5 cm.

hat. The dancing hats of these Indians have the forms of truncated cones. To the top are attached a series of rings, mostly made of basketry, which indicate the social rank of the owner, each ring symbolizing a step in the social ladder. The top of the hat, therefore, does not belong to the decorative field, which is confined to the surface of the cone. The artist found it necessary, therefore, to open the back of the sculpin far enough to make room for the gap in the decorative field. He has done so by representing the animal as seen from the top, but split and distended in the middle, so that the top of the hat is located in the opening thus secured.

Fig. 40 represents a dish in the shape of a seal. The whole dish is carved in the form of the animal; but the bottom, which corresponds to the belly, is flattened, and the back is hollowed out so as to form the bowl of the dish. In order to gain a wider rim the whole back has been distended so that the animal becomes inordinately wide as compared to its length. The flippers are carved in their proper positions at the sides of the dish. The hind flippers are turned back, and closely join the tail. A similar method of representation is used in decorating small boxes. The whole box is considered as representing an animal. The front of its body is painted or carved on the box front; its sides, on the sides of the box; the hind side of its body, on the back of the box. The bottom of the box is the animal's stomach; the top, or the open upper side, its back. These boxes, therefore, are decorated only on the sides, which are bent of a single piece of wood (Fig. 41). When we unbend the sides we find the decoration extended on a long band, which we may consider as consisting of two symmetrical halves. The center is occupied by the front view of the animal, the sides by a side view, and the ends by one-half of the hind view at each end of the board. An actual unbending of the sides of the box would not give a symmetrical form; but, since the ends are necessarily sewed at the corner, the hind view of the body will occupy one end.

In the decoration of silver bracelets a similar principle is followed, but the problem differs somewhat from that offered in the decoration of square boxes. While in the latter case the four edges make a natural division between the four views of the animal—front and right profile, back and left profile—there is no such sharp line of division in the round bracelet, and there would be great difficulty in joining the four aspects artistically, while two profiles offer no such difficulty. When the tail end of each profile is placed where the ends of the bracelet join, then there is only one point of junction; namely, in the median line of the head. This is the method of representation that the native artists have adopted (Figs. 42, 72, 73, 74). The animal is cut in two from head to tail, so that the two halves cohere only at the tip of the nose and at the tip of the tail. The hand is put through this hole, and the animal now surrounds the wrist. In this position it is represented on the bracelet. The method adopted is therefore identical with the one applied in the hat (Fig. 39), except that the central opening is much larger, and that the animal has been represented on a cylindrical surface, not on a conical one.

An examination of the head of the bear shown on the bracelet (Fig. 42) makes it clear that this idea has been carried out rigidly. It will be noticed that there is a deep depression between the eyes, extending down to the nose. This shows that the head itself must not be considered a front view, but as consisting of two profiles which adjoin at mouth and nose, while they are not in contact with each other on a level with the eyes and forehead. The peculiar ornament rising over the nose of the bear, decorated with three rings, represents a hat with three rings (see p. 78), which designate the rank of the bearer.

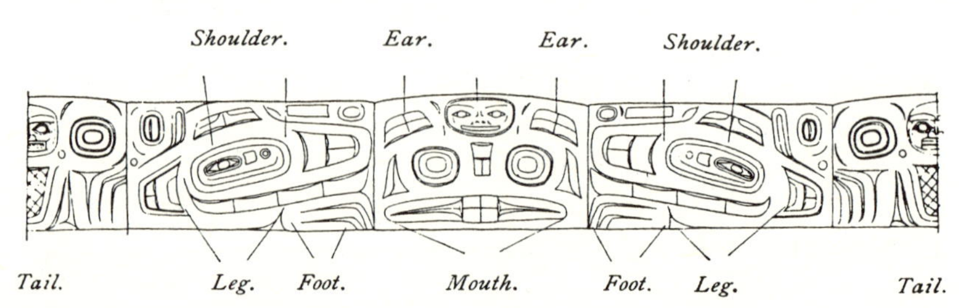

FIG. 41 (19/953). Carving on the sides of a dish representing a beaver. The sides of the dish are bent of a single piece of wood, and are shown here flattened out. Tribe, Tlingit. Length of short sides, 29 cm; length of long sides, 31.5 cm; greatest height of sides, 16 cm.

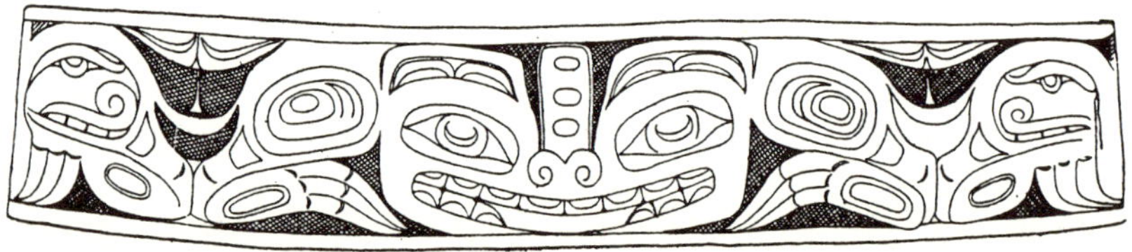

FIG. 42 (E/2428). Design on a bracelet representing a bear. Tribe, Nass River Indians. Height, 3.5 cm.

We have thus recognized that the representations of animals on dishes and bracelets (and we may include the design on the hat, Fig. 39) must not be considered as perspective views of animals, but as representing complete animals more or less distorted and split.

The transition from the bracelet to the painting or carving of animals on a flat surface is not a difficult one. The same principle is adhered to; and either the animals are represented as split in two so that the profiles are joined in the middle, or a front view of the head is shown with two adjoining profiles of the body. In the cases considered heretofore the animal was cut through and through from the mouth to the tip of the tail. These points were allowed to cohere, and the animal was stretched over a ring, a cone, or the sides of a prism. If we imagine the bracelet opened, and flattened in the manner in which it is shown in Fig. 42, we have a section of the animal from mouth to tail, cohering only at the mouth, and the two halves spread over a flat surface. This is the natural development of the method here described when applied to the decoration of flat surfaces.

It is clear that on flat surfaces this method allows of modifications by changing the method of cutting. When the body of a long animal, such as that of a fish or of

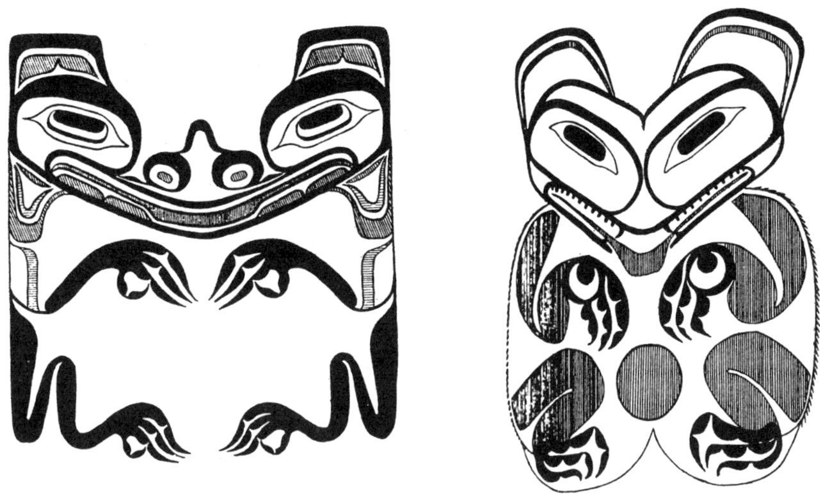

FIG. 43. Painting representing a bear. Tribe, Haida.

FIG. 44. Painting from a housefront representing a bear. Tribe, Tsimshian.

a standing quadruped, is cut in this manner, a design results which forms a long narrow strip. This mode of cutting is therefore mostly applied in the decoration of long bands. When the field that is to be decorated is more nearly square, this form is not favorable. In such cases a square design is obtained by cutting quadrupeds sitting on their haunches in the same manner as before, and unfolding the animal so that the two halves remain in contact at the nose and mouth, while the median line at the back is to the extreme right and to the extreme left.

Fig. 43 (a Haida painting) shows a design which has been obtained in this manner. It represents a bear. The enormous breadth of mouth observed in these cases is brought about by the junction of the two profiles of which the head consists.

This cutting of the head is brought out most clearly in the painting (Fig. 44), which also represents the bear. It is the painting on the front of a Tsimshian house, the circular hole in the middle of the design being the door of the house. The animal is cut from back to front, so that only the front part of the head coheres. The two halves of the lower jaw do not touch each other. The back is represented by the black outline on which the hair is indicated by fine lines.

In a number of cases the designs painted on hats must also be explained as formed by the junction of two profiles. This is the case in the painted wooden hat (Fig. 45), on which the design of a sculpin is shown. It will be noticed that only the mouth

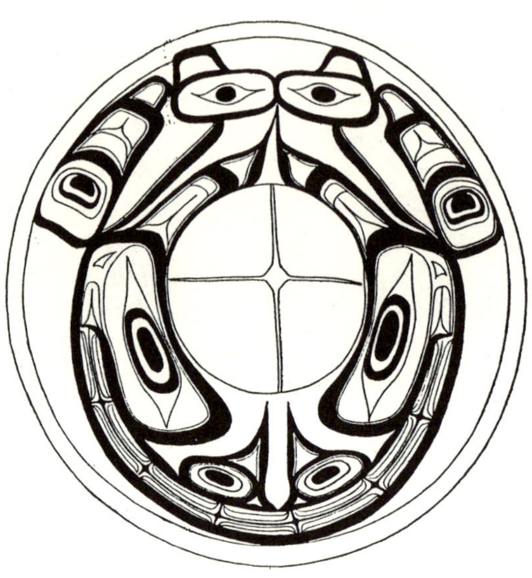

FIG. 45 (16/281). Wooden hat painted with the design of a sculpin. Tribe, Haida. Height, 17 cm; width, 41 cm; depth, 42.5 cm.

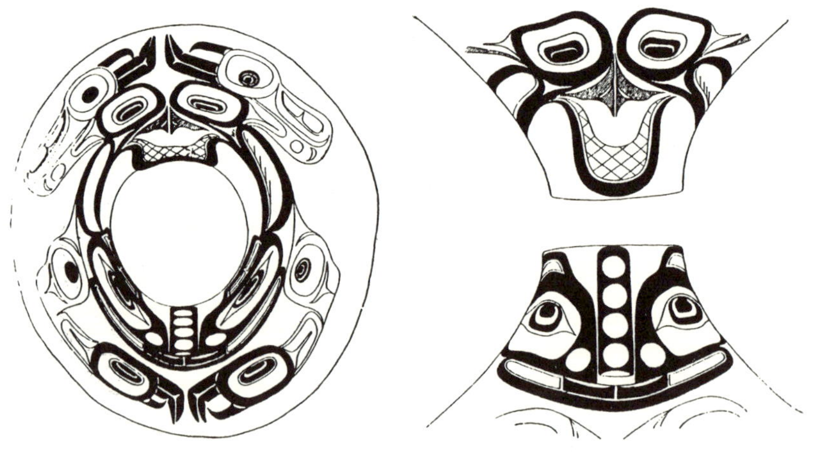

FIG. 46 (16/692). Hat made of spruce roots painted with the design of a beaver. Tribe, Haida or Tsimshian. Height, 16 cm; diameter, 36.5 cm.

of the animal coheres, while the eyes are widely separated. The spines rise immediately over the mouth. The flippers are attached to the corners of the face, while the dorsal fin is split into halves, each half being joined to an eye.

The beaver (Fig. 46) has been treated in the same manner. The head is split down to the mouth, over which rises the hat with four rings. The split has been carried back to the tail, which, however, is left intact, and turned up toward the center of the hat. The importance of the symbols becomes very clear in this specimen. If the two large black teeth, which are seen under the four rings, and the tail with the cross-hatchings were omitted, the figure would represent the frog.

In other designs the cut is made in the opposite direction from the one described heretofore. It passes from the chest to the back, and the animal is unfolded so that the two halves cohere along the middle line of the back. This has been done in the Haida tattooings (Figs. 47 and 48), the former representing the duck, the latter the raven. In both the tail is left intact. The duck has been split along the back so that the two halves of the body do not cohere except in their lowest portion, while the two halves of the raven are left in contact up to the head.

Fig. 49 is a dancing apron woven from mountain-goat wool, and fastened to a large piece of leather, the fringes of which are set with puffin beaks. The woven design represents the beaver. Its symbols, the two pairs of incisors and the scaly tail, are clearly represented. While in most carvings and paintings the tail is turned upward in front of the body, it is hanging down here between the two feet. The meaning of the ornaments in the upper part of the apron to the right and to the left of the head are not quite clear to me, but I believe they must be considered as the back of the body split and folded along the upper margin of the blanket. If this explanation is correct, we have to consider the animal cut into three pieces, one cut running along the sides of the body, the other one along the back.

Fig. 50 is one of a pair of leggings embroidered with quills on a piece of leather. The design, which represents the sea monster described in Fig. 24, must also be explained as a representation of the animal split along its lower side, and flattened. In the lower portion of the legging the two profiles are seen, which are joined on a level with the eyes, while the two mouths are separated. The nostrils are shown in the small triangle below the line connecting the two eyes. Owing to the shape of the legging, the arms are not attached to the body, but to the upper part of the head. They appear at the right and left margins of the legging, and are turned inward along the lower jaws, the three-toed paws touching the lower margin. The fins, which are supposed to grow out of the upper part of the arms, adjoin the elbows, and are turned upward. Another pair of fins, which do not appear in most representations of this monster, are attached to the upper part of the back, and form the two flaps to the right and left of the upper margin. On the back we see a series of circles, which probably represent the dorsal fins. The tail occupies the center of the upper margin.

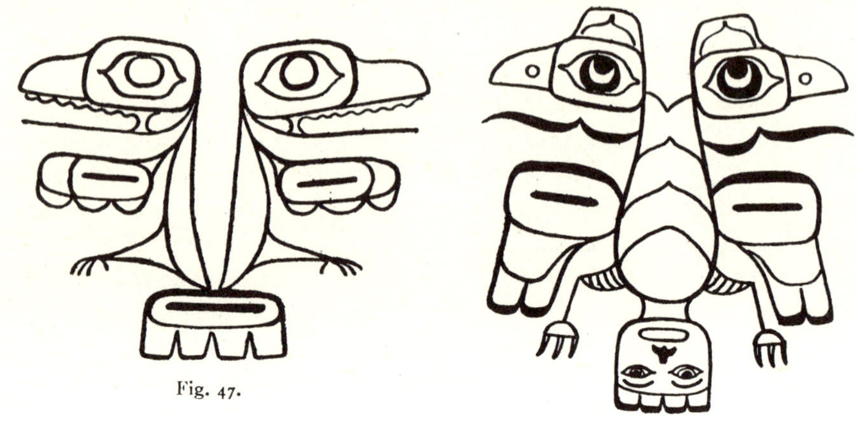

Fig. 47.

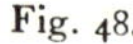

Fig. 48.

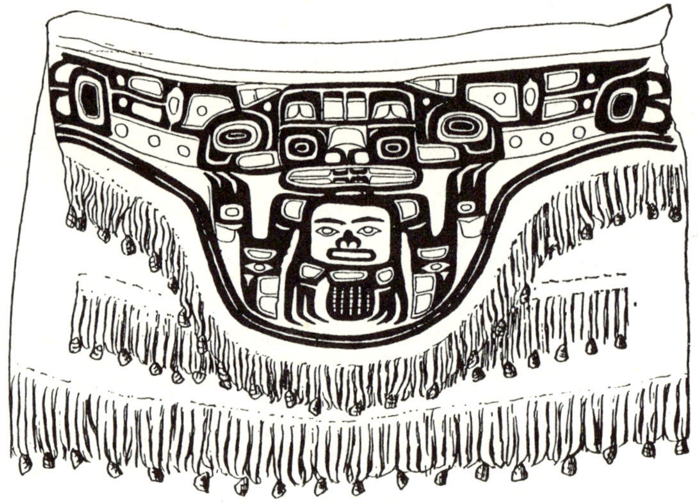

Fig. 49.

FIG. 47. Tattooing representing a duck. Tribe, Haida.

FIG. 48. Tattooing representing a raven. Tribe, Haida.

FIG. 49 (16/349). Dancing apron woven of mountain-goat wool, design representing a beaver. Tribe, Tsimshian. Height of design, 38 cm; width, 91 cm.

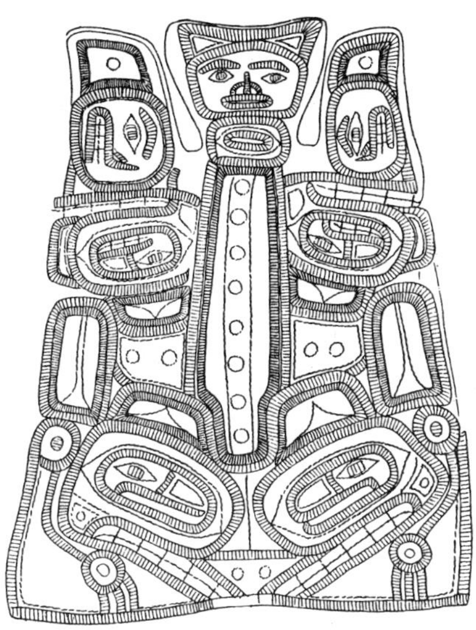

FIG. 50 (16/334). Embroidered legging representing a sea monster with a bear's head and body of the killer whale. Tribe, Haida. Height, 37.5 cm; greatest width, 31 cm.

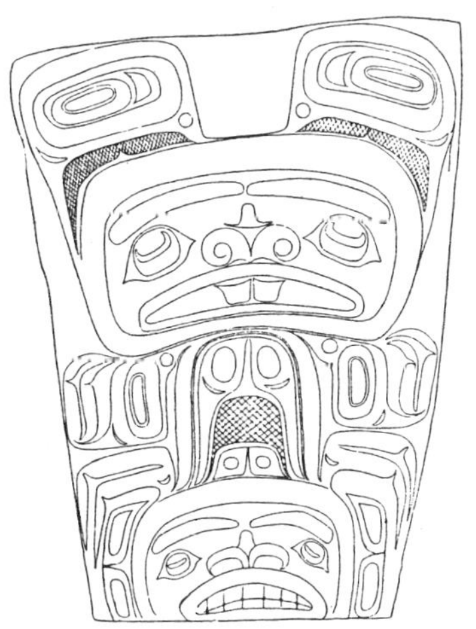

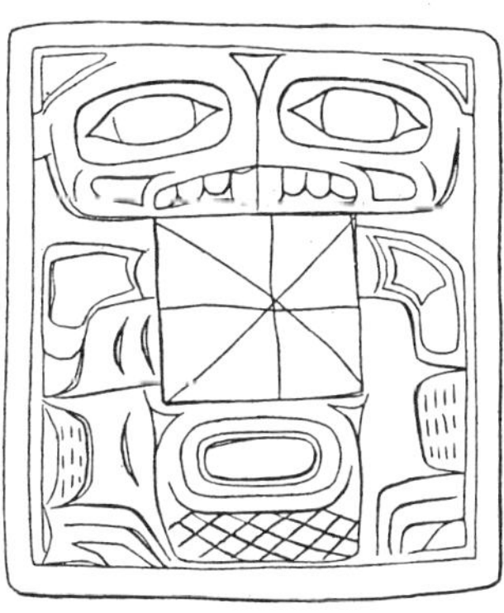

FIG. 51 (16/330). Painted legging with design representing a beaver sitting on a man's head. Tribe, Haida. Height, 22 cm; greatest width, 19 cm.

FIG. 52 (19/1057). Gambling leather with engraved design representing a beaver. Tribe, Tlingit. Height, 18.5 cm; width, 17 cm.

The smaller ornaments in the outside corners of the head, adjoining the mouth, probably represent the gills.

Fig. 51 represents a leather legging painted with the design of a beaver squatting on a human head. In this specimen we observe that the proportions of the body have been much distorted owing to the greater width of the legging at its upper part. The head has been much enlarged in order to fill the wider portion of the decorative field.

The gambling leather (Fig. 52) is treated in a similar manner. It represents the beaver, and must probably be explained as the animal cut in two. The symbols—the large incisors and a scaly tail—appear here as in all other representations of the beaver, but the lower extremities have been omitted. It might seem that this design could be explained as well as a front view of the animal, but the deep depression between the two eyes is not in favor of this assumption. The head consists undoubtedly of two profiles, which join at the nose and mouth; but the cut has not been continued to the tail, which remains intact.

In the following figures we find a new cut applied. Figs. 53 and 54 represent the shark. I explained, when discussing the symbols of the shark, that in the front view of the animal the symbols are shown to best advantage. For this reason side views of the face of the shark are avoided, and in representing the whole animal a cut is made from the back to the lower side, and the two sides are unfolded, leaving the head in front view.

The painting (Fig. 53) has been made in this manner, the two halves of the body being entirely separated from each other, and folded to the right and to the left. The heterocerc tail is cut in halves, and is shown at each end turned downward. The pectoral fins are shown unduly enlarged, in order to fill the vacant space under the head.

The shark which is shown in Fig. 54 is treated in a slightly different manner. Again the head is left intact. The cut is made from back to chest, but the two halves of the animal are not separated. They cohere at the chest, and are unfolded in this manner, so that the pectoral fins and dorsal fins appear to the right and left of the body. The heterocerc tail is not clearly indicated in this specimen.

The method of section applied in Fig. 55 is still different. The figure represents a painting on the margin of a large leather blanket. The animal here represented is the killer whale. The upper painting clearly represents the profile of the animal. The lower painting represents the other profile, so that both the right and the left halves of the animal are shown. Since there was not room for showing the dorsal fin on the lower painting, it is indicated by a curved line on one of the series of wider fringes at the lower margin of the blanket. It is remarkable that the tails in the two halves of the animal are not drawn symmetrically; but it is possible that this is due to a mistake on the part of the painter, because the design is repeated on the opposite

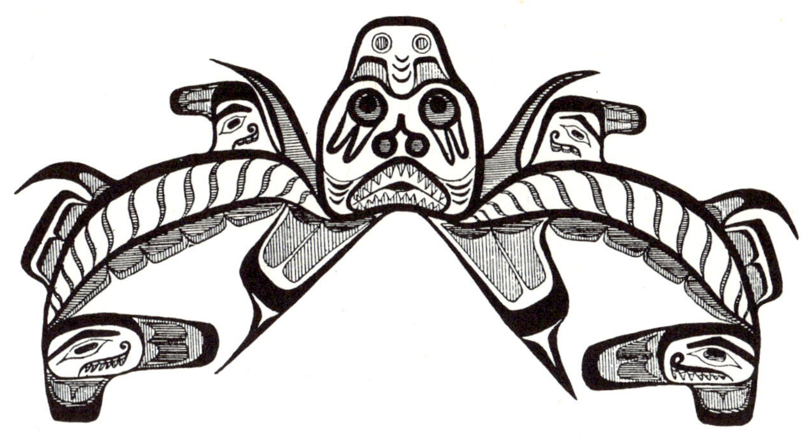

FIG. 53. Painting representing a shark. Tribe, Haida.

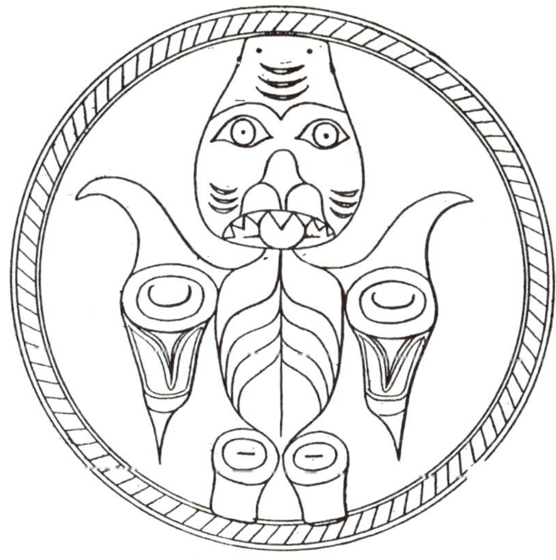

FIG. 54 (16/603). Slate dish with carved design representing a shark. Tribe, Haida. Diameter, 27.5 cm; depth, 3.5 cm.

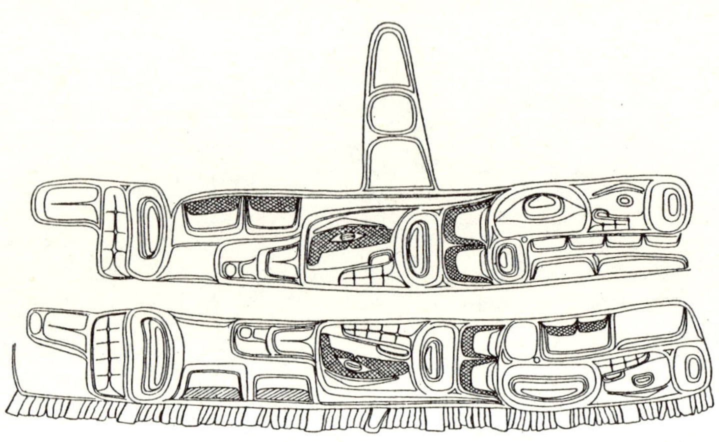

FIG. 55 (E/1502). Painting on edge of a blanket representing a killer whale. Tribe, Tlingit. Length, 124 cm.

margin of the blanket in the same manner, but with symmetrical tails. The two halves of the body differ in details, but their main features are identical. The flipper is shown on a very large scale. It is attached immediately behind the head, and extends to a point near the tail. Its principal part is occupied by a face, in front of which an eye is shown.

Animals are represented by means of sections not only on flat surfaces, but also in round carvings in which one side cannot be shown. This is the case on all totem poles, the hind part of which is not carved. Whenever all the symbols of the animal can be shown on the front of the totem pole, the animals are apparently represented in their natural position. But representations of animals, the symbols of which would be placed on the rear side of the totem pole, make it clear that the artist actually splits the animals along the rear of the totem pole, and extends this cut in such a way that the animal is spread along the curved front of the pole. This will become clear by a consideration of the following figures.

Fig. 56 represents a sea monster with a whale's body and bear's paws. It differs from the monster discussed before in that it has a whale's head, and no fins attached to the forepaws. It has, however, one large dorsal fin. The blowhole of the whale is shown over its eyebrows. The tail is turned up in front of the body, and the paws are raised in front of the chest. The dorsal fin will be recognized in the narrow strip, ornamented with a small ring, which slants downward from the elbow toward the tail. An ornament of this sort is shown on both sides of the carving. We see, therefore, that the dorsal fin has been split, and is turned down along each side of the body. This shows that the right and left margins of the carved portion of the totem pole must be considered as the medial line of the back, which has been split and pulled apart.

The sculpin shown on the totem pole (Fig. 57) is treated in the same manner, but in this case the cut is made along the lower side of the animal. The head is turned upward, so that the front view of the face is seen when looking down upon the back of the fish. The spines rise over nose and eyebrows. The pectoral fins are shown over the eyebrows on the edge of the carved portion of the pole, while the hind portion of the lower part of the body occupies the upper part of the margin of the pole.

The exceedingly intricate central figure on the pole shown in Fig. 58 must be explained in the same manner as Fig. 56. We see here the sea monster described before in Fig. 24. It has a bear's head. In each ear is placed a small human figure, the hands of which grasp the eyelid of the monster, which they are lifting. The tail is turned upward in front of the body, immediately over a beaver's head, which is the next lower figure on the column. The dorsal fin has been split, and one-half of it is seen under the mouth of the bear, indicated by a projection which is decorated with a double circle. The forepaws of the animal are raised in front of its chest, and appear under the mouth. The fins which are attached to them are shown to the right and to the left of the tail. The animal is swallowing another being, but it is not clear what animal is meant. A fish tail and a hand are seen protruding from the mouth. The space between the forepaws and the tail of the sea monster is occupied by an inverted bird, which will be seen clearly when the figure is reversed. Its head is shown with beak resting between the feet. The two wings are extended, and reach from the fins of the forearm of the monster to its dorsal fin. The particular point brought out by this figure is the same as that which I tried to make clear in considering Fig. 56; namely, that the two edges of the carved pole must be considered as the extended medial line of the back of the animal that is represented on the pole.

These carvings make it clear that in paintings on hats, such as shown in Figs. 39, 45, and 46, and in flat figures, such as Fig. 12, we must consider the outer rim of the figure as the distended sides of a cut made along the lower side of the animal. All these distortions and sections of animals may be explained by the necessity the artist felt of showing all the symbols of the animal in his works.

In most cases the symbols appear clearly in profiles of animals. For this reason the artist, when representing profiles, has not endeavored to show both sides of the body. I will give here a series of figures illustrating this point.

Fig. 59 represents the top of a box on which is carved the sea monster Wasku. It has a wolf's head and body, and a large dorsal fin. It is able to hunt in the sea as well as on land. The artist has shown a profile of the animal with one foreleg and one hind leg, the tail curled up over the back. The dorsal fin, which in most representations of this animal stands out vertically from the body, has been laid down along the back in order to fit it into the decorative field.

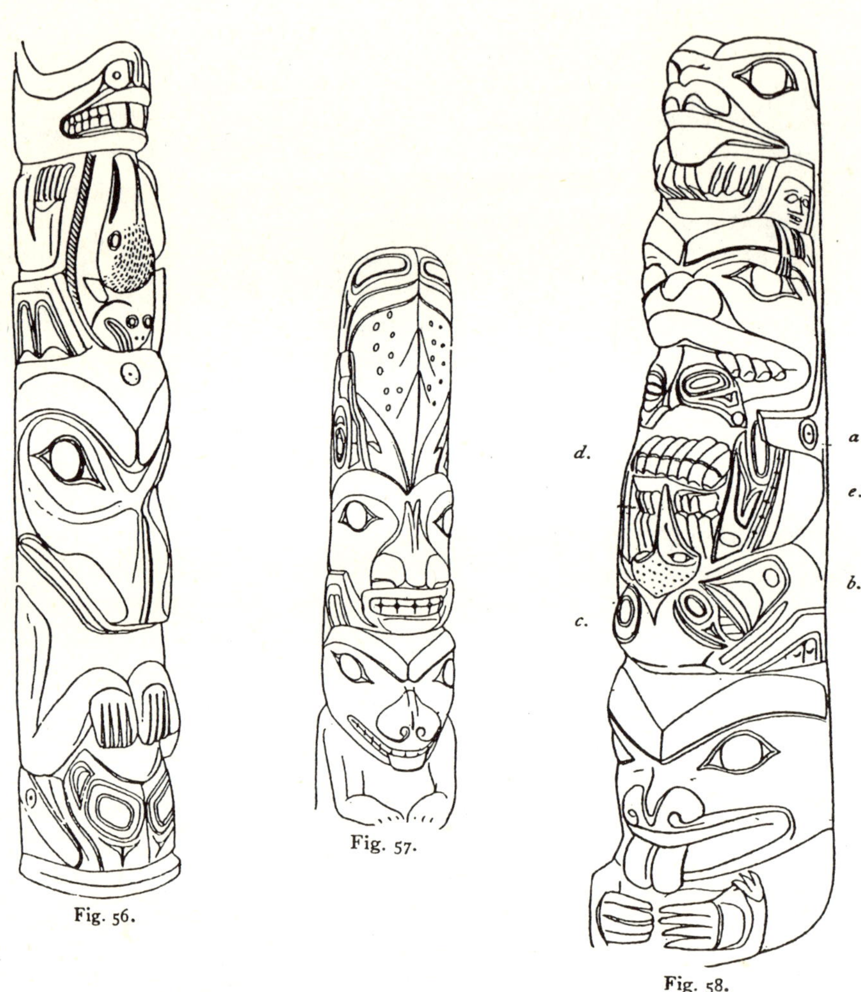

FIG. 56 (16/544). Part of model of a totem pole with design representing a sea monster. Tribe, Haida. Height of figure, 23 cm; width, 7.5 cm; depth, 6 cm.

FIG. 57 (16/1155). Part of model of a totem pole with design representing a sculpin. Tribe, Haida. Height of figure, 15 cm; width, 5.5 cm; depth, 5.5 cm.

FIG. 58. Part of a totem pole with design representing a sea monster devouring a fish: *a*, dorsal fin; *b*, fin of forearm; *c*, tail of monster; *d*, paws of monster; *e*, wing of bird. Tribe, Haida. Height of figure (excluding ears), 13 cm; width, 5.5 cm; depth, 5 cm.

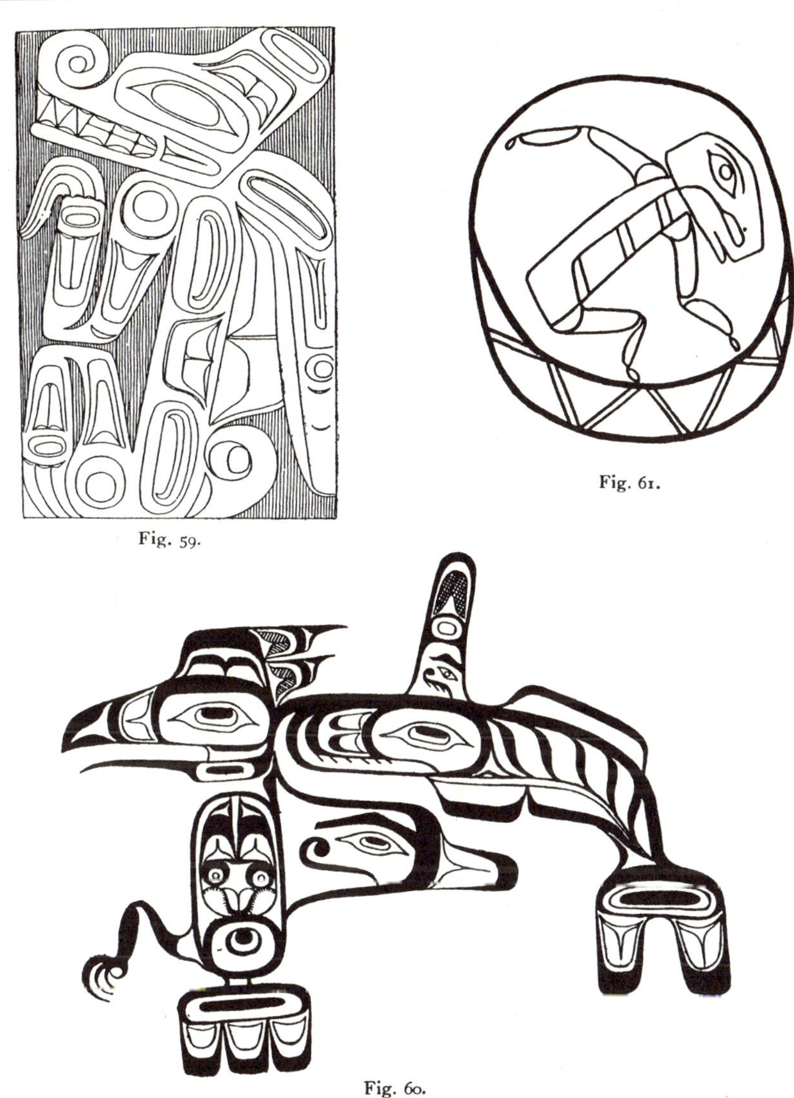

Fig. 59.

Fig. 61.

Fig. 60.

FIG. 59 (16/687). Slate carving representing the sea monster Wasku. Tribe, Haida. Size, 29.5 × 19.5 cm.

FIG. 60. Tattooing representing the fabulous sea monster Tsem'aks. Tribe, Haida.

FIG. 61. Tattooing representing the moon. Tribe, Haida.

Fig. 60 is a tattooing representing the sea monster Tsem'aks, which has a raven's body with a whale's body attached to its head, and a fin attached to the raven's back. It is shown in profile with one leg, the dorsal fin, and the tails of raven and whale twisted around so as to be seen from the side.

Fig. 61 is a tattooing representing the moon. In its lower portion the crescent will be seen. In the dark portion of the moon a semihuman figure is shown in profile, with one leg. One arm is extended downward, and one backward, as though he were lifting a heavy weight.

In Fig. 62, which represents the design on a circular slate dish, we see a good case of the adaptation of a profile to the decorative field. The design represents a killer whale with two dorsal fins. The animal is bent around the rim of a dish so that the head touches the tail. The two dorsal fins are laid flat along the back, while the large flipper occupies the center of the dish.

Fig. 63, which is the painting on the head of a drum, is a combination of front and side views. It is a system of representation with which we are familiar in the art of ancient Egypt. Here the head is turned sideways, while the body, the outstretched wings, and the feet are shown in front view. It is found very rarely in the art of the Indians of the North Pacific coast, and, so far as I am aware, almost exclusively in representations of the eagle. The painting on the outer ring of the drumhead is difficult to explain. It will be noticed that the tail of the eagle occupies the lower center of the ring. On top we see the front view of a human figure, the arms of which are placed near the lower corners of the face, and are of diminutive size, while the hands are of very large size. The two sitting figures below the two hands probably represent the back of the man who is shown on top, but their connection with the peculiar finlike figures on the lower portion of the painting is not clear.

There are very few designs which can possibly be interpreted as full-face views of animals. I explained before that the face of the shark is always shown in this manner, because its symbols appear best in this position. The only other animal which is painted or carved on flat surfaces in full front view is the hawk or thunderbird, whose symbol is the long beak which descends to the chin. A number of carvings representing the thunderbird were given in Figs. 13–16.

We find full-face representations of the thunderbird very frequently used on dishes, on which the beak is indicated by a long wedge which separates the mouth into two halves. It is, however, not certain whether the artists consider this face always as a full front view, because we often find (Fig. 64) a depression between the two eyes, corresponding to the depression which I described before when referring to the joining of the profiles of animals. It may be that the long central wedge must be considered as the two halves of the long descending beak, which join in the middle. It might be expected, however, that in this case the beak would, at least sometimes, be carried on outward to the right and to the left below the chin,

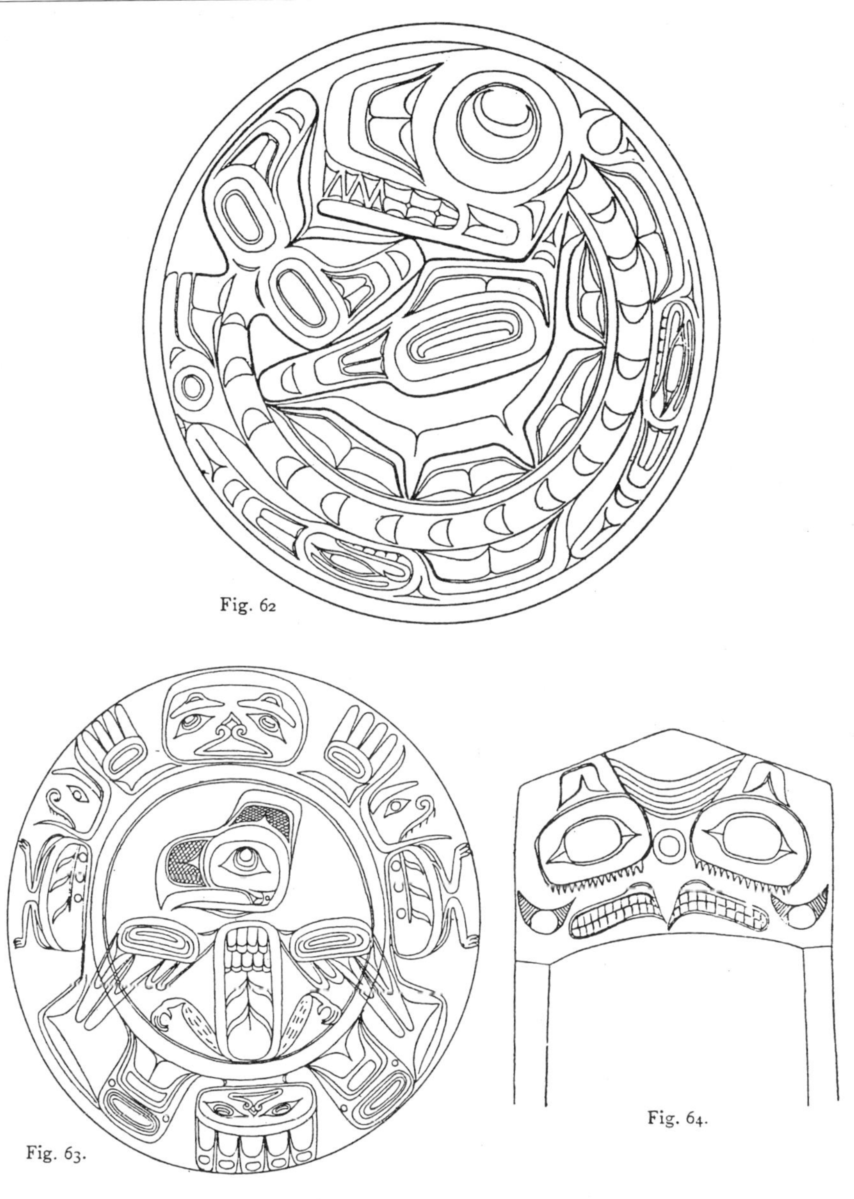

FIG. 62 (16/605). Slate dish with design representing a killer whale. Tribe, Haida. Diameter, 41.5 cm; depth, 6.5 cm.

FIG. 63 (16/748). Drum painted with design of an eagle. Tribe, Tsimshian. Diameter, 58 cm.

FIG. 64 (E/1236). Carving on the end of a food tray representing a hawk. Tribe, Tlingit. Width, 20 cm.

corresponding to one-half of the beak seen in Fig. 13. I have not observed a single specimen in which this is the case, and therefore I am rather inclined to consider the carvings of thunderbirds as full front views.

This ornament may have originated in the following manner: Many grease and food dishes have the form of canoes. The canoe symbolizes that a canoe-load of food is presented to the guests; and that this view is probably correct is indicated by the fact that the host in his speeches often refers to the canoe filled with food which he gives to his guests. The canoe form is often modified, and a whole series of types can be established forming the transition between canoe dishes and ordinary trays. Dishes of this sort always bear a conventionalized face at each short end, while the middle part is not decorated. This is analogous to the style of the decoration of the canoe. On the whole the decoration of the canoe is totemistic. It may be that it is only the peculiar manner in which the beak of the hawk is represented which has given rise to the prevalence of this decoration. The upper jaw of the hawk is always shown so that its point reaches the lower jaw and turns back into the mouth. When painted or carved in front view the beak is indicated by a narrow wedge-shaped strip in the middle of the face, the point of which touches the lower margin of the chin. The sharp bow and stern of a canoe with a profile of a face on each side, when represented on a level or slightly rounded surface, would assume the same shape. Therefore it may be that originally the middle line was not the beak of the hawk, but the foreshortened bow or stern of the canoe. This decoration is so uniform that the explanation given here seems to me very probable.

In Fig. 65 we see a painting representing a full front view of the thunderbird. Its principal symbol is the long beak, which in front view appears like a long line descending from the nose over the mouth. It is doubtful if in this case the body may be considered as being split along the back. On account of the fact that the face is certainly represented as a full-face view, it seems to me more likely that the animal is represented with spread wings, similar to the eagle in Fig. 63.

I have described a number of sections applied in representing various animals. Heretofore we have had cases only in which the sections were rather simple. In many cases in which the adaptation of the animal form to the decorative field is more difficult, the sections and distortions are much more numerous and far-reaching than those described before.

The cut that has been applied in the totem pole (Fig. 66) is also much more intricate than the preceding ones. The upper figure represents a bird which is shown in the form of a human being, to the arms of which wings are attached. Under this figure we find a representation of the killer whale. The hind part of its body is more easily recognized than the head. A small human figure is seen riding on the dorsal fin. The tail, which appears at the lower margin of the figure, is turned backward over the back of the animal. We must therefore imagine that the head has been

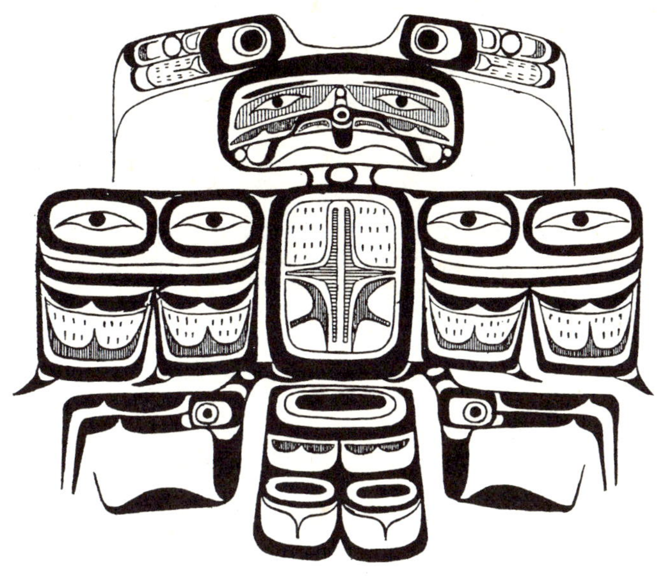

FIG. 65. Painting from front of a house representing a thunderbird. Tribe, Kwakiutl.

turned downward behind the human figure riding on the dorsal fin. We must remember that the part of the animal which is turned downward will be placed on the back of the totem pole, which is not carved, and that consequently, according to what was stated before, the artist will split it and distend it so that the middle line will appear at each edge of the carved portion of the pole. Thus the right half of the head will be brought into view on the right side of the totem pole, the left half on the left. This is the explanation of the whale's head with its teeth, which is seen in our figure next to the tail, the lower jaw being omitted. The flipper, which adjoins the head, is laid over the back of the whale, immediately under the feet of the human being riding on the dorsal fin of the whale. The figure must therefore be explained in such a way that the animal is twisted twice, the tail being turned up over the back, and the head being turned down under the stomach, the head being then split and extended outward.

Fig. 67 is a copy of a painting on the front of a box. It represents a frog. By far the greater portion of the box front is occupied by the head of the animal, which, according to what was said before, must be considered as consisting of two adjoining profiles. The symbol of the frog's head is its toothless mouth. The two black portions extending downward from the lower corners of the face are two halves of the body.

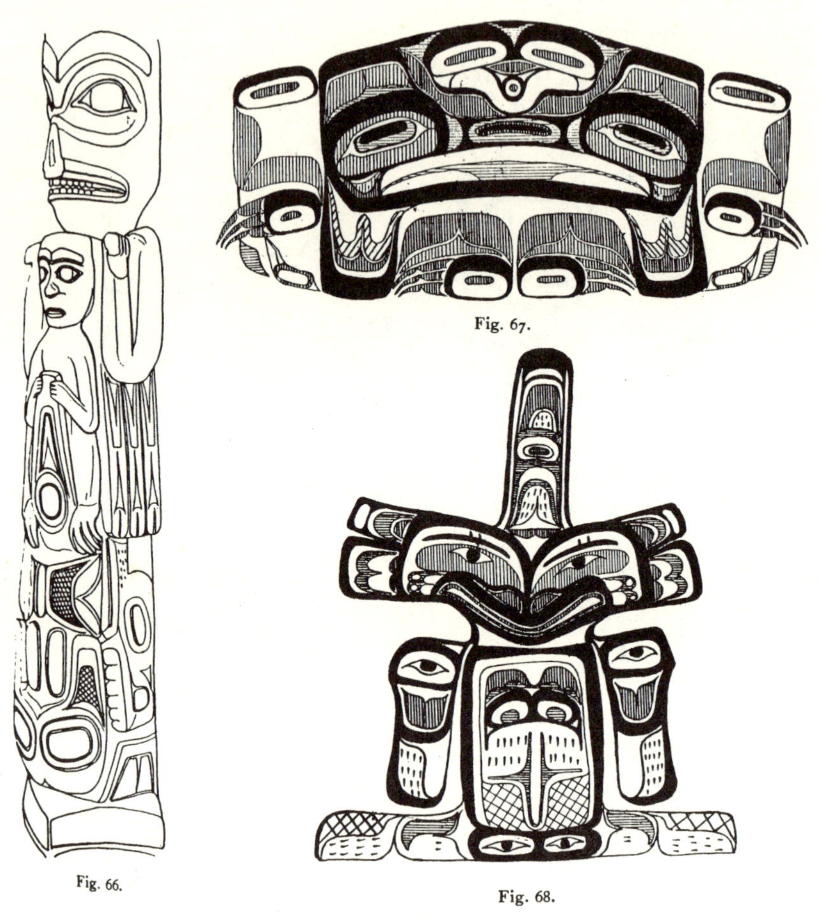

Fig. 66. Fig. 67. Fig. 68.

FIG. 66 (16/1166). Part of a model of a totem pole with design representing a killer whale. Tribe, Haida. Height from whale upward, 35 cm; width, 8 cm; depth, 6.5 cm.

FIG. 67. Painting from a box front, design representing a frog. Tribe, Haida.

FIG. 68. Painting from a housefront with design representing a killer whale. Tribe, Kwakiutl.

To these are joined the forepaws, which occupy the space below the mouth; the upper arm and forearm being turned inward, the forefeet being turned outward under the arm. The hind legs occupy the lateral field on both sides of the head. They are not connected in any way with the body of the animal.

In Fig. 68 we find a novel representation of the killer whale, which is copied from the painting on a house of the Kwakiutl Indians. The sections that have been used here are very complicated. First of all, the animal has been split along its whole back toward the front. The two profiles of the head have been joined, as described before. The painting on each side of the mouth represents gills, thus indicating that a water animal is meant. The dorsal fin, which according to the methods described heretofore would appear on both sides of the body, has been cut off from the back before the animal was split, and appears now placed over the junction of the two profiles of the head. The flippers are laid along the two sides of the body, with which they cohere only at one point each. The two halves of the tail have been twisted outward so that the lower part of the figure forms a straight line. This is done in order to fit it over the square door of the house.

In Fig. 69 the same animal has been treated in still a different manner. The figure is also the painting from a housefront of the Kwakiutl Indians. The central parts of the painting are the two profiles of the head of the killer whale. The notch in the lower jaw indicates that it also has been cut, and joined in its central part. The cut on the upper part of the face has been carried down to the upper lip. The body has disappeared entirely. The cut of the head has, however, been carried along backward the whole length of the body as far as the root of the tail, which latter has been cut off, and appears over the junction of the two profiles of the head. The dorsal fin has been split, and the two halves are joined to the upper part of the head, from which they extend upward and outward. Immediately below them the two halves of the blowhole are indicated by two small faces, the upper parts of which bear a semicircle each. The flippers are attached to the lower corners of the face. The painting on the face next to the mouth represents the gills.

Fig. 70 is another house painting of the Kwakiutl, representing the raven. The same principle has been adhered to by the artist who made this painting. The central portion of the figure is occupied by the head of the raven split from its lower side upward so that the two halves cohere along the upper edge of the beak. Then the two halves of the head have been folded upward, so that the two halves of the tongues and the two lower jaws appear on each side of the central line. The two halves of the lower side of the body are shown extending in a curved line from the corners of the mouth toward the tail, which latter has not been cut. The wings have been considerably reduced in size, and pulled upward so that they appear over each upper corner of the head. The legs occupy the right and left lower parts of the painting, the feet being disconnected from the thin legs.

In Fig. 71, which is a painting on the margin of a blanket, the sea monster described in Fig. 24 is represented. The animal is shown here as split in two along its back; but all its parts, except the head, the paws, and the tail, are much reduced in size. The two enormous eyes, and between them the nose, will readily be recognized. The teeth are indicated by a series of slanting lines under each eye, but the lower jaws of both halves have been omitted. The whole body is represented by the thin

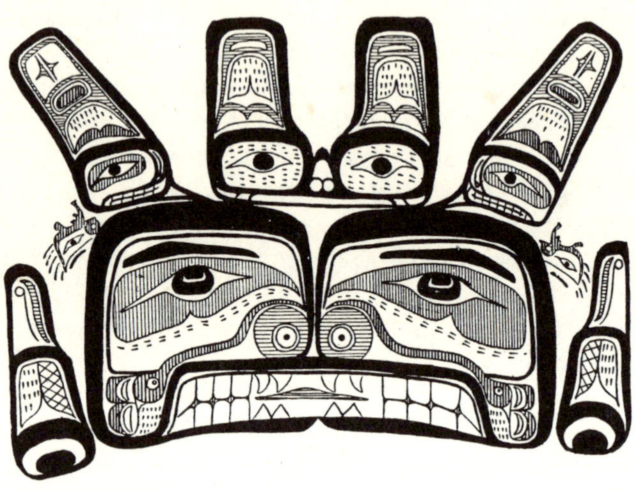

FIG. 69. Painting from a housefront, design representing a killer whale. Tribe, Kwakiutl.

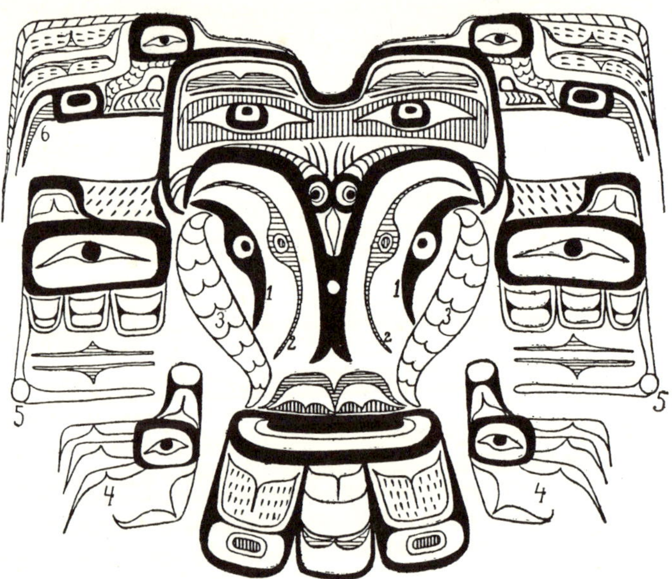

FIG. 70. Painting from a housefront representing a raven. Tribe, Kwakiutl. (1) Lower jaw; (2) tongue; (3) chest; (4) feet; (5) legs; (6) wings.

line extending from the lower outer corner of the eyes upward, then along the upper margin of the painting, and downward again. The three dorsal fins are shown over this line—one-half of each on each side of the back. The arms are indicated by two curves under the line indicating the back. The fin of the arm is shown under the forearm. While all these are of small size, the paw which adjoins the forearm is shown on a very large scale, the claws turned toward the face. The line representing the body runs toward both ends of the painting along the lower margin until it is merged into the tail, one-half of which is shown on each side. In this specimen the proportions of the body are much more distorted than in any previous case.

The following series of figures are designs found on a number of silver bracelets. The animals represented on these are also shown very fragmentarily.

In Fig. 72 we see the beaver cut in two along its back. The face does not need any further explanation. The forelegs adjoin it on each side, the toes being turned inward; but the whole rest of the body has been omitted, except the two halves of the tail, which the artist was compelled to show, because they are symbols of the animal.

In Fig. 73 we recognize the sea monster, with a bear's head and a whale's body. Here also by far the greater portion of the etching represents the head and forearms of the monster. The fins, which are attached to the upper arms near the elbow, are shown on a rather small scale. The whole rest of the body is of very small size, the two halves of the body, with the adjoining half of the tail, occupying only the outer upper margin of the bracelet. I am not quite clear whether the artist intended to represent the two halves of the dorsal fin by the curved ornament adjoining the hat which rises over the nose of the monster.

The hawk which is shown in Fig. 74 has been cut in a different manner, namely, from the beak backward, the two halves being then turned outward. The center of the design is occupied by the two halves of the head, and the two talons which adjoin it. The wings are cut off from the body, and occupy the outer corners of the design.

The designs on the following series of carvings are no less conventionalized. Fig. 75 is a sea monster adjusted to a circular slate dish. The carving is perfectly symmetrical; but, owing to an accident, the drawing appears asymmetrical because it has been taken from an eccentric point of view. Here also the center is occupied by the head of the animal. The tail is seen under the lowest part of the mouth, turned upward in front of the body. The arms are shortened considerably. They are attached to the lower corners of the mouth, the paws touching the chin. The fins are joined to the upper part of the arms, and are turned upward so that they lie close to the sides of the face and about on a level with the ears.

In Fig. 76, which represents the front of a small box carved in slate, the same sea monster is shown. Again we see the animal cut in two, the section separating

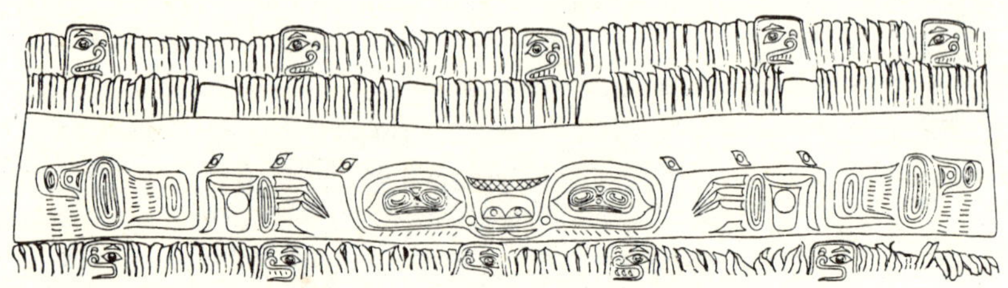

FIG. 71 (16/355). Painting from the edge of a blanket representing a sea monster. Northern British Columbia. Length, 139 cm.

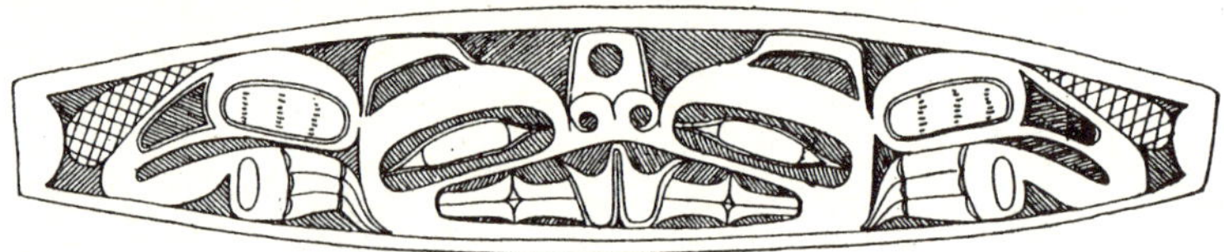

Fig. 72.

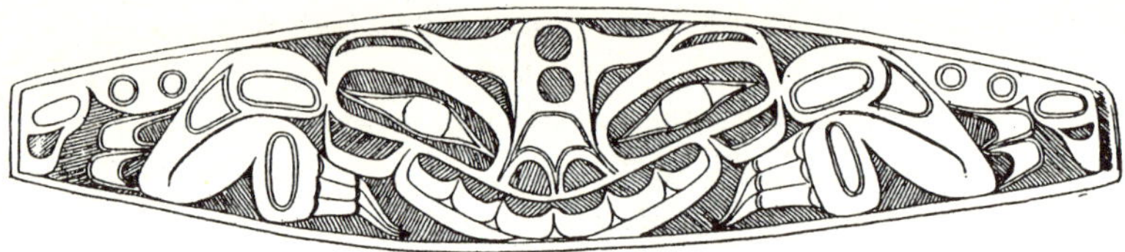

Fig. 73.

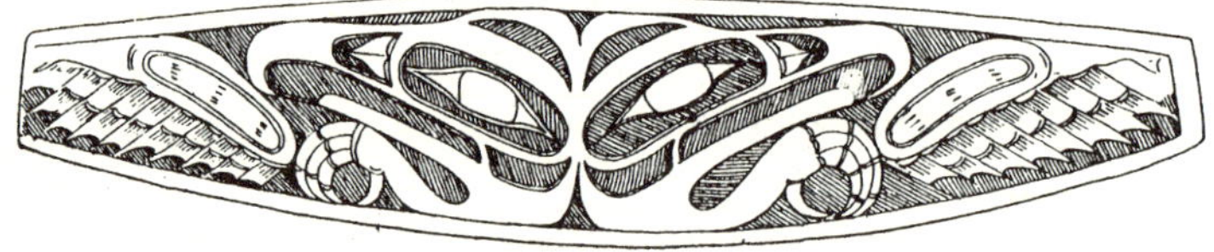

Fig. 74.

FIG. 72 (E/2462). Design on a silver bracelet representing a beaver. Tribe, Haida. Height, 3.5 cm.

FIG. 73 (E/2461). Design on a silver bracelet representing a sea monster. Tribe, Haida. Height, 3.5 cm.

FIG. 74 (E/2463). Design on a silver bracelet representing a hawk. Tribe, Haida. Height, 3.5 cm.

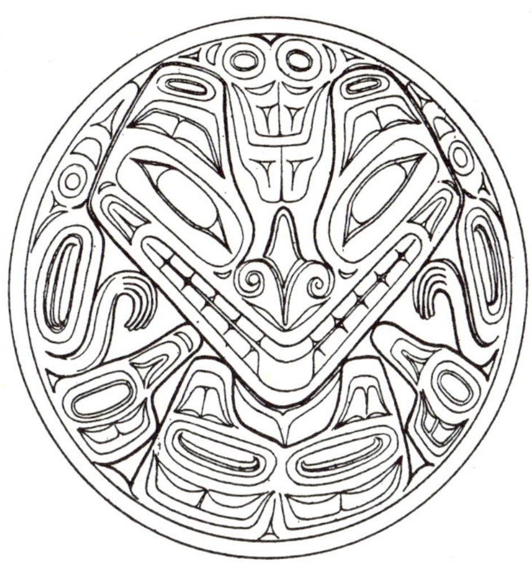

FIG. 75 (16/611). Slate dish with design representing a sea monster. Tribe, Haida. Diameter, 36.5 cm; depth, 7.5 cm.

the eyes and the ears, the mouth, however, being left intact. Here the whole body has been omitted, with the exception of the paws, to which the fins are attached. The paws will be recognized turned inward under the mouth, while the fins extend upward along the outer margins of the slab. The dorsal fin has been bisected, and one-half is shown in each upper corner. The ornament in the center of the upper margin probably represents the tail turned upward over the back so that it almost touches the head.

Fig. 77 represents the carving on a slate slab. We have here a different representation of the sea monster, which is also, as we might say, very much abbreviated. The head occupies by far the larger portion of the carving. The body, which is seen underneath the head, occupying the center of the slab, is indicated by a comparatively small square with rounded edges, which is decorated with two fins. The rest of the decoration on the lower edge of the slab must be interpreted as the arms of the monster, the large face on each corner representing an elbow. The whole arm, extending from the elbow to the hand, is omitted. The latter is indicated by an oval the center of which is occupied by an eye. From it rise the three fingers or claws. The important symbols of the monster, the fins, which are attached to the forearm, are shown adjoining the elbow, and rise along the sides of the slab, outside of the

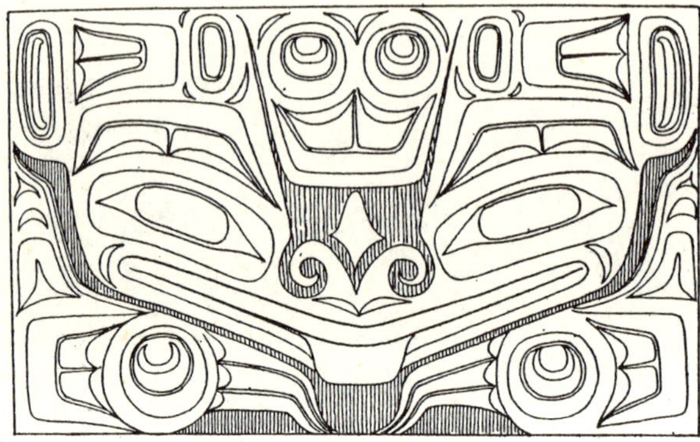

FIG. 76 (16/687). Front of a slate box with design representing a sea monster. Tribe, Haida. Size, 18.5 × 30 cm.

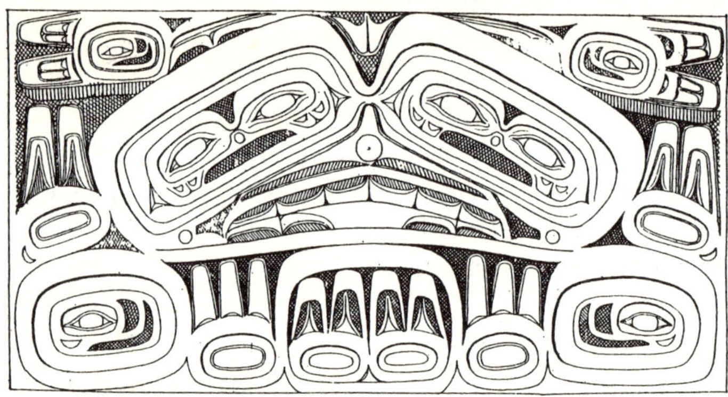

FIG. 77 (16/1149). Slate slab with design representing a sea monster. Tribe, Haida. Size, 14 × 26.5 cm.

eyes. The two ornaments occupying the upper corners of the slab are undoubtedly the tail of the monster.

The shark which is shown in Fig. 78 is found on one end of a small food tray. I do not need to repeat the description of the shark's face, on which the characteristic symbols will be recognized. I have introduced this figure here in order to show that the whole body of the animal has been omitted with the sole exception of its pec-

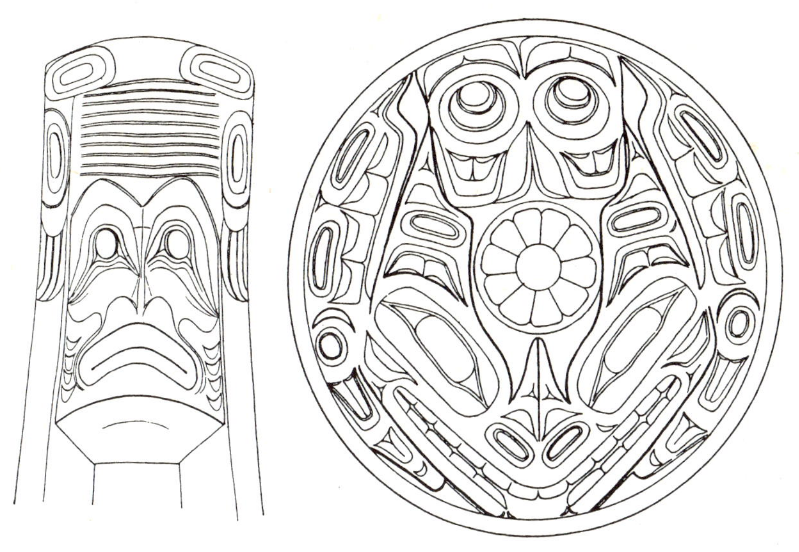

FIG. 78 (16/1187). Design from the end of a food tray representing a shark. Tribe, Tlingit. Central length of design, 12.5 cm.

FIG. 79 (16/882). Slate dish with design representing a sculpin. Tribe, Haida. Diameter, 34 cm; depth, 6.5 cm.

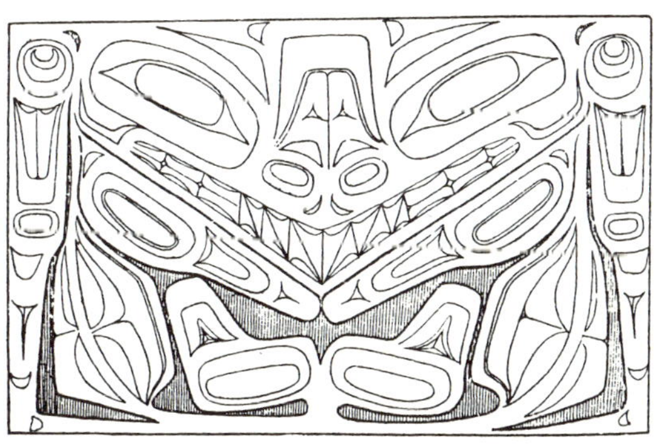

FIG. 80 (16/687). Front of a slate box with design representing a sculpin. Tribe, Haida. Size, 18.5 × 30 cm.

toral fins, which are carved on the rim of the tray on both sides of the forehead. Their position is somewhat analogous to the one found on the totem pole (Fig. 33).

In Figs. 79 and 80 we find the representations of the sculpin distorted and dissected in the same manner as the sea monster on the preceding figures.

In Fig. 79 the sculpin has been adapted to a circular slate dish. The center of the design is occupied by a rosette, which has undoubtedly been copied from European designs. In the drawing the outlines of the various parts of the body have been strengthened in order to make their relations somewhat clearer. It will be noticed that the head is split in two, cohering only at the nose and the upper jaw. The two spines rise immediately from the nose. The two halves of the body extend from the corners of the face upward along the rim of the dish. There they grow thinner, indicating the thin portion of the fish body near the tail. The tail has not been split, and is turned upward and backward so that it touches the central rosette. A comparison between this design and the design at the center of the upper margin in Fig. 76 will show a great similarity between the two, thus making it probable, that, as stated before, the latter design is intended to represent the tail of the monster. The pectoral fins of the sculpin are shown in a rather abnormal position. They are turned forward from the body so that they adjoin the lower jaw. They will be recognized between the jaws and the rim of the dish. The dorsal fin is indicated by the long pointed ornaments extending from the eye toward the tail.

In the design of Fig. 80, the sculpin has been dissected in a somewhat different manner. The head occupies the upper margin of the slab. It has a remarkably triangular shape. The body has been bisected from head to tail, and turned and twisted in such a manner that each half extends in a curve downward from the corners of the face to the middle of the lower margin of the slab. The pectoral fins have been left in contact with the corners of the mouth, and are placed in the same position as in the preceding figure, namely, adjoining the lower jaw. They meet just below the chin of the animal. I believe the ornaments which are stretched along the right and left margins of the slab represent the dorsal fins of the sculpin.

Our last figure (Fig. 81) shows the design of a beautiful Chilcat blanket. In this specimen the distortion and dissection of the animal have been carried further than in any of the preceding specimens. On the design are shown the two profiles of the head, the dorsal fin, the tail, the flippers, and the chest of the killer whale. In order to understand the design, we must imagine the whale placed head downward, the chest toward the observer. The design on the chest is the large face which occupies the center of the upper margin of the blanket. Then we must imagine that the head has been cut off, and split and twisted in such a way that the two halves of the mouth are turned outward. Next we must imagine the body of the animal cut through just above the chest, and turned backward so that the tail is placed behind the head. Then the two halves of the head have been moved to the right and to the left in

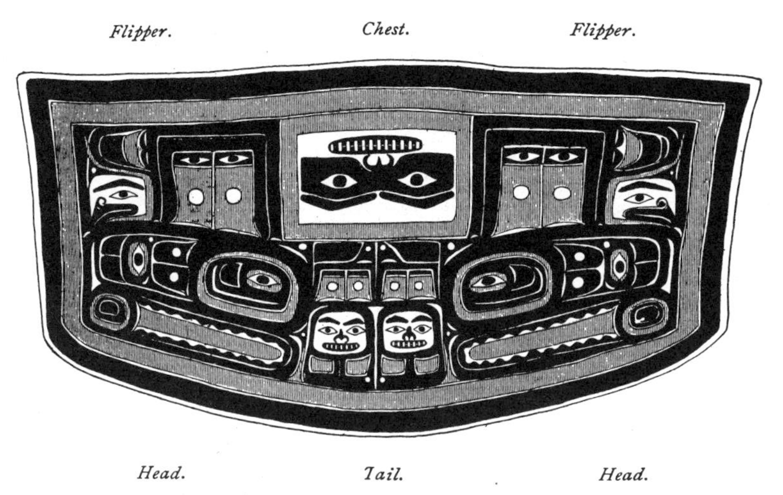

FIG. 81. Chilcat blanket representing a killer whale. Tribe, Tlingit. Width, 156 cm; height, 77 cm.

order to allow the tail to appear between the two halves. In this position the dorsal fin would be hidden behind the chest of the animal. In order to make it visible it has been cut off from the back and moved toward the tail until it appears just above the tail; it has been split and flattened so that both halves, the left and the right, are seen under the chest. Finally the two flippers have been considerably enlarged and twisted in such a way that they occupy the two upper corners of the blanket.

I will add a remark in regard to the frequent occurrence of the eye ornament on all these designs. An examination of our figures will show that in most cases it is used to indicate a joint. Shoulder, elbow, hand, hips, knees, feet, the points of attachment of fins, tails, and so forth, are always indicated by eyes, which, I believe, may best be interpreted as representations of the surfaces of ball-and-socket joints.

We can now sum up the results of our considerations. In the first part of this paper I described the symbols of a number of animals, and pointed out that in many cases there is a tendency to substitute the symbol for the whole animal. The works of art which I described in the second part of my paper may be said to illustrate a principle which is apparently diametrically opposed to the former. While the symbolism developed a tendency to suppress parts of the animal, we find in the efforts of the artist to adapt the form of the animal to the decorative field a far-reaching desire to preserve, so far as feasible, the whole animal; and, with the exception of a few profiles, we do not find a single instance which can be interpreted as an endeavor to give a perspective and therefore realistic view of an animal. We have found a variety of methods applied which tend to bring the greatest possible part of the animal form into the decorative field. I conclude from this that it is the ideal of the native artist to show the whole animal, and that the idea of perspective representation is entirely foreign to his mind. His representations are combinations of symbols of the various parts of the body of the animal, arranged in such a way that if possible the whole animal is brought into view. The arrangement, however, is so that the natural relation of the parts is preserved, being changed only by means of sections and distortions, but so that the natural contiguity of the parts is preserved.

The success of the artist depends upon his cleverness in designing lines of dissection and methods of distortion. When he finds it impossible to represent the whole animal, he confines himself to rearranging its most characteristic parts, always of course including its symbols. There is a tendency to exaggerate the size of the symbols at the expense of other parts of the subject. I presume this is the line in which the two principles of the decorative art of the Indians of the North Pacific coast of America merge into each other. The gradual emphasizing of the symbol at the expense of other parts of the body leads in many cases to their entire suppression, and to designs in which the animal is indicated only by its symbols.

5. Facial Paintings of the Indians of Northern British Columbia

In this essay, originally published as part of the Jesup North Pacific Expedition memoirs, Boas continues to investigate the relationship between the representation of an image and the shape of the object on which it appears. He had addressed this question at some length the year before in "The Decorative Art of the Indians of the North Pacific Coast." Here, he focuses on how artists adjust the images that they paint upon the most "difficult" surface, the human face. He arranges examples of facial paintings drawn by the famous Haida artist Charles Edenshaw (identified here as Ē´dEnsâ), according to their relative realism.

The art of the Indians of northern British Columbia shows a peculiar development that has for a long time attracted the attention of investigators. While among most primitive people we find a tendency to the development of geometric designs, the Indians of northern British Columbia use for decorative purposes almost exclusively animal motives. The animal forms are highly conventionalized, and may be recognized by a number of symbols characteristic of the various animals that the artists try to represent. The Indians have adopted a peculiar method of adapting the animal form to the decorative field. There is no endeavor to represent the form by means of perspective, but the attempt is made to adapt the form as nearly as possible to the decorative field by means of distortion and dissection. The more clever an artist is in designing methods of distortion and dissection which fill the decorative field and bring into view all the important parts of the animal body, the greater is his success.[1] It will be seen, therefore, that the greater the difference between the form of the decorative field and the form of the animal to be represented, the greater will be the difficulty of adaptation. When an animal is to be represented on a bracelet, it is shown as though it were cut from head to tail, and as though the arm were pushed through the opening, the whole animal thus surrounding the wrist. The same method is followed in the decoration of dishes, where the sides of the animal are shown on the sides of the dish, while the opening of the dish represents the back of the animal, its bottom the lower side of the animal. When the animal form is to be shown on flat surfaces, the body is generally represented as split in two, and spread in both directions, so that it appears like two profiles placed side by side.

The peculiarities of the conventionalism of these tribes appear most clearly

Reprinted from *American Museum of Natural History Memoirs*, vol. 2, pp. 13–24, 1898.

1. I have explained in another place the fundamental ideas underlying this art [Boas 1897a; chap. 4, this volume].

where the difficulty of adaptation of the subject to the decorative field is greatest. I concluded, therefore, that if I could obtain a series of representations on very difficult surfaces, the principles of conventionalism would appear most clearly. No surface seems to be more difficult to treat, and to adapt to animal forms, than the human face. For this reason I resolved to make a collection of facial paintings such as are used by the Indians when adorning themselves for festive dances.

The subjects that are used for this purpose are largely the crests of the various families. These are laid on in black, red, blue, and green; the colors being mixed with grease, and put on with the fingers, with brushes, or by means of wooden stamps cut out for this purpose.

The collection which is discussed in the present paper was obtained from Ē´dᴇɴsâ [Edenshaw], a Haida chief from Masset, one of the most famous artists of the tribe. I have arranged the material in such an order as to begin with the most realistic, and proceed to higher and higher degrees of conventionalism, until in the last group of paintings we find a number of purely geometrical designs representing animal forms.

One interesting point was brought out in the beginning of my investigation. The decorations differ according to the rank and wealth of the wearer. The full and rather realistic representations of animals are considered of greater value, and as indicating higher rank, than conventional representations which consist of symbols of the animals.

Before I begin to discuss the meanings of the facial paintings, it may be well to make a brief statement explaining the social organization of the Haida. The tribe is divided into two clans—the Raven clan, or Q'oā´la; and the Eagle clan, or G˙it'ina´—which are exogamous. Each of these clans is subdivided into a great number of families, many of which derive their names from the localities at which they are believed to have originated. Each family has a number of crests. A few of these are common to all the families of the clan. All the G˙it'ina´, for instance, have the eagle, and almost all the Q'oā´la have the bear and the killer whale. But besides these, each family has a number of special crests, all of which are derived from certain traditions setting forth the adventures of an ancestor of the family. Most of these traditions tell of his encounter with an animal or a spirit, which, from that time on, became the crest of his family. The Haida have maternal institutions counting descent in the female line; that is to say, the child belongs to its mother's clan, and inherits its maternal uncle's rank and property. Not all the members of the family use all its crests. In the beginning the youth seems to possess the most general crest of the clan only—the G˙it'ina´ the eagle, and the Q'oā´la the bear and the killer whale. As he reaches higher social rank by repeated distributions of property among the members of the opposite clan, he becomes entitled to the privilege of using other crests; but the use of the total number belonging to the family seems to be restricted to its chief.

I shall now proceed to a description of the designs represented on Plates I–VI.[2]

Fig. 1, Plate I, represents on the left side of the face the killer whale; on the right side of the face, the right whale. The form of the animal is to a certain extent adapted to the form of the eyebrow. The Indian considers heavy, regular eyebrows a sign of beauty. Naturally the eyebrow of the Indian is very wide, covering part of the upper eyelid, and ascending rather high on the temples. In order to give the eyebrow line the desired shape, the Indians, particularly the women, sometimes pluck the hair from the eyelid, so as to procure a sharp line along the upper rim of the orbit. A comparison of Fig. 2, Plate II, and Fig. 3, Plate V, shows that the two animal forms are intended to emphasize the eyebrows of the dancer. The designs of the killer whale and of the right whale are identical. They are identified by their color, red being the color of the right whale, black that of the killer whale. The same use of red and black for identifying right whale and killer whale may be observed in Figs. 14 and 15, Plate III, the first of which represents the back of the right whale, while the second represents the dorsal fin of the killer whale. Red is also used for symbolizing the eyes of the whale in Fig. 11, Plate IV. The right whale and killer whale design in Fig. 1, Plate I, is supplemented by the red painting on the lips. This painting symbolizes copper, one of the most valuable possessions of the Haida. It was used by Chief Skidegate, from whom the village ʟqā´gîlt received its current name. He also wore, on festive occasions, a single bristle of a sea lion, placed upright in his hair, which was tied in a knot on the top of his head. This single bristle indicated that there was no one of equal rank in the whole tribe.

Figs. 2 and 3, Plate I, represent the halibut, and require no further remarks. The whole series from Fig. 2 to Fig. 13 are rather realistic representations of whole animals or of the larger portion of animals. The designs are not always placed in the position shown on the plate. The red sun with its black rays (Fig. 8) was worn sometimes between the eyes, sometimes covering the mouth and the lower part of the nose. It was also made of wood, and worn on the forehead. In this case the rim of the red disk was inlaid with pieces of abalone shell. This was the ornament used by the chief of the Kits'adê´s of the Stakinqoan of the Tlingit. It was called the "house of the sun." The rainbow (Fig. 9, Plate I) was also placed in different positions. Sometimes it was worn extending from the ear on one side to the posterior corner of the jaw on the other, the concave side turned upward; the blue line running from the ear downward to the jaw, following the lower border of the jaw, while the green line formed the upper margin. Sometimes it was placed on the forehead, the green

2. From drawings by Mr. Rudolph Weber.

EXPLANATION OF PLATE I

FIG. 1. Left eyebrow: killer whale; black. Right eyebrow: whale; red. Lips painted red, representing copper. Used by the Yak[u]g'it'inai' of ʟqā'gîlt or Skidegate. (G'it'ina')

FIG. 2. Halibut; red and black. Used by the Sta'stas of K''iū'st'a, the Yê'das of the Kaigani; the Ts'āʟlānas of lā'k'ō. (G'it'ina')

FIG. 3. Halibut; red and black. Used by the Sta'stas of K''iū'st'a,, the Yê'das of the Kaigani; the Ts'āʟlānas of lā'k'ō. (G'it'ina')

FIG. 4. Devilfish; red and black. Used by the Yak[u]lā'nas of lā'k'ō and Nanaā'ri of the Tlingit. (Q'oā'la)

FIG. 5. Dog salmon; red and black. Used by the Sk'a'g'nas xa'edra (dog salmon house people) of the Kaigani. (G'it'ina')

FIG. 6. Dog salmon; red and black. Used by the Sk'a'g'nas xa'edra (dog salmon house people) of the Kaigani. (G'it'ina')

FIG. 7. Starfish; red. Used by the S'ale'ndas of lā'k'ō. (G'it'ina')

FIG. 8. Sun; red and black. Used by the Kits'adê's of the Stakinqoan of the Tlingit. (G'it'ina')

FIG. 9. Rainbow; upper margin green, body red, lower margin blue. Used by the Stastasqēowai of Lga'it or Gold Harbor. (Q'oā'la)

FIG. 10. Moon; crescent on chin red; ornaments on cheeks made of abalone shell glued on to the skin. Used by the Yak[u]lā'nas of lā'k'ō and ʟqēnōʟlā'nas of Q'u'na or Skidans. (Q'oā'la)

FIG. 11. Dog salmon; red and black. Used by the Sk'a'g'nas xa'edra of the Kaigani. (G'it'ina')

FIG. 12. Halibut; red and black. Used by the Sta'stas of K''iū'st'a, the Yê'das of the Kaigani; the Ts'āʟlānas of lā'k'ō. (G'it'ina')

FIG. 13. Halibut; red and black. Used by the Sta'stas of K''iū'st'a, the Yê'das of the Kaigani; the Ts'āʟlānas of lā'k'ō. (G'it'ina')

FIG. 14. Woodpecker; red and black. Used by the Taslā'nas of Dā'dens. (Q'oā'la)

FIG. 15. On forehead: sea lion blowing; black. On chin: throat of killer whale; red. Used by the Skoā'ʟ'adas of Lga'it or Gold Harbor. (Q'oā'la)

FIG. 16. Wolf; red and black. Used by the Q'adasqē'owai of T'ano' or Tlo. (Q'oā'la)

border following the hairline. Fig. 10 represents the crescent of the moon. Abalone shells are glued to the cheeks. These are intended to represent the faint light of the moon illuminated by the reflection from the earth. Sometimes the design is supplemented by a crescent-shaped neck ring made of wood inlaid with large pieces of abalone shell. In Figs. 11, 12, and 13, large portions of the dog salmon and halibut are represented.

The following three figures (Figs. 14, 15, 16, Plate I) symbolize animals by means of their heads. In Fig. 14 is seen the head of the woodpecker in black and red. Fig. 15 is the sea lion. It is shown reclining backwards, indicating that the sea lion is blowing. The chin is daubed with red. The same design is found frequently in the series of facial paintings represented here; for instance, in Figs. 11 and 12, Plate II, and Fig. 8, Plate V, it represents the throat of the killer whale. The teeth and the long snout in Fig. 16 signify the wolf.

In all the preceding figures the face was treated like a flat surface; the whole figure, or an important part of the figure, being placed in a convenient position. The only cases in which a certain amount of adaptation to the human face is found are

Memoirs Am. Mus. Nat. Hist., Vol. II. Plate I.

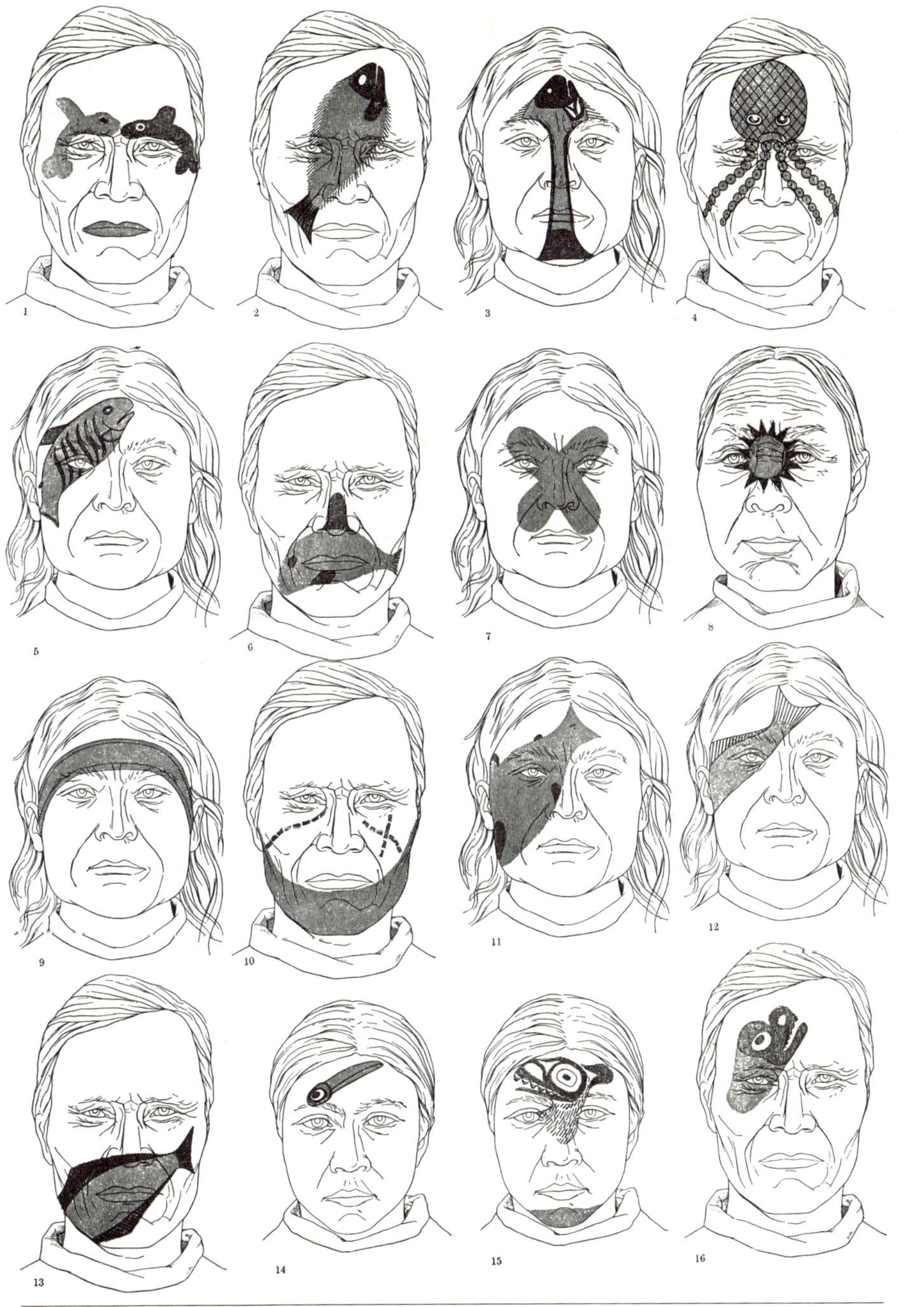

EXPLANATION OF PLATE II

FIG. 1. Beaver; red and black. Over nose: hat; over eyebrows: ears; on cheeks: paws; on chin and lips: tail. Used by the Sta´stas of K·'iū'st'a. (G·it'ina')

FIG. 2. Raven; red and black. Over nose: hat; over eyebrows: beak split in two; on upper eyelids: tongue; on left cheek: tail; on right cheek: wing; on chin and lips: belly. Used by the G·it'ina´.

FIG. 3. Killer whale; black and green. On right cheek: head; on forehead: dorsal fin; on left cheek: tail. Used by women of the Sta´stas of K·'iū'st´a. (Q'oā´la)

FIG. 4. Dogfish; red. On forehead: head with nostrils; under eyes: gills; on right cheek: fin; under note: tail split in two. Used by the Q'onaq'ē´owai of T'ano´ or Tlo. (G·it'ina')

FIG. 5. Sculpin; black, blue, lips red. The lips represent the mouth; on upper lip: the spines; nostrils represented by circles on each side of mouth; on nose: dorsal fins; on forehead: tail. Used by the G·it'ina´ of Sga'nguai or Ninstance. (G·it'ina')

FIG. 6. Starfish; red. The arms placed side by side. Used by the S'ale'ndas of lā'k·ō. (G·it'ina')

FIG. 7. Mouth of the sea monster Ts'anxō´utsē (sea bear); red and black. Used by the Yak[u]lā´nas of lā´k·ō and the Nanaā´ri of the Stakinqoan of the Tlingit. (Q'oā´la)

FIG. 8. Proboscis of mosquito; black. Tsimshian. (Laxskī'yek)

FIG. 9. Beak of hawk; black and red. Used by the Slêngalā'nas of la'an. (Q'oā´la)

FIG. 10. Mouth of frog; red. Used by the Q'onaq'ē´owai of Q'u'na or Skidans. (G·it'ina')

FIG. 11. On nose and cheek: paw and tail of sea lion; black. Tail under right eye. On chin: throat of killer whale; red. Used by the Skoā'l'adas of ʟga´it or Gold Harbor. (Q'oā´la)

FIG. 12. On forehead: paw of sea lion; black. On chin: throat of killer whale; red. Used by the Skoā'l'adas of Lga´it or Gold Harbor. (Q'oā´la)

FIG. 13. On cheeks and forehead: tracks of bear; red and black. On chin: tail of bear; red. Used by the Yak[u]lā´nas of lā´k·ō and Nanaā´ri of the Stakinqoan of the Tlingit. (Q'oā´la)

FIG. 14. Paws of the sea monster Ts'anxō´utsē; black. Used by the Yak[u]lā´nas of lā´k·ō and by the Nanaā´ri of the Stakinqoan of the Tlingit. (Q'oā´la)

FIG. 15. Paws of wolf; red and black. Used by the Q'adasqē´owai of T'ano´ or Tlo. (Q'oā´la)

FIG. 16. Talons of eagle; black. Used by the Q'onaq'ē´owai of T'ano´ or Tlo. (G·it'ina')

the whales in Fig. 1, the rainbow as described before, and the crescent of the moon (Fig. 10).

In the series of designs represented on Plate II (Figs. 1–5), a different principle has been made use of. In some of these the face itself is utilized as part of the conventionalized design. In Fig. 1, Plate II, we see the beaver. One of the principal symbols of the beaver is the scaly tail, which is indicated by hachure lines. The tail is generally represented as being raised in front of the beaver's body. It is shown in this manner in the present design, extending from the chin upward to the nose. The eyes of the person represent at the same time the eyes of the beaver. I explained, in the paper quoted before, that the ears of all animals are shown surmounting the eyes. For this reason the beaver's ears are here shown immediately over the eyebrows. The beaver's hat is also painted on the face, and represented in the usual conventional manner by means of three circles, which represent the rings on the hat. The paws are shown on the cheeks. Their position intimates that they are represented as though they were raised up to the mouth, in the same manner in which the beaver

Plate II.

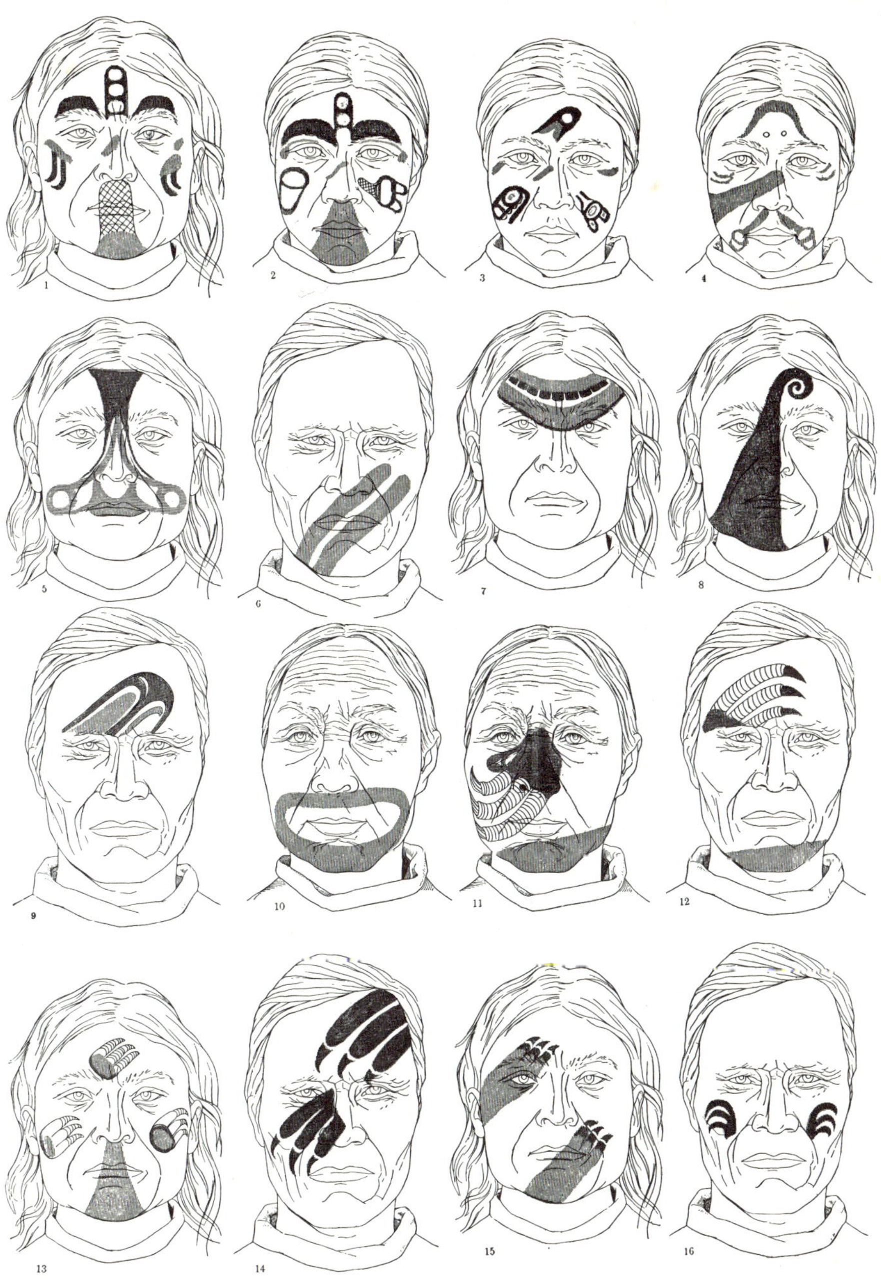

is usually represented on the carvings and paintings of the Haida. Fig. 2, Plate II, represents the raven. The eyebrows are here utilized to represent the beak cut in two. The two profiles of the beak are shown in such a way that their tips are placed at the inner angles of the eyebrows. The tongue is shown in red on the upper eyelids, its base being near the outer corners of the eyes. The raven's hat rises on the forehead, over the nose. It is represented by two circles. The wing is shown in black on the right cheek, the tail on the left cheek. The lower side of the body is symbolized by the red painting extending from nose to chin. In this case the peculiar method of dissecting the body, and showing parts of it in such an arrangement as to fill the decorative field, has been applied. Fig. 3, Plate II, shows the killer whale in profile, dissected so as to fit the face. This design is used principally by women. The head of the animal, with its large teeth, is shown on the right cheek; the tail on the left cheek; and the dorsal fin on the forehead. The green paint with which the base of the dorsal fin, the joint of the tail, and the eye are shown is used exclusively by the family Sta´stas. Sometimes, instead of showing dorsal fin, head, and tail, the dorsal fin alone is used to symbolize the killer whale.

In Fig. 4, Plate II, we have a representation of the dogfish, arranged also on the principle of dissection. In this case, as in Fig. 1, Plate II, part of the face is utilized to represent the animal. The eyes of the person are the eyes of the dogfish. On the forehead, over the eyes, rises its peculiar long snout with the two nostrils. The gills are shown by two curved lines just below the outer corners of the eyes. The tail is represented as cut in two, one half extending from the right nostril downward, the other from the left nostril downward. The asymmetrical form of the tail is shown clearly in each half. The dorsal fin is placed on the right cheek, extending from the ear up to the nose. Sometimes this painting is supplemented by black daubs on both cheeks. The color of the dogfish is red, like that of the whale, as may be seen from a comparison of the present figure and Fig. 16, Plate III.

The characteristic colors of the sculpin are red, blue, and black, as may be seen in Fig. 5, Plate II, and Figs. 5–8, Plate IV. Fig. 5, Plate II, must be interpreted as an adaptation of the whole figure of the sculpin to the human face. The mouth is painted red, representing the mouth of the sculpin. On the upper lip rise the two spines which are found over the mouth of the sculpin. The round nostrils are placed on the cheeks, adjoining the outer corners of the mouth, and the continuous dorsal fin is indicated by the blue triangle extending along the bridge of the nose. The tail is shown in black on the forehead. A comparison with the representations of the sculpin on Plate IV shows that in the latter case only a few of the symbols applied here have been made use of to represent the fish.

The two red bars of Fig. 6, Plate II, are the arms of the starfish, which are shown in the form of a cross in Fig. 7, Plate I.

In the following series of paintings the animals to be represented are shown by means of symbols. I have arranged them in such a way as to bring out the various parts of the body that have been utilized. In Fig. 7, Plate II, we find the large mouth of the sea monster Ts'ānxō´utsē in red and black, with its enormous teeth. The characteristic colors of the monster are red and black, with black dorsal fin. The name may be translated as "grizzly bear of the sea." It is identified with the sea monster Hagulâ´q of the Tsimshian. It is represented as half bear and half killer whale. It has two tails—a bear's tail and a whale's tail—and an enormous dorsal fin perforated at its base. Very often a human face is shown at the base of the fin. The Indians maintain that this face is characteristic of the sea monster; but it must be borne in mind that in all the representations of animals we find a tendency to indicate joints by means of eyes, which often develop into faces, and that fins and tails are always shown as connected to the body by means of joints. Fig. 8 is the long proboscis of the mosquito. In Fig. 9 the beak of the hawk is shown, characterized by the returning point of the beak [see chap. 4, this volume; Boas 1897:131]; the red line under the beak represents the tongue of the bird. In Fig. 10 we see the large toothless mouth of the frog. Sometimes the lips are reddened as a symbol of the frog, also symbolizing its toothless mouth. It is interesting to note that the last-named painting is utilized for a variety of purposes. I mentioned before, in describing Fig. 1, Plate I, that this painting represented copper, the symbol of wealth. This seems to be the most frequent interpretation. In the present case it represents the frog, while in other cases it seems to indicate the blood of the slave killed during the celebration of the festival, and buried under a post of the house; but it seems that in the last-named case the painting is not confined to the lips, but extends slightly beyond their margins.

In the following series of figures the feet of the animals are used as symbols. In Figs. 11 and 12 we see the feet of the sea lion. In Fig. 11 its tail is shown attached to the base of the foot, extending over the cheek, under the right eye. Fig. 13 represents the tracks of the bear, and the bear's tail on the chin. In Fig. 14 we have the feet of the sea-monster Ts'ānxō´utsē; in Fig. 15, the feet of the wolf; and in Fig. 16, the talons of the eagle. The last named are also used in a variety of ways. Sometimes, instead of painting the cheeks with the eagle's talons, the hair is put up in a bunch on top of the head, tied with cedar bark dyed red in a decoction of alder bark, and an eagle's talon protruding from the knot forward. A large square piece of an abalone shell is fastened to it in such a way that the eagle's talon appears to hold the shell. Still another method of wearing the eagle's talons is as follows: A head ring is made of twisted cedar bark dyed red in a decoction of alder bark, and the eagle's talons are tied to the sides of the ring in such a way that they extend from the sides toward the middle on the forehead. This ornament is used by the chief of the Yak^{u}lā´nas when celebrating the erection of a new house. On this occasion slaves are killed, and buried under the house post. This ceremony is symbolized by the red painting of the lips, and of the skin immediately surrounding the lips. Women wear the sym-

EXPLANATION OF PLATE III

FIG. 1. Feet of mountain goat; black. Used by the ʟqenoʟlā´nas of Q'u´na or Skidans. (Q'oā´la)
FIG. 2. Tail of the monster Wasx; red. Used by the G'it'i'ns of ʟqā´gîlt or Skidegate. (G˙it'ina´)
FIG. 3. Tail of wolf; red and black. Used by the Qadasqē´owai of T'ano´ or Tlo. (Q'oā´la)
FIG. 4. Tail of hawk; red and black. Used by the Sʟêgalā'nas of la'an. (Q'oā´la)
FIG. 5. Tail of woodpecker; red and black. Used by the Taslā'nas of Dā'dᴇns. (Q'oā´la)
FIG. 6. On forehead: tail of raven; red and black. On neck: throat of raven; red. Used by the G˙it'ina´.
FIG. 7. Tail of raven; red and black. Used by the Yak[u]lā´nas of lā'k˙ō, and the Yēʟnasxā´edra of Kaigani. (G˙it'ina´)
FIG. 8. Raven wings; copper tips glued on to skin, bases green paint. Used by the G'itk'amga'n (G˙itsē´es) of the Tsimshian. (Qanha'da)
FIG. 9. On face: raven's wing; black. On neck: raven's throat; red. Used by the G˙it'ina´.
FIG. 10. Feathers of the bird Ts'ā'gul; red. Painting used by Nenk'ilsʟasʟingai´.
FIG. 11. Tuft of puffin; red and black. Used by the Q'oā´la of the Kaigani.
FIG. 12. Tuft of puffin; red and black. Used by the Q'oā´la of the Kaigani.
Fig. 13. Arm of devilfish; red and black. Used by the Sk'ag'nas xā'edra of the Kaigani. (G˙it'ina´)
FIG. 14. Back of right whale; red. Used by the Q'oā´la.
FIG. 15. Dorsal fin of killer whale; black. Used by the Q'oā´la.
FIG. 16. Back and fin of dogfish; red. Used by the Q'onaq'ē´owai of T'ano´ or Tlo. (G˙it'ina´)

bol of the eagle in the form of ear ornaments made of abalone shell, which are cut in the shape of eagle's talons. Fig. 1, Plate III, shows the hoofs of the mountain goat.

The next series of paintings symbolize the animals by means of their tails. In Fig. 2, Plate III, we see the tail of the fabulous monster Wasx. This monster is believed to be half wolf and half whale. It is capable of hunting on land as well as in the waters. Its favorite game is whales; and when returning from hunting it carries one whale under each arm, one in its mouth, one behind each ear, one under its dorsal fin, and one held in its long tail. For this reason the curved tail in which it holds the whale is one of its symbols. Fig. 3 is a rather realistic representation of the wolf's tail. The chief of the Yak[u]lā´nas, instead of the painting, wears two wolves' tails tied to the topknot of his hair, fastened by means of red cedar bark. With this he wears a twisted ring of red cedar bark.

The following series of birds' tails is largely characterized by the form of individual feathers. The hawk's tail (Fig. 4) is shown spreading, with pointed feathers, while the tails of the woodpecker (Fig. 5), and of the raven (Figs. 6, 7) are shown with rounded tips and parallel feathers. Since the symbol of the raven's tail (Fig. 6) is not clear, it is supplemented by the additional symbol of the raven's throat, represented by red paint on the throat of the dancer. Fig. 7 represents the raven's tail split in two, the body being indicated by the red paint extending from nose to chin, and one-half of the tail being shown extending upward from each side of the mouth. This painting is used by the chief of the Yak[u]lā´nas, and is supplemented by a carved

Plate III.

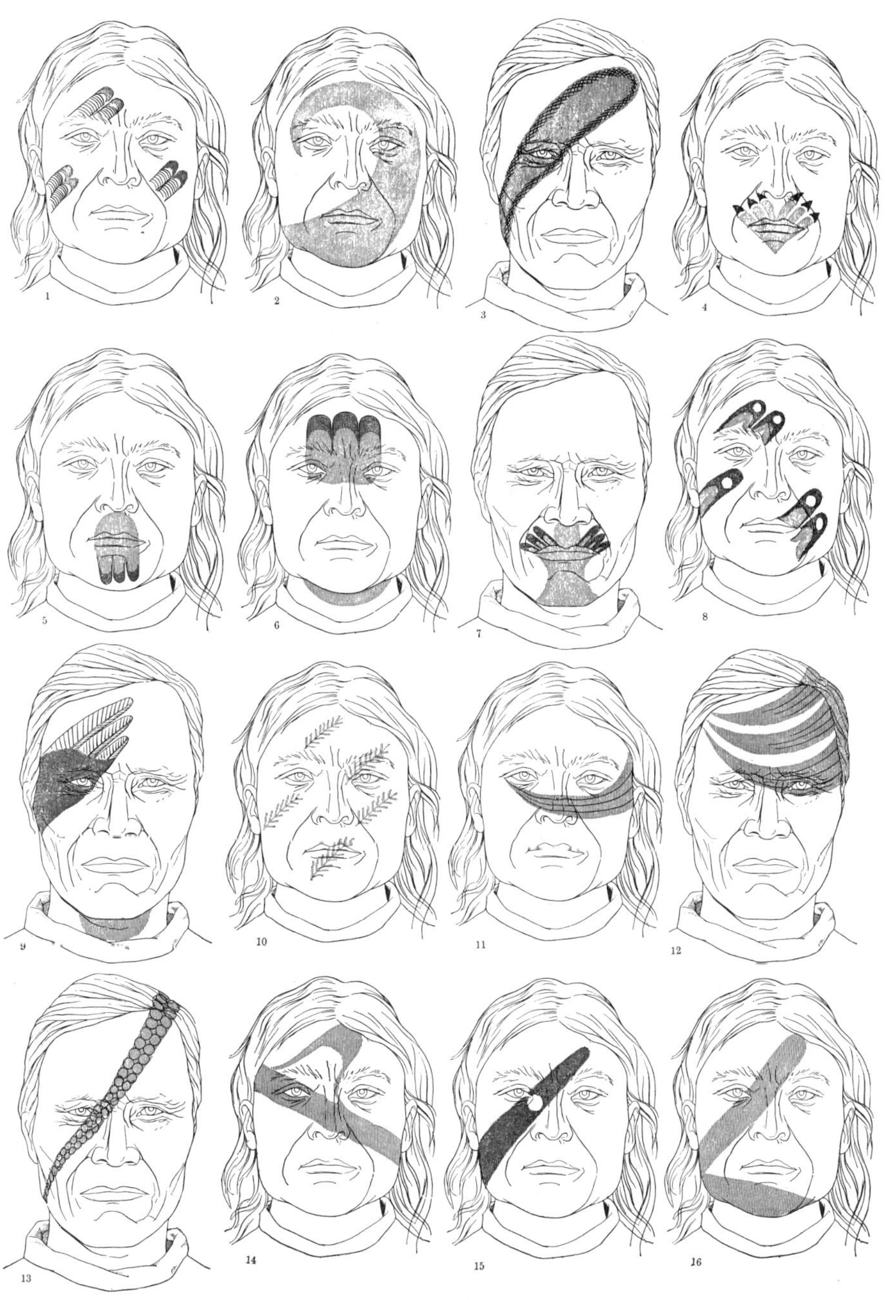

raven head, which is attached to the topknot. Three ermine skins are placed in its beak. Fig. 8 shows the wings of the raven on forehead and left cheek; a single feather, perhaps a tail feather, on the right cheek. This design is used by the G˙itsē´es, a Tsimshian tribe. The tips of the feathers are cut out of copper and glued to the skin, while the bases are painted green. In Fig. 9 we find a rather realistic representation of a raven's wing, supplemented by the red throat of the raven.

Fig. 10 is a painting that is not used by the present Indians, but is found on the mask representing Nenk˙ilsLasLîngai´; that means "the future Nenk˙ilsLa´s." Nenk˙ilsLa´s is the mythical name of the uncle of the Raven. The name was later on inherited by the Raven himself, who for this reason is called "the future Nenk˙ilsLa´s." According to tradition he killed the bird Ts'ā´gul, put on its skin, and flew up to heaven, where he liberated the sun [recorded in Dawson 1878–79: 149 ff.]. The painting represents the feathers of the bird Ts'ā´gul.

In Figs. 11 and 12 we find the red tuft of the puffin. This is also used in various positions. It is sometimes worn on cheek and forehead, as shown in the present figures. Sometimes it is placed on the chin. Fig. 13 is the arm of the devil fish, set with sucking cups. In Figs. 14, 15, and 16, we have the backs and dorsal fins of the right whale, the killer whale, and the dogfish. The right whale is characterized by its red color; the killer whale, by the black color and a perforation in the middle of the fin. Fig. 1, Plate IV, represents the dorsal fin of the Wasx (see p. 116). It differs from the fin of the whale and of the shark in that its tip is turned backward. Fig. 2 shows the same fin in a different position, occupying the whole chin and lower part of the cheeks. Fig. 3 shows the dorsal fin of the sea monster Ts'ānxō´utsē. Its peculiar characteristic is the black color, and its great width as compared to the dorsal fin of the killer whale. Fig. 4 is the short bear's tail of the same sea monster, characterized by the two colors black and red. Figs. 5–8 are all symbols of the sculpin. In all of them the lips are painted red, representing the mouth of the fish. In Fig. 5 the spines of the back are represented in blue on upper lip and nose. In Fig. 6 the two spines which rise over the mouth are shown in blue, diverging upward from the mouth. In Fig. 7 the vertebrae of the fish are added to the mouth. They are represented by a series of four blue circles extending upward from nose to forehead, each circle representing one vertebra. In Fig. 8 the pectoral fins are placed on each side of the mouth.

Fig. 9 is difficult to explain. It is said to symbolize the raven's hat; but the form of the ornament does not agree with the typical conventionalized hat design, which consists of a series of rings, as in Figs. 12 and 13. The significance of the painting is therefore doubtful. In Fig. 10 we find the horns of the mountain goat; in Fig. 11, the large eyes of the whale, indicated by a red painting all round the eyes.

Fig. 12 represents another sea monster called Ts'Em'â´s. It is symbolized by its hat and two large red ears, which are painted over the eyebrows, and extend down over the upper eyelids. The tradition of the Ts'Em'â´s has evidently been borrowed from the Tsimshian, among whom the same monster is called Ts'EM'a´ks, which means "in the water." It is said to live in rivers, and to be a dangerous foe to travelers. The traditions rather suggest that the Ts'EM'â´s is the personified snag. This opinion is supported by the painting shown in Fig. 10, Plate VI, in which the Ts'EM'â´s is represented by a long bar, broadening at its lower end. Fig. 13 was described originally as the mountain goat, the ears being placed over the eyes, and the ornament in the middle representing a single horn. It is not certain that this interpretation is correct. At a later date I revised the collection, and asked the Indian to repeat the names of the beings whom he intended to represent in his sketches. His answers were in almost all cases identical with the first descriptions; but in the present painting he said first that it represented the Ts'EM'â´s. He interpreted it as identical with Fig. 12; but later on he corrected himself, saying that the ears of the Ts'EM'â´s are not black. The interpretation of the central ornament on the forehead as the horn of the mountain goat remained doubtful, however. It resembles in type the representations of the hat; but it is likely that the rings surrounding the horn of the mountain goat would be represented in the same manner as the rings of the hat, or the vertebrae of the sculpin in Fig. 7, Plate IV. It seems that circular ornaments surrounding a long object, when represented on a flat surface, are turned up, so that the actual representation resembles a row of cross sections of the object. In Fig. 14 we have the feet of a bear, placed so that the heel portion surmounts the eyebrows. By this means the heel portion of the foot is made to serve two purposes. It represents both part of the foot and the ears of the animal.

The conventional symbols applied in the following figures are of such a character that, without a full explanation, it would not be possible to discover what animal they are intended to represent. The small triangle on the nose, shown in Fig. 15, is intended to symbolize the mouth of the devilfish. In Fig. 16 the large teeth of the sea lion rise over the eyebrows, while the chin is painted red, symbolizing the throat of the killer whale. In Fig. 1, Plate V, we see a large red oval in the middle of the face, which represents the bladder of the sea lion. This painting is also supplemented by the red chin symbolizing the throat of the killer whale. The combination of colors is the characteristic symbol in Figs. 2 and 3. In Fig. 2 we find the tail of the sea monster Ts'ānxō´utsē, which is in form identical with the tail of the killer whale. The latter, however, is black on both sides. In Fig. 3 we have one black and one red eyebrow of the same sea monster. In Fig. 4 we find a curious principle applied. The painting represents the tail of the halibut protruding from the mouth of the dancer. This painting is not intended to symbolize the halibut, but the sea lion swallowing a halibut; that is to say, the whole face of the dancer is intended as a representation of the sea lion, which is characterized by the food it is eating. The chin is again painted red, indicating the throat of the killer whale. The crossing black lines in Fig. 5 symbolize the ribs of the bear. We have here reached a purely geo-

EXPLANATION OF PLATE IV

FIG. 1. Dorsal fin of Wasx; red. Used by the G·it'i'ns of ʟqā'gîlt or Skidegate. (G·it'ina')
FIG. 2. Dorsal fin of Wasx; red and black. Used by the G·it'i'ns of ʟqā'gîlt or Skidegate. (G·it'ina')
FIG. 3. Back and dorsal fin of the sea monster Ts'anxō'utsē; black. Used by the Yak[u]lā'nas of Iā'k·ō and the Nanaā'ri of the Stakinqoan of the Tlingit. (Q'oā'la)
FIG. 4. Short bear's tail of the sea monster Ts'anxō'utsē; black and red. Used by the Yak[u]lā'nas of Iā'k·ō and the Nanaā'ri of the Stakinqoan of the Tlingit. (Q'oā'la)
FIG. 5. The lips represent the mouth of the sculpin; red. Over mouth and on nose: spines; blue. Used by the G·it'i'ns of ʟqā'gîlt or Skidegate, and of Sga'nguai or Ninstance. (G·it'ina')
FIG. 6. The lips represent the mouth of the sculpin; red. Over the mouth: spines; blue. Used by the G·it'i'ns of ʟqā'gîlt or Skidegate, and of Sga'nguai or Ninstance. (G·it'ina')
FIG. 7. The lips represent the mouth of the sculpin; red. On nose and forehead: vertebrae of the sculpin; blue. Used by the G'it'i'ns of ʟqā'gîlt or Skidegate, and of Sga'nguai or Ninstance. (G·it'ina')
FIG. 8. The lips represent the mouth of the sculpin; red. Over the mouth: flippers; blue. Used by the G·it'i'ns of ʟqā'gîlt or Skidegate, and of Sga'nguai or Ninstance. (G·it'ina')
FIG. 9. Hat of raven; blue. Used by the G·it'ina'.
FIG. 10. Horns of mountain goat; black. Used by the ʟqenoʟlā'nas of Q'u'na or Skidans. (Q'oā'la)
FIG. 11. Eyes of whale (red). (Q'oā'la)
FIG. 12. Over nose: hat of the sea monster Ts'ᴇm'â's; black. Over the eyebrows: its ears; red. Used by the Lgaiolā'nas of ʟqā'gîlt or Skidegate. (Q'oā'la)
FIG. 13. Over nose: horn of mountain goat. Over eyebrows: its ears; black. Used by the ʟqenoʟlā'nas of Q'u'na or Skidans. (Q'oā'la)
Fig. 14. Feet of bear; black and red. The part of the painting over the eyebrows represents the ears. Used by the xoa'dōs of Naēku'n. (Q'oā'la)
FIG. 15. Nose of devilfish; red. Used by the Sk'ag'nas xā'edra of Kaigani. (G·it'ina')
FIG. 16. Over eyebrows: teeth of sea lion; black. On chin: throat of killer whale; red. Used by the Skoā'ʟ'adas of ʟga'it or Gold Harbor. (Q'oā'la)

metrical design intended to symbolize an animal form—a development which has never been found heretofore in the art of the North Pacific tribes. The head of the dancer shown in Fig. 6 is daubed all over with red. It represents the white head of the eagle. The color red is used to represent the white parts of the animals. The upper part of the head of the dancer is here identified with the upper part of the head of the eagle. Similar to this is the symbol of the red-headed woodpecker, which consists in a liberal application of red paint all over face and hair.

In Fig. 7 we notice a narrow red line on each side of the face. This is intended to represent the red feathers in the wings of the woodpecker. In this case the sides of the head are identified with the sides of the animal. The painting represented in Fig. 8 has been discussed before. It is the throat of the killer whale, which appears so often in combination with other designs. The long bar, with a series of five crescents, shown in Fig. 9, represents the throat of the monster Ts'ānxō'utsē, which is characterized by a series of white spots. In Fig. 10 we find a broad red band surrounding the whole face. This is intended to represent the eagle's nest. In Fig. 11 we find one side of the face painted black, the other side painted red. This is also

Plate IV.

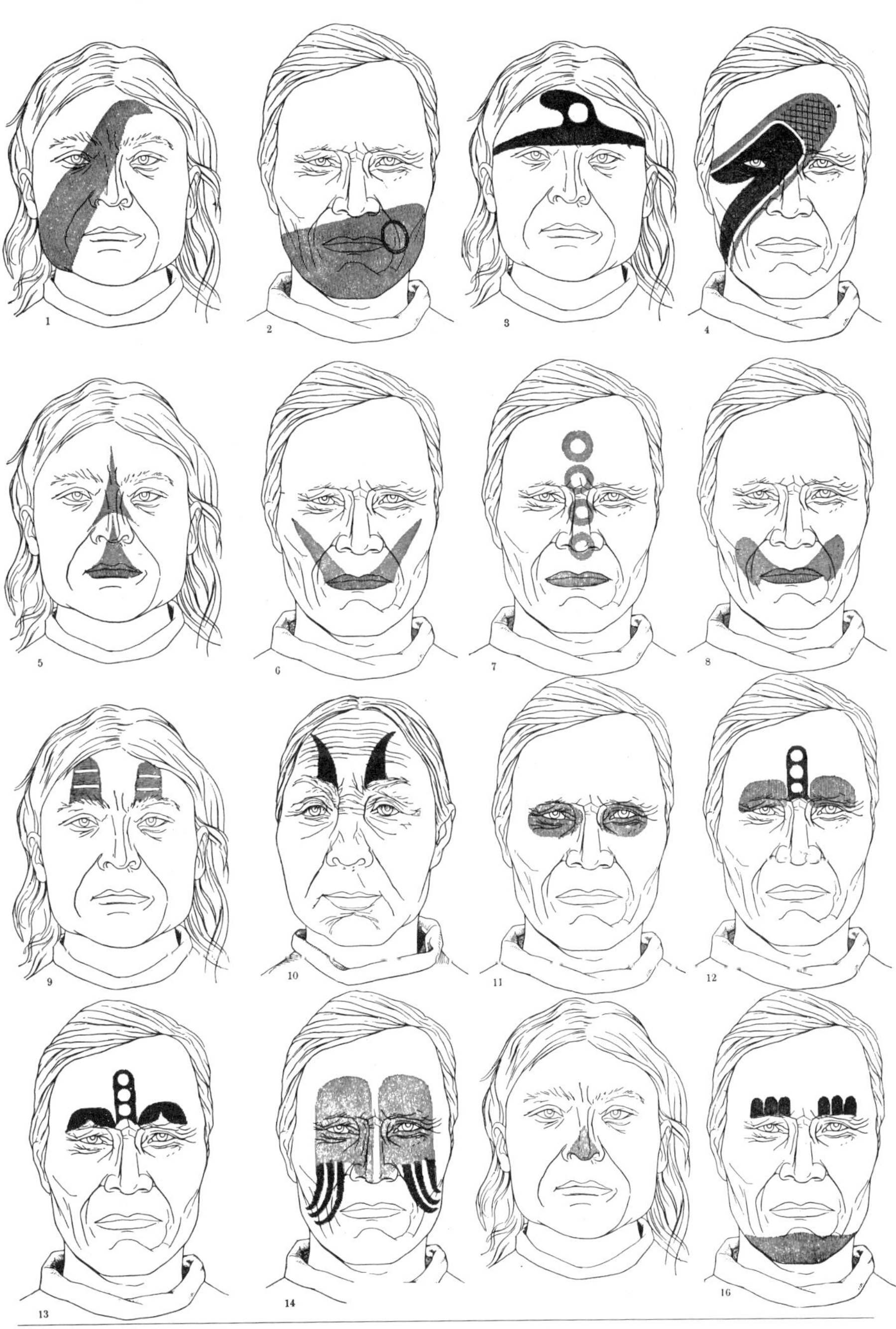

EXPLANATION OF PLATE V

FIG. 1. On face: bladder of sea lion; red. On chin: throat of killer whale; red. Used by the Skoā'ʟ'adas of ʟga'it or Gold Harbor. (Q'oā'la)

FIG. 2. Tail of the sea monster Ts'anxō'utsē; red and black. Used by the Yak^{u}lā'nas of lā'k'ō and the Nanaā'ri of the Stakinqoan of the Tlingit. (Q'oā'la)

FIG. 3. Eyebrows of the sea monster Ts'anxō'utsē; red and black. Used by the Yak^{u}lā'nas of lā'k''ō and the Nanaā'ri of the Stakinqoan of the Tlingit. (Q'oā'la)

FIG. 4. Face: sea lion devouring a halibut. Fish tail; black. On chin: throat of killer whale; red. Used by the Skoā'ʟ'adas of ʟga'it or Gold Harbor. (Q'oā'la)

FIG. 5. Bear's ribs; black. Used by the Yak^{u}lā'nas of lā'k'ō. (Q'oā'la)

FIG. 6. Head of white-headed eagle; red. Used by the G'it'ina'.

FIG. 7. Red wing-feathers of the woodpecker; red. Used by the Taslā'nas of Dā'dens. (Q'oā'la)

FIG. 8. Throat of the killer whale; red. Used principally by the women of the Q'oā'la.

FIG. 9. Throat of the sea monster Ts'anxō'utsē; red. Used by the Yak^{u}lā'nas of lā'k'ō and the Nanaā'ri of the Stakinqoan of the Tlingit. (Q'oā'la)

FIG. 10. Nest of eagle; red. Used by the G'it'ina' .

FIG. 11. Halibut; black and red. The left side of the face represents the dark upper side of the fish; the right side of the face represents the light lower side of the fish. Used by the Ts'āʟlānas of lā'k'ō. (G'it'ina')

FIG. 12. Mosquito bites; red. (G'it'ina')

FIG. 13. Tree with holes pecked by the woodpecker; black and red. Used by the Qaoqē'owai of lā'k'ō. (Q'oā'la)

FIG. 14. Vertical bar of copper; red. Used by the Sta'stas of K''iū'st'a. (G'it'ina')

FIG. 15. Vertical bar of copper; red. Used by the Sta'stas of K''iū'st'a. (G'it'ina')

Fig. 16. Trees carried down by a rock slide; black. Used by the ʟqenoʟlā'nas of Q'u'na or Skidans. (Q'oā'la)

the symbol of an animal. It represents the halibut, the left side of the face indicating the upper dark side of the animal, while the right side of the face represents the light lower side of the animal. This painting is generally used in connection with a peculiar hair dress, the whole hair being tied up in a knot on top of the head, and ten ermine skins being placed inside the knot, which is fastened by means of red cedar bark. Fig. 12, which represents mosquito bites, requires no explanation; but in Fig. 13 we see a principle applied which becomes evident in many carvings of totem poles [see this volume, Chap. 4; Boas 1897a:156]. Since in many cases the rear side of the object cannot be decorated, the subject of the decoration is split along its rear, and spread over the front of the object. In this manner the trunk of a tree, with holes made by a woodpecker, is utilized in this figure. We notice two vertical black bars in the middle of the face, representing the outlines of the tree. The holes made by the woodpecker on both sides of these lines must be explained in the following way: The tree has been split on the rear side, and both halves of the rear portion have been extended in such a way as to cover both sides of the face; so that the fields to the left and to the right represent the rear of the tree.

Figs. 14 and 15 symbolize copper plates, which are considered the most valuable property by the Indians. The copper plates have an almost rectangular form, being

Plate V.

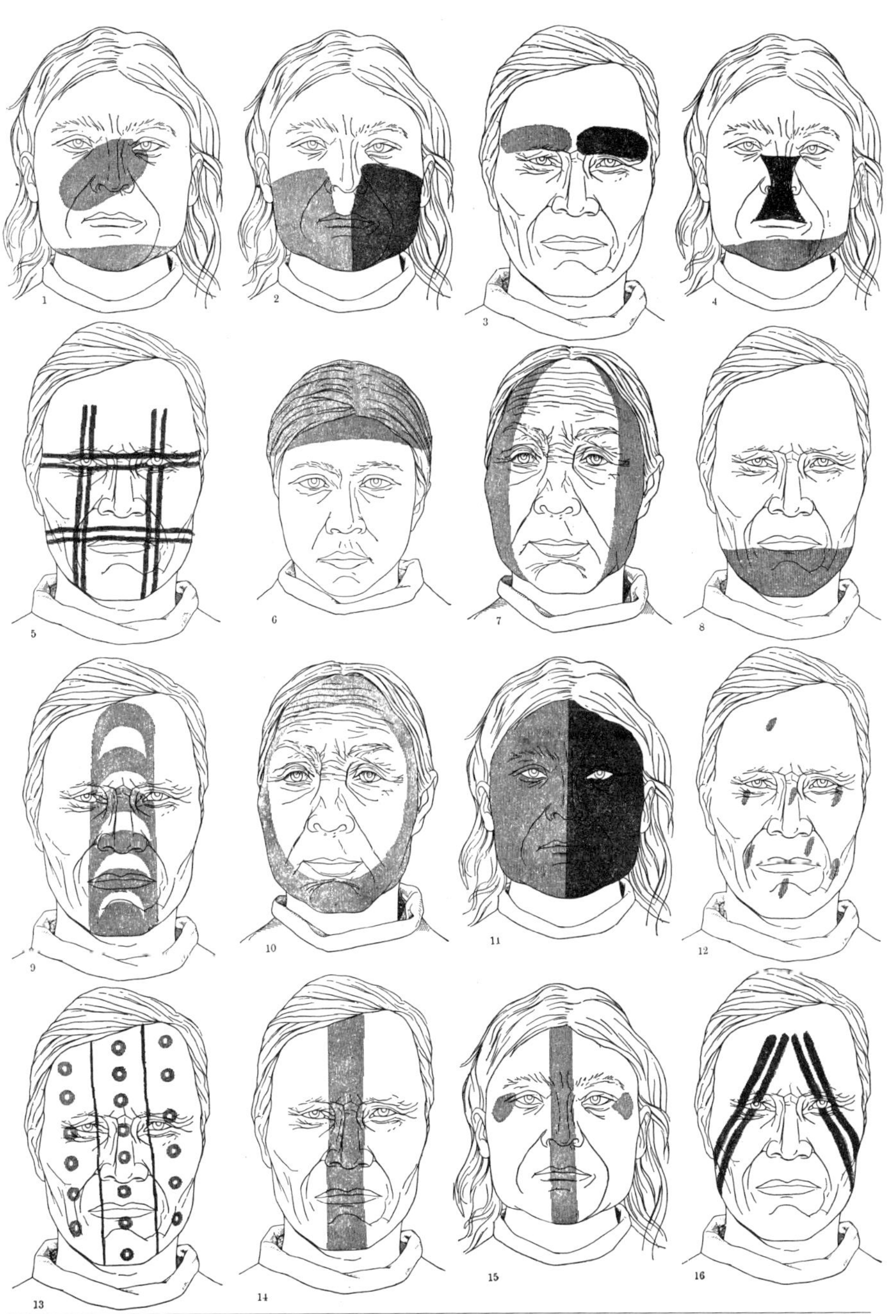

EXPLANATION OF PLATE VI

FIG. 1. Evening sky; red. Used by the S'ale'ndas of lā'k'ō. (G'it'ina')
FIG. 2. Cirrus clouds on the horizon of the ocean; red. Used by the Taslā'nas of Dā'dens. (Q'oā'la)
FIG. 3. Cirrus clouds on the morning or evening sky; red. Used by the ʟqenoʟlā'nas of Q'u'na or Skidans. (Q'oā'la)
FIG. 4. Cumulus clouds; red and black. Used by the ʟqenoʟlā'nas of Q'u'na or Skidans. (Q'oā'la)
FIGS. 5 and 6. Cumulus clouds; red and black. Used by the Ya'dasg'it'inai' of (?). (G'it'ina') The two paintings supplement each other, and are worn by two persons who appear before the tribe together.
FIG. 7. Stratus cloud; black. Used by the xoa'dōs of Naēku'n. (Q'oā'la)
FIG. 8. Afterimage of the sun; red. Used by the Kits'adê's of the Stakinqoan of the Tlingit.
FIG. 9. Painting of the Mē'lem dancer; red and black. The painting around the mouth represents blood.
FIG. 10. The monster Ts'ᴇm'â's; red. Used by the Skoā'l'adas of ʟga'it or Gold Harbor, and the Qogā'ngas of Lqā'gîlt or Skidegate.
FIG. 11. Fishnet; red and black. Used by the G'itsē'es, a Tsimshian tribe. (Qanha'da)
FIG. 12. Beaver; red and black. The lines drawn from the eyes downward represent tears. The ornament on the chin represents the beaver's tail. Used by the Sta'stas of K''inu'sta.
FIG. 13. Sea otter tattooing. Used by the Kunlā'nas of la'gen.

about twice as high as wide. They are strengthened by means of a ridge running from the middle of one long side to the middle of the opposite side. One of the squares is divided by another ridge, the two ridges forming a T. The red bar on the faces in Figs. 14 and 15 represents the second ridge, which is considered the most valuable portion of the copper plate. The Indians have a custom of breaking the coppers and distributing them among the members of the tribe. When thus broken up the second ridge is kept until the last, and has a much higher value than all the other portions of the copper. The ridge is sometimes extended over the hair, which in this case is tied up in two knots, one on each side of the bar. The knots are tied with red cedar bark, to which a large square piece of abalone shell is attached. In Fig. 16 we find two pairs of parallel black lines, which remind us of Fig. 5, Plate V. Their meaning is, however, entirely distinct from the meaning of the previous figure. They represent a rock slide, more particularly the trees uprooted by the falling masses of stone.

Fig. 1, Plate VI, is identical with Fig. 6, Plate V, but it has a different meaning. It represents the red clouds of the evening sky, the clouds being symbolized by the red paint covering the top of the head. In Fig. 2 the outlines of the face represent the horizon; and the red spots all round it, the cirrus clouds on the horizon. The same kind of cloud scattered over the morning or evening sky is shown in Fig. 3. Fig. 4 represents the dark cumulus cloud of a thunderstorm, the red sections indicating the blue sky between the dark clouds, which are symbolized by the black sections of the face. Figs. 5 and 6 are always used in conjunction. They also symbolize the cumulus cloud of a thunderstorm; the red line in Fig. 6 corresponding to the red sections in Fig. 4, and the black lines to the black sections. In Fig. 7 we observe again two black bars resembling those shown in Figs. 5 and 16, Plate V. In this case

Plate VI.

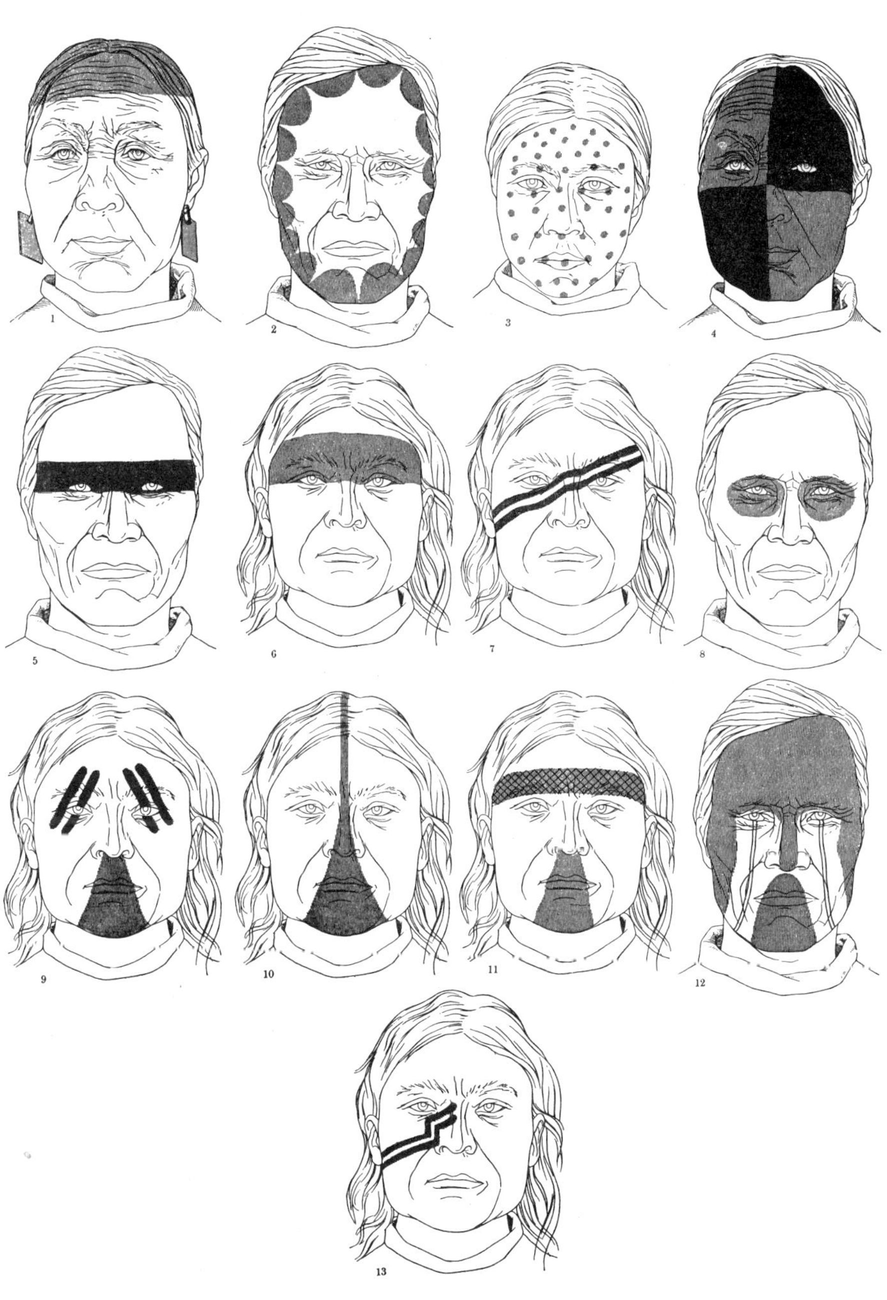

they are intended to represent dark stratus clouds. Fig. 8, Plate VI, which consists of red painting around the eyes, is identical with Fig. 11, Plate IV, which represents the large eyes of the whale. The present figure signifies the afterimage of the rising sun. The person using this design wears earrings made of abalone shell, which are cut in the form shown in Fig. 8, Plate I. A very interesting modification of this painting consists of a single large red circle placed on the right or left temple, which is also intended to represent the afterimage of the sun.

The painting shown in Fig. 9 is not used in the same class of ceremonials to which all the preceding paintings apply. It is employed in a religious ceremonial in which live dogs are torn and devoured. I have not been able to discover any meaning in the two pairs of black bars placed over the eyes, while the painting on the chin and mouth is explained as the blood of the dogs. In Fig. 10 we have a representation of the monster Ts'ᴇᴍ'â´s. Fig. 11 is a painting used by G˙itsē´es, a tribe of the Tsimshian, and is said to represent a fishnet.

The Indian who made the series of painting for me was not able to give any explanation of Figs. 12 and 13, which represent the beaver and the sea otter respectively. He explained that Fig. 12 was principally used during mourning ceremonials, and that the black lines extending from the eyes downward represented the beaver's tail, but he was not certain in regard to that point. Fig. 13 is a tattooing used by the family Kunlā´nas. He was unable to explain why it represents the sea-otter, but merely stated that it was obtained by the family immediately after the Deluge, when they landed at Naēku´n.

The explanations given here show that while a considerable series of facial paintings are no more conventionalized than the paintings found on other objects, the intricacy of the decorative field has led the Indians to develop geometrical designs, although no other cases are known in which such designs are applied by these tribes to symbolize animal forms. It is of importance to note that the same decorations may symbolize a variety of objects. Thus the design for the whale's eye and that for the afterimage of the sun are identical. The head of the eagle and the evening sky are expressed by the same painting. The ribs of the bear, the rock slide, and the stratus cloud are so much alike that, without a statement on the part of the Indians, it would be impossible to know what is meant. The collection is of theoretical interest mainly because it shows that the difficulty of adapting the subject of decoration to the decorative field has been a most powerful element in substituting geometrical forms for less conventional designs, and in showing a series of important transitional forms. We find here also the first steps in the development of color symbolism, which plays an important part in the arts of other tribes, while it hardly occurs at all in the more realistic decorative motives of the Indians of the North Pacific coast.

6. Art of the Thompson Indians

Boas added these sections to the Jesup North Pacific Expedition monograph on the Thompson Indians by James Teit. In his analysis of their decorative art, Boas compares the art of this interior Salish group with that of the Coast Salish. Unlike the Northwest Coast artists, the Thompson decorate their implements with images that are not related to the shape of the object. Moreover, unlike the images which most Northwest Coast Natives can decipher, those of the Thompson are often ambiguous and abstract. In his conclusion, Boas draws on other cultural elements in addition to art, pointing to similarities between the Thompson and Plains Indians that are probably due to historical factors. He suggests that the Salish speakers who migrated to the coast borrowed certain art forms from their neighbors there, while those on the plateau were influenced by peoples inhabiting the plains.

DECORATIVE ART

The almost complete absence of works of plastic art among the Thompson Indians is most striking, particularly when compared with the highly developed art of the neighboring Coast tribes, who model almost all their implements in animal forms. Their dishes, spoons, hammers, lances, clubs, fishhooks, harpoon points and canoes represent animals, distorted and adapted to the shape of the objects. Among the Thompson Indians very few carvings of this kind are found. For example, one stone vessel represents a frog (Fig. 1), and another represents a snake coiled around a cup (Fig. 2). Here also belongs a spoon with a head of an animal carved at the end of the handle (Fig. 3). A few hammerstones show an animal head instead of a knob at the upper end (Fig. 4). Plastic decoration was rare in prehistoric times also. Mr. Harlan I. Smith has figured a fragment of a steatite pipe from Lytton representing an animal's head, and two remarkably well-executed carvings in bone—according to the Indians, toggles of dogs' halters—representing animal figures (Fig. 5). Excavations at Kamloops also have yielded but few specimens of this character. Notable among these are a sacrificial stone vessel in the shape of a man, and two beautiful war clubs made of antler, the handles of which represent heads of warriors. . . . Carvings representing human or animal figures are also very rare in this area. The only ones known to me are the crude figures erected over graves (Figs. 6–8). Here may also be mentioned the rude stone ornaments placed on top of houses. Fig. 9 shows one of these, representing a man. Hawk feathers are glued to

"Art" and "Conclusion" from "The Thompson Indians of British Columbia," by James Teit, *American Museum of Natural History Memoirs*, vol. 2, pp. 376–90, 1900.

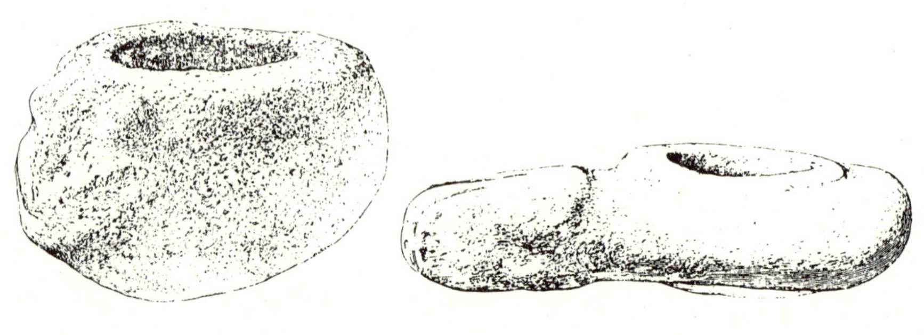

FIG. 1 (16/1291). Stone vessel representing a frog

FIG. 2 (16/1292). Stone vessel representing a cup with snake coiled around it

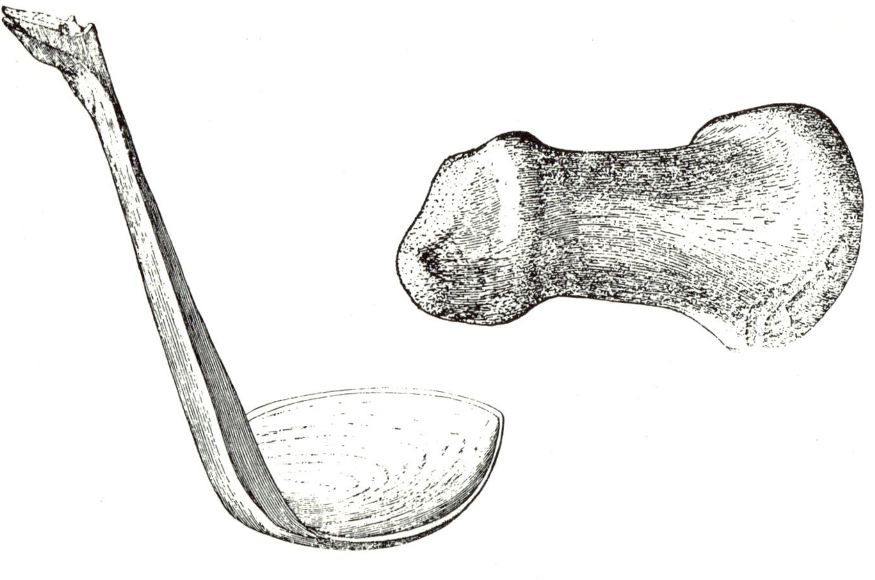

FIG. 3 (16/1329). Wooden spoon

FIG. 4 (16/6951). Hammerstone with animal head

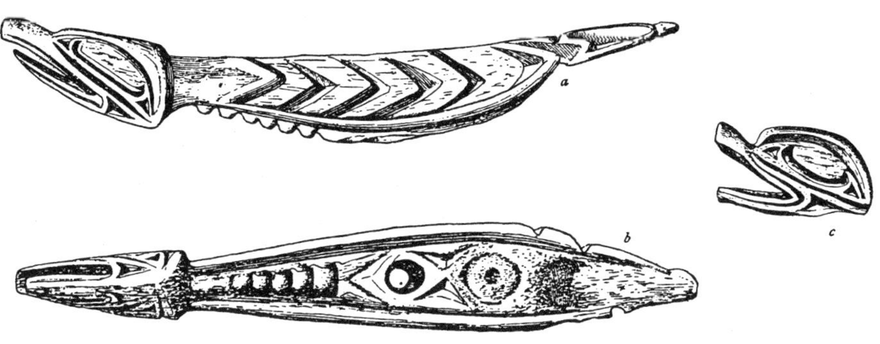

FIG. 5*a*, *b* (16/3030), *c* (16/3029). Bone carvings

the back of the head, and the clothing is indicated by red painting. None of these carvings can compare with the beautiful work of the Coast Indians.

The principle of decorative art of the Thompson Indians is quite distinct from that of the Coast tribes. The former have the conception of animals adapting themselves to the use of man, and assuming the form of implements. The whale becomes a canoe, the seal a dish, the crane a spoon. The latter adopt this idea very rarely, but decorate their implements with symbolic designs placed on a suitable surface, but without any immediate connection with the form of the implement. In the former, the decoration depends upon form; in the latter, form and decoration have no intimate connection. Comparatively few designs are primarily decorative. Their fundamental idea is symbolic. For this reason by far the greater number of designs may be described as pictographs rather than as decorations. Nevertheless the symbol is often used for purposes of decoration.

The symbols are mostly painted, etched, or etched and filled with colors. The Thompson Indians have not developed any great skill in graphic art. Their designs are largely attempts at a realistic representation, but the difficulties of execution have led them to adopt a number of conventional expedients to express certain ideas. They use a number of conventional designs, the meaning of which is always understood. These are shown in Fig. 10.

Another important expedient is the substitution of relation in space for an actual representation of the object. A cross represents the crossing of two trails; dots near such a cross, offerings made near the crossing of trails (Fig. 11*n*). A single or double straight line signifies a trench; and lines or dots placed near its ends, sacrifices placed there (Fig. 11*f*). The object sacrificed is further suggested by the form of the line or dot. A line signifies something long, such as a pole (Fig. 11*l*), while dots suggest

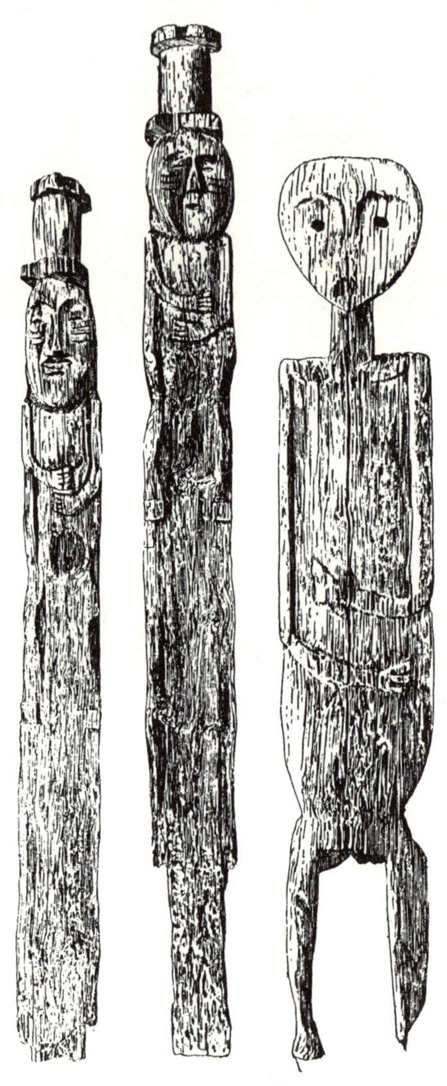

FIGS. 6 (16/1378); 7 (16/1379); 8 (16/1380). Grave figures

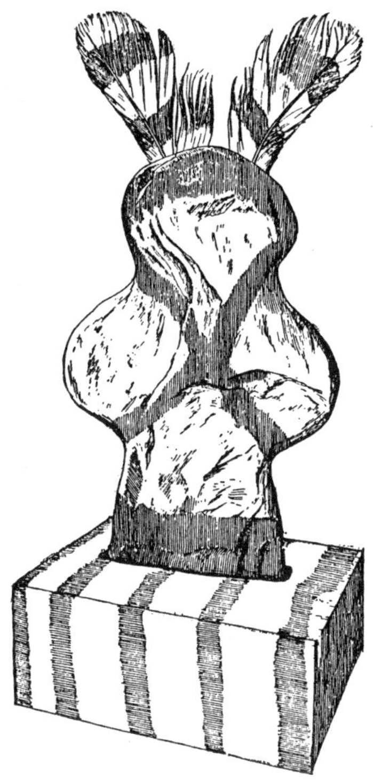

FIG. 9 (16/4872). House ornament representing a man

food and painted boulders. A line connecting a number of designs designates that they belong together or are near each other. Thus in Fig. 11, *a* represents the grizzly bear, going by way of *b* to the lake *c*. . . .

It will be seen that some of the conventional signs are ambiguous. When found on implements, the use of the latter often determines the meaning of the designs, because they are always symbolic of the use of the implement; while in ceremonial implements they represent the dreams of the owner. In other cases the accompanying figures define the significance of the ambiguous design. On the pipe shown in Fig. 12 we see on the left-hand side of the upper side of the stem a circle with a long line. It signifies a lake and a river flowing into it. This meaning is determined by the beaver and otter running toward the river from the right-hand side next to it. On the tongs (Fig. 13), we see almost the same design, but there it represents a basket and ladle.

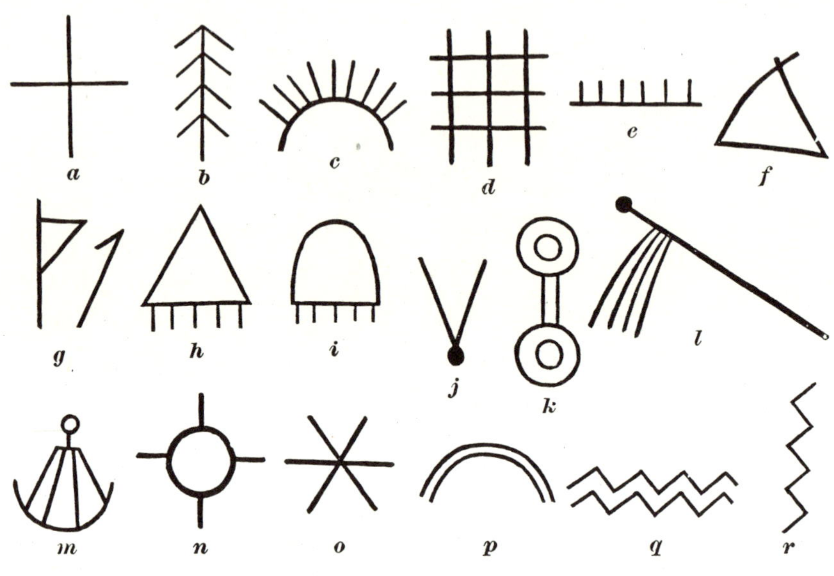

FIG. 10. Conventional designs: *a*, The crossing of trails; *b*, Fir branches used by girls in their puberty ceremonials; *c*, Unfinished basketry or a pile of fir branches; *d*, Matting; *e*, A trench with earth thrown to one side; *f*, Underground house with protruding ladder; *g*, Grave poles; *h*, Tracks of grizzly bear; *i*, Tracks of bear cub; *j*, Loon; *k*, Two lakes connected by a river, the inner circle representing the water; *l*, Cascade; *m*, Mountain, the curved lower line representing the earth, the lines running down the sides of the mountain representing gulches, and the circle on top representing a lake on the mountain; *n*, Sun; *o*, Star; *p*, Rainbow; *q*, Mountains and valleys or track of a snake; *r*, Lightning

In some cases where the use of the implement determines the significance of the design, all attempt at reproducing the form of the object, or even of its conventional sign, is abandoned. Thus the red ornament on a stirrer (Fig. 14) represents food. The red tip signifies salmon; the lines in the middle, roots; the red on the handle, trout. The red at the end of tongs (Fig. 13) represents the spring from which water is obtained, and the lines on the back of the tongs are water snakes.

The symbolism of designs is well expressed in the decorations of weapons. On the inner side of a bow (Fig. 15) we find two rattlesnakes, represented by a red zigzag band and white crosslines for the tail, crawling into their den, which is represented by a red band in the middle of the bow. On another bow (Fig. 16) are represented a hunter and two dogs, and a warrior decorated with feathers. The red ends of the bow represent trees; four lines on one end, woodworms under the bark. These are rubbed by young men on their arms to gain strength for spanning bows. Lances were often painted with the design of a skeleton (Fig. 17). The lance head represents the

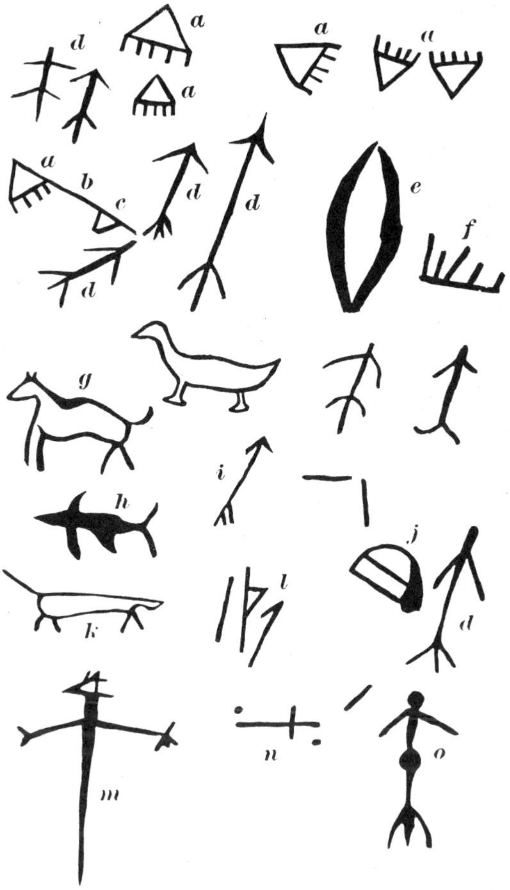

FIG. 11. Rock-paintings from a boulder called "The Coyote's Wife." *a*, grizzly bear; *b*, grizzly bear's tracks; *c*, pool of grizzly bear; *d*, fir tree branch; *e*, vulva of coyote's wife; *f*, trench with poles; *g*, coyote; *h*, fish; *i*, arrow; *j*, cap with fringe; *k*, otter; *l*, grave poles; *m*, insect; *n*, crossing of trails, sacrifice of food and pole; *o*, insect *kilaxwa'us*

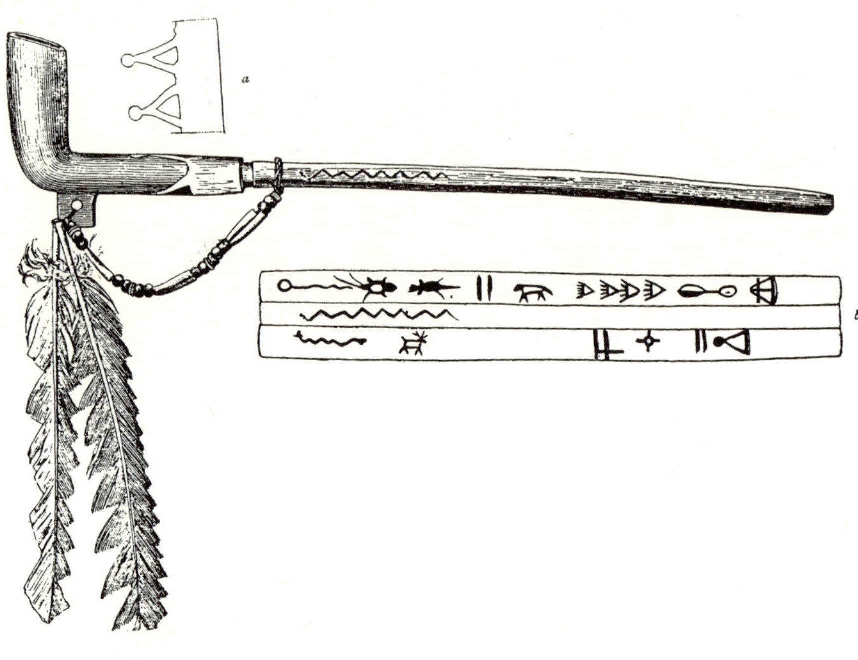

FIG. 12 (16/4561). Shaman's pipe: *a*, inlaid design on bowl; *b*, designs on stem

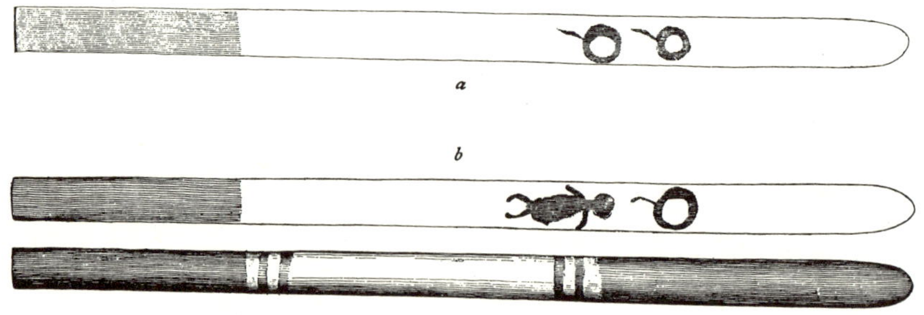

FIG. 13 (16/1351a, 16/1351b). Pair of tongs: *a*, inner view; *b*, inner and outer views.

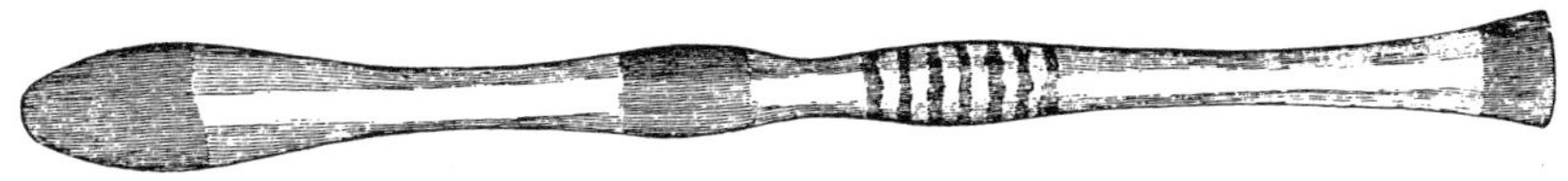

FIG. 14 (16/1352). Stirrer

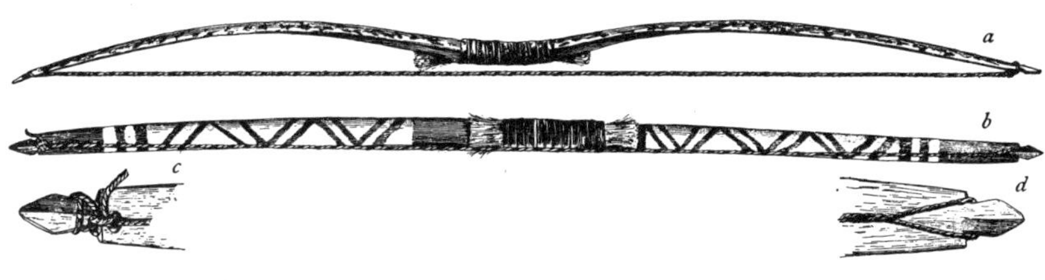

FIG. 15 (16/1341). Bow covered with snakeskin: *a*, side; *b*, front; *c*, *d*, ends

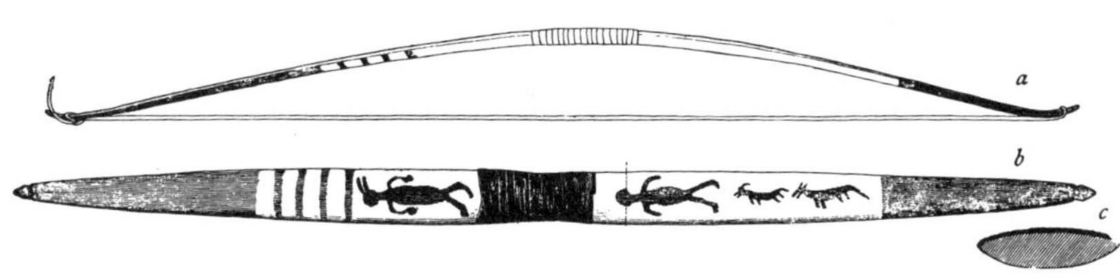

FIG. 16 (16/1340). Sinew-backed bow: *a*, side; *b*, front; *c*, cross section

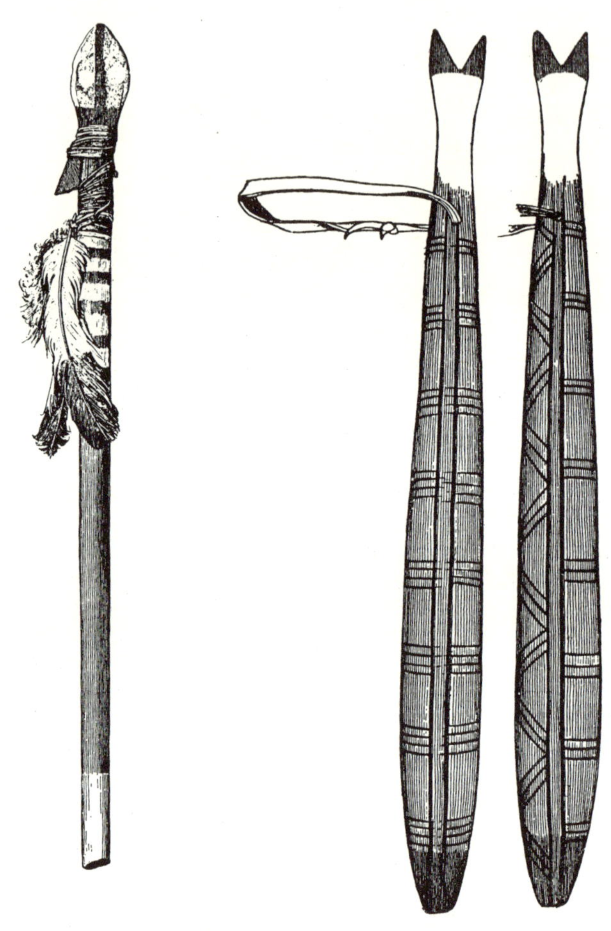

FIG. 17 (16/1343). Short spear with stone point

FIG. 18 (16/1070). Birch-wood club

skull, indicated by the two orbits and the aperture of the nose. The rings on the shaft represent the ribs. The stone war axe (Fig. 26) represents a woodpecker. The point of the axe is to be as powerful in piercing skulls as the beak of the woodpecker is in piercing the bark of trees. A wooden club (Fig. 18) is decorated with designs representing the ribs of a skeleton. Drinking tubes used by girls during the puberty ceremonials (Fig. 19) are often decorated with symbols of the crossings of trails at which they staid, of trenches which they dug, or of other objects connected with their ceremonials. The crosses on the holes of the tube are said to represent stars,

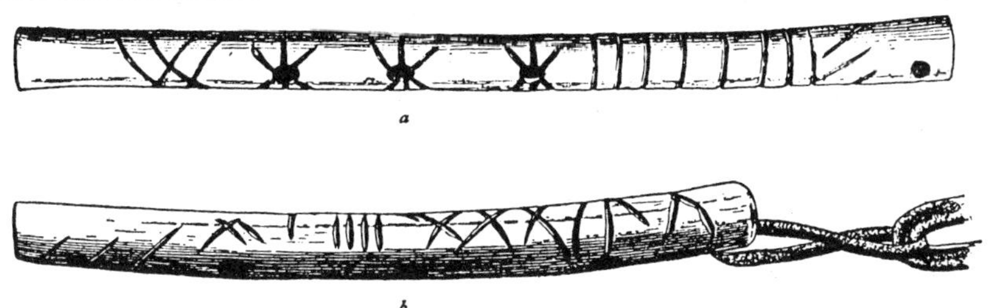

FIG. 19*a* (16/4871); *b* (16/1355). Drinking tubes with holes

while those at the ends represent crossings of trails. The design shown in Fig. 20 is an old design found on robes and pouches made of buffalo-skin. Its meaning is unknown.

Designs representing the guardian spirits and supernatural dreams of the owner are very frequent. These were believed to be the means of endowing the implements with supernatural powers. Men decorated their clothing according to instructions received from their guardian spirits, and painted their dreams on their blankets. In Fig. 21 a mountain range resting on an earth line is shown above the fringe. On the upper part of the blanket two suns are shown, outside of which there are two large beetles called "kokaum" (June bugs). In the center is a buck deer pursued by two Indians. The figures near the right and left margins are grizzly bears. On the lower part of the blanket two loons are shown. They are painted on a large scale, because they are the principal guardian spirits of the wearer. Between them there is a lake with trees around one side, and a canoe and a man in the center. The trail lines under the loons indicate that they belong to the lake. The owner's pipe is painted in the lower right-hand corner.

Boys, during the puberty ceremonials, painted their aprons and blankets in the same manner. In Fig. 22 a painted apron of this kind is shown. The central top figure is the lad himself in the attitude of a dancer, with a feather headdress and his apron. The bow and arrow painted at his side are symbolic of his future professions of hunting and war. Two moons and six stars painted around him suggest his nightly travels. He must become familiar with the deer and salmon, the pursuit of which will occupy much of his time in future years, and furnish him with most of his food; therefore the figures of a buck or an elk and of a salmon are painted beneath him. Under them is painted a lizard, of which he has dreamed, or which he has already obtained, or is anxious to obtain, for his guardian spirit. On the left of the apron is a picture of the Dawn of the Day, to which he prays, and which he awaits daily in his solitude. The light-colored cloudy portion is the daylight rising from the dark line, which

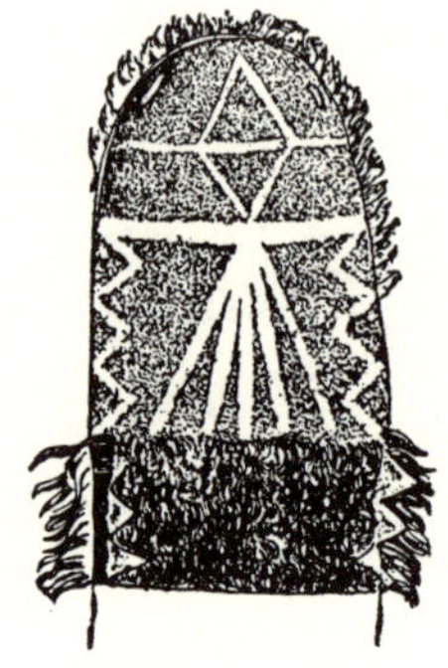

FIG. 20 (16/8723). Design on flap of a pouch

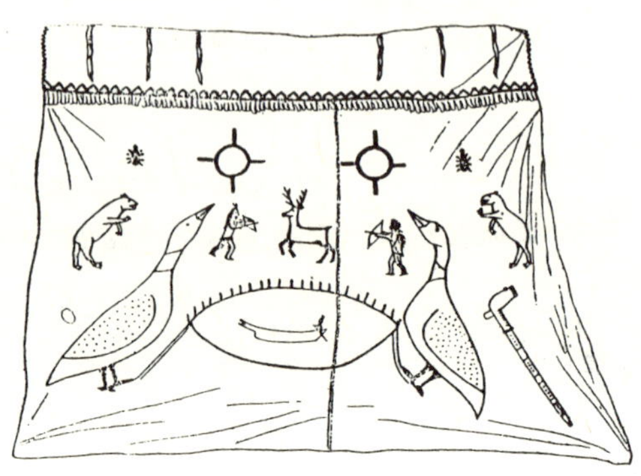

FIG. 21 (16/4577). Blanket with dream design

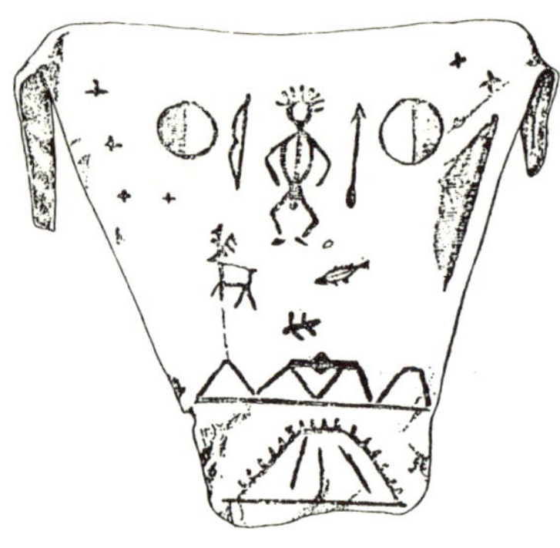

FIG. 22 (16/4536). Painted apron

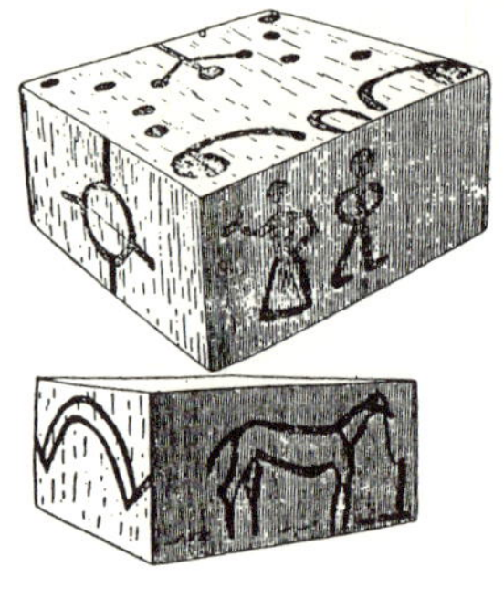

FIG. 23 (16/4575). Drum

means the horizon. Underneath are pictured four mountains resting on an earth line, with a lake between two of them. These are the mountains over which he travels. At the bottom are the principal mountains where he resides while trying to obtain a guardian spirit. The short spikes around the edges represent trees; and the long lines inside, gulches.

Another example of a pictographic design is shown on the drum, Fig. 23. The drum was made to be used at a potlatch. On one side is a dancing man and a woman. The horse represents the commonest gift at a potlatch, which is generally given away after a man or woman has danced. The other paintings have no special significance

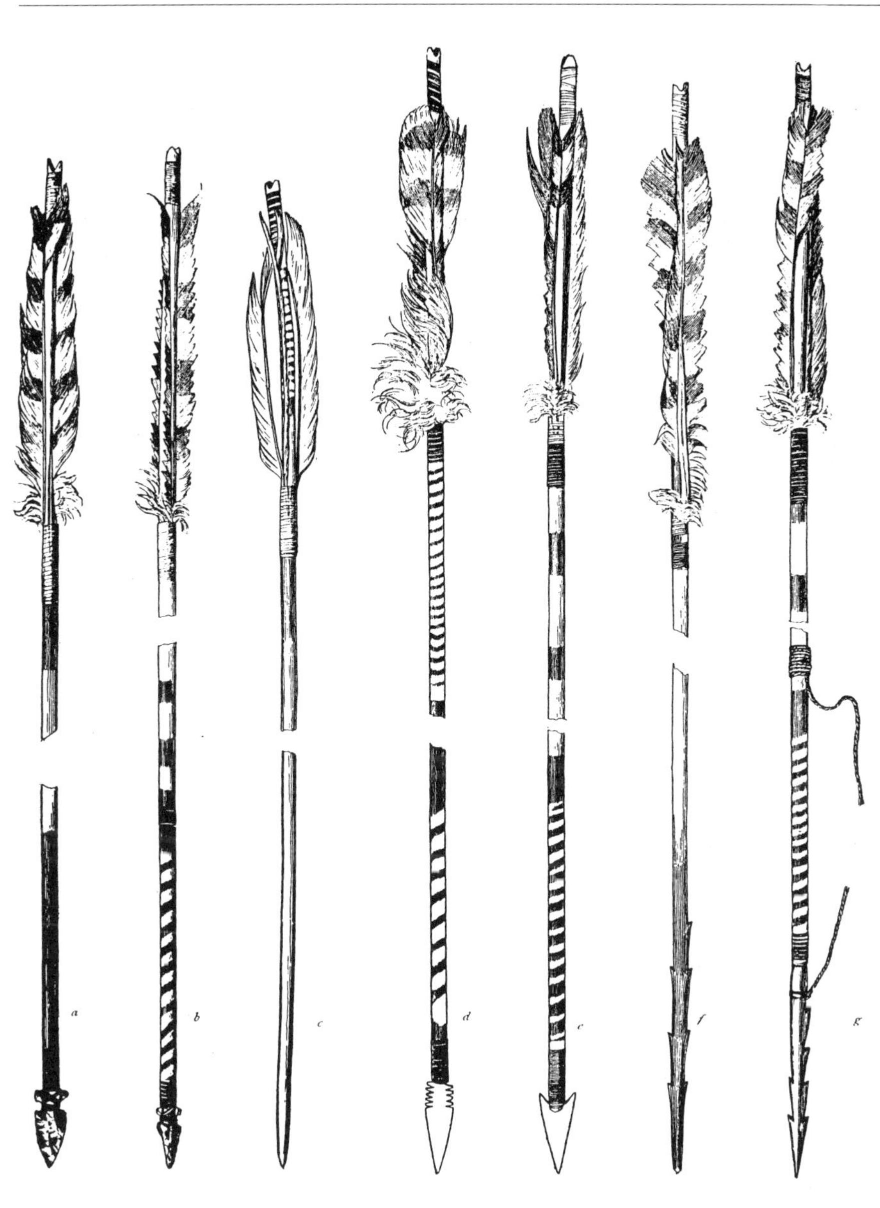

FIG. 24*a* (16/1278); *b* (16/1276); *c* (16/1036b); *d* (16/1342); *e* (16/1300); *f* (16/1299); *g* (16/1301). Arrows

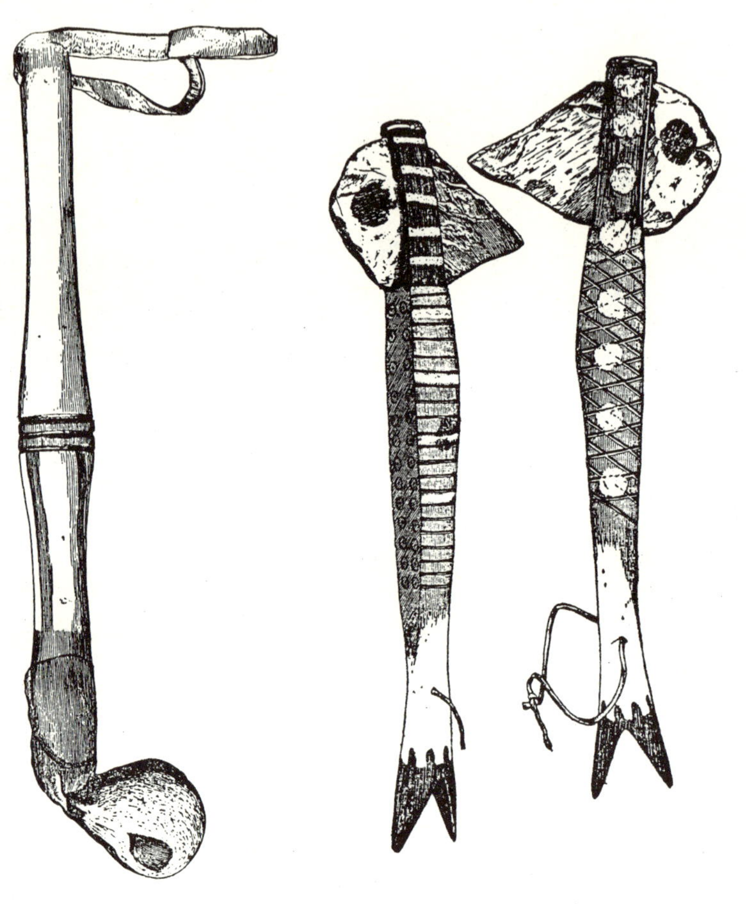

FIG. 25 (16/4560). War club with design of sky, earth, and thunderbird

FIG. 26 (16/4559). War axe representing woodpecker

in reference to the potlatch, but were painted on the drum to suit the fancy of the men who made it.

Clubs were often decorated with designs representing the owner's guardian spirits. On the arrow in Fig. 24*d*, the water snake is represented. On the war club (Fig. 25), we see sky and the thunderbird. The black and red lines on the handle represent the earth, and the four lines connecting earth and sky represent lightning. The quiver is painted red and black, with mountains rising over a line representing the earth, and two suns.

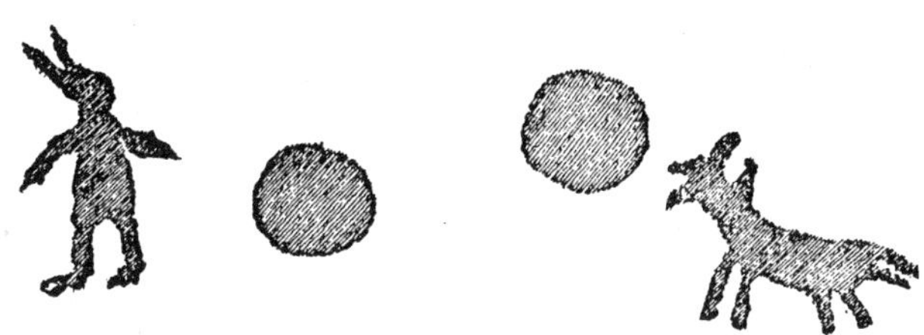

FIG. 27 (16/1345). Painting on shaman's headband

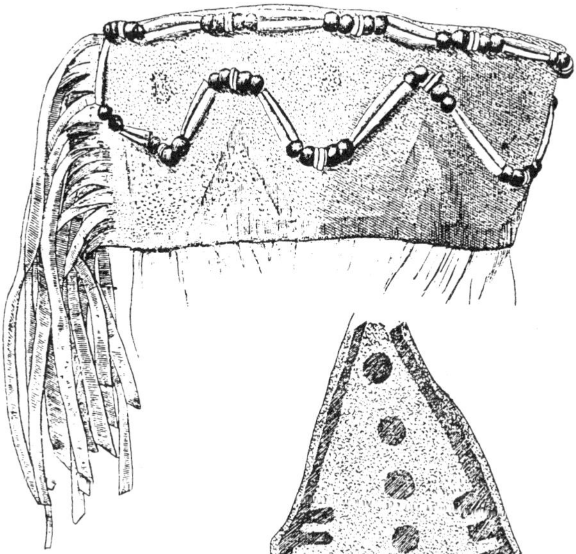

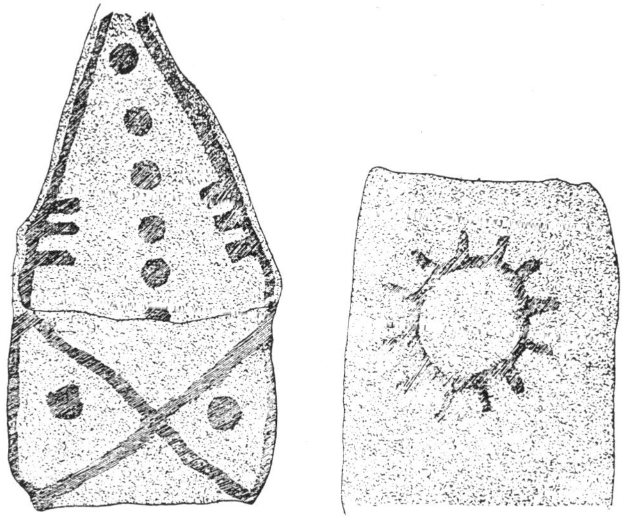

FIG. 28 (16/4596). Maiden's headband

FIG. 29 (16/4584). Front and back of a pouch for birch-bark cards, with design of sun, stars, and crossing of trails

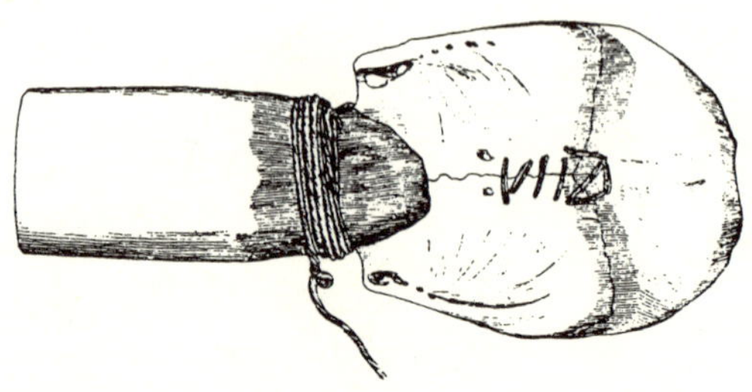

FIG. 30 (16/4831). Spoon made of skull cap of a deer

In Fig. 27 is represented the painting on a shaman's headband. On one side the wolf and a star are shown, and on the other a star and the shaman himself wearing a feather headdress.

Gambling implements were decorated with designs supposed to secure luck. On the pouch holding a set of birch-bark cards, Fig. 29, is the figure of the sun. The dots signify stars; the cross means either the crossing of trails or a reel for winding string.

Handles of digging sticks often had carvings representing the dreams of the owner. . . .

The shaman's pipe, Fig. 12, shows inlaid in the stone stem the loon necklace design, which signified the necklace with pendant loon's head that was sometimes worn by shamans. On the stem are shown the following: on top, at the left, a lake, and a river flowing into it; a beaver; an otter; two earth lines; a wolf; track of the grizzly bear; two mysterious lakes of several colors, connected by a river; a mountain with fog on top. On the side is a snake; underneath, at the left, a rattlesnake; then a buck deer, earth lines, the sun, earth lines, and a loon necklace. On the appendage of another pipe (Fig. 31) is carved, on one side the sun, on the other a man with a spear in his hand. On still another (Fig. 32), the appendage is given the shape of a canoe. On one side is carved in relief the head of a big-horn sheep, on the other an otter. On the stem, ribs are represented in red. The pipe represented in Fig. 33 shows the design of ribs inlaid in the stem of the bowl.

To this class of designs belong most of the rock paintings found so frequently in the country inhabited by the Thompson Indians. Almost all of these were made by boys and girls during their puberty ceremonials. The figures composing each painting were generally made by different individuals and at different times, and consequently the figures are disconnected. On Figs. 34 and 35, some of these paintings

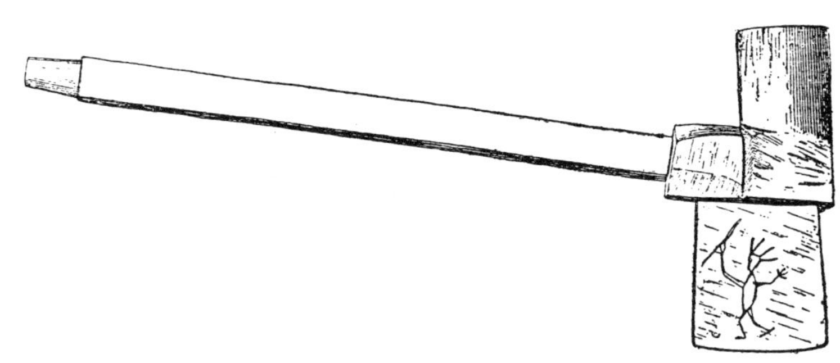

FIG. 31 (16/4563). Pipe design of man

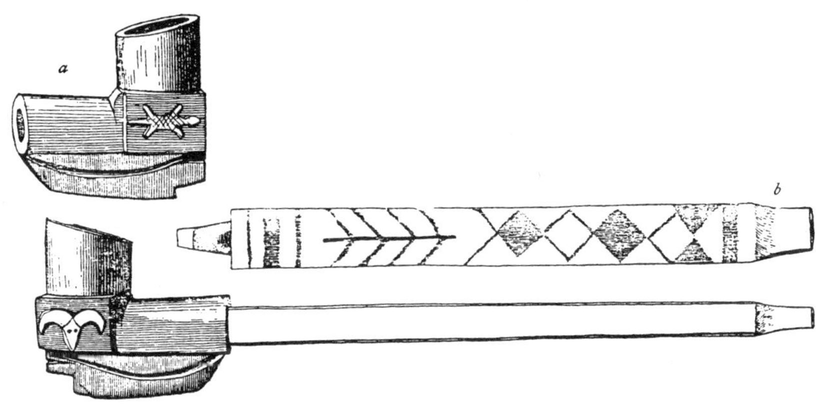

FIG. 32 (16/4564). Pipe design of otter and bighorn sheep: *a*, reverse of bowl; *b*, top of stem

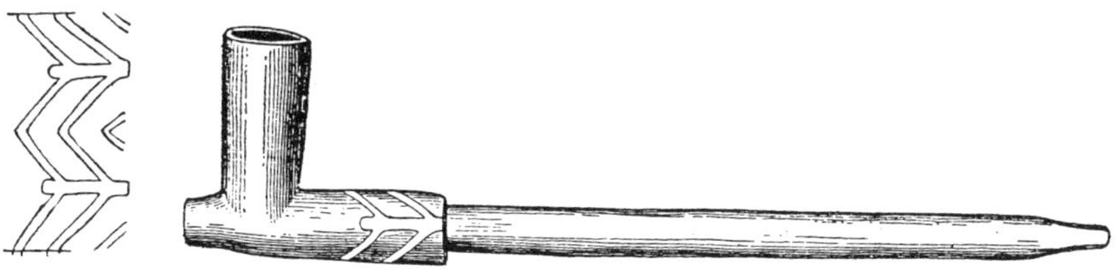

FIG. 33 (16/4565). Pipe design of ribs

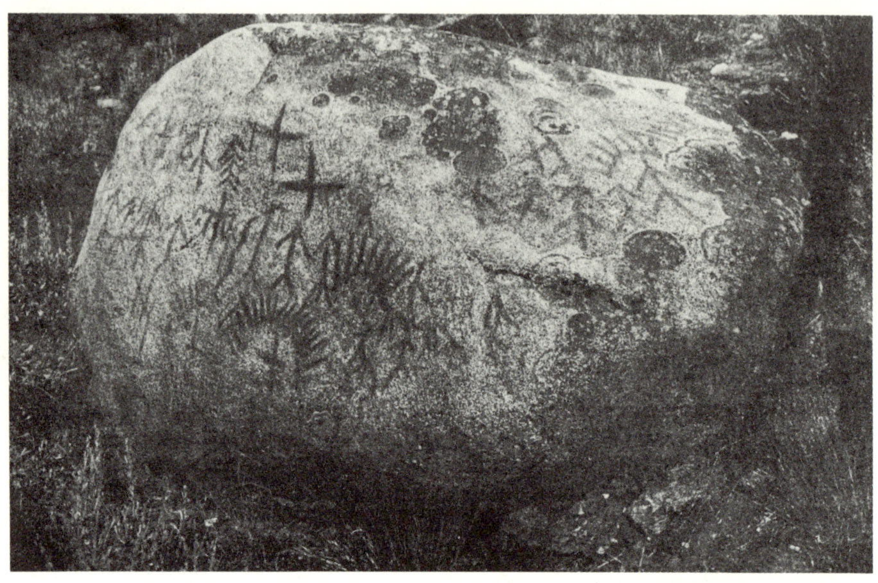

FIG. 34. Boulder near Spences Bridge

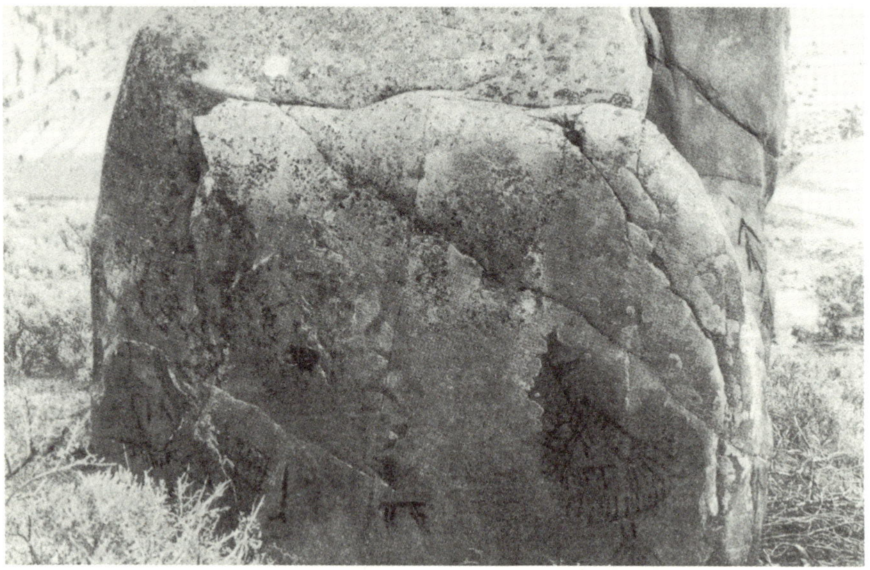

FIG. 35. Boulder near Spences Bridge called "The Basket of Coyote's Wife"

will be found that have been reproduced from photographs. Others, such as Fig. 11, have been reproduced from drawings collected by Messrs. James Teit, Harlan I. Smith, and John Oakes, in the region between Lytton and Spences Bridge, and in Nicola Valley. All the explanations were obtained by Mr. Teit.

Sometimes the connection between ornamentation and object is difficult to understand. A cap (Fig. 28) shows a series of lodges on a line representing the earth, and dentalia sewed on in a mountain design over the earth line. The dots on the cap represent stars. A piece of skin (Fig. 36) for playing the stick game we find surrounded by a line, inside of which is a circle. These represent the world. The short lines extending inward are clumps of trees. Two men and a dog are seen in the center of the world. A bat for playing ball (Fig. 37*a*) represents a small water snake. On a tobacco pouch (Fig. 38) is represented a lizard in appliqué skin.

Many objects are decorated with the "butterfly" or "eye" design; for instance, an arrow flaker (Fig. 39) and tweezers (Fig. 40). The design of the woodworm was also frequently used. It consists of a series of short parallel lines, the ends of which are sometimes connected by long straight lines.

The specimens in which the painted or etched designs are closely adapted to the form of the object are very few. The butterfly design just mentioned is often adjusted in such a way as to bring about a decorative effect. The same is the case with the arbitrary symbols of food and trees on a stirrer, tongs, and bows (Figs. 13–16), while the less conventional designs are little influenced in form and position by the decorative field. The only exceptions to this rule are the basketry and weavings of the Lower Thompsons and the beadwork which evidently developed from the former. . . . The woven carrying straps (Fig. 41) show the arrow pattern adapted to a long narrow band. Fig. 42 represents a snake pattern in beads. . . .

The rhythmic arrangement of beaded strings is often very elaborate, as illustrated in Fig. 43, which shows the grouping of strings composing the fringe on a pair of trousers. When worn, the fringe hangs down so that the arrangement of the strings cannot be seen. Nevertheless the same motive is applied throughout, which consists of five elements—one string of one glass bead and two bone beads in alternating order, one undecorated string, one of alternating glass and bone beads, one undecorated, one of one glass bead and two bone beads in alternating order.

MUSIC

The Thompson Indians used very few musical instruments. Their songs and dances were accompanied by the drum, which consisted of a round wooden frame covered with skin. That of a one-year-old deer was considered best, and was often worn before being used on the drum, because this was believed to improve the sound. The drums were generally painted with symbolic designs. Those made for use at pot-

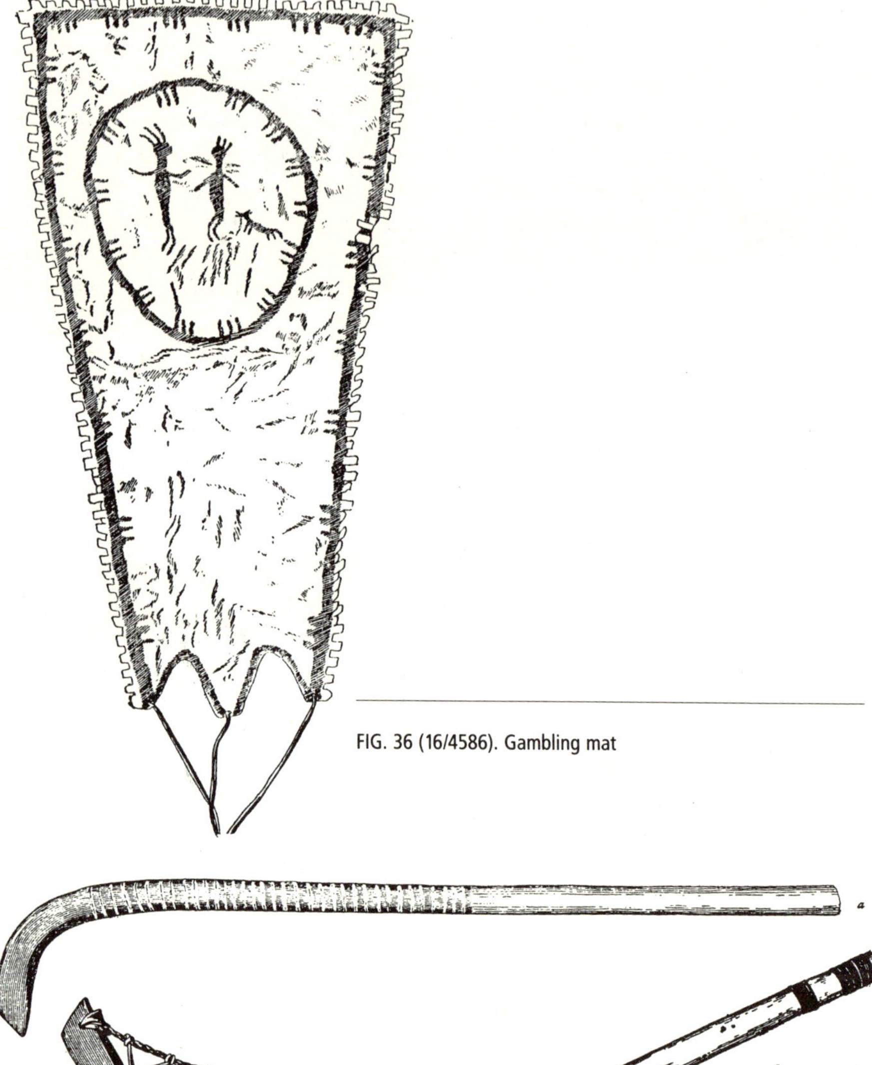

FIG. 36 (16/4586). Gambling mat

FIG. 37*a* (16/4857); *b* (16/4871). Lacrosse sticks

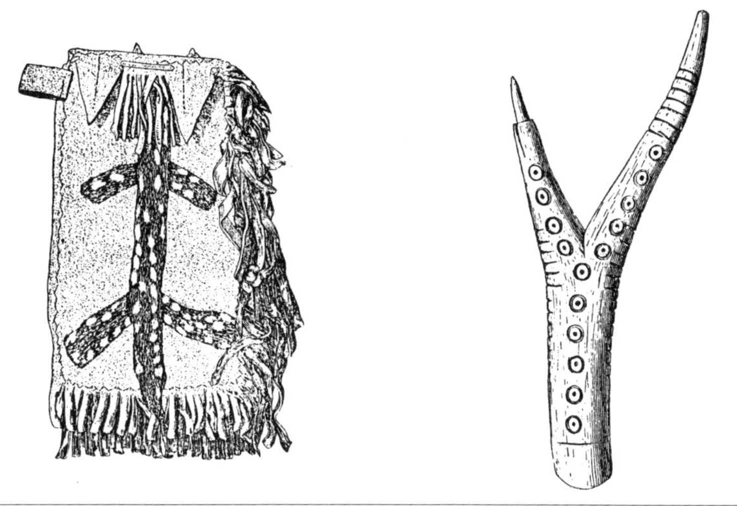

FIG. 38 (16/6720). Tobacco pouch with design of a lizard

FIG. 39 (16/4835). Arrow flaker

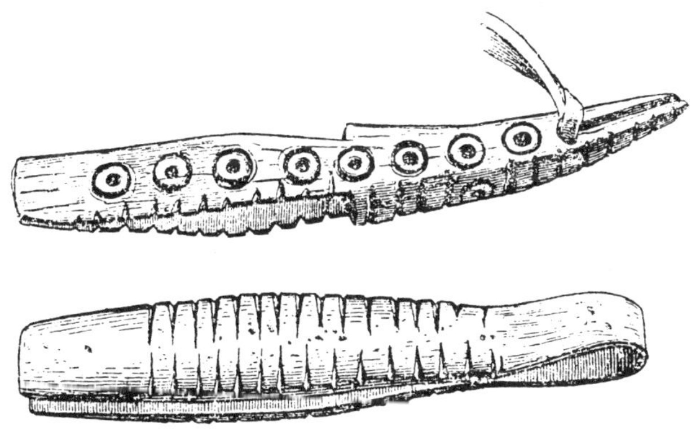

FIG. 40 (16/4570, 16/4569). Tweezers

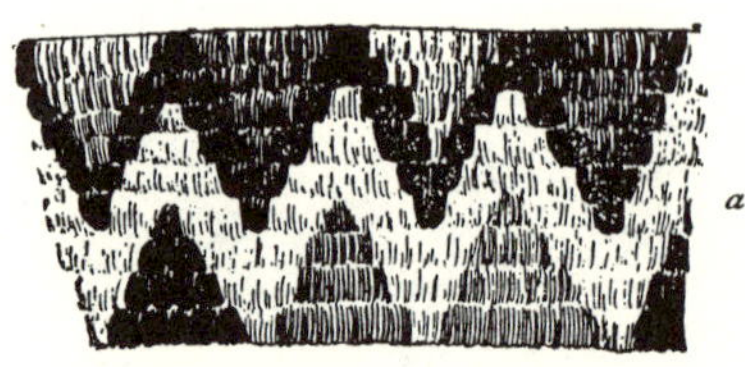

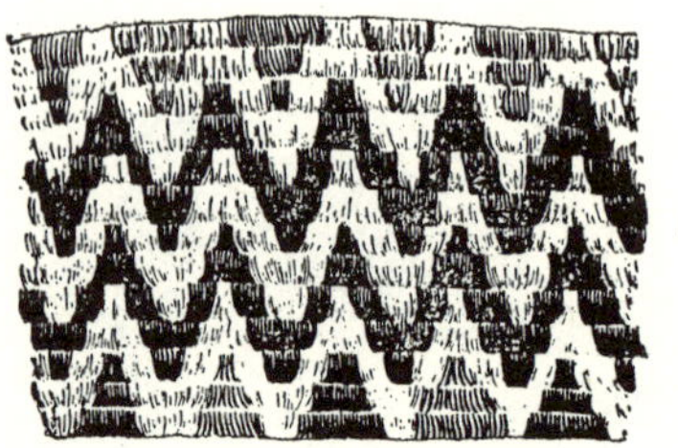

FIG. 41 (16/4631). Arrow designs on carrying straps

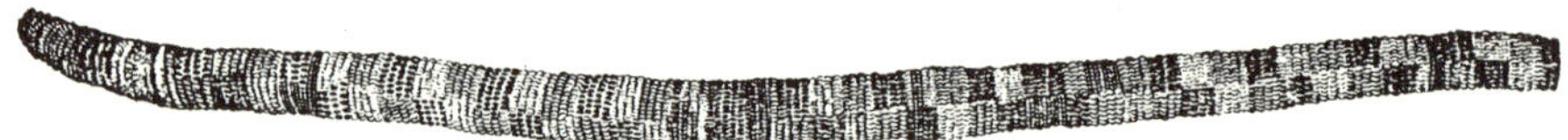

FIG. 42 (16/1333). Beaded necklace with snake design

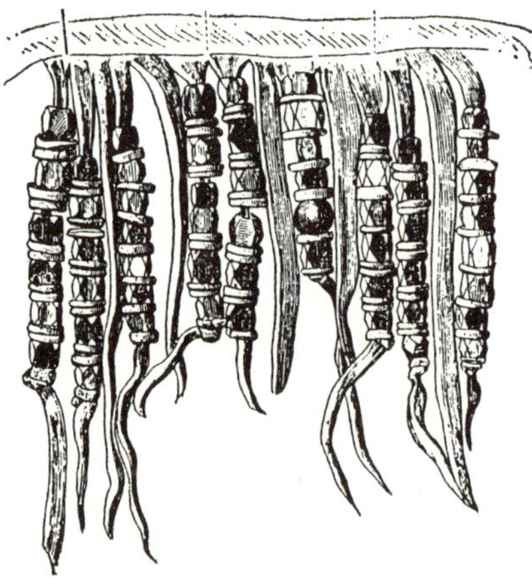

FIG. 43 (16/1353). Fringe showing rhythmic repetition of five elements

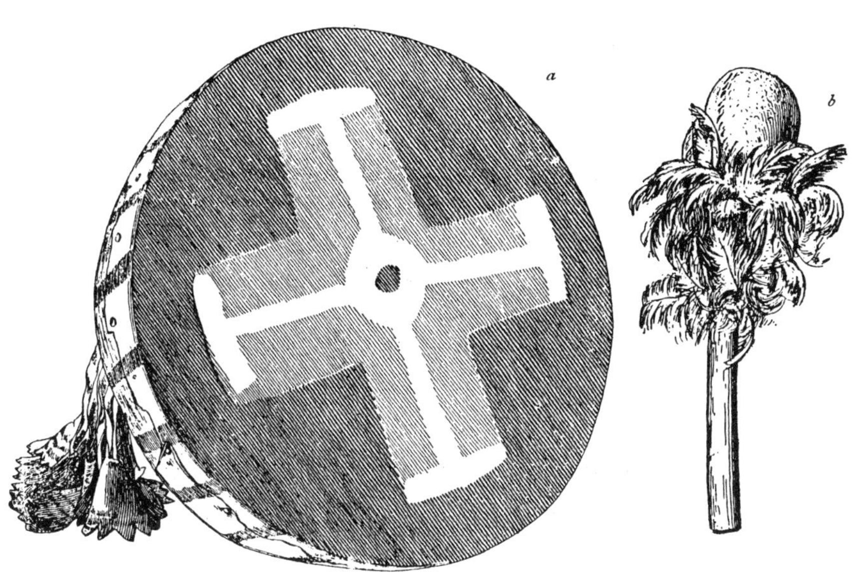

FIG. 44 (16/1380) *a*, *b*. Drum, drumstick

latches had designs referring to those festivals. Such a one is shown in Fig. 23. It is only recently that square drums, like the present specimen, have been made, a box being used for the frame. The paintings represent, on the sides, the rainbow, the sun, a male and female dancer, and a horse tied to a post, to be given away as a present. On the top is painted a grave post with attached sacrifices, stars, and on the upper part a deer trap, the curved lines representing the spring poles. On another drum (Fig. 44) is seen a cross painted in red, which represents the points of the compass. The four white lines are said to represent bridges, more particularly the one at Botani, from which Coyote fell (see *Traditions of the Thompson River Indians*, by James Teit, p. 26). The white crosslines at the ends of the long white lines represent the ends of the bridges. No explanation has been obtained for the rest of the painting. The drumstick in Fig. 44 is made of skin padded with deer hair and decorated with hawk feathers.

The Thompson Indians used no rattles except rattling anklets made of deer hoofs, which were worn at dances.

The Indians have a great many songs, which they divide into classes. The principal classes of songs are the lyric song, treating of love, deeds of valor, etc.; the dance song; the war song; the shaman's song; the song sung in sweat houses; the mourning song; the prayer or religious song; the gambling song for the game *lehal*; and the cradle song. One song is called the cricket song. The tune is an imitation throughout of the cricket's chirp. The cricket is supposed to say, "Mend the fire," or "Put fuel on the fire," consequently the words of the song are the same.

DANCING

Dances also take place at potlatches and other festivals. One or more (generally women, perhaps three or four at a time) get up and dance. Many of these dance as long as they have the breath to do so, after which they hold out a present of a dress or a blanket, saying, "This is because you have seen me dance." This present is then handed over to the guests. Sometimes a man gets up and dances, holding a rifle in his hands, with which he goes through many maneuvers, uttering at the same time grunts and exclamations, and then the rifle is given to the guests. At times some of these men and women imitate in their dances certain birds and animals, such as prairie chicken, hare, or goose, in sound and gesture. Sometimes the whole actions and motions of the birds or animals while feeding, etc., and the hunting of them, were gone through, causing much merriment to the onlookers. These particular animals were selected because their motions were well suited to this kind of dance; and, besides, these animals or birds were seldom the guardian spirits of any person. They were not the guardian spirits of the persons who imitated them. The particular songs or tunes for those dances were called by the names of the birds and animals. In the majority of feast dances, no animals or birds were imitated. Some Indians think that the custom of imitating birds, etc., in these dances, may have been copied from the northern Shuswap, who carried it to greater perfection than any other tribes. When trading parties of the northern Shuswap wintered in the Spences Bridge country, as they did sometimes, the latter gave feasts to the former, and vice versa. When the former entertained the Spences Bridge band, they frequently gave exhibitions of these animal dances on a grand scale. The favorite animals imitated were the moose and the caribou; the dancers being dressed to resemble these animals, even to the antlers. All the actions of the animals in the rutting season were gone through; and the whole process of hunting them, and their final death, were all acted by several men. Generally one or two men acted as hunters, showing how they hunted the animals, and finally shooting and skinning them all. The hunters painted their faces in perpendicular stripes of red and black. Many of the actors held in their hands rattles made of cow's or sheep's horn, with shot inside. Each person danced separately at a considerable distance from the others, never moving from one place while dancing. Occasionally some of the women danced close together, facing the guests. They remained stationary, moving only the body, head, and arms, or went forward and receded, accompanying their motions with a hissing sound.

Sometimes they danced one behind the other. In the latter case, the dancers were women, who advanced slowly toward the speaker, and either gave him presents or received them from him. Sometimes the principal of the party giving presents arose and danced to the accompaniment of drum and song. A guest who praised the dancer was entitled to a present. The chief or best singers, both male and female, sat in a circle round the drummer or leader of the singing.

Formerly, when dancing at the potlatch, some of the men and women put birds' down on their hair. Any kind of down was used, except that of the eagle, which was looked upon as being the peculiar property of the shaman. Some people kept this down in bags made of bow-snake's skin. Some used to paint their faces red or with perpendicular red stripes.

CONCLUSION

The culture of the Thompson Indians, which has been described in the preceding pages, resembles in many respects the culture of other tribes of the western plateaus, and bears evidence of having reached its present stage under the influence of the culture of both the Plains Indians and the tribes of the North Pacific coast, although the affiliations with the former seem to be by far the stronger.

The Salish tribes, of whom the Thompson Indians are one, are remarkable not only on account of their far-reaching linguistic differentiation and the diversity of physical types represented in the various groups, but also on account of the great variation in their cultural status. While the most northern Salish tribe, the Bella Coola, have absorbed all the important elements of the culture of the Northwest Coast, which they have developed in their own peculiar way, we find that the tribes farther to the south have adopted this culture to a much less extent. The most northern tribe of this group are the Comox, who live on the central part of the east coast of Vancouver Island. While they still possess many of the characteristic features of the culture of the Northwest Coast—such as totemism, highly developed plastic art, and a peculiar mythology—these decrease in number as we proceed southward, until on the coast of the State of Washington most of them are found to have disappeared. The most southern tribe of Salish affiliation, the Tillamook, who live in northern Oregon, have developed a culture which is strongly influenced by that of the tribes of northern California. East of the Cascade Range and of the Coast Range of British Columbia we find Salish tribes who, partly on account of different environment, partly on account of eastern influence, resemble in their culture, in many respects, the tribes of the Plains. The Lillooet, who live in one of the large valleys of the Coast Range of British Columbia, are the only one among the Salish tribes of the interior, to whom they belong according to their linguistic affiliation, who have absorbed many elements of Coast culture.

All this tends to show that the Salish tribes have been subject to foreign influence rather than that they themselves have exerted a strong influence upon the tribes with whom they have come in contact. This may have been due to a low stage of development of their early culture, or to social conditions unfavorable to a continued growth of their own culture.

One of the most important questions in regard to the early history of the Salish tribes is whether the home of the tribe was situated on the coast or east of the mountains. On the whole, the evidence seems to be in favor of an inland origin of the present Coast tribes of Salish affiliations. Archaeological investigation of the coast region indicates that in very early times the culture of the southern coast of British Columbia was quite similar to the culture of the northern coast. While at the present time the type of man found in that area is characterized by very broad head and face, we find in the earlier period, which is indicated by the lower strata of the shell heaps, interspersed among the broad-headed type, a peculiar type with narrow face and narrow head, which has no analogue on the coast. These finds indicate a period of mixture of two distinct tribes. The vocabularies and grammatical forms of the Coast Salish dialects prove clearly that at an early time the tribes speaking these dialects must have formed one group of the Salish people, and that they must have differentiated after their arrival on the coast. This is shown most clearly by the fact that theirs alone, among the Salish languages, possess pronominal gender, and that a number of terms referring to the sea are common to most of them. The phonetic disintegration of these dialects, on the other hand, suggests the effect of profound cultural revolutions, many of which may have been due to mixture with foreign tribes. That such mixture has taken place is also borne out in the variety of physical types represented in this area, in the variety of cultural forms, and in the changes of mode of life which are evidenced by the changes in burial customs that have taken place in some of these districts in prehistoric times. The existence of small isolated foreign tribes, such as the Chemakum and Athapascan of Washington, substantiates these views. All this is the more striking in comparison with the uniformity of physical type, of dialect, and of culture, which we find among the tribes of the interior.

When comparing the culture of the Coast Salish with that of the interior, we find that both have a number of features in common, and that these points are the ones in regard to which the Coast Salish show a marked difference from their northern neighbors. This is particularly true of their social organization, of their art, and of their mythology. While the northern tribes are characterized by a division into exogamic totems, the Salish tribes consist of a number of village communities of very loose social structure. Only the Bella Coola and the tribes north of Puget Sound have adopted to a limited extent the more elaborate organization of their neighbors. I have tried to show elsewhere how the totemic system of the north was probably introduced among the Salish and Kwakiutl tribes [Boas 1897b:333; 1898c:120], and that we may assume that originally all the Salish tribes were as loosely organized as we find the Thompson Indians of today. I have also tried to show that the mythology of the Coast Salish has not been much affected by the myths of the northern tribes [Boas 1895:346]. We may therefore conclude that the period of contact between the two groups of people does not cover an excessively long time.

This view is corroborated by a consideration of the art of the Coast Salish, whose works are much cruder than those of the northern tribes. They have never adopted to its fullest extent the method of the latter, of adjusting decoration to the decorative field, but adhere more or less to the pictographic style of the interior. Even on their totem poles we find a number of figures carved on a board rather than a succession of intricately connected figures covering the whole post. The petroglyphs of southern Vancouver Island particularly are of the same pictographic character as those of the east and as the rock paintings of the interior of British Columbia, while those of the northern coast resemble in style the conventional paintings and carvings of the Northwest Coast art. We must also mention here that a number of objects, particularly pipes, found in southern Vancouver Island and on the Lower Fraser River, are identical in type with specimens found among the archaeological remains of the interior.

When analyzing the culture of the Thompson Indians, we find much evidence of a strong influence of eastern culture by way of the Nicola Valley. The style of dress, the use of feather ornaments, the cradle of the Nicola band, are decidedly due to contact with the east. The Nicola band have always been in close contact with the Okanagon; and eastern products, such as pipes and painted buffalo hides, and eastern fashions and customs, such as styles of dress and the method of building round tents instead of square lodges, have been introduced in this manner. Even the first vague traces of Christianity seem to have found their way to the tribe along this route.

In many respects these resemblances between their culture and eastern culture are common to them and to other tribes of the western plateaus. The sinew-lined bow, the occurrence of the tubular pipe, the peculiar woven rabbit-skin blanket, the high development of the coyote myths, and the loose social organization, combined with the lack of elaborate religious ceremonials, characterize them as resembling still more closely the culture of the western highlands.

The decorative art of the Thompson Indians is quite similar to the art of the Indians of the plains and of the plateaus, in that it consists in the application of pictographs for decorative purposes. It is, however, much simpler than the elaborate art of the eastern tribes.

Their manufactures show many affiliations with those of the coast. Sagebrush-bark fabrics are of the same make as the cedar-bark garments of the coast; the tools for woodwork used by the Lower Thompsons are evidently copies or importations from the coast region. Ornaments made of dentalia and abalone shell must be considered as evidence of trade rather than as copies of ornaments worn on the coast. The hand hammer, harpoon, and fish knife may also be counted as copies of implements used by the Coast tribes.

One of the elements of their culture that is most difficult to explain is the occurrence of the beautiful basketry made of cedar bark, and of woven fabrics made of mountain-goat wool, among the Lower Thompsons. Coiled basketry of this type is found in many places along the Pacific coast. Professor Otis T. Mason [1883–84: 295] has pointed out that the coiled basketry of the Arctic Athapascans, which belongs to this type, may be related to the coiled basketry of the Apache and Navajo. Since the publication of his paper, much material has been gathered which is strongly in favor of this view. The same type of basketry is found not only among the Athapascan tribe of the Mackenzie Basin, as Professor Mason points out, but also among the Chilcotin of British Columbia. It occurs all along the Coast Range and the Cascade Range in British Columbia and in Washington, and attains its greatest beauty in California. Isolated Athapascan tribes are found throughout this area. Their existence proves that at one time a wave of Athapascan migration must have swept southward along the coast. It would seem, therefore, that this art originated among the tribes who now practice it, at the time of the Athapascan migration. It is remarkable, however, that such basketry is not found in Nicola Valley, which at one time was the home of an Athapascan tribe. It may be that the scarcity of wood in this area is responsible for the restriction of the art to the western portion of the country. The style of weaving applied in the woollen blanket of the Lower Thompson Indians suggests that its origin is due to the application of the technique of weaving found in the interior to a different material. The method of weaving these blankets is the same in principle as that applied by the Upper Thompsons in making rabbit-skin blankets and mattings.

In a general way, we may say, therefore, that the Thompson Indians are in appearance and culture a plateau tribe, influenced, however, to a great extent by their eastern neighbors, to a less extent by the tribes of the coast. Their whole social organization is very simple; and the range of their religious ideas and rites is remarkably limited, when compared to those of other American tribes. This may be one of the reasons why, in contact with other tribes, the Salish have always proved to be a receptive race, quick to adopt foreign modes of life and thought, and that their own influence has been comparatively small.

7. The Decorative Art of the North American Indians

In this essay Boas investigates the relationship between style and interpretation by illustrating the process by which ethnic groups appropriate artistic motifs from other ethnic groups and impose upon those motifs meanings appropriate to their own culture. As an example he describes similar images explained quite differently by different groups of Plains Indians; these motifs, he suggests, originated among the Pueblos.

The extended investigations on primitive decorative art which have been made during the last twenty years have clearly shown that almost everywhere the decorative designs used by primitive man do not serve purely esthetic ends, but that they suggest to his mind certain definite concepts. They are not only decorations, but symbols of definite ideas.

Much has been written on this subject; and for a time the opinion prevailed that wherever an ornament is explained as a representation of a certain object, its origin has been in a realistic representation of that object, and that it has gradually assumed a more and more conventionalized form, which often has developed into a purely geometrical motive [see Haddon 1895]. On the other hand, Cushing [1886] and Holmes [1886] have pointed out the important influence of material and technique in the evolution of design, and, following Semper [1861–63], have called attention to the frequent transfer of designs developed in one technique to another. Thus, according to Semper, forms developed in wood architecture were imitated in stone, and Cushing and Holmes showed that textile designs are imitated on pottery.

The origin of certain designs from technical forms is now recognized as an important factor, and it must therefore be assumed that in many cases the interpretation has been read into the design. The existence of this tendency has recently been pointed out by H. Schurtz [1906] and by Professor A. D. F. Hamlin [1898], who has treated in a series of essays the evolution of decorative motives.

In speaking of the process of conventionalization or degeneration of realistic motives, Professor Hamlin says: "Indeed, this degeneration may reasonably be accepted as suggesting that the geometric forms which it approaches were already in habitual use when it began, and that the direction of the degeneration was determined by a preexisting habit or 'expectancy' (as Dr. Colley March calls it) of geometric form acquired in skeuomorphic decoration" [1898:93] (i.e., in a form developed from

Reprinted from *The Popular Science Monthly*, vol. 63, pp. 481–498, 1903.

technical motives). At another place [1898:35] he says: "After having undergone in its own home such series of modifications, the motive becomes known to the artists of some race or civilization through the agency either of commerce or of conquest. It is carried across seas and lands, and in new hands receives still another dress in combinations still more incongruous with its original significance. It is no longer a symbol, but an arbitrary ornament, wholly conventional, modified to suit the taste and the arts of the foreigners who have adopted it. In many cases it undergoes modification in two or more directions, resulting in divergent developments, which in time produce as many distinct motives—cousins, as it were, of each other—each of which runs its own course independently of the others. This phenomenon we may call 'divergence.' A common cause of divergence is the tendency to assimilate a borrowed motive to some indigenous and familiar form, usually a natural object, thus setting up a new method of treatment quite foreign to the origin of the motive."

I intend to show in the following pages that the same processes, which Professor Hamlin traces by historical evidence in the art of the civilized peoples of the old world, have occurred among the primitive tribes of North America.[1]

Before taking up this subject, I wish to call attention to a peculiar difference between the decorative style applied in ceremonial objects and that employed in articles of everyday use. We find a considerable number of cases which demonstrate the fact that, on the whole, the decoration of ceremonial objects is much more realistic than that of ordinary objects. Thus we find the garments for ceremonial dances of the Arapaho covered with pictographic representations of animals, their sacred pipe covered with human and other forms, while their painted blankets for ordinary wear are generally adorned with geometrical designs. Among the Thompson Indians ceremonial blankets are also covered with pictographic designs, while ordinary wearing apparel and basketry are decorated with very simple geometrical motives. On the stem of a shaman's pipe we find a series of pictographs, while an ordinary pipe shows geometric forms. Even among the eastern Eskimo, whose decorative art, on the whole, is very rudimentary, a shamanistic coat has been found which has a number of realistic motives, while the ordinary dress of the same tribe shows no trace of such decoration (Fig. 1*a* and *b*). Perhaps the most striking examples of this kind are the woven designs of the Huichol Indians of Mexico. All their ceremonial weavings are covered with more or less realistic designs, while all their ordinary wearing apparel presents geometrical motives. In fact, the style of the two is so different that it hardly seems to belong to the same tribe (Fig. 2). The same

1. The examples and illustrations here represented are taken, unless otherwise stated, from specimens in the American Museum of Natural History. The information and material used were collected by Dr. Roland B. Dixon, Professor Livingston Farrand, Dr. A. L. Kroeber, Dr. Berthold Laufer, Dr. Carl Lumholtz, Mr. H. H. St. Clair, Mr. James Teit, and Dr. Clark Wissler, all of whom have contributed to the systematic study of decorative art undertaken by the museum.

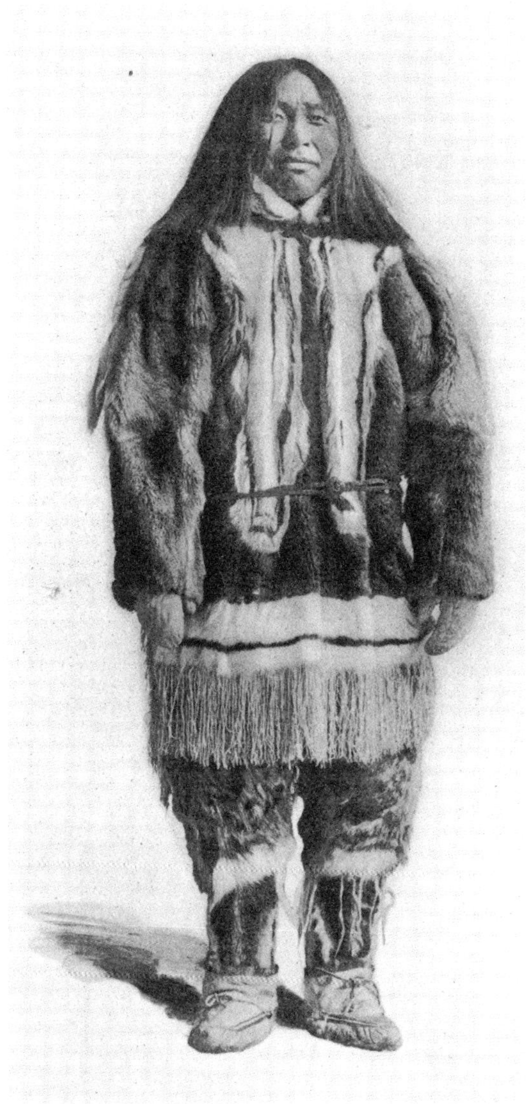

FIG. 1*a*. Eskimo in ordinary dress

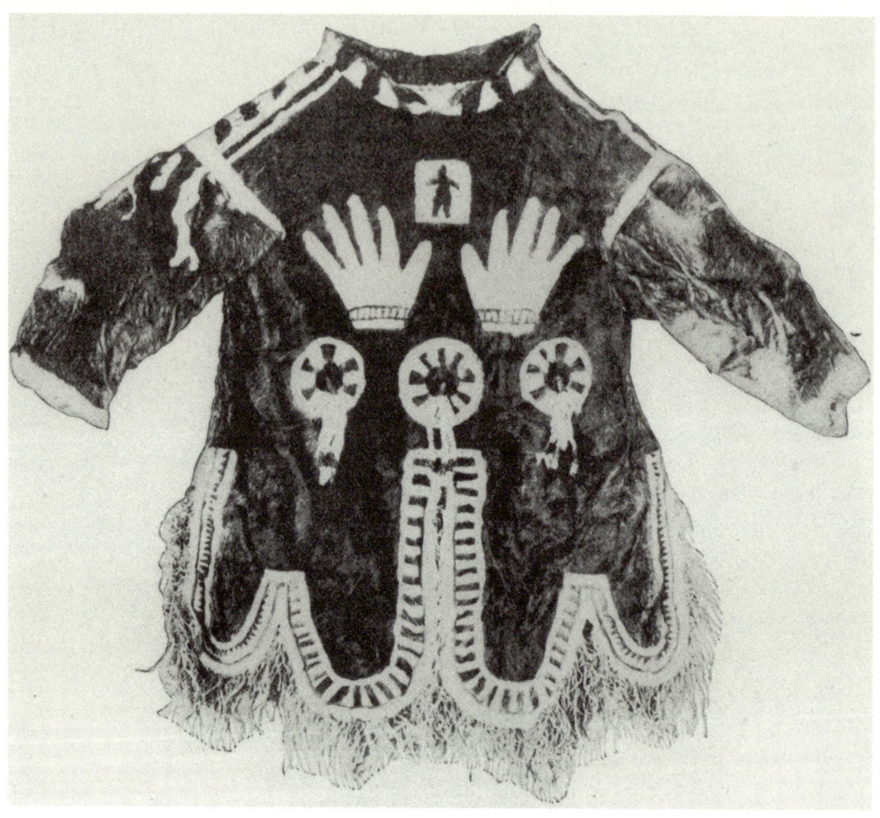

FIG. 1*b*. Shamanistic coat of Eskimo

phenomenon may be observed outside of America, as is demonstrated by the difference in style between the shaman's coat and the ordinary coat of the Gold of the Amur River (Fig. 3*a* and *b*). We may perhaps recognize the same tendency in the style of decoration of modern dwelling rooms and in that of public buildings. The designs on the stained glass of house windows are usually arranged in geometrical forms; those of churches represent pictures. The wall decorations of houses are wall papers of more or less geometrical character; those of halls devoted to public uses are generally adorned with symbolic pictures.

This difference in the treatment of ceremonial and common objects shows clearly that the reason for the conventionalization of motives cannot be solely a technical one, for if so, it would act in one case as well as in the other. In ceremonial objects the ideas represented are more important than the decorative effect, and it is intel-

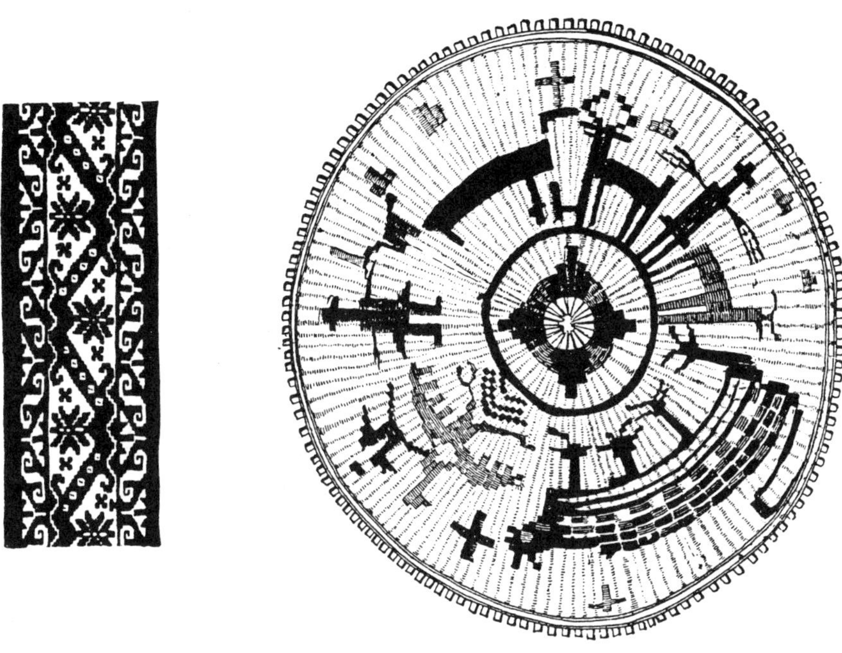

FIG. 2. Woven designs of the Huichol Indians (after Dr. Carl Lumholtz)

ligible that the resistance to conventionalism may be strong; although in some cases the very sacredness of the idea represented might induce the artist to obscure his meaning intentionally, in order to keep the significance of the design from profane eyes. It may, therefore, be assumed that, if a tendency to conventionalization exists, it will manifest itself differently, even among the same tribe, according to the preponderance of the decorative or descriptive value of the design.

On the other hand, the general prevalence of symbolic significance in ordinary decoration shows that this is an important aspect of decorative art, and a tendency to retain the realistic form might be expected, provided its origin were from realistic forms. If, therefore, the whole decorative art of some tribes shows no trace of realism, it may well be doubted whether their ordinary decorative designs were originally realistic.

The history of decorative design can best be investigated by analyzing the styles of form and interpretation prevailing over a limited area. If the style of art were entirely indigenous in a given tribe, and developed either from conventionalization of realistic designs or from the elaboration of technical motives, we should expect

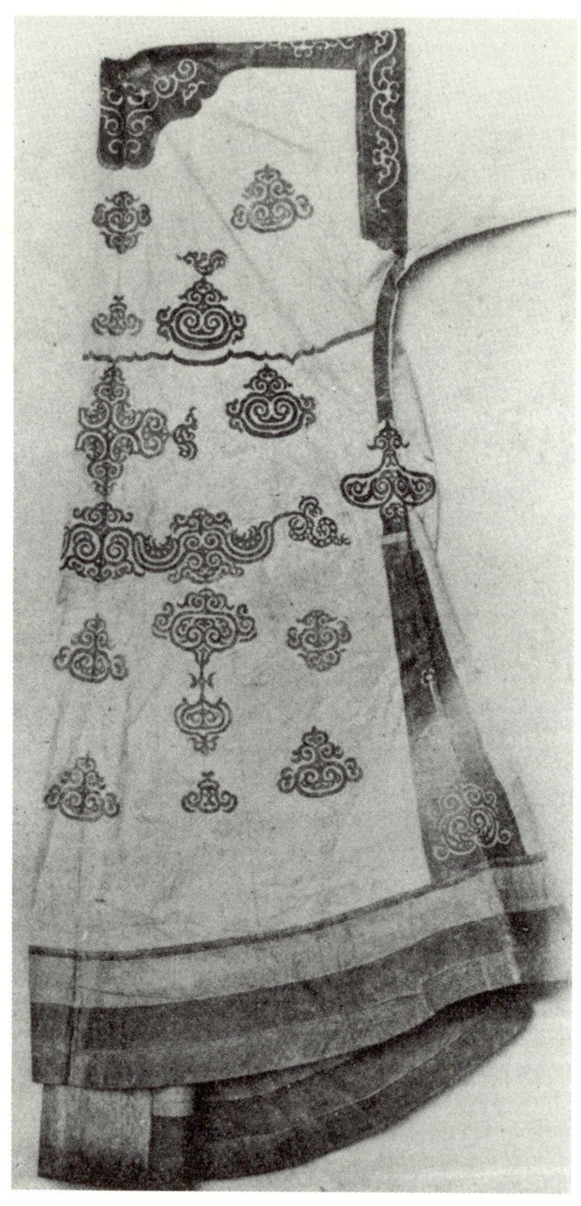

FIG. 3*a*. Ordinary coat of the Gold of the Amur River (after Dr. Berthold Laufer)

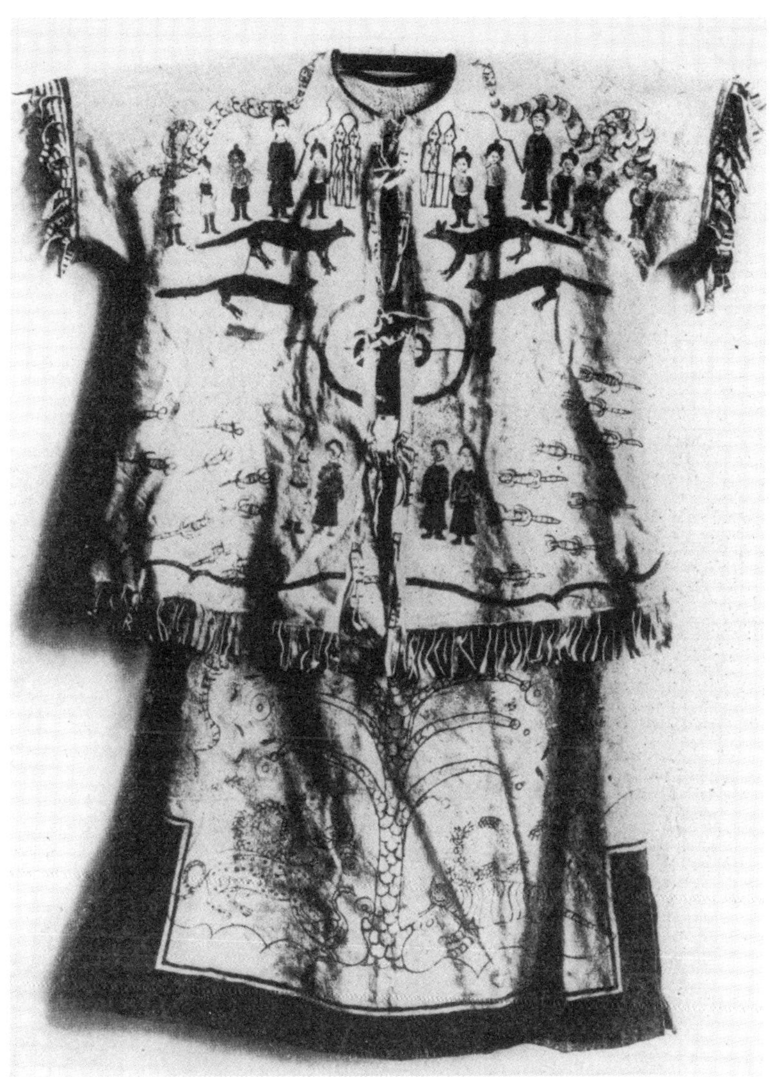

FIG. 3*b*. Coat of a shaman of the Gold of the Amur River

to find a different style and different motives in each tribe. The general customs and beliefs might be expected to determine the subjects chosen for decoration, or the ideas that are read into the technical designs.

As a matter of fact, the native art of North America shows a very different state of affairs. All over the Great Plains and in a large portion of the western plateaus an art is found which, notwithstanding local peculiarities, is of a uniform type. It is characterized by the application of colored triangles and quadrangles in both painting and embroidery in a manner which is found in no other part of the world.

The slight differences of styles which occur are well exemplified in the style of painted rawhide bags or envelopes, the so-called parfleches. Mr. St. Clair has observed that the Arapaho are in the habit of laying on the colors rather delicately, in areas of moderate size, and of following out a general arrangement of their motives in stripes; that the Shoshone, on the other hand, like large areas of solid colors, bordered by heavy blue bands, and an arrangement in which a central field is set off rather prominently from the rest of the design (Fig. 4). This difference is so marked that it is easy to tell a Shoshone parfleche that has found its way to the Arapaho from parfleches of Arapaho manufacture. In other cases the most characteristic difference consists in the place on the parfleche to which the design is applied. The Arapaho and the Shoshone never decorate the sides of a bag, only its flaps, while the tribes of Idaho and Montana always decorate the sides. Another peculiarity of Arapaho parfleche painting, as compared to that of the Shoshone, is the predilection for two right-angled triangles standing on the same line, their right angles facing each other—a motive of common occurrence all over the southern part of the Plains and in the southwestern territories; while the Shoshone generally place these triangles with facing acute angles. A detailed study of the art brings out many minor differences of this sort, although the general type is very uniform.

Certain types of designs are so much alike that they might belong to one tribe as well as to another. A series of moccasins of the Shoshone, Sioux, and Arapaho (Fig. 5) will serve as a good example. The characteristic forms of all of these are a cross on the uppers, connected with a bar on the instep, from which arise at each end two short lines. These designs are so complex that evidently they must have had a common origin. It is of great importance to note that nevertheless the explanations given by the various tribes are quite different. The design is interpreted by the Arapaho as the morning star; the bar on the instep, as the horizon; the short lines, as the twinkling of the star. To the mind of the Sioux the design conveys the idea of feathers, when applied to a woman's moccasin; when found on a man's moccasin, it symbolizes the sacred shield suspended from tent poles. The identical design was explained by the Shoshone as signifying the sun (the circle) and its rays; but also the thunderbird, the crossarms of the cross evidently being the wings; the part nearest the toe, the tail, and the upper part, the neck with two strongly conventionalized

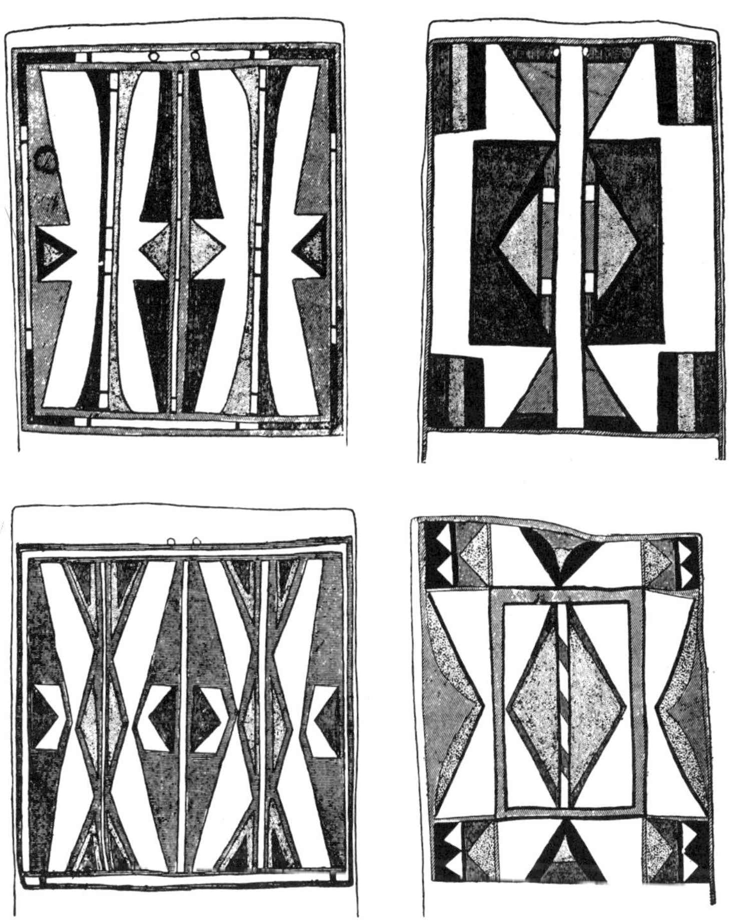

FIG. 4. Painted rawhide bags (after A. L. Kroeber and H. H. St. Clair). *Left:* Arapaho; *right:* Shoshone

heads attached. If these are the ideas conveyed by this design to the weavers, it is clear that they must have developed after the invention or introduction of the design; that the design is primary, the idea secondary, and that the idea has nothing to do with the historical development of the design itself.

It may be well to give a few additional examples of such similarity of design and difference of symbolism. One of the typical designs of this area is a cross to the ends of which deeply notched squares are attached (Fig. 6). Dr. Kroeber [1902] received the following explanation of this design from an Arapaho: the diamond in the center

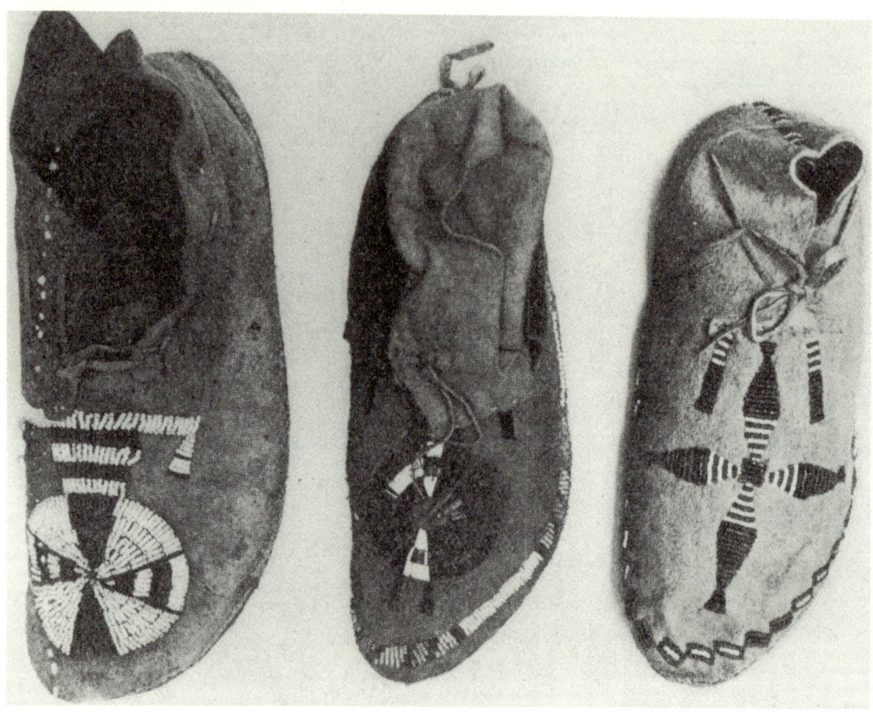

FIG. 5. Moccasins. *From left:* Shoshone, Sioux, Sioux and Arapaho

represents a person; the four forked ornaments surrounding it are buffalo hoofs or tracks. Dr. Wissler found the design on a pair of woman's leggings of the Sioux. In this case the diamond-shaped center of the design represents the breast of a turtle; the green lines forming the cross indicate the four points of the compass; the forked ornaments symbolize forks of trees struck by hailstones, which are indicated by small white rectangles. Mr. St. Clair came across the same design among the Shoshone, where it was found on a cowhide bag. The central diamond was interpreted as the sun and clouds; the notched designs were explained as mountain-sheep hoofs. There is a certain similarity in this case between the explanations given by the Arapaho and those of the Shoshone, while the Sioux connect ideas of a different type with the design.

Such differences of interpretation are also found on painted designs. The Shoshone sometimes imagine they see a battle scene in the squares and triangles of their parfleche designs. The square in the center of Fig. 7 was explained to Mr. St. Clair

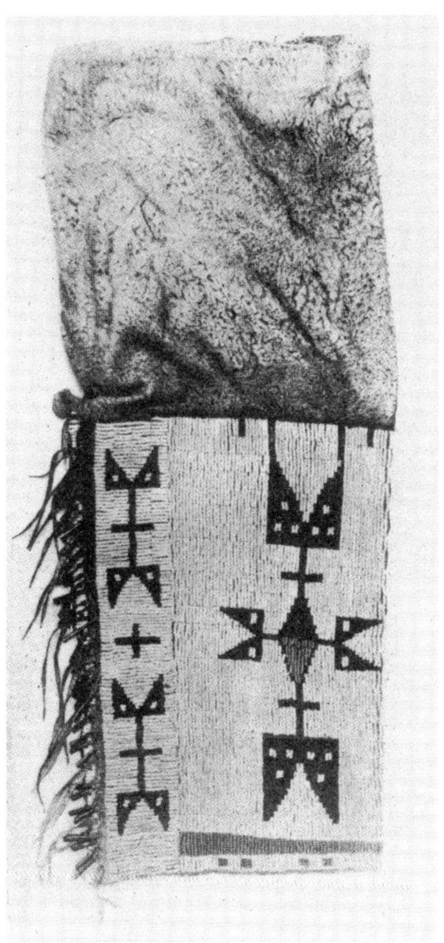

FIG. 6. Legging with bead embroidery

as an enclosure in which the enemy was kept by a besieging party, represented by the marginal squares. The narrow central line is the trail by which the enemy made good his escape. Many others represent geographical features, such as mountains and valleys. Such geographical ideas are represented on some Arapaho parfleches, while others exhibit a more complex symbolic significance. Battle scenes, however, are not found in interpretations given by the Arapaho.

The similarity of complex designs, combined with dissimilarity of interpretation, justifies a comparison of simpler forms. These might be believed to have originated

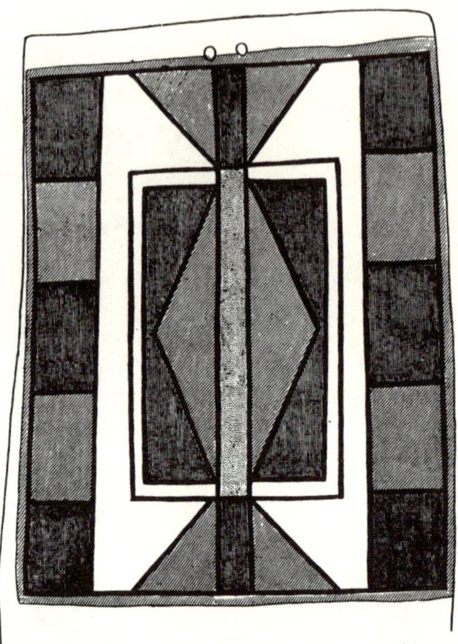

FIG. 7. Shoshone parfleche design

independently; but the sameness of the complex forms proves that their component elements must have had a common origin, or at least have been assimilated by the same forms. One of the striking examples of this kind is the cross. Among the Arapaho it signifies almost invariably the morning star. To the mind of the Shoshone it conveys the idea of barter. The Sioux recognizes in it a man slain in battle and lying flat on the ground with arms outstretched. The Thompson Indians of British Columbia recognize in it the crossing trails at which sacrifices are made.

The simple straight red lines with which skin bags are decorated are another good example. A specimen was collected by Dr. Kroeber among the Arapaho (Fig. 8*a* and *b*) in which he explains the stripes on the beaded design on the narrow sides and on the flaps of the bag as camp trails; the shorter transverse stripes intersecting these longitudinal lines, as ravines, that is, camping places. On the front of the bag the horizontal lines of quillwork, which resemble the lines on buffalo robes, are paths. Bunches of feathers on these lines represent buffalo meat hung up to dry. Adjoining the beadwork are small tin cylinders with tufts of red hair; these represent pendants or rattles on tents. Mr. St. Clair obtained the following explanation of a Shoshone bag of almost identical design: The porcupine quillwork on the front of the bag rep-

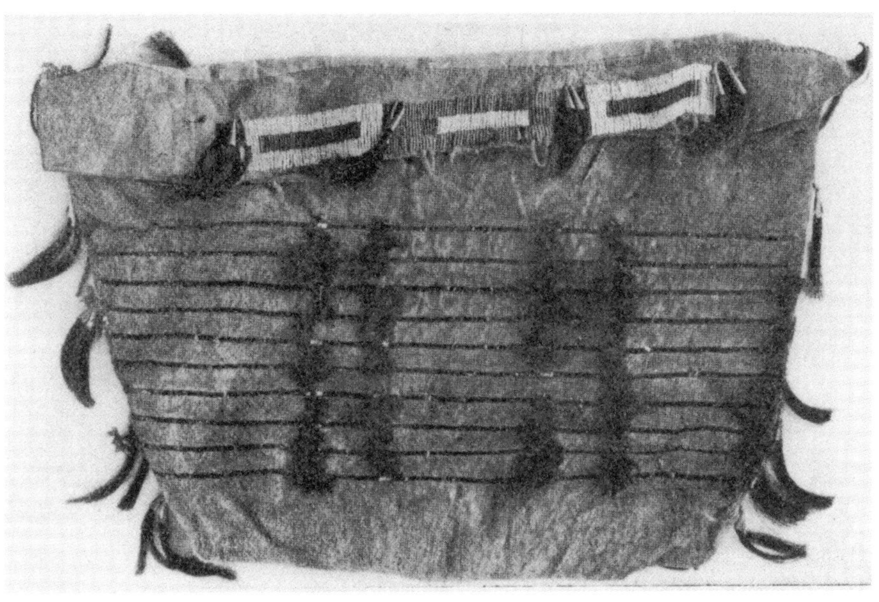

FIG. 8*a*. Skin bag of the Arapaho (after A. L. Kroeber)

resents horse trails. The red horsehair tassels at each side are horses stolen by people of one village from those of another, the villages being represented by the beadwork at the sides of the bag. The beadwork on the flap represents the owners of the horses indicated by the horsehair tassels on the flap. Among the Sioux the same design is used in the puberty ceremonial, and symbolizes the path of life.

It must not be believed that the interpretation of a certain motive, or even of a complex figure when used by the members of one tribe, is always the same. As a matter of fact, the number of ideas expressed by it is often quite varied. We find, for instance, the obtuse triangle with enclosed rectangle (Fig. 4) explained by the Arapaho as the mythic cave from which the buffalo issued, as cattle tracks, as a mountain, cloud, brush hut, and tent; an acute triangle, with small triangles attached to its base, as a bird's tail, frog, tent, and bear's foot.

Nevertheless the explanations given by various tribes show peculiar characteristics in which they differ from those of other tribes. The explanations possess no less a style of their own than the art itself. Triangles are explained as tents by all tribes, and mountains or hills form a prominent feature of their descriptions; but among the three tribes mentioned, only the Sioux see wounds, battle scenes with moving masses of men, horses, the pursuit of enemies, the flight of arrows, in their

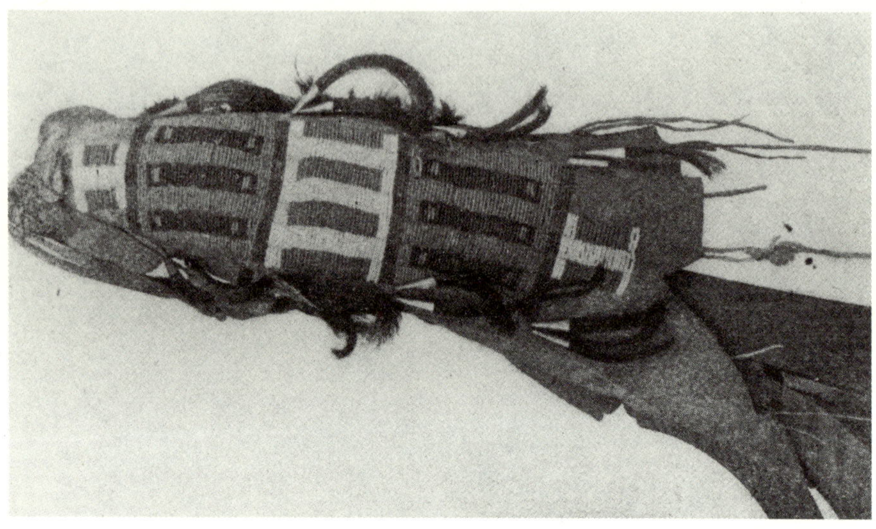

FIG. 8*b*. Side of Arapaho bag

conventional designs; only the Shoshone see in them pictures of forts and stones piled up in memory of battles; only the Arapaho recognize in them prayers for life directed to the morning star.

We find, therefore, that in this area the same style of art is widely distributed, while the style of explanation differs materially among its various tribes.

It may be worthwhile to review briefly the distribution of the style of art here discussed. On the whole, it is confined to the Plains Indians, west of the eastern wooded area. It would seem that it has been carried into the plateau region rather recently, where, however, it has affected almost all the tribes east of the Cascade Range and of the Sierra Nevada. We find the acute triangle with small supporting triangles, and the obtuse triangle with enclosed rectangle, in the characteristic arrangement of the parfleches, on a bag of the Nez Percés (Fig. 10) collected by Dr. Livingston Farrand. At first glance, the art of the Pueblos seems quite different from the one that we are discussing here: but I believe that an intimate association of the two may be traced. The old pottery described by Dr. Fewkes, for instance, shows a number of the peculiar triangle and square motives which are so characteristic of the art of the Indians of the Plains. The same triangle with supporting lines, the same triangle with the enclosed square (Fig. 10), is found here. It seems very plain to my mind that the transfer of this art from pottery to embroidery and painting on

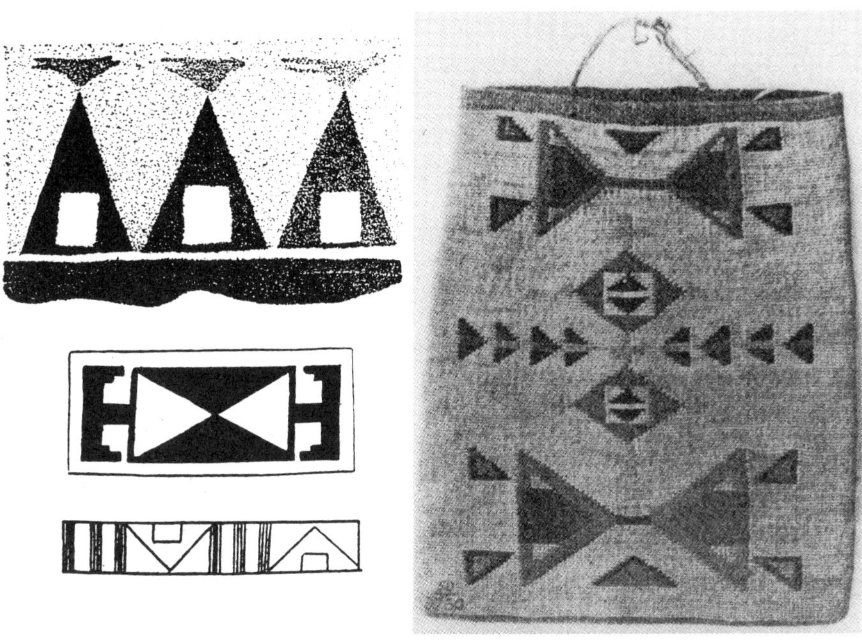

FIG. 9. Decorative motives of the Pueblo Indians (after Dr. W. F. Fewkes from specimens in the U.S. National Museum)

FIG. 10. Woven bag of the Nez Percés

flat surfaces has brought about the introduction of the triangular and rectangular forms which are the prime characteristic of this type of art.

In the prehistoric art of the northern plateaus, in California, on the North Pacific coast, in the Mackenzie Basin, in the wooded area of the Atlantic coast, we find styles of art which differ from the art of the Plains, and which have much less in common with Pueblo art. Therefore I am inclined to consider the art of the Plains Indians in many of its traits as developed from the art of the Pueblos. I think the general facts of the culture of these tribes are fairly in accord with this notion, since it would seem that the complex social and religious rites of the Southwest gradually become simpler and less definite as we proceed northward. If this opinion regarding the origin of the art of the Plains is correct, we are led to the conclusion that the tent with its pegs is the same form in origin as the rain clouds of the Pueblos, so that the scope of interpretations of the same form is still more enlarged. Under these conditions, we must conclude that the interpretation is probably secondary throughout, and has become associated with the form which was obtained by borrowing. With this we are brought face to face with the skeuomorphic origin of the triangular design from basketry motives, which has been so much discussed of recent years.

The so-called quail-tip design of California is another example of the continuous distribution of a motive over a wide area, the occurrence of which in the outlying districts must be due to borrowing. The characteristic feature of this design, which occurs in the basketry of California and Oregon, is a vertical line, suddenly turning outward at its end. This motive occurs on both twined and coiled basketry, and with many explanations [Dixon 1902:2 ff.]. In some combinations it is explained as the lizard's foot (Fig. 11*a*, *b*), in others as the pinecone or the mountain (Fig. 11*c*). The gradual distribution of this motive over a wide area can best be proved in this case by a comparison with the distribution of the technique in which it is applied. The design occurs all over central and northern California. On the Columbia River it is found on the Klickitat baskets. These are of the peculiar imbricated basketry which is made from this point on, northward. While the designs on imbricated basketry found in British Columbia are of a peculiar character, the Klickitat baskets of the same make (Fig. 11*d*) have the typical California designs which also occur on the twined bags of this district (Fig. 11*e*).

Thus we find not only that the distribution of interpretations and that of motives do not coincide, but also that the distribution of technique does not agree with that of motives. I think we can also demonstrate that the limits of styles of interpretation in some cases overlap the limits of styles of art. We have seen that on the Plains the style of art covers a wider area than the style of interpretation. It would seem that in other regions the reverse is the case. For instance, the style of art of the Nootka tribes differs very much from that of the Kwakiutl. Although both apply animal motives, the Nootka use very little surface decoration consisting of combinations of characteristic curved lines, which play an important part in Kwakiutl art, and which serve to symbolize various parts of the body. Nootka art is more realistic and at the same time cruder than Kwakiutl art. The ideas expressed in the art of both tribes, however, are practically the same. In the Southwest we find that the culture of the Pueblos has deeply influenced the neighboring Athapascan and Sonoran tribes, while at the same time the decoration of their basketry bears a close relation to that of Californian basketry. Although I do not know the interpretations of designs given by the Apache, Pima, and Navajo, it seems probable that they have been influenced by the ideas current among the Pueblos. Among the Pueblos themselves—and in these I include the tribes of northern Mexico, such as the Huichol—there are well-marked local styles of technique and of decoration, and a general similarity of interpretation. I think the marked prevalence of geographical interpretations found among the Salish tribes of British Columbia, the Shoshone, and the Arapaho is

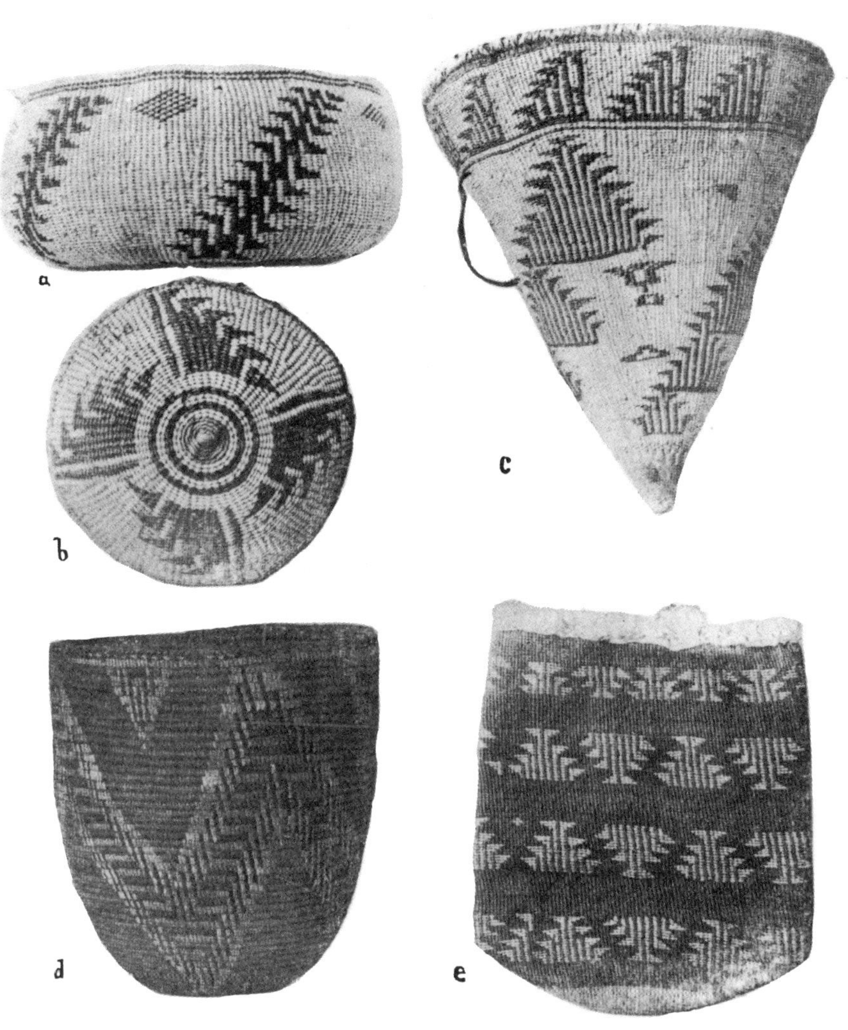

FIG. 11. Baskets from the Pacific Coast: *a*, *b*, Pit River, California; *c*, Maidu, California; *d*, Klickitat, Washington; *e*, Nez Percés, Idaho (*a*, *b*, and *c* after Dr. Roland B. Dixon)

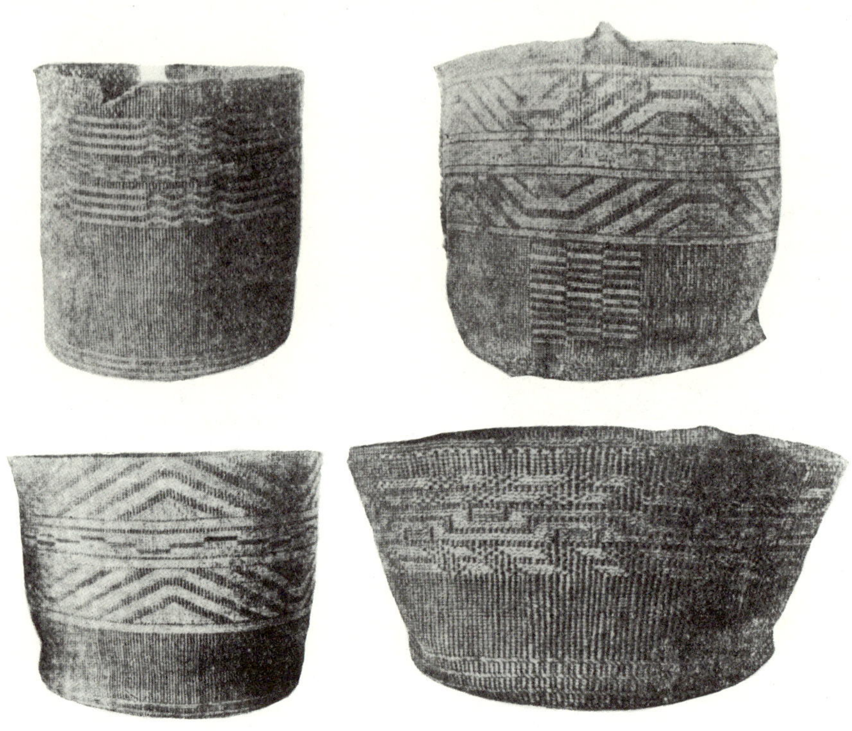

FIG. 12. Tlingit baskets (specimens in the possession of G. T. Emmons)

another instance of distribution of a style of interpretation over an area including divers styles of art.

In a few cases it seems almost self-evident, from a consideration of the interpretations themselves, that they cannot have developed from realistic forms. The multiplicity of Arapaho explanations for the triangles which I mentioned before suggest this. According to G. T. Emmons [1903:263 ff.], the zigzag and the closely allied meander in Tlingit basketry have a variety of meanings. The zigzag may represent the tail of the land otter (Fig. 12*a*), the hood of the raven (Fig. 12*b*), the butterfly (Fig. 12*c*), or, when given a rectangular form (Fig. 12*d*), waves and floating objects. It is evident, in view of the data here discussed, that these must be different interpretations of motives of similar origin.

We conclude from all this that the explanation of designs is secondary almost throughout and due to a late association of ideas and forms, and that as a rule a gradual transition from realistic motives to geometric forms did not take place. The two groups of phenomena—interpretation and style—appear to be independent. We may say that it is a general law that designs are considered significant. Different tribes may interpret the same style by distinct groups of ideas. On the other hand, certain groups of ideas may be spread over tribes whose decorative art follows different styles, so that the same ideas are expressed by different styles of art.

We may express this fact also by saying that the history of the artistic development of a people, and the style that they have developed at any given time, predetermine the method by which they express their ideas in decorative art; and that the type of ideas that a people is accustomed to express by means of decorative art predetermines the explanation that will be given to a new design. It would therefore seem that there are certain typical associations between ideas and forms which become established, and which are used for artistic expression. The idea which a design expresses at the present time is not necessarily a clue to its history. It seems probable that idea and style exist independently, and influence each other constantly.

For the present it remains an open question why the tendency to form associations between certain ideas and decorative motives is so strong among all primitive people. The tendency is evidently similar to that observed among children who enjoy interpreting simple forms as objects to which the form has a slight resemblance; and this, in turn, may bear some relation to the peculiar character of realism in primitive art, to which I believe von den Steinen [1894:250 ff.] was the first to draw attention. The primitive artist does not attempt to draw what he sees, but merely combines what are to his mind the characteristic features of an object, without regard to their actual space relation in the visual image. For this reason he may also be more ready than we are to consider some characteristic feature as symbolic of an object, and thus associate forms and objects in ways that seem to us unexpected.

It may be worthwhile to mention one general point of view that is suggested by our remarks. The explanations of decorative design given by the native suggest that to his mind the form of the design is a result of attempts to represent by means of decorative art a certain idea. We have seen that this cannot be the true history of the design, but that it probably originated in an entirely different manner. What is true in the case of decorative art is true of other ethnic phenomena. The historical explanation of customs given by the native is generally a result of speculation, not by any means a true historical explanation. The mythical explanation of rites and customs is seldom of historical value, but is generally due to associations formed in the course of events, while the early history of myths and rite must be looked for in entirely different causes, and interpreted by different methods. Native explanations of laws, of the origin of the form of society, must have developed in the same manner, and therefore cannot give any clue in regard to historical events, while the association of ideas of which they are the expression furnishes most valuable psychological material.

8. Primitive Art

This brochure available to visitors to the American Museum of Natural History served the dual purposes of directing their attention to certain important objects and of communicating to the public some of Boas's theories about art. Here Boas directs the visitor to art displayed in the Northwest Coast Hall (First Floor, Hall 108), the Plains and Eastern Woodlands Hall (First Floor, Hall 102), and the Californian and Mexican Hall (Second Floor, Hall 202). In his text, Boas illustrates how realistic forms are often gradually transformed into geometric ones, but that such transformation sometimes occurs when one group borrows a motif from another and ascribes to it a new meaning appropriate to its own culture.

I have not included the illustrations from this brochure because most appear in other essays in this volume.

INTRODUCTORY NOTE

A visit to the ethnological halls of the Museum shows that the primitive tribes whose manufactures are exhibited in the cases delight in ornamenting all the objects which are used in ordinary life, in festivals, and in sacred ceremonials. Many of the ornaments may seem crude to our taste, but undoubtedly they are applied to the objects for the same purpose as that for which we apply decorative ornamentation.

Studies of the forms of primitive decoration, which have been carried on by many students, demonstrate the fact that almost everywhere decorative designs, no matter how simple their forms may be, are significant. In many cases we find animal forms and plant forms used for decorative purposes, and in these the significance is at once given by the design. In other cases the ornament consists of nothing but geometrical elements, such as straight lines, triangles and rectangles, or curves and spirals. These designs also are interpreted by primitive man as representing certain natural forms, and thus they express definite ideas.

It may therefore be said that most primitive decoration is symbolic. The style of decoration by means of which ideas are expressed differs very much in various parts

Reprinted from *American Museum Journal*, vol. 4, no. 3, supplement: Guide Leaflet No. 15, 1904. At the end of this pamphlet, Boas provides a short bibliography of papers that describe in detail the collections to which he refers—for the Northwest Coast (Hall 108): Boas 1897a and 1900a, Emmons 1902, Farrand 1900; for the Plains Indians and Siberia: Kroeber 1902, Wissler 1904 (in preparation), Laufer 1902; for the California Indians and the Huichol: Dixon 1902, Lumholtz 1904 (in press). He also writes that "the following general works on primitive art are recommended to students": Grosse 1897, Haddon 1895.—Ed.

of the world. The groups of ideas that are expressed by ornamental designs are also different, according to the characteristic culture of each tribe.

The collections to which this Leaflet refers may be found in Halls 108 [Northwest Coast], 102 [Plains and Eastern Woodlands], and 202 [California and Mexico].

HALL 108: CASES C, D, AND 3

The Coast Tribes of Alaska and British Columbia These tribes use throughout animal forms for purposes of decoration. Some of their masks show that they have the power of producing good realistic representations of human and animal forms (Case C 12); but more frequently the characteristic forms of the animal to be represented are exaggerated in size, as, for instance, the beak of the hawk and the incisors of the beaver.

Sometimes the characteristic feature is represented alone, and thus becomes the symbol of the animal. In Case 3c the symbols of several animals are exhibited. The beaver . . . is characterized by two large incisors, by a broad tail on which scales are indicated by means of hachure, and sometimes by the stick which it holds in its paws [see Fig. 6, chap. 4]. The killer whale is symbolized by its long dorsal fin; the shark or dogfish, by its long, pointed snout, which is represented as rising over its forehead, by its large mouth with depressed corners and many teeth, and by the gill lines which appear on its cheeks. The sculpin is symbolized by spines which rise over its mouth; the eagle, by its crooked beak; the squid, by the suckers which appear attached to the eyebrows or to other parts of the body; the raven, by its long beak; the sea monster, by its large head and by flippers attached to its elbows.

The method of distorting the animal form in order to make it fit the decorative field is illustrated in the specimens in Case C 13. The decorated wooden dish in the bottom of the case represents an animal. It is so shown that the front of the dish represents the animal's head; the sides of the dish, the sides of the body; while the narrow end in the rear represents the tail. Thus it will be seen that the dish actually represents the body of the animal hollowed out from the back. The animal forms are placed in a similar manner on painted hats . . . ; the whole animal being laid around the conical hat, and, as it were, being pulled over the head. In some cases the adaptations require material changes in the form of the animal. When, for instance, a fish is to be painted or carved on the front of a square box, the body of the fish must be so distorted as to fill as nearly as possible the whole decorative field. This is done by cutting the fish along its whole back from head to tail, by exaggerating the size of the head, twisting half of the body along each side of the decorative field and placing the tail so that its end comes just under the head. In still other cases the form of the decorative field necessitates great reduction in the size of certain parts of the body. Thus we find in Case 3c a blanket border representing a sea monster [see Fig. 71, chap. 4]. The animal is shown split in two along its back; but all its parts—except its head, the paws, and the tail—are much reduced in size. The teeth are indicated by a series of slanting lines under each eye, but the lower jaw has been omitted. The body is represented by a fine line extending from the lower outer corners of the eye, around, then along the upper margins and finally down again. The arms and the fins, which are believed to be attached to the elbows of the monster, are of very small size, while the paw is painted on a very large scale. The wide strips in the fringe represent the dorsal fins of the monster. This reduction of parts of the body has evidently given rise to the elimination of all except the characteristic symbols, whenever this was necessary. We find a similar reduction of the sea-monster design on a bracelet in Case C 13 [see Fig. 73, chap. 4], and the complete omission of parts of the body on another bracelet representing the eagle, of which only head, talons, and wings are shown.

Sometimes, in the effort to bring the animal form into the decorative field, the animal is dissected and distorted in a most astonishing manner. This is particularly true in the case of the large ceremonial blankets woven by these tribes, in which various parts of the animal body seem to be combined in the most irregular manner, although really each part represents a definite portion of the animal represented. The blanket above Case D 3 and the explanatory model in that section illustrate this dissection. Similar distortions occur in paintings. For instance, in the copy of a painting from a housefront (Case D 3), representing the killer whale, the central part of the figure represents the head of the whale [see Fig. 69, chap. 4]. The flippers are shown close to the corners of the jaws, half of the blowhole and half of the dorsal fin in the right- and left-hand upper corners, while the tail is shown just over the head.

A collection of designs representing various animals, indicated by their symbols and distorted so as to fit the decorative field, is shown in the exhibition cases. The lower part of Case 3c contains representations of the dogfish or shark. Case 3b contains representations of a mythical sea monster. In case D 1 the sea lion, sculpin, raven, crane, frog, and seal are shown. Case D 2 contains representations of the beaver, all of which are characterized by the large incisors and the tail with hachure. Case D 3 contains representations of the killer whale, characterized by the long dorsal fin; D 4, representations of the bear, which is characterized by its large mouth, often represented with protruding tongue, and its large paws; D 5, those of the raven; D 6, those of the thunderbird or hawk and the eagle, the thunderbird being characterized by the hooked beak, which turns back into the mouth.

One of the peculiar characteristics of the decorative art of the North Pacific coast is the frequent occurrence of the "eye." A form similar to an eye, consisting of an inner and an outer circle, is applied to indicate all joints, evidently to signify the socket and the head moving in the socket. Often this eye is elaborated as a whole face, which then makes the interpretation of the animal form very difficult.

The essential features of the decorative art of the coast Indians of Alaska and British Columbia may thus be characterized as a representation of animal forms by means of distortion and omission, the decorative forms being somewhat realistic representations of parts of the body, preference being given to those parts which are symbolic of each animal.

Purely geometrical decoration is found in only one place on the North Pacific coast. It is applied to the basketry of the Tlingit Indians (Case E 3–8), who, however, in their painting and carving, use the style of art described before. This geometrical style was probably developed in imitation of the porcupine embroidery of the tribes of the interior. Most of the ornamented baskets are made of spruce root, and are embroidered with grass. The ornaments are generally arranged in two broad parallel stripes of the same design, separated by a narrow band containing a different design. The motives consist of rectangular and triangular forms. The people interpret each motive as the representation of some realistic object. The meander pattern is interpreted as waves and as objects floating in the waves, while a similar design executed in obtuse angles is interpreted as the butterfly. Diagonal rows of small rectangles are interpreted as a string tied around the basket, while two such lines meeting in a similar way represent goose tracks. Rectangles divided diagonally into two sections are interpreted as bear's feet, one half representing the sole of the foot, while lines in the other indicate the claws. In many cases, both the design and the figure cut out of the background are given names [see Fig. 12, chap. 7].

It is important to note that the interpretations given to the designs on some baskets seem to be entirely disconnected. This suggests that the combination of the patterns has no distinct symbolic significance, but that the so-called interpretations are rather pattern names.

HALL 108: CASES 0, 12, AND P

Coast Tribes of Washington and Tribes of the Interior of British Columbia The general character of the decorative art of this region is entirely different from that of the coast tribes of Alaska described before. The ornamentation applied by the tribes of the interior to their garments and to objects of everyday use is throughout pictographic; that is to say, it consists of realistic representations of natural objects, which are connected, and tell a complete story. We notice, for instance, on a painted blanket in Case 12j [see Fig. 21, chap. 6], a number of animal and human figures. A mountain range rising on the earth is shown above the fringe. On the upper part of the blanket, two suns are shown, outside of which are two beetles. In the center is a stag pursued by two Indians. The figures near the right and left margins are grizzly bears. On the lower part of the blanket two loons are shown. These are painted on a large scale because they are the guardian spirits of the wearer. Between them there is a lake with trees around one side, and a canoe and a man in the center. Trail lines between the loons indicate that they belong to the lake. The owner's pipe is painted on the lower right-hand corner. The idea expressed by these figures is a prayer for success in hunting on mountain and lake. The hunters and the canoe man represent the wearer of the blanket; the suns, beetles, and loons are his guardian spirits.

In many cases these pictographs become more geometrical in character, so that they may be called ornamental designs. Such is the case, for instance, in a young woman's headband made of buckskin (Case 12d) [see Fig. 28, chap. 6], painted red with designs representing lodges in the lower part and stars in the upper. In some cases the whole form of the object is given a symbolic interpretation. Thus we find a stone war axe (Case 12c) representing the woodpecker. This design symbolizes the idea that the point of the axe is to be as powerful in piercing skulls as the beak of the woodpecker is in piercing the bark of trees. The point of the axe represents the beak of the bird; the red dot on the rounded part of the stone, its eye; the handle, its body. In the pictographic art of this tribe, certain motives have obtained a conventional meaning. Such is the case, for instance, with the triangles on the girl's headband mentioned before, which always represents lodges. Crosses, like those on the drinking tubes in Case 12d, represent the crossing of trails; parallel lines represent ditches, and a circle with four equidistant rays symbolizes the sun.

The pictographic art of these tribes tends to assume a geometrical character particularly on their woven bags and on their imbricated basketry. The merging of the pictographic and purely decorative elements may be observed very clearly in a bag (Case 12d), on which a series of diamonds represents isolated lakes, and lakes connected by streams. Near these lakes are shown ducks flying toward the water. Designs half pictographic and half geometrical may also be seen on the baskets in Case O 9, in which the figures of birds, men, and dogs may be recognized. A striking interpretation is given for two baskets in Case O 11. The peculiar rectangular forms which face each other are each interpreted as a head. In one of these, the short lines on the back represent the hair, while the two pairs in each opening represent teeth. In the other one these attachments have entirely disappeared, but the form is still interpreted as that of two heads facing each other.

A great variety of geometrical forms may be observed in these brackets (Case P 1–3). Almost all of them are also given realistic interpretations. One interesting basket, the design of which consists of alternating large and small diamonds, is explained as the beaver design, the large central pattern being interpreted as the body of the beaver; the small diamonds at the lower end, its tail; the one at its upper end, the head; while the black lines forming one side of the intermediate diamond are the fore and hind legs of the animal.

It is fairly evident that this type of basketry has influenced that of the coast tribes of Washington, who also have geometrical designs on their baskets. We find among these tribes a good many baskets imported from the interior, while their own baskets show a different type of manufacture, but somewhat similar designs. Here a meandering pattern is interpreted as ripples of water, while a design consisting of zigzags is interpreted as mountains and valleys (Case O 7). Attention is called to the peculiar designs composed of hooks (Case O 8), which will be referred to in the description of Californian designs. These designs also occur in the basketry from the interior of the state of Washington (Case R 12).

The forms which we observe on the coast of Washington have also influenced the type of basketry of the tribe of Cape Flattery, a branch of the Nootka, whose culture is similar to that of the more northern coast tribes. Among them we find many fine baskets with geometrical designs (Case N 10). These baskets are made on a foundation of cedar bark, while the designs are executed in colored and bleached grass stems. Most of the designs resemble in character the geometric designs of the southern coast tribes. It is, however, peculiar to this tribe, that on some of these baskets, whaling and fishing scenes, with canoes and their crew, are represented. Such scenes were also used in the ornamentation of the old type of hats that were worn in the eighteenth century, but which have gone out of use.

HALL 102: CASES 17–29

Plains Indians The decorative art of the Plains Indians resembles in some characteristic features that of the tribes of the interior of British Columbia, although its technique is much better and more elaborate. Its fundamental character is pictographic. In objects which serve ceremonial purposes, this character is strictly maintained. Thus we find on buffalo hides which are records of events, and even on blankets, pictographic representations of battle scenes, or of other events in the daily life of the Indian. On garments used in ceremonial dances, paintings occur which represent birds, sun, and moon, and are similar in character to those described before.

These, however, are not, strictly speaking, decorative designs. In most cases where ornamentation is the prime object, the forms which are utilized are arranged more or less symmetrically; and with the development of symmetry we find that the occurrence of realistic forms disappears. Almost all the decorative work of the Indians of the Plains is made in bead embroidery, and is probably an outgrowth of the embroidery in porcupine quills which was characteristic of the Indians before they came in contact with the whites. The forms which are the constituent elements of decorative motives are very simple and characteristic. They consist throughout of regularly arranged triangles and rectangles, most in brilliant and strongly contrasting colors, and often also showing sections of varying color. Sometimes the decoration is applied to the whole surface, sometimes only a particular part of the object is decorated. Much of the painting is done on rawhide, but most of the embroidery is made on soft skin. The background of the painting is usually rawhide, while the beaded designs are often set off against a background of white or colored beads.

The manner of combination of triangles and rectangles is so peculiar, that decorated objects obtained from the Plains Indians can readily be distinguished from objects from any other part of the world. Although there is a certain sameness among all of them, each tribe has certain peculiarities of its own. The most characteristic form, which occurs over and over again in Indian decorative art, is the somewhat pointed triangle, either divided into halves of different color, or including another triangle of different color. This form is generally explained as the tepee, the tent of the Plains Indians. Another form which is almost as frequent is a very obtuse triangle, often with a small rectangle in the middle. This is interpreted as a hill, while the center figure is often called a cave in the hill. We find also very often designs consisting of parallel lines, sometimes broken up by equidistant short patterns of different color. These lines are generally interpreted as trails; and breaks in the lines, as camping sites or other interruptions of the continuous trail.

The decorative forms applied by the Indians may, on the whole, be described as a variety of combinations of the acute tent triangle and of the obtuse hill triangle with rectangles and straight lines. Circles divided into sections occur also quite frequently. All these forms are executed in a variety of color, which is generally included in the symbolic interpretation of the design.

The detailed arrangement of the decorative motives shows some characteristic differences among different tribes. Thus, we find that the Arapaho (Case 20h) like to arrange their patterns on hide bags in a number of parallel stripes, and that in the painted designs they put on the color in rather small areas. The Shoshone (Case 26e), on the other hand, like to arrange the decorative field in such a way as to lay out a wide border which cuts out a central field. The designs in these areas are laid on in strongly contrasting colors, without leaving any white background to speak of. Similar differences may be observed in the beadwork of different tribes. Some—for instance, the Comanche (Case 26d)—prefer to arrange their patterns in delicate narrow bands; while others, like the Sioux, utilize large beaded surfaces. These may be observed on moccasins, bags, and pouches, on which white or colored beads form the background, from which the designs are set off. It seems, however, that some beaded and painted designs are common to all the tribes of the Great Plains.

Interpretation of Arapaho Designs The characteristics of Indian interpretations will best appear from a description of a few specimens. The square design near the lower edge of a small pouch (Case 20e) is the bear's foot, generally conventionally represented by the Arapaho with only three claws. Square pink spots on the body of the design are the bare skin on the sole of the foot. The white beadwork is sand or soil. The curved band on the flap is a mountain. The leather fringe at the bottom of the pouch represents trees.

White beading on another pouch represents sand: the green beads at the edges, on account of their color, represent timber; two compressed crosses, the morning star; and squares on the flaps, rocks. The large figure near the bottom is a mountain with a tree on its summit. Below it are four small red and blue rectangles, which denote little streams flowing from a spring near the foot of the mountain. The spring is represented by a green square in the large triangle.

Paint pouches, amulets, and head ornaments are often given animal forms. [One] pouch represents a lizard. The large ornament at about the middle of the bag represents a butterfly. The triangles are its wings, and the rhomboidal figure of beadwork projecting on the leather surface is its body. On the flap is the dragonfly. The detached, somewhat triangular figures at the sides of the dragonfly are its wings.

On an Arapaho moccasin (Case 20h), a wide stripe embroidered on the instep represents the path on which the wearer travels. The two pieces of the transverse stripe, which duplicate in miniature a part of the main stripe, are insects or worms which the wearer desires to avoid, and which, for this reason, are placed by the side of his path. The upper portion of the large stripe is light blue, which signifies, as in many other cases, haze. The red and dark-blue bands that edge the white portion of the stripe represent day and night. The winged triangle, which appears twice, signifies sunrise, and also the passage over a mountain.

The explanation of painted designs of the Arapaho is quite similar to that of beaded designs. Thus, on one hide bag (Case 19c) three wide blue stripes represent rivers, both form and color being symbolic. The red rectangles in them are islands, and the white border around these is sand. The triangles are bears' feet; the red portions of the triangles represent the bare skin of the sole of the foot; the projections at the base of the triangles are the claws. The unpainted background represents the prairie; the black spots in them are coyotes. Blue lines enclosing the whole design are buffalo paths; the white lines between them, antelope paths; the yellow line is an elk path; and red lines are deer paths.

It will thus be seen that the interpretation of the designs given by the Arapaho is partly realistic, while a part of the designs express abstract ideas. The morning star, the life symbol, the path of life, and other concepts which are intimately associated with the religious ideas of the people appear frequently in their interpretations of their designs. Purely animal forms are, comparatively speaking, rare; while geographic features—such as mountains, valleys, and rivers—tents, parts of the body, and plant designs occur very frequently.

CASE 17C

Interpretation of Blackfoot Designs Among the Blackfoot we find the same type of decorative designs as among the Arapaho, triangles and diamonds being the most important elements, but they are purely decorative, without symbolic significance. These geometric forms, however, have pattern names as constituent elements of the complex designs, for example: the diamond-shaped figures are known as "spavin" patterns. The idea is, not that the design represents a "spavin," but that it resembles this affection as it appears upon a horse's foot.

CASES 24, 25

Interpretation of Sioux Designs The decorative art of the Siouan tribes comprises geometrical designs in beadwork, and pictographic designs in paintings. The geometric designs are both symbolic and decorative. The pictographic designs are usually symbolic. Most of the geometric designs are made by the women; the pictographic, by the men. The art of the women is especially interesting, because we find them using simple geometrical forms as design elements; for example, all triangular designs of a certain size are known as "tent" patterns; all rectangular designs are known as "bag" patterns; all small triangular designs are known as "point" patterns, or "leaf" patterns; diamond-shaped designs are known as "arrow-point" patterns. Complex geometrical designs are built up from these simple elements, and the names given above are the technical names for these designs. The complex designs are best represented in the decoration of tobacco pouches, as illustrated in Case 25a.

These complex designs, taken as a whole, often have special names; for example, a diamond-shaped figure with forked appendages, as shown in the adjoining illustration (Case 25a), is sometimes spoken of as the "turtle" design, or "turtle" pattern. So far as the makers of these designs are concerned, the name "turtle" is simply the pattern name, and in no wise a representation of the animal specified. Thus we have a series of decorative designs in which the motive is not the representation of objects or ideas, but merely an appeal to the esthetic sense. However, these design elements may be combined into wholes which do represent definite objects or ideas, and so become symbolic designs; but the use of designs to represent any particular idea does not conform to any rule, it depends rather upon the fancy of the maker. A good example of this type of design is illustrated in Case 25a. It represents a decoration seen by the maker in a dream. It is thus a picture of the dream design. But there are certain geometrical forms which are symbolic, and are looked upon as sacred. One of the most common of these designs is that of a spider-web, which may be seen on the pouch shown in Case 25c. This design is looked upon as too sacred to be used for mere decorative purposes.

There is another type of design midway between the sacred symbolic one and the merely decorative one, such as the design of the turtle upon the dresses of women. This is simply a U-shaped figure placed on the breast and the back. It appears on most of the beaded dresses, and is placed there partly for decoration, and partly because it is the prevailing style. The old women know that in former times the design of the turtle was placed on the dress as a kind of prayer to the mythical turtle, who was believed to be the guardian spirit watching over the lives of women. Now they say that the design is placed on the dress simply because "that is the way." Thus we have a design which was formerly sacred and symbolic, but is now chiefly decorative. The painted decorations upon the buffalo robes of men and women are of this type also.

In general, the decorative art of the Sioux presents three types, or perhaps stages, in the development of primitive art—a purely decorative type, a purely symbolic type, and an intermediate conventional type. The men employ the same simple and combined geometrical designs as are used by the women, but for the presentation of military ideas. Thus, the moccasin shown in Case 24g represents a battle in which the wearer participated. The triangular designs around the sole (the tent pattern) represent hills; the small rectangles (the box pattern), enemies standing between the hills; the small marks upon each hill design, bullets striking. The instep of the moccasin is colored red to represent blood, and the triangular design within the red area represents an arrow. The idea to be conveyed is, that the owner engaged in a battle in which the enemy took refuge in the hills, and that blood was shed.

Thus we have among the same people identical geometrical designs, with identical technical names, used to convey different ideas. The military symbolism of the men differs from the symbolism of the women in one respect; namely, that anyone familiar with the mode of presentation can interpret the designs used by men with considerable exactness.

In a general way the interesting characteristic of Sioux art is the existence of two schools—that of the women and that of the men—each of which makes use of the same design elements, but to different ends.

CASES 28, 29

Tribes of the Eastern Woodlands Very little of the ancient art of the Indians of the eastern woodland area remains. Under the influence of modern patterns, the old style of porcupine quill and beadwork has practically disappeared, and plant patterns have taken its place. Only on woven pouches and mats do some of the old patterns persist. These designs are partly of geometrical character; partly they consist of very stiff conventional reproductions of animal and human forms (Case 29a). The favorite design seems to be that of a bird with spread wings, the shape of which has also influenced the manner of representing the human form (Case 28e). The geometric designs (Cases 28e, 31) are mostly arranged in bands, and consist of triangles, zigzags, and diamonds, which show only slight relation to those of the Indians of the Plains, while they remind us somewhat of the designs of the Indians of the state of Washington. We may perhaps recognize in some of the triangles with points under their bases the tent design so common among the Plains Indians. The whole makeup, however, of the geometric forms is quite distinctive. If there ever has been any interpretation of these geometric designs, it seems to have been forgotten, and the designs are considered purely as ornamental, not as symbolic. The only striking exception is the same spiderweb design that we find among the Sioux Indians, and which occurs here practically in the same form (Case 28h).

Painted decorations are much rarer among these tribes than among those of the Great Plains. In place of the hide bags, which are so common among all the Prairie tribes, hide trunks are used which are painted with patterns similar to those described before. Probably these hide trunks are modern forms of ancient bark boxes.

It is interesting to note that in the modern woven beadwork of these tribes the realistic flower designs which have been in vogue for a considerable period tend to assume geometrical shapes. The series of beaded belts exhibited in Case 28h brings out clearly the fact that the leaves and fruits tend to assume the forms of diamonds, while the flowers tend to develop in the direction of crosses.

SECOND FLOOR, HALL 202

On the second floor are found collections from California and Mexico which illustrate some of the characteristics of the decorative art of these regions.

HALL 202: CASES 1–6

California Indians The decorative art of the California Indians, more particularly that of the Indians of southern California, is almost entirely confined to basketry. Their baskets are mostly round, rather rarely oblong, many of them quite shallow: consequently we find a tendency to arrange the decorative designs in radial groups or in spirals. The designs themselves are rarely realistic, but consist always of more or less intricate geometrical designs. The similarity of these designs on various baskets is quite striking. Their interpretations, however, differ considerably. A collection illustrating the similarity of design and the diversity of their meaning has been assembled in Case 2a, b. There we find on one basket a design representing a squirrel's foot. A similar design on another basket represents mountains and pinecones; on still another, the bear's foot; and on a fourth the owl's claw.

In the same case are shown a number of baskets illustrating one of the most common ornamental motives found in California, the so-called quail tip, a design consisting of a slender line with a small heavy hook standing off from the end at right angles. This design was described before as found on baskets from the state of Washington (Case R 12 in Hall 108), and it seems probable that it has spread along the Pacific coast from tribe to tribe. This seems the more likely, since it is found in entirely different weaves, according to the district in which it occurs. While it is found on many Californian weaves, it is applied in the state of Washington on the peculiar imbricated basketry the characteristic designs of which are illustrated by baskets of the Thompson and Lillooet Indians (see Cases O and P, Hall 108).

The interpretations given to designs by the Californian Indians vary greatly. The designs often represent plants, while some represent fish teeth, snakes, worms, millipedes, butterflies, etc. Designs symbolic of larger animals are absent. One of the most frequently occurring designs on Californian, and perhaps on all, basketry is the feather and arrow-point design (Cases 2, 3). Realistic designs are found only in the extreme southern part of California and in the adjoining portions of Arizona.

In northern California the interpretation of designs seems to be almost absent. The patterns of this district are called "striped," "zigzag," etc., terms which are evidently names, not interpretations (Case 6f).

HALL 202: CASE 15

Huichol Indians, Mexico The decorative art of the modern tribes of Mexico has evidently been much influenced by Spanish art. The most elaborate decorative work of the present period is done in textiles, particularly in weaving and in embroidery, while modern pottery designs are of a crude character. The designs found in various regions of Mexico and of Central America, and also those of South America, consist to a great extent of geometrical elements, but also of somewhat angular representations of birds, mammals, and men, all more or less conventionalized. The color combinations differ also considerably in various regions. [See Fig. 2, chap. 7.]

One of the designs found most frequently on textile work is a series of triangles which are similar in their arrangement to the arrow design on Californian basketry. This type of design is found on the belts of the Pueblo Indians of New Mexico and Arizona is well as in Mexico. A comparison with ancient Mexican designs, in so far as they have been preserved on ancient Mexican codices, or as they may be recognized on the garments of ancient sculptured figures, shows that these types of weaving did not exist before the advent of the Spaniards and the introduction of European fabrics.

For this reason it is interesting to note that by some tribes the designs are at present given interpretations quite analogous to those found among the Prairie Indians and among other primitive tribes. A collection of belts, ribbons, and pouches from the Huichol tribe of western Mexico (Case 15) illustrates this point. The zigzag triangle, described by the Californian Indians as the arrow design, is called here the "double water-gourd" design. The Indians compare the hourglass figure, which originates from a combination of two triangles, to the double gourd, which has two thick ends and a constriction in the middle. The X-shaped form, also quite common, is interpreted as a brush made of loose fibers tied together in the middle or at one end. A series of scrolls is an element which occurs very frequently in their weaving. It is called the "bridle," because Mexican bridles have on either side of the bit a figure resembling one of these scrolls. It is also interpreted as the linking of hands. One decorative element . . . is interpreted as the steel for striking fire. It is considered as an ornamental elaboration of the form of steel used in this region. The arbitrary character of the interpretations given by these people may be seen in the elaboration of this design, which is sometimes developed into a continuous band, and is then explained as a vine and flowers. A very frequent element of decoration is . . . interpreted as roots of plants. The transition from these forms to more realistic ones is very gradual. The simple geometrical forms are combined into plant designs, and, in their most symmetrical arrangement, to flower designs. To these are added sometimes realistic representations of double-headed birds, or mountain lions and other animals. Long narrow ribbons covered with designs of this character are generally described as serpents, the design indicating the marks on the serpent's back.

A comparison of the decorative designs exhibited in Case 15 with the designs on ceremonial objects which will be found in Cases 13 and 14 shows a marked difference between the two styles. The execution of the purely ornamental objects is careful—the designs are regular in outline, and the conventionalism in interpretation and in form is strong. The decoration on sacrificial objects, on the other hand, is, on the whole, crude; it is throughout pictographic in character. The crudeness of these designs is partly due to lack of skill in the use of the brush and of the carving tool, and in the application of beadwork by means of wax—an art which is undoubtedly a survival of the ancient turquoise mosaics. All carved and painted designs of the Huichol Indians seem to be crude, and many of the embroidered designs on sacrificial objects are also poorly executed; but this may be partly due to their temporary character. A few of them, however, are carefully woven; but their designs are pictographic, not geometrical. The interpretation of the conventional decorative designs of the Huichol is, on the whole, in line with the ideas expressed on their ceremonial objects. Their constant thought is the need of rain for their crops; and the water gourd, the flowers, the vines, and serpents are all considered as symbols of rain or of the vegetation produced by rain.

In this respect the interpretation of the geometrical designs given by the Huichol resembles very much that given by the Pueblo Indians of the arid Southwest. Some of the favorite motives of their decorative art are interpreted in the same manner, terraced triangles with lines descending from them being always interpreted as rain clouds and falling rain; while zigzag lines represent lightning.

SUMMARY

The description of these collections shows that in many remote parts of the world primitive people interpret the ornamental designs which they use for decorating objects of everyday use as representations of realistic ideas. Investigations among other peoples, from whom the Museum has no collections, show that the same tendency may be found all over the world. In some cases it has been found possible to bring together a series of decorative motives which show at one end an almost realistic representation of a certain object, while at the other end of the series may be seen a purely conventional form. From this observation the conclusion has been drawn that, on the whole, geometrical ornaments originated from realistic forms by gradual transformation.

On the other hand, we have seen that in many cases the same form was transferred from one tribe to another by borrowing, as, for instance, among the Indians of the Plains; and that different interpretations were given to the same forms by different tribes. This seems to indicate that the interpretation may also be adapted to the design, or, as we may say, that, according to the favorite concepts of the people, an idea has been "read into" the design.

9. Notes on the Blanket Designs

Following a discussion of the use of Chilkat blankets and their manufacturing technique written by George Emmons for this Jesup North Pacific Expedition monograph, Boas analyzes in minute detail the imagery on these textiles. He points out that all blankets have a tripartite composition, with the central field being the largest. That central field contains the principal representation of the animal or animals depicted, while the two symmetrical flanking fields illustrate the sides and back of the central animal, split down the middle, its den, or smaller animals. Included here as well is information on the use of the pattern board in the fabrication of the blanket and its formal relationship to box designs and dancing aprons. Boas discusses the ambiguities that exist in explanations of the images on Chilkat blankets, and he concludes that these result from the artistic conventions that dictate the manner by which the weaver represents her subject.

The designs on the Chilkat blankets take a unique position among woven designs in America, as well in their technical execution as in the forms that are represented. While ordinarily designs in weaving are made by the use of different colors in warp and woof, the Chilkat blankets, somewhat like the weavings of Peru, are made up of separate units, which are sewed or woven together as described by Lieutenant Emmons in the preceding pages. The designs used in the woven fabrics of North America are either geometric designs or strongly conventionalized representations of animals, in which apparently the difficulty of applying the technique of weaving to the representation of realistic figures becomes evident. In the Chilkat blanket we have, on the other hand, the clearest evidence that the blanket pattern is merely a painted design, which is transferred without any change to the technique of weaving. Hence we find here numerous curved lines which are ordinarily absent in weaving.

The clearest evidence of the transfer of the painted design to the blanket is given by the method of weaving. The pattern is prepared by the men, who paint it on pattern boards. These pattern boards are placed by the woman by the side of the blanket, and are transferred directly to the weaving, as described by Lieutenant Emmons. Examples of pattern boards and of blankets copied from them are shown in Figs. 1 and 2. All the pattern boards are made in the same way as the one here illustrated; namely, only part of the whole middle pattern and one wing are shown, the other side being symmetrical with the one shown on the pattern board. The

Reprinted from "The Chilkat Blanket" by George T. Emmons, *American Museum of Natural History Memoirs*, vol. 3, pp. 351–400, 1907. Except where noted otherwise, all specimens illustrated in this volume are from the collection of the American Museum of Natural History.—Ed.

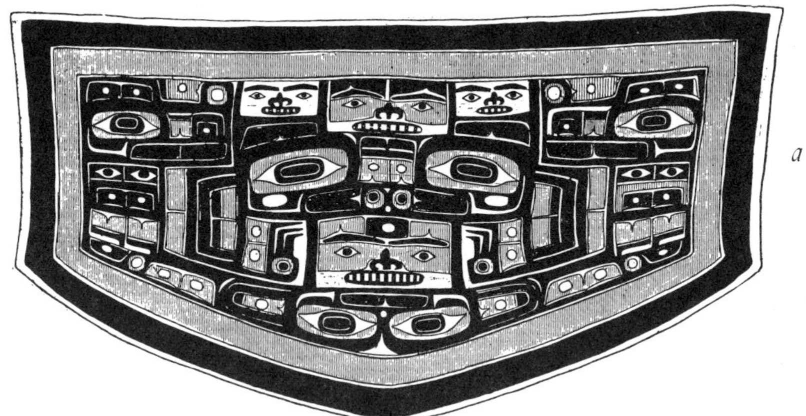

a

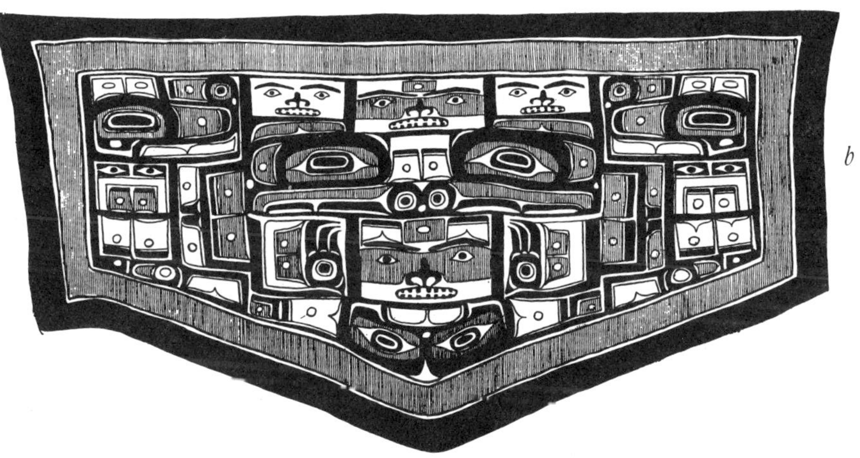

b

FIG. 1*a* (16/958), *b* (from Klukwan, Alaska; 16/351). Blankets. Width, 157 cm, 152 cm, respectively.

According to Emmons, the design represents a bear with young. The large central figure represents the male bear; the two inverted eyes in the middle of the lower border, with the adjoining round wing designs, the hindquarters of the bear; the three heads in the middle, the female and two young bears; the lateral fields, each a young bear; the design along the lower border of the lateral field, a freshwater stream on which the bear lives; the round wing design adjoining the medial eyes on the lower border, paws; the central head on the upper margin, the forehead of the bear.

According to Swanton, it shows the sea grizzly bear. The explanation is the same, except that the three heads in the middle along the upper border are explained, the middle one as the top of the head, the lateral ones as parts of the ear; the wing design which extends sideways from the body, cutting into the lateral fields, as part of the front leg; the wing field which cuts into the lateral field, probably the fins, which are believed to be attached to the arms of the sea grizzly bear; the two wing designs on the lower border, outside of the round wing design adjoining the medial eye, the paws.

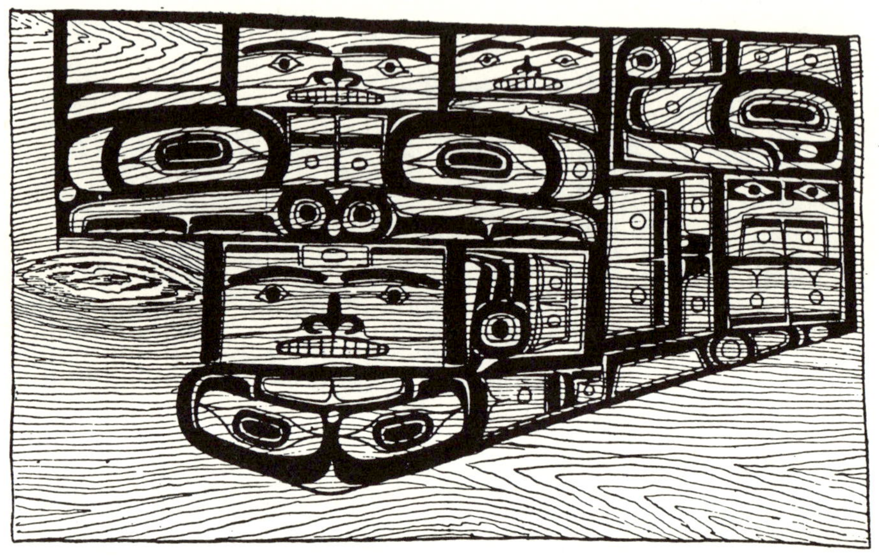

FIG. 2. Pattern board for blanket shown in Fig. 1*b*

symmetry of the design is brought about by the use of bark patterns in the same way as these are used in obtaining symmetry in painted designs. It will be seen, therefore, that the blanket design cannot be considered in any sense a textile design, but is a strict imitation of a painted design, no liberties for its adaptation to the technique of weaving being allowed. It is interesting in this connection to note that a considerable number of blankets are found identical in type, as might be expected, if we consider that the blanket design is produced as an accurate copy from a painted board. Thus the two blankets in Fig. 1 *a* and *b* are practically identical in design and agree with the pattern board (Fig. 2), which is reproduced from a photograph taken by Lieutenant Emmons.

There is still another blanket of the same type in the Peabody Museum, Cambridge, Mass. It resembles practically in all details Fig. 1*a*, with the sole exception of the fields adjoining the large eyes on the lower border, which consist of a single wing design. Further, the lateral fields differ in that the ring over the bird's beak is missing; that the goggle design is moved slightly toward the middle, leaving room at the outer border under the upper head for a single wing design, and under this for the eye which is so often found in this position (see, for instance, Fig. 16). The lower border of the lateral field consists of an eye design close to the border of the middle field, to which are attached a series of wing designs stretching along the lower border upward.

We shall see presently that other pairs of blankets show even better agreement among themselves. The present example, however, is selected here because not only the two blankets are available, but also the pattern board. It is quite obvious that sometimes the pattern boards have been copied, and that thus slight deviations in the details of a design are introduced. This probably accounts for the differences among patterns which in their whole plan must be considered as identical. The two specimens here described show a considerable number of minor differences. Thus, taking the figure in the upper right-hand corner of the blanket Fig. 1*a*, which represents apparently the profile of a bird's head, it will be seen that the portion in front of the eye is occupied by two separate designs; while in the blanket Fig. 1*b*, the same space is occupied by a single curved design with black tip and central white spot. The design occupying the space over the bird's head shows also certain variations. While in the blanket *a*, the circle which probably represents the nostril, and which is placed just over the tip of the beak, has a white center, it has a black center in *b*. Similar differences may be noticed in the field under the beak just discussed, and occupying the middle part of the lateral field. In *b* a number of circular white spots are indicated here which are not present in *a*. A detailed examination of the whole blanket designs brings out similar differences.

A better example of two blankets made from the same pattern board is shown in Fig. 3 *a* and *b*. Here the agreement of the two specimens is practically perfect. It will be noticed that even the details of the ear, eye, body, foot, and tail, as indicated in *a*, are also repeated in *b*. Other sets of blankets made from the same pattern board, or from pattern boards that must have been copies of the same original, are shown in Figs. 19, 21, and 23.

Before discussing the significance of design elements and of the whole designs as explained by the Indians, it seems best to discuss the general style of decoration of the blankets, without reference to their symbolic signification and to the pattern names, but only in regard to the objective forms of the designs. An examination of the first twenty-four blankets (Figs. 1, 3, 15–27) shows very clearly that the general form of the blanket is the same in every case, and that it is divided into three fields of unequal size—a wide middle one, occupying approximately one-half of the surface of the blanket, or sometimes a little more; and two narrow lateral fields, each occupying about one-fourth of the whole width of the blanket. On almost all the blankets here mentioned, the line of division of these fields is perfectly clear, and indicated by black and white lines, the designs of the lateral fields and that of the central field being entirely distinct. These twenty-four blankets may again be divided into two groups. The fundamental pattern of the central field of the first

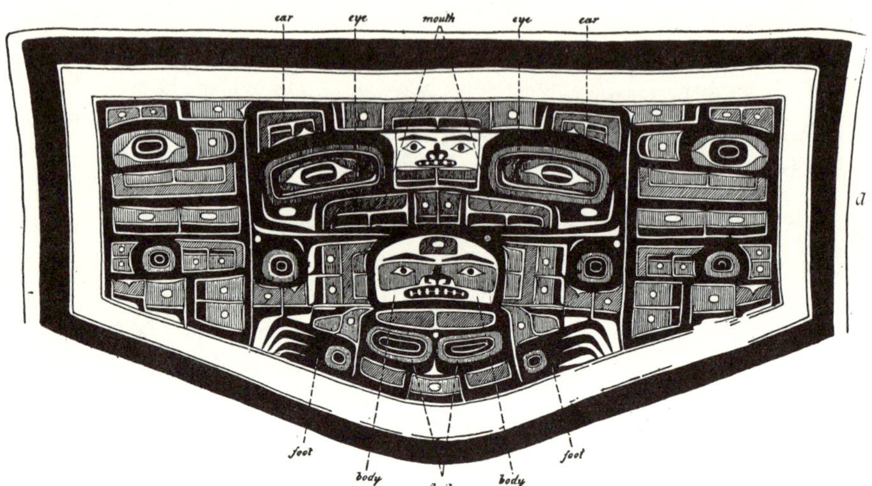

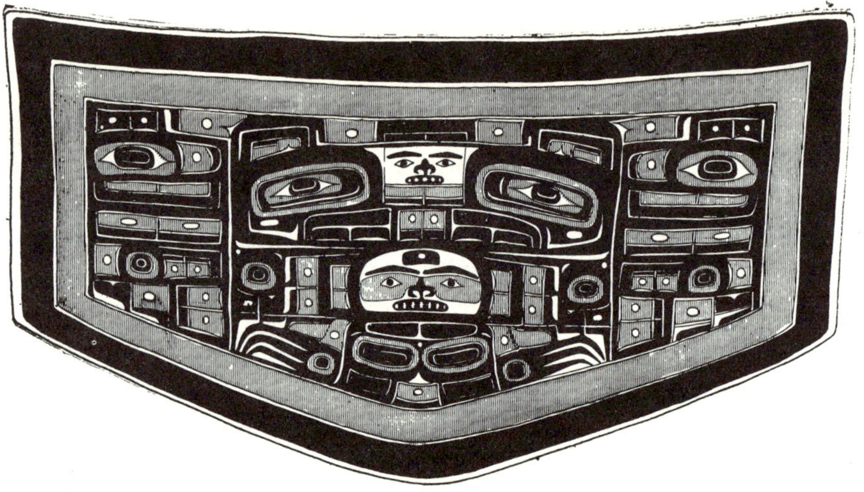

FIG. 3. Blankets.

b (T/25542). Width, 172 cm. According to Emmons, the design represents the osprey or thunderbird standing with outspread wings. The lateral fields represent clouds, and at the same time the body of the thunderbird and also the raven in profile.

According to Swanton, it represents the beaver. The two designs under the corners of the jaw represent the alder, which is the beaver's food; while the wing designs next to the body represent the forelegs. The middle portion of the mouth is interpreted as the two incisors of the beaver. The lateral fields are the beaver's house.

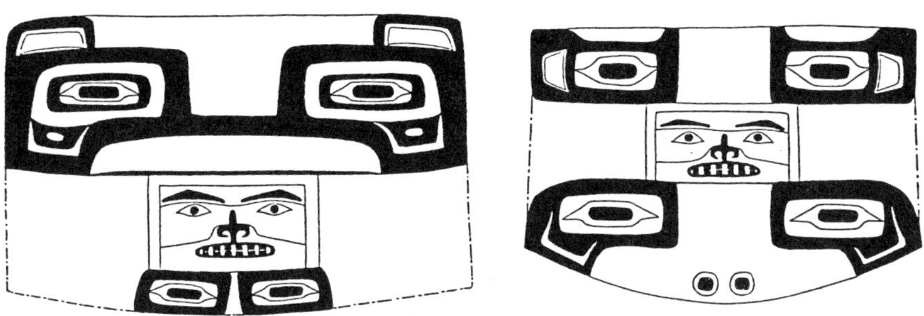

FIG. 4. Schematic representation of the design of blankets, Type 1.

FIG. 5. Schematic representation, Type 2.

twelve is indicated by the schematic representation shown in Fig. 4. The fundamental trait of the design consists evidently of two large eyes—one in each upper corner of the central field—a face in the middle, and two eyes turned upside down in the middle at the bottom. An examination of the twelve figures (Figs. 1, 3, 15–18) will show that this trait is common to all these designs. The two large eyes on top are always surmounted by ears, and have underneath a long, wide mouth, which varies considerably in form. The central face is always immediately under the mouth; while the two lower eyes vary somewhat in their position, being sometimes directly under the central face, sometimes moved out slightly toward the sides (see Figs. 16, 17). According to the characteristic art of the Northwest Coast, these three elements in conjunction naturally represent an animal: the eyes, with the adjoining ears, jaws, and mouth, being the head; the central face being the body; while the two inverted eyes below are the double joint of the tail, every joint being represented by an eye design.

The second group of blankets (Figs. 19–27) represents a quite distinct type, which is shown in Fig. 5. Here the fundamental type of the middle field is the same central face that we found in the preceding type; but in place of the large eyes on top we find two large inverted eyes, often without the adjoining jaw design. In the corresponding corners below, we find two large eyes with jaw design, while the center of the lower border is occupied by two small circular designs. In this way a much more symmetrical pattern is obtained, consisting of a rectangular face, around which the four eyes are arranged fairly symmetrically.

In both types of designs the intervening spaces are filled with a variety of patterns, which depend upon the selection of the animal to be represented, but partly also upon the fancy of the artist.

The general scheme of the narrower lateral designs is also quite definite. We find on practically all the blankets an eye design—part of the profile of an animal head—in the upper outer corner of the lateral field, and another eye design near the lower border, generally approximately in the middle of the lateral field (see Figs. 3, 17*b*, and 18*a*). The position and occurrence of this lower eye design is much more irregular than that of the upper eye design. It is missing, for instance, in Fig. 1, and it is placed near the outer border in Fig. 18*b*.

It is of interest to investigate the origin of this peculiar arrangement of the blanket pattern. It seems likely, as Lieutenant Emmons points out, that the regular occurrence of a middle field and of the narrower lateral fields may be partly due to the manner in which the blanket is worn. When it is put on, the wide central field covers the back, and the narrow flaps are on both sides in front of the body. When the dancer is at rest, the sides of the central design would naturally be on the sides of the body; but when dancing and shaking his rattle, the elbows are often lifted, and by this motion the whole back is extended, and the whole central design may be seen in rear view.

The first of the central patterns is evidently closely related to the box patterns shown in Figs. 6–8. In all of these the large face with the two eyes, the depression between the eyes, the large mouth, and the small body will be recognized, leaving the same lateral fields open that are found in the first type of the blankets. In some cases the body is decorated with the same face pattern that is found in the blanket (Figs. 6*a* and 8*d*); but the eye pattern will be noticed also in the body design of Figs. 6*b*, 7, and 8*b*. The box patterns have, in addition to the central figure with large head, an eye design in each corner. This is seen clearly in the broad box fronts in Figs. 6 and 7, and also in the broad sides of the boxes in Fig. 8, except in that marked *a*, in which the body is omitted entirely, and only the eyes in the upper corners are shown. It seems quite possible that the narrow lateral fields of the blanket are related to these eye designs in the corners: at least, a comparison between the lateral fields of the blanket designs and the lateral strips on the box fronts containing the two eyes, brings out a certain analogy in the position of the decorative designs. We find, for instance, in Fig. 6*a*, the eyes in the upper corners, to which is attached a finlike design extending along the upper edge toward the middle, which may be compared to the beak part of the heads in the upper part of all the lateral blanket fields. That portion which lies along the side of the head on the box front seems to correspond to the portion of the lateral blanket field between the upper and the lower eye (see, for instance, Figs. 15*a* and 17*b*); while the lower eye in the blanket, with its attachments, corresponds somewhat to the lower eye in the box design. This similarity becomes perhaps even more apparent when we compare the design on the central field of the blanket with the designs on the narrow sides of boxes, as shown in Figs. 7 and 8. We recognize in all these cases (see particularly Fig. 8*c* and *d*) a somewhat narrower head, large as compared to the body, but without the eye designs in the

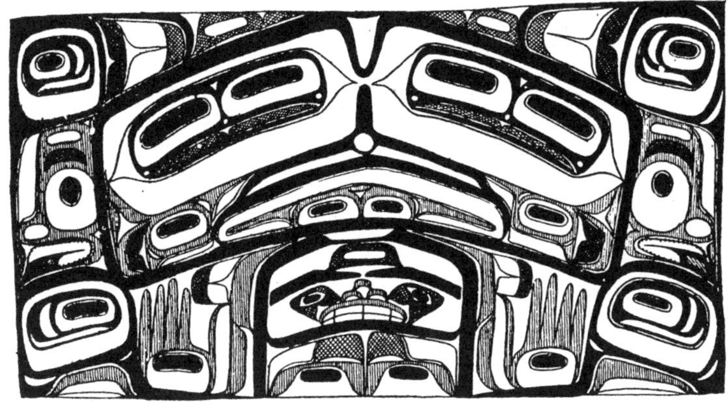

a

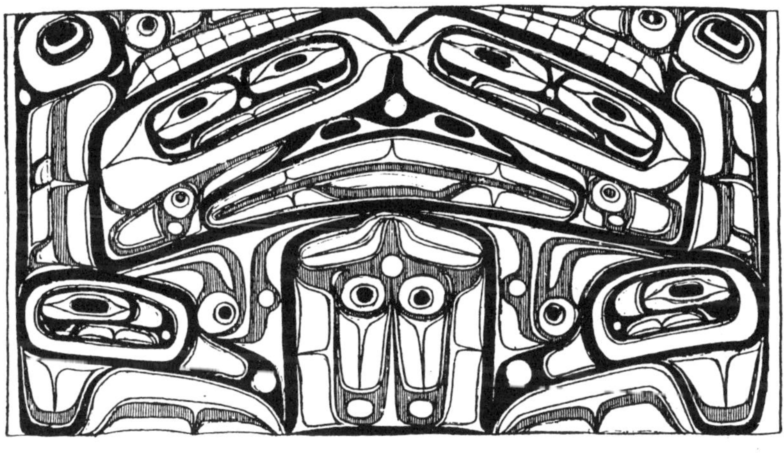

b

FIG. 6*a* (E/652), *b* (19/1287). Painted and carved box fronts. Length, 53 cm, 73 cm.

upper and lower corners. These occur only in the upper corners of the box side shown in Fig. 8*a*, which, as pointed out before, consists of heads only, without the body.

The exaggeration of the head as compared to the body is a common trait of Northwest Coast art, and occurs frequently in painted designs as well as in incised designs and in reliefs, while it is not so characteristic of sculptures in the round. It

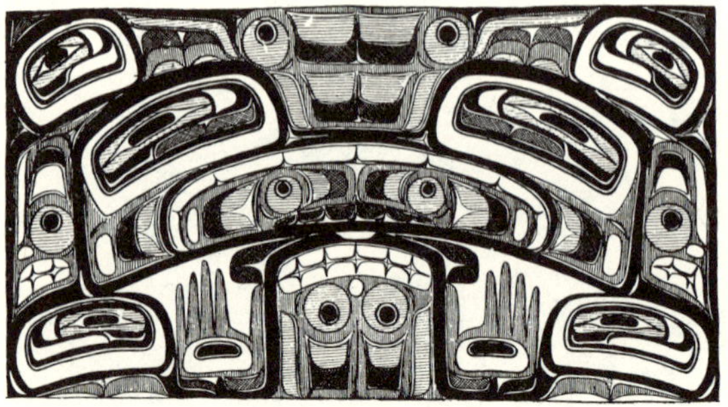

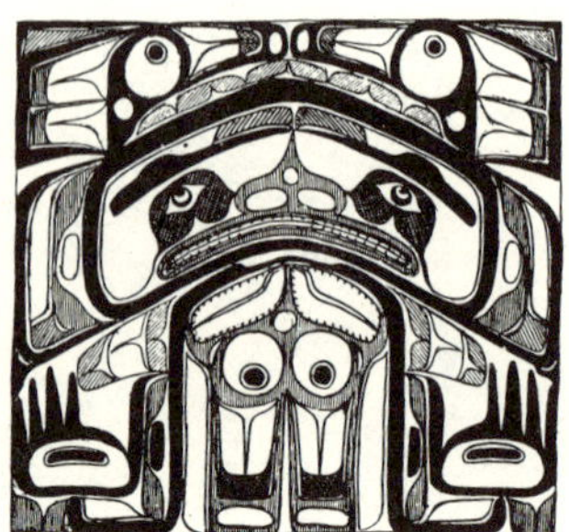

FIG. 7 (19/1286). Front (*a*) and side (*b*) of carved and painted box. Length, 82 cm.

is commonly found on head masks of the Tsimshian and Haida.[1] The incised designs on bracelets[2] exhibit the same peculiarity, which may also be observed on painted designs on blanket borders.[3] This exaggeration may be partly due to the tendency to represent the head as consisting of two profiles. The peculiar type of head here discussed is found on all the ends of food trays of the Tsimshian which are shown in Figs. 9 and 10. I do not feel certain whether the form of this kind of food tray, which among the more southern tribes occurs also without decoration, has had an influence upon the development of the decorative form of the head which is so commonly used, or whether the head was applied to this surface because its form coincides with it so well.

In judging the characteristic style of the blanket design, attention should be called also to the absence of curved chin lines seen on many trays. Figs. 1, 3, and 15 show that the line forming the lower border of the mouth and lower jaw is almost always a straight line, and that the upper border of the head has a very slight curvature only. On the box designs Figs. 6 and 7, on the other hand, the chin line is always considerably higher in the middle than at the sides. This tendency is even more marked on the narrow side of the box shown in Fig. 7*b*. On the other hand, the boxes shown in Figs. 8*d* and 11*a* and *b* show the same straight lower edge which is characteristic of the blanket designs. Taking this in connection with the tray designs shown in Figs. 9 and 10, it becomes evident that the form of the head is not determined alone by the form of the decorative field. Both box and blanket have a straight upper edge, near which the head is placed. Nevertheless we often find in

1. See *Bulletin of the American Museum of Natural History*, vol. 9, fig. 13, p. 131; fig. 17, p. 132. [This volume, chapter 4]

2. Ibid., fig. 42, p. 147; figs. 72–74, p. 169. [This volume, chapter 4]

3. Ibid., fig. 71, p. 168. [This volume, chapter 4]

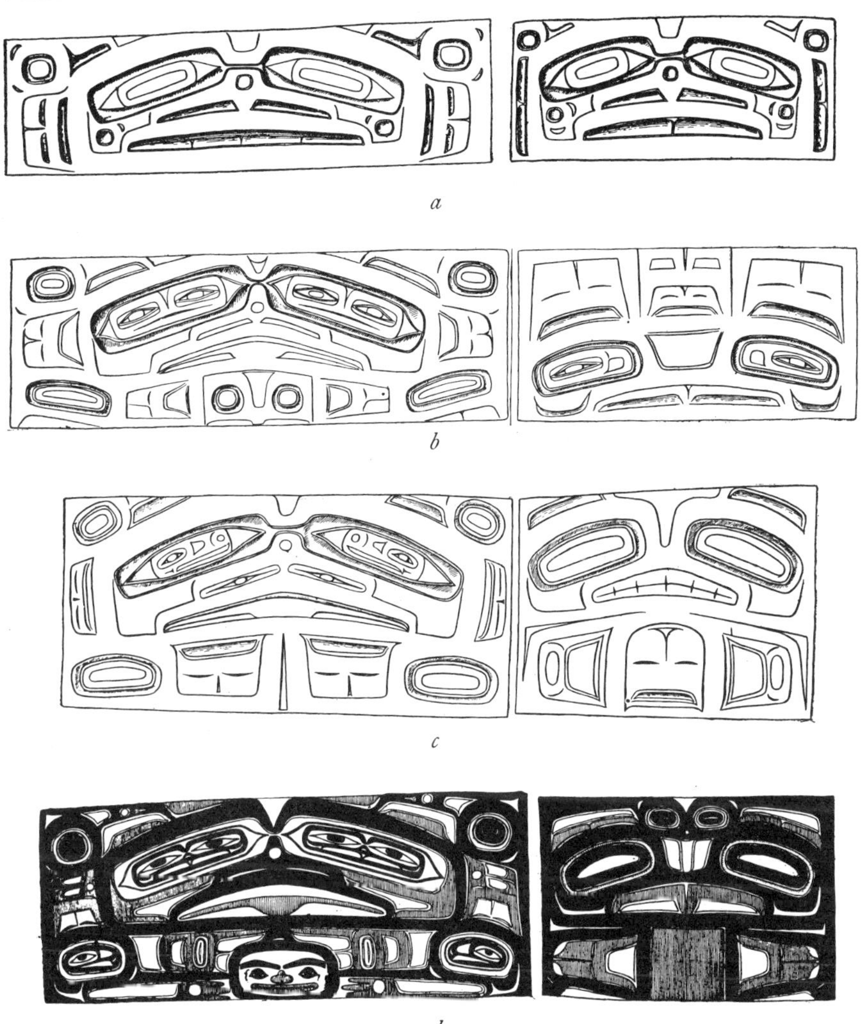

FIG. 8*a* (E/2220), *b* (E/1292), *c*, *d*. Fronts and sides of carved and painted boxes. Length, *a–c*, 61 cm, 60 cm, 57 cm.

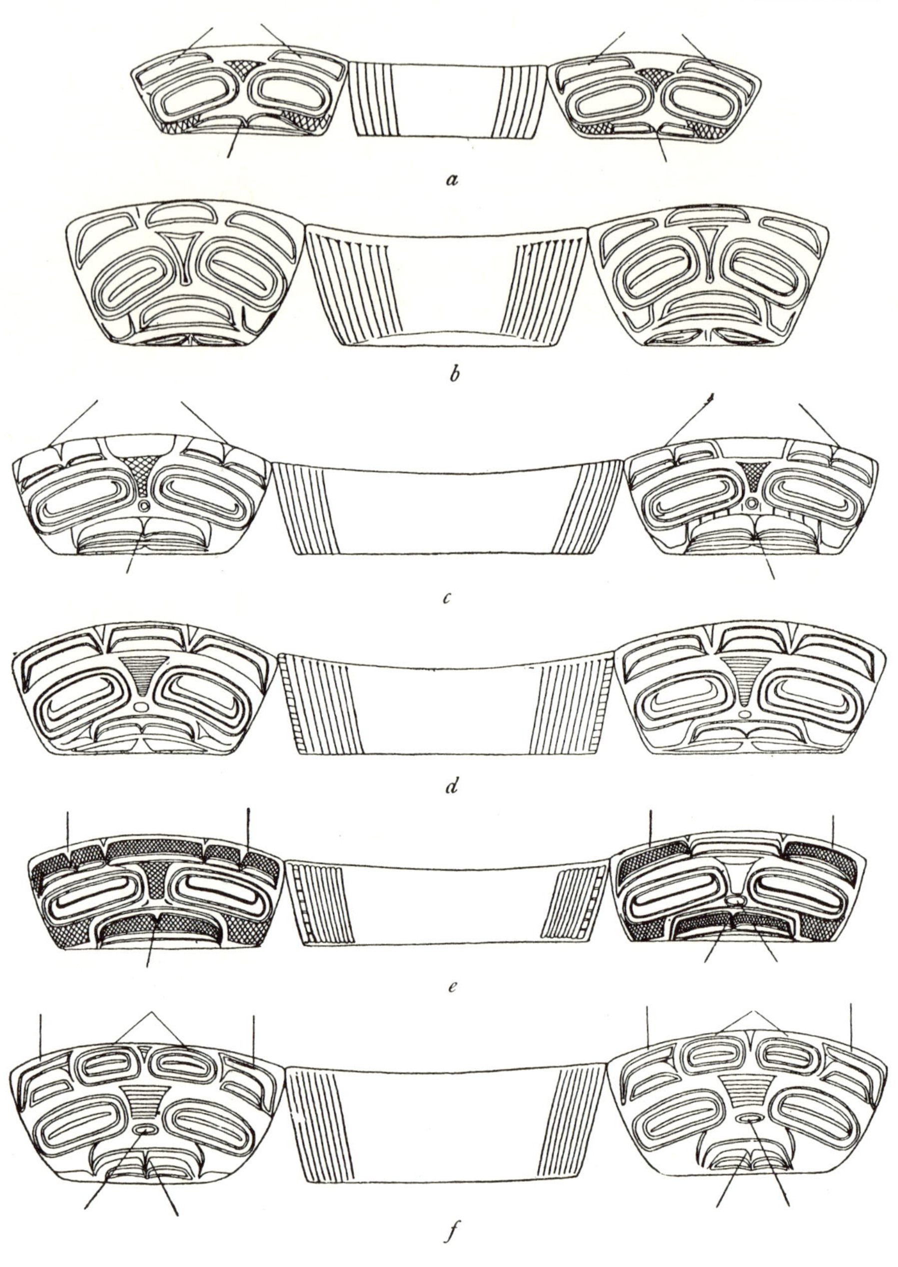

FIG. 9*a* (16/77), *b*, *c*, *d* (19/941), *c* (16/62*a*), *f* (E/365). Carved trays. Length, *a*, 12 cm; *d–f*, 63 cm, 40 cm. The lines indicate ears, forehead, nose, and mouth.

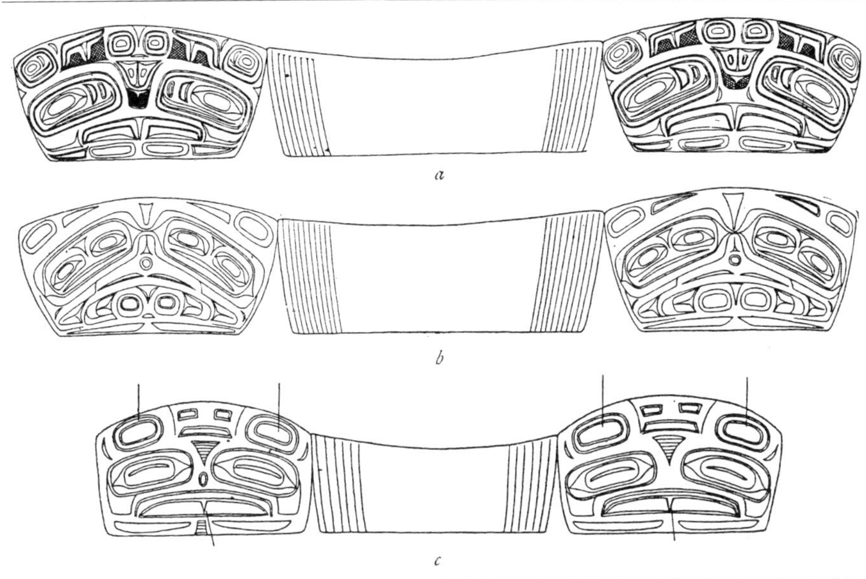

FIG. 10*a* (E/260), *b* (E/35), *c* (E/1146). Carved trays. Length, *a*, 53 cm, *b*, 45 cm; *c*, 17 cm.

the boxes slanting eyes and curved lower rim of the mouth, while in the blanket not a single case of a markedly slanting eye and of a curved mouth line has come to my notice. In the tray designs there seems to be a marked influence of the curvature of the upper rim, which has the effect of compressing the lateral portions of the design, while the inner corners of the eyes are drawn upward, thus giving it a more slanting position.

Attention may be called here to the peculiar application of the design consisting of the large head and small body in the two boxes shown at *a* and *b* in Fig. 11. In both these cases the box is made of a single board, and one head is placed on two adjoining sides, each pair of sides representing the design heretofore discussed, and corresponding, in proportions as well as in arrangement, to the front of the long box (Figs. 6 and 7).

I have added here illustrations of some other types of boxes which illustrate clearly certain definite types, the variations consisting in modifications of details. The three boxes shown in Fig. 11*c*–*e* represent animals, the face and tail ends being shown on the short sides, while the side of the body is shown on the long sides. In these three cases the shoulder joints and hip joints are indicated by inverted eyes. For this reason the long sides of the boxes assume the form of an inverted face, and all the details which are intended to represent the side of the body and the feet are

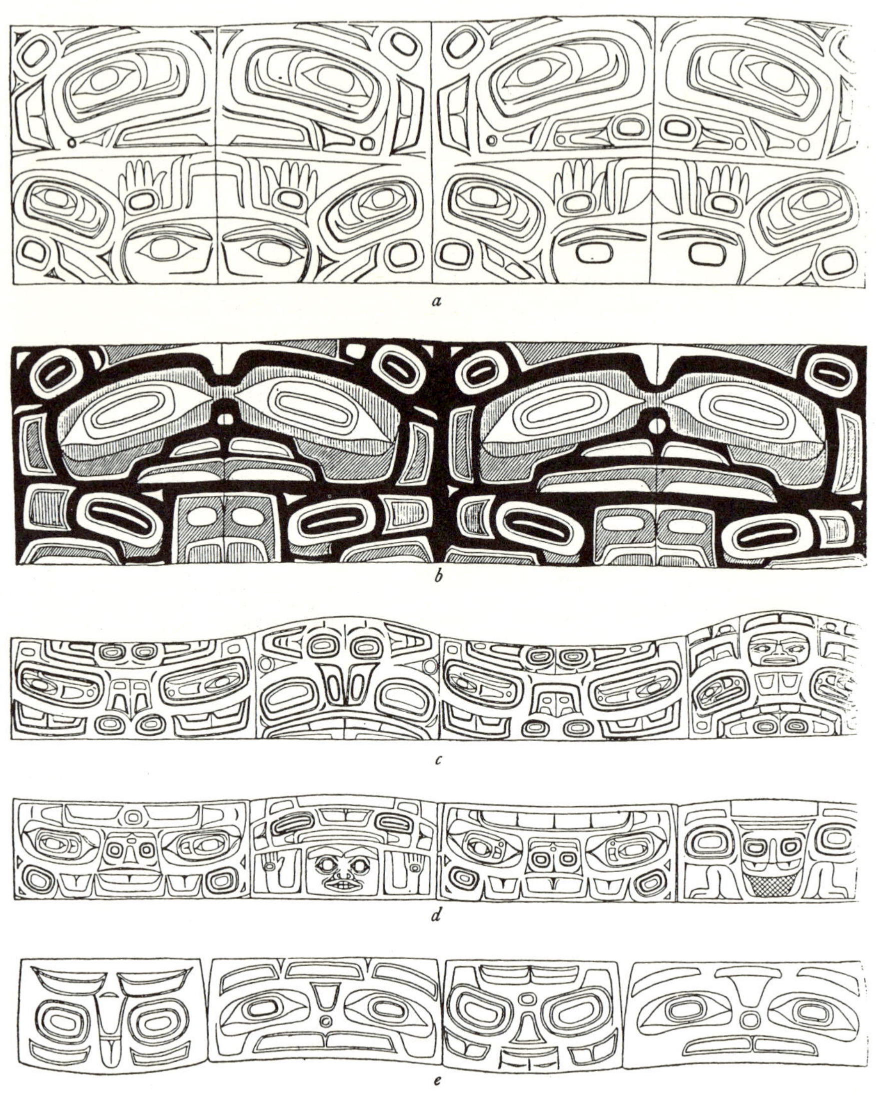

FIG. 11*a* (E/1228), *b* (E/1496), *d* (E/1561), *e* (16/245). Carved boxes. Length, *a*, *b*, 23 cm, 18 cm; *d*, *e*, 44 cm, 17 cm.

modified so as to bring out clearly the idea of the inverted face. In Fig. 11*c* the two groups of concentric circles on the upper rim of the long side will readily be recognized as the nostril, which is placed in the middle of the mouth. The vertical lines in *d* on one of the long sides are the large teeth of an animal, while on the opposite side the peculiar beak design divides the mouth into two parts. In *e* both sides are represented as hawk faces, which are characterized by the division of the mouth into two parts. It is interesting to note that in all these cases the two long sides exhibit slight differences. The box illustrated in Fig. 11*d* represents the beaver, which is symbolized by the hind legs and the scaly tail, shown on one of the short ends. There is a certain contradiction to the sides in the hip and leg designs on the short end, which also shows the tail.

The boxes shown in Fig. 12 are decorated on a different plan. Here the front and the hind end of the body are shown on the short sides in the same manner as on the preceding group of boxes. The sides, however, show only the shoulder joint and the arm, represented here in upright position as a profile. The form is particularly clear in Fig. 12*c*, where the shoulder joint may be recognized distinctly in the large eye near the middle short front. The smaller eye nearer the outer side is the foot joint, while the paws are placed under this foot joint. In Fig. 12*b* the details are not quite so distinct, but the wing feathers attached to the shoulder joint may readily be recognized. The small eye in each lower corner of the side of the box probably represents the foot joint, while the talons are turned up between the foot joint and the shoulder joint. The principles of arrangement of Fig. 12 *a* and *d* will be best understood by comparing these two figures with *e*, where the arrangement of shoulder joint and arm is perfectly plain. It seems fairly clear that the ornaments placed along the lower rim of the box represent the forearm and the foot.

Fig. 12*f* takes a position intermediate between the two last groups. The sides show both shoulder and hip joint, but not in the inverted position characteristic of the boxes shown in Fig. 11.

The box designs shown in Fig. 13 are so intricate that I have not succeeded in analyzing the irregular grouping of eyes, arms, and feet. The box shown in Fig. 13*a* consists of four profile designs. I am not certain, however, which of these is intended to represent the face, and which ones the sides of the body. In *b* the leg designs on those two sides which are carved down to the bottom are quite distinct, but the rest of the figure is not clear. The same is true in regard to the significance of the leg and feet designs, which are quite distinct in Fig. 13*d*.

The fixed character of the form of the head on the blanket, and its difference as compared to the heads on trays and boxes, suggest that the whole animal figure as such, in its general proportions, is a fundamental characteristic of the blanket design without any reference to its significance. We shall see presently that the various forms which have in common the traits heretofore discussed are interpreted as var-

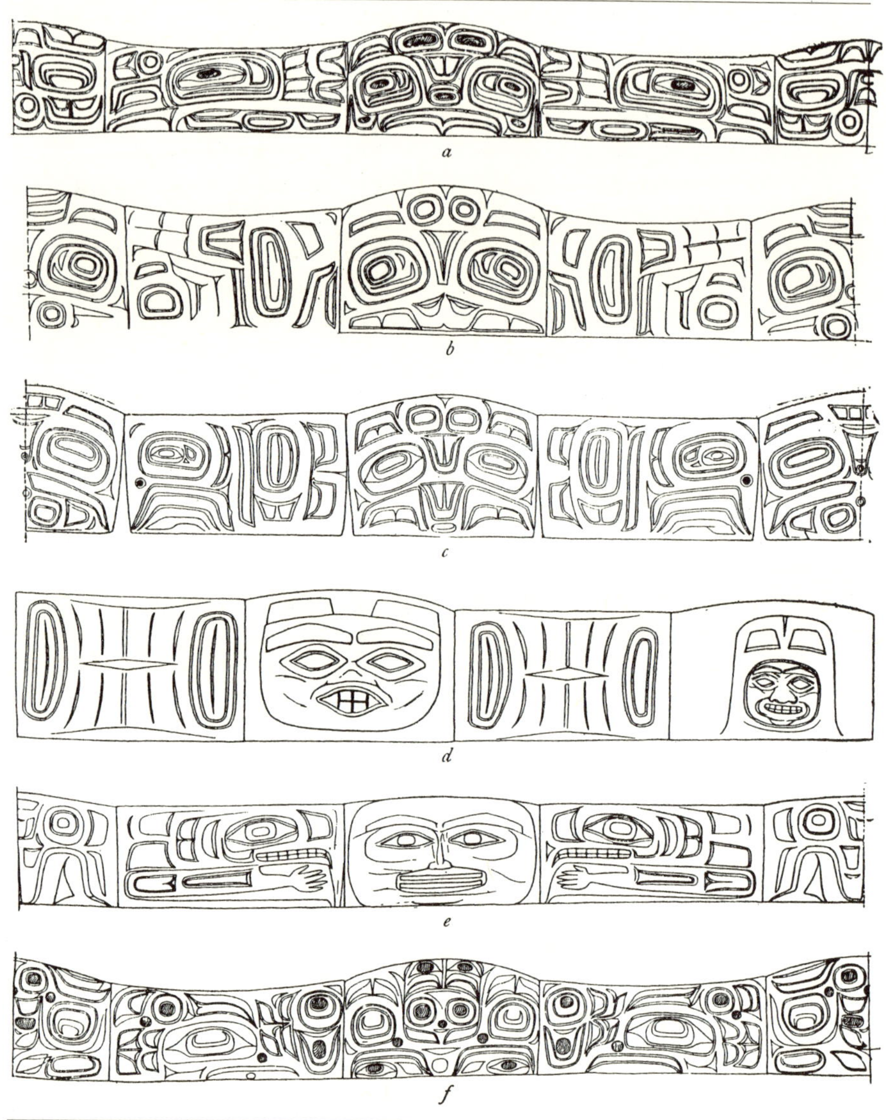

FIG. 12*a* (16/69), *b* (E/394), *d* (16/73), *f* (19/945). Carved boxes. Length, *a, b, d, f,* 43 cm, 14 cm, 23 cm, 24 cm.

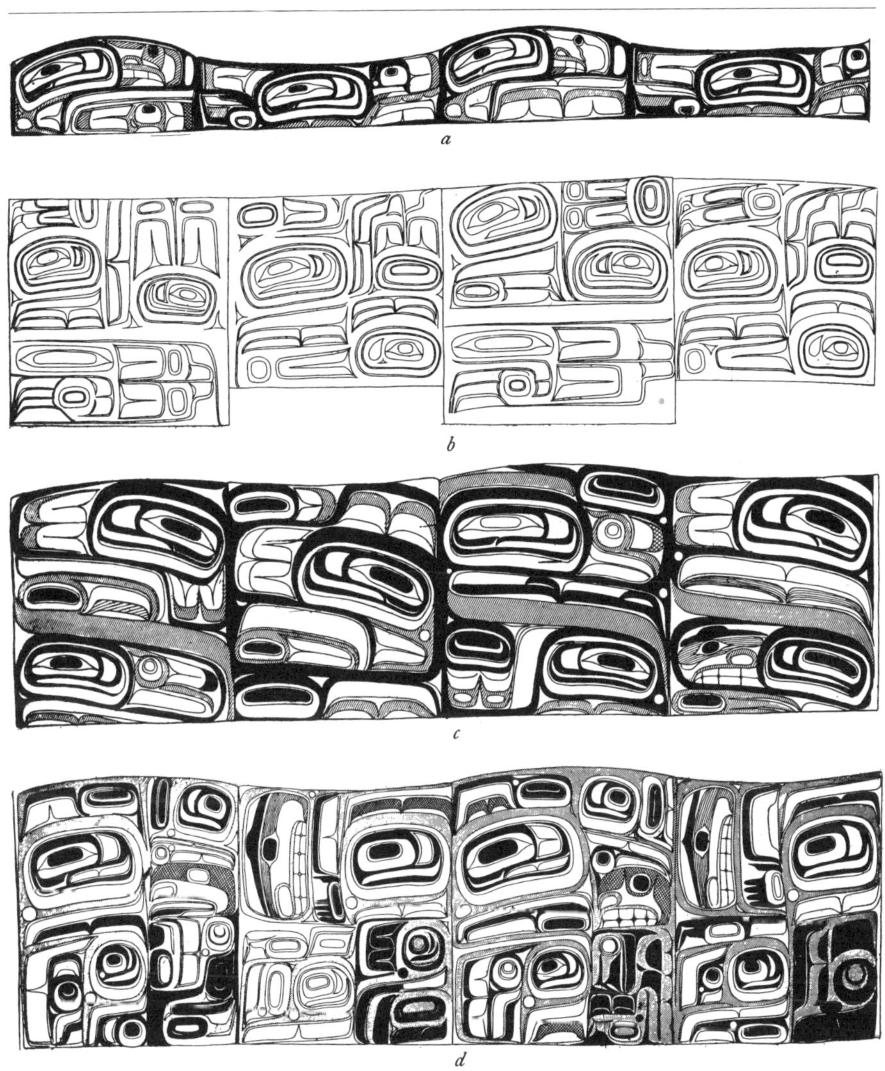

FIG. 13*a* (16/67), *b* (16/950), *c* (16/1074), *d* (16/1233). Carved and painted boxes. Length, 38 cm, 27 cm, 32 cm, 36 cm.

ious animals; while the same animals, when represented on boxes and trays, have forms different from those on the blanket, but characteristic of the object on which they appear.

In order to illustrate more fully the arrangement of the designs, it seems desirable to discuss here the significance of the various design elements. The various parts of the patterns which enter into the composition of blanket designs are given definite names by the Tlingit. These have been collected by Lieutenant Emmons, and are illustrated in Fig. 14. In our further descriptions of designs, the pattern names here given, and their numbers, will be applied. It will appear, however, that many of these patterns, notwithstanding their definite names, are used merely as ornamental elements, without any reference to their signification. All the patterns are well-known elements in painted designs. Thus the eyes of figures found on painted and carved boxes have the same forms which we find here in designs 3, 6, and 8; and, although the third design is called the head of the salmon trout, it is almost always used to indicate the eye of some creature.

Attention is also called to the similarity of the mouth design (10) and eyebrow design (5). When viewed independently, the two are apparently quite identical. The same is true in regard to the design "one within another" (15), the nostril (12), and some of the simpler forms of the eye design (7). The ear (13) is identical with some of the designs called the wing feather of the red flicker (20). It is also impossible to draw a definite line between the white part of the jaw design (11), the hair-ornament design (18), and the slit design (19).

It is important to note the significance of the simpler form of the eye design on the blanket patterns as well as in other designs. In Fig. 3 the eye design appears at the base of the foot near the lower edge of the blanket. In Fig. 1, two eyes appear in a similar way in the talons at the sides of the central body. The two characteristic eyes near the lower edge in the middle of the blanket are interpreted as a part of the tail of the animal here represented. Another good case of the application of the eye design in a similar connection is shown in Fig. 17*a*, where it again appears near the base of the paws in the center of the design. According to the statement of the natives, which is corroborated by the objective evidence of the designs, these eyes are intended throughout to indicate joints. According to a statement that Dr. Farrand received from some Bella Bella Indians, it is more particularly the ball-and-socket joint viewed in cross section, the inner circle being the ball, the outer circle the socket. According to the Kwakiutl theory of art, the joint is applied in the same manner. Thus its significance in all the cases where it appears in the base of paws is perfectly evident. It is intended to represent the wrist or ankle joint. In the same way the two eyes, which are characteristic of the first type of design under the body, must always be explained either as the joint of the tail or as the hip joints, according to the forms constituting the rest of the figure. From this point of view, the face on the body also becomes intelligible. I called attention before to the relation between the face on the body as shown in the blankets, and on the box Fig. 6*a*, and the designs shown on the body in Figs. 6*b* and 7. Here it is quite apparent that the two dark eyes are thought of in the position of the shoulder blades; and it does not seem unlikely that from this initial concept, which will result in two eyes placed in a somewhat square field, the face on the body has been developed by a natural elaboration of this design. It is, however, just as possible that the face may be simply intended to fill in a vacant space, as appears to be the case in a considerable number of instances. In accordance with this method of explanation, the two inverted eyes near the upper edge of the second type of blankets are explained almost throughout as the joints of a tail. It will be noticed that in this case the size of the tail joints is entirely out of proportion as compared to the eye which is shown in the lower portion of the blanket. In the first type of blankets the eye is always much larger than any of the joint designs.

The wing feathers of the red-winged flicker are used very commonly as decorative designs, evidently also in cases where they are intended to represent quite different objects. Thus, the double flicker feather, which will be found as the third design from the end in the table of named patterns (Fig. 14), occurs in Fig. 3 as the beak of a bird, occupying the middle of the mouth design between the two large eyes. It occurs also between the ears along the upper border of the design as the single flicker feather. Here, as well as over the beak of the bird, in the lateral fields, it is used only for filling in parts of the design which otherwise would remain undecorated. In Fig. 1 the same design occurs between the eyes, just over the nostril, and here also it obviously has nothing to do with the red-winged flicker. Many other cases of this application of the wing-feather design, simply for the purpose of filling in spaces, may be observed in practically all the blankets. A comparison of Figs. 15*b* and 17*a* with the box designs Fig. 6, shows that the wing-feather design serves to express the forearm and the upper arm. In Fig. 6*a* we have the two hands placed in a position similar to the paws in Figs. 1, 15*a*, and 17*a*. On the box the parts are connected with the body by a narrow red strip, which is divided by characteristic curves into two parts. A comparison of this design with Figs. 43 and 51, *Bulletin of the American Museum of Natural History*, vol. 9 [see chapter 4, this volume], shows very clearly that they are meant to represent the upper arm. In the blanket design Fig. 15*a*, the two sections connecting the paw with the body may be recognized distinctly as upper arm and forearm, in the same way as in the blanket Fig. 39. In the blanket designs Figs. 1 and 17*a*, the space that is available for the upper arm is still more condensed; but it is nevertheless quite obvious that the two wing-feather designs which lie on the outer sides of the paws must be interpreted here also as the forearm and upper arm. Judging by this analogy, I think there can be very little doubt that the two wing-feathers placed by the sides of the body in Fig. 3 may be considered in the same way

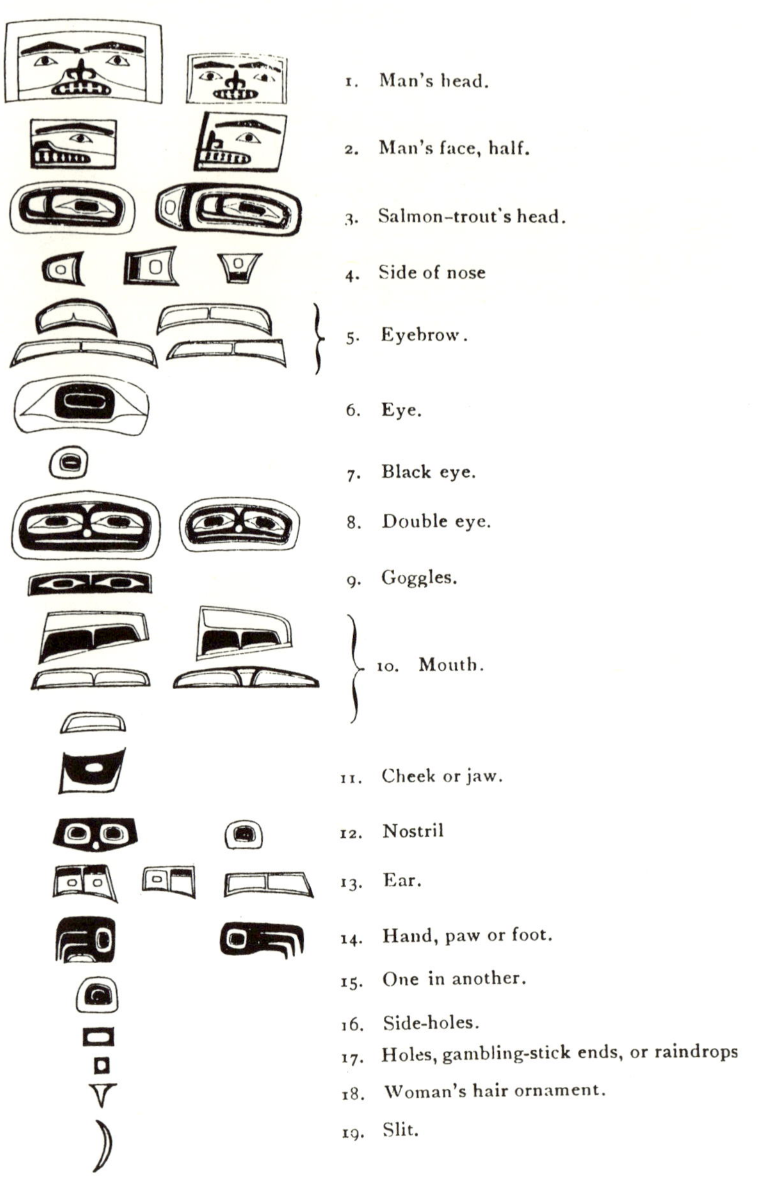

FIG. 14. Names of elements of patterns, according to G. T. Emmons

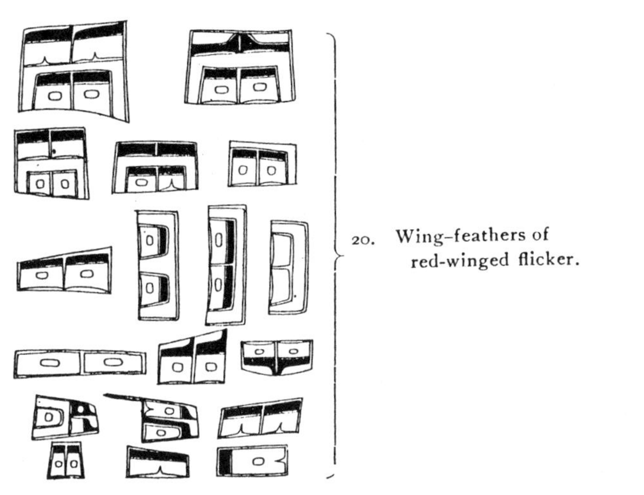

FIG. 14 continued.

as the two parts of the arm of the animal here represented. Since the animal here shown is a bird, these feathers are in this way made to represent the bones of the wing.

Similar considerations have determined the distribution of ornaments in the design Fig. 15*b*. Here the two feet will be recognized at the lower edge of the design. Adjoining it are two long white flicker-feather designs, which obviously represent the legs. Each of the two inverted double eyes under the jaws must be interpreted as a shoulder joint, to which is attached the lower part of the arm in the form of a flicker-feather design.

The forms here discussed are interpreted as various kinds of animals—birds, quadrupeds, sea monsters—but never as the red-winged flicker, nor can the parts be interpreted as ornaments made of flicker feathers. It is obvious that we are dealing here with a fixed form, which has a conventional name, and which is used for a variety of purposes.

It will be noticed that this design occurs in three principal forms. In one of these the design is cut off square in the upper end. Most of those shown in Fig. 14 are of this type. Another characteristic form of this design has the pointed wing feather, as the second one in the series. A third form, which is not given in the series of named designs, seems to be quite common. It has a rounded tip, and may be observed, for instance, in the beak part in front of the upper eye in the lateral fields

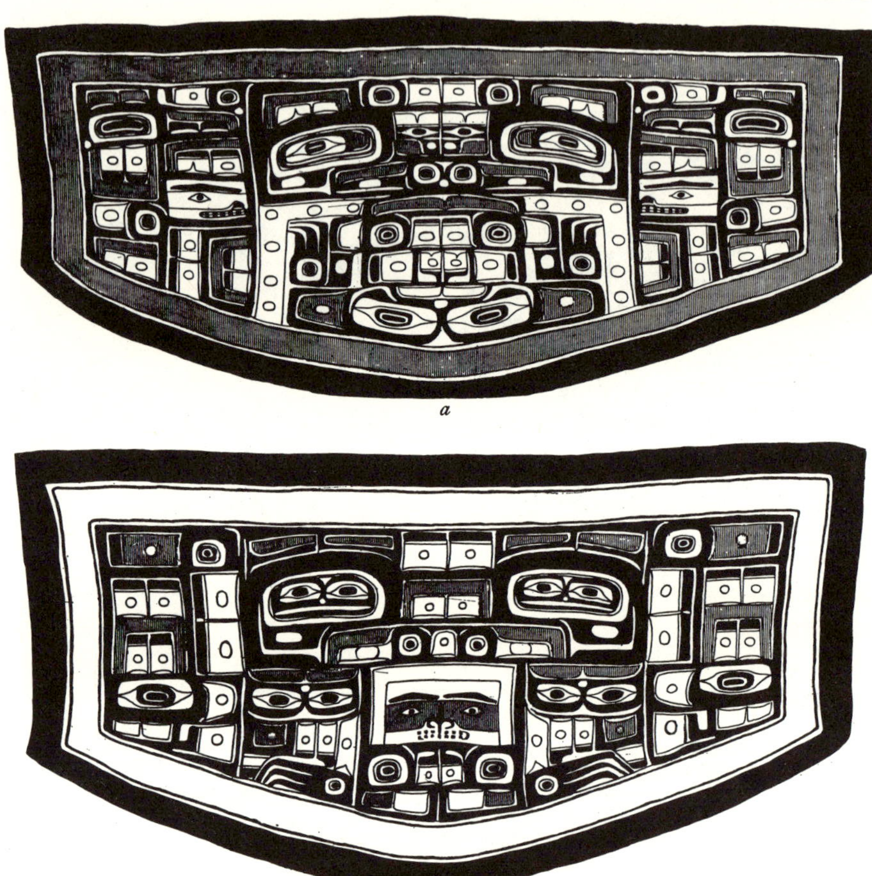

FIG. 15. Blankets.

a. The design represents a bear sitting up. The eyes and the adjoining round wing designs represent the tail. The body is not decorated with the usual face design, but has instead the design of the mouth, two eyes, and wing designs. The lateral fields represent the bear's body and at the same time the raven in profile (Emmons). (Field Museum of Natural History, cat. no. 19586.)

b. The design represents a bear under water. The inverted faces under each jaw, with adjoining wing design, represent the forehead with attached dippers; the lateral fields, the raven sitting, the beak turned outward, the wing on the middle outer part; while the foot is represented by the inverted eye and the adjoining round wing design below, and the tail by the wing designs along the lower border (Emmons).

of Fig. 3, also in front of the lower lateral eye in Fig. 1*b* and in the central field in Fig. 27.

The wing design is applied wherever a somewhat oval or rectangular field which is situated laterally has to be filled in, particularly when the field adjoins another design which is surrounded by heavy black lines, and which forms part of an animal body. For this reason the design appears very commonly in front of, over, or under the eye design. It is used to fill in the ears; it appears at the side of the body, as in Figs. 3 and 16; and it is used to fill in small fields which adjoin black lines, as, for instance, in the lowest section of the lateral fields in Fig. 3*a*. The white circle on a yellowish background, black tip, and small white segment at the base, are almost ever-present. The white segment at the base is limited very often by a pointed double curve—like a brace—which divides the adjoining yellow field more or less distinctly into two halves. These may be observed, for instance, in one of the ear designs in Figs. 1 and 3, and also in the design over the nose in Fig. 16.

Judging from the general application of this design, it is quite obvious that it is not primarily a feather design, but that it is a decorative element used throughout in certain definite positions for the purpose of filling in.

Flat black curves seem to be used quite often for indicating the teeth. These may be observed in Figs. 1*b*, 3, on the body of Fig. 17*b*, in the lowest face in Fig. 18*a*, in the lower face of Figs. 19 and 25*a*. It will be noticed that in the design in the blankets of the second type the place of these teeth designs is very often taken by flicker-wing designs (see Fig. 21).

Attention has been called before to the fact that the face may be used simply for the purpose of filling in the field occupied by the body of the animal. The use of faces for the purpose of filling in appears much more clearly in those cases where the profile is used. In Fig. 27*b*, for instance, where the distinct line between the central field and the lateral fields of the blanket is missing, it is obvious, even at first glance, that the profiles of faces found on both lateral wings are only intended to fill an empty space in the design. Commonly the space, which in this case is occupied by a face, is occupied by the wing feather design, as may be seen by a comparison between the closely related patterns *a* and *b* of Fig. 27. The face is quite common in this position, but it is not always so distinctly marked as a design intended to fill in an empty space. It occurs in this position on Figs. 15*a*, 16 *a* and *b*, 17 *a* and *b*, 19 *a* and *b*, 25*b*, and 27*b*.

According to the interpretation given by the Indians, it would seem that the essential concept of the lateral field is that of a sitting bird, the head stretching in profile across the whole upper part of the field, the central part of the field on the outer side being occupied by the body, while the tail and feet stretch along the lower border. Thus an empty field is always left between the beak and the tail, which is occupied either by the face design just discussed or by various forms of wing-feather

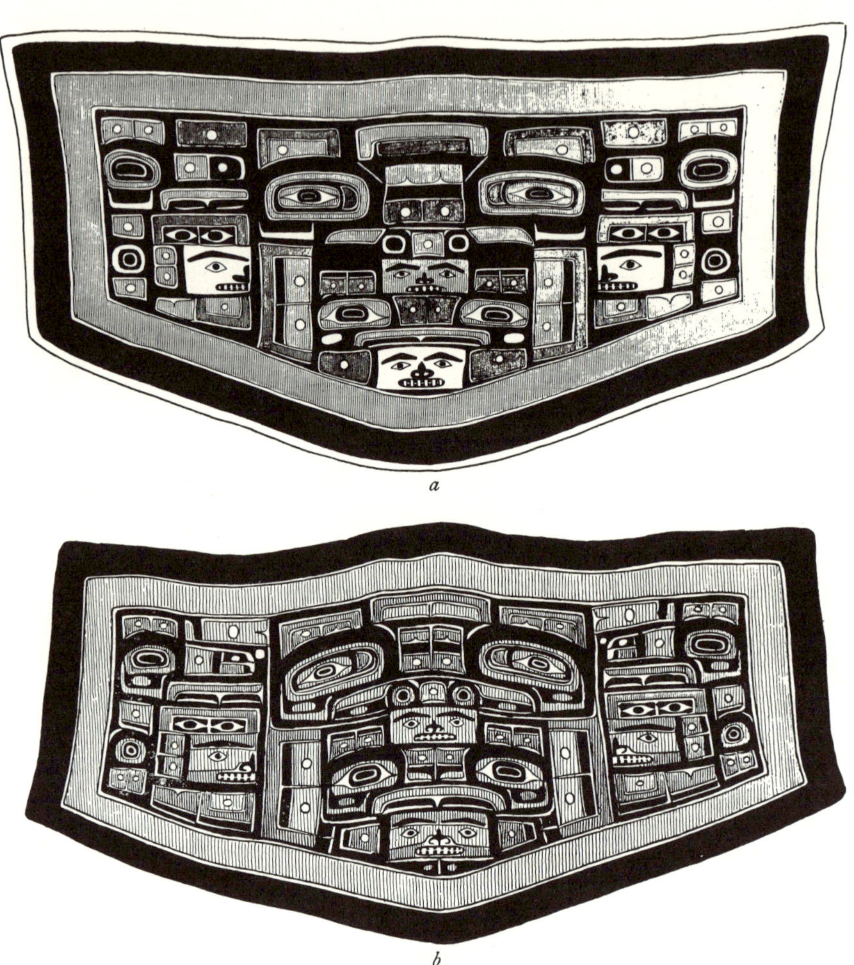

a

b

FIG. 16. Blankets.

a (E/1501). Length, 168 cm. According to Emmons, the design represents a female wolf and young one. The body of the wolf has the form of a hawk; the two eyes and the double wing design between them, near the lower border of the blanket, being the face of the hawk; the double feather design over these eyes, the hawk's ears; the lower white face, the body of the hawk; the wing-feather designs extending downward under the jaw of the wolf, the wings of the hawk. The lateral fields represent the young wolf sitting up, probably at the same time the sides and back of the wolf's body.

According to Swanton, it shows a young raven. The body of the raven is occupied by two profiles of ravens. The face at the bottom is the raven's tail; the lateral wing designs extending downward from under the corners of the jaw are the wings of the raven. The lateral fields represent two young ravens in profile.

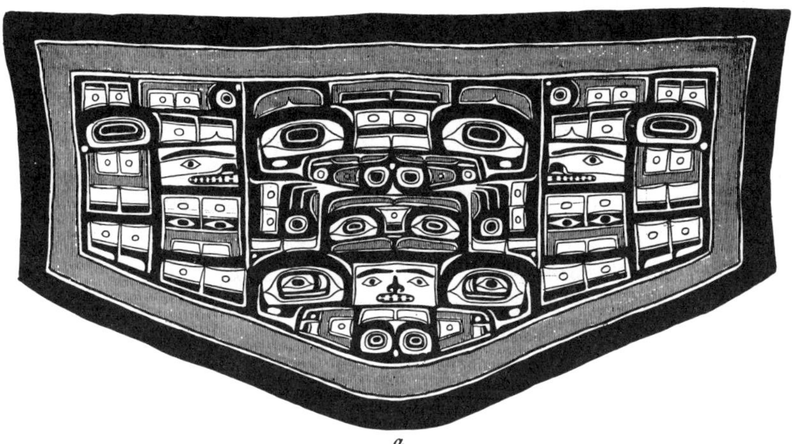

a

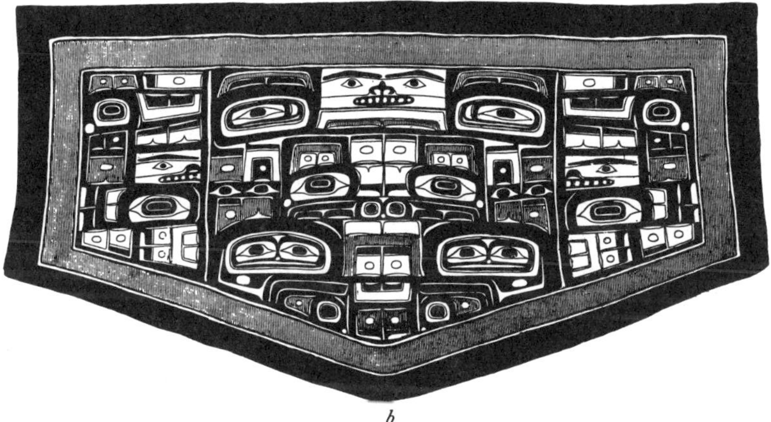

b

FIG. 17. Blankets.

a. According to Emmons, the design represents either a wolf sitting or a whale diving. When viewed as a wolf, the head is on top; the central face is the body, on each side of which are the forepaws. The two eyes below are the head; the central face, the back of the whale; the two eyes above, the fluke of the whale's tail; and the paws on each side, the whale's fins. The lateral fields are explained as a raven.

b. The design represents a whale diving, the head shown at the bottom, the tail on top. The face in the middle represents the body of the whale; the lateral fields, the sides and back of the body, at the same time a raven sitting; the lower eye in the side field, with attached wing designs, being the foot, the wing designs along the lower border, the tail of the raven (Emmons). (Field Museum of Natural History, cat. no. 19595.)

designs. Even if this explanation of the lateral fields should be secondary, the fact remains that in every single case a somewhat rectangular middle field may be distinguished, which is occupied either by the face design or by wing-feather designs.

It would seem that these considerations make it quite clear that the blanket pattern is fixed in all its essential features without any particular reference to its interpretation, and that in any attempt to represent a definite animal the freedom in the arrangement of motives or of symbols of the animal is quite limited; and that, on the whole, the fundamental traits of the pattern remain the same, no matter what animal is to be represented.

We will now revert to the discussion of the blanket types. In the blankets shown in Fig. 15*b* and Fig. 48, the eye design under the jaw of the principal figure has been elaborated into a wing, the joint of which is indicated by a double eye. In the latter specimen there are important modifications of the lateral fields, into which the central figure cuts deeply, while the upper part is more distinctly used as a wing design belonging to the central figure than is the case in other blankets. Evidently the profile of the human face shown in the lower portion of the lateral fields is inserted here in imitation of the profile seen in a similar position in Fig. 15*a*. The displacement of the goggle design under the profile is also peculiar. Figs. 16–18 must be classed with the first type, the fundamental pattern of which is shown in Fig. 4. The two blankets shown in Fig. 16 are evidently made from pattern boards which were originally copies of the same original board. All the essential traits of the two designs are the same, but there are deviations in the details. The mouth of the central animal figured, which is perfectly plain in *b*, is indistinct in *a*, on account of the great width of the black lines which form part of the body and of the head. There are also differences in the elaboration of the wing design, in the ears of the central figure, in the beak of the profile head in each upper lateral corner, and in the form of the wing design over the nostril of the central animal. This specimen differs from those previously described (Figs. 1, 3, 15) in that the two eyes near the lower border are not inverted, and are placed a little higher than usual and farther apart. It would seem that this change in position is related to the process by which the whole lower part of the central field has been combined into a single animal head, in which the human face which in the preceding specimens represents the body appears now simply as a forehead ornament of the same character as the upper human face found in Fig. 3. In this manner the human face near the lower border may also be understood as the body of that animal which occupies the lower portion of the middle of the central field. If this explanation is correct, then the slight modification of the fundamental design must be considered as due to the endeavor to represent an additional animal in the lower part of the blanket design. The modification of the fundamental plan found in Figs. 17 and 18 is even more marked. Here the two lower eyes have been moved out toward the corners of the middle field, and are in size equal to the upper eyes. Owing to this process, the middle field becomes somewhat similar to the second type of blankets, with the exception that the upper two eyes are upright, not reversed. It does not seem improbable that in this case an assimilation with the more symmetrical second type has taken place. Hand in hand with this change goes the treatment of the central face as an animal head in place of the usual human head. The peculiarity of arrangement in the two blankets represented in Fig. 18 lies particularly in the treatment of the field on each side of the central body, which is here developed as an eye almost equal in size to the two upper and lower eyes. It seems likely that this eye is related in its origin to the small central eye design on each side of the body in Fig. 3; but it has been so much enlarged that the whole central face has been reduced very much in size. There is a specimen in the Peabody Museum of American Archaeology in Cambridge, Mass. (cat. no. 56679), which is practically identical with the one shown in Fig. 18*b*.

Turning from these blankets to those of the second type, we may recognize, on the whole, much greater uniformity of treatment. The two designs in Fig. 19 are so closely related, that we are probably not mistaken if we ascribe them to the same original pattern board. The three designs in Figs. 21 and 22 are also so nearly alike that they must be ascribed to the same pattern board; and the same is true of the designs in Fig. 23 *a* and *b*. Among these three sets, the two types shown in Figs. 21–23 seem to be particularly closely related. The essential points of difference consist in the inversion of the wing design in the center of the upper border, the lack of the goggle design under the central face in Fig. 23, and the different arrangement of the eye and wing design under the central face. The adjoining wing patterns are also slightly different. The lateral fields in the two styles are very much alike, except for a few minor differences in wing patterns. The six blankets (Fig. 22 representing two specimens) probably go back to the same original pattern board. While the two blankets shown in Fig. 25 are not so readily reducible to the two patterns of this type so far discussed, they are evidently closely related to them. It would appear that Fig. 25*a* is related to the pattern Fig. 19. It has in common with it the tooth pattern and the central nostril pattern along the middle part of the lower border and the peculiar position of the lower eye in the lateral field close to the outer border. The wing designs above and below this eye are also the same in the two types. The essential difference consists in the occurrence of the eye and nose of moderately large size at the sides of the body, where in the pattern shown in Fig. 19 only wing designs occur, and in the absence of the face design in the lateral fields. It is worth remarking that the eye design at the sides of the body agrees with the form in Fig. 23. On the other hand, the blanket shown in Fig. 25*b* seems to be closely related to the type shown in Figs. 21–23, particularly in regard to the treatment of the central part of the lower border. The field at the sides of the body, between the lower and upper eyes, is treated in a way similar to the type in Fig. 19.

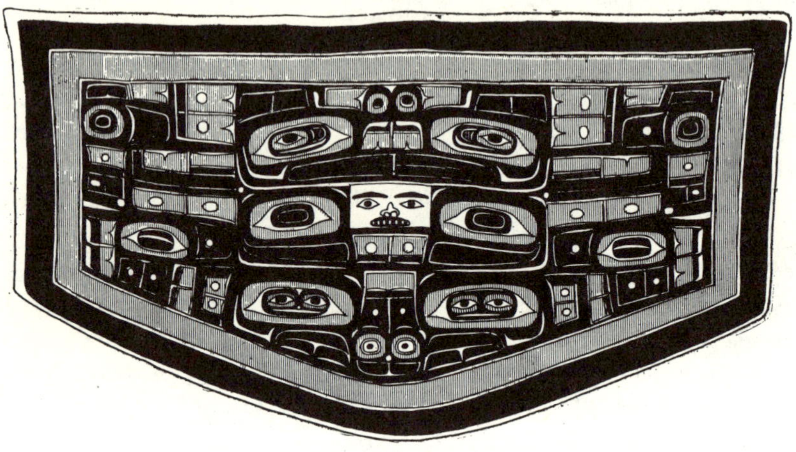

a

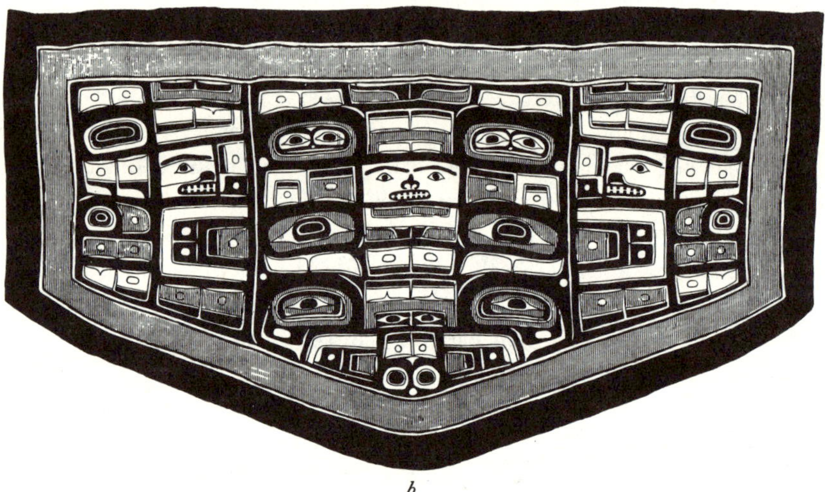

b

FIG. 18. Blankets.

a (16/351). Length, 158 cm. According to Emmons, it represents on top a brown bear sitting up. On the body of the bear is a raven's head; the hindquarters are treated as a whale's head, the eyes being the hip joints, the mouth the feet, of the bear. The principal figure is also explained as a whale; the head is below. The body, which is turned up, is treated as a raven's head, and its tail as a bear's head. The side panels are the sides and back of these animals, but also an eagle in profile on top, and a raven in profile below.

According to Swanton, the whole blanket represents a halibut; the head is below; the whole large middle face, the body; the face near the upper margin, the tail; the wing design next to the lowest head, the small pectoral fins; the rest of the lateral fields, the continuous border fin.

b. According to Emmons, the design represents a whale; the side panels, a sitting raven in profile. (U.S. National Museum, cat. no. 168292.)

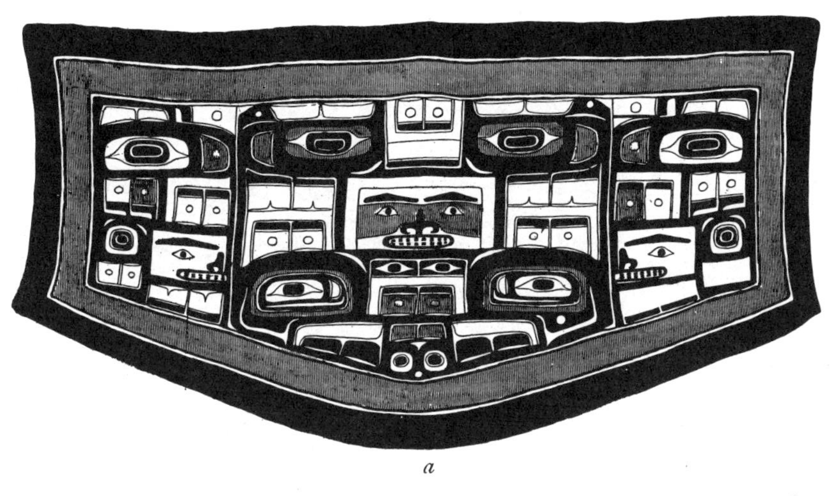

a

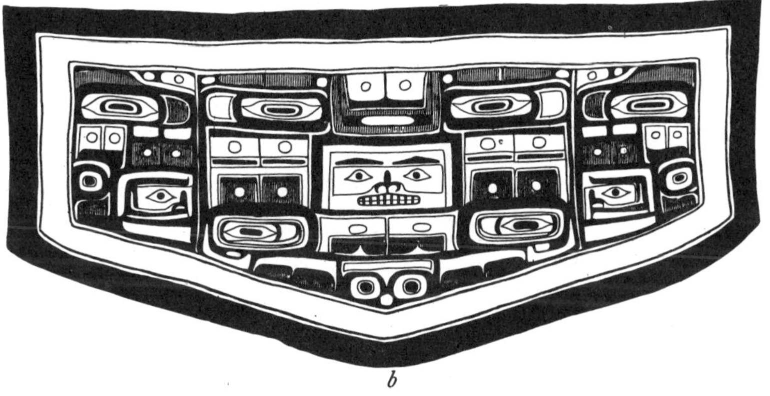

b

FIG. 19. Blankets.

a. According to Emmons, the design represents a whale. The head, with nostrils and mouth, is shown below. The central face represents the body; the eyes near the upper border are the flukes of the tail; the large wing designs at the sides of the body, the fins. The lateral fields represent a young raven sitting, at the same time the sides and back of the whale. (U.S. National Museum.)

b. According to Emmons, it represents a whale diving, the details of explanation being the same as in Fig. 19*a*. The lateral fields represent a young raven sitting.

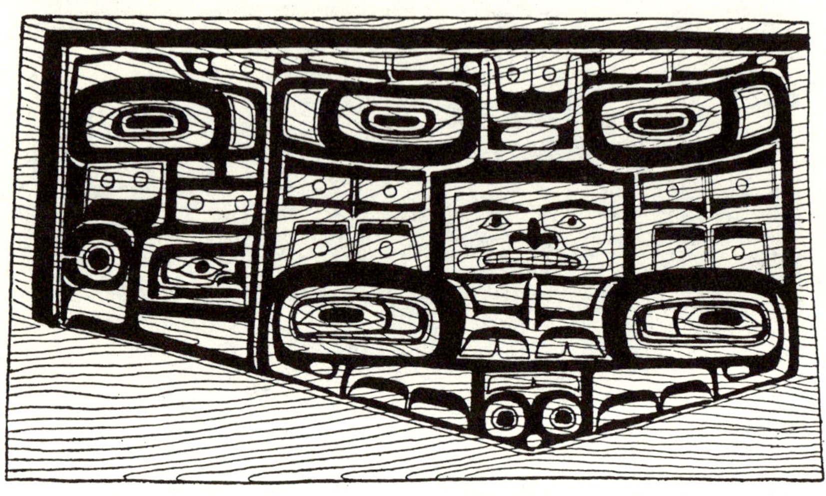

FIG. 20. Pattern board for blanket shown in Fig. 19*b*.

Lieutenant Emmons has found one more blanket of this type which is closely related to the type shown in Fig. 25*b*. The whole lower portion of the central field agrees in the two specimens, the only exception being that, in the blanket which is not illustrated, the two eyes on the upper border of the blanket are drawn apart, and resemble most closely, in their arrangement, Fig. 22. They differ, however, in that the outer portion of the eye is considerably extended, and encroaches upon the lateral fields, thus condensing the two birds' heads in each upper corner. Thus it will be seen that the lateral fields are not clearly defined in this specimen. In place of the angular wing design which occupies the region under the beak in the lateral field in Fig. 22, we have here a raised paw in the same position as the raised paw in Fig. 15*a*, which occupies the corresponding position just under the outer extension of the middle eyes on the upper margin. This is the only blanket of this type in which paw designs are found, and it is obviously a modification of the group of designs just described.

The following group of blankets (Figs. 26 and 27) still belong to the same type. They differ, however, in that the sharp division between the central field and the lateral fields is broken. Owing, however, to the prominence of the large eye designs in the middle field and the smallness of the designs in the lateral fields, the central field stands out fairly prominently. In Fig. 27*a* the same change of arrangement has

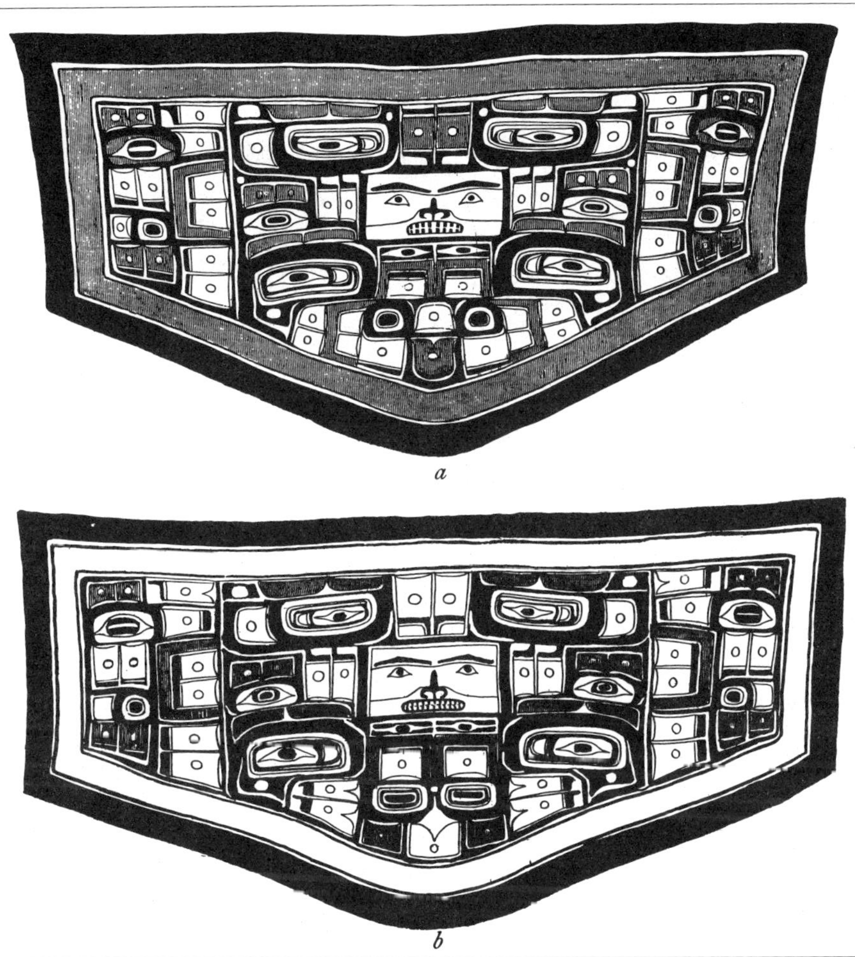

a

b

FIG. 21. Blankets.

According to Emmons, the design represents a whale diving, the explanation being the same as that of Fig. 19*a*. The lateral fields represent the sides and back of the whale, at the same time a young raven sitting.

occurred that may be observed in Fig. 25*b*. The inverted eyes near the upper border have been moved together, so that they come in contact with the middle.

Fig. 26 shows a blanket in which a modification of the type of design here discussed has taken place, which is somewhat similar to the modification of the first type shown in Figs. 16 and 17. The fundamental difference consists in the substitution of an animal head for the human face in the middle of the central field. Thus

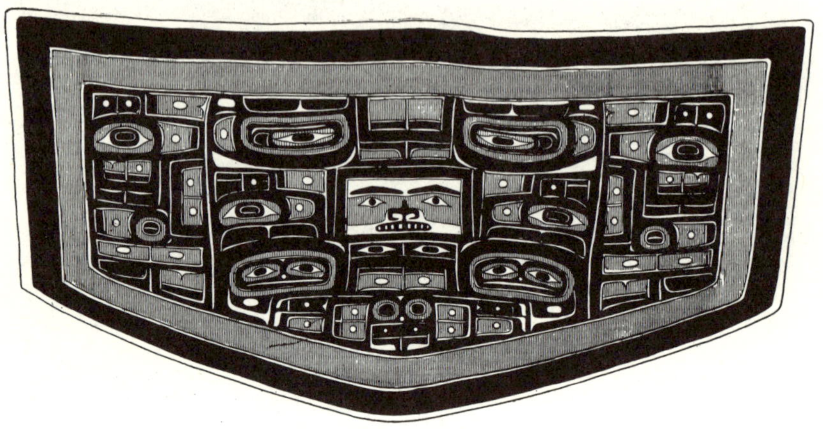

FIG. 22 (16/350). Blanket. Width, 166 cm.

According to Emmons, it represents a whale diving, and in the lateral fields a raven sitting. The details of the explanation are the same as given before.

According to Swanton, it represents a wolf with young. The head is shown below. The hind legs and hip joints are represented by the two large eyes and the adjoining ornaments along the upper border, the two dark segments just over the eye being the feet. The face in the middle of the design represents, as usual, the body of the animal. The small eye designs, with adjoining ear and wing-feather designs, in the middle on each side of the body, are interpreted as front, leg, and foot. The lateral designs are explained as a young wolf sitting.

the human face, which still persists, is much reduced in size, and may be compared to the human face in Fig. 3, over the nostril of the central figure. The enlargement of this head has reduced the size of the space at the side of the body and between the upper and lower eye, which is here filled with an eye design, with adjoining wing designs. The lateral field is also considerably modified. The upper eye, to which, in almost all the preceding blankets, an ear design was attached, touches the upper border; and the lower eye is placed in the same way, upside down. The line setting off the central field from the lateral fields is not quite so sharp as in the blankets previously described.

In the two blankets shown in Fig. 27 the field at the side of the body, between the upper and lower eyes, is treated in a peculiar manner, being occupied by a single rounded wing design, which is interpreted as the dorsal fin of a whale. There is little doubt that this characteristic symbol is used here to replace the designs previously described, on account of the endeavor on the part of the artist to represent the killer whale. Attention may also be called to the difference in form of the upper attachments to the outer corners of the eye designs at the middle of the upper border,

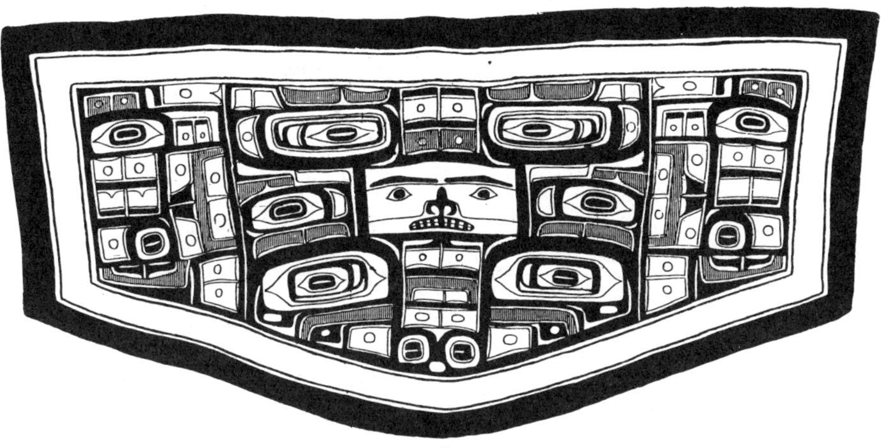

a

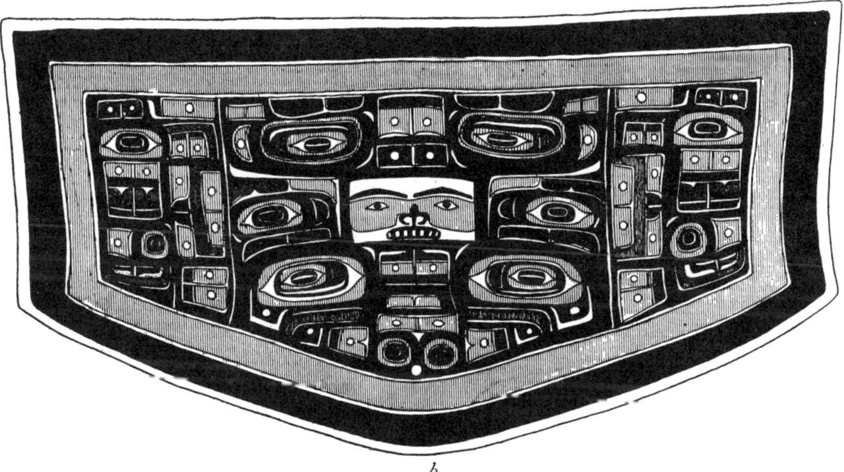

b

FIG. 23 (16/952 and 16.1/126). Blankets. Width, 168 cm.

a. According to Emmons, the design represents a whale, and in the lateral fields the side and back of the whale, at the same time an eagle sitting. The details of the explanation are the same as those given before.

According to Swanton, this blanket represents a killer whale; the central design on each side of the body, each one-half of the dorsal fin; the small wing designs in the lateral fields on each side of the lower face, the side fins; the rest of the lateral fields, the ribs and other inner parts of the body.

b. According to Emmons, the design represents a whale diving, and in the lateral fields a raven. The details of the explanation are the same as those given before.

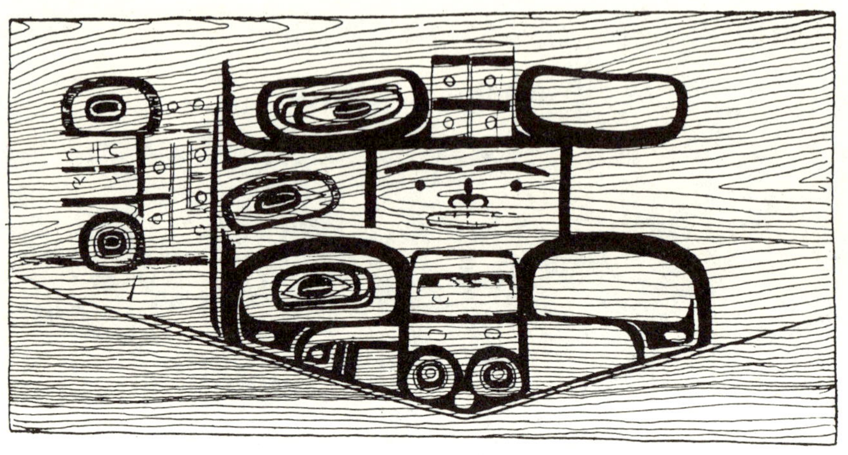

FIG. 24. Pattern board for blanket shown in Fig. 23*b*.

which are here circular in form, while in all previous cases they resemble the jaw design.

In Fig. 27*b* a radical rearrangement of the designs along the lower border in the lateral field has been made, by means of which the lateral field is connected entirely with the middle field. In Fig. 27*a* the fundamental traits of the lateral fields, as heretofore described, persist more clearly.

The following series of blankets have been separated because certain of the fundamental traits of the patterns heretofore described are not found in them. A few of them only are old blankets representing peculiar designs, while most of them are evidently modern products which show the gradual degeneration of the old blanket patterns. The blanket and blanket board shown in Figs. 28 and 29 are closely related to the blanket shown in Fig. 15*b* and belong to the first type. A comparison of the two illustrates clearly their relationship. The essential difference between the two patterns consists, however, in the fact that the design of the blanket Fig. 28 is not divided into the three fields, as all old blankets are, and that the whole figure is much more realistic, and resembles much more closely the modern paintings of the Indians of the Northwest Coast than do older blankets. The apparent realism of this figure is perhaps brought about most strongly by the reduction of the size of the head as compared to the spread wings, the better definition of the tail, and the clearness with which the legs are set off from the wing feathers. The realism of the figure is much helped also by a yellow band with white circles setting off the whole central figure from the lateral fields. The upper part of the lateral field is also much more

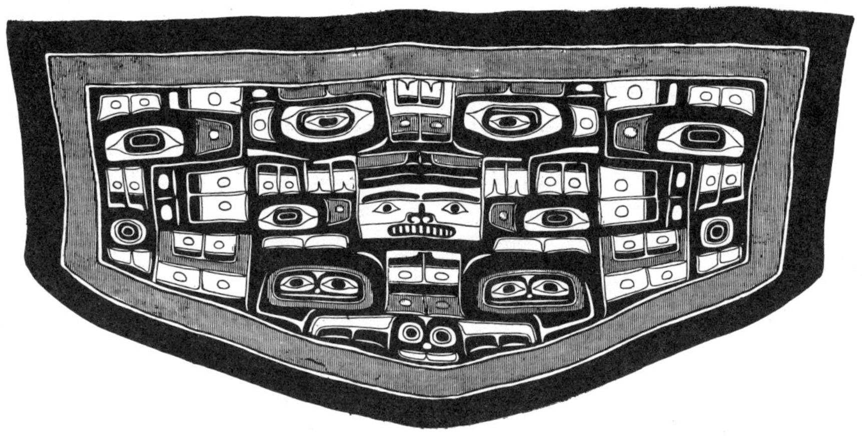

a

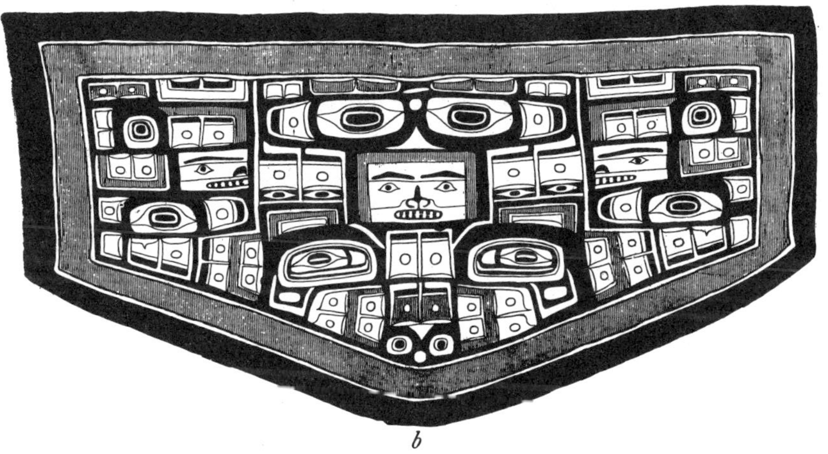

b

FIG 25. Blankets.

a. According to Emmons, the design represents a whale diving, the explanation being the same as that of Fig. 19*a*. The lateral fields represent the sides and back of the whale, at the same time a young raven sitting. (U.S. National Museum, cat. no. 20804.)

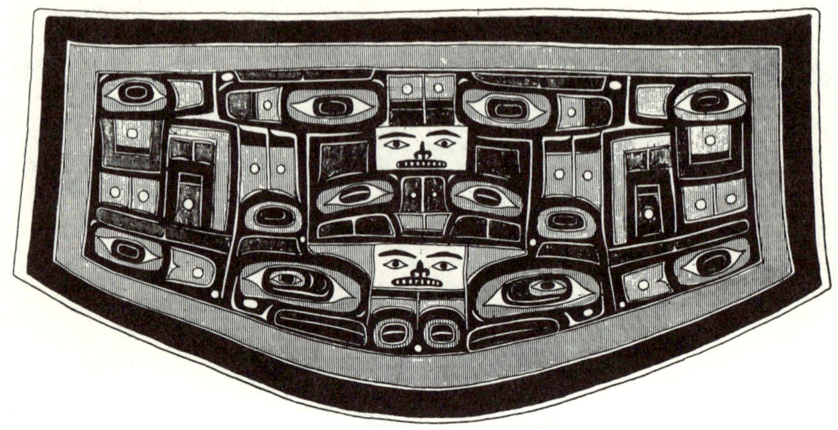

FIG. 26 (16/955). Blanket. Width, 152 cm.

According to Emmons, the design represents a whale. The explanation is the same as given before, except that the body is indicated here by a larger face, which in its details represents a raven. The lateral fins are indicated by the eye design over the lower head, with the attached wing designs. The lateral fields represent a raven sitting, the eye and adjoining wing design along the lower border representing the tail.

According to Swanton, it represents a whale. The two fins on the side of the body and over the lower eyes are explained as two fins on the back of the whale; the eyes with adjoining wing design in each upper corner of the blanket, as the side fins; the inverted eye in the lateral fields at the lower border, as whale bone; the rectangular space in the lateral fields between the upper and lower eyes, as the ribs of the whale.

strongly subordinated to the central figure than is the case in the blankets previously described. The upper corners contain no heads, but simply wings—designs which appropriately represent the feathers on the back of the bird.

To the same type belongs Fig. 30, which is closely related to the blanket shown in Fig. 1. The essential difference in the central design is found in the position of the feet and in the occurrence of wing designs in place of feet at the sides of the body. The tail is also a little more realistic than usual. The lateral fields in this blanket differ entirely from all those in the first two groups. The two characteristic eyes still occur in their relative positions, but they are used in entirely new combinations. The lower part of each of the lateral fields is worked out as a whale's head with open mouth. The characteristic rectangular field which cuts into the middle part of the lateral field from the central field, and which is found in all the designs previously described, does not occur here; and instead of it, we find two vertical fields side by side rising over the whale's head. These are taken up entirely by eye and wing-feather designs.

To the same type belongs the blanket shown in Fig. 32, which, however, cannot

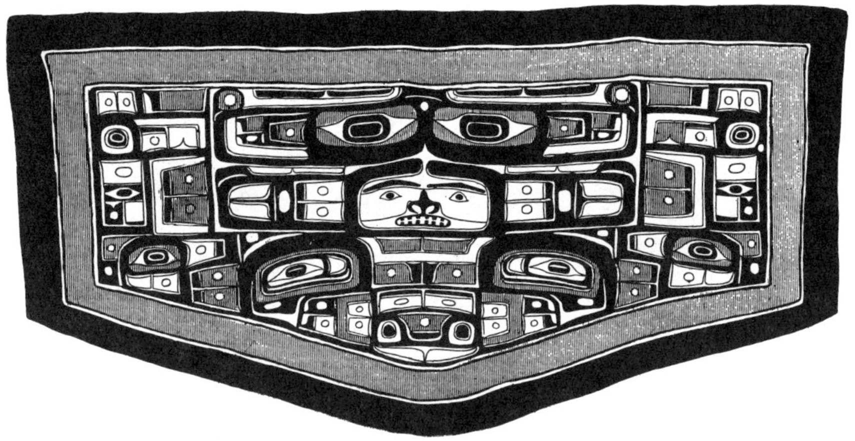

a

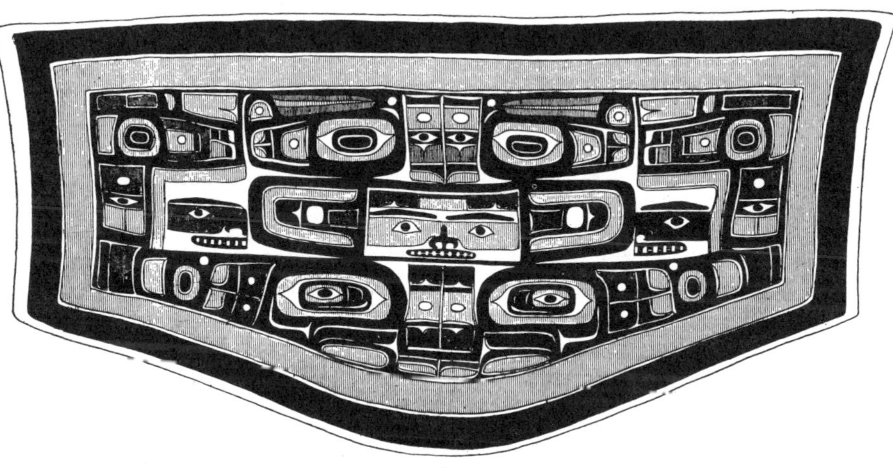

b

FIG. 27. Blankets. Width, 156 cm.

a. The design represents a killer whale. Below, the head is shown. The face in the middle represents the body, while the flukes of the tail are shown along the upper border. The two lateral rounded wing designs represent the two halves of the dorsal fin; the lateral fields, the sides and back of the whale, and at the same time an eagle sitting, the wing being placed in front of the body toward the middle field (Emmons). (U.S. National Museum).

b (16/956). Same explanation.

According to Swanton, this figure represents a killer whale, but some of the details are differently explained. The large rounded wing designs extending from the eyes along the lower border of the blanket are explained as the side fin of the killer whale; the two faces on each side of the dorsal fin, as the blowhole. The rest of the lateral design represents the intestines.

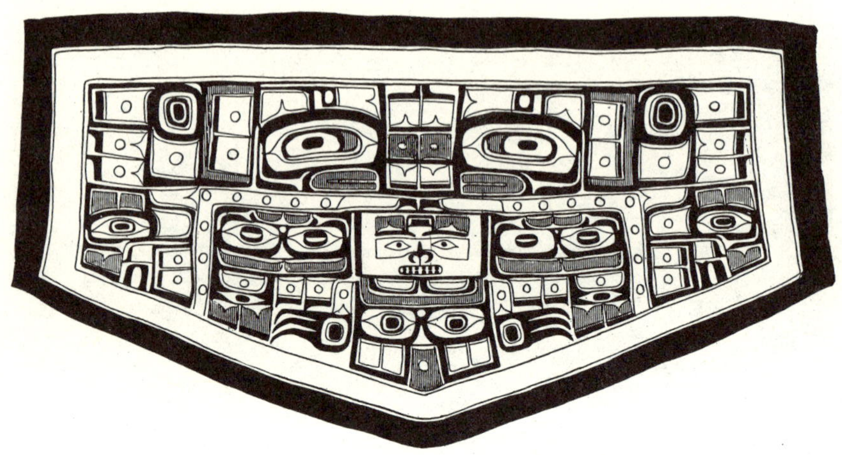

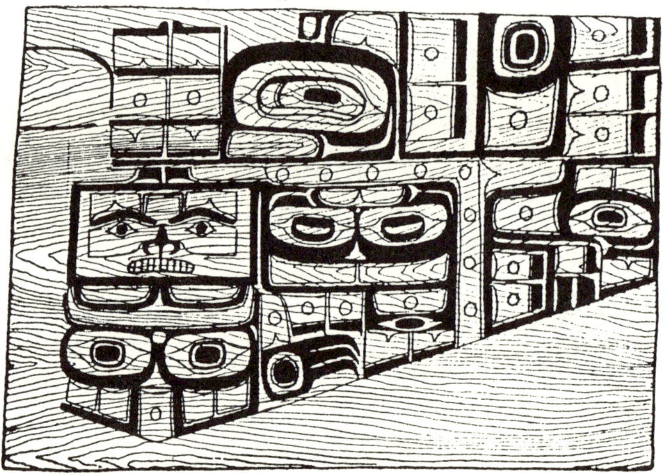

FIG. 28. Blanket.

According to Emmons, it was originally the property of Chartrich, and represents a sea bear; the upper central part being the head of the bear; the wing designs between the eyes, the rings on his hat; the space below, enclosed by a white line with rings, the body of the bear; the field in each upper corner, the side fins; the field in each lower corner, the back, which is ornamented as a wolf's head.

The figure represents at the same time an eagle standing with outspread wings; the human face in the middle being the eagle's body; the inverted double eyes on each side, with adjoining feather ornaments, the wings. The ornament in each upper corner is then interpreted as an eagle; the eye design, and the asymmetrical wing design under it, being the head of the eagle; the feather design on the outer border being the eagle's wing.

FIG. 29. Pattern board for blanket shown in Fig. 28.

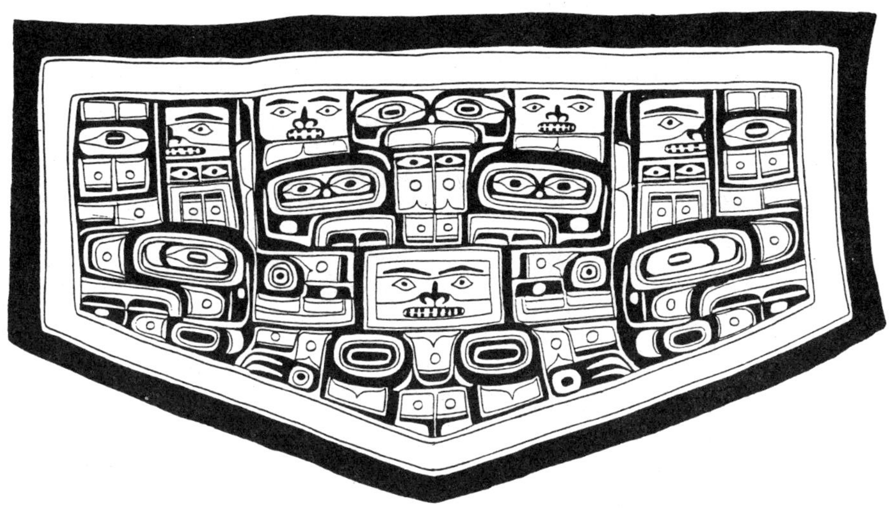

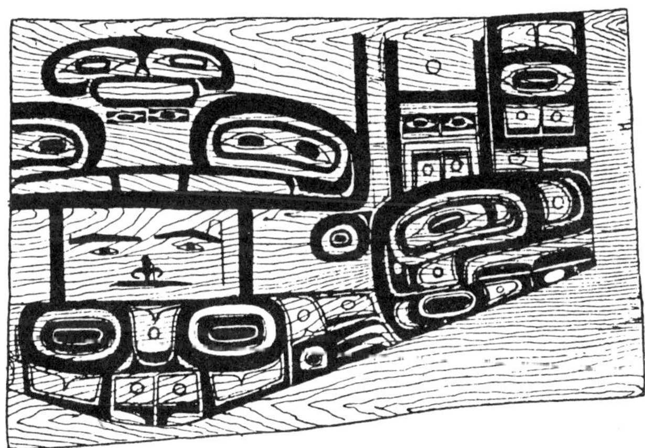

FIG. 30. Blanket.

According to Emmons, the design represents a thunderbird catching two whales. The central figure is explained in the same way as Fig. 1, to which it is closely related. The difference in the two designs consists in the different elaboration of the lateral fields, which are occupied in the present specimen by the whale head below, while the upper part represents the whale's body, but at the same time the back of the bird.

FIG. 31. Pattern board for blanket shown in Fig. 30.

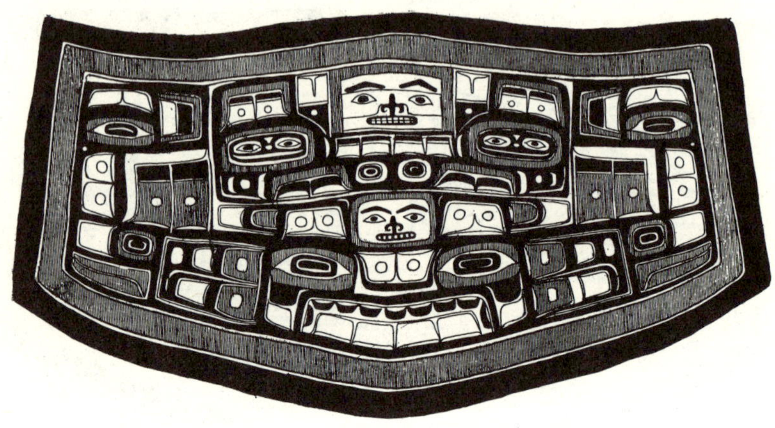

FIG. 32. Blanket. (Field Museum of Natural History, cat. no. 19570.)

According to Emmons, it represents a killer whale. The head with open mouth and teeth is shown below, while the two large eye designs on top represent the fluke of the tail. The small face in the middle is the body, in each side of which is one-half of the dorsal fin. The lateral fields represent the back of the body, at the same time ravens. The wing of the raven is shown by the feather design in the space under the beak. The lower eye, with the adjoining white field toward the border, is the foot, while the tail is shown at the lower border.

readily be associated with any of the blankets of the first series. On the whole, the impression given by this design is that of an old blanket. The difference between the design and the first groups lies largely in the absence of clearly defined lateral fields and in the development of the two lower eyes into the form of a large open mouth, with numerous teeth in the upper jaw, which does not occur in any of the other designs. The space at the sides of the body, which is so characteristic, is here very much reduced in size. The essential traits of the lateral fields are the same as those found in the first two types of blankets.

Quite a unique form is shown in the blanket Fig. 33 and in the apparently related form Fig. 34. Both of these seem to be good old blanket designs. Although both are distantly related to the second type of blankets, they show so many peculiarities that they cannot readily be grouped with them. The line setting off the lower part of the middle field from the two inverted eyes on top recalls the similar line in Fig. 15. Attention may be called to the occurrence of numerous wing designs with central circles in a similar arrangement on the pattern board in Fig. 34, which suggests that perhaps the rectangular figure with white dots may have originated by an amalgamation of many wing designs which happen to be placed in a rectangular order surrounding the double head designs. The lateral field in Fig. 33 shows the regular

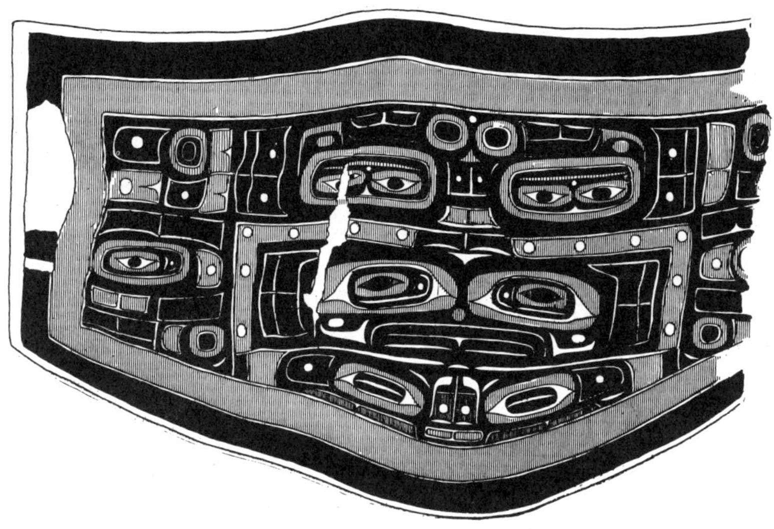

FIG. 33 (16/329). Blanket. Width, 127 cm.

According to Emmons, the design is that of an inverted whale, the head on the upper border, the side fins on either side of the head in the lateral field, the tail below the fins. Below, in the space surrounded by a yellow stripe with white circles, is the dragonfly—the large head in the middle, and the wings on each side of the head. Below is the body bisected. Its head is like that of the hawk without ears.

According to Swanton, this blanket represents a killer whale. The head is shown inverted on the upper border. The wing design between the two eyes represents the backbone. On either side of the head, extending into the lateral field along the upper border of the blanket, is the dorsal fin. The large head in the middle of the blanket is the body of the killer whale, on each side of which the side fin is shown. The two eyes at the bottom represent the tail. The lower spaces in the lateral fields, occupied by an inverted eye, and the adjoining wing designs, are interpreted as the ribs of the animal.

arrangement; while the lateral field in Fig. 34 is entirely broken up, although the two eyes still persist in their old position.

The three following specimens, shown in Figs. 35 and 36, bear apparently hardly any relation to the more common blanket types, although all of them are apparently good old specimens, which are treated with unusual freedom. The realism of Fig. 36*a* is particularly remarkable. The specimen shown in Fig. 36*b* consists of repetitions of a conventional face design.

In the remaining blankets the patterns are so much broken up that they can be explained only by considering the design in relation to the animal that it is intended to represent. Before taking up these modern designs, it may be well to add a few remarks relating to the interpretation of the whole series of designs here given.

In the legends to our illustrations the explanations obtained by Lieutenant Em-

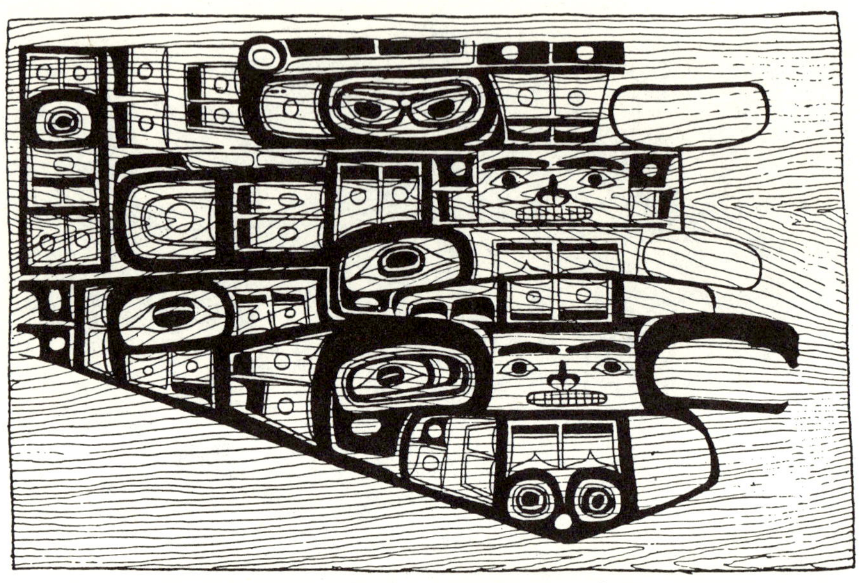

FIG. 34. Pattern board for blankets.

According to Emmons, the design represents a killer whale catching a hair seal. The head of the killer whale is shown in the middle of the design. Between its eyes, and just over them, is a human face representing the blowhole. Extending sideways into the lateral fields, which are not well set off from the middle field, is the dorsal fin. The two eyes along the upper border are the tail of the killer whale. The vertical field extending along the upper part of the side border is the fluke of the tail. The whole lower part of the design represents the seal; the two large eyes being in the middle, under the eyes of the killer whale; the large mouth, in the lowest part of the blanket. Adjoining the eyes is a double wing design representing the flipper of the seal. The hind flippers are represented by the yellow design near the outer lower corners, with the adjoining wing designs.

mons are given. A number of additional explanations were obtained by Dr. John R. Swanton, who had the kindness to submit to the Indians of Sitka a number of photographs which I gave him. It will be noticed that some of the explanations obtained by both authorities agree, while others show characteristic differences.

On the whole, the central field of the blanket is considered as the principal design. It represents a single animal or a combination of animals; while the lateral fields are conceived of as the sides and back of the animal, which is imagined to be split in two along its back. At the same time, however, the sides are regularly explained either as small animals, or, in some cases, as the den of the animal shown in the middle. The contradictions in the explanations given to Lieutenant Emmons and to Dr. Swanton are so great that it is quite obvious that no fixed type of con-

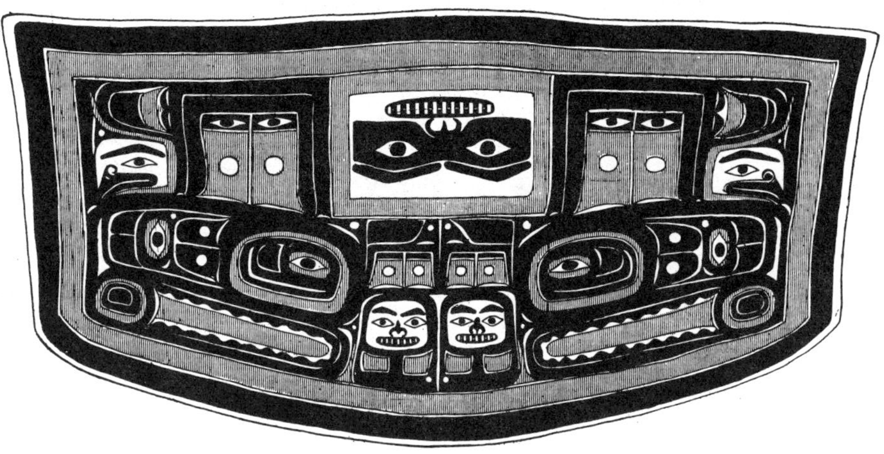

FIG. 35 (E/627). Blanket. Width, 154 cm.

According to Emmons, the design represents a killer whale. In each lower corner is one-half of the head, with the teeth; right in front of the teeth, the nostril; between the two halves of the head, at the lower border of the blanket, the tail. The inverted face in the middle above represents the body. The large square designs containing the goggle design on each side are interpreted as the water blown out from the blowhole. One-half of the dorsal fin is indicated by the small round wing-feather design in each upper corner, the human face in profile under it representing one-half of the blowhole.

According to Swanton, the Gonaqadē't is represented. One-half of the head is shown in each lower corner, the eye design in front of the tongue being interpreted as the chin. The two faces in the middle of the lower border are interpreted as the young ones of the Gonaqadē't; the flicker-feather designs over them, as the inner part of the body of the old animal. The inverted large face in the middle, at the upper border, is interpreted as its hat; the large square design on each side of this face, containing the goggle design, as the dorsal fin. The two human faces in profile near the upper corners are young ones, the body shown by the round feather design over the face.

Another interpretation of this design, obtained by Franz Boas, is a killer whale in the two halves of the head in each lower corner; the food of the killer whale represented by the eye design in front of the mouth; the tail below, in the middle; the two halves of the dorsal fin just over the tail. The chest is represented by the inverted face in the middle of the upper border; the flippers, by the adjoining square designs and the attached round feather designs. According to this description, the profile faces near the upper corners should be the blowholes (see *Bulletin of the American Museum of Natural History* 9:174 [this volume, chapter 4]).

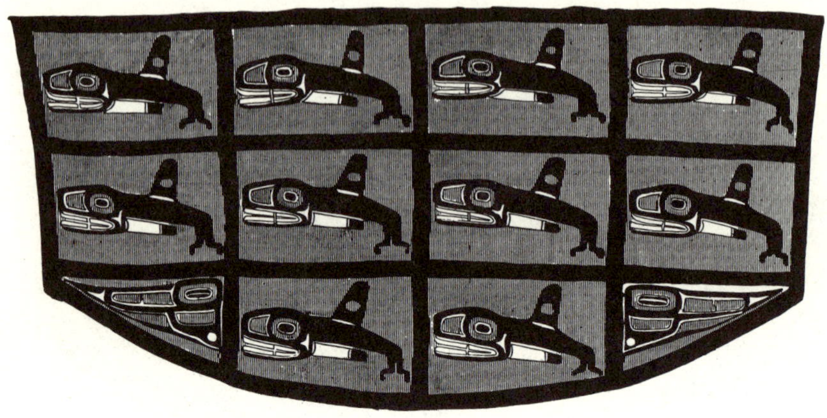

a

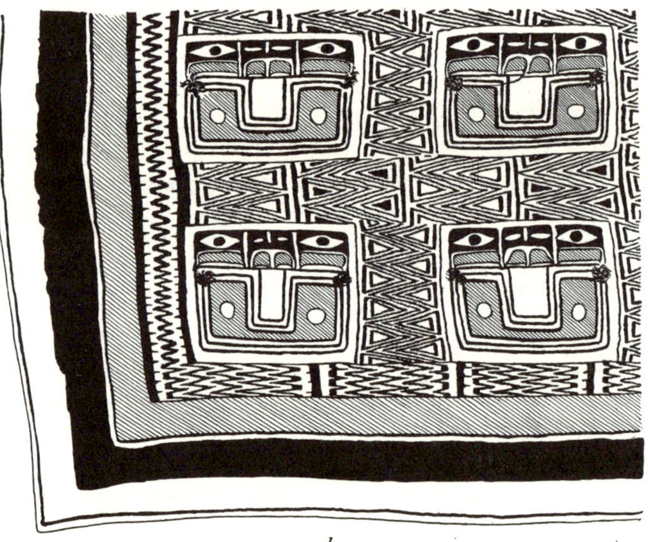

b

FIG. 36. Blanket.

a. The design represents a school of killer whales. (Field Museum of Natural History, cat. no. 19571.)

b. Part of shirt with face designs. (Museum of the Geological Survey of Canada.)

ventionalization exists, but that rather the design is inferred in accordance with the position of the various parts of the body and certain symbolic traits. These, however, are often ambiguous. It is very characteristic, for instance, that the very distinct figure shown in Fig. 3 should be explained to Lieutenant Emmons as an osprey, to Dr. Swanton as a beaver. The reason for this discrepancy is quite obvious. The informant of Lieutenant Emmons had in mind particularly the typical front views of the eagle which are found on trays (see Figs. 9 and 10). One of the characteristic traits of the osprey is the hooked beak, which in front view—or, perhaps better, in the representation of the animal by two profiles in contact at the point of the beak—appears like a point separating the long mouth into two parts. In this beak the nostrils are marked. The animal shown in Fig. 3 may be considered in this manner. The two wing-feather designs which separate the wide mouth would in this case be considered as the beak with its nostrils. On the other hand, they may be considered as the large incisors of the beaver which are represented in the same manner, and in which the circular eye design is merely inserted for decorative purposes. The conception of this animal as the beaver would be helped by the curved black lines in the mouth, which are interpreted as tooth designs, which do not properly belong to the osprey. On the other hand, the absence of the forepaws would rather favor the conception of the whole form as a bird. Dr. Swanton's informant, however, did not see the connection of the shoulder joint under the corners of the jaw with the wings, and for this reason interpreted this part as the stick which the beaver is gnawing.

The ambiguity of the explanation of Fig. 16 is also easily intelligible. The figure which was explained to Lieutenant Emmons as a female wolf, to Dr. Swanton as a raven, lacks all the traits which would definitely symbolize any particular animal; and the uncertainty due to this fact is expressed also by the statement made to Lieutenant Emmons, that the lower portion of the animal represents a hawk. The same vagueness is brought out in the two explanations of Fig. 18*a* given to Lieutenant Emmons, and to the entirely different one given to Dr. Swanton. In these cases the essential cause of ambiguity lies in the selection of the various eye designs, all of which are of a size equal to the principal head of the figure represented. When the two upper eye designs are taken as the principal head, the whole design may be looked at as one certain kind of an animal. If the middle or lower eye designs are taken as the principal head, an entirely different animal results. Another characteristic discrepancy in explanation is that of Fig. 22, which was explained to Lieutenant Emmons as a whale diving, while Dr. Swanton was told that it was intended to represent a wolf.

While we have seen that most of the old designs may be classed in two principal styles, and that the number of old designs is very small, attention should be called to the fact that a few independent types seem to belong to the oldest specimens of woven blanket designs with which we are familiar. For instance, Fig. 35 represents

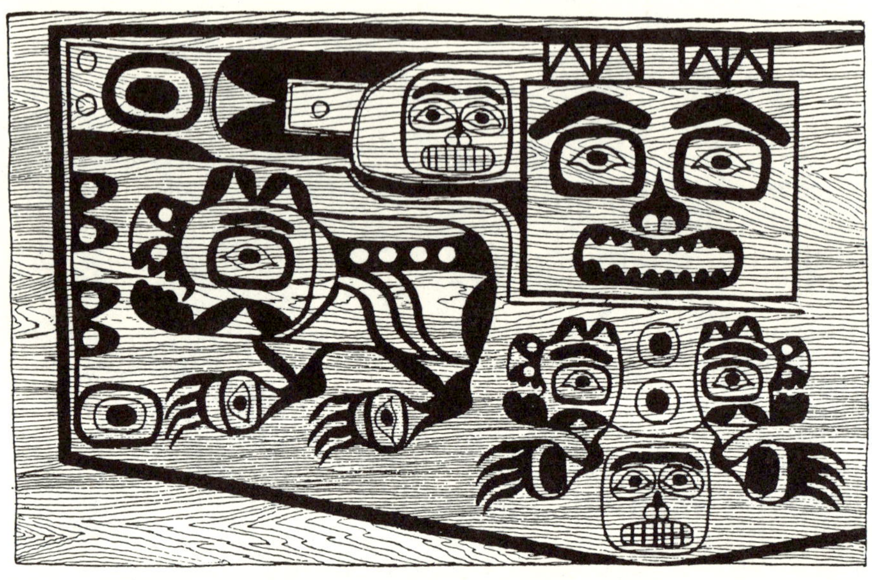

FIG. 37. Pattern board for blanket. The design represents a young brown bear below, in the middle; on each side, an old female brown bear. The face above, in the middle, with adjoining designs, is interpreted as the bear's den.

a blanket which, according to Lieutenant Emmons, was at one time the property of Chartrich, chief of the Qagontan family and the principal chief of the Chilkat tribe. Lieutenant Emmons states that this was the first blanket ever woven by the Chilkat people, and that it was copied from the original blanket obtained from the Tsimshian more than a century and a half ago. The peculiar blanket shown in Fig. 36*a*, which is also quite different in type from all the others, was collected by me, through Mrs. Morison, among the Tsimshian Indians. It might seem, therefore, that the old styles of blankets, which differ from the ordinary two types, were perhaps originally Tsimshian patterns, and that the development of the peculiar Chilkat types took place after the introduction of the blanket industry among the Tlingit.

In more modern blankets the indefiniteness of the old conventionalism is breaking down entirely. The pattern board Fig. 37, for instance, reminds us only very slightly of the typical blanket designs. The small animals figured in the middle near the lower edge are like the tattooed designs of the Haida.[4] The large bear on each

4. See Swanton, "Contributions to the Ethnology of the Haida" (*Publications of the Jesup North Pacific Expedition*, vol. 5, plate XX, nos. 13, 14); and F. Boas, "Decorative Art of the Indians of the North Pacific Coast" (*Bulletin of the American Museum of Natural History*, 1897:151). [This volume, chapter 4]

side is analogous to the slightly conventionalized paintings of the Northwest Coast Indians, while the upper border may be compared to the apron borders, Figs. 42 and 43, which will be described later on.

In some of the blankets there is a peculiar adherence to the old style, while the breaking-up of the conventionalization takes place only in parts of the blanket. For instance, the blanket Fig. 38*a* belongs undoubtedly to the first type of Chilkat blankets. The central figure may still be readily recognized, and the position of the eyes in the lateral fields remains the same as that previously described. Instead of the body of the central animal, we have, however, the same realistic representation of a double killer whale with adjoining flukes, probably a killer whale cut in two lengthwise, which breaks into the blanket design, making it impossible to connect the rest of the designs in any way with these small representations of animals. It may perhaps be justifiable to compare the use of these small animal forms on the large conventionalized face with the small animal carvings of northern Tlingit tribes, which they are in the habit of attaching to their masks. While it is impossible to say that the idea expressed in this case and expressed in the mask is the same, the similarity of these two processes seems striking. The breaking-up of the first design has proceeded even farther in the blanket shown in Fig. 38*b*. Here practically the whole central field is broken up, with the exception of the two lower eyes. The whole upper portion is occupied by semirealistic representations of killer whales. It is noticeable that the upper part of the lateral field of this specimen agrees in all details with the corresponding portion of Fig. 38*a*. In the design shown in Fig. 39 all the elements of the old blanket design have disappeared, and we have simply a painting such as is found frequently on modern housefronts and planks. It is peculiar to note that even these blankets have their pattern boards (Fig. 39*a*), which shows that the designs as applied by the women are never more than an accurate copy of men's paintings.

Lieutenant Emmons has called attention to the tendency of Tlingit carvings to be more realistic than those of the Haida and Tsimshian. I quite agree with him in the opinion that many of the carvings of the Tlingit, like their bird rattles and the masks with attached animals and helmets, have a tendency to be realistic in form. There is also quite a large number of paintings on leather that have a fairly strong realism, although their style conforms strictly to the characteristic style of the Northwest Coast art. I think the preceding discussion shows clearly, however, that the realistic forms of the blankets shown on the last few pages cannot be considered as more typically Tlingit in character than the strictly conventional blankets discussed on the earlier pages. The persistency with which characteristic features of the conventional types reappear in these more realistic blankets seems to me satisfactory proof of the theory that all the more realistic blankets that conform in their

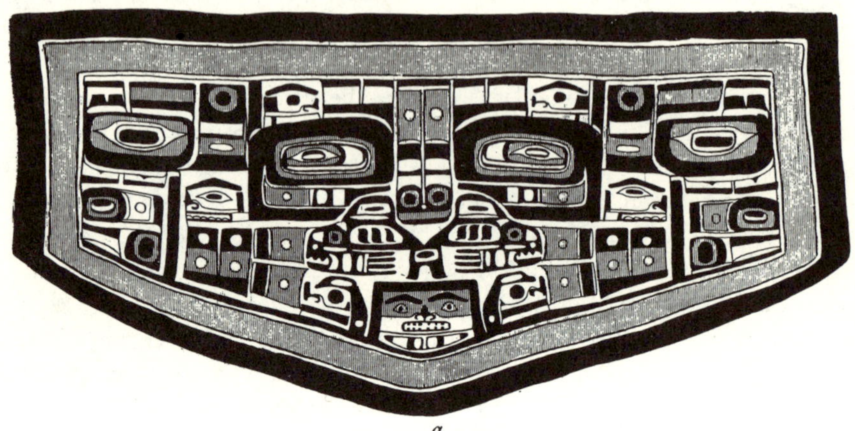

a

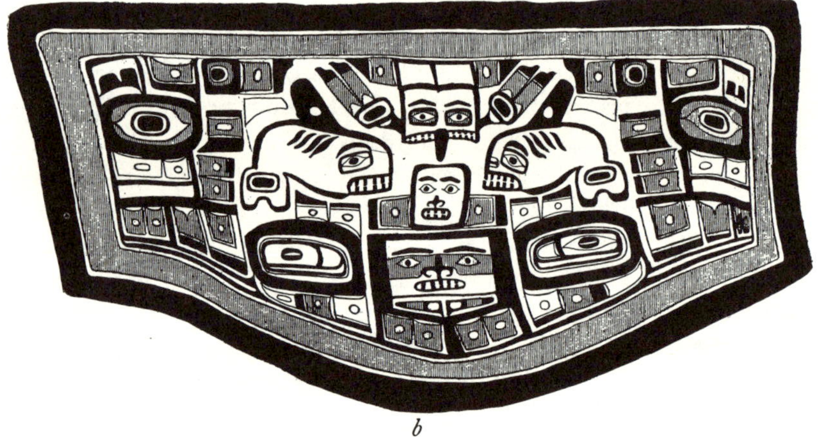

b

FIG. 38. Blankets.

a. The design represents, in the lower portion of the middle field, two killer whales catching two hair seals (represented by the profile faces under the whales). The human face separating these two seals is interpreted as a rock in the ocean on which the seals bask. The large head on top, in the middle, is that of a raven, while no particular explanation is given for the rest of the design.

b. From Klukwan, the design representing two killer whales. The rest of the design is said to be purely ornamental.

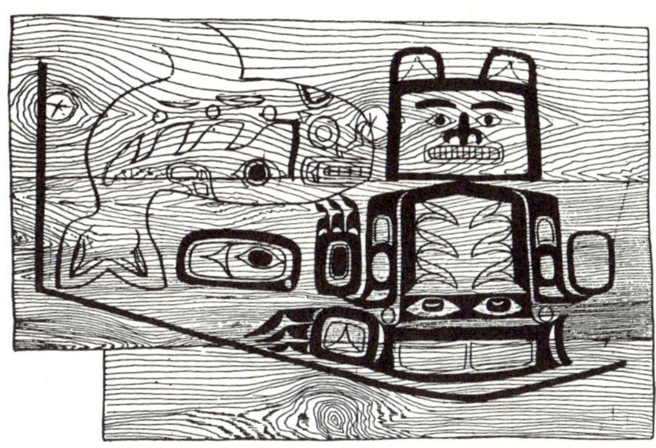

a

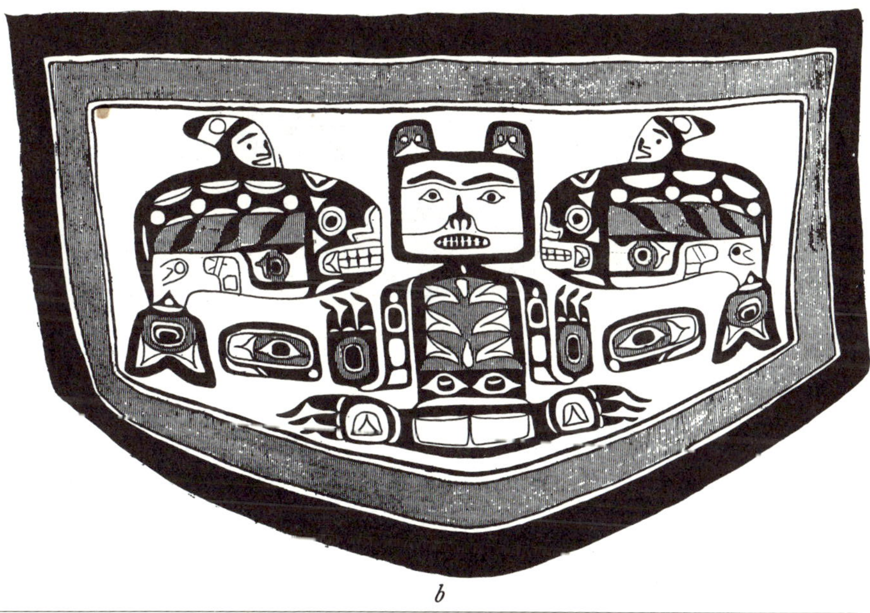

b

FIG. 39. Blanket and pattern board from Klukwan, representing a bear and two killer whales.

general plan to the conventional blanket designs originated later, when the conventional type began to lose its hold upon the minds of the people.

In Figs. 40–43 a number of dancing aprons are represented which are woven in the same technique as the dancing blankets. A characteristic feature of many of these aprons is that the design is put on so that it is upside down when the apron is

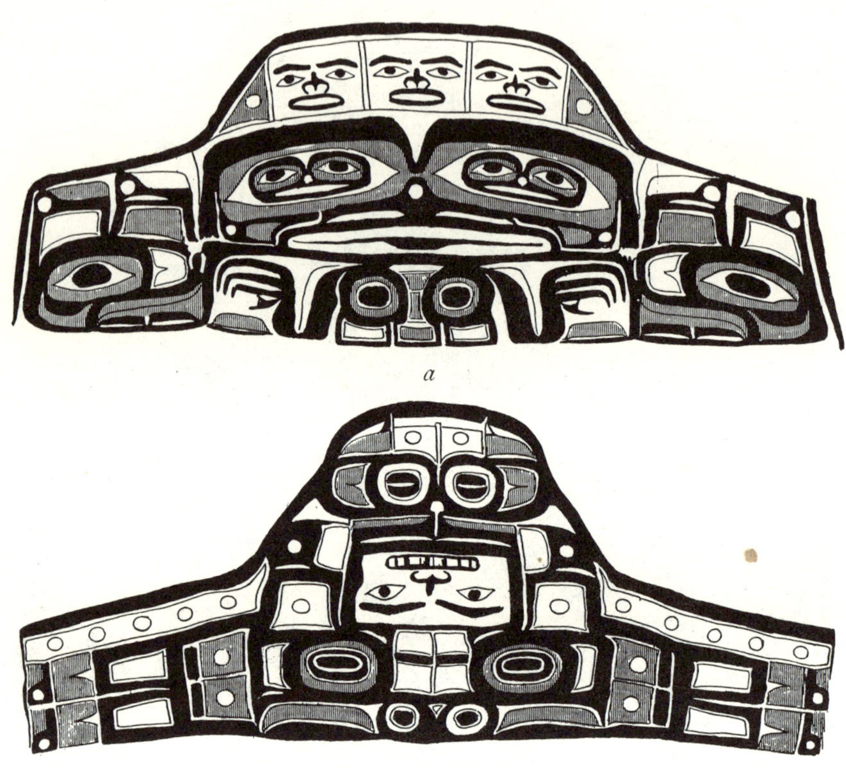

FIG. 40. Dancing aprons (inverted).

a (16/348). Width, 99 cm. According to Emmons, the design represents Gonaqadē't rising out of the sea, and is so applied that when the apron is worn, the head of the animal turns downward. The center of the apron is occupied by the large head with protruding tongue, under which are the arms and the shoulder joints. The three small designs near the lower border represent the body. In each lateral field is shown one-half of the beak, the two wing designs on the top representing the double dorsal fin. Over the head of the central figure are three human heads.

According to Swanton, the explanation is the same, except that the lateral fields are interpreted as the inner part of the body, showing two ribs above. The human faces are interpreted as small people who surround Gonaqadē't.

b. The design represents two profile views of killer whales, which meet in the middle line of the apron. The design is again shown inverted, as in Fig. 40*a*. That portion under the inverted human face in the middle, and extending on either side to the end of the middle field, is the head of the killer whale; the part extending outward from here to the border of the apron, the side fin; while the dorsal fin is indicated by the portion between the outer edge of the blanket and the inverted face in the middle. The inverted face represents the lower side of the body, while the tail is shown in the narrow field on top. (Field Museum of Natural History.)

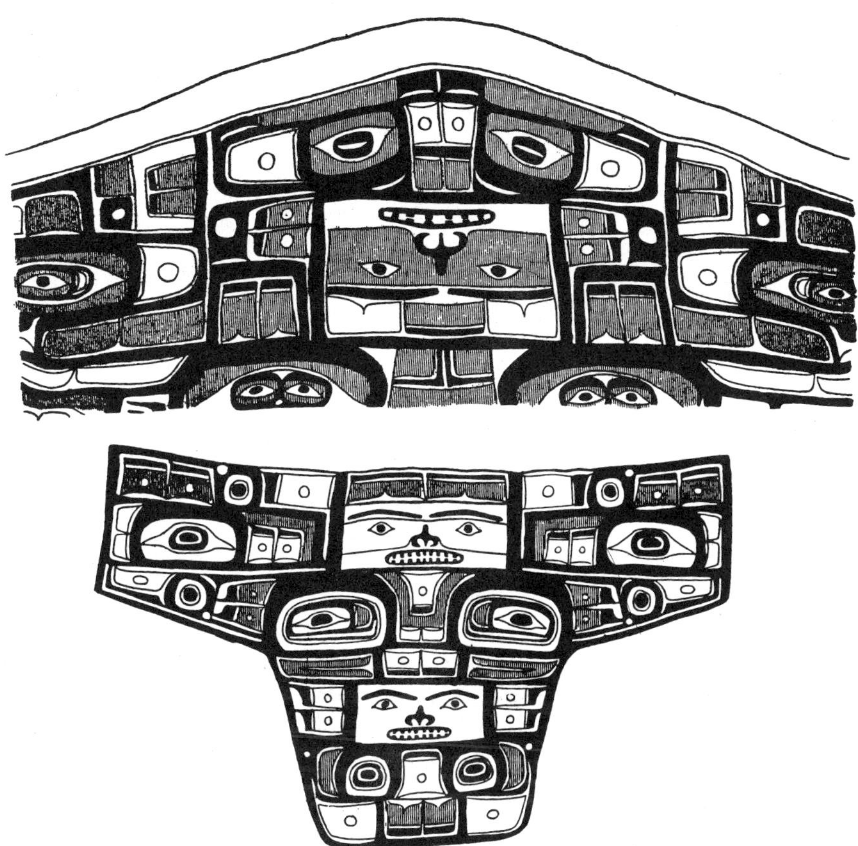

FIG. 41. Dancing apron (inverted). Width, 107 cm. (Museum of Natural History.)

According to Emmons, the design represents a killer whale. It is here also placed on the blanket in an inverted position. The half eyes on the lower border of the illustration represent the eyes of the killer whale. Over them rises the side fin, and over this, on each side, is one-half of the dorsal fin. The inverted face in the middle represents the under side of the body; and the inverted eyes on top, the fluke of the tail. The lateral fields are each one-half of the body of the whale.

According to Swanton, the half eyes have the same interpretation. The portion outside of the eyes, along the lower edge of the illustration, is the mouth. The double feather design over the eyes is interpreted as the blowhole; the inverted eyes at the upper border of the illustration, as the tail. The double feather design between these eyes is interpreted as the dorsal fin, while the side fins are between the blowhole and the tail. The large eye design in the lateral field is interpreted as the inner parts of the body.

FIG. 42. Dancing apron. From Klukwan.

The design represents a raven; the two large eyes in the middle, and the whole portion of the design underneath, being the raven's head; the two eye designs near the lower part of the design, the nostrils; the human face on top, the tail; the field on each side of the tail, the wing, which represents at the same time a raven's head in profile. Under the wings are the feet of the raven.

worn. A consideration of the designs shows that the woven blanket is a modification of the older painted skin apron, in which the conventionalism of the blanket design has been used to modify the old and more realistic painted designs.

I am inclined to believe that in this case the probability is in favor of the assumption that the aprons which resemble the style of the blankets most are not older forms, but are due to the strong influence of the whole group of ornamental ideas connected with the blanket technique, which were applied to the apron design. My principal reason for this opinion is the lack of fixity of design in the most conventionalized forms of woven aprons, and the comparatively great frequency of excellent old pieces which are highly realistic. The inverted position of the conventional design in the woven apron is evidently borrowed from the manner of painting the skin aprons.

The woven aprons shown in Figs. 43 and 44 resemble in their general style more closely the painted aprons, while the specimens Figs. 40–42 resemble in many respects the blanket designs, particularly in that the more decorative field is filled in with wing designs and the like, wherever an open space remains. Among the conventional apron designs, Fig. 40 shows a strong resemblance to the painted carved box designs, although in other respects features of the blankets may also be recognized in this specimen. The flatness of the mouth and the three small heads over the forehead belong to the features which it has in common with the blankets. The manner in which the middle field is set off from the two lateral fields is also evidently due to the influence of the blanket design. In the apron shown in Fig. 40*b*, the middle field is also laid out somewhat like the blankets of the second type, although in detail it resembles much more strongly the arrangements of eye and body designs which are interpreted as the sculpin or other fish, and which are used as dancing leggings;[5] but the treatment of the details, particularly the arrangement of white circles and of wing designs, conforms to features of the Chilkat blanket. Special attention may be called to the similarity of Fig. 41 and of the blanket design Fig. 33, on the one hand, and the second type of blanket designs on the other. The double eye on top and the peculiar form of the eye design below, as well as the arrangement of the lateral field, are very much like Fig. 33, while the central face, in its relative position to the surrounding eye designs, agrees with the forms found in the second type. The apron shown in Fig. 42 is also highly conventionalized, but differs from the others in that the figure is upright; and no very close relation between the apron design and the blanket design can be traced, except in the elements and composition of the smaller parts of the whole design.

The two realistic designs shown in Fig. 43 are very closely related. Both represent

5. See Boas, "Decorative Art of the Indians of the North Pacific Coast" (Bulletin), fig. 50, p. 152. [This volume, chapter 4]

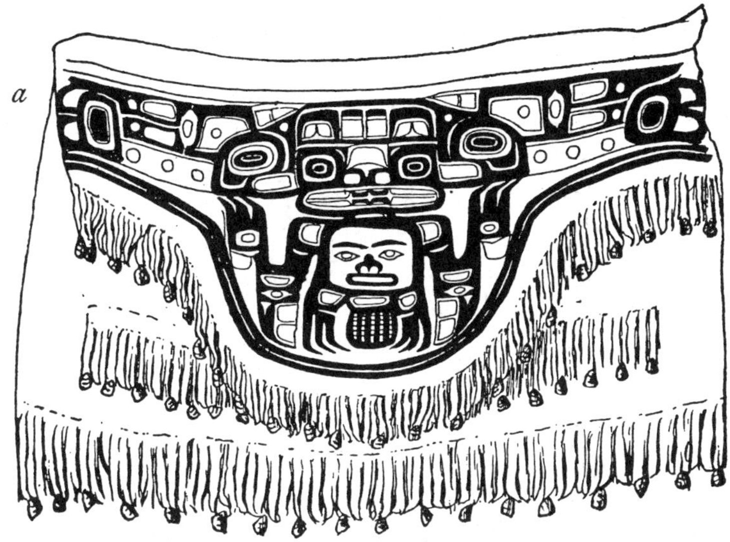

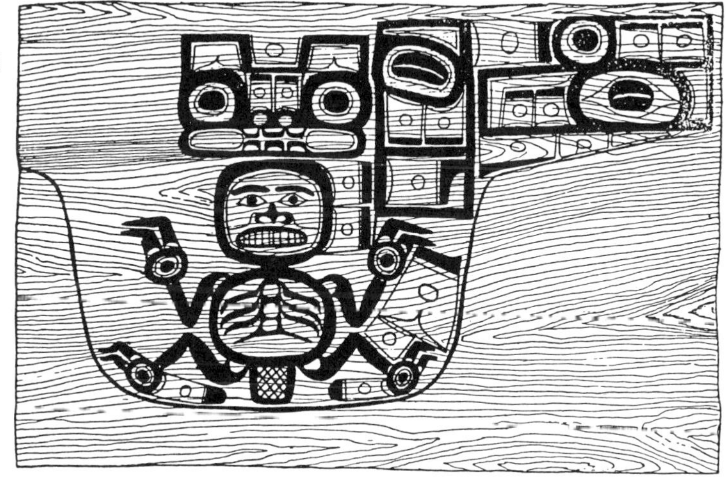

FIG. 43. Dancing apron and pattern.

a (16/349). Width, 93 cm. According to Emmons, the design represents a beaver sitting up. The eye ornament on each side of the beaver's head represents the beaver's house; the lateral extension of this ornament, the beaver dam and water.

According to Swanton, the eye ornament next to the head, and the adjoining leather ornaments, represent the trees that are the beaver's food, while the eye ornaments at each end of the upper edge represent its house.

b. The design represents a beaver sitting up. At each side of the beaver's head are the beaver's house and the beaver dam.

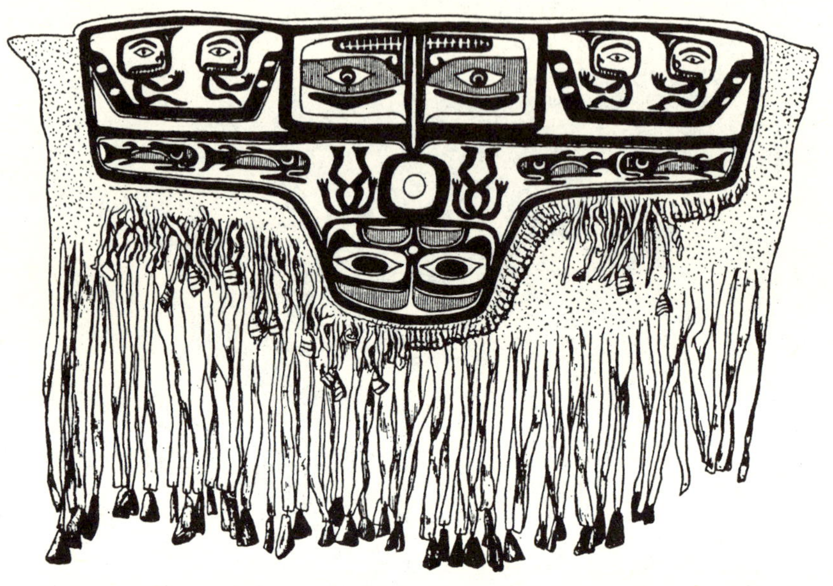

FIG. 44 (E/2602). Dancing apron.

the beaver, and in both cases the outer borders are treated somewhat apart from the middle portion of the design. It is curious to note that in the pattern board the body of the beaver is represented as a man with head and body, while, according to the analogy in all other similar cases, the human face would be expected to represent the body of the beaver. While in the pattern board the lateral fields are set off sharply from the middle field, this is not the case in the woven apron. I have indicated before that the designs stretching along the upper border outward are not a feature that belongs to the blanket alone; but these may be compared also to the position of similar designs on painted boxes and on painted borders of blankets.[6] The closest resemblance between woven and painted designs may be seen in the apron shown in Fig. 44, which in all its details resembles the painted skin aprons. The realistic manner in which the two pairs of fishes are shown, the manner of representing the men in their canoes in the right- and left-hand upper corners, and the peculiar position and form of the face in the lower part of the middle, with the two small bodies under it, are characteristic of painted designs of the Tlingit.

The same type of blanket design is also used on a number of shirts, one of which

6. See Boas, "Decorative Art of the Indians of the North Pacific Coast" (Bulletin), fig. 71, p. 168. [This volume, chapter 4]

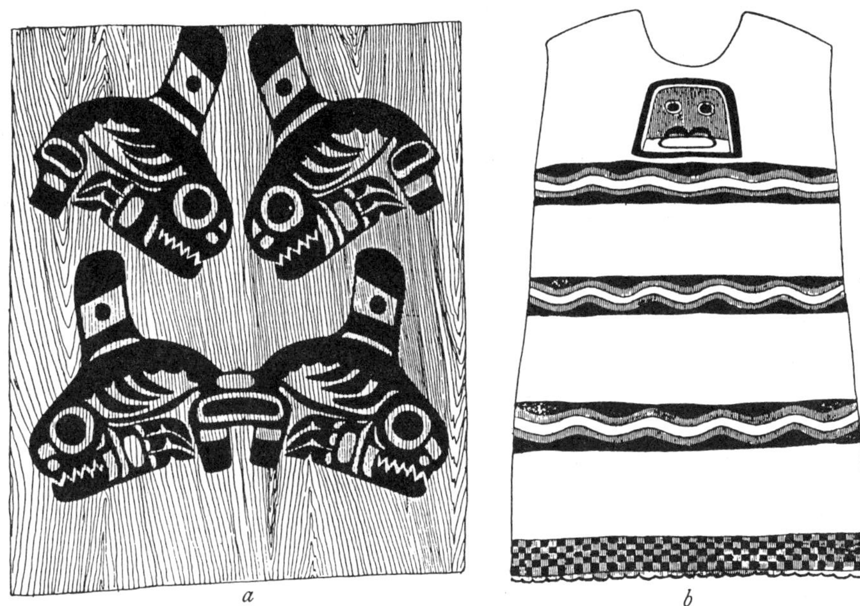

FIG. 45. Pattern board for dancing shirt and back of dancing shirt.
a. From Klukwan. The design represents killer whales.
b (19/1048). According to Emmons, the face on the back represents a shark's head.
According to Swanton, the zigzag lines on the back of the shirt are called the spinal column. The face on the back is interpreted as Gonaqadē't's face.

is represented in Fig. 46. Owing to the difference in shape of the decorative field, the details of arrangement of the figures differ considerably from those found in the blankets, but the sameness of general principle will readily be recognized. According to Lieutenant Emmons, the shirt made in this weave and decorated in this manner is, comparatively speaking, a new invention. It has evidently not flourished for a long time, for modern shirts are degenerating even more than the blanket designs, and realistic forms are quite commonly found on them. A pattern board for a shirt is shown in Fig. 45.

The same kind of weave is also used for making leggings, and the same style of conventionalism prevails in these specimens (Fig. 47).

The following observations on the colors of the blankets are based only on the specimens preserved in the American Museum of Natural History. In the photographs from which most of the illustrations have been drawn, the distinction between white, yellow, and blue is often not clear, which is largely due to the fact that

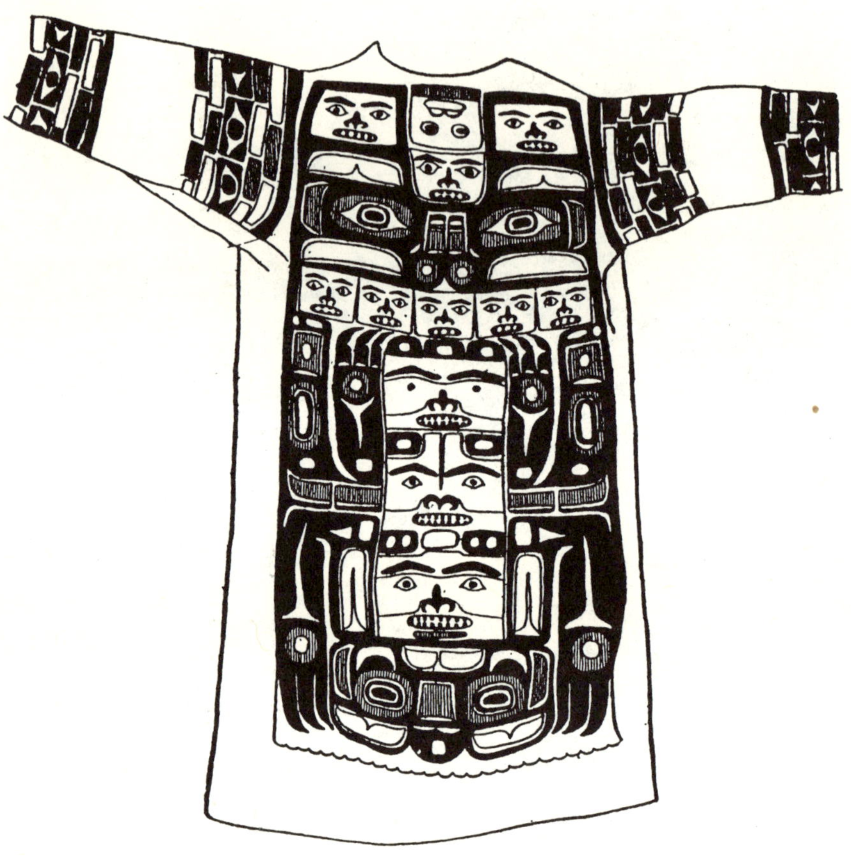

FIG. 46. The design represents a brown bear, its face being shown on top; the two human faces near the neck representing the ears of the bear; the row of five human faces across the shirt front, the mouth of the bear; the series of three faces under the mouth, the body of the bear, at the side of which the forelegs are shown turned upward, while the hind legs are turned downward, the eyes under the lower face being the hip joints of the bear. At the same time the whole lower portion of the shirtfront is interpreted as the frog; the hip joints of the bear being the head of the frog, the body of the bear being the back of the frog, and legs of the bear being at the same time the legs of the frog.

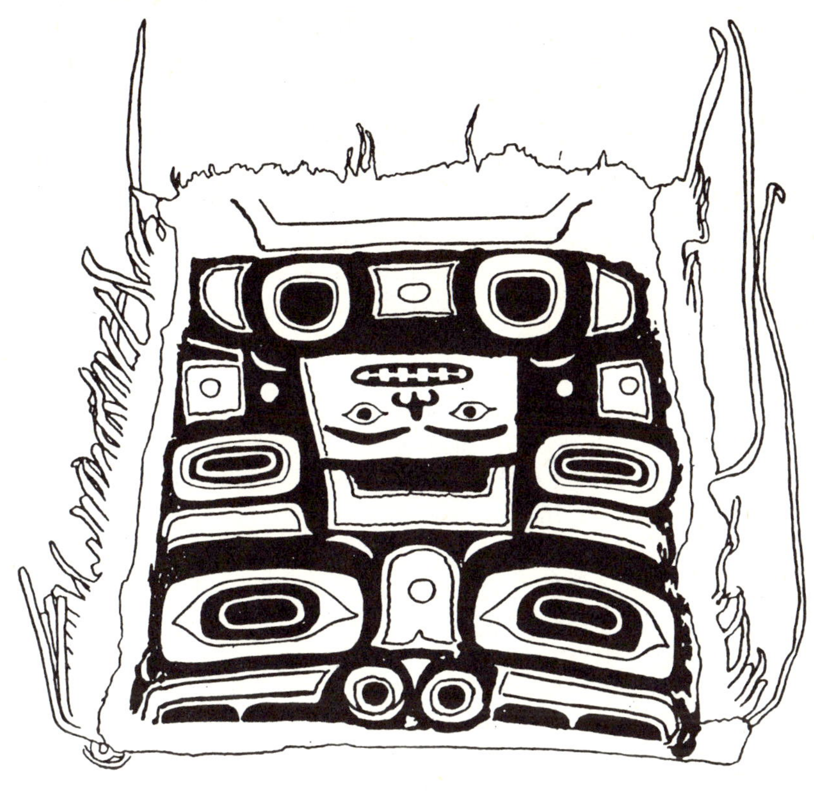

FIG. 47. Dancing legging (inverted). Field Museum of Natural History.

According to Emmons, the design represents a whale. In the illustration the head is shown below. The inverted human face represents the back; the eye designs with adjoining feather designs on each side are the fins; and the two eyes near the upper border, the tail.

in older blankets these three colors tend to become a brownish yellow, and are difficult to distinguish. Most of the blankets contain, besides black and white, yellow and blue, but a few are woven only in white, black, and yellow. As Lieutenant Emmons has remarked, red is rare, and seems to be used only in more recent blankets. Lieutenant Emmons has stated before that white must be considered as the background of the blanket design, and that the outer border is always black and yellow.

The pupil and the white of the eye are always white. When the eye is framed by a black border, forming an oval, the inner portion around the white of the eye is always filled in in yellow. When the eye is elaborated so that there is a small semicircular design at the inner corner of the eye, this is done in blue. In one case (Fig.

26) this semicircular design is developed into a wing design, which is yellow at the base and blue at the tip. In other cases, where the semicircular design is larger, being developed into a wing design or beak design, these are generally yellow. In many cases, wing designs are enclosed in rectangular framework, which occurs with particular frequency in the middle part of the lateral fields, as in Figs. 1*a*, 16*a*, and 22, but also in other positions, as in the ears in Figs. 16*a* and 3*b*, also setting off the profile beak in the lateral field of Figs. 3*b* and 1*b*, surrounding the goggle design in Fig. 16*a*, and in various places surrounding wing designs, as in Fig. 35 and under the human faces in Fig. 16*a*. All these are done in blue, while the inner field is yellow. There are a few exceptions in which the frame appears yellow, while the wing design in the frame is done in blue, as in the lateral fields of Fig. 26, where perhaps the contrast with the adjoining blue rectangular frame has led to the peculiar arrangements of colors. This inversion, however, has not taken place in the similar juxtaposition of wing designs of rectangular frames in the lateral field of Fig. 22. A similar contrast may have led to the adoption of a yellow square frame in the middle of the upper border of Fig. 16*a* and in the middle of the lateral borders of Fig. 1*a*.

The circles in all the wing designs are done in white.

Almost without exception, the color design representing the mouth and the ear of any head is done in blue. This accounts often for the occurrence of blue designs over and under inverted eyes, which must be interpreted as mouths and ears.

In almost all blankets there is a tendency to color the wing designs in the extreme upper and lower corners blue. Exceptions may be observed in the lower corners of Fig. 1*b* and in all the corners of Fig. 16*a*. In this latter specimen there are so many exceptional traits that it seems justifiable to consider it as a new and inferior product. Apparently in the better specimen of the same type (Fig. 16*b*) the corners were blue. Since, however, this specimen was drawn from a photograph, the colors cannot be determined with certainty.

Many of the human faces have the part around the eyes colored. This coloring is always done in yellow, except in Fig. 34 where it is blue. The forehead designs of these faces, when colored, are either yellow or blue, or, if consisting of three parts, blue in the middle and yellow at the sides, or vice versa.

I have observed only one case in which blue is apparently used for filling in a background. This is in the wing designs of the lower middle part of Fig. 35, and in the left and right hand upper corner of Fig. 48. The jaw slits and the round spots in the jaw design are always white. Wherever a yellow, blue, and white field adjoin, the outlines are marked by a narrow black line. Yellow and blue fields are generally set off from adjoining black fields by a narrow white strip, from which the yellow or blue is again divided by a narrow black band. Exceptions to this rule are the yellow fields in eyes and some of the blue rectangular frames surrounding wing designs. The intervening black and white occur regularly in wing designs.

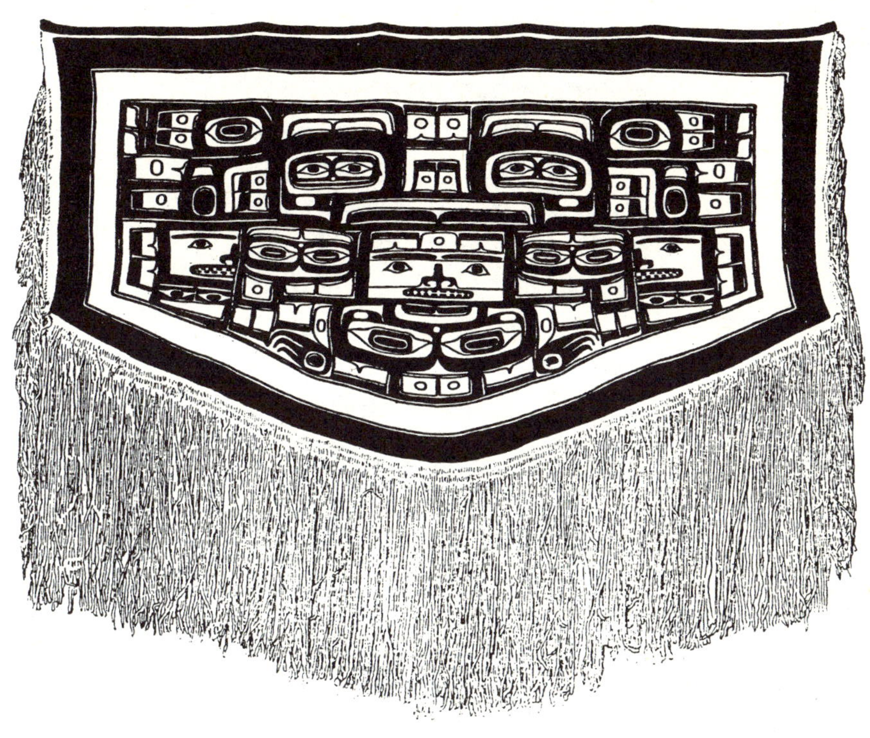

FIG. 48. Chilkat blanket. The design represents a bird. The two double eyes in the middle, near the upper border, are the eyes of the bird; the human face in the middle is the body; the two inverted eyes in the middle at the bottom are the hip joints, to which are joined the thighs and feet; the two inverted double eyes at the sides of the body with adjoining wing designs are the wings of the bird; the tail seems to be represented by the eye design with adjoining wing designs in the upper corners; under these an elaboration of the bird's wings is shown; the human faces in profile near the lower corners are analogous to the human faces in similar position occurring in the lateral fields of other blankets.

The same color scheme may be observed on the woven shirt shown on Fig. 49. On the whole, the wing designs are treated in yellow, while the semicircular spaces in the eyes, ears, and rectangular frames of wing designs are all done in blue. The lower human face, around the eyes, is also blue.

EDITOR'S NOTE

All the illustrations and explanations in the preceding paper, unless otherwise stated, have been collected by Lieutenant G. T. Emmons, who obtained the ma-

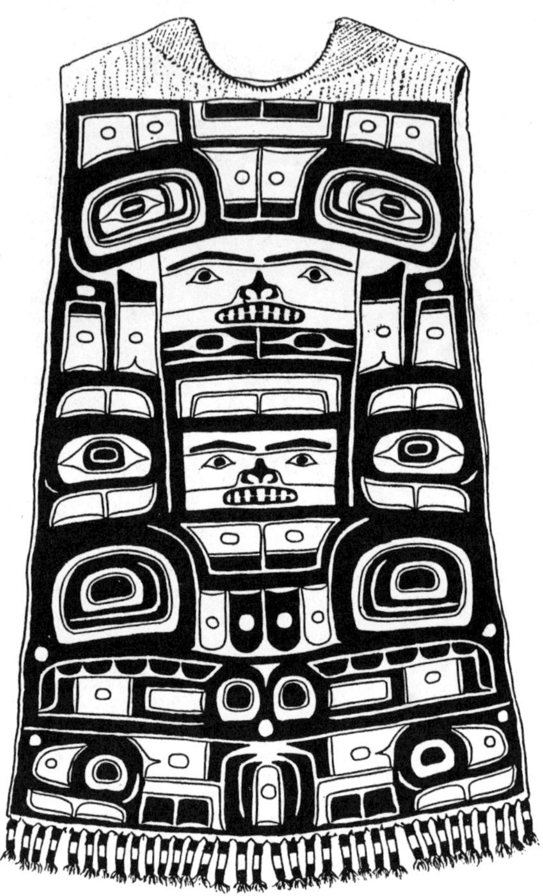

FIG. 49 (19/1048). Dancing shirt. According to Emmons, the design represents a killer whale. Its head is shown by the two large eye ornaments in the lower part of the blanket, under which the mouth with its teeth extends right across the front of the shirt, the nostrils being in the middle of the mouth; the blowhole, by the human face in the middle of the shirtfront, over the eyes; water spouted out from the blowhole, by the feather designs under this face; the body, by the face above the central human face. At each side of the blowhole is one eye representing the joint of the side fin, which extends upward along the sides as a feather ornament. The feather ornament between the side fin and the upper face (the body) represents one-half of the dorsal fin. The two eyes on top are the tail of the whale. Under the mouth of the killer whale two young kites are shown in profile, the head turned outward, the tail turned down under the body, and represented by two black tooth designs just behind the mouth. The single rounded feather design in the center, between the two tails, is the dorsal fin.

According to Swanton, the shirtfront represents Gonaqadē't; the design under the mouth being interpreted as the forelegs; the clawlike designs in the middle being the forefeet. The two human faces with adjoining designs are interpreted as the belly; the designs on the sides of this, as the side fins; the two eyes and adjoining designs on top, as the hind legs. The monster is here shown swimming.

terial through the courtesy of the several museums noted, or from original photographs taken in Alaska during the past twenty years. It seems desirable to express here appreciation of the valuable services rendered by Lieutenant Emmons in collecting photographs of all the accessible blankets, whether in the possession of museums or in that of Indians. Particularly interesting is also the collection of photographs of pattern boards, almost all of which are the property of the Chilkat weavers. The patient collection of information and interpretation among the natives, such as is presented in Lieutenant Emmons's memoir on the basketry designs of Alaska and in the present memoir, will be highly valued by all ethnologists.

Franz Boas

10. Decorative Designs of Alaskan Needlecases: A Study in the History of Conventional Designs, Based on Materials in the U.S. National Museum

This detailed analysis of the style of Alaskan needlecases, which range from naturalistic to quite abstract, proves to Boas that sequences arranged according to similarities prove nothing about the artwork's history; the series could have begun in a realistic mode and ended in a conventional one or begun in a conventional mode and ended realistically. He suggests that the imagination of the artist and the pleasure in the artistic process play significant roles in the creation of an artwork.

In 1877, Professor F. W. Putnam [1886] described in detail the decorative designs found in the pottery of the Chiriqui Indians, and was the first, I believe, to propound clearly the theory that conventional designs develop from attempts at realistic representations, which gradually degenerate so that ultimately a purely conventional design remains, in which the realistic origin can hardly be recognized. Since that time this theory has been independently stated by a number of investigators, particularly by H. Stolpe [1892:19 ff.] and H. Balfour [1893]. It has been applied extensively to explanations of primitive designs. The most noteworthy contributions on this subject are those by Karl von den Steinen [1894:258 ff.], on the art of the Brazilian Indians, and by A. C. Haddon [1895], on the art of the natives of New Guinea.

Opposed to this view has been the theory propounded by Semper, who emphasizes the influence of material upon the development of the design, and that proposed by Cushing [1886] and Holmes [1888:223], who emphasize the importance of technique upon the development of geometrical design. More recently Karl von den Steinen [1905] has also emphasized the importance of technical conditions upon the development of design, and his arguments have been followed and elaborated by Max Schmidt in discussions of South American designs. Th. Koch [1906] follows the same line of argument, showing that at least in Brazil a considerable number of cases may be found in which designs that have developed from technical motives receive a realistic significance.

Reprinted from *Proceedings of the U.S. National Museum*, vol. 39, pp. 321–44, 1908.

From a wider point of view, the secondary development of motives and their reinterpretation as realistic designs have been claimed by Heinrich Schurtz [1900] and by Professor Hamlin [1898] in a discussion of the development of architectural decorative designs. The secondary character of symbolic interpretation has also been set forth by A. L. Kroeber [1901:329], Clark Wissler [1904:231 ff.], and by myself [1903:481 ff.].

We have therefore at the present time three distinct theories regarding the development of decorative design: First, the theory of the realistic origin of conventional motives; second, that of the technical origin of conventional motives; and, third, the theory that the explanations of conventional motives are essentially secondary in character, and due to a later association of the existing decorative forms with realistic forms.

I shall discuss in the following pages the decorative designs of Alaskan needlecases, largely from the region between the mouth of the Yukon River and the western part of Norton Sound, which seem to throw considerable light upon the history of decorative design, and illustrate the applicability of these various theories.

Among the carvings of Alaskan Eskimo we find a very large number of needlecases of peculiar form. They are of the characteristic tubular type of the Eskimo needlecase, in which the needle is inserted in a strip of skin pulled into a tube, which protects the needle against breakage. The peculiar type to which I here refer has, on the whole, a tube slightly bulging in the middle, and expanding into two wings or flanges at the upper end. It is characteristic of almost all these specimens that at a short distance below the flanges there are two small knobs on opposite sides of the tube. In some cases these are well marked, while in other cases they are so diminutive that they cannot be seen at all, although they can be felt when moving the finger gently over the surface of the tube. They must be considered as one of the characteristic features of this type, which is so well defined, and whose distribution is so restricted that there cannot be the slightest doubt as to the unity of its origin.

These needlecases have also a characteristic decoration. On the whole, there is a tendency to set off a slightly concave surface, which extends along the faces of the tube, between the flanges and farther down. This concave face may be observed on many of the needlecases shown in Figs. 1 and 2 (see Fig. 1, nos. 6, 7, 9, 10; Fig. 2, nos. 1–4, 6, 8, 9, 11, 12). The flanges and the upper border of the tube are generally decorated by a design consisting of a number of parallel lines, which is repeated near the lower end of the flanges, where the parallel lines almost always slope slightly downward toward the tube. Similar line designs are also found on the concave face of the tube. In many cases these lines meet the lower lines on the flanges at an angle, being incised so that they slope downward from the middle line of the tube outward (Fig. 1, nos. 1–6). In other cases they continue in the same direction as the lines on the flanges (Fig. 1, nos. 7, 8; Fig. 2, nos. 2–4, 6–12). Many of the needlecases

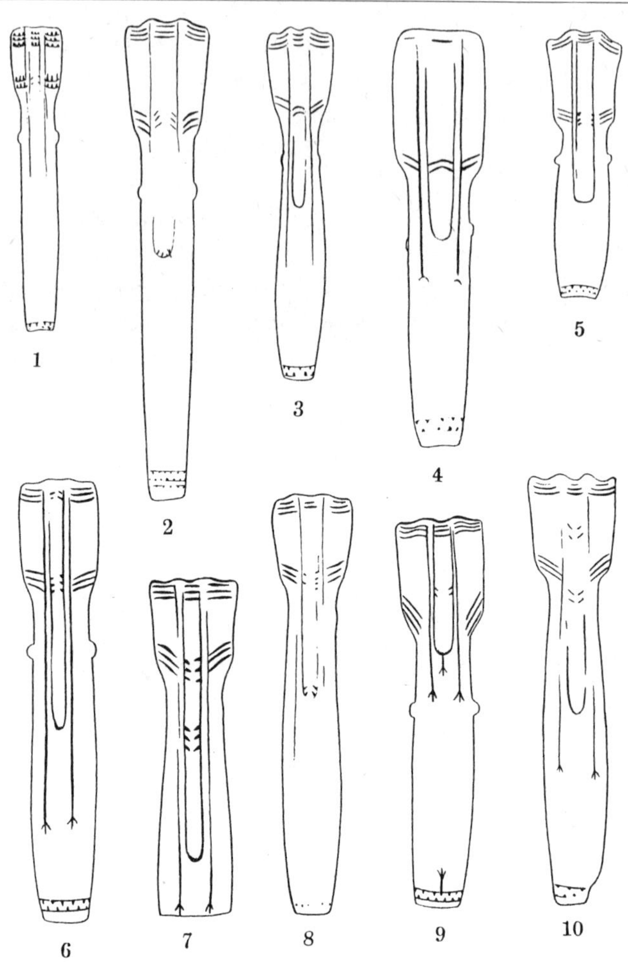

FIG. 1. Decorated Alaskan Needlecases

1. Ancient specimen from the mouth of the Yukon River, Alaska. Cat. no. 38758, USNM
2. From Razboinski, a village on the Lower Yukon River, Alaska. E. W. Nelson, collector. Cat. no. 48802, USNM
3. From Cape Darby, Norton Sound, Alaska. E. W. Nelson, collector. Cat. no. 44172, USNM
4. From Kwikpak, Lower Yukon River, Alaska. E. W. Nelson, collector. Cat. no. 38096, USNM
5. From St. Michael, Norton Sound, Alaska. Lucien M. Turner, collector. Cat. no. 24490, USNM
6. From Paimut, Kuskokwim River, Alaska. E. W. Nelson, collector. Cat. no. 38362, USNM
7. Upper part of a needlecase. From Mission, Lower Yukon River, Alaska. E. Q. Nelson, collector. Original no. 4249, USNM
8. From Razboinski, Lower Yukon River, Alaska. E. W. Nelson, collector. Cat. no. 48801, USNM
9. From St. Michael, Norton Sound, Alaska. E. W. Nelson, collector. Cat. no. 33700, USNM
10. From Pikmiktalik, a village south of St. Michael, Alaska. E. W. Nelson, collector. Cat. no. 33695, USNM

are so much polished and rubbed off by use that the design lines cannot be recognized distinctly. In other cases broken ends have been cut off (Fig. 1, no. 7), with the result that the characteristic decorative traits have become obscure. It would seem, however, that in all the better specimens of this simple type the central concave face of the needlecase is set off more definitely by two parallel incised lines, which extend downward to about the middle of the tubing, and which end at this place in two or three small spurs (Fig. 1, nos. 4, 6, 7, 9, 10; Fig. 2, nos. 2, 6, 8–12). The border design on the flanges is not continued over the space between the lines just referred to and the concave face of the tube. The parallel lines near the lower border of the flanges are also generally interrupted at this place. There is only a single specimen, among the simple needlecases, on which they run continuously (Fig. 2, no. 7).

Another characteristic decorative design of these needlecases is a narrow band extending around the lower end. This consists always, wherever it can be distinctly recognized, of two parallel lines with short alternating spurs directed toward the space between the two lines. Whenever these spurs are given a greater width this design assumes more or less the form of a zigzag band. A comparison of a considerable number of these designs shows clearly, however, that the primary idea is not the zigzag band, but rather the two lines with alternating spurs. This is best shown by the fact that in those cases where the lines are thin the alternation is often quite irregular. This may be observed, for instance, in the specimen shown in Fig. 1, no. 2. On the whole, however, an alternation is observed. Bands of this kind may be recognized clearly in Fig. 1, nos. 3–6, 9, 10; Fig. 2, nos. 6, 8–10. Sometimes the band at the lower end appears doubled, or elaborated by the addition of short vertical lines with short spurs at their ends (Fig. 1, no. 9; Fig. 2, nos. 11, 12; Fig. 3, nos. 1, 2; Fig. 4, nos. 2, 3, 5, 6). These lines are four in number, except in the last three cases. In the specimen shown in Fig. 4, no. 5, two of these lines are absent, because their space is occupied by a long alternate-spur band which runs down the whole side of the needlecase. In the specimen shown in Fig. 4, no. 6, one of them is absent, probably because the ivory at the place where it would be shows the soft inner part of the tusk, and has besides other defects. In Fig. 4, no. 3, there is one of these lines on each side of the needlecase. In one specimen in the Royal Ethnographical Museum in Berlin the number of these lines is more than four (Fig. 5).

A partial doubling of the spur band may be observed in Fig. 1, no. 2; Fig. 2, no. 11; Fig. 4, nos. 3, 5, 7.

The features here enumerated comprise those of the most generalized type of these needlecases. They may be briefly summed up as (1) a tube slightly bulging in the middle, (2) flanges at the upper end, (3) small knobs under the flanges, (4) a long concave face at the upper end of the tube, (5) long parallel lines with small forks at their lower ends setting off the concave face, (6) border designs consisting

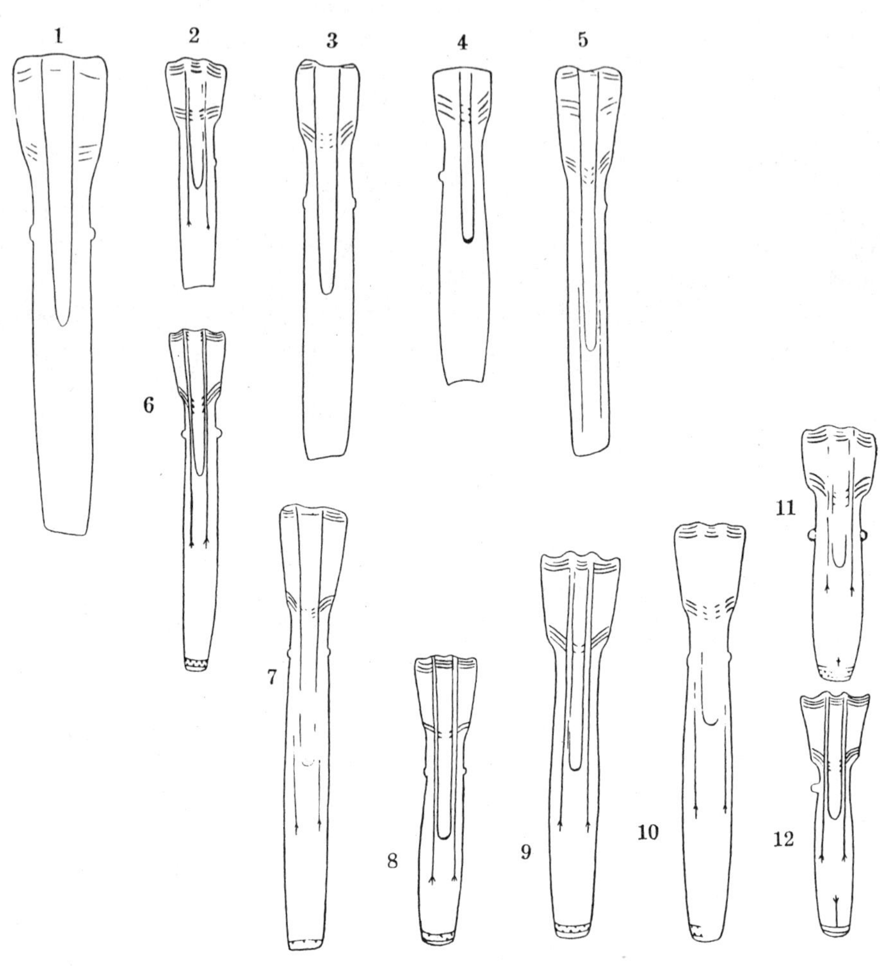

FIG. 2. Decorated Alaskan Needlecases

1. From Razboinski, Lower Yukon River, Alaska. E. W. Nelson, collector. Cat. no. 48806, USNM
2. From Razboinski, Lower Yukon River, Alaska. E. W. Nelson, collector. Cat. no. 48812, USNM
3. From St. Michael, Norton Sound, Alaska. E. W. Nelson, collector. Cat. no. 33694, USNM
4. From Sledge Island, west of Cape Nome, Alaska. E. W. Nelson, collector. Cat. no. 44744, USNM
5. From Razboinski, Lower Yukon River, Alaska. E. W. Nelson, collector. Cat. no. 48811, USNM
6. From St. Michael, Norton Sound, Alaska. Lucien M. Turner, collector. Cat. no. 24495, USNM
7. From St. Michael, Norton Sound, Alaska. Lucien M. Turner, collector. Cat. no. 24470, USNM
8. From Kaviag, near Port Clarence, Alaska. E. W. Nelson, collector. Cat. no. 33703, USNM
9. From St. Michael, Norton Sound, Alaska. Lucien M. Turner, collector. Cat. no. 24476, USNM
10. From St. Michael, Norton Sound, Alaska. Lucien M. Turner, collector. Cat. no. 24477, USNM
11. From Cape Nome, Norton Sound, Alaska. E. W. Nelson, collector. Cat. no. 176290, USNM
12. From Pikmiktalik, south of St. Michael, Alaska. E. W. Nelson, collector. Cat. no. 33702, USNM

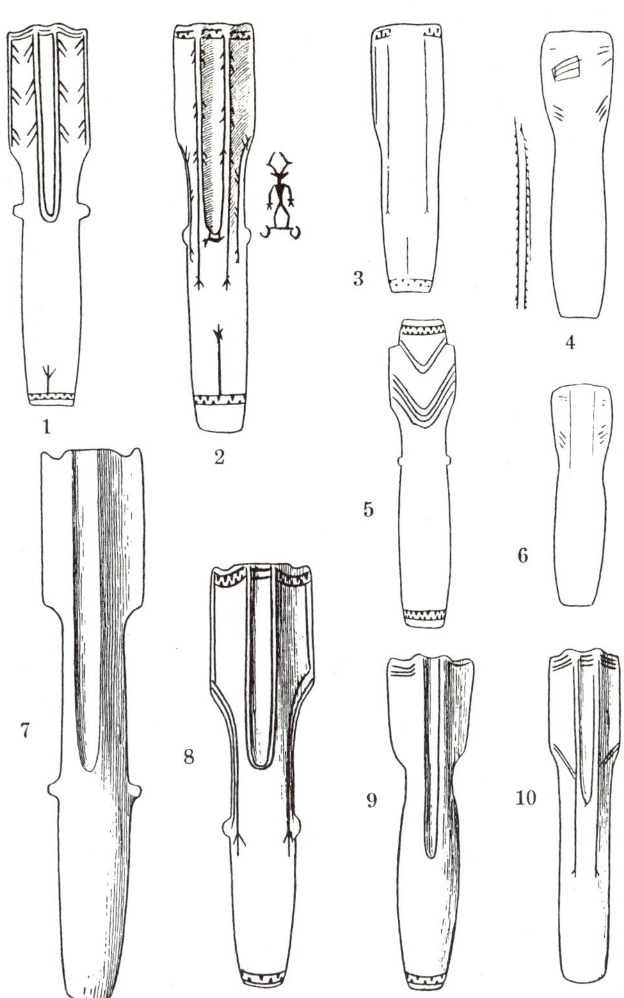

FIG. 3. Decorated Alaskan Needlecases

1. From Kwikpak, Lower Yukon River, Alaska. E. W. Nelson, collector. Original no. 3972, USNM
2. From Cape Darby, Norton Sound, Alaska. E. W. Nelson, collector. Cat. no. 44171, USNM
3. Western Alaska. J. Henry Turner, collector. Cat. no. 153830, USNM
4. From Kotzebue Sound, Alaska. E. W. Nelson, collector. Cat. no. 48569, USNM
5. From St. Michael, Norton Sound, Alaska. Lucien M. Turner, collector. Cat. no. 129293, USNM
6. From Kaviag, near Port Clarence, Alaska. E. W. Nelson, collector. Cat. no. 33693, USNM
7. From Kaviag, near Port Clarence, Alaska. E. W. Nelson, collector. Cat. no. 33697, USNM
8. From Kaviag, near Port Clarence, Alaska. E. W. Nelson, collector. Cat. no. 33699, USNM
9. From Cape Nome, Norton Sound, Alaska. E. W. Nelson, collector. Cat. no. 45338, USNM
10. From Cape Nome, Norton Sound, Alaska. E. W. Nelson, collector. Cat. no. 176289, USNM

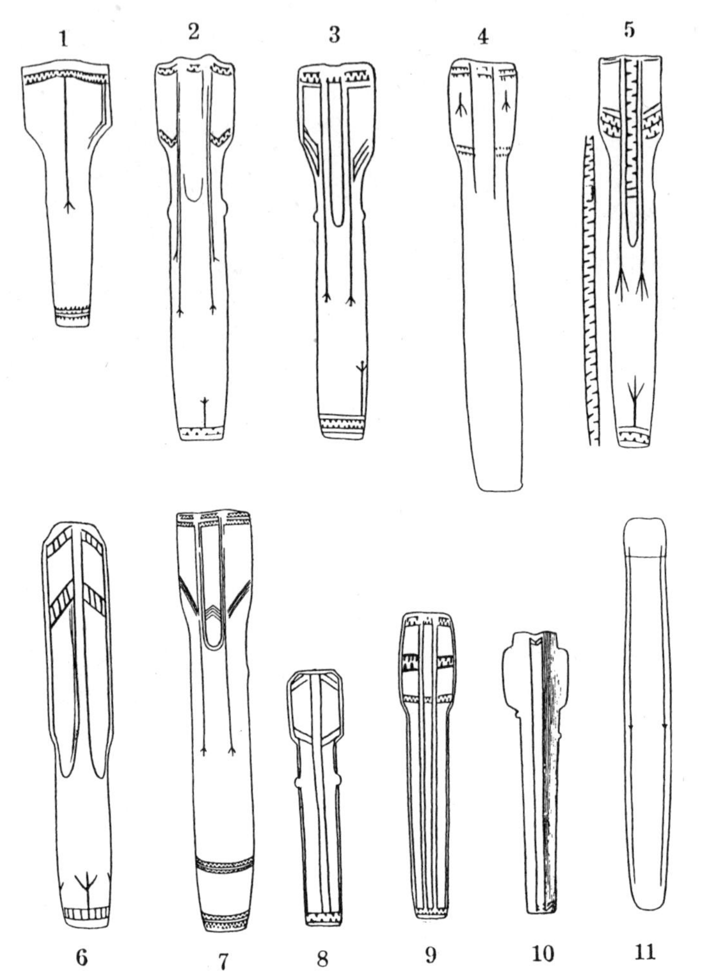

FIG. 4. Decorated Alaskan Needlecases
1. From St. Michael, Norton Sound, Alaska. Lucien M. Turner, collector. Cat. no. 176289, USNM
2. From St. Michael, Norton Sound, Alaska. Lucien M. Turner, collector. Cat. no. 129239, USNM
3. From Shaktoiik, eastern part of Norton Sound, Alaska. E. W. Nelson, collector. Cat. no. 39094, USNM
4. From St. Michael, Norton Sound, Alaska. Lucien M. Turner, collector. Cat. no. 24466, USNM
5. From mouth of Yukon River, Alaska. E. W. Nelson, collector. Cat. no. 38758, USNM
6. From St. Michael, Norton Sound, Alaska. Lucien M. Turner, collector. Cat. no. 24483, USNM
7. From Unalaklik, eastern shore of Norton Sound, Alaska. E. W. Nelson, collector. Cat. no. 33696, USNM
8. From St. Michael, Norton Sound, Alaska. Lucien M. Turner, collector. Cat. no. 24494, USNM
9. From Sledge Island, west of Cape Nome, Alaska. E. W. Nelson, collector. Cat. no. 44732, USNM
10. From St. Michael, Norton Sound, Alaska. Lucien M. Turner, collector. Cat. no. 24484, USNM
11. From Ooglamie, Point Barrow, Alaska. P. H. Ray, collector. Cat. no. 56575, USNM

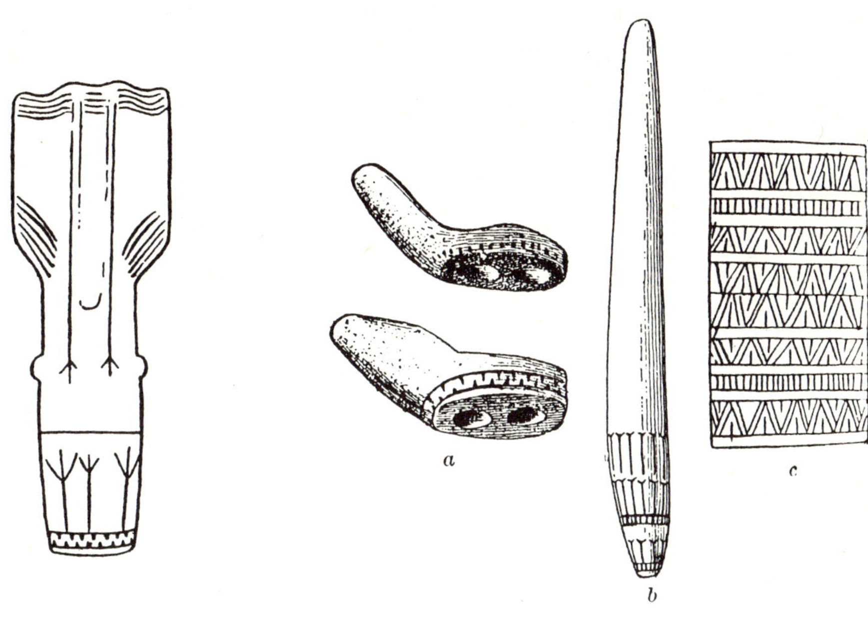

FIG. 5. Needlecase (Royal Ethnog. Mus. Berlin, no. IV A 5892).

FIG. 6 *a* (60/5375). Ivory attachment to line, west coast of Hudson Bay; *b* (60/5152), creaser, Iglulik (from Boas, "Eskimo of Baffin Land and Hudson Bay," *Bull. Amer. Mus. Nat. Hist.*, XV, pp. 458, 459); *c*, design of needlecase, King Williams Land (no. 10405, USNM).

of lines at the upper and lower ends of the flanges and on the concave face, and (7) an alternate-spur band at the lower end of the tube.

In order to understand the significance of this peculiar type of needlecase, we must bear in mind that the two design elements which are most characteristic of this specimen—namely, the line design with short branches and the alternate-spur design—are characteristic Eskimo motives over the greater part of the Arctic coast. The alternate-spur band design has been found by me on a number of very old specimens from Southampton Island and Lyons Inlet, collected by Captain G. Comer, which are reproduced here in Fig. 6 *a* and *c*. In the same region the forked-line design is found on bone engravings (Fig. 6*b*) and it may be observed in a few of the specimens found by Parry in Fury and Hecla Strait in 1820. Besides this, this design is commonly found in tattooings, the form of which is almost everywhere very stable. It occurs in the tattooings from the west coast of Hudson Bay, as well as in those from Baffin Land (Fig. 7). Unfortunately I have not had an opportunity to examine extensive collections from Greenland, in order to ascertain the occurrence of these

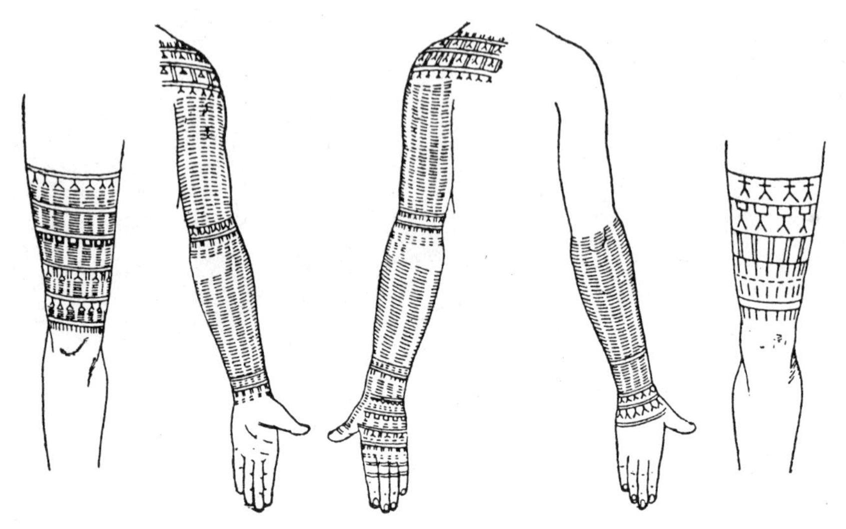

FIG. 7. Tattooings from the west coast of Hudson Bay and from Hudson Strait (from Boas, "Eskimo of Baffin Land and Hudson Bay," *Bull. Amer. Mus. Nat. Hist.*, XV, p. 473).

designs. In view of their wide distribution over the whole Eskimo area, it seems justifiable to consider them as a very old possession of the Eskimo, and to assume that originally they bore no relation to the needlecases on which they are found in such great regularity. Incidentally it may be remarked that the explanations of these forms as bushes and whales' tails, which are given by the Alaskan Eskimo, appear so one-sided that they cannot be accepted as a general interpretation.

It is important to note that the designs here mentioned do not seem to occur in parts of America or Asia which are outside of Eskimo influence. I have not been able to discover them on any objects of Indian manufacture except on a few specimens from the Yukon River made by Athapascan tribes directly under Eskimo influence. In Asia the same designs occur among the Koryak and Chukchee (Fig. 8), while farther to the west and south I have not been able to find them. I am not certain whether the alternate-spur-line design does occur in the art of the Samoyed, but I have not discovered a single example in a large collection of Yakut specimens brought together by Mr. Jochelson; and it does not seem to occur among the Gilyak, Ainu, and southeastern Tungus tribes. It seems that the design occurs occasionally in Polynesian and Micronesian art, but I should not venture to conclude from this an historical relation, notwithstanding the rather large number of peculiar analogies

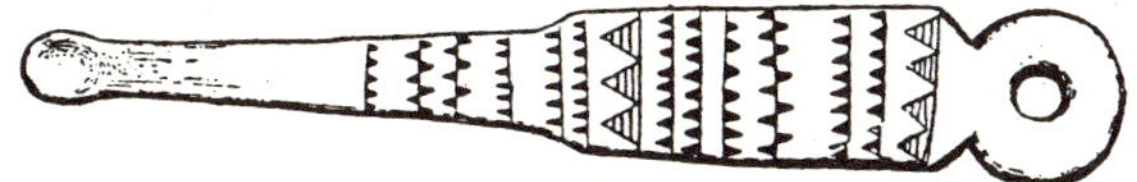

FIG. 8 (70/7226). Ear spoon, Northern Kamokatka (from W. Jochelson, *The Konyak*, Jesup North Pacific Expedition Publications, VI, p. 673.

between the northeast coast of the Pacific Ocean and the islands northeast of Australia.

Considering the continuous area in which the two designs occur, we may say that their essential home seems to be the Eskimo region, beginning with Alaska, and extending eastward and northeastward to Hudson Bay and Smith Sound, and that a few of the neighboring Indian tribes may have adopted them, and that they also occur among the neighboring Chukchee and Koryak.

One needlecase that has been found in the region of Southampton Island seems to me of particular importance in this connection (Fig. 9*a*). It will be seen that this needlecase also consists of a tube, like most Eskimo needlecases; that it expands into wide flanges near its upper end, the whole tube being flattened; and that near the middle there are two large wings, which correspond in their position to the small knobs of the Alaskan needlecases. This specimen has also the characteristic alternate-spur band of the Alaskan needlecases at its upper end, and the decoration is repeated here in two parallel lines. Attention may be called to the occurrence of the same pattern at the same place, in a number of the more complex specimens from Alaska, shown in Fig. 3, nos. 2, 5, 8; Fig. 4, nos. 1–3, 7, 9; Fig. 5, no. 4. These and other similar occurrences show that the Eskimo often substituted this design for the single parallel lines.

The alternate-spur-band design is related to the single spurred line, a pattern which is very common in many parts of the world. In the decorative art of the Eskimo it appears often in place of the alternate-spur band: for instance, on some needlecases of the type here discussed (see Fig. 10; also Fig. 1, no. 1 and Fig. 4, no. 4). In other cases the alternate-spur band is replaced by a ladder design (Fig. 4, no. 6), which, on account of its rarity, may be considered as a degenerate form of the alternate-spur band.

A group of needlecases similar to the one just described from Southampton Island has been found in the district between Southampton Island and Smith Sound. The

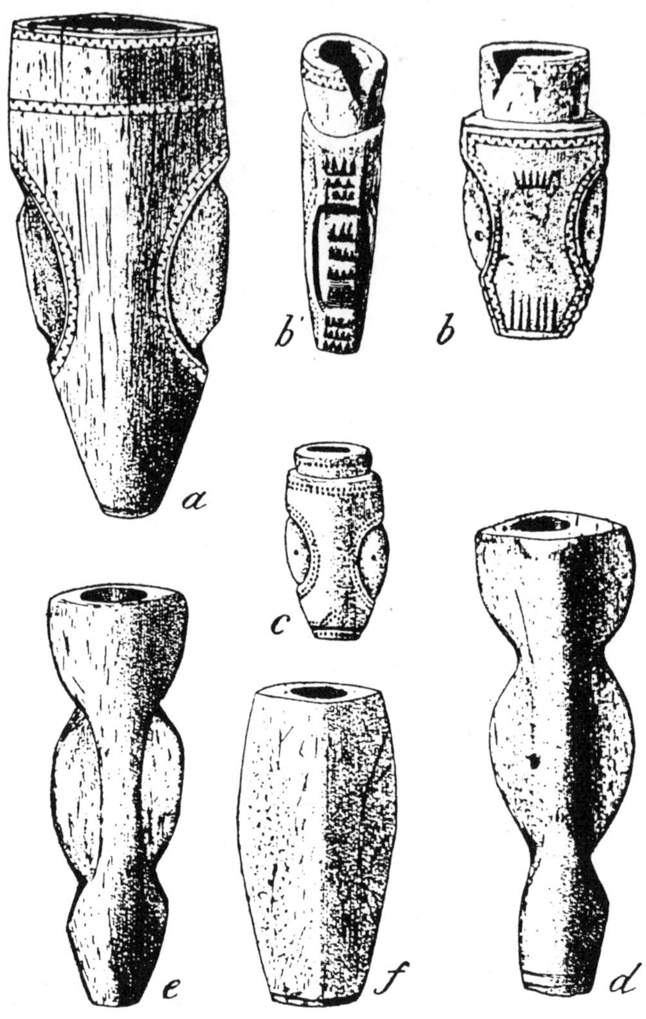

FIG. 9 (60/4153, 60/5154, 60/5155, 60/5165, 60/5167, 60/5156). Needlecases. Frozen Strait except *c* (Ponds Bay) and *f* (Aivilik) (from Boas, "Eskimo of Baffin Land and Hudson Bay," *Bull. Amer. Mus. Nat. Hist.*, XV, p. 433).

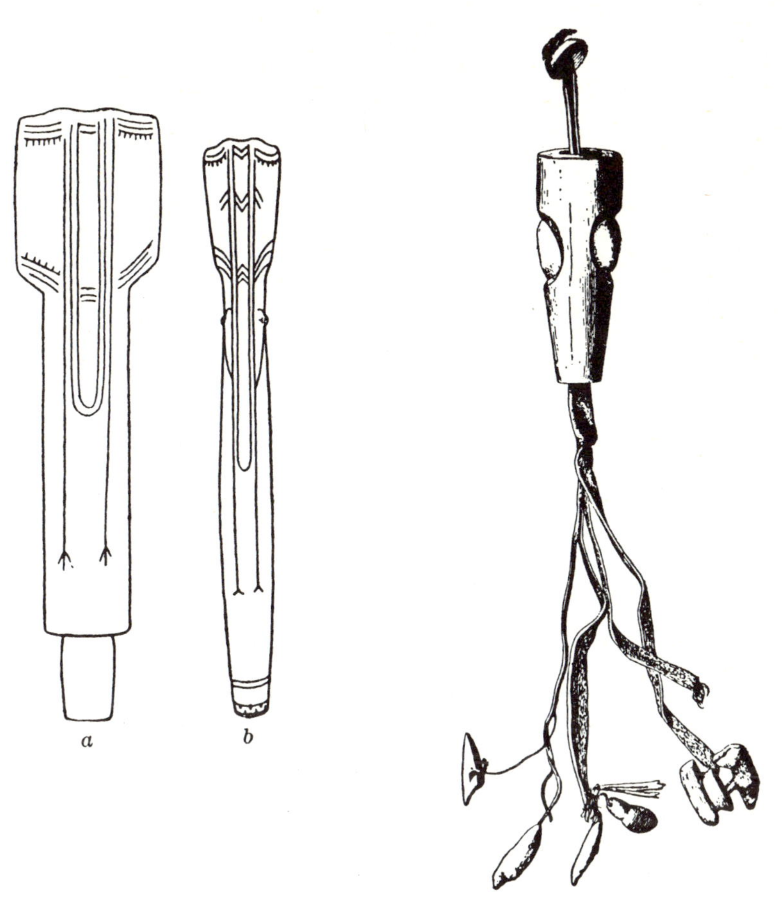

FIG. 10. Needlecases. *a*, Peabody Mus. Amer. Arch., Cambridge, no. 50264; *b*, Royal Ethnog. Mus., Berlin, no. IV, A 3988).

FIG. 11 (60/5). Needlecase. Smith Sound (from Kroeber, "The Eskimo of Smith Sound," *Bull. Amer. Mus. Nat. Hist.*, XII, p. 287).

only type of needlecase known from Smith Sound has this peculiar character. Unfortunately the specimens which I have seen are all exceedingly rough; but they all consist of a flattened tube, very wide at the upper end, and small and round at the lower end, provided at the sides with two characteristic wings (Fig. 11). The same type with some dot decorations has been collected at Ponds Bay in the northern part of Baffin Land (Fig. 9c), while the older specimens from the northern part of Hudson Bay are much more elongated, and have the wings and flanges set off more clearly from the body of the needlecase (Fig. 9 *d* and *e*).

It seems to me very plausible that the Alaskan type and the Eastern type represent specialized developments of the same older type of needlecase, and that the flanges and diminutive knobs of the Alaskan specimens are homologous to the flanges and large wings of the Eastern specimens. When the first specimens of this kind were collected, Professor O. T. Mason, according to information which he has kindly given to me, was inclined to believe that they were of foreign origin. In a note on the specimen shown on Fig. 4, no. 2, he wrote at that time:

This specimen is a needlecase from St. Michael, Alaska. It is made of walrus ivory and carved in a form which suggests the butt end of an arrow, with two feathers projecting from opposite sides on the shaft. The likeness is made more striking by the fluting on the butt end, which resembles the nock of the arrow. A little in front of the two feathers are projecting bosses. The tube of the needlecase is slightly expanded in the middle and contracted at the smaller end. The ornamentation consists of narrow bands across the shaft, and the feathers at their extremities cut out in zigzag line very much in the style of Polynesian ornamentation. At the smaller end there is also a similarly ornamented band from which rise four symbols of shrubs. An exactly similar piece is figured in Nordenskiöld [1881:241] and labeled "knife handle from Port Clarence." There are four of these objects in the U.S. National Museum, and, compared with hundreds of others, they place themselves unmistakably in the class of needlecases. There is no doubt that these six specimens—five in the U.S. National Museum and one shown by Nordenskiöld—are not aboriginal in form or ornament; that they belong to a style of art introduced into Alaska after the advent of the Russians.

In Seebohm [1882:56] will be seen the figure of a Samoyed needlecase with a tube of metal, inclosed at its top in a belt, and riveted along the side. The suggestion is here thrown out that the Eskimo artist has endeavored to reproduce, in ivory, a facsimile of this metal tube and a portion of the leather belt, even to the projecting rivets. The Nordenskiöld specimen has, in addition, walrus heads and seals carved on the side of the tube.

This Polynesian style of ornamentation is common on hundreds of Eskimo objects in and about St. Michael; for, after the advent of the Russians and intercourse with sailors of the Pacific Ocean, the arts of the two areas became very much entangled.

Considering the antiquity of the Eastern specimens, it does not seem plausible that the Alaskan specimens are a newly developed type. Their great frequency and the fixity of the type are also not in favor of this view.

It might perhaps also be argued that the knobs serve for firmly attaching the needlecase to a skin strap, but there is no evidence whatever that the needlecases were thus suspended. On the contrary, they seem to have been carried like all other Eskimo needlecases, by an attachment to the strip of skin into which the needles are inserted.

It seems certain, therefore, that the diminutive knob of the Alaskan needlecase serves no practical end whatever, and that it is a purely conventional feature in the form of the utensil. It is true that the large wings and flanges of the Eastern needlecases also serve no practical end; but it seems well to bear in mind the close resemblance of the two types.

It is important and interesting to compare the simple types heretofore described to a number of more complex needlecases which clearly belong to the same type.

It would seem that, first of all, the strong inclination of the Alaskan Eskimo to decorate carved objects by means of incised designs has led to further developments of the patterns heretofore described. Examples of this kind may be observed in Figs. 3 and 4. In Fig. 3, no. 2, the same typical arrangement of flanges, knobs, and faces may be observed; but the concave face and vertical line are further decorated by oblique spurs placed in pairs, and the lower border design of the flange is elaborated into a single line with double oblique spurs also. On both sides of the needlecase, and surrounded by the line running downward along the lower border of the flange and on the body of the tube, is a design of what seems to be a human being with a caribou head, which stands on a line extending across the side of the needlecase, just over two knobs, the single knob on each side being doubled in this case. On the lowest point of the line surrounding the concave face stands a quadruped with long body and bent legs. Another type of elaboration and modification of the design is shown in Fig. 3, no. 1, where the lines with pairs of oblique spurs have also been made use of. The needlecases illustrated in Fig. 3, nos. 3, 4, 6, are so much worn down that the designs have become very indistinct; but in these specimens, as well as in the one shown in the same figure, no. 5, the middle concave face was never well marked. In the last-named specimen the border lines of the flanges are continued across the whole needlecase (compare Fig. 2, no. 7). While these specimens resemble in general shape the characteristic designs, the forms are rounded off and have lost many of their decorative traits. On the reverse side of the specimen shown in Fig. 3, no. 4, a double line with oblique spurs running outward from the lines is shown, but not in the middle of the needlecase. Its position is so irregular that it cannot be compared with the decorations of the specimens heretofore described. It will be observed that the same specimen has quite an irregular line decoration on the flanges. Fig. 3, no. 7, is a roughly finished specimen of the usual type. The concave face is hollowed out deeply, and the flanges are set off more markedly than in the majority of specimens. The knobs have been moved very far downward. This specimen seems to be modern and very roughly finished. Fig. 3, no. 8, also seems to be a modern specimen, in which the vertical border lines of the concave face have been moved toward the border of the flange, and where the upper border is replaced by an alternate-spur band. In this specimen the knobs are also moved very far downward. The specimen shown in Fig. 3, no. 9, resembles in many respects the one shown in no. 7 of the same plate, particularly in the depth of the concave faces and in the sharp angle formed by the flanges where they are set off from the body of the tube.

Fig. 4, no. 1, represents a specimen which is also presumably quite modern and shows material deviations from the type. Here, instead of the middle concave face, we have a narrow flat surface with a single vertical forked line, the occurrence of which is obviously a survival of the older concave field with its two-forked border lines. On the sides of this needlecase, just under the flanges, is also a vertical forked line, which extends a little lower than the medial forked line. The knobs on the sides are very indistinct and marked only by the sudden transition of the faces cut out under the flanges on each side into the tubular lower portion of the specimen. In Fig. 4, no. 2, the border lines of the concave face consist of two forked lines on each side, and the border lines of the flanges have been transformed into alternate-spur bands. In no. 4 of this figure, the same lines are etched as spur bands and the forked-line design is placed on the flanges. There is no indication of knobs. In the specimen shown in no. 5 we find on the concave face of the tube an alternate-spur band added, which ends below, on the reverse and the obverse, with two parallel crosslines. On the lower part of the flanges is shown, on one side a double alternate-spur band, while the opposite side is laid out on the same plan, with the only exception that the crosslines between the lowest pair of border lines are drawn right across (as in the bands in Fig. 4, no. 6). The whole side of this needlecase is flattened, beginning under the flange, down to the lower border. This flat field is occupied in its whole length by an alternate-spur band.

The bands in Fig. 4, no. 6, are occupied by ladder designs instead of alternate-spur designs. Presumably this is the result of careless execution of the older spur design. No. 7 shows a very careful technique, and it is characterized by a strict adherence to the general type, extreme smallness of the knobs, and elaboration of the single decorative motives. Thus the upper border consists here of two alternate-spur bands; the lower border of the flanges of a number of parallel lines which are very close together. The same kind of lines occur on the middle field. The decorative band at the lower end is also doubled, and repeated at a short distance above the lower end.

Other modifications are found in the following specimens. In Fig. 12 there is no middle concave face, but in its place we find two parallel lines which are carried down to the lower border. There are also two parallel lines on each side running down from the flanges to the lower border, and to the upper and lower border lines of the flanges are added vertical border lines, so that the whole flanges appear framed. The cross section of this specimen is angular. In Fig. 13 two parallel lines

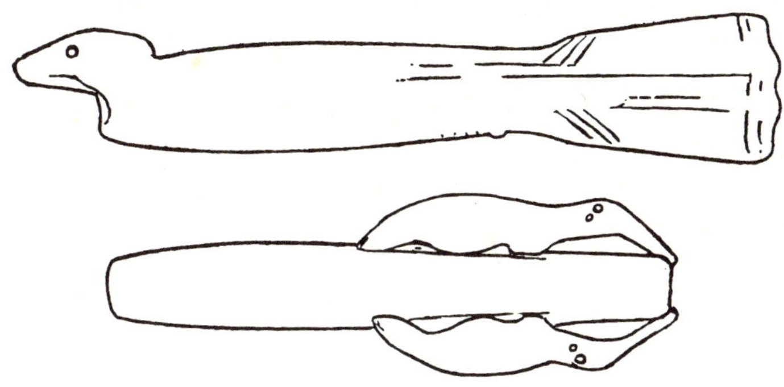

FIG. 12. Needlecase (Royal Ethnog. Mus., Berlin, no. IV A 3987).

FIG. 13. Needlecase (Royal Ethnog. Mus., Berlin, no. IV A 5491).

are substituted for the concave face, as in the specimen just described. The sides of this needlecase are also flat, while the back shows no vertical design and a rounded surface. Its only decoration consists of a continuous alternate-spur band design on top and at the lower end of the small flanges, continuing the corresponding bands on the front of the specimen and on the narrow sides of the flanges. This specimen has no indication of knobs.

Fig. 4, no. 10, is in many respects peculiar, particularly in so far as the two small knobs are not on the same level. The middle concave field is carried down to the lower end of the needlecase, as in the two preceding cases, and the whole needlecase is angular in cross section. It has eight faces, which taper down toward the lower end. On the three faces on the right-hand side is the small double-angle decoration which has been indicated in our illustration. A double angle turned with its apex downward is also found on the lateral face of the right-hand side. As shown in the illustration, the flanges do not extend up to the top of the needlecase, as is the case in most specimens.

The needlecase represented in Fig. 4, no. 11, illustrates a very peculiar reduction in the general form. The flanges have almost disappeared, and with them the upper and lower decorative border, as well as the border at the lower end of the tube; and all that remains to remind us of the form here discussed are four parallel forked lines, which, however, are continued beyond the forks. Nevertheless the impression given by the specimen in connection with the whole series is such that I do not doubt for a moment that it belonged originally to the series under discussion.

The series represented in Figs. 14–16 seems to me of special importance, and interesting from a theoretical point of view. The identity of the types of needlecases here shown and the preceding ones is perfectly obvious. The specimens collected in Fig. 14 show with perfect distinctness the bulging tube, the flange with its decoration, the knobs, and the concave face of the tube. Here part of the specimen seems to be conceived of as an animal. The bulging tube is the body of the animal, whose head has been added at the lower end of the tube. Although the transformation of the lower end of the needlecase into an animal has been perfected, it does not seem likely that the whole object was conceived as an animal form. If this were the case, the flanges, when transformed into the tail of a sea mammal, would probably have been modified, and the position of the head would be so changed as to be in proper relation to the tail.

It seems to my mind entirely artificial to assume that in this case the animal form as such could possibly have preceded the typical needlecase as before described, but that we are dealing here evidently with a secondary interpretation of the design, which finds expression in the addition of the animal head and in other later additions to the whole form. In Fig. 14, nos. 2, 3, 5, 6, and 7, the entire old design may be recognized in all its details; even the alternate-spur band remains, although it interferes with the form of the seal's head which has been added. In no. 3 the head of the animal has been turned, so that the lower part of the needlecase looks like a sea animal swimming on its back. A similar specimen from the Royal Ethnographical Museum in Berlin is shown in Fig. 12. It has a unilateral small knob. In no. 1 of Fig. 14 we find what may be a still further development of the original design here described. The seal's head has disappeared again, and in its place we find a simple knob. There are three parallel lines near the lower end of this knob, which make the whole area, seen from the top, look a little like a small crustacean. The knobs in this specimen are very small. I consider it quite possible that here we may have a case where, under the stress of older forms of the needlecases, a partial reversion to the original type has taken place.

The strong tendency of the Eskimo to utilize animal motives has found expression in another manner in the specimen represented in Fig. 14, no. 4. Here the small lateral knobs have been considerably enlarged and have been given the form of seals' heads (see also Fig. 13). I believe that here also there can be no doubt in regard to the question whether the seal's head or the knobs are older. If the knob had to be considered as a degenerate form of the seal's head, it would hardly be intelligible why only one or two specimens out of a great number should retain the heads in this place, while in practically all other cases the reduction to a simple knob, sometimes so small that it can hardly be felt, should have occurred. It seems quite evident that in this case the imagination of the artist was stimulated by the traditional knob, and that it has been developed, owing to a desire to further decorate the utensil, into seals' heads. The modification of the central concave face of this specimen is quite

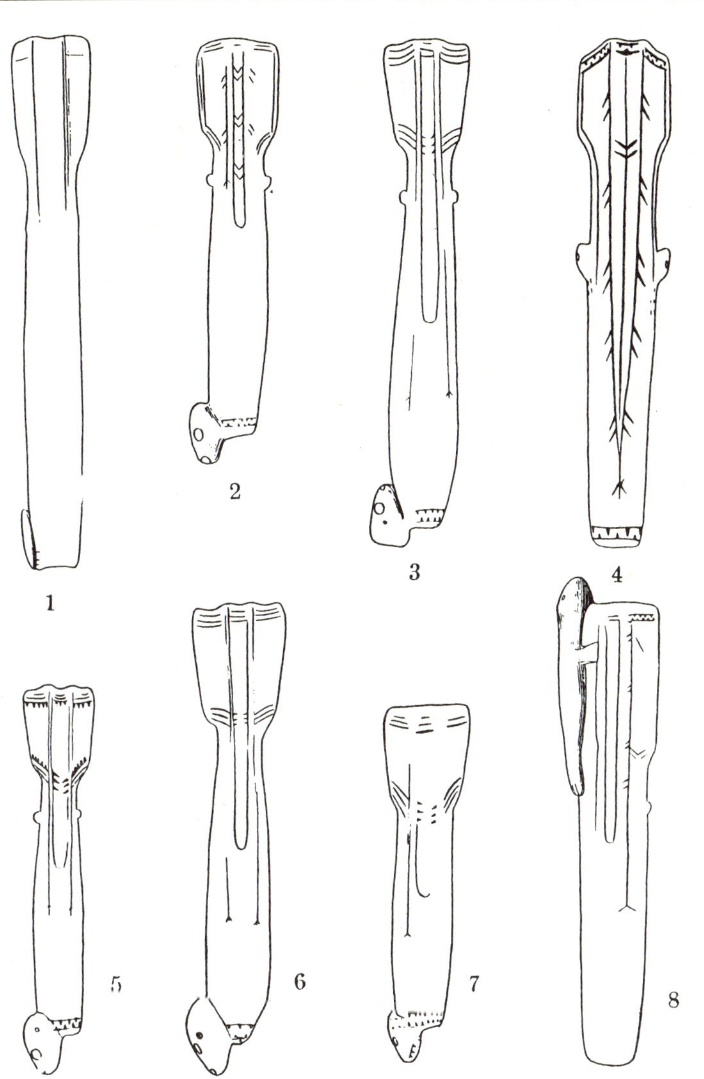

FIG. 14. Decorated Alaskan Needlecases

1. Peabody Museum, Cambridge, Mass. Cat. no. 63563
2. From St. Michael, Norton Sound, Alaska. Lucien M. Turner, collector. Cat. no. 24487, USNM
3. From Lower Yukon, Alaska. E. W. Nelson, collector. Cat. no. 33698, USNM
4. From Cape Nome, Norton Sound, Alaska. E. W. Nelson, collector. Cat. no. 176230, USNM
5. From Paimute, Kuskokwim River, Alaska. E. W. Nelson, collector. Cat. no. 37150, USNM
6. From St. Michael, Norton Sound, Alaska. Lucien M. Turner, collector. Cat. no. 24473, USNM
7. From Razboinski, on the Lower Yukon River, Alaska. E. W. Nelson, collector. Cat. no. 48860, USNM
8. From Norton Sound, Alaska. Lucien M. Turner, collector. Cat. no. 24469, USNM

in accord with other modifications of the same surface, which have been described before. On the reverse of this needlecase the pairs of oblique spurs attached to the converging lines are directed toward the upper part of the needlecase.

In Figs. 15 and 17 a number of specimens have been collected, in which another part of the needlecase has been modified through the general tendency of the Eskimo artists to introduce animal designs. Instead of the lower end, the flange has been thus developed. The procedure appears perhaps clearest in the specimen shown in Fig. 15, no. 3, where on one side the flange shows a number of perforations and modifications, by means of which it has been developed into a quadruped, while on the other side a walrus head has been developed by making a long slit along the body of the tube and by inserting an eye, the lines indicating nostrils and mouth, near the upper border. Thus the outer sides of the flanges form the tusks of the walrus head, while the top forms the head itself. The specimen here referred to shows clearly its close relation to the original type of needlecase. The decoration of the lower part, and the concave face, may still be observed. The characteristic decorations of the concave face are also indicated. In nos. 1, 5, and 6 of the same figure we find the same type of needlecase with a double walrus head at the top. It would seem that in most of the specimens the tusks have been broken off. In no. 5 the small knobs under the lower end of the tusks may be observed quite distinctly. In this specimen traces of the vertical forked lines bordering the middle field also remain. In these three specimens the middle concave face is quite distinct. In nos. 2 and 4 of Fig. 15, two specimens are represented which combine a modification of the lower end of the needlecase with that of the upper end. At the lower end a seal head is represented at one side, as in the specimens previously discussed, while in the upper end the double walrus head is found. In these specimens also the middle concave face is well marked, although in no. 4 it is not bordered by an incised line.

The next group of modifications of the old type of needlecase follows out the same direction as those just described, the flanges being modified so as to represent an animal on each side. A specimen of this type is shown in Fig. 13, where a walrus with head stretched forward is shown. The tusks touch the upper end of the tube, while the two flippers are shown at the lower end. Two seals are shown in the same position in Fig. 16 and in Fig. 17, no. 7, while two quadrupeds occupy the position of the flanges in nos. 1 and 6 of Fig. 17. In no. 4 of Fig. 17 the quadrupeds appear doubled; and in no. 8 the seals have so much increased in size that they occupy the whole side of the needlecase. However, in this case also, the close relation between all these types can easily be demonstrated by an examination of Fig. 17, nos. 4 and 7, which retain all the characteristic traits of the simple type. The two animals in no. 6 of this figure seem to represent lemmings. They are placed somewhat differently from the ordinary form of the flanges, but are evidently developed from forms like these shown in nos. 1 and 7 of this figure. A specimen in which the one side

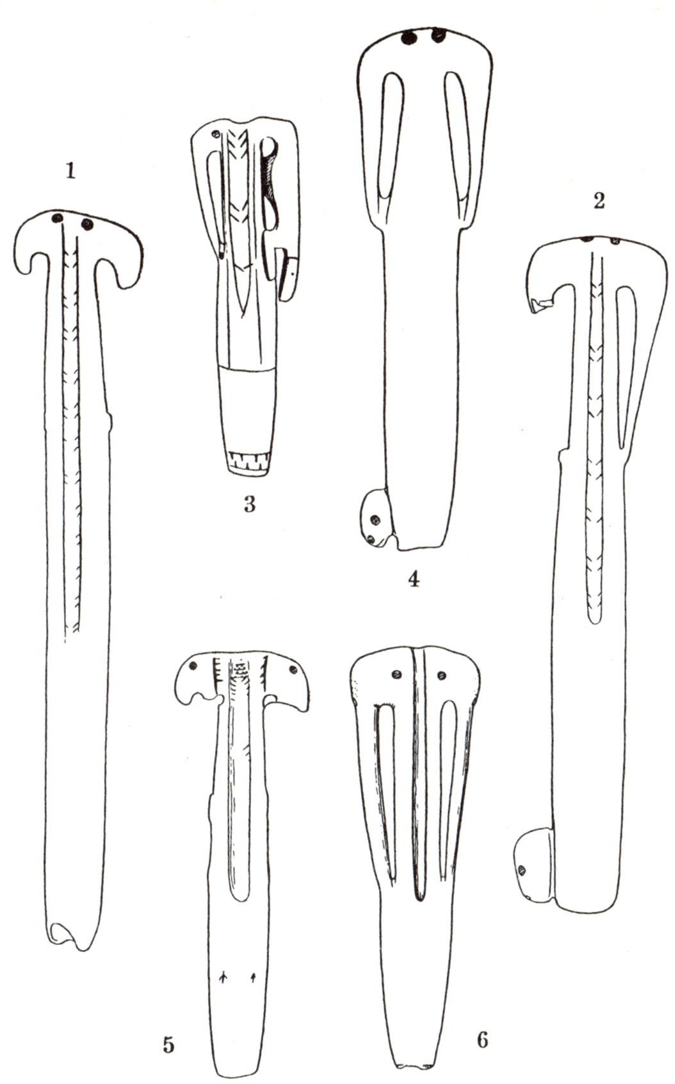

FIG. 15. Decorated Alaskan Needlecases

1. From the Lower Yukon River, Alaska. E. W. Nelson, collector. Cat. no. 38363, USNM
2. From St. Michael, Norton Sound, Alaska. Lucien M. Turner, collector. Cat. no. 24488, USNM
3. From St. Michael, Norton Sound, Alaska. E. W. Nelson, collector. Cat. no. 43792, USNM
4. From Lower Yukon River, Alaska. E. W. Nelson, collector. Cat. no. 38448, USNM
5. From Razboinski, on the Lower Yukon River, Alaska. E. W. Nelson, collector. Cat. no. 48817, USNM
6. From St. Michael, Norton Sound, Alaska. Lucien M. Turner, collector. Cat. no. 24465, USNM

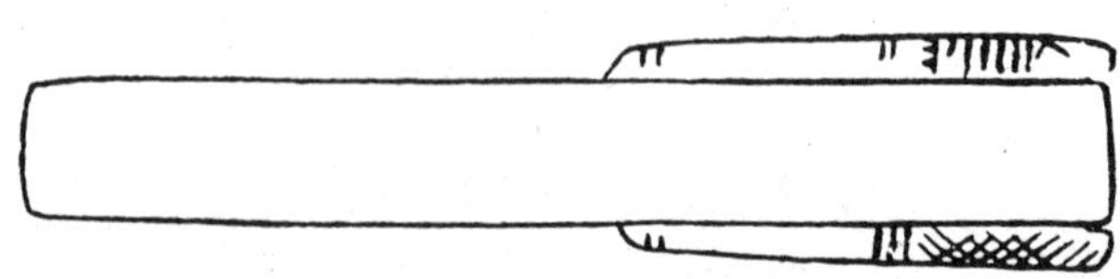

FIG. 16. Needlecase (Royal Ethnog. Mus., Berlin, no. IV A 2991).

of the needlecase retains the ordinary shape, while the opposite side of the flange has been transformed into an animal, is represented in Fig. 14, no. 8.

In this case also it would seem exceedingly difficult to interpret the simple geometrical form of the needlecase as a later development from the animal representations here discussed. In this case, similarities of the decorative designs on the tubings would be entirely unintelligible, while the assumption that the animal forms have developed from the geometrical forms seems to give a very plausible explanation of the forms of these specimens.

The specimens in which the upper end has been so modified as to become a double walrus head lead us to another group in which the walrus head is repeated a number of times along the sides of the tube. Specimens of this kind are represented in Fig. 17, nos. 2 and 3. In both of these traces of the old upper and lower border decoration remain, and no. 3 also shows the typical oblique spurs in pairs in the same position which has been described several times. It therefore seems perfectly natural to interpret nos. 2 and 3 as the result of repetitions of the animal design, which was first developed from the flanges of the old needlecase. Nos. 3 and 5 differ from other specimens of their kind in that they have the walrus head developed only on one side, while on the opposite side the flange is suppressed.

As has been indicated, the geometrical decorations of the typical flanged needlecases reappear in many of these highly modified specimens. Attention may also be called to the forked-line designs which rise from the lower border in the usual number in the specimens shown in nos. 4, 6, and 7 of Fig. 17. In no. 7 the number of these lines is five. The specimen, however, is very crude and quite modern, and the deviation in number may be due to inaccuracy in laying out the ornament. In no. 4 there are two forked designs on opposite sides, while from the tails of the animals down to the lower border runs an alternate-spur band. Between the alternate spur-bands and the long forked lines there are short forked lines, as indicated in the illustration. Only in no. 8 do we find an important modification of the lower end of the needlecase, which forms a ring that in our specimen has been broken. The backs of the two needlecases shown in nos. 3 and 5 are somewhat flat. It is of interest to

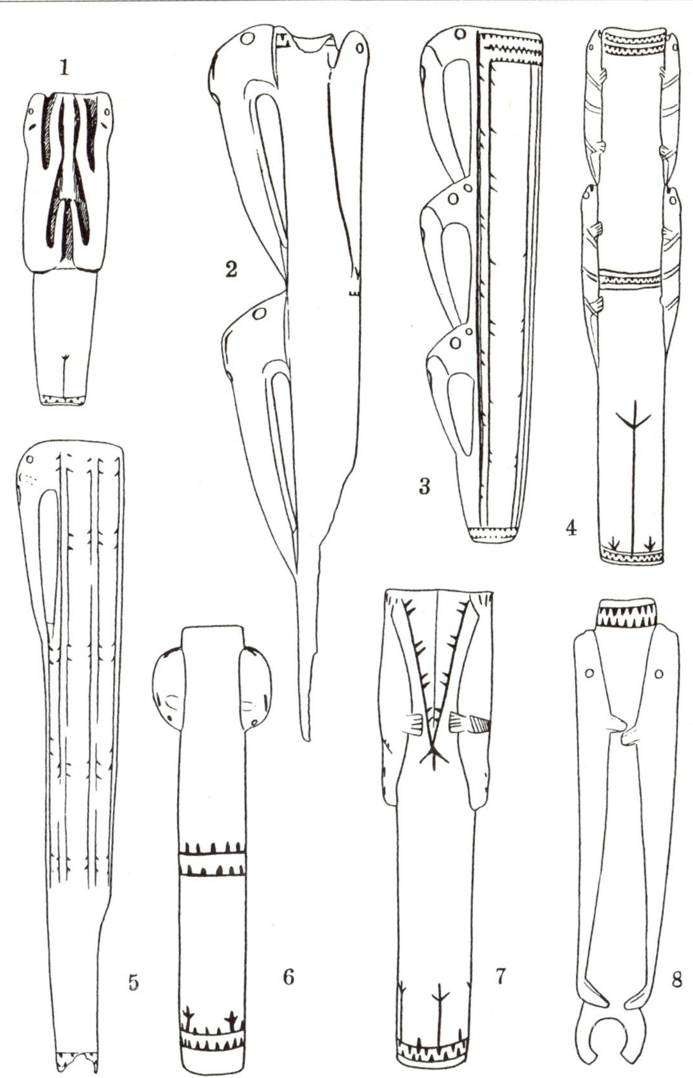

FIG. 17. Decorated Alaskan Needlecases

1. From Sledge Island, west of Cape Nome, Alaska. E. W. Nelson, collector. Cat. no. 44731, USNM
2. From Nubviakehukaluk, Alaska. E. W. Nelson, collector. Cat. no. 43942, USNM
3. From western Alaska. J. Henry Turner, collector. Cat. no. 153832, USNM
4. From western Alaska. J. Henry Turner, collector. Cat. no. 153831, USNM
5. From Norton Sound, Alaska. E. W. Nelson, collector. Cat. no. 33615, USNM
6. From Hotham Inlet, east of Kotzebue Sound, Alaska. E. W. Nelson, collector. Cat. no. 64164, USNM
7. From Norton Sound, Alaska. Lucien M. Turner, collector. Cat. no. 24468, USNM
8. From Sledge Island, west of Cape Nome, Alaska. E. W. Nelson, collector. Cat. no. 45168, USNM

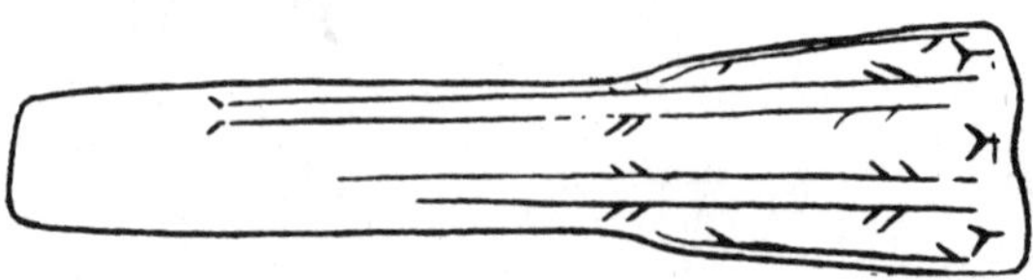

FIG. 18. Needlecase (Royal Ethnog. Mus., Berlin, no. IV A 3992).

compare the line decoration of the latter needlecase with the one in Fig. 18, which is a simple modification of the fundamental type.

The illustrations, nos. 1 and 2 in Fig. 19, of two needlecases in human form, are not quite as convincing as the specimens themselves; but a comparison of these forms with the other needlecases of this series seems to me to suggest with great force that the human figures here shown are related to the same type of needlecase that we are discussing here. The whole human figure is treated as a tube, and it is my opinion that the bulging hips correspond to the bulging middle part of the needlecase, while the arms correspond to the flanges, and perhaps more particularly to developments of the flanges similar to the walrus-head developments, while the head is a later development of the upper border, suggested by the perception of the similarity of the whole form to a human figure. I do not wish to imply that the human figure in this case has necessarily developed from the type of needlecase first discussed; but it seems plausible to me that an assimilation between the human figure and this type has taken place in the two specimens here illustrated. It seems likely that the animal figure shown in Fig. 20 must be considered in a similar manner. There is no doubt that the vivid representation of the animal lying down has very little to do with our type of needlecase; but nevertheless I cannot free myself from the impression that the artist, in his treatment of the subject, has been influenced by the treatment of the flanges of needlecases and by the general form of this utensil. There is a certain similarity between the position of the feet and the positions of the walrus tusks down in Figs. 15 and 17, which is not explained by a realistic treatment of the animal alone; and the same is true of the position of the neck and head and of the curves in the hind part of the body.

The similarities which I am discussing here are even less clear in some of the other specimens represented in Fig. 19. No. 3 of this figure evidently represents a human leg, the design on one side being a representation of tattooing. In this case faint traces of the upper border design and of the lower border design remain, and the outline of the whole specimen still recalls to a certain extent the bulging tube below and the wider part with its flanges above. If we agree to consider this specimen

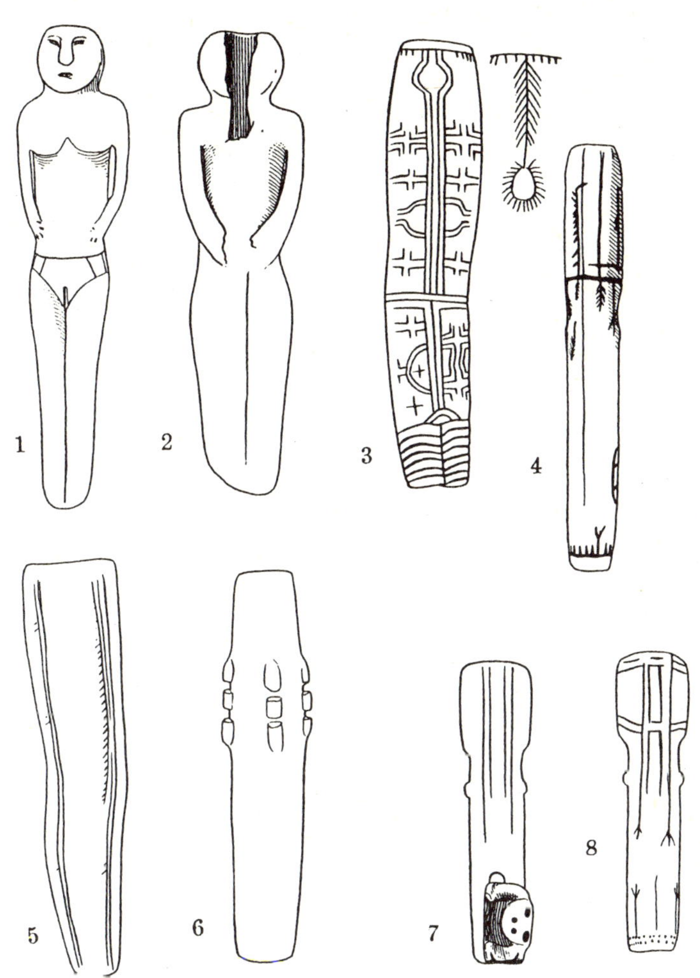

FIG. 19. Decorated Alaskan Needlecases
1. From the Lower Yukon, Alaska. E. W. Nelson, collector. Cat. no. 38364, USNM
2. From Alaska. E. W. Nelson, collector. Cat. no. 43945, USNM
3. From St. Michael, Norton Sound, Alaska. Lucien M. Turner, collector. Cat. no. 129219, USNM
4. From Alaska. Lucien M. Turner, collector. Cat. no. 24493, USNM
5. From Razboinski, on Lower Yukon River, Alaska. E. W. Nelson, collector. Cat. no. 48815, USNM
6. From Koyuk River, Norton Sound, Alaska. E. W. Nelson, collector. Cat. no. 44069, USNM
7, 8. From Alaska. Lucien M. Turner, collector. Cat. no. 24467, USNM

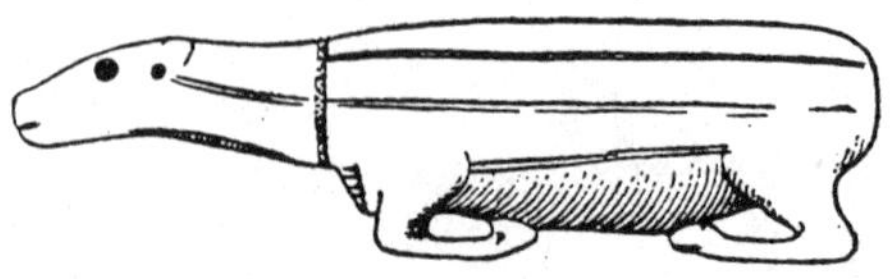

FIG. 20. Needlecase (no. 33619), St. Michaels, E. W. Nelson.

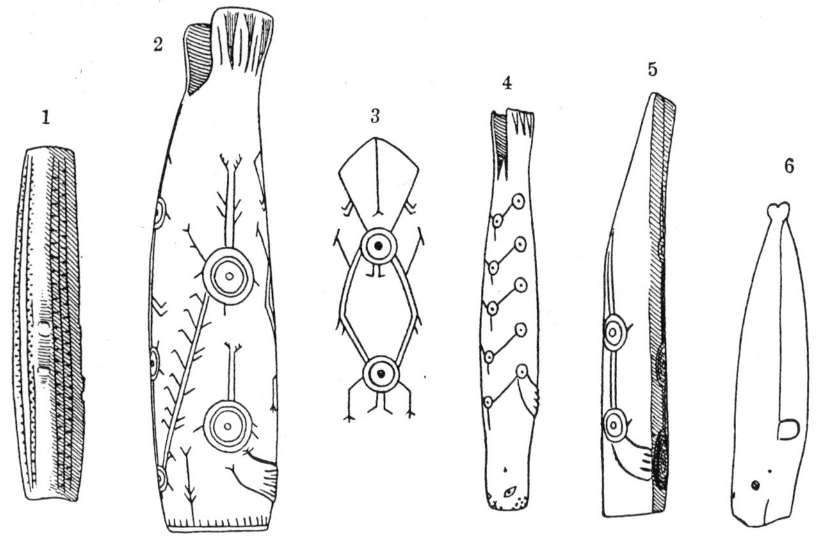

FIG. 21. Decorated Alaskan Needlecases
1. From Sledge Island, west of Cape Nome, Alaska. E. W. Nelson, collector. Cat. no. 55167, USNM
2, 3. From St. Michael, Alaska. Lucien M. Turner, collector. Cat. no. 129229, USNM
4. From Togiak River, north of Bristol Bay, Alaska. I. Applegate, collector. Cat. no. 127443, USNM
5. From Nunivak Island, eastern shore of Bering Sea, Alaska. E. W. Nelson, collector. Cat. no. 43699, USNM
6. From St. Michael, Norton Sound, Alaska. Lucien M. Turner, collector. Cat. no. unknown, USNM

as belonging to the present series, the specimen shown in no. 5 must be considered as belonging here also. There is no doubt that no. 4 of this figure belongs to our series. The tube and the knobs are the same as those occurring in the most typical specimens. Instead of the concave faces, we have merely flat surfaces, and the flanges have been much reduced in size, but are perfectly distinct and sharply set off. The ornamentation, however, differs on the flanges and concave faces from the ordinary decoration. Besides the designs shown in the illustration, we have, on the back of the flange to the right, a line with two pairs of one-sided oblique spurs running downward and a forked line running down from the black ring, like the one shown on the right-hand side of the illustration. On the right-hand side of the lower part of the needlecase an etched design, representing a quadruped with long tail, will be observed. No. 6, Fig. 19, shows a simple tube with four groups of knobs, which may have been suggested by the knobs of the specimens here described. Nos. 7 and 8, Fig. 19, represent a needlecase, which on one side shows the typical form of the flanged specimens, while on the opposite side the head, neck, and forepaws of an animal are set off.

Another geometrical development of the ordinary type is represented in Fig. 21. In this specimen the general outline of the flanged tube is readily recognized, but all the other characteristic features have disappeared.

In Fig. 22 five specimens are illustrated whose relation to the flanged type is very doubtful. The knobs in no. 1 of this figure, which are doubled in the axial direction and appear on four sides of the tube, are analogous to those shown in no. 6 of Fig. 19, and these two types are undoubtedly closely related. Attention may be called to the awl-like implement illustrated in Fig. 23 which shows the same four knobs here described, and which therefore in its origin may well be related to the decorative designs on the needlecases. The animal types in Fig. 22, nos. 2–6, and in Fig. 24, diverge so much from the flanged type that their relationship seems very doubtful. Still I cannot free myself from the impression of a certain influence of the flanged types upon these forms also. This becomes apparent by a comparison of the needlecase shown in Fig. 24 with the animal types here discussed. It is quite evident that this specimen has its affiliations both with the animal types and the walrus-head types. It is, however, also possible that its form has originated by assimilation of two distinct types.

The conclusion which I draw from a comparison of the types of needlecases here represented is that the flanged needlecase represents an old conventional style, which is ever present in the mind of the Eskimo artist who sets about to carve a needlecase. The various parts of the flanged needlecase excite the imagination of the artist; and a geometrical element here or there is developed by him, in accordance with the general tendencies of Eskimo art, into the representation of whole animals or of parts of animals. In this manner small knobs or the flanges are developed into heads or animals. After this modification has once set in, the animal figures may be repeated in other parts of the implement. Besides this, associations between animal forms and the form of the whole needlecase seem to have taken place, which have to a certain extent modified the manner of representing animals which were adapted to use as needlecases; so that the old form and style of the needlecase determined the treatment of the animal form.

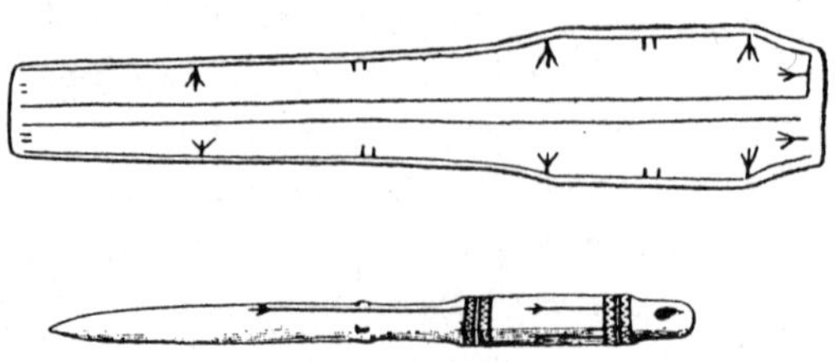

FIG. 22. Needlecase (Peabody Mus. Amer. Arch., Cambridge, Mass., no. 146).
FIG. 23. Awl (no. 43837). Unalakleet, Norton Island, E. W. Nelson.

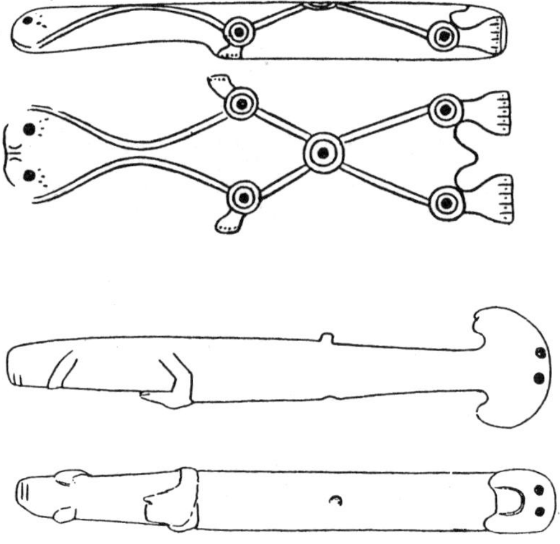

FIG. 24. Needlecase (Royal Ethnog. Mus., Berlin, no. IV A 3986).
FIG. 25. Needlecase (Royal Ethnog. Mus., Berlin, no. IV 3985).

If we were to apply to the present series the theory of the origin of conventional form from realistic motives, it would be exceedingly difficult to account for the general uniformity of fundamental type. It seems to me that, on the basis of this theory, we could not account for the diversity of realistic forms and the uniformity of general type. Neither does it seem possible to account for the series of types by assumption of any influence of technique; and my impression is that the only satisfactory explanation lies in the assumption that the multifarious forms are due to the play of the imagination with a fixed old conventional form, the origin of which remains entirely obscure. This I freely acknowledge. If, however, we are to form an acceptable theory of the origin of decorative designs, it seems a safer method to form our judgment based on examples the history of which can be traced with a fair degree of certainty, rather than on speculations in regard to the origin of remote forms for the development of which no data are available.

I believe a considerable amount of other evidence can be brought forward sustaining the point of view that I have tried to develop, namely, that decorative forms may be largely explained as results of the play of the imagination under the restricting influence of a fixed conventional style. Looking at this matter from a purely theoretical point of view, it is quite obvious that in any series in which we have at one end a realistic figure and at the other end a conventional figure, the arrangement is due entirely to our judgment regarding similarities. If, without further proof, we interpret such a series as a genetic series, we simply substitute for the classificatory principle which has guided us in the arrangement of the series a new principle which has nothing to do with the principle of our classification. No proof whatever can be given that the series selected according to similarities really represents an historical sequence. It is just as conceivable that the same series may begin at the conventional end and that realistic forms have been read into it, and we might interpret the series, therefore, as an historical series beginning at the opposite end. Since both of these tendencies are active in the human mind at the present time, it seems much more likely that both processes have been at work constantly, and that neither the one nor the other theory really represents the historical development of decorative design.

The assumption of a development from realistic design to conventional design also omits the consideration of one exceedingly important element, namely, the style of convention that prevails in the types of art of different areas. If geometrical designs developed from realistic motives the world over, it still would remain to be proved why a certain style of conventionalism belongs to one art and another style to another art; and in order to explain in a satisfactory way the different styles of art, we should have to accept these as given at a very early stage during the process of conventionalization of realistic designs.

The attempt to explain the processes of conventionalization by the theory of the influence of technical motives does not seem to offer an entirely adequate solution of this problem. It is true that certain very simple designs seem to be due almost entirely to the influence of technique upon simple decorative tendencies. This influence, however, does not reach so far as to determine in detail the character of design in the same kind of material or in the same technique. As an example of such differences may be mentioned, for instance, the designs in woven checkered mattings from West Africa, where peculiar realistic figures alternate with geometrical band designs; the designs of cedar-bark mattings of the Ojibwa and of those of the North Pacific coast, and of designs made in the same technique by the South American Indians. In all these cases the technical conditions are practically the same, but the styles differ vastly. It seems necessary, therefore, to assume in the development of design the existence of tendencies which are due to causes different from the technique, and unrelated to the realistic motives which may be current or may have been current.

I have no theory to offer in regard to the origin of these types of convention, which presumably was connected with a whole series of activities determining the perception and reproduction of forms; but it seems desirable to point out by a number of instances the fixity of these conventional forms and the deep influence that they have had even in apparently realistic forms. I have pointed out in the discussion of the designs of the blankets of the Chilkat Indians that a great many of the older forms can be reduced to two fundamental types, and that, no matter what animal may be represented in the art to the weaver, it is almost always reduced to one of these two forms [Boas 1907:355]. In the same place I have shown that the treatment of the animal figure on carved boxes of the Tlingit has other fixed conventional forms, which, although closely related to the blanket design, are quite permanent and applied only in the manufacture of boxes [Boas 1907:357 ff.].

In a quite different region, among the Tungus tribes of the Amur River, Dr. Berthold Laufer has shown that one of the essential types determining the whole arrangement of decorative designs, which consist of realistic figures as well as of curved lines, is based on the type of "cocks combatant" [Laufer 1902:22 ff.].

It is also important to note that figures conforming to such fundamental types may be interpreted in a great variety of ways by the people who use them. I have pointed out such a similarity of type and fundamental difference of interpretation in explanations given by the Huichol Indians [Lumholtz 1904:287, figs. 451 and 465]. Here we find practically the same figure once interpreted as the freshwater crab, and then as oak leaves and stems. Other more extended series of such ambiguous interpretations may be found in the art of the Plains Indians as well as in those of other parts of the world [Kroeber 1902, Wissler 1904].

I have suggested before that in many cases these forms seem to compel us to assume that the interpretations of many simple forms are entirely secondary; that often the forms have been borrowed; and that later on, according to their use in the life of the people, they have been given a fitting interpretation [Boas 1903].

I think evidence can be brought forward also to show that the tendency to play, and the play of the imagination with existing forms, have deeply influenced the decorative art of primitive tribes as we find it at the present time.

The first of these traits appears with particular clearness in the tendency to use rhythmic repetitions of varying forms. Bead necklaces are one of the most striking examples of the pleasure that man receives through the use of rhythmic repetition of colors and forms. It is very important to notice that among primitive tribes the rhythmic and symmetrical order of such arrangements are often exceedingly complex—so complex, in fact, that they can be recognized by us only by a close study of the arrangement. A case of this kind occurs in the fringe on a pair of leggings collected among the Thompson Indians, which I have described [Boas 1900b:384, fig. 313]. In this specimen we have a fringe which hangs down in a very disorderly fashion, so that the constituent elements cannot be seen distinctly. Nevertheless a most painstaking arrangement of the component elements is adhered to, the rhythmic unit consisting of five elements—one string having one glass bead and two bone beads in alternating order, one undecorated string, one having alternating glass and bone beads, one undecorated, and one having one glass bead and two bone beads in alternating order. I have found still more complex rhythmic repetitions and symmetrical arrangements on the embroidered borders of coats of the Koryak. These contained sometimes ten and more elements in one group [Jochelson 1908: 689 ff.]. Still another case of similar kind, from Peru, has been described by Mr. Mead [1906]. Here a rhythmic repetition of six units seems to be very common.

I consider it particularly important to observe that in the first of these specimens the rhythmic repetition cannot be seen when the leggings are in use, because this suggests strongly that the reason for the application of the rhythmic repetition is not the esthetic pleasure in the effect which it produces, but the pleasure felt by the maker. If this is true, then we do not need to assume that in the other cases a much more highly developed appreciation of complex rhythm is found among primitive people than the one we possess. Corroborative evidence in regard to this point is offered by the basketry of the Thompson and Lillooet Indians. I have noticed that here, where in a fine imbricated technique color bands are produced, the basket weavers tend to use with great regularity certain groupings of the number of stitches belonging to each color, although, owing to the irregularity of the size of the stitches, these modifications can hardly be observed [Teit 1906:206]. If these facts have a wider application, it would seem that on the whole the pleasure given by much of the decorative work of primitive people must not be looked for in the beauty of the finished product, but rather in the enjoyment which the maker feels at his own cleverness in playing with the technical elements that he is using. In other words, one of the most important sources in the development of primitive decorative art is analogous to the pleasure that is given by the achievements of the virtuoso.

Examples may also be given illustrating the effect of the play of imagination upon the development of design. One of the best examples of this kind is offered by the decorated bag of the Thompson Indians illustrated by Professor Farrand [1900:pl. 33, fig. 1]. The analogy of this soft rectangular bag, which is decorated with rows of large diamonds, to other similar bags shows quite clearly that the rows of diamonds have the same origin as the rows of diamonds which are painted on parfleches of the Plains Indians. In this case the diamonds suggested the idea of ponds; and, in order to emphasize this idea, which came to the mind of the woman who used the bag, she added a number of birds flying toward these ponds. Other examples of this kind have been mentioned by Doctor Koch in his observations on the drawings of South American Indians. The development of the triangles in the designs of the Plains Indians to tent designs or cloud designs brings out similar points.

Thus it would seem that the development of decorative designs cannot be simply interpreted by the assumption of a general tendency toward conventionalism or by the theory of an evolution of technical motives into realistic motives by a process of reading in, but that a considerable number of other psychic processes must be taken into consideration if we desire to obtain a clear insight into the history of art.

11. Clubs Made of Bone of Whale

This essay, which follows Harlan Smith's contribution to the Jesup North Pacific Expedition memoirs, deals with the clubs—many of which are Nuu-chah-nulth (Nootka)—found in the southern Northwest Coast area. Boas here describes the clubs Smith collected, and classifies them according to how closely they adhere to the "fundamental type" upon which the handle depicts a bird's head.

One of the most characteristic types of specimens from the region between Vancouver Island and Columbia River is the war club made of bone of whale or of stone, broad and rather thin, of lenticular cross section, and generally with a carved head. This type of club, which is represented in Figs. 1–7, bears a certain resemblance to the clubs of Hawaii and New Zealand, and it has been claimed that their occurrence proves direct relationship between Northwest American culture and that of the Polynesian Islands. I believe that the group of clubs brought together here by Mr. Smith, and representing practically all the specimens of which he has been able to gain information, will clearly show that this type of club has developed independently in America. A comparison of the localities from which the clubs have been obtained will show that the majority are from the west coast of Vancouver Island, a number having been obtained in Indian villages, where they were probably in use until recent times. The clubs made of bone of whale from the more outlying districts, as Columbia River and the interior of British Columbia at Kamloops, do not deviate sufficiently from the fundamental type to justify the assumption that they are of independent origin.

I have combined in Figs. 1–7 clubs made of bone of whale, and these are arranged according to the definiteness with which they represent the fundamental type. Fig. 1 *a–c* shows clearly that the handle is conceived of as the head of the eagle or thunderbird represented in the type commonly found in the art of the Nootka, with a bird headdress of the type of the eagle-head masks so commonly used by the Nootka Indians. In Fig. 1*b*, the eye and beak of the headdress are not marked, so that possibly this portion of the handle might be conceived of as the ear and forehead of the eagle; but a comparison with Fig. 1*a* brings out the practical identity in outline, showing that the origin of the form must have been the same. Fig. 1 *c* and *d* exhibits again clearly the bird headdress; *c*, however, differs from the others in the smallness of the eye, which gives the head a somewhat human shape, and which modifies the section ordinarily occupied by the eye in such a way that it appears like human hair.

Reprinted from "Archaeology of the Gulf of Georgia and Puget Sound," by Harlan Smith, *American Museum of Natural History Memoirs*, vol. 4, pp. 403–12, 1908.

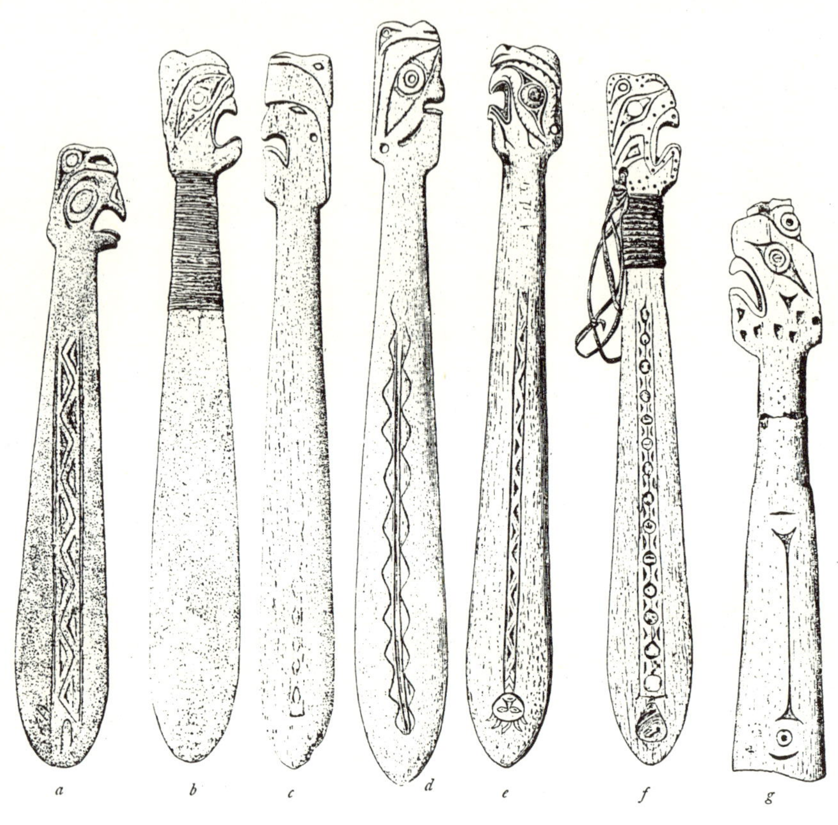

FIG. 1. Clubs made of bone of whale. *a*, From Nootka, collected by Captain Cook (British Museum, Cat. no. N.W.C. 42); *b*, From Nootka (British Museum, Cat. no. N.W.C. 47); *c*, From Columbia River (Oregon Historical Society, Cat. no. 385, List 38); *d*, From Nootka, collected by Captain Cook, 1778 (Ethnographical Museum, Florence); *e*, From Barclay Sound, collected by Mr. A. Jacobsen (Royal Ethnographical Museum, Berlin, Cat. no. IV A 1574); *f*, From Nootka, collected by Captain Cook (British Museum, Cat. no. N.W.C. 41); *g*, From shell heap at Cadboro Bay, collected by Mr. J. Maynard (Provincial Museum, Victoria, Cat. no. 769).

Even if this had been the idea that the artist intended to elucidate, the cut of the mouth, and the similarity of the field occupied by the hair to what is ordinarily the eye field, show that the fundamental type is the same, although it may have been interpreted somewhat differently here. It will be noticed that this specimen, which differs somewhat in interpretation from the others, is from the Columbia River, a point far distant from the center of distribution of these clubs. The clubs represented

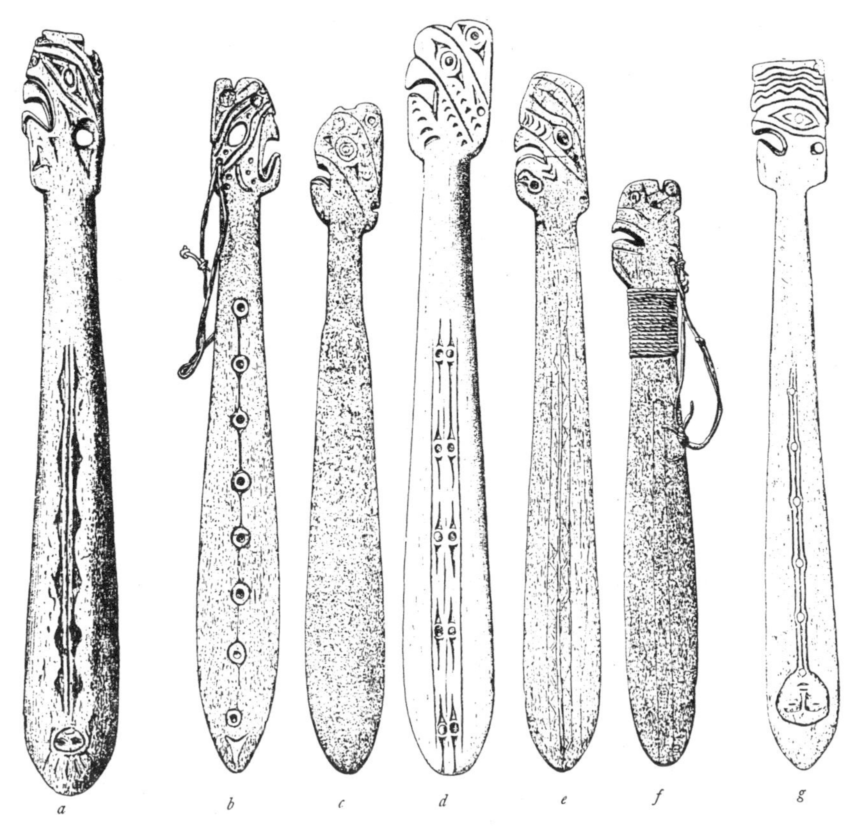

FIG. 2. Clubs made of bone of whale. *a*, From Neah Bay, collected by Hon. James Wickersham (U.S. National Museum, Cat. no. 198032); *b*, Collected by Vancouver (British Museum, Van. 93); *c*, From Nootka (collection of Mr. W. Sparrow Simpson, British Museum, Cat. no. 9383); *d*, From Upper Columbia River, collected by Colonel Brooks, U.S.A., about 1810, property of Mr. M. F. Savage, New York (American Museum of Natural History, 16/4578); *e*, British Museum, Cat. no. 78-11-1.623; *f*, From Nootka (British Museum, Cat. no. 8766); *g*, University Museum, Cambridge, Eng., Cat. no. R. D. 112 d.

in *e*, *f*, and *g* of this figure are also quite realistic representations of the eagle head surmounted by a bird headdress. Attention may be called to the line and scallop designs on *e*, which, according to the interpretation of the modern Indians, indicate feathers. Feathers are also indicated by the dot design on *f* and the triangular incisions on *g*, an old specimen from Cadboro Bay.

The group of clubs combined in Fig. 2 *a–d* differ from the preceding group only in having the eye field set off more definitely from the headdress and the lower part of the face. In these specimens also (except in *c*) dots and grooved lines indicate feathers.

The specimens of Fig. 2 *e–g* retain all the fundamental features of the preceding types, except that the bird headdress (except in *f*) disappears; nevertheless the form of the beak and the general outline of the club are so nearly the same as those of the preceding types that there can be no doubt of the fundamental identity of these designs. In *e* we observe the trait characteristic of modern Northwest Coast art of indicating the body of the animal on the head by a representation of the foot with its joint on the lower jaw.

The forms combined in Fig. 3 are more degenerate representations of the same type. The indistinctness of *a* may be due to the imperfect condition of the handle. In *b* and *c* the identity of type is brought out particularly by the form of the beak. The club illustrated in *d* had probably originally a lower jaw, which seems to have been broken off. In both this and the following the bird headdress is indicated, although not with the usual clearness. The modern specimen shown in Fig. 3*f* and the old one in Fig. 3*g* deviate considerably from the preceding types, the handle being carved simply in the shape of a bird's head. The specimen represented in Fig. 3*h* is made of serpentine, and is inserted here for the purpose of comparison. The incised design on the handle is crude, but resembles so much in type the handles heretofore described that it must probably be considered as a copy of this type. The specimen represented in Fig. 3*i* presumably does not belong to this series, but seems to be a dagger.

In Fig. 4*a*, another specimen is represented which is quite typical, showing clearly the crooked beak, the eye, and the headdress. In this specimen we find, however, a peculiar displacement of the eye, which, instead of being placed over the beak, has been made just behind it. This and the exaggeration of the curvature of the beak lead to the series of types represented in Fig. 4 *b–e*, in which, in place of an upright head, we have a curved beak placed in the axis of the club. That this is the correct interpretation of these forms is illustrated particularly by the occurrence of the peculiar notch in the upper termination of *b* and by the eye in the upper termination of *c*.

The two human forms illustrated in Fig. 4*f* and Fig. 5*a* may be considered as strong modifications of the original type. Possibly the common form of the forehead in the typical forms explains the excessive bulge of the forehead in Fig. 4*f*.

The remaining clubs cannot be readily classified with the preceding types, partly on account of the differences of the form of blade, partly on account of difference in form of the handle. None of the typical handles have the blade shaped and incised so as to represent the whole animal, while the clubs shown in Fig. 5 *b* and *c* are thus treated. Notwithstanding the strong curvature of the beak of the animal

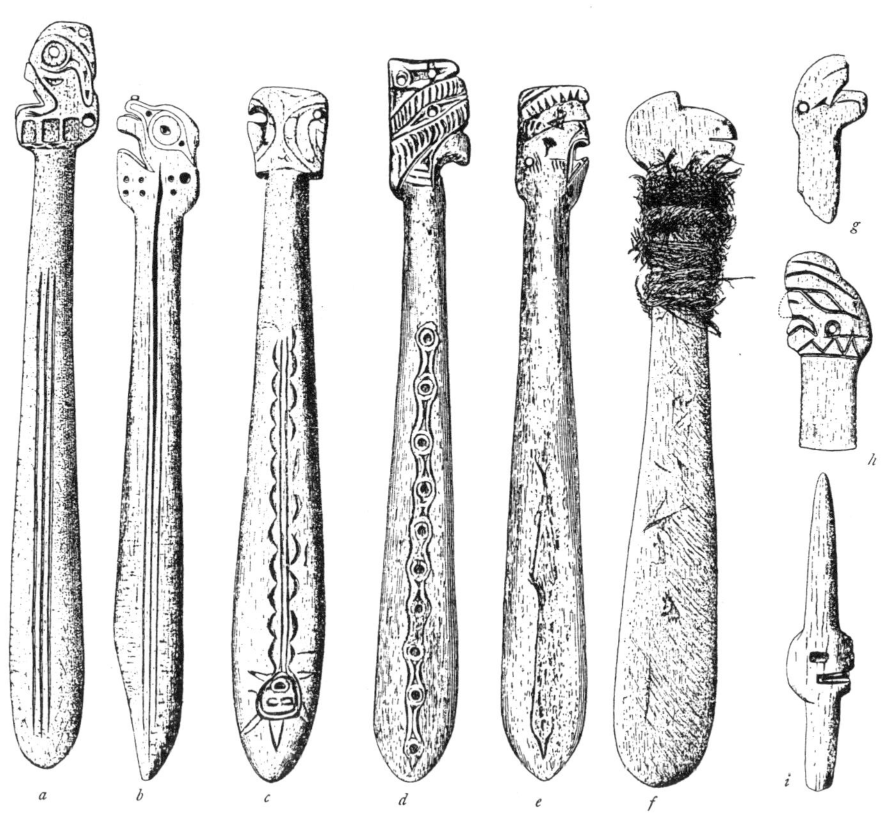

FIG. 3. Clubs made of bone of whale (except *h*). *a*, From Quamichan Indians, collected by Dr. C. F. Newcombe (Field Museum of Natural History, Chicago, Cat. no. 85345); *b*, From shell heap, Plumper's Pass, collected by Mr. Eduard Lomas (Provincial Museum, Victoria, Cat. no. 770); *c*, From Neah Bay, collected by Hon. James Wickersham (U.S. National Museum, Cat. no. 198033); *d*, From Nuchatlath, collected by Mr. A. Jacobsen (Royal Ethnographical Museum, Berlin, Cat. no. IV A 1215); *e*, From Hesquiath, collected by Mr. A. Jacobsen (Royal Ethnographical Museum, Berlin, Cat. no. IV A 1573); *f* (16/2106), From Clayoquath, collected by Mr. Fillip Jacobsen; *g* (16/912), Bishop Collection from British Columbia; *h* (260/1471), Made of serpentine, from Blalock Island, Wash., opposite Umatilla, Ore., collected by Mr. D. W. Owen; *i*, From Cadboro Bay, collected by Mr. James Deans (Provincial Museum, Victoria, Cat. no. 774).

represented in Fig. 5*b*, I presume it is intended for a killer whale with a fin extending backward from the head. The curvature of the head itself is rather suggestive of a bird's head. The treatment of the handle is somewhat interesting, the notches suggesting a correspondence to the outlines of the typical eagle-head handles. Without some such analogy, the peculiar notching of the handle would be difficult to un-

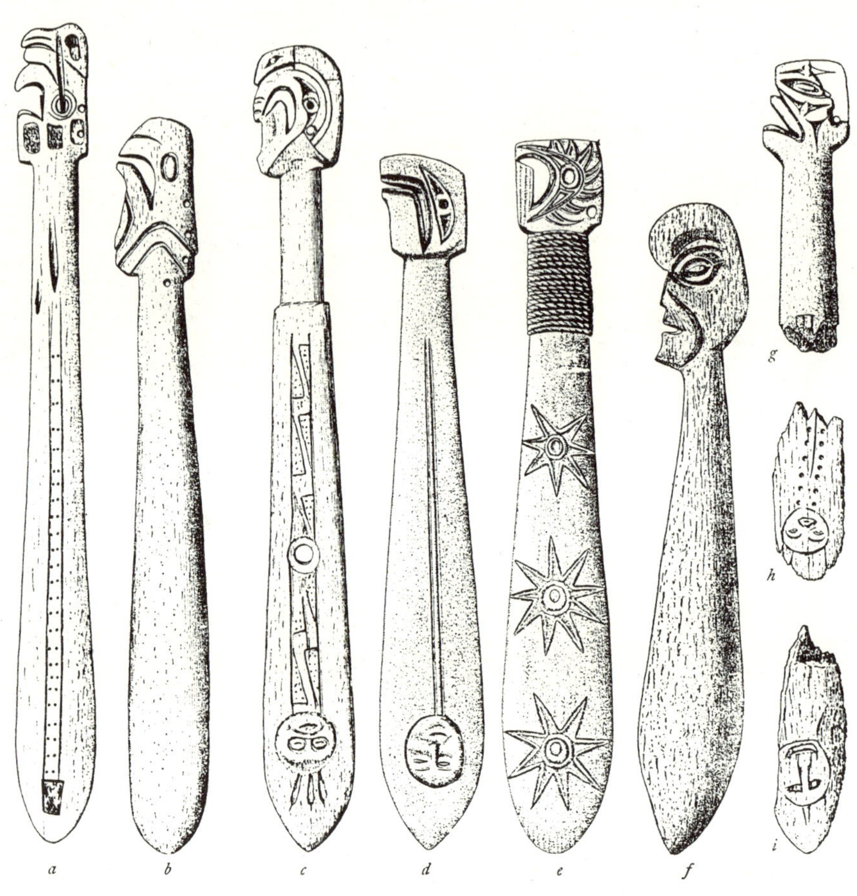

FIG. 4. Clubs made of bone of whale. *a*, From Fort Vancouver, Wash., about 1830 (Academy of Natural Sciences, Philadelphia); *b*, From Neah Bay, collected by Hon. James Wickersham (from cast in U.S. National Museum, Cat. no. 198031); *c*, Peabody Academy of Sciences, Salem, Mass., Cat. no. E 6640; *d*, *e*, From Nootka, collected by Capt. James Magee about 1794 (Peabody Museum, Cambridge, Mass., Cat. nos. 256, 255); *f*, From Neah Bay, collected by Hon. James Wickersham (from cast in U.S. National Museum, Cat. no. 198030); *g* (16/855), From shell heap at Cadboro Bay; *h* (16/911), Bishop Collection; *i* (16/1100), Excavated on Songish Reservation.

derstand. The following specimen (Fig. 5*c*) has simply the square knob, and the blade is carved in the form of a killer whale with fin turned down. Obviously the fundamental idea of decoration in this specimen is quite distinct from that applied in the eagle clubs. The club shown in Fig. 5*d* is quite different in essential form from the preceding ones. It is rounder in section, and curved. The handle end shows very

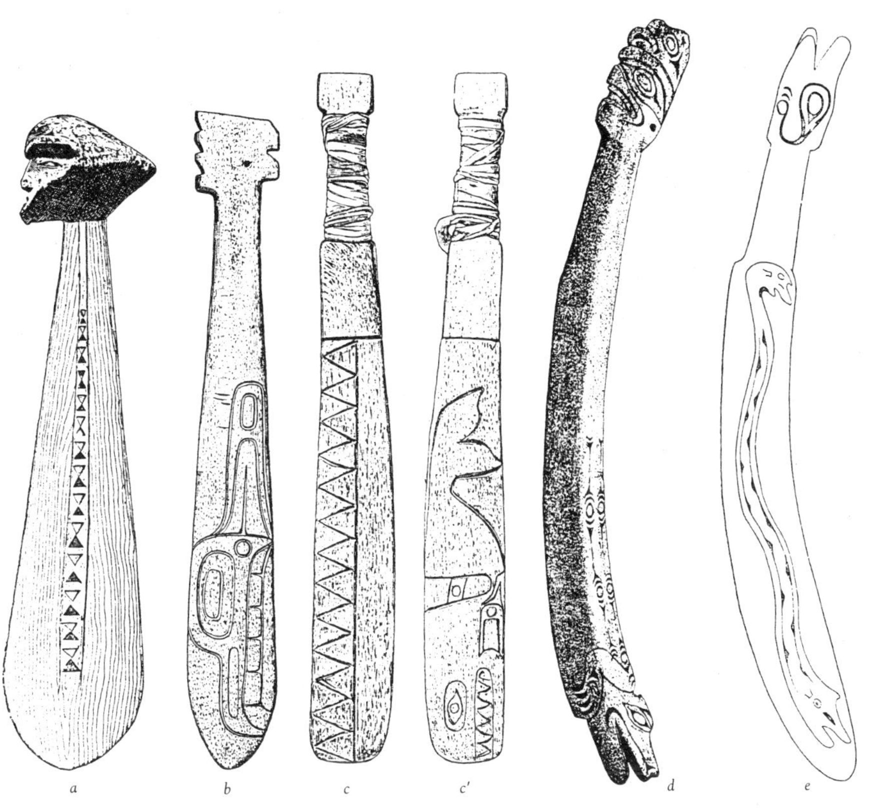

FIG. 5. Clubs made of bone of whale (except *a*). *a*, Made of wood, from Nootka (British Museum, Cat. no. N.W.C. 39); *b*, Collected by Mr. A. Jacobsen (Royal Ethnographical Museum, Berlin, Cat. no. IV A 1575); *c*, *c′*, From Hopitchisath, collected by Professor K. von den Steinen (Royal Ethnographical Museum, Berlin, Cat. no. IV A 7108); *d*, British Museum, Cat. no. 9382, collection of Mr. W. Sparrow Simpson; *e*, From west coast of Vancouver Island, collected in 1790 by Professor E. H. Giglioli, Florence (from drawing and photos by Mr. D. I. Bushnell, Jr.).

clearly the fundamental idea of the typical handle; namely, a bird's head surmounted by a bird headdress. The bird's head here, however, is very much more elaborate, and does not show the typical curved profile cut of the open beak. The opposite end clearly represents a wolf with foreleg carved immediately behind the head. This is obviously also the idea of the similar club shown in Fig. 5*e*. In this case the wolf's head is put at the upper end, and the foreleg is joined to the eye in a manner quite common in the art of the North Pacific coast. The incised design on the blade represents the double-headed serpent of the Nootka, the symbol of lightning.

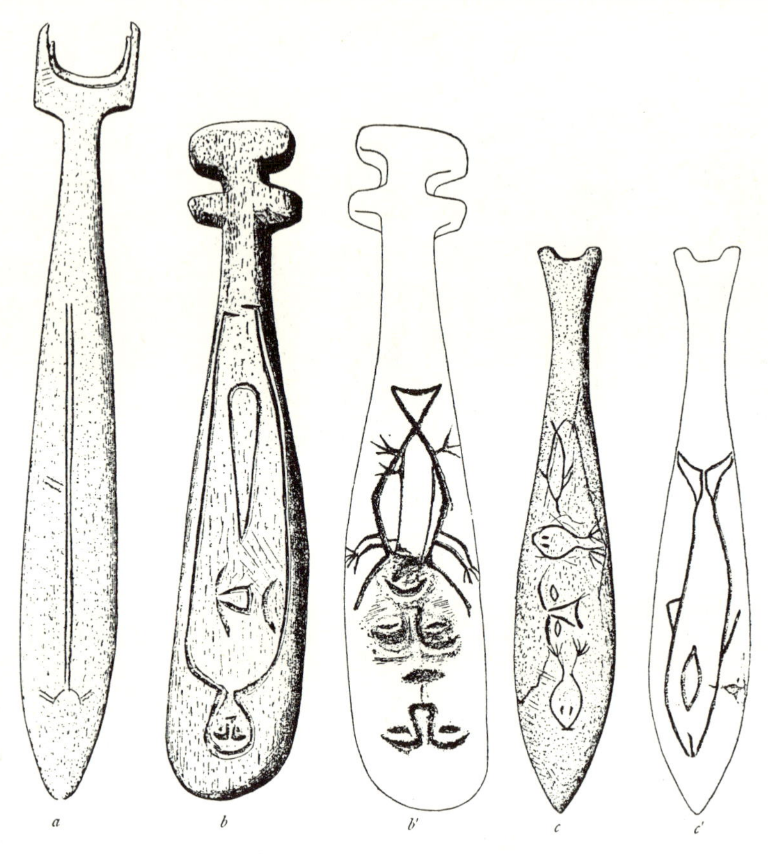

FIG. 6. Clubs made of bone of whale. *a*, From Nootka, collected by Captain Cook in 1778 (Ethnographical Museum, Florence); *b*, *b'* (16/2107), *c*, *c'* (16/2108), From Clayoquath, collected by Mr. Fillip Jacobsen.

The three clubs shown in Fig. 6 *a–c* have blades of the characteristic type. The handles, however, are quite distinct.

The first three specimens shown in Fig. 7 differ from the typical clubs in not being symmetrical, but being clearly used on one edge only, probably as bone swords. They are introduced here for the purpose of comparison with the handles of the preceding specimens. The last group (Fig. 7 *d–f*) represents two clubs found at Kamloops [Smith 1900: 422] and one of doubtful provenience. The last of these was purchased in Victoria from a curio dealer, who claimed that it came from Douglas Channel. No weight, however, can be attributed to his statement. In type these three specimens are identical. The handles represent human faces surmounted by a headdress

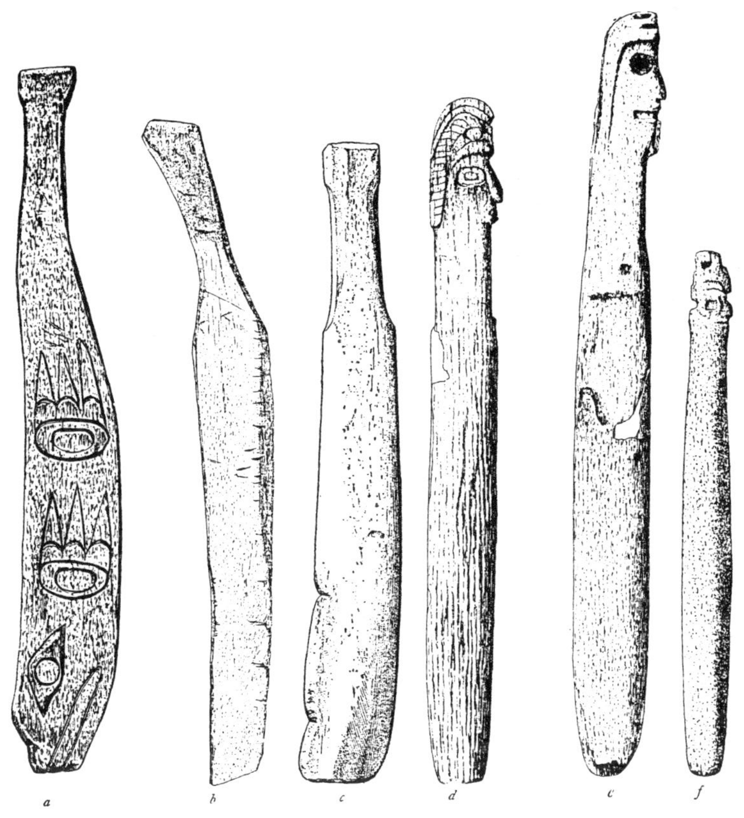

FIG. 7. Clubs made of bone of whale. *a*, From Hopitchisath, collected by Professor K. von den Steinen (Royal Ethnographical Museum, Berlin, Cat. no. IV A 7109); *b* (16/2670), From Quatsino Sound, collected by Dr R. B. Dixon; *c*, From Tongass Indians, collected by Hon. James Wickersham (from cast in U.S. National Museum, Cat. no. 19S029); *d* (16/2475), *e* (16/2474), From Kamloops; *f* (16/8377).

in which eye and beak clearly reappear. It is of course possible that these specimens may represent warriors in war costume, but it seems to me more probable that they are related to the type here discussed.

The blades of the clubs are not less characteristic than the handles. In general outline the characteristic clubs are very much alike. While a few are undecorated, most of them show a decoration which consists either of a central geometrical band usually present on both sides of the club or of a human head combined with this conventional geometrical decoration. The most common type of geometric decoration is that of a row of triangles, either alternating, and thus producing a zigzag band (Fig. 1 *a* and *e*), or in opposition along a medial line forming a series of lozenges (Fig. 1*c*, *d*; Fig. 2*a*, *e*; Fig. 3*c*). Probably related to these are the circular designs often inlaid with haliotis, accompanied by rounded or somewhat triangular incisions (Fig. 1*f*; Fig. 2*b*, *d*, *g*; Fig. 3*d*).

The characteristic combination of this geometrical design with the human face may be observed in Fig. 1*e*; Fig. 2*a*, *g*; Fig. 3*c*; Fig. 4*c*, *d*; and in the fragments Fig. 4*h*, *i*.

The strong influence of this method of decoration upon inland art is clearly exhibited in a copper club from Spuzzum which bears the same type of incised design, consisting of a human face connected with long central lines [Smith 1899:150]. The two modern specimens illustrated in Fig. 6*b* and *c*, show incised designs on the blades which are probably, at least in part, influenced by the human head on the older clubs. This is particularly true of the human figure on *b*, while the incised designs on *c*, representing fishes, a human face, and a killer whale, are purely pictographic in character.

12. Representative Art of Primitive Peoples

After a brief discussion of the roles of technical skill and the artist's virtuosity in the creation of artworks, Boas focuses on representative art, specifically of the graphic variety. He analyzes the problem an artist confronts when depicting a three-dimensional object on a two-dimensional surface. The primitive artist often solves this problem by representing all the essential traits of his subject, a solution also used by certain medieval and Dutch artists.

When studying the graphic and plastic arts of primitive people, two aspects have to be distinguished—the type of art which develops from the mastery of technique, and the other which develops from the attempts at a graphic representation of objects which interest the people.

When we speak of art, we have to bear in mind that all art implies technical skill. It is therefore an improper use of the term to speak of primitive art when we refer to objects in which the producer does not possess that mastery of technique that makes the product of his labors a work of art. A basket, a pot, or a wooden object, crudely made and irregular in outline, cannot claim the term of a product of artistic activity. On the other hand, the increase in skill brings it about that the products of the handicraft of man attain an artistic value. An inexperienced basket maker who does not control the movements of her hands will produce an uneven fabric, the stitches of which will be different in size and different in texture, and which will for this reason possess an irregular surface. On the other hand, the expert basket weaver will have such control over her movements that all the various operations will be performed in an automatic manner; so that the intensity of pull and the manner of twisting that are necessary in these operations will be performed with even intensity. For this reason the stitches will be absolutely regular, and the regularity itself will produce an esthetic effect. The same is true in the case of woodwork, where the use of the axe or of the adz in the hands of the expert workman will be so automatic that perfectly regular lines and surfaces will be produced. This virtuosity in the handling of tools and of materials is the very essence of artistic skill; and we may safely say that in many cases the esthetic effect of the manufactured objects is not due to a primary intention on the part of the manufacturer, but is a secondary product of the possession of masterly skill.

While this skill may produce regularity of outline, it does not necessarily result in designs. As soon, however, as the workman begins to play with his technique—

Reprinted from *Holmes Anniversary Volume*, Washington, D.C., pp. 18–23, 1916.

an occupation that is enjoyed by every virtuoso—then the opportunity is given for the origin of design. The potter who in turning her pot gives it regular impressions with the nail of her thumb, the basket maker who in playing with her technique develops the art of twilling, or the woodworker who varies the form of the surfaces over which he works with his adz, are led at once, by this very play with the technique, to the creation of decorative designs.

In all these matters we do not presuppose any impulse that has for its primary object the creation of esthetic forms: the esthetic forms appear rather as secondary products of virtuosity. Neither do we need to presuppose in this line of activities any desire to represent forms, and to convey ideas by means of decorative forms.

It is obvious, however, that these technical activities do not exhaust the range of forms that are found as products of the artistic skill of primitive man. We find everywhere attempts to convey definite meanings by means of graphic outlines or sculptural forms. These may be simply what has been called *Augenblickskunst* by Wilhelm Wundt; that is, forms which are intended only for the use of the moment, and that are designed to represent to the mind of the maker or to that of others certain impressions received from the experience of the moment. In these productions the artistic element is practically absent, because the outlines are always crude, and there is no technical skill exhibited in their execution.

It is characteristic of the development of representative art, however, that the technical skill which is acquired in the development of technical art is applied also to the execution of representative forms; and it is in this case that we actually find the beginnings of representative art.

It is not my purpose to discuss in the following lines the intimate relations between decorative art and representative art that do develop in many cases, and that are found with particular strength in primitive life. This subject has been discussed fully and extensively in many publications, among which must be mentioned the excellent contributions by Professor William H. Holmes, published in the Annual Reports of the Bureau of American Ethnology. It may be sufficient to point out that, according to our present point of view, it seems futile to discuss the question whether representative decorative art is older than geometrical decorative art, but that it rather appears that we are dealing here with two different sources of artistic activity, which tend to merge into the development of graphic and plastic arts. We may recognize both a tendency to geometrical conventionalization of representative design whenever it is used for decorative purposes, and we may also recognize the tendency to read meaning into geometrical decorative design when it is given representative value.

Considerable interest attaches to the question of the characteristics of both the crude and the more highly developed representative designs that occur in various cultural stages.

We will direct our attention here particularly to the attempts at representation on a surface; that is to say, to the graphic arts of drawing, engraving, and painting.

It is clear that whenever man tries to represent objects of nature in this manner, he is confronted with the problem of showing a three-dimensional object on a surface. The complete presentation of the object in all its aspects cannot be given; and the question therefore arises of solving the problem how to represent in an adequate way a three-dimensional object in a two-dimensional space.

When we examine the products of the art of primitive people, we find that on the whole a method is used which is apparently quite foreign to our modern feeling. While in our modern perspective drawing the painter tries to give the visual impression of the object, showing only what we believe we see at any given moment, we find that in more primitive forms of art this solution of the problem appears unsatisfactory, for the reason that the momentary position of the object will not exhibit certain features that are essential for its recognition. For instance, if a person is seen from the back, the eyes, the nose, and the mouth are not visible; but at the same time we know that eyes, nose, and mouth are essential characteristic elements of the human form. This idea is so fundamental in the view of most primitive people that we find practically in every case the endeavor to represent those elements that are considered as essential characteristics of the object to be represented. It is obvious that when this is to be done, the idea of rendering the momentary impression must be given up, because it may not be possible to see all these different features at the same time; and thus we find that one of the characteristic traits of primitive art is the disregard of the relative position of the essential elements of the object of representation.

It is interesting to note that the same problem presents itself to the child when it first tries to draw, and that the solution of the problem generally follows the same line that is adopted by primitive man; namely, the endeavor to represent all those elements that are considered as essential and characteristic rather than the actual spacial relations as they appear at any given moment. We must explain from this point of view the profiles with two eyes, or the outlines of the body under the garments, which occur in the drawings of both children and primitive tribes.

However, it must not be assumed that this tendency is independent of certain traditional characteristics that impress a style upon every particular area. This may be observed even in cases where we are dealing with realistic representations executed in very crude outlines. Thus the human form as represented in certain South American drawings consists very often of a triangle with point downward, the two descending sides of the triangle being continued as legs, while the horizontal line on top represents the shoulder line, and is continued outward so as to represent the arms. In other regions we find that the human body is often represented by a curved line which is open below and terminates in the legs and feet. The Eskimo, on the other hand, never utilize a form of this kind, but always execute their drawings in the form of silhouettes. On account of their tendency to show silhouettes, attention is directed only to the outlines, which are executed in many cases with a remarkable degree of fidelity to nature. On the other hand, the artist of the Magdalenian period was not satisfied with the mere outline, but tried to fill in details that the Eskimo habitually disregards. The treatment of the body by the Bushman shows again other characteristics. Cases of this kind indicate that we have to speak of traditional style even in those cases in which the forms seem at first glance to be a result of the naïve attempt at representing essential elements of the object to be represented. This stylistic character is expressed both in the outline and in the traits which are selected for representation.

The fundamental idea that in the representation of an object its essential traits must be shown has led to the development of artistic styles, which demonstrate a high technical skill, but which are quite foreign to our feeling. Perhaps the most characteristic case is that of the art of the Indians of the North Pacific coast of America, in which the principle of the representation of an object by means of symbols is carried to extremes. The conventional form in which an animal body is represented does not differ much for various types of animals; but the fundamental rule underlying the art is that the characteristic parts of the animals *must* be shown. Thus a beaver, which is characterized by the large incisors and by the tail, *must* contain these elements, no matter how the rest of the body may be treated. The killer whale *must* show the large dorsal fin, no matter how the rest of the body may be treated.

Since the art of the Northwest Coast is at the same time, on the whole, a decorative art, in which definite principles have developed in regard to the treatment of the decorative field, we find that the method of representation consists always in the attempt to squeeze the symbols of the animal that is to be represented into the decorative field and follow the rules of the treatment of surfaces that are presented by the style of the Northwest Coast art.

When we compare the art of the North Pacific coast, which has developed this tendency to an extreme degree with our modern art, it might appear that the principles are fundamentally opposed to each other. Nevertheless it is easy to show that modern art is only slowly and by degrees emancipating itself from the idea that the representation of a three-dimensional object should contain essential permanent characteristics of the object. If we remember that the imagination of the primitive artist is given its direction by the desire to represent all the essential parts of his subject, no matter whether they may be visible at a given moment or not, we can see that the paintings of the Middle Ages, in which different scenes of the same incident are represented in the same painting, follow out to a certain extent the same idea. Thus if we see in one painting Adam and Eve in Paradise on the left, the serpent in the middle, and the expulsion from Paradise on the right, it is clear that the artist followed in a way the same principle of showing the essential scenes in the same painting, although they do not belong to the same visual impression. But we can go a step farther. Large groups, like those of the Dutch painters, in which, on a large canvas, many individuals are shown with equal distinctness, do not represent the momentary visual impression. We see with distinctness only a small part of the visual field, while the rest appears blurred, and the painting therefore represents, not a momentary visual impression, but a picture reconstructed from a succession of impressions that are obtained when the eye moves over the whole field of vision. The discrepancy between the momentary impression and the painting is particularly striking in those cases where the picture itself is small and can be taken in at a single glance. Then the sharpness of outline with which all the figures stand out is contradicted by our everyday experience. It is only quite recently that pictorial art has used this phenomenon to any extent in order to compel the viewer to direct his attention to that point that is prominent in the mind of the painter.

Similar observations may be made in regard to color. We find that almost throughout, the colors which are utilized are those in which an object appears to us permanently. It is only with difficulty that most of us get accustomed to green faces, such as appear in the shadow of a tree, or red faces that may be produced by red curtains or the reflection of a brick wall. In these cases the abstraction from the momentary impression is so strong that most of us are not even aware that we actually do see these passing color effects.

It appears from this point of view that the principle of painting what may be called the permanent characteristics of an object have not by any means disappeared from modern art, and that, although the conflict between the momentary visual impression and what we consider the permanent form is not as fundamental as it is in many forms of primitive art, its effect may be traced even into modern times.

It is easy to show that the absence of realistic forms in the representative art of primitive tribes is not due to lack of skill. For instance, in those rare cases in which it is the object of the artist to deceive by the truthfulness of his representation, we find that the narrow lines imposed by conventional style may be broken through. Thus the wood carvers of the North Pacific coast, who are hemmed in so rigidly by the conventional style of that region, succeed in carving heads remarkably true to nature, which are used in their winter ceremonies, and which are intended to give the impression that a certain person has been decapitated. A remarkable specimen of this kind has been illustrated in the Annual Report of the United States National Museum for 1895 (page 504). Equally convincing are some attempts of these Indians to reproduce in wood carving classical statues that have been shown to them. We must rather seek for the condition of their art in the depth of the feeling which demands the representation of the permanent characteristics of the object in the representative design.

13. Introduction to *Primitive Art*

In this introduction to his 1927 Primitive Art, *Boas identifies technical perfection as a principal characteristic of artistic excellence and the foundation of the "stable" or "fixed" forms that characterize style. Boas then discusses the expressive component of art, stating that the inspiration to express ideas through art is not older than the inspiration to create form. He ends with a criticism of those writers who give priority to the expressive qualities of art.*

No people known to us, however hard their lives may be, spend all their time, all their energies in the acquisition of food and shelter, nor do those who live under more favorable conditions and who are free to devote to other pursuits the time not needed for securing their sustenance occupy themselves with purely industrial work or idle away the days in indolence. Even the poorest tribes have produced work that gives to them esthetic pleasure, and those whom a bountiful nature or a greater wealth of inventions has granted freedom from care, devote much of their energy to the creation of works of beauty.

In one way or another esthetic pleasure is felt by all members of mankind. No matter how diverse the ideals of beauty may be, the general character of the enjoyment of beauty is of the same order everywhere; the crude song of the Siberians, the dance of the African Negroes, the pantomime of the California Indians, the stone work of the New Zealanders, the carvings of the Melanesians, the sculpture of the Alaskans appeal to them in a manner not different from that felt by us when we hear a song, when we see an artistic dance, or when we admire ornamental work, painting or sculpture. The very existence of song, dance, painting and sculpture among all tribes known to us is proof of the craving to produce things that are felt as satisfying through their form, and of the capability of man to enjoy them.

All human activities may assume forms that give them esthetic values. The mere cry, or the word, does not necessarily possess the elements of beauty. If it does so it is merely a matter of accident. Violent, unrestrained movements induced by excitement, the exertions of the chase, and the movements required by daily occupations are partly reflexes of passion, partly practically determined. They have no immediate esthetic appeal. The same is true of all products of industrial activity. The daubing of paint, the whittling of wood or bone, the flaking of stone do not necessarily lead to results that compel our admiration on account of their beauty.

Nevertheless, all of them may assume esthetic values. Rhythmical movements

Reprinted from *Primitive Art*, pp. 9–17. New York: Dover Publications, Inc., 1955. (Originally published in 1927.)

of the body or of objects, forms that appeal to the eye, sequences of tones and forms of speech which please the ear, produce artistic effects. Muscular, visual and auditory sensations are the materials that give us esthetic pleasure and that are used in art.

We may also speak of impressions that appeal to the senses of smell, taste and touch. A composition of scents, a gastronomical repast may be called works of art provided they excite pleasurable sensations.

What then gives to the sensation an esthetic value? When the technical treatment has attained a certain standard of excellence, when the control of the processes involved is such that certain typical forms are produced, we call the process an art, and however simple the forms may be, they may be judged from the point of view of formal perfection; industrial pursuits such as cutting, carving, molding, weaving; as well as singing, dancing and cooking are capable of attaining technical excellence and fixed forms. The judgment of perfection of technical form is essentially an esthetic judgment. It is hardly possible to state objectively just where the line between artistic and pre-artistic forms should be drawn, because we cannot determine just where the esthetic attitude sets in. It seems certain, however, that wherever a definite type of movement, a definite sequence of tones or a fixed form has developed it must become a standard by which its perfection, that is, its beauty, is measured.

Such types exist among mankind the world over, and we must assume that if an unstandardized form should prove to possess an esthetic appeal for a community it would readily be adopted. Fixity of form seems to be most intimately connected with our ideas of beauty.

Since a perfect standard of form can be attained only in a highly developed and perfectly controlled technique there must be an intimate relation between technique and a feeling for beauty.

It might be said that achievement is irrelevant as long as the ideal of beauty for which the would-be artist strives is in existence, although on account of imperfect technique he may be unable to attain it. Alois Riegl [1893] expresses this idea by saying that the will to produce an esthetic result is the essence of artistic work. The truth of this assertion may be admitted and undoubtedly many individuals strive for expression of an esthetic impulse without being able to realize it. What they are striving for presupposes the existence of an ideal form which the unskilled muscles are unable to express adequately. The intuitive feeling for form must be present. So far as our knowledge of the works of art of primitive people extends the feeling for form is inextricably bound up with technical experience. Nature does not seem to present formal ideals—that is, fixed types that are imitated—except when a natural object is used in daily life; when it is handled, perhaps modified, by technical processes. It would seem that only in this way form impresses itself upon the human mind. The very fact that the manufactures of man in each and every part of the world have pronounced style proves that a feeling for form develops with technical activities. There is nothing to show that the mere contemplation of nature or of natural objects develops a sense of fixed form. Neither have we any proof that a definite stylistic form develops as a product purely of the power of the imagination of the workman, unguided by his technical experience which brings the form into his consciousness. It is conceivable that elementary esthetic forms like symmetry and rhythm, are not entirely dependent upon technical activities; but these are common to all art styles; they are not specifically characteristic of any particular region. Without stability of form of objects, manufactured or in common use, there is no style; and stability of form depends upon the development of a high technique, or in a few cases on the constant use of the same kind of natural products. When stable forms have been attained, imaginative development of form in an imperfect technique may set in and in this case the will to produce an esthetic result may outrun the ability of the would-be artist. The same consideration holds good in regard to the esthetic value of muscular movements used in song and dance.

The manufactures of man the world over prove that the ideal forms are based essentially on standards developed by expert technicians. They may also be imaginative developments of older standardized forms. Without a formal basis the will to create something that appeals to the sense of beauty can hardly exist.

Many works of art affect us in another way. The emotions may be stimulated not by the form alone, but also by close associations that exist between the form and ideas held by the people. In other words, when the forms convey the meaning, because they recall the past experiences or because they act as symbols, a new element is added to the enjoyment. The form and its meaning combine to elevate the mind above the indifferent emotional state of everyday life. Beautiful sculpture or painting, a musical composition, dramatic art, a pantomime, may so affect us. This is no less true of primitive art than of our own.

Sometimes esthetic pleasure is released by natural forms. The song of a bird may be beautiful; we may experience pleasure in viewing the form of a landscape or in viewing the movements of an animal; we may enjoy a natural taste or smell, or a pleasant feeling; grandeur of nature may give us emotional thrill and the actions of animals may have a dramatic effect; all of these have esthetic values but they are not art. On the other hand, a melody, a carving, a painting, a dance, a pantomime are esthetic productions, because they have been created by our own activities.

Form and creation by our own activities are essential features of art. The pleasure or elevation of mind must be brought about by a particular form of sense impression, but this sense impression must be made by some kind of human activity or by some product of human activity.

It is essential to bear in mind the twofold source of artistic effect, the one based on form alone, the other on ideas associated with form. Otherwise the theory of art will be one-sided. Since the art of man, the world over, among primitive tribes as well as among civilized nations, contains both elements, the purely formal and the significant, it is not admissible to base all discussions of the manifestations of the art impulse upon the assumption that the expression of emotional states by significant forms must be the beginning of art, or that, like language, art is a form of expression. In modern times this opinion is based in part on the often observed fact that in primitive art even simple geometrical forms may possess a meaning that adds to their emotional value, and that dance, music and poetry almost always have definite meaning. However, significance of artistic form is neither universal nor can it be shown that it is necessarily older than the form.

I do not intend to enter into a discussion of the philosophical theories of esthetics, but will confine myself to a few remarks on the views of a number of recent authors who have treated art on the basis of ethnological material, and only in so far as the question is concerned whether primitive art is expressive of definite ideas.

Our views agree fundamentally with those of Fechner [1876] who recognizes the "direct" appeal of the work of art on the one side and the associated elements that give a specific tone to the esthetic effects on the other.

Wundt [1919:5] restricts the discussion of art to those forms in which the artistic work expresses some thought or emotion. He says, "For the psychological study art stands in a position intermediate between language and myth. . . . Thus the creative artistic work appears to us as a peculiar development of the expressive movements of the body. Gesture and language pass in a fleeting moment. In art they are sometimes given a higher significance; sometimes the fleeting moment is given a permanent form. . . . All these relations are manifested principally in the relatively early, although not in the very earliest stages of artistic work in which the momentary needs of expression of thought dominate art as well as language."

Max Verworn [1920:8] says: "Art is the faculty to express conscious processes by means created by the artist himself in such a manner that they may be perceived by our sense organs. In this general sense language, song, music and dance are art, just as well as painting, sculpture and ornamentation. The graphic and plastic arts in the narrow sense of the term result from the ability of making conscious processes visible in permanent materials."

Richard Thurnwald [1926:211] accepts the viewpoint of Wundt when he says, "Art, however inadequate its means may be, is a means of expression that belongs to mankind. The means employed are distinct from those used in gesture, language and writing. Even when the artist is intent only upon the repetition of what he has in mind he does so with at least the subconscious purpose of communicating his ideas, of influencing others."

The same one-sidedness may be recognized in Yrjö Hirn's [1900:29] opinion, who says: "In order to understand the art impulse as a tendency to esthetic production we must bring it into connection with some function from the nature of which the specifically artistic qualities may be derived. Such a function is to be found, we believe, in the activities of emotional expression."

It will be seen that all these authors confine their definitions of art to those forms which are expressions of emotional states or of ideas, while they do not include in art the pleasure conveyed by purely formal elements that are not primarily expressive.

Ernst Grosse [1894:292] expresses similar views in somewhat different form. He stresses the practical purpose of artistic forms which appears to him as primary. However, he assumes that these forms, while devoted first of all to practical purposes, are intended at the same time to serve an esthetic need that is felt by the people. Thus, he says, that primitive ornament is by origin and by its fundamental nature not intended as decorative but as a practically significant mark or symbol, that is to say as expressive. If I understand him correctly this practical significance implies some kind of meaning inherent in the form.

Emil Stephan [1907:51ff.] concludes from his detailed discussion of Melanesian art that technical motives offer no sufficient explanation for the origin of artistic forms. He considers all ornament as representative and sees the origin of art in that unconscious mental process by which the form appears as distinct from the content of the visual impression, and in the desire to give permanence to the form. For this reason he considers the artistic forms also as equivalents of the way in which the form appears to the primitive artist.

Alfred C. Haddon [1895] and W. H. Holmes [1886:443ff.] seek the origin of all decorative art in realism. They discuss the transfer of technical forms to ornament but they see in these also results of the endeavor to reproduce realistic form, namely, technical details. Henry Balfour [1893] agrees, on the whole, with this position but he stresses also the development of decorative motives from the actual use of technical processes.

Gottfried Semper [1860] emphasizes the importance of the form as determined by the manner of use. He also stresses the influence of designs developed in weaving and of their transfer upon other forms of technique, particularly upon architectural forms.

Alois Riegl [1923:2ff.] is also inclined to stress the representative character of the most ancient art forms, basing his argument essentially upon the realistic paleolithic carvings and paintings. He sees the most important step forward in the attempt to show the animals in outline, on a two-dimensional surface which necessitates the substitution of an ideal line for the three-dimensional form that is given to us by everyday experience. He assumes that geometric ornament developed from the treatment of the line, obtained by the process just mentioned, according to formal principles.

Setting aside the assumed sequence of these two aspects, his viewpoint is distinguished from that of the authors referred to before, by the recognition of the principle of form as against that of content.

The principle of form is still more energetically defended by van Scheltema [1923] who tries to prove definite developmental processes through which the formal treatment of North European art has passed, first in the Neolithic period, then in the bronze age and finally in the iron age.[1]

Alfred Vierkandt [1925:338ff.] also emphasizes the fundamental importance of the formal element in the esthetic effect of all manifestations of art.[2]

1. For a comprehensive review of works on primitive art up to 1914, see Martin Heydrich [1914]; also the bibliography in Eckert von Sydow [1923] and Herbert Kühn [1923]. An excellent review of the subject has been given by Elizabeth Wilson [n. d.]

2. See also *Jahrbuch für historische Volkskunde*, vol. 2; Vom Wesen der Volskundt, Berlin 1926; Rafael Karsten [1926].

Conclusion to *Primitive Art*

These remarks summarize the main points Boas makes in Primitive Art. *These include the twofold origins of art—technique and ideas, the aesthetic "joys" of mastering technique, and the universals of style—symmetry, rhythm, and emphasis on form. He reviews some of the characteristics that identify individual art styles, stressing the uniformity of reaction to artistic images within an ethnic group. Reviewing the different occurrences of naturalistic and stylized art, he disputes the assumption that art styles were originally naturalistic and became stylized. For Boas, realism and stylization develop from different sources, and the relative naturalism or stylization of an artwork is in large measure due to the importance the culture assigns to these characteristics. The art style of a group is the product of a long and complex process influenced by many factors. Boas concludes with a statement that the differences between the art and the appreciation of art in primitive and western societies is the result of cultural rather than mental differences.*

We have now completed our review of the forms of primitive art and we shall try to sum up our inquiry.

We have seen that art arises from two sources, from technical pursuits and from the expression of emotions and thought, as soon as these take fixed forms. The more energetic the control of form over uncoordinated movement, the more esthetic the result. Artistic enjoyment is, therefore, based essentially upon the reaction of our minds to form. The same kind of enjoyment may be released by impressions received from forms that are not the handiwork of man, but they may not be considered as art, although the esthetic reaction is not different from the one we receive from the contemplation or the hearing of a work of art. When speaking of artistic production they must be excluded. When considering only esthetic reactions they must be included.

The esthetic effect of artistic work developing from the control of technique alone is based on the joy engendered by the mastery of technique and also by the pleasure produced by the perfection of form. The enjoyment of form may have an elevating effect upon the mind, but this is not its primary effect. Its source is in part the pleasure of the virtuoso who overcomes technical difficulties that baffle his cleverness. As long as no deeper meaning is felt in the significance of form, its effect is for most individuals, pleasurable, not elevating.

We have seen that in the various arts definite formal principles manifest them-

Reprinted from *Primitive Art*, pp. 349–56. New York: Dover Publications, Inc., 1955. (Originally published in 1927.)

selves, the origin of which we did not try to explain, but which we accepted as present in the art of man the world over, and which for this reason we considered as the most ancient, the most fundamental characteristics of all art. In the graphic and plastic arts these elements are symmetry, rhythm and emphasis of form. We found symmetry to be very generally right and left and suggested that this may be due to the symmetry of manual movements as well as the observation of right and left symmetry in animals and in man. We also observed that rhythmic repetition runs ordinarily in horizontal bands and pointed out the general experience that natural objects of the same or similar kind are arranged in horizontal strata, such as woods, mountains, and clouds; legs, body, and limbs. Rhythmic form seems to be closely related to technical processes, although other causes of rhythmic repetition are revealed in poetry. The simplest technical processes produce a simple repetition of the same motives, while with increasing virtuosity more complex orders become the rule. The more virtuosity is developed, the more complex are the rhythms that are liable to make their appearance. The ability of primitive artists to appreciate rhythm seems to be much greater than our own.

The desire to emphasize form made itself felt in the application of lines to the rim. We also observed the tendency of the rim designs to become exuberant and to encroach upon the decorative field. No less important is the tendency to attach ornament to prominent places of the decorated object and to divide the decorative field according to fixed principles.

While the features so far considered are common characteristics of art the world over, they do not explain the style of separate areas. We considered this problem in some detail in the field of decorative art. Here our attention was first arrested by the fact that purely formal art, or perhaps better, art that is apparently purely formal, is given a meaning endowing it with an emotional value that does not belong to the beauty of form alone. It is an expressionistic element that is common to many forms of primitive art. It is effective because in the mind of the tribes certain forms are symbols of a limited range of ideas. The firmer the association between a form and a definite idea, the more clearly stands out the expressionistic character of the art. This is true in the graphic and plastic arts as well as in music. In the former a geometrical form, in the latter a sound cluster, a particular type of musical phrasing, if associated with a definite meaning, evokes definite emotions or even concepts. A study of these conditions shows also that a uniform reaction to form is indispensable for the effectiveness of an expressionistic art, a condition which is not fulfilled in our own modern society, so that an expressionistic art can appeal only to a circle of adepts who follow the lines of thought and feeling developed by a master. Symbolic art can still be applied successfully in the case of a few symbols that have fixed associations which are valid for all of us.

The wide distribution of symbolic forms and the remoteness of their resemblance to the objects they symbolize led us to a consideration of the question of their history. We examined particularly the theory that all artistic reproduction is by origin naturalistic and that geometrization grows up only when the artist tries to introduce ideas that are not inherent in the object itself. We saw that this theory cannot be maintained, because realistic representation and geometrization spring from distinctive sources. In plastic art the contrast between the two tendencies does not appear as clearly as in graphic art. In the former it is found more in surface treatment than in general outline. In graphic art the matter is complicated by the difficulties involved in representing a three-dimensional object on a two-dimensional surface, a problem which the artist has to solve. This may be done in one of two ways. Either a perspective representation of the object as it appears at a given moment may be attempted, or the artist may decide that the essential point is to show all its characteristic parts, no matter whether they are visible in a single view or not. The former method lays stress upon the accidental features, it is impressionistic; the latter stresses those elements that are felt to constitute the fundamental qualities of the object, it is expressionistic. The two methods which we called the symbolic and the perspective are absolutely distinct and the one cannot be developed from the other. We have also seen that the consistent application of the perspective method is reached only when we introduce also the principle of indistinctness of those points that are removed from the center of the field of vision and that of dependence of color upon environment. Both of these have been tried in our day, without having found general acceptance. The symbolic method is always more or less wavering in the application of its principle. Sometimes perspective correctness of outline is attempted with a considerable degree of freedom in regard to the detailed treatment of those symbols that are considered important. Of this character are the Egyptian paintings with their vacillation between front and side views. In other cases the realism of outline is entirely sacrificed and the form may be reduced to a mere assembly of symbols.

The theory has been advanced that geometric ornament developed through the degeneration of perspective designs, in part perhaps also through that of symbolic designs. It is assumed that the symbol, or the object represented, was misunderstood and that in course of time through a process of slurring, by careless and inaccurate representation the forms became fragmentary and finally lost all semblance to the original. It is not possible to accept this theory, because the conditions under which the supposed slurring occurs are seldom realized. Slovenly work does not occur in an untouched primitive culture. Misunderstandings may happen in cases of borrowing of designs or in that of a gradual transformation of those concepts that find expression in decorative art. Actual slurring is found in factory production. By an examination of a few cases of this kind we were able to show that it does not lead to geometrization, but to the growth of an individualism akin to that of our handwriting. It cannot be denied that in such cases occasion for re-interpretation with consequent changes of form occur, but these are not frequent. On the other hand we were able to show that reading-in of realistic meanings into geometric forms is quite common. We proved this by means of a detailed comparison of the style of painting and embroidery of the North American Plains Indians which we found to be practically identical everywhere, while the interpretations varied from tribe to tribe. This phenomenon agrees with the general tendency to keep intact the form, but to endow it with new meaning according to the chief cultural interests of the people. We pointed out the prevalence of the same tendency in folktales and ritual. As a general explanation the geometrization of realistic patterns is, therefore, unacceptable. In the majority of cases it seems to be rather due to the inclination of man to give a meaning to geometric form, as we enjoy reading meanings into the forms of clouds and mountains. We were also able to describe a few cases in which the process of reading-in has actually been observed.

Another act prevents us from considering geometrization as a general historical process. It is very seldom only that the steps are found so distributed that they can be proved to follow one another in time. Much oftener all are found at the same time among the same people.

Considering all these points we reached the conclusion that the stylistic form, which contains to a greater or lesser extent constant geometrical elements, is decisive in determining the manner in which representations are rendered. We were thus led to the attempt to find the principles underlying art styles.

We approached this subject by the study of a few art forms. We compared a number of art styles that make use of the spiral and found in each characteristic traits, as well regarding the form of the spiral as in the handling of the decorative field. In the same way we observed that in the art of the North American Indians the same kind of triangles and rectangles are used by all the tribes, but that there exist typical differences in the treatment of the decorative field. The problem was carried through in some detail by means of a study of the decorative art of the North Pacific coast which is highly symbolic in character. This example taught us an additional point, namely that in symbolic art the selection of symbols is of decisive importance in defining the style and that the arrangement of the symbols is subject to the same formal treatment of the decorative field which controls the arrangement of geometrical motives.

On the basis of this study we conclude that the particular types of geometrical motives that enter into the representative form, as well as the treatment of the decorative field determine the character of the design and that the degree of realism depends upon the relative importance of the geometric and representative elements. When the purely decorative tendency prevails we have essentially geometrical, highly conventionalized forms; when the idea of representation prevails, we have, on the contrary, more realistic forms. In every case, however, the formal element that characterizes the style is older than the particular type of representation. This does not signify that early representations do not occur, it means that the method of representation was always controlled by formal elements of distinctive origin.

The pattern of artistic expression that emerges from a long, cumulative process determined by a multiplicity of causes fashions the form of the artwork. We recognize the permanence of pattern in those cases in which a useful form that has lost its function persists as a decorative element; in the imitation in new materials of natural forms used at one time as utensils, and in the transfer of forms from one technique to another. The fixity of the pattern does not permit the artist to apply natural forms unmodified to decorative purposes. His imagination is limited by the pattern. In cases of greater freedom the representative value may not be seriously encroached upon. Such is the case for instance, with the oriental palmetto and the ear ornaments of the Marquesas Islands, on which in olden times two deities were represented, back to back, while nowadays two girls in a swing are carved, in exactly the same special arrangement. When the pattern is highly formal and not adapted to representation, an apparent geometrization may be the result. The distinction between these two aspects appears clearly in those cases in which pictography and symbolic geometric art appear side by side.

The art of the North Pacific coast proved also that we must not assume that the style of a tribe must always be uniform, but that it is quite possible that in different industries, particularly when carried along by different parts of the population, quite distinctive styles may prevail. The excellence and consistency of a style as well as the multiplicity of forms depend upon the perfection of technique. We found, therefore, that in those cases in which technical work is done by the men alone, they are the creative artists, that when the women do a great deal of technical work they are no less productive, and that when the two sexes carry on different industries they may develop distinctive styles. It is, however, more frequent that the style of a dominant industry may be imposed upon work made by other processes. Weaving in coarse material seemed to be a most fertile source of patterns that are imitated in paintings, carvings, and pottery.

A comparison of the fundamental elements that are found in the graphic and plastic arts—the arts of space—as contrasted with those of poetry, music, and dance—the arts of time—brings out certain differences and similarities. Common to both are rhythm, and it seems likely that the rhythm of technique is merely a spacial expression of the rhythm of time, in so far as the rhythmic movements result in rhythmic forms when applied to technical pursuits. We may perhaps also speak in both types of art of attempts to emphasize closed forms, for often we find musical phrases, and single ideas in poetry closed by what might be called a decorative end, consisting of burdens and of codas. Similar elements may also appear as introductions in the beginning. Completely lacking in the pure arts of time is symmetry, because an inverted time order does not convey the impression of symmetry, as is the case in the arts of space. It occurs only in a symmetrical arrangement of phrases. Dance contains elements of both the spacial order and time arts. Therefore, the principles of the former may be clearly observed in dance forms. Rhythmic movements and rhythmic spacial order, symmetry of position and of movement, and emphasis and balance of form are essential in esthetic dance forms.

The graphic and plastic arts owe much of the emotional value to the representative and symbolic values of form. This is no less true in literature, music and dance. Narrative and poetry so far as they contain intelligible words, always have a meaning which may have a deep significance because they touch upon those aspects of life that stir the emotions. Frequently there is an added meaning, when the words have a symbolic, ulterior significance related to religious beliefs or philosophical ideas. In music and dance also symbolic significance is often attached to form.

We are at the end of our considerations, but one question remains to be answered. We have seen that the desire for artistic expression is universal. We may even say that the mass of the population in primitive society feels the need of beautifying their lives more keenly than civilized man, at least more than those whose lives are spent under the urgent necessity of acquiring the meager means of sustenance. But among others also the desire for comfort has often superseded the desire for beauty. Among primitive people the καλὸν κ'ἀγαθόν coincide. Goodness and beauty are the same. Do they then possess the same keenness of esthetic appreciation that is found at least in part of our population? I believe we may safely say that in the narrow field of art that is characteristic of each people the enjoyment of beauty is quite the same as among ourselves: intense among a few, slight among the mass. The readiness to abandon one's self to the exaltation induced by art is probably greater, because the conventional restraint of our times does not exist in the same forms in their lives. What distinguishes modern esthetic feeling from that of primitive people is the manifold character of its manifestations. We are not so much bound by a fixed style. The complexity of our social structure and our more varied interests allow us to see beauties that are closed to the senses of people living in a narrower culture. It is the quality of their experience, not a difference in mental make-up that determines the difference between modern and primitive art production and art appreciation.

The Boasian Legacy in Northwest Coast Art Studies

ALDONA JONAITIS

Franz Boas's writings have informed every study of Northwest Coast art written in the twentieth century. On the most fundamental level, he provided the raw material for research. During his tenure as curator at the American Museum of Natural History from 1895 to 1905, Boas oversaw the acquisition of vast quantities of Northwest Coast art, coordinated the activities of the Jesup North Pacific Expedition, and rearranged the American Museum's North Pacific Hall.[1] Boas's work in four major areas of art history—iconographic, formal, historical, and psychological—laid the groundwork for every subsequent analysis of Northwest Coast art. His key to identifying animals was essential for later iconographic studies, including those informed by structuralist theory.[2] Inspired in part by his writing on style are sophisticated formal analyses of Northwest Coast art that go well beyond his explanation of split representation and characterization of designs on Chilkat blankets and bentwood boxes.[3] Boas's focus on history anticipated later, more nuanced reconstructions of the history of Northwest Coast style within the region and the more radical diffusionism of transpacific contact. And, his interest in the psychology of creativity led to research on individual artists within the Northwest Coast tradition.

Scholars in the United States, Canada, and abroad have acknowledged Boas's pioneering contributions to Northwest Coast art. One of the most appreciative is Leonard Adam who, in *Nordwest-Amerikanische Indianerkunst* (1923), says: "We owe to Boas our first unravelling of the unique decoration" and later singles him out as the "true decoder [*wahrhafter erschliesser*] of Northwest Coast Indian culture" (pp. 6, 17). Raymond Firth applauds Boas's treatment of symbolic art in which Boas demonstrates how people in the same community can interpret the same motif differ-

1. See Boas's categories of art history, pages 36–37, this volume. See Jacknis 1985 and Jonaitis 1988a for more on Boas and the American Museum; see Cole 1985 for more on Boas's collecting.

2. Many publications utilize Boasian explanations of animal imagery. See, for example, Inverarity 1960:41; Drucker 1963:182–84; Harner and Elsasser 1965:15; Gunther 1966:8–9; Holm 1967; Malin and Feder 1968:24–27; Stewart 1979:42–81; Haberland 1979; Wyatt 1984:15; Reid 1987:226; Stewart 1990:37–39.

3. A good number of writers describe split representation in a Boasian fashion. See, for example, Garfield and Wingert 1950:60, Inverarity 1960:37–38; 44–48; Drucker 1963:181–85; Drucker 1965:131; Holm 1965; Harner and Elsasser 1965:14–15; Gunther 1966:6–7; Malin and Feder 1968:27–28; Wardwell 1978:18; Stewart 1979:36–40; Anderson 1979:59–63.

ently (1973: 128). Firth finds Boas's analysis of the emotional appeal of symbols such as flags and swastikas in modern society especially valuable. In his review article on "Ethnoart," Harry R. Silver (1979:272) praises Boas's measured critique of evolutionism: "Boas's approach still stands as a model of balanced reasoning and careful research." In particular, according to Silver, Boas successfully disputed extreme evolutionist points while not himself falling into an extreme diffusionist position, and insisted that several factors including materials, technique, and psychology must be taken into account before art can be understood (1979:272).

Helen Codere (1966) is probably the most enthusiastic commentator on Boas's writings on art. Answering those critics who accuse Boas of never having synthesized his vast materials, Codere suggests that these critics have failed "to recognize [his conclusions] as conclusions or to understand the nature of their significance" (1966:xx). Codere believes that Boas's analysis of art provides the basis for an observer to distinguish between genuine and fake Northwest Coast art. By following Boasian stylistic principles, Codere suggests, one can identify what is wrong with pieces that purport to be Northwest Coast art, such as commercial copies of totem poles, and produce what appears to be "authentic" Northwest Coast art. Codere is probably too lavish in her praise here, for later refinements of Boas needed to be done in order for Northwest Coast style to be understood completely. Michael Ames (1992:61–62) supports Codere's view, but credits Bill Holm's work with complementing Boas's. As Holm himself points out (1983a:34), Boas never recognized the full significance of the formline in Northwest Coast art; only by understanding this key feature could an artist genuinely reconstruct this style.[4]

Codere finds Boas's analysis of art helpful in understanding Northwest Coast Indian "ways of thinking and imagining" (1966:xxi). She is most intrigued by the split representation. At first trying to imagine a body split in two and joined at the mouth and nose was "extremely unpleasant"; soon, however, she realized that this is not an art of "butchered things" but one that represents with real vitality a living being. This "trick of Kwakiutl visual imaging" is, to Codere, "not a matter of dissecting,

4. The question of Boas's understanding of the formline is interesting. Holm writes that "[Boas] certainly did recognize 'formlines' when they were narrow and black, but he apparently didn't realize that they were ubiquitous, and didn't see them when they were very broad and massive and especially if they were unpainted or the paint had worn away. Just to check this out, I reread parts of *Primitive Art* (and found lots of notes scribbled in the margins 30 or more years ago!). Among them was another noted clue to his misunderstanding. On page 254, referring to Emmons's list of blanket pattern names, in a single paragraph, he proves both that he understood the principles of formlines and that he didn't understand them. 'Another characteristic pattern, the narrow crescent, has presumably also originated from the desire to break the monotony of continuous areas. *It appears particularly when it is desired to set off two merging patterns against each other* [proof for]. Here also design names obtained by Emmons, "woman's hair ornament" (r) and "Slit"(s) *have nothing to do with its function and significance as part of the whole pattern* [proof against!]' " (pers. com. 1992; italics Holm's).

then perceiving; it is one of perceiving in the case of split representation from three viewpoints rather than one and arranging these three separate perceptions into one that is connected and unified" (1966:xxi–xxii).[5]

Douglas Fraser, in an interesting assessment of Boas's artistic writings, commends Boas's "devastating critique of the Evolutionist School" (1966:1) and briefly describes his analysis of representative and geometric decorative art, as well as his treatment of the significance of environment, technique, and function in the creation of an art style. But he criticizes Boas for ignoring the communicative and expressive features of art. Suggesting a psychological reason for this omission, Fraser states:

> *Technical mastery, for Boas, was both a hallmark of true art and a source in itself of aesthetic pleasure. Thus he concerned himself primarily with the study of* form *and tended to leave aside questions of content or expressive intention. In many ways these preferences are consistent with his personal ideal of self-control, indefatigable labor, meticulous attention to detail, and a liking for the measurable and the orderly, with a corresponding distaste for the subjective or chancy side of art* (1966:3).

A careful reading of Boas reveals that he did acknowledge the "subjective or chancy" aspects of art; while he gave considerable weight to technique, he recognized on many occasions the communicative function of art.

STYLE AND HISTORY

Boas concentrated on the formal qualities of art in many of his writings. Subsequent scholars, drawing on his detailed work on Northwest Coast art, refined our understanding of this complex style and its history. In 1918, Boas's student Herman Haeberlin identified an area of Northwest Coast art that had not yet been adequately studied, "the relations of form in the art products themselves" (1918:259).[6] The Boasian treatment of Northwest Coast art, which both identifies features of the rep-

5. In their introduction to the Museum of Modern Art's 1941 exhibition catalogue, *Indian Art of the United States*, Rene d'Harnoncourt and Frederic Douglas assert that the split representation in Northwest Coast art was not meant to depict a "mythical monster" but instead, because it shows the "two sides of one and the same animal . . . illustrate a tendency toward realism, not a desire to express mystic powers. The Northwest Coast people always considered all aspects of their model, and used this device to give a complete rendering of their subject when they portrayed it on a two-dimensional plane" (1941:11–12). The authors, trying very hard to convince a New York audience that Northwest Coast art was accessible and comprehensible, assert that the split representation demonstrates the "realism" so appreciated by so many viewers of western art.

6. Despite his clear allusions to his mentor's writings, Haeberlin did not once mention Boas's name in this essay, which has no footnotes or references.

resented animals and also describes the manner in which they fit into the space being decorated, deals, Haeberlin argues, primarily with content not style. In order to analyze style, Haeberlin lists several topics meriting further investigation: relationships between the motifs within figures, such as the eyes and the brows; the formal qualities of the plastic surface modeling of three-dimensional objects; the principles that govern the combination of different animals on artworks such as totem poles and spoon handles; and "the persistency with which painted lines are given artistic 'character' by making them lighter and heavier at different points, as for instance in the outlines of the eyes which represent joints" (1918:260).[7] Anthropologist Haeberlin's questions about style have profound art historical significance.

Haeberlin suggests further analysis as well of the imagination and psychology of the artist, particularly with respect to the process in which the artist adapts a subject to the surface being decorated. To arrive at such an understanding of the creative process, Haeberlin urges scholars to approach "primitive art" using methods employed in western art criticism, and not treat it solely as an "ethnographic element":

. . . the aesthetic study of our [western] art is privileged by being able to become individualistic and biographical, so to say, thanks to the detailed documentary evidence bearing on its historical development. . . . But in the study of primitive art it is just this biographical feature of the history of modern art that we need for stimulation. We tend too much towards conceiving the art of a primitive people as a unit instead of considering the primitive artist as an individuality. It is necessary to study how the individual artist solves specific problems of form relations, of the combination of features and of spatial compositions in order to understand what is typical of an art style (1918:263–64).[8]

This statement deserves underlining; here, in 1918, Haeberlin is encouraging scholars to treat Native artists as individuals who use creativity and aesthetic judgment in the production of artworks. What is so interesting is that this challenge to treat primitive artists like those of the West was virtually ignored for decades.[9]

Haeberlin was by and large correct about the limitations of Boas's approach to style. It was to be almost half a century before anyone attempted a serious study of the formal qualities of Northwest Coast art. Bill Holm, in *Northwest Coast Indian Art: An Analysis of Form* (1965), accomplished a genuine reconstruction of "the rules upon which this system of principles was based" (p. v). In this original book, the "other" classic of Northwest Coast art, Boas's influence comes through clearly. Holm credits Boas with having made major contributions to our understanding of

7. Holm (1965) later identified these as formlines and ovoids.

8. Note that it took some time for Northwest Coast art to be treated as "art." See Jonaitis 1981, 1988:237–40.

9. Haeberlin died in 1918, and unfortunately never pursued this significant issue.

representation in Northwest Coast art but points out that, with the exception of symmetry, Boas concentrates on "principles of representation rather than of composition, design organization, or form" (1965:8). Holm goes on to precisely define the formal elements of northern Northwest Coast two-dimensional style. Holm begins his analysis with a refinement of Boas's ideas on the stylization of imagery, first reviewing the representational ambiguity characteristic of Chilkat blankets and bentwood boxes, and the difficulties inherent in identifying some of the more abstract motifs such as those on Edenshaw's gambling sticks (Swanton 1909:149–54, Boas 1927:210–16). Then he classifies three degrees of realism in two-dimensional work: configurative, where the animal appears with a relatively naturalistic silhouette; expansive, where, although split, its parts are rearranged with some consideration of their natural anatomical relationships; and distributive, where the abstracted parts fill the space in so complex a fashion that identification becomes virtually impossible.

The body of Holm's book consists of a study of the formal elements of Northwest Coast art. Perhaps his most important contribution is the identification of the formline as "the characteristic swelling and diminishing linelike figure delineating design units." "These formlines," he writes, "merge and divide to make a continuous flowing grid over the whole decorated area, establishing the principal forms of the design. . . . To call [the formline] line only would be to minimize its importance as a formal element. The constantly varying width of the formline gives the design a calligraphic character" (Holm 1965:29, 35).

The primary formline, usually black, outlines the major elements of the image, while secondary formlines, often in red, denote other elements. A tertiary color—blue, green, or blue-green—is sometimes used for additional elements. Other components of these designs include ovoids, eyelids, U-forms, and split U-forms, all of which work in harmony with the formlines to create the distinctive Northwest Coast two-dimensional image. Further on, Holm identifies hands, feet, and claws, supplementing Boas's identification of the animals upon which those body parts can appear.

Holm (1965:69) comments that identifying the formal characteristics of this art is simpler than analyzing their organization, "for here the Indian artist demonstrated his great sensitivity and mastery of the idiom. The very fact that 'art' is involved makes objective analysis difficult." Holm here seems to be in agreement with Boas on the importance of technical mastery, as well as on the significance of an individual artist's genius and creativity as he or she works within the culturally determined parameters of a stylistic system. To characterize the system, Holm proceeds to study boxes much like those Boas dealt with in *Primitive Art* (1927:265–77), pointing to the significance of the degree of realism in the representation of the animal image. In addition to the formline, other key features that contribute to the overall appearance of this style are horizontal symmetry and avoidance of parallelism (two elements Boas had identified[10]), "semiangularity of curves," avoidance of concentric lines in ovoids and U-forms, and the use of elegant transitional devices. "The total effect of the system was to produce a strong, yet sensitive, division of the given shape by means of an interlocking formline pattern of shapes related in form, color, and scale" (Holm 1965:92). Another arena for consensus between Holm and Boas involves their assessment of the pleasure artists take in the creative process. Boas (1927:349) credits the "joy engendered by the mastery of technique and also the pleasure produced by perfection of form" as key to an artwork's aesthetic effect. Holm, who unlike Boas became a master Northwest Coast–style artist, describes from a personal point of view the satisfaction derived from the physical activity of carving and painting (1965:92–93).[11]

So useful is it for understanding the formal qualities of the northern style that *Northwest Coast Indian Art* can be considered a "textbook" on the subject. As such, it could be criticized by those who object to a rigid codification of style that does not give room for individual creativity. Because of this, it is worth noting Holm's concluding paragraph (1965:93):

. . . it is certain that no system could ever, of itself, produce the masterworks of Northwest Coast art which are the inspiration and the object of this study. As in all art it remained for the imagination and sensitivity of some of the most imaginative and sensitive of men to give life to a list of rules and principles and produce the wonderful compositions that came from the northern coast. It is precisely because each piece was the creation of the mind of a man that it can be analyzed only superficially in terms of elements and principles, while that quality which raises the best of Northwest Coast design to the status of art remains unmeasured.

Here again, Holm demonstrates his kinship to Boas.

Numerous scholars, including Holm, refined the characterization of this system of two-dimensional design and identified regional differences. As early as 1950, Paul Wingert and Viola Garfield discussed certain stylistic characteristics of different Northwest Coast groups. In *Northwest Coast Indian Art* (1965:24), Holm briefly differentiates the manner in which different groups applied painting decorations on three-dimensional objects such as masks. In his description of Haida, Tlingit, and Tsimshian mask painting, Holm refers to facial painting that Boas studied (1898b), noting that the artist's designs have little or no relation to the form upon which they

10. Boas (1927:263) explains the curved lower lines of faces on bentwood boxes as "a desire to avoid excessive parallelism."

11. Holm (1965:92–93) also agrees with Boas (1927:335) on the relationship of art production to dance.

appear and thus are independent of form. In contrast, Kwakwaka'wakw mask paintings accentuate the sculptural forms, while those of the Bella Coola "deliberately cross the carved forms."[12] Later, Holm (1967, 1974) continued his discriminations of regional two-dimensional styles and also studied one of the most complex examples of that genre, the Chilkat blanket (1982). In other works Holm addresses the differences among the sculptures of different Northwest Coast groups (1972, 1983a, 1987, 1990a). Peter Macnair (Macnair, Hoover, and Neary 1980) sensitively characterizes the two- and three-dimensional styles of the British Columbian coastal peoples, including in his analysis twentieth-century works up to the present.

Boas had briefly ventured into the topic of regional distinctions as early as 1888 when he used them to reconstruct Northwest Coast history. In *Primitive Art* (1927:279) Boas proposed that the symbolic style—what we now call the formline style—developed relatively recently in the area of northern British Columbia and southern Alaska; the older style was a geometric form of decoration found on Vancouver Island among the Kwakwaka'wakw and Nuu-chah-nulth. His speculations have provided the groundwork for several major contributions to the understanding of the history of Northwest Coast art. Indeed, while Boas's scheme has been modified in subsequent literature, much of his general outline remains intact.

Being most concerned with questions of naturalism and stylization in two-dimensional renderings, Boas paid relatively little attention to Northwest Coast sculpture. Later scholars, concentrating as much on sculpture as on two-dimensional design, proposed a more detailed reconstruction of the development of Northwest Coast regional styles. The first professionally trained art historian to study this region was Paul Wingert (1949). In his analysis of the stylistic characteristics of Salish sculpture, he accepts Boas's opinion that this style is older than the monumental and decorative northern traditions. An interesting hypothesis Wingert puts forth is that this old Salish sculptural style, with its "simplicity and clarity of carved shapes" (1949:119), was either shared in earlier times with the Kwakwaka'wakw and Nuu-chah-nulth, or actually influenced those two Wakashan groups. Wingert goes on to make a statement that he acknowledges runs counter to the more widely held theory that cultural influence spread from the Kwakwaka'wakw to the Salish: "It seems likely . . . [that] the Kwakiutl especially, who were a northern people, appropriated an art form with which they came into contact in the southern part of the Northwest Coast, and, with the acquisition of metal tools, developed it and imprinted upon it certain northern elements" (1949:121). Because of this, he proposed that the Kwakwaka'wakw and the Nuu-chah-nulth represent transitional styles between north and south. The next year in their publication on the Tsimshian, Wingert and Viola Gar-

12. Because this essay brings us to the present, I use the name preferred by the group that Boas called Kwakiutl.

field (1950) offered further refinements of the stylistic differences between the various Northwest Coast peoples.

Subsequent scholars took interest in exploring regional differences from which they could further Boas's history of the region. Philip Drucker (1963:177–78, 187–89; 1965:128–31, 153–54) described as the older "Wakashan" the realistic, naturalistic, and more three-dimensional style of the Kwakwaka'wakw and Nuu-chah-nulth, calling the highly conventionalized surface decorative style the northern style. Drucker (1965:154) points out that the Tlingit, with their lesser use of conventionalism and two-dimensional decoration and greater realism and "power," share an archaic style with the Wakashan groups. Later in the historic period, the Haida influenced the Kwakwaka'wakw and to a lesser extent the Nuu-chah-nulth, which resulted in "a hybridization [that] combines the serenity and simplicity of the northern style with the vigor of Wakashan art." Wilson Duff (1967a) hypothesizes that two older artistic traditions which he labeled Old Wakashan and Northern Graphic were ultimately blended to create two historic styles: northern and Kwakiutl. In the first, two-dimensional designs dominate the carved surfaces they decorate (as in masks and totem poles); the Kwakiutl style has freer use of decorative images and bolder sculptural forms (Duff 1967a; Holm 1972). Macnair refines the picture in his careful description of precontact, southern two-dimensional art and the inventive fashion in which the Kwakwaka'wakw translated the northern style in their art (Macnair, Hoover, and Neary 1980:36–42). Boas and some of his historically oriented successors did not have access to the more recently excavated archaeological material from the coast which has modified the history of Northwest Coast art somewhat (see Borden 1983, Carlson 1983, MacDonald 1983). As Holm (1990a:602–3) summarizes it, certain elements of Northwest Coast style such as pinched eyes, skeletal details, and a prototype of the formline existed among all the peoples from Washington to northern British Columbia hundreds of years prior to contact. By the late eighteenth century, two complex systems of two-dimensional decoration existed, one, the more familiar northern style, the other, the less widely recognized Central Coast Salish style. The existence of the Salish type of formline is worth noting.

The arts of the Nuu-chah-nulth and Coast Salish people have received relatively little attention in the literature. Several possible reasons for this can be suggested. Compared with the abundance of carving and painting among the Kwakwaka'wakw and their northern neighbors, the Nuu-chah-nulth and Salish produced less art. Moreover, the flamboyance of Kwakwaka'wakw art and the greater elegance and refinement of the northern style, tend to overshadow the simpler, more direct southern art styles. Finally, it may be that Boas and his successors, by giving northern Northwest Coast material a privileged position, have overlooked the corpus of work they would characterize as archaic.

Wayne Suttles has addressed the neglect of Salish materials in art studies in two ways.[13] In "Productivity and Its Constraints: A Coast Salish Case" (1983), Suttles suggests that certain ritually connected constraints resulted in a relatively small corpus of art among the Coast Salish. Later, in an assessment of the underlying assumptions that he sees having characterized Northwest Coast art studies, Suttles (1989) identifies as "essentialism" the condition in which one culture is considered peripheral to others. For Suttles, essentialism represents the "view that types are real and that the variations we see in the world around us are imperfections;" in such a view, certain tribes are envisioned as the "type," while surrounding ones are peripheral, derivative, and, in Suttles's words, imperfect. The Salish and Nuu-chah-nulth have, with few notable exceptions (see Wingert 1950), suffered from this type of essentialism, if not explicitly then implicitly. Indications exist that this may be changing. Recently, Holm (1990a:613) has called attention to the presence of a formline style among the Central Coast Salish that has considerable antiquity and sophistication, characterized by the representation of animals in shallow relief "by excising the background around the figure and by defining the positive forms of body parts by negative, carved relief slits in crescent and T or wedge shapes." Although this system is related to the northern formline tradition, Holm suggests it is not derivative but a parallel development from "a common body of concepts."

DIFFUSIONISM AND TRANSPACIFIC CONTACT

In his efforts to prove the weaknesses of evolutionism, Boas demonstrated that art styles change as artistic motifs were diffused from one culture to another, in a process similar to that of the diffusion of features of mythology and social organization between neighboring groups. Boas substituted history for evolutionism in favoring diffusion as an explanation for similarities that occurred in contiguous or relatively close cultures. The use of stylistic similarities to reconstruct artistic developments over time brings us to the topic of the more radical kind of diffusionism that became popular in some circles during the first half of the twentieth century.

Boas readily accepted the concept of the diffusion of artistic styles from one group to another within the Northwest Coast region and neighboring areas. During the first half of the twentieth century, a group of scholars, mainly Europeans, promoted a less cautious version of diffusionism that they believed explained similarities in cultures separated by considerable spatial and temporal distances. Some of these, such as adherents of the Kulturkreis school of Vienna, were of the opinion that all world cultures developed from movements of peoples from a finite number of culture centers.[14] Although Boas never approved of such extreme diffusionism, several

13. See Suttles (1982) for an interesting article on the Swaixwé mask.

14. See Kluckhohn 1936 for a detailed analysis of the Kulturkreis school.

scholars used certain features of Northwest Coast art to support their claim that ancient Chinese art of the Zhou and Shang periods influenced the development of Northwest Coast art. This claim has produced a rich, although ultimately flawed, body of literature based in large measure on visual materials taken from Boas's works.

Out of the major figures in the question of transpacific contact is Leonard Adam, who wrote several significant works on Northwest Coast art. In 1923, Adam published a small book, *Nordwest-Amerikanische Indianerkunst*, in which he suggested that instead of being "primitive," this material represented a most accomplished style; here he agrees with both Boas and Haeberlin. In separate chapters, Adam described Northwest Coast design and ornament, stylized sculpture, and realistic sculpture. In the last section of his text, "Die Beziehungen der Nordwestkunst zu Anderen Kunstgebieten" [The Relations of Northwest Art to Other Art Provinces] (1923:32), Adam describes the similarities of Northwest Coast art to the art of other regions and poses the question of their origins. This question, he feels, must address two issues: (1) the resemblance of northeast Asian art to that of the Pacific Northwest, and (2) the cultural dissimilarity between the Indians of the Northwest Coast and their Native American neighbors.[15]

Unlike several later scholars who interpret such data as indicative of transpacific contact, Adam cautions that drawing conclusions about the origins of Northwest Coast style on the basis of parallels with Chinese art "would be dilettantism without any scientific value for the real state of the question." Instead of advancing such a flawed argument, Adam proposes a more Boasian historical reconstruction that first investigates the relationships between the Northwest Coast Indians and nearby Indian groups. He points to the linguistic research of Pliny Goddard and Edward Sapir which, by identifying certain similarities between the Tlingit language and Athapaskan, suggests that the Northwest Coast was not in reality so very isolated from its neighbors.[16] Adam then states that only when those relationships had been thoroughly investigated could the scholar begin to examine the connections to the more remote peoples such as those of ancient Mexico. And, "only when these tasks have been accomplished will both the possibility and methodological justification be at hand to permit the comparative look at the Northwest Coast to the south seas and beyond that to the West" (Adam 1923:32).

15. See Kroeber 1923 for a discussion of the lack of similarities between the Northwest Coast cultures and the surrounding Indian cultures. In this essay, Kroeber concludes that the case for Asian origins is weak and that the Northwest Coast is "aloof" from both Asia and America.

16. Thompson and Kinkade (1990:42) have the following to say on this issue: "A number of linguistic features occur over the Northwest Coast culture area and tend to define it as a distinct linguistic diffusion area. However, most of these features extend into the Plateau, California, or Subarctic culture areas. On the other hand, some features are found only in northwestern North America and are rare elsewhere in the world; the combination of a number of these features makes the overall region (as a whole) unique in the world."

In "Das Problem der Asiatisch-Altamerikanischen Kulturbeziehungen mit besonderer Berücksichtigung der Kunst" [The Problem of Asiatic–Old American Culture Relations with Special Consideration of Art], Adam (1931) expands on the similarities between the art of ancient China and the Northwest Coast. Adam enumerates the eight features of Northwest Coast decorative style gleaned from the writings of Boas, Emmons (1907), and Swanton (1905):[17]

1. *The principle of stylizing (as a contrast to realistic representations);*
2. *The principle of schematic characterization, or symbolism:*
   a. *by way of accentuating certain characteristic features of the body;*
   b. *by adding characteristic attributes (e.g., a stick held by the beaver in its forepaws);*
3. *The principle of splitting the body;*
4. *The principle of dislocating the split details;*
5. *The principle of representing* one *animal by two profiles;*
6. *The principle of symmetry (with exceptions!);*
7. *The principle of reducing (representations 'pars pro toto' [part by the whole]);*
8. *The principle of illogical transformation of details into new representations which were originally not provided for (e.g., two toes of a paw becoming a bird's beak whereby the* eye ornament *which is, properly speaking, no eye, but simply indicates a joint, becomes an eye in the proper sense of the term) (Adam 1936:8–9)*[18]

Certain of these features, specifically "splitting" and "illogical transformation of details," appear on carved vessels from Honduras dating from circa A.D. 1300, as well as on artworks of ancient China, dating from the second and first century B.C. (Adam 1931:63). Despite these similarities, Adam feels that the time span between ancient China, pre-Columbian Honduras, and the nineteenth century-cultures of the Northwest Coast (cultures which he feels, like Boas, developed relatively recently) is simply too great for a connection to be made. A Chou bronze found in the New World would, Adam asserts, not prove artistic influence:

. . . even if someone were to show me a genuine Chou bronze found on American soil dating from before the European era, I would not admit the possibility that the striking similarity between Northwestern American ornamentation and that of the Chou dynasty

17. Emmons actually contributed very little to an understanding of style per se in his part of the Chilkat blanket monograph; most of Emmons's section deals with technique of manufacture. Swanton's chapter on art is primarily an identification of imagery on Haida art. Much of the material he presents was collected by Boas. In addition, Boas worked closely with Swanton as the latter was writing this chapter (see Jonaitis 1992). Thus, while Adam credits Emmons and Swanton, the stylistic characteristics he lists are largely from Boas.

18. This list is the English version of Adam's principles as published in 1936 in *Man*.

derived from cultural borrowing. For although Northwest ornamentation manifests the same principles of design as Chou ornamentation, for all its refinement the American work represents, in my opinion, a more primitive stage of a stylistic development in the evolution of which—and this is the crux of the issue—we can discern in the [American] land itself (1931:64).

In his concluding paragraph, Adam once again repeats the suggestion, made as well in his 1923 book, that cultural development within the New World must be investigated before one can raise the question of foreign influence. Then he suggests an alternative explanation for Chinese–Northwest Coast similarities: an "ancient racial kinship" [*rassenmassige Urverwandtschaft*] of the Mongoloid people which reveals itself in a similar sensibility and psychology that generates similar art among people of distant time and place.

In 1936, Adam published "North-West American Indian Art and Its Early Chinese Parallels" in English, where he summarizes his points made in 1931. This is the article most frequently cited in the English literature; in it he repeats the eight characteristics of Northwest Coast style, emphasizing the split image and accepting Boas's technical explanation for the motif. After pointing to the similarities between this style and that of Chou art, he states that he "does not suggest a historical connection between these two styles created by so different peoples and with a chronological distance of about 3,000 years" (Adam 1936:10). Once again Adam's explanation for these parallels is not diffusion but "a similar mentality to the psychological background of corresponding artistic ideas" (1936:11).

The same year that Adam published an essay in English urging caution in historical reconstructions, Carl Hentze promoted the concept of migrations from China to the Northwest (1936). In *Objets rituels, croyances et dieux de la Chine antique et de l'Amérique* [*Ritual Objects, Beliefs and Gods of Ancient China and America*], Hentze asserts that although similarities do not necessarily indicate direct influences, cultural independence is quite rare, for cultures are most often influenced by other cultures. In order to hypothesize real influence from one to another culture, there must exist in each a cultural complex that shares many of the same features; Hentze believes that the appearance of such complexes in different societies indicates migrations of peoples from one area to another. This, Hentze says, seems to have been the case with ancient China and the Americas (1936:12–13).

Unlike Adam, who focuses on formal qualities, Hentze concentrates on iconographic images that he interprets as having dualistic, and sometimes even lunar and solar, significance. Using Boasian texts as his documentation, Hentze describes the similarity between the Sisiutl image and that of a double-headed serpent in Chinese art, drawing heavily on Gottfried Locher's *The Serpent in Kwakiutl Religion* (1932) that argued that the Sisiutl embodies a dualism of good and evil, upper and lower worlds (1936:39–40).[19] Hentze also makes a connection between Old and New World representations of a raptorial bird holding a human, using Kwakw*a*k*a*'wakw images as one of his examples (1936:65–67) and once again interpreting the motif as manifesting dualism.

A book that numerous Americans read with considerable interest was *The Birth of China* by Herrlee Glessner Creel (1937). Although the book concerned China, Creel does point to "certain definite and close resemblances between Shang design and the decorative art of certain North American Indians" (1937:47), and goes on to state that "there is a very considerable likelihood" that influences spread from a center, which in his view could only have been in Asia and not in the New World. In the discussion of Shang bronzes, Creel comments that both Shang art and Northwest Coast art represent animals and use isolated eyes for decoration, and describes the split image that occurs in both areas, strongly concluding that "these are the only two areas in the world in which this technique is used, according to my present information. This may be another indication of the Pacific affinities of Shang civilization" (p. 122).

Carl Schuster, in "Joint Marks" (1951), agrees that historical documentation on transpacific contact has not yet been found, but suggests that one day such documents may be unearthed (1951:3). In the meantime he suggests that scholars continue to gather evidence of artistic correspondences between the Old and New Worlds. He proposes that joint marks, which are decorations or accentuations of the joints of figures found in the art of certain peoples of South America and Mesoamerica, Oceania, ancient China, and the Pacific Northwest indicate historic connections between those regions. Schuster refers to Boas for support of his contention that joint marks are "a conspicuous feature" of Northwest Coast art: "As early as 1897 Boas recognized the special function of the eye as a joint-mark in the art of the Northwest Coast: 'An examination . . . will show that in most cases it [the eye] is used to indicate a joint. Shoulder, elbow, hand, hips, knees, feet, the points of attachment of fins, tails and so forth, are always indicated by eyes' " (1951:17). The significance of joint marks among the Northwest Coast peoples provides evidence, in Schuster's mind, of transpacific contacts.

In 1949, Robert Heine-Geldern, an Austrian ethnologist whose field of study was Southeast Asia, presented a paper to a New York audience on the Chinese influence in the Pacific and in America that many found compelling. Miguel Covarrubias summarized Heine-Geldern's argument in the most complete statement of transpacific contact, *The Eagle, the Jaguar, and the Serpent* (1954). Early in this book

19. See Boas's review of Locher's book (1933) in which he argued against Locher's interpretation of the Sisiutl.

on Native American art (p. 31), Covarrubias repeats Heine-Geldern's theory that the similarities between the art of ancient China and the New World are due not to coincidence or similar psychological foundations, but instead to migrations of peoples. As early as the third millennium B.C., according to both Heine-Geldern and Covarrubias, the basic prehistoric culture, the "Old Pacific Style" that underlay the Shang and Chou cultures of China, spread to the Northwest Coast (as well as to other areas). Characteristic of this culture were heraldic totem poles, as well as the joint marks, serpent cults, and split representations described by Adam, Hentze, and Schuster.

Covarrubias's analysis of Northwest Coast art (1954:164–91) draws heavily on Boas, particularly his description (though not his explanation) of the split image. Covarrubias repeats Boas's historical reconstruction of Northwest Coast style, based on the assumption that the geometric decorative style is older than the complex symbolic style, then asserts that this theory "leaves unexplained the source of the super-stylized totemic motifs, made of curves and irregular rounded shapes, more reminiscent of the arts of pre-Buddhist China and the Marquesas Islands than of the arts of the American Indians" (1954:188). Like Adam several decades earlier, Covarrubias claims that Northwest Coast art is more like that of ancient China and less like that of the neighboring Indian peoples. Since migration across the Pacific is no longer considered impossible, "it becomes more and more difficult to believe that this great art is purely a local development," despite the uncertainty as to how the migration actually occurred (1954:191). To support his claim, Covarrubias explains the presence of two distinct types of art on the Coast by asserting that the simple geometric art is the style of the original inhabitants of the Northwest Coast, while the elaborate totemic style resulted from the influence of "a foreign people of higher culture" (1954:191).[20]

Covarrubias makes explicit what is implicit in the work of other diffusionists, the supposition that only a more evolved society could have created this complex style. It is of interest that Boas's identification of what he believed to be the older and newer decorative styles of Northwest Coast art, which inspired the more sophisticated stylistic analyses and historical reconstructions of Holm, Wingert, Drucker, and Duff, also provided justification for Covarrubias's theory that more "advanced" foreigners were responsible for the more ornate style. Despite the favor with which the transpacific contact theory was held by some well up to the 1970s, today it has few adherents. Opposing the diffusionist bias that it took influence from a more "civ-

20. The persistence of the diffusionist model is represented by Badner (1963, 1966) and Coe (1972) and Fraser (1968). It is worth mentioning at this point the ideas put forth by Marius Barbeau on the notion of cultural development on the Northwest Coast. He believed that several elements of culture including mythology and crests came in relatively recent times from Asia via the Aleutian Islands. See Barbeau 1932, 1934, and 1945. See also Duff 1964 for an assessment of these ideas.

ilized" culture to inspire the development of the extraordinary Northwest Coast style, most scholars now assume that the Indians themselves invented this elaborate art. Where they do hypothesize diffusion, it is in the more scientifically founded, more credible fashion of *Crossroads of Continents: Cultures of Siberia and Alaska* (Fitzhugh and Crowell 1988), a reconstruction of movements of art and ideas across the Bering Sea.

ICONOGRAPHY AND STRUCTURALISM

Boas repeated on several occasions that two factors contribute to an artwork: style and meaning. As is the case with style, the meaning of Northwest Coast art has been the subject of a large number of publications. As Haeberlin and Holm point out, much of what Boas wrote dealt with content rather than style; his classification of animal images is, of course, the first step or primary level of any iconographic interpretation of Northwest Coast art, in the Panofskyian sense. One of the earliest forays beyond Boas into meaning was written by T. T. Waterman (1923). Basing much of his discussion on materials from Boas's publications, Waterman found certain conundrums in the art that pose questions. The first conundrum is a peculiar triangle area above the forehead of the animal Boas identifies as "shark." Using several illustrations from Boas and from Swanton (1905), and invoking the Boasian interpretation that the artist desires to represent all significant features of the animal, regardless of how those features are situated on the natural animal, Waterman concluded that "all drawings of the shark . . . whether including the whole length of the fish or just the head end, represent the fish as he would look from the under side, plus the addition of two eyes" (1923:439). In this example, Waterman provides one additional clue to the configuration of component parts on the representation of an animal, but does not attempt to ask the cultural significance of the shark.

His next conundrum is the meaning of the copper, a shield-shaped plate of beaten metal often containing an etching or painting of a crest animal. Although Boas described the copper in several publications, he did not explain why it is so prized by the Northwest Coast people. Basing his argument on Tlingit mythology, Waterman suggests that the copper depicts the wealth-giving monster Gonakadet.[21] This association of the copper and Gonakadet is an early example of conjoining art and myth to answer the question so often asked about Northwest Coast art: What does it mean? Indeed, later scholars including Lévi-Strauss (1982), MacDonald

21. The two other conundrums Waterman discusses are architecture and totem poles. In connection with these, Waterman speculates on the presence of house pits from Prince William Sound to California, as well as the meaning of totem poles.

(1984), and Jonaitis (1986) use Waterman's interpretation as support for more complex analyses of the copper.[22]

An iconographic interpretation goes beyond the identification of imagery and investigates its deeper significance to the culture's world view. Two major and interconnected approaches to deciphering meaning in Northwest Coast art are those put forth by the surrealists and by the structuralists.[23] During and directly after World War II, the surrealists "discovered" this art and attributed to it profound meaning.[24] One of the most poetic interpretations of Northwest Coast art can be found in "Totem Art," written in 1943 by surrealist Wolfgang Paalen. In addition to stressing what he felt was the mystical nature of this art and its dualistic foundations, Paalen makes clear his opposition to the notion of transpacific contact, noting that if resemblances exist between art made in ancient China and art made in the New World, they are due to "mythological conceptions that resemble one another [which] can achieve rather similar plastic expression without the intervention of any direct influence" (Paalen 1943:11).[25] This is of course not unlike Adam's assessment of these same similarities.

Paalen's interpretations of the art itself are sometimes quite fanciful; unlike Waterman, who based his brief interpretation of the copper on ethnographic evidence, Paalen explains some Northwest Coast art without regard for evidence. In his drive to interpret Northwest Coast art as a manifestation of totemism, Paalen resorts to what we might call a psychological evolutionism. "Totemic thought," he argues, is a prelogical cognitive process in which "communication is communion," in which a magical climate pervades, where distinctions are not made between the subjective and objective, nor between the self and the world. All this has inspired the creation of totem art:

Through dances, sacrifices, cannibal repasts, orgies, and divinatory and incantatory rites the great communion is accomplished—in a frenetic choreographic action is conjured the power of the ancestor, of the beast-demon. Action into which enter as components and accessories all kinds of artistic creations that are not considered separately as "works of

22. It is of interest to note that Marcel Mauss, in *The Gift* (first published in 1927), made the same connection.

23. It is beyond the scope of this essay to review the other streams of thought that contributed to the structuralist analyses of art. See Carroll 1979.

24. See, for example, Cowling 1978, Rushing 1988, and Mauze 1992. Some early abstract expressionists, influenced in large part by the surrealists, had similar readings of Northwest Coast art and can be included in this discussion.

25. For the surrealists with their romantic attachment to the primitive, the notion that artistic concepts flowed from a "high" to a "low" culture would have been quite unacceptable. See Winter (1992) for an essay on Paalen.

art," for at the magic stage art is still a means and a vehicle of direct action (Paalen 1943:20).

It should be noted here that Paalen's words are motivated by great admiration for this kind of mysticism; he and his surrealist associates agreed that the West had lost the enviable cosmic unity they believed to be so prevalent in the primitive world.[26] Paalen barely mentions Boas in this article (although he does call him "one of the greatest anthropologists" (1943:19) in a reference to Boas's attempts to intervene on behalf of the Indians in respect to the antipotlatch law), omits Boas's books from the short bibliography, and only notes in passing that a frontlet he has used as an illustration was also published by Boas in 1897 (1943:13, 23).

In contrast, a friend of the surrealist circle of European refugees in New York City during World War II, Claude Lévi-Strauss, has sincere praise for Boas in his surrealist-inspired article "Art of the Northwest Coast at the American Museum of Natural History" (1943). He points out that the most important works on Northwest Coast art were by Boas as well as by Swanton, and pays homage to "the great Boas, who died a few months ago."[27] Lévi-Strauss takes the initial description of split representation from Boas, but then expands upon it, making it poetically Lévi-Straussian:

A rigid conformism obeying fundamental rules permits, however, the representation of a bear, a shark, a beaver without any of the limits which elsewhere confine the artist. The animal is represented altogether in full face and in profile, from the back and at the same time from above and from below, from without and from within. A butcher draftsman, by an extraordinary mixture of convention and realism has skinned and boned, even removed the entrails, to construct a new being coincident of its anatomy with the parallelopiped or rectangular surface and the object created is at once a box and an animal—many animals, and a man (1943:181).

In this article, Lévi-Strauss briefly discusses transpacific contact, pointing to the lack of any evidence for such diffusionism. He addresses this issue in far greater depth in "Le Dédoublement de la représentation dans les arts de l'Asie et de l'Amérique" published the next year, and translated in 1963 as "Split Representation in the Art of Asia and America." In the 1968 catalogue of a photographic exhibition on transpacific contact, *Early Chinese Art and the Pacific Basin*, Douglas Fraser states that in

26. As I have demonstrated (Jonaitis 1981), this is a common occurrence in Northwest Coast scholarship, which often reflects the values of the writer or of the period in which she or he writes more than any "truth" about the art.

27. In what we might term a poetic irony of history, Boas died in Lévi-Strauss's arms during a lecture in New York City in 1942 (Lévi-Strauss, pers. com. 1988).

this essay, Lévi-Strauss offers the only real alternative to Boas's and the diffusionists' explanations of the split image (1968:97). In this highly significant piece, Lévi-Strauss first reviews Hentze and Adam, repeating Adam's descriptions of the characteristics of Northwest Coast style. He notes that in addition to similarities with Chinese art, Northwest Coast art resembles that of the New Zealand Maori and the Brazilian Caduevo. He suggests that when history cannot yield a satisfactory answer, as it does not here, then one must look to "psychology, or the structural analysis of forms; let us ask ourselves if internal connections, whether of a psychological or logical nature, will allow us to understand parallel recurrences whose frequency and cohesion cannot possibly be the result of chance" (1963:242).

Lévi-Strauss compares split representation in the art of all four groups, pointing out that in each, leaders used art to validate ranking. Then he goes into a complex argument that interprets split representation from several interrelated perspectives: (1) as a reference to the "splitting" of the personality between the "dumb" biological person and the social being; (2) as a reference to a series of dualities, such as representational/nonrepresentational art, the human face/its manmade decoration, person/impersonation, the existence of the individual/function of society, community/hierarchy, plastic expression/graphic expression; (3) as a type of motif that occurs in societies in which masks are used to validate social hierarchies. Lévi-Strauss concludes that even if diffusion did occur, it would be "a diffusion of organic wholes wherein style, esthetic conventions, social organization, and religion are structurally related" (1963:260). Thus structure subsumes history.[28]

In his subtle and complex structuralist study, *Way of the Masks* (a 1982 translation of *La Voie des masques* [1979]), Lévi-Strauss investigates the unusual form of the Salish Swaixwé mask by analyzing related mythic beings and their plastic representations from other neighboring tribes. In a comment with which Boas would agree, Lévi-Strauss disputes those functional anthropologists for whom tribes exist in isolation, without significant contact with other people (1982:144–45). By analyzing a group of mythically related masks from different peoples, it is possible not only to understand the artworks themselves, but also to glimpse the cultural history of the region. The Swaixwé mask, Lévi-Strauss argues, alludes to a mythological complex that addresses the universal disorder associated with natural disasters such as earth-

28. A brief discussion of art and social organization on the Northwest Coast is offered by Frances Morphy in "The Social Significance of Schematization in Northwest Coast American Indian Art" (1977). Morphy points out that most students of Northwest Coast art study the type of art Boas called symbolic, describing the use of pieces, the myths, the context; few, she says, have addressed the issue of formal rules of representation going from realistic to symbolic, which he calls "schematic." In this short essay, Morphy suggests that a fruitful field of investigation would be why the artist selects certain key symbols (such as incisors and cross-hatched tail for a beaver) when he wishes to illustrate a particular being. Morphy proposes that since crests identify groups, the symbols were selected to "differentiate the social groups who won the crest from one another" (p. 767).

quakes and storms and the social disorder of incest, and concludes that to be civilized a group must have orderly rules of marriage. Elements of this mythological and artistic complex are found among the Kwakiutl, Haida, and Tsimshian, as well as the Coast Salish, implying a complicated historical movement, "to which it would be unwise to assign a privileged direction" (1982:226). Thus although Lévi-Strauss cannot actually reconstruct the events which led to this dispersal of the complex, he does acknowledge the significance of history in the process.

Lévi-Strauss influenced several other scholars who endeavored to understand meaning by employing what is generally classified as a structuralist approach. The majority of these writings tend to ignore the time depth that Lévi-Strauss recognizes in *Way of the Masks*, and focus instead upon deeper messages within the art.[29] Wilson Duff (1981b), who was a leading structuralist scholar, justifies his attempts to penetrate the significance of Northwest Coast art with a reference to Boas:

Boas (1927:12) once said that it is essential to bear in mind the two-fold source of artistic effect, the one based on form alone, and the other on ideas associated with form, otherwise the theory of art will be one-sided. I think that what Boas meant by "idea associated with form" is what I mean by "meaning." Today thanks to Bill Holm we are in a position where we can describe with great detail and great sensitivity the form of Northwest Coast Indian art. . . . However, to describe the form is not to explain the meaning. It seems to me that the description of Northwest Coast art has suffered from the dangers Boas forecast and has become a little bit one-sided, because we can say a lot about form but not very much about meaning (Duff 1981:210).

In *Images: Stone: B.C.* (1975), Duff hypothesizes that the Northwest Coast artist adhered to a system of logic informed by dualisms such as life-death, inner-outer, and, most significant in art, male-female. Thus in addition to representing images of social or sacred meaning and decorating useful implements, the artist engaged in a kind of "abstract thinking, a half-secret dialogue, a self-conscious system for diagramming logical paradoxes and therefore a medium for exploring by analogy the living paradoxes in myth and life" (Duff 1975:14). Much of what the artist does as a result, Duff argues, is create images associated with the universal concerns of sexuality.

One of Duff's students, Carol Sheehan McClaren, in "Moment of Death, Gift of Life: A Reinterpretation of the Northwest Coast Image 'Hawk' " (1978), assesses Boas's influence on Northwest Coast art scholarship. According to McClaren, Northwest Coast studies have followed two anthropological traditions—the historical-particularism of Boas and the structuralism of Lévi-Strauss. She is positive

29. See, for example, MacDonald 1981, 1984; Jonaitis 1986; Penney 1981.

about Boas's contributions in that "little escaped his clear eye for detail, his systematic organization and collation of data" (p. 66); complementing this approach is the Lévi-Strauss structuralism which endeavors to understand the logic within the image itself. McClaren analyzes the image that Boas identified as the hawk from a structuralist perspective "that probes the structural logic ensconced in the image itself" (p. 67).

Boas's flaw, McClaren argues, is that he "separated ideas from things. . . . Clearly, his persistence in asking 'What does it represent?' was designed to elicit a nominal response—i.e., 'this visual image represents such and such a crest'—without inquiring into the logic making such images appropriate elements for a crest" (p. 71). Until recently, most scholars have uncritically accepted Boas's identification of animal imagery in Northwest Coast art. McClaren then presents an interesting argument that the so-called "hawk" image represents not a bird but a salmon. Although she is correct in stating that Boas identified this image as the hawk, she does not acknowledge, in her accusations of his inflexibility, that Boas himself frequently recognized the possibility of ambiguity in imagery.

The premise of intellectual equality among diverse groups informs the structuralism of Lévi-Strauss and those he has influenced. One reason scholars find the diffusionism promoted by Covarrubias and others disquieting is its premise that culture is transmitted from a more advanced to a less advanced group. In contrast, according to the structuralists, if two cultures independently invent similar artistic motifs because of similar thought processes, it follows that they are intellectually equal. As Wilson Duff argues in *Images: Stone: B.C.* (1975:25), by appreciating Northwest Coast art, non-Natives should "begin to grant [the Northwest Coast] artist-philosophers credence as people of intellect and mature wisdom." These comparisons of Northwest Coast art with that of "high culture," as well as Duff's assertion that the very sophistication of the thought processes evident in Northwest Coast art signifies the advanced nature of the culture, promote the intellectual equality of all races. Although much of the structuralist literature is purely hypothetical in its interpretations of Northwest Coast art, and purports to explain what and how Native people think, the goal of structuralism, to prove that all people have equal intellects, is comparable to that of Boas.

THE ROLE OF THE ARTIST

The artist as a creative individual has become a major topic in Northwest Coast art historical literature in recent years, and signifies an important breakthrough based on Boas's effort to elevate the status of the Native artist. Audrey Hawthorn summarized Boas's contribution to the literature by describing his focus on the experience of the individual artist (referred to by Boas as "he"): the artist must understand his craft and technique; he must understand his material; he must understand the forms he is to make; and he must create forms in a manner recognizable to his culture. The conclusion is that once the craftsman has met these requirements and has been properly apprenticed to a master, he becomes an artist, capable of creating real works of art; "his imagination and his ability to achieve have come together" (Hawthorn 1979:20–21).

Although Boas did not himself publish much on specific artists, he frequently made the point that Native artists, as they worked within the constraints of tradition, were in every way creative and original. He recognized the considerable talent of Haida artist Charles Edenshaw, whom he described as "one of the best artists among the Haida" (1927:275) and who drew and explained Northwest Coast images such as Haida face paintings (Boas 1898b) and gambling sticks (Boas 1927:210–12; Swanton 1905:147–54). Boas and Swanton asked Edenshaw to carve model totem poles and houses to serve as illustrations in Swanton's Jesup Expedition memoir (Swanton 1905; see also Jonaitis 1992a). Their public interest in a Native American artist helped dispel the myth of the primitive artisan working within a prescribed form and lacking originality.

While Boas did not write biographies, many coming after him pursued the topic of the Northwest Coast artist as individual. Marius Barbeau (1957) picked up on the importance of Edenshaw and sought to identify his art and that of other Haida masters in what turned out to be an ambitious process, flawed by occasional lapses of sloppy scholarship (see Hoover 1984:201). We now know a good deal more about Edenshaw, Mungo Martin, Willie Seaweed, the Haida Nunstins, as well as several anonymous yet individualistic Tlingit and Haida masters.[30]

The literature on living Northwest Coast artists is expanding as well.[31] Some of these studies are biographical, some focus on iconography, and some identify the artist's unique stylistic signature. From a perspective of western art history, to identify the artists as individuals removes them from the category "anonymous" and places them in the category of "fine artists." This change of category, of course, also serves to elevate the status of the artists in the minds of those who read this literature. Thus starting with Boas and continuing to the present, there has been a shattering of the stereotype of an Indian so totally integrated into a group that she or he lacks the individualism and creativity characteristic of Euro-American artists.

30. For more on Edenshaw, see Duff 1967b, Holm 1981, Thomas 1982, Hoover 1983, and Jonaitis 1992a; on Martin, see Hawthorn 1964, Duff 1981a, Nuytten 1982; on Willie Seaweed, Holm 1974 and 1983b; on Nunstins, Gessler 1981; on anonymous Haida and Tlingit masters, Wright 1983, Brown 1987.

31. Some examples of literature on contemporary Northwest Coast art are Macnair, Hoover, and Neary 1980, Blackman and Hall 1986, and Gerber and Katz-Lahaigue 1989, Danford 1990. For contemporary Northwest Coast artists' own statements, see Davidson 1992, Hamilton 1991, Neel 1991, Paul 1992, Point 1988.

BOAS AND BEYOND

I began this book by suggesting that Boas's art history warrants serious consideration as a classic corpus resonant with contemporary intellectual trends. An underlying theme of postmodernism is its critical challenge to the hierarchical assumptions of white male privilege that have in the past informed much scholarship. If we accept the premise that ideas should be judged within the contexts of their times, it is evident that Boas was posing a similar challenge. In his art historical as well as his anthropological writings, Boas succeeded in validating Native cultures during a time when many judged these cultures as inferior. He used carefully thought out examples to disprove logically the nineteenth-century premise that human races progressed in a lock-step fashion from simplicity to complexity. Later, he began to focus on the psychology and creativity of artists, thus allowing them the individuality of their western counterparts. He also made connections between the styles of western and primitive art, thus equating the artists of all cultures. Although the inspiration behind these efforts is still relevant to the contemporary world, their underlying assumptions need to be scrutinized.

Much of the literature on Northwest Coast art that Boas inspired either implicitly or explicitly used art to promote the equality of Indians and whites. The celebration of the excellence of Northwest Coast art apparent in the literature on style and on history, the promotion of the intellectuality of the artist in structuralist analyses, and the acknowledgment of the individual in works on specific artists convey the message that this art, these people, these traditions are worthy of respect. This worthiness is, however, in some cases based on a similarity of some sort with the art of more "advanced" cultures, including that of twentieth-century Euro-American traditions. Although the battle for social equality of all races must continue to be fought, the method of proving the value of Native cultures by equating them with that of the West is today less valid. Modern-day Northwest Coast artists no longer need their works or their culture validated by such comparisons. Northwest Coast peoples have a keen sense of their own history, acknowledge what they have accepted from white culture as well as what they have unfortunately given up, and celebrate what is theirs.

The deeper issue that faces contemporary Northwest Coast Native peoples, as well as the anthropologists and art historians who study them, is that of control over their own legacy. Native people are empowered when they assume the right not only to control their own artistic legacy but also to insist on their privileged voice—although not a sole voice—in its interpretation. The last decade of the twentieth century is forcing scholars to confront critical questions: Who has the right to speak? What can that speaker speak about? With the discrediting of the sole voice of white authority, it is for some no longer acceptable for a non-Native scholar to speak, as the unquestioned authority, for Native people. As Jeanette Armstrong asserts, in a call for Native self-determination (1990:143–44):

> . . . *imagine the writer of [the] dominating culture berating you for speaking out about appropriation of cultural voice and using the words "freedom of speech" to condone further systematic violence, in the form of entertainment about your culture and your values and all the while yourself being disempowered and rendered voiceless through such "freedoms." . . . Imagine interpreting for us your own people's thinking towards us, instead of interpreting for us, our thinking, our lives, our stories. We wish to know, and you need to understand, why it is that you want to own our stories, our art, our beautiful crafts, our ceremonies, but you do not appreciate or wish to recognize that these things of beauty arise out of the beauty of our people.*

For some, the belief that only the oppressed can represent their own history produces as its next logical step a denial to the non-Native the right to produce any scholarship on Native cultures. Others make efforts to modify the anthropological discourse in such a way that voices of Native people can be heard directly, not through the homogenizing and de-individualizing filter of the ethnographic monograph. By speaking for themselves, Native people avoid being positioned as ethnographic subjects and also assume the universally recognized privilege of being "the authority." One of the most vocal spokespersons for empowering Native people, literary critic Gayatri Chakravorty Spivak, has a somewhat different approach to this issue. She urges the non-Native to rage against the "history that has written such an abject script that [the non-Native] is silenced" (1990:62) and challenges us to earn the right to speak by critiquing the histories of our relationships to Native peoples. While no simple answer to this complex question presents itself, we can take Boas once again as a challenging departure point for promoting the cause of serious and ethical scholarship. Certain topics suggestive of future research are those that combine an acceptance of the privileged position of the Native voice with an ongoing effort to deconstruct the grand narratives that maintain the asymmetrical position of native peoples in the postcolonial world.

Despite Boas and his successors' contributions to the history of Northwest Coast art, considerable gaps in the story remain. Some of these gaps exist because Boas ignored certain aspects of Northwest Coast art, while others exist in spite of him. For example, because he credited the northern groups with originating the luxurious formline style over the more archaic style found in the southern groups, and because he concentrated so heavily on the Kwakiutl, more has been written about the art of the Kwakwaka'wakw, Tsimshian, Haida, and Tlingit than on the more southerly Salish and Nuu-chah-nulth. Recently scholars have begun to pay closer attention to the outstanding artistic products of those neglected groups without whom a true history of Northwest Coast art is impossible.[32]

Boas pointed to the significance of female creativity in the artistic process, and there are some studies of Tlingit and Salish textiles, button blankets, basketry, labrets, and the role of women in Kwakwaka'wakw ceremonialism.[33] Few scholars, however, have attempted to analyze the interplay between male and female art, the central role of women in the artist culture of the Northwest Coast, and the contributions of present-day women on the Northwest Coast. It is perhaps a reflection more of our own culture's disregard of the significance of women's art that Boas's suggestive comments on female creativity have not been picked up by twentieth-century analysts of Northwest Coast art. Although one might criticize Boas for imposing the notion of tradition and authenticity upon some facets of Northwest Coast art, we can only blame ourselves for this major omission.

THE DISAPPEARING PRIMITIVE

Boas was not entirely innocent of intellectual activities that we today consider disempowering to Native people. Part of his research agenda was the pursuit of the pristine Indian whose "pure" culture was not adulterated by contact with non-Natives. In his instructions to George Hunt and other collectors in the field, he repeatedly asked for the oldest artifacts, the oldest stories. He was not particularly interested in what happened to Northwest Coast peoples when missionaries, white officials, and settlers entered their lives, for he saw his task as recording for historical analysis the last remnants of what on numerous occasions he called "dying" or "disappearing" cultures. This quest for the unacculturated in which Native peoples were nostalgically perceived as dying primitives, their authentic cultures mourned as victims of progress, ignored their ability to respond creatively and with flexibility to outside cultural influences.

In recent years the myth of the vanishing Indian has been discredited. Anthropologists have begun questioning the nature of their research and writing about aboriginal peoples, realizing how apparently innocuous descriptions of culture can reinforce imperialist ideologies no longer acceptable in the postcolonial era. But if the "vanishing savage," a victim of the contemporary age, is no longer mourned by anthropologists, he still often is by a public unaware of the connection between this

32. As I have already pointed out, Wayne Suttles (1982, 1983) has made major contributions to our understanding of Salish art. See also Kew 1980. As for the Nuu-chah-nulth, see Jonaitis and Inglis 1992.

33. For Chilkat blankets, see Samuel 1982, 1987 and Holm 1982; for weaving, see Gustafson 1980; for button blankets, Jensen and Sargent 1986; for basketry, Jones 1968, Lobb 1978, Corey 1983, La Foret 1984; for the Tlingit labret, Jonaitis 1988a; and for the role of women in Kwakwaka'wakw ceremonialism, Jonaitis 1992b.

perception of a nonchanging native who should remain pristine and primitive and the imperialist agenda. The "yearning for singularization" that Igor Kopytoff (1986) identifies, the "longing" central to Susan Stewart's analysis of collecting, Renato Rosaldo's "imperialist nostalgia" (1989), and Nicholas Thomas's "ideology of primitivism" (1991), all contribute to a stereotype of stability, unchangeability, and tradition of non-western cultures.

Boas's efforts to salvage what was disappearing sometimes led to his dismissing what remained. Adherence to what I might call the "purity paradigm" prevented him from recognizing some very creative responses to the acculturative process. In his analysis of the Chilkat blanket, Boas mentions and then disregards the more contemporary versions of these textiles in which the formal conventions are dismantled. And in *Primitive Art*, he refers to the influence of European ware on Native art as "contamination" (p. 144). It is worth noting, however, that despite this, Boas uses models of totem poles, silver bracelets, and argillite carvings as major examples in his analysis of Northwest Coast art.[34] Although he said that he privileged history in his interpretation of culture, he sometimes chose to ignore the history that continued after contact with non-Natives. Although he himself was unable to envision the perpetuation of the Indian cultures he and his colleagues studied, he did lay the groundwork for later investigations of how artworks reflect ongoing Native accommodation to the situation in the colonial and the postcolonial world.

With the discarding of the purity paradigm, we have been freed to expand the definition of Northwest Coast art to include art made for tourists, art that displays stylistic changes resulting from contact with non-Natives, and art made in recent years. One of the exciting features of the new Native art history is a recognition that such arts of acculturation are not signifiers of a disappearing primitive but instead present fascinating examples of Native accommodation and cultural endurance in the colonial and postcolonial world. As a result of the expansiveness that has come to categorize contemporary scholarship, we have been freed to embrace within the definition of "authentic" Northwest Coast art works as varied as argillite made for sale to ship captains and tourists, blankets made from trade wool textiles and decorated with Chinese buttons, contemporary carvings and prints, and the thousands of model totem poles found in curio shops, airport stores, and fine art galleries.[35]

If we reject the concepts of precontact purity and postcontact contamination,

34. See Graburn 1976 for an early positive statement on the value of tourist art. The most interesting recent works on this theme focus on the Eastern Woodlands. See Phillips 1988, 1991, in press.

35. Part of the current reassessment of how we look at Native art includes a scrutiny of the notion of "authenticity." See for interesting insights on this issue Ames 1992, Clifford 1987, Dominguez 1987, MacCannell 1986, Miller 1991, Howell 1991. An early and notable discussion is found in Benjamin 1969. For Northwest Coast arts of acculturation, see for argillite, Kaufman 1976, Sheehan 1981, Macnair and Hoover 1984, Wright 1983, 1985, and 1987; for button blankets, Jensen and Sargent 1986; for a general discussion of acculturated art, Blackman 1976.

we can see that such artworks make eloquent statements about cultural survival within an historical context.[36] As Boas went to great pains to demonstrate, Native groups never existed in pristine isolation from each other; on the Northwest Coast, evidence of interactions and mutual influences appear in the archeological and historical records. Indeed, Boas explicitly based his reconstruction of Northwest Coast art history on these very interactions and influences. Although he might have overlooked the consequences of contact with whites once more distant travelers appeared on the scene, Native history did not cease.[37]

Present-day scholars identify continuities of past traditions as well as those newly invented traditions that represent legitimate expressions of a Native presence in the contemporary world. Doing so constitutes not only a scholarly, academic endeavor but also makes a political statement. As I discussed in the introductory essay in this book, by segregating Native people into timeless "primitives" incapable of responding with creativity and strength to new and often difficult conditions, narratives that announced the death, or at least the deterioration, of their cultures have contributed to their disempowerment.[38] By depicting the forces of progress overwhelming Native peoples, one accepts unquestioningly (although usually unconsciously) the dominant society's cultural hegemony over those it colonized. Today, such messages of disintegrating cultural presences succumbing to a superior and victorious colonizing force have been discredited, happily replaced by a more liberating discourse of postcolonial cultural endurance in the global community.

Although Boas did not celebrate acculturated art, an analysis of such art is by no means foreign to his perspectives on culture history. Indeed, including such works would be a logical step in his historical project, which characterizes the creative process as, on the one hand, originality within the constraints of culture and, on the other hand, a response to ongoing external influences. Fundamental to Boas's notion of history is the acceptance by one group of art elements generated by another group, with appropriate reinterpretations and reconfigurations. In keeping with his pervasive distrust of simple explanations for cultural phenomena, Boas cau-

36. It is noteworthy that a major scholar of the Haida, Margaret Blackman, observed as early as 1976 that there exists "an unacknowledged but nonetheless extant attitude among anthropologists which holds the aboriginal cultures as inherently more worthy of investigation, more interesting, and somehow more 'real' than the cultures which evolved under subsequent culture change" (1976:389).

37. Blackman (1977:2) comments how "despite earlier pronouncements of the decline of Northwest Coast ceremonialism in the first half of the 20th century," a considerable number of traditions persisted in contemporary Northwest Coast ceremonials. It would be wrong to consider the movement of influences only from the non-Natives to the Natives. In an interesting work, Thomas (1991) studies the reciprocal relationships that native peoples in the Pacific established with their colonizers.

38. One example of an alternative to the image of total cultural destruction is Guy Brett's comment: "Another outcome of the resurgence of the Third World has been to reveal unmistakably that peoples responded to colonialism not as passive victims but as active subjects, making their own representation of the experience from their point of view, as part of a survival struggle" (1991:116).

tioned scholars not to assume too rigid a cultural constraint over creativity; thus he paved the way for us to appreciate innovative responses to changing conditions. Just because certain art elements that become part of a Native repertoire came from non-Natives, as is the case with button blankets, or were developed in response to non-Natives, as was the case with argillite made for sale to outsiders, does not make them less valid as Northwest Coast artworks. These artists did not lose their ethnic identity when they interacted with non-Natives in the marketplace, both as consumers of materials and as manufacturers of commodities; as the constraints of culture changed, their creative responses changed as well.

The relationship of the Northwest Coast artist to the international market merits further discussion. As early as the 1820s, Haida artists were selling argillite sculptures to foreign traders. By the late nineteenth century, Native artists participated in a lively sale of carvings, baskets, and other artworks to the tourists who traveled up and down the coast by steamer. And, certainly, today Northwest Coast artists make masks both for use at their own community ceremonials and for sale in commercial galleries. The manufacture of art specifically as a commodity to be sold to outsiders could be disturbing to some, as it denies any intimate association between artistic creations and their function within the community. This is of course yet another version of the purity paradigm which stereotypes the "genuine" Indian making "authentic" Indian art within the constructed concept of "tradition." Today, scholars who recognize the imposition of such inappropriate stereotypes are investigating how Native cultures functioned in the past and function today in a cosmopolitan and international context.[39]

Haida art provides an example of this. Up until quite recently, the standard representation of northern Northwest Coast art history described the great flourishing of Tlingit, Haida, and Tsimshian art during the nineteenth century, then the disappearance of this sophisticated style during the early decades of the twentieth century, and finally its "renaissance" in the 1960s, inspired in large part by Bill Holm and Bill Reid.[40] I have recently (Jonaitis 1993) analyzed the history of Haida art, focusing on the narrative of despair that characterized the perceived demise of Haida art after the death of Charles Edenshaw in 1920. At that time, although artists did cease producing sculptures in the classic formline style of their ancestors, they nonetheless continued to create model totem poles for sale to curio shops and tourists. The fact that some carvers—even if just a few—continued making art, crude as it

39. James Clifford (1992) refers to this as studying "traveling cultures." Kopytoff (1986) suggests scholars analyze the "cultural biography of things" to interpret how they are accepted, understood, and redefined as they circulate beyond their originating communities. Nelson et al. (1992:8) encourage application of the concept of articulation, which analyzes the "continual severing, realignment, and recombination" of cultural phenomena.

40. The Kwakwaka'wakw, because they never stopped producing art and never ceased potlatching during the twentieth century, are exempted from this narrative of disappearance.

appeared, was of greater relevance than their abandonment of formline canons. In addition, the commoditization of their art made for the curio market was not substantially different in nature from the nineteenth-century artists who made argillite carvings for sale to ship captains and tourists; thus, it would not be incorrect to expand the definition of "traditional" Haida art to *include* rather than exclude art intended for use outside the community.[41]

Non-Natives must continually be alert to the pitfalls of imposing stereotypes of purity and authenticity upon Native artworks. For example, by denying the validity of the noncanonical Haida art made between 1920 and 1960, we implicitly stifle the voices of those who thought it acceptable and appropriate to make art for sale. While the reappearance of the canon in the 1960s was a positive feature of Northwest Coast art history, it does not follow that noncanonical art warrants dismissal. In this age when many voices, especially those of Native people themselves, speak and are listened to, we need not—indeed we must not—be exclusionary. Similarly, we must recognize that space exists for many versions of the Northwest Coast artistic legacy: elegant, refined examples and cruder, more direct pieces; artworks meant to be used within the community and those intended to circulate beyond its borders; creations that adhere to formal and iconographic canons and those which ignore, deviate from, or intentionally reject artistic traditions.[42]

The relevance of Franz Boas's work to the modern-day Kwakwaka'wakw demonstrates with clarity how he ultimately allowed space for new expressions of cultural resilience, autonomy, and vitality. This is evident both in terms of artistic creativity and Native scholarship. At different times during the months of preparation for "Chiefly Feasts," Kwakwaka'wakw artists Tony Hunt, Richard Hunt, and Calvin Hunt traveled to New York where they saw their artistic heritage in museum storerooms and on display, and could read George Hunt's detailed collection notes. During the time the exhibition was in New York and then in Victoria, British Columbia,[43] other artists had the opportunity to see these treasures. Back in their studios (where many have copies of Boas's publications), some of these artists created new artworks inspired by old ones. One example of this was the Nulami'sta dancer's apparatus from New Vancouver (Jonaitis 1991, figs. 1.36–38, pp. 62–64). I had commissioned a copy of this double curtain by Calvin Hunt because the original was too delicate to travel to the other exhibition venues. So fascinated was

41. See Appadurai 1986 and Kopytoff 1986 for interesting insights into the process of commoditization.

42. This of course allows room for Northwest Coast Native artists to work in stylistic modes other than those clearly of Northwest Coast origin.

43. "Chiefly Feasts" was on exhibition at the American Museum of Natural History from October 1991 to February 1992 and at the Royal British Columbia Museum in Victoria, B.C., from May 1992 to November 1992.

Hunt by the artistry of the Nulami'sta that he created a silkscreen print of the double dancer's apparatus which was sold in the American Museum and Royal British Columbia Museum gift shops as well as other Northwest Coast art galleries. In addition, one of the artists in Hunt's studio, Tommy Hunt, created a wooden version of the Nulami'sta which is now in the collection of a Washington State corporation.

Although these various new versions of the curtains were intended for exhibition outside the community, the artworks themselves have profound meaning for the Kwakwaka'wakw; when the delegation of ten Kwakwaka'wakw elders visited the American Museum of Natural History in spring of 1990 to assist us with the "Chiefly Feasts" exhibit, Agnes Cranmer performed a dance she owned that was associated with a version of the Nulami'sta. Then, before the version carved by Tommy Hunt was sold, his family performed a dance at which they validated their claim to its privilege.[44] The "cultural biography" of this dancer's apparatus includes its collection by George Hunt for Franz Boas; its representation in an exhibition created in partnership with the Kwakwaka'wakw people; its meaning to the contemporary descendants of its creators; its two-hundred-fold replication in a silkscreen print, copies of which are in collections from the East to the West coasts; and its appearance in a new wood version in the headquarters of an international corporation.

Art is not the only vehicle for Native expressions of endurance in the postcolonial world, as is evident in the scholarly contributions of Gloria Cranmer Webster, George Hunt's great-granddaughter. Webster was curator of the "Potlatch Today" section of "Chiefly Feasts," a consultant on the project from its outset, and the author of the essay in the catalogue on the contemporary potlatch (Webster 1991). A museum professional who directed the U'mista Cultural Centre in Alert Bay for ten years and an active participant in contemporary potlatches, Webster has contributed substantially to Northwest Coast scholarship, drawing both on Boas's anthropology and on her own experience of her culture.[45] In her compelling essay, "From Colonization to Repatriation" (1992), she directs our attention to the historic interrelationship of an anthropologist (Boas) with a Native community that have ramifications to this day. She quotes a chief's famous challenge "to a first-time visitor at Fort Rupert in 1886" with respect to the antipotlatch law that had recently been passed by the Canadian government:

44. Another example is the new version of the Whale mask from Hopetown (Jonaitis 1991, fig. 6.4, p. 260) that Richard Hunt carved for a private collector. The original artwork—like the dancer's apparatus—was determined by the conservator to be too delicate to travel; since it was central to the story of Siwidi (see Ostrowitz and Jonaitis 1991), it was fortuitous that this collector agreed to allow his newly carved version to travel with the show. For a discussion of this replication, see Ostrowitz 1993.

45. Webster 1991 contains the most lucid statement of the contemporary Kwakwaka'wakw potlatch. For an equally valuable description of contemporary Kwakwaka'wakw society, see Webster 1990. See also Webster 1993.

Do we ask the white man, "Do as the Indian does"? No, we do not. Why then do you ask us, "Do as the white man does"? It is a strict law that bids us dance. It is a strict law that bids us distribute our property among our friends and neighbors. It is a good law. Let the white man observe his law, we shall observe ours. And now, if you are come to forbid us to dance, be gone, if not, you will be welcome to us (1992:30).

Webster then contextualizes this quote, and concludes her essay with a forceful statement of cultural endurance:

That visitor was Franz Boas, an anthropologist who was to devote most of his professional life to working with George Hunt of Fort Rupert. Together, they documented every aspect of the life of the Kwagul', leaving a valuable legacy for the descendants of Hunt as they strengthen their culture in the contemporary world (p. 31).

Webster concludes her essay with a forceful statement of cultural endurance that includes another allusion to Boas:

To paraphrase the challenge made to Franz Boas in 1886, "Let the white man observe his celebrations, we shall observe ours." While the white people celebrate Columbus's five hundredth anniversary, we celebrate our survival in spite of everything that has happened to us since the white people first came to this continent (p. 37).

Boas never purposefully said, "Here it is. Here is the truth about Northwest Coast art." He couldn't do that, for his method was to demonstrate the flaws of any master narrative that purported to represent the "truth." As a result, he never foreclosed the possibility of new insights into the artistic process. Boas also recognized and used art history to work against the silent but forceful messages inherent in some kinds of scholarship that positioned Native people as inferior to whites. Because of his insistence on avoiding premature theory, coupled with his profound sensitivity to issues of power, his art historical writings seem more relevant today than they did a few decades ago. We can read Boas differently now from the way we read him twenty years ago; that reading, I propose, is far more positive as a result of our reassessment of his contributions. Boas's work allows us to reexamine the meaning of the words "classic" and "canon," the "c" words of postmodern theorists. By writing of Native American culture in an open and liberating fashion, Boas has given us an early model of how values and tolerance coupled with openness and critical judgment can coexist without grinding down or dismissing the Native people studied. A classic is something that continues to be relevant despite the passage of time; by that definition, Boas's art history is classic.

Bibliography

Abu-Lughod, Lila

1991 "Writing Against Culture," in *Recapturing Anthropology: Working in the Present*, ed. R. Fox, pp. 137–62. Santa Fe: School of American Research Press.

Adam, Leonard

1923 *Nordwest-Amerikanische Indianerkunst*. Orbis Pictus Band 17. Berlin: Ernst Wasmuth.

1931 "Das Problem der Asiatisch-Altamerikanischen Kulturbeziehungen mit besonderer Berücksichtigung der Kunst," *Wiener Beiträge zur Kunst und Kultureschichte Asiens* 5:40–64.

1936 "North-West American Indian Art and Its Early Chinese Parallels," *Man* 36:8–11.

Alexander, Jeffrey C., and Steven Seidman, eds.

1990 *Culture and Society: Contemporary Debates*. Cambridge: Cambridge University Press.

Ames, Michael

1992 *Cannibal Tours and Glass Boxes: The Anthropology of Museums*. Vancouver: University of British Columbia Press.

Anderson, Richard

1979 *Art in Primitive Societies*. Englewood Cliffs: Prentice-Hall.

Appadurai, Arjun

1986 "Introduction: Commodities and the Politics of Value," in *The Social Life of Things: Commodities in Cultural Perspective*, ed. A. Appadurai, pp. 3–63. Cambridge: Cambridge University Press.

Appiah, K. Anthony

1991 "Is the Post- in Postmodernism the Post- in Postcolonial?" *Critical Inquiry* 17:336–57.

Armstrong, Jeanette

1990 "The Disempowerment of First North American Native Peoples and Empowerment through Their Writings," *Gatherings: The En'owkin Journal of First North American Peoples*, no. 1.

Asad, Talal, ed.

1973 *Anthropology and the Colonial Encounter*. New York: Humanities Press.

Atkinson, Paul

1990 *The Ethnographic Imagination: Textual Constructions of Reality*. London and New York: Routledge.

Badner, Mino

1963 "The Protruding Tongue Motif in the Sculpture of the Northwest Coast of America." Master's thesis, Columbia University.

1966 "The Protruding Tongue and Related Motifs in the Art Styles of the American Northwest Coast, New Zealand and China," *Weiner Beiträge zur Kulturgeschichte und Linguistik* 15:5–44.

Balfour, Henry

1893 *The Evolution of Decorative Art*. London: Percival.

Barbeau, Marius

1932 "Asiatic Migrations into America," *Canadian Historical Review* 13:403–17.

1934 "The Siberian Origin of Our Northwestern Indians," *Proceedings of the Fifth Pacific Science Congress, 1933*, pp. 2777–89.

1945 "The Aleutian Route of Migration into America," *Geographical Review* 35:424–43.

1953 "Haida Myths Illustrated in Argillite Carvings," Anthropological Series 32, *National Museum of Canada Bulletin* 127.

1957 "Haida Carvers in Argillite," Anthropological Series 38, *National Museum of Canada Bulletin* 139.

Baxandall, Michael

1974 *Painting and Experience in Fifteenth-Century Italy*. Oxford: Oxford University Press.

Belting, Hans

1987 *The End of the History of Art?* trans. C. Wood. Chicago: University of Chicago Press.

Benjamin, Walter

1968 "The Work of Art in the Age of Mechanical Reproduction," in *Illuminations*, ed. H. Arendt, pp. 217–52. New York: Schocken Books. (First published 1936).

Berger, Maurice

1992 *How Art Becomes History: Essays on Art, Society, and Culture in Post-New Deal America*. New York: Harper Collins.

Berlo, Janet Catherine

1992 "Introduction: The Formative Years of Native American Art History," in *The Early Years of Native American Art History: Politics of Scholarship and Collecting*, ed. J. Berlo, pp. 1–21. Seattle: University of Washington Press.

Berlo, Janet Catherine, and Ruth B. Phillips

1992 " 'Vitalizing the Things of the Past': Museum Representations of Native North American Art in the 1990s," *Museum Anthropology* 16:29–43.

Bhabha, Homi

1984 "Of Mimicry and Man: The Ambivalence of Colonial Discourse," *October* 28:125–33.

1992 "Postcolonial Authority and Postmodern Guilt," in *Cultural Studies*, ed. L. Gossberg, C. Nelson, and P. Treichler, pp. 56–65. New York and London: Routledge.

Blackman, Margaret

1973 "Totems to Tombstones: Culture Change as Viewed through the Haida Mortuary Complex, 1877–1971," *Ethnology* 12:47–56.

1976 "Creativity in Acculturation: Art, Architecture and Ceremony from the Northwest Coast," *Ethnohistory* 23:387–413.

1977 "Continuity and Change in Northwest Coast Ceremonialism: An Introduction," *Arctic Anthropology* 14:1–4.

1981 "Windows on the Past: The Photographic Ethnohistory of the Northern and Kaigani Haida," National Museum of Man, Mercury Series, Canadian Ethnology Service, Paper no. 74.

1990 "Haida: Traditional Culture," in *Handbook of North American Indians*, vol. 7: *Northwest Coast*, ed. W. Suttles, pp. 240–60. Washington, D.C.: Smithsonian Institution Press.

Blackman, Margaret, and Edwin Hall

1986 "Snakes and Clowns: Art Thompson and the Westcoast Heritage," *American Indian Art* 11:30–45.

Boas, Franz

1888a "The Development of Culture in Northwest America," *Science* 12:194–96.

1888b "The Houses of the Kwakiutl Indians, British Columbia," *Proceedings of the United States National Museum* 11:197–213.

1888c "On Certain Songs and Dances of the Kwakiutl of British Columbia," *Journal of American Folklore* 1:49–64.

1889 "Tattooing of the Haida," *Transactions, New York Academy of Science, 1889*, pp. 115–16.

1890a "The Use of Masks and Head-ornaments on the Northwest Coast of America," *Internationales Archiv für Ethnographie* 3:7–15.

1890b "The Indians of British Columbia. Sixth Report of the Committee on the North-Western Tribes of Canada; The Lku'ngen, Houses and Boats; the Nootka," *Report of the British Association for the Advancement of Science for 1890*, pp. 563–66, 582–85.

1891a "The Indians of British Columbia: Seventh Report of the Committee on the North-Western Tribes of Canada; The Bilqula, Secret Societies and the Potlatch," *Report of the British Association for the Advancement of Science for 1891*, pp. 408–17.

1891b "Distribution of Tales among the Natives of North America," *Journal of American Folk-Lore* 4:13–20.

1894 "Human Faculty as Determined by Race," *Proceedings of the American Association for the Advancement of Science* 63.
1895 *Indianische Sagen von der Nord-Pacifischen Küste Amerikas*. Berlin: A. Asher.
1896 "The Decorative Art of the Indians of the North Pacific Coast," *Science* 4:101–3.
1897a "The Decorative Art of the Indians of the North Pacific Coast," *Bulletin of the American Museum of Natural History* 9:123–76.
1897b "The Social Organization and the Secret Societies of the Kwakiutl Indians," *Report of the U.S. National Museum for 1895*, pp. 311–788.
1898a "The Jesup North Pacific Expedition," *American Museum of Natural History Memoirs* 2:1–11.
1898b "Facial Paintings of the Indians of Northern British Columbia," *American Museum of Natural History Memoirs* 2:13–24.
1898c "The Mythology of the Bella Coola Indians," *American Museum of Natural History Memoirs* 2:25–127.
1899 "Summary of the Work of the Committee in British Columbia. Twelfth and Final Report on the North-Western Tribes of Canada, 1898," *Report of the British Association for the Advancement of Science, 1898*, pp. 40–61.
1900a *Ethnological Collections from the North Pacific Coast of America: Being a Guide to Hall 108 in the American Museum of Natural History*. New York: American Museum of Natural History.
1900b "Art," in "The Thompson Indians of British Columbia" by James Teit, *American Museum of Natural History Memoirs* 1:376–90.
1903 "The Decorative Art of the North American Indians," *Popular Science Monthly* 63:481–98.
1904 "Primitive Art," *American Museum Journal* (supp.), vol. 4, no. 3: guide leaflet 15:1–39.
1907 "Notes on the Blanket Designs," in George T. Emmons, "The Chilkat Blanket," *American Museum of Natural History Memoirs* 3:351–400.
1908a "Clubs Made of Bone of Whale," in Harlan I. Smith, "Archeology of the Gulf of Georgia and Puget Sound," *American Museum of National History Memoirs* 4:403–12.
1908b "Decorative Designs of Alaskan Needlecases: A Study in the History of Conventional Designs, Based on Materials in the U.S. National Museum," *Proceedings of the U.S. National Museum* 34:321–44.
1909 "The Kwakiutl of Vancouver Island," *American Museum of Natural History Memoirs* 8:301–522.
1916 "Representative Art of Primitive Peoples," Holmes Anniversary Volume, Washington, D.C., pp. 18–23.
1921 "Ethnology of the Kwakiutl," *Bureau of American Ethnology Thirty-fifth Annual Report*, pts. 1 and 2.
1927 *Primitive Art*. Oslo: Instituttet for Sammenlignende Kulturforskning, H. Aschehoug.
1933 Review of G. Locher, *The Serpent in Kwakiutl Religion*, in *Journal of American Folklore* 46:418–21.
1940 *Race, Language and Culture*. New York: Macmillan.

Bogoras, Waldemar
1904 "The Chuckchee," *American Museum of Natural History Memoirs* 11:1–733.

Boon, James
1982 *Other Tribes, Other Scribes: Symbolic Anthropology in the Comparative Study of Cultures, Histories, Religions and Texts*. Cambridge: Cambridge University Press.

Borden, Charles E.
1983 "Prehistoric Art of the Lower Fraser," in *Indian Art Traditions of the Northwest Coast*, ed. R. Carlson, pp. 131–65. Burnaby, B.C.: Simon Fraser University Press.

Boyd, Robert T.
1990 "Demographic History, 1774–1874," in *Handbook of North American Indians*, vol. 7: *Northwest Coast*, ed. W. Suttles, pp. 135–48. Washington, D.C.: Smithsonian Institution Press.

Brett, Guy

1991 "Unofficial Versions," in *The Myth of Primitivism: Perspectives on Art*, ed. S. Hiller, pp. 113–36. London and New York: Routledge.

Brinton, Daniel G.

1890 *Races and Peoples: Lectures on the Science of Ethnology*. New York: N. D. C. Hodges.

Brown, Steve

1987 "From Taquan to Klukwan," in *Faces, Voices and Dreams: A Celebration of the Centennial of the Sheldon Jackson Museum*, ed. P. Corey, pp. 157–76. Sitka: Division of Alaska State Museums and Friends of the Alaska State Museum.

Bunzel, Ruth L.

1929 *The Pueblo Potter: A Study of Creative Imagination in Primitive Art*. New York: Columbia University Press.

Carlson, Roy

1983 "Prehistoric Art of the Central Coast of British Columbia," in *Indian Art Traditions of the Northwest Coast*, ed. R. Carlson, pp. 121–29. Burnaby, B.C.: Archaeology Press.

Carpenter, Edmund

1975 "Introduction," in Bill Holm and Bill Reid, *Form and Freedom: A Dialogue on Northwest Coast Indian Art*, pp. 9–27. Houston: Institute for the Arts, Rice University.

Carroll, Michael

1979 "Lévi-Strauss on Art: A Reconsideration," *Anthropologica* 21: 177–88.

Clifford, James

1987 "Of Other Peoples: Beyond the 'Salvage' Paradigm," in *Dia Art Foundation Discussions in Contemporary Culture*, ed. H. Foster, pp. 121–30. Seattle: Bay Press.

1988 *The Predicament of Culture: Twentieth-Century Ethnography, Literature, and Art*. Cambridge: Harvard University Press.

1992 "Traveling Cultures," in *Cultural Studies*, ed. L. Grossberg, C. Nelson, and P. Treichler, pp. 96–111. New York and London: Routledge.

Clifford, James, and George E. Marcus, eds.

1986 *Writing Culture: The Poetics and Politics of Ethnography*. Berkeley: University of California Press.

Codere, Helen

1966 "Introduction," in *Kwakiutl Ethnography* by Franz Boas, ed. H. Codere, pp. xi–xxxii. Chicago: University of Chicago Press.

Coe, Ralph T.

1972 "Asiatic Sources of Northwest Coast Art," in *American Indian Art: Form and Tradition*, pp. 85–92. New York: E. P. Dutton.

Cohn, Bernard S.

1981 "Anthropology and History in the 1980s," *Journal of Interdisciplinary History* 12:227–52.

Cole, Douglas

1982 "Franz Boas and the Bella Coola in Berlin," *Northwest Anthropological Research Notes* 16:115–24.

1983 "The Value of a Person Lies in His *Hertzenbildung*," in *Observers Observed: Essays on Ethnographic Field Work*, ed. G. W. Stocking, Jr., pp. 13–52. *History of Anthropology 1*. Madison: University of Wisconsin.

1985 *Captured Heritage: The Scramble for Northwest Coast Artifacts*. Seattle: University of Washington Press; Vancouver, B.C.: Douglas and McIntyre.

Cole, Douglas, and Ira Chaiken

1990 *An Iron Hand upon the People: The Law against the Potlatch on the Northwest Coast*. Seattle: University of Washington Press; Vancouver, B.C.: Douglas and McIntyre.

Cole, Douglas, and David Darling

1990 "History of the Early Period," in *Handbook of North American Indians*, vol. 7: *Northwest Coast*, ed. W. Suttles, pp. 119–34. Washington, D.C.: Smithsonian Institution Press.

Comaroff, John, and Jean Comaroff
1992 *Ethnography and the Historical Imagination*. Boulder: Westview Press.
Coombes, Annie E.
1991 "Ethnography and the Formation of National and Cultural Identities," in *The Myth of Primitivism: Perspectives on Art*, ed. S. Hiller, pp. 189–214. London and New York: Routledge.
Corey, Peter
1983 "Tlingit Spruce Root Basketry since 1903," in *The Box of Daylight: Northwest Coast Indian Art*, ed. B. Holm, pp. 137–38. Seattle: Seattle Art Museum and University of Washington Press.
Covarrubias, Miguel
1954 *The Eagle, the Jaguar, and the Serpent*. New York: Alfred Knopf.
Cowling, Elizabeth
1978 "The Eskimos, the American Indians, and the Surrealists," *Art History* 1:484–500.
Creel, Herrlee Glessner
1937 *The Birth of China*. New York: Frederick Ungar.
Crosby, Marcia
1991 "Construction of the Imaginary Indian," in *Vancouver Anthropology: The Institutional Politics of Art*, ed. S. Douglas, pp. 267–94. Vancouver: Talon Books.
Cushing, Frank Hamilton
1886 "A Study of Pueblo Pottery," *Fourth Annual Report of the Bureau of American Ethnology*. Washington, D.C.
Danford, Joanne B.
1990 *From Periphery to Centre: The Art of Susan and Krista Point*. Thunder Bay, Ont.: Thunder Bay Art Gallery.
Davidson, Robert
1992 "The World is as Sharp as the Edge of a Knife," *Robert Davidson Exhibition: "A Voice From the Inside."* Vancouver: Derek Simpkins Gallery of Tribal Art, pp. 7–10.
Dawson, George
1880 *Geological Survey of Canada. Report of Progress for 1878–1879*. Montreal.
de Laguna, Frederica, ed.
1991 *The Tlingit Indians: George Thornton Emmons*. Seattle and New York: University of Washington Press and the American Museum of Natural History.
Dixon, Roland B.
1902 "Basketry Designs of the Indians of Northern California," *Bulletin of the American Museum of Natural History* 17:1–32.
Dominguez, Virginia
1987 "Of Other Peoples: Beyond the 'Salvage' Paradigm," in *Dia Art Foundation Discussions in Contemporary Culture*, ed. H. Foster, pp. 131–37. Seattle: Bay Press.
1992 "Invoking Culture: The Messy Side of 'Cultural Politics,'" *The South Atlantic Quarterly* 91:19–42.
Douglas, Frederic, and Rene d'Harnoncourt
1941 *Indian Art of the United States*. New York: Museum of Modern Art.
Doxtoder, Deborah
1988a "The Home of Indian Culture and Other Stories for the Museum," *Muse* 6:26–31.
1988b *Fluffs and Feathers*. Brandford, Ont.: Woodlands Cultural Centre.
Drew, Leslie, and Douglas Wilson
1980 *Argillite: Art of the Haida*. Vancouver, B.C.: Hancock House.
Drucker, Philip
1963 *Indians of the Northwest Coast*. Garden City: Natural History Press.
1965 *Cultures of the North Pacific Coast*. San Francisco: Chandler.
Duff, Wilson
1964 "Contributions of Marius Barbeau to West Coast Ethnology," *Anthropologica* 6:63–96.

1967a "Contexts of Northwest Coast Art," in *Arts of the Raven*. Vancouver, B.C.: Vancouver Art Gallery.

1967b "Charles Edenshaw: Master Artist," in *Arts of the Raven*. Vancouver, B.C.: Vancouver Art Gallery.

1975 *Images: Stone: B.C.: Thirty Centuries of Northwest Coast Indian Sculpture*. Seattle: University of Washington Press.

1981a "Mungo Martin, Carver of the Century," in *The World Is as Sharp as a Knife*, ed. D. Abbott, pp. 37–40. Victoria: British Columbia Provincial Museum.

1981b "The World is As Sharp as a Knife: Meaning in Northern Northwest Coast Art," in *The World Is as Sharp as a Knife*. ed. D. Abbott, pp. 209–24. Victoria: British Columbia Provincial Museum.

Duffek, Karen, and Tom Hill

1989 *Beyond History*. Vancouver, B.C.: Vancouver Art Gallery.

Durham, Jimmie

1991 "The Search for Virginity," in *The Myth of Primitivism: Perspectives on Art*, ed. S. Hiller, pp. 286–91. London and New York: Routledge.

Dürr, Michael, Erich Kasten, and Egon Renner

1992 *Franz Boas: Ethnologe–Anthropologe–Sprachwissenschaftler. Ein Wegbereiter der modernen Wissenschaft vom Menschen*. Berlin: Staatsbibliothek zu Berlin, Preussischer Kulturbesitz.

Erliade, Mircea

1960 *Myths, Dreams and Mysteries*, trans. P. Mairet. New York: Harper Torchbooks.

Emmons, George T.

1902 "The Basketry of the Tlingit Indians," *American Museum of Natural History Memoirs* 3:229–77.

1907 "The Chilkat Blanket. With Notes on the Blanket Design by Franz Boas," *American Museum of Natural History Memoirs* 3:329–401.

1991 *The Tlingit Indians*. Edited by Frederica de Laguna. Seattle and London: University of Washington Press.

Fabian, Johannes

1983 *Time and the Other: How Anthropology Makes Its Object*. New York: Columbia University Press.

Farrand, Livingston

1900 "Basketry Designs of the Salish Indians," *American Museum of Natural History Memoirs*, 2:391–99.

Fechner, G. T.

1876 *Vorschule der Aesthetik*. Leipzig: Britkopf und Härtel. (New edition, 1925.)

Firth, Raymond

1973 *Symbols Public and Private*. Ithaca: Cornell University Press.

Fitzhugh, William, and Aaron Crowell, eds.

1988 *Crossroads of Continents: Cultures of Siberia and Alaska*. Washington, D.C.: Smithsonian Institution Press.

Foucault, Michel

1972 *The Archaeology of Knowledge and the Discourse of Language*. New York: Harper Colophon.

1978 *Discipline and Punish*. New York: Pantheon.

1984 *The Foucault Reader*, ed. P. Rabinow. New York: Pantheon

Fox, Richard G.

1991 "For a Nearly New Culture History," in *Recapturing Anthropology: Working in the Present*, ed. R. Fox, pp. 93–114. Santa Fe: School of American Research Press.

Fraser, Douglas

1966 Introduction to Boas's "Representative Art of Primitive People," in *The Many Faces of Primitive Art*, ed. D. Fraser, pp. 1–3. Englewood Cliffs: Prentice-Hall.

1968 *Early Chinese Art and the Pacific Basin*. New York: Intercultural Arts Press.

Freed, Stanley A., and Ruth S. Freed
1983 "Clark Wissler and the Development of Anthropology in the United States," *American Anthropologist* 85:800–25.
Garfield, Viola, and Paul Wingert
1966 *The Tsimshian Indians and Their Arts*. Seattle: University of Washington Press. (First published 1950.)
Geertz, Clifford
1988 *Works and Lives: The Anthropologist as Author*. Cambridge: Polity.
Gerber, Peter R., and Vanina Katz-Lahaigue
1989 *Susan A. Point, Joe David, Lawrence Paul: Indianische Kunstler der Westküste Kanadas*. Zurich: Volkerkundemuseum der Universitat Zurich.
Gessler, Trisha
1981 *The Art of Nunstins*. Queen Charlotte Islands Museum.
Goldman, Irving
1975 *The Mouth of Heaven: An Introduction to Kwakiutl Thought*. New York: John Wiley.
Goldwater, Robert
1986 *Primitivism in Modern Art*. Cambridge, Mass.: The Belknap Press of Harvard University Press. (First published 1938).
Gossett, Thomas F.
1972 *Race: The History of an Idea in America*. Dallas: Southern Methodist University Press.
Graburn, Nelson
1976 *Ethnic and Tourist Arts: Cultural Expressions from the Fourth World*. Berkeley: University of California Press.
Grant, Madison
1916 *The Passing of the Great Race*. 2d ed. New York: Scribner's Sons.
Grosse, Ernst
1897 *The Beginnings of Art*. New York: Appleton. (Translation of *Die Anfänge der Kunst* [1894]).
Gunther, Erna
1966 *Art in the Life of the Northwest Coast Indian*. Portland, OR: Portland Art Museum.
Gustafson, Paula
1980 *Salish Weaving*. Seattle: University of Washington Press.
Haberland, Wolfgang
1979 *Donnervogel und Raubwal: Indianische Kunst der Nordwestküste Nordamerikas*. Hamburg: Hamburgisches Museum für Völkerkunde und Christians Verlag. "'Diese Indiners Sind Falsch': Neun Bella Coola im Deutschen Reich 1885/86," *Archiv für Völkerkunde* 42:6–67.
Haddon, Alfred
1895 *Evolution in Art*. London: Walter Scott.
Haeberlin, Herman
1918 "Principles of Esthetic Form in the Art of the North Pacific Coast," *American Anthropologist* 20:258–64.
Haeberlin, H. K., James A. Teit, and Helen H. Roberts, under the direction of Franz Boas
1928 "Coiled Basketry in British Columbia and Surrounding Region," *Bureau of American Ethnology Forty-first Annual Report*, pp. 19–484.
Hall, Stuart
1990 "The Whites of Their Eyes: Racist Ideologies and the Media," in *The Media Reader*, ed. M. Alvarado and J. O. Thompson, pp. 7–23. London: BFI Publishing.
Haller, John
1971 *Outcasts from Evolution: Scientific Attitudes of Racial Inferiority, 1859–1900*. Urbana: University of Illinois Press.
Hamilton, Ron
1991 "I Invite Honest Criticism: An Introduction," and "A Biography of Sorts," in *In Celebration*

of Our Survival: The First Nations of British Columbia, ed. D. Jensen and C. Brooks, pp. 89–103. Vancouver: University of British Columbia Press.

Hamlin, A. D. F.

1898 "Development of Decorative Motifs," *The American Architect*. New York.

1916 *History of Ornament, Ancient and Modern*. New York: Century.

Harner, Michael J., and Albert B. Elsasser

1965 *Art of the Northwest Coast*. Berkeley, CA: Robert H. Lowie Museum of Anthropology.

Harris, Marvin

1968 *The Rise of Anthropological Theory*. New York: Thomas Y. Crowell.

Harvey, David

1989 *The Condition of Postmodernity*. Cambridge: Basil Blackwell.

Hawthorn, Audrey

1964 "Mungo Martin: Artist and Craftsman," *The Beaver*, Summer, pp. 4–12.

1979 *Kwakiutl Art*. Seattle: University of Washington Press.

Hawthorn, Harry

1961 "The Artist in Tribal Society: The Northwest Coast," in *The Artist in Tribal Society*, ed. M. Smith, pp. 59–70. London: Routledge and Paul.

Heine-Geldern, Robert

1949 "Chinese Influence in the Pacific and in America." Lecture given at the Viking Fund, February 25, 1949, New York.

Henshaw, Henry

1883 "Animal Carvings from Mounds of the Mississippi Valley," *Second Annual Report of the Bureau of Ethnology*. Washington, D.C.

Hentze, Carl

1936 *Objets rituels, croyances et dieux de la Chine antique et de l'Amérique*. Antwerp: Editions De Sikkel.

Herskovits, Melville J.

1953 *Franz Boas: The Science of Man in the Making*. New York: Scribner's Sons.

Heydrich, Martin

1914 "Afrikansche Ornamentik," *Internationales Archiv für Ethnographie* 22:supplement.

Higham, John

1963 *Strangers in the Land: Patterns of American Nativism, 1860–1925*. New York: Atheneum.

Hiller, Susan, ed.

1991 *The Myth of Primitivism: Perspectives on Art*. Ithaca: Cornell University Press.

Hinsley, Curtis

1891 *Savages and Scientists: The Smithsonian Institution and the Development of American Anthropology*. Washington, D.C.: Smithsonian Institution Press.

Hirn, Yrjö

1900 *The Origins of Art*. London: Macmillan.

Holm, Bill

1965 *Northwest Coast Indian Art: An Analysis of Form*. Seattle: University of Washington Press.

1967 "The Northern Style—A Form Analysis," in *Arts of the Raven*. Vancouver, B.C.: Vancouver Art Gallery.

1972 "Heraldic Carving Styles of the Northwest Coast," in *American Indian Art: Form and Tradition*, pp. 77–84. New York: E. P. Dutton.

1974 "The Art of Willie Seaweed: A Kwakiutl Master," in *The Human Mirror*, ed. M. Richardson. Baton Rouge: Louisiana State Press.

1975 *Form and Freedom: A Dialogue on Northwest Coast Indian Art*. Houston: Rice University Press. (Reprinted as *Northwest Coast Indian Art*. Seattle: University of Washington Press.)

1981 "Will the Real Charles Edenshaw Please Stand Up? The Problem of Attribution in Northwest Coast Indian Art," in *The World Is as Sharp as a Knife*, ed. D. Abbott, pp. 175–200. Victoria: British Columbia Provincial Museum.

1982 "A Wooling Mantle Neatly Wrought: The Early Historic Record of Northwest Coast Pattern-twined Textiles," *American Indian Art Magazine* 8:34–47.
1983a "Form in Northwest Coast Art," in *Indian Art Traditions of the Northwest Coast*, ed. R. Carlson, pp. 33–45. Burnaby, B.C.: Simon Fraser University Press.
1983b *Smoky-Top: The Art and Times of Willie Seaweed*. Seattle: University of Washington Press.
1987 *Spirit and Ancestor: A Century of Northwest Coast Art at the Burke Museum*. Seattle: University of Washington Press.
1990a "Art," in *Handbook of North American Indians*, vol. 7: *Northwest Coast*, W. Suttles, ed., pp. 602–3. Washington, D.C.: Smithsonian Institution Press.
1990b "Kwakiutl: Winter Ceremonies," in *Handbook of North American Indians*, vol. 7: *Northwest Coast*, W. Suttles, ed., pp. 378–86. Washington, D.C.: Smithsonian Institution Press.

Holmes, William Henry
1888 "The Origin and Development of Form and Ornament in Ceramic Art," *Sixth Annual Report of the Bureau of Ethnology*, pp. 189–252.
1890 "On the Evolution of Ornament: An American Lesson," *American Anthropologist* 3:137–46.
1903 "Aboriginal Pottery of the Eastern United States," in *Twentieth Annual Report of the Bureau of American Ethnology*.

Hoover, Alan
1983 "Charles Edenshaw and the Creation of Human Beings," *American Indian Art Magazine* 8:62–67, 90.
1984 "A History of the Study of Argillite," in *The Magic Leaves: A History of Haida Argillite Carving*, ed. Peter L. Macnair and Alan L. Hoover, pp. 199–207. Victoria: British Columbia Provincial Museum.

Horowitz, Helen
1975 "Animals and Man in the New York Zoological Park," *New York Historian* 56: 426–55.

Houle, Robert
1992 "The Spiritual Legacy of the Ancient Ones," in *Land Spirit Power: First Nations at the National Gallery of Canada*, ed. D. Nemiroff, R. Houle, and C. Townsend-Gault, pp. 43–75. Ottawa: National Gallery of Canada.

Howell, Signe
1991 "Art and Meaning," in *The Myth of Primitivism: Perspectives on Art*, ed. S. Hiller, pp. 217–37. London and New York: Routledge.

Inverarity, Robert Bruce
1960 *Art of the Northwest Coast Indian*. Berkeley: University of California Press.

Jacknis, Ira
1984 "Franz Boas and Photography," *Studies in Visual Communication* 10:2–60.
1985 "Franz Boas and Exhibits," in *Objects and Others: Essays on Museums and Material Culture*," ed. G. W. Stocking, Jr., pp. 75–111. *History of Anthropology* 3. Madison: University of Wisconsin Press.
1991 "George Hunt, Collector of Indian Specimens," in *Chiefly Feasts: The Enduring Kwakiutl Potlatch*, ed. A. Jonaitis, pp. 177–226. Seattle: University of Washington Press.
1992 "'The Artist Himself': The Salish Basketry Monograph and the Beginnings of a Boasian Paradigm," in *The Early Years of Native American Art History: Politics of Scholarship and Collecting*, ed. J. Berlo, pp. 134–61. Seattle: University of Washington Press.

Jacobsen, Johan Adrian
1884 *Capt. Jacobsen's Reise an der Nordwestküste Amerikas, 1881–1883*. Edited by A. Woldt. Leipzig: M. Spohr.
1977 *Alaskan Voyage, 1881–1883: An Expedition to the Northwest Coast of America*, trans. E. Gunther. Chicago: University of Chicago Press.

Jameson, Fredric
1991 *Postmodernism, or, the Cultural Logic of Late Capitalism*. Durham: Duke University Press.

Jencks, Charles
1991 "Postmodern vs. Late-Modern," in *Zeitgeist in Babel: The Postmodernist Controversy*, ed. I. Hoesterey, pp. 4–21. Bloomington: Indiana Univesity Press.

Jencks, Charles, ed.
1992 *The Post-Modern Reader*. New York: St. Martin's Press.

Jensen, Doreen, and Polly Sargent
1986 *Robes of Power: Totem Poles on Cloth*. Vancouver: University of British Columbia Press.

Jochelson, Waldemar
1908 "The Koryak," *American Museum of Natural History Memoirs* 10:1–842.
1926 "The Yukaghir and the Yukaghirized Tungus," *American Museum of Natural History Memoirs* 13:135–342.

Jonaitis, Aldona
1981 "Creations of Mystics and Philosophers: The White Man's Perceptions of Northwest Coast Indian Art from the 1930s to the Present," *American Indian Culture and Research Journal* 5:1–48.
1986 *Art of the Northern Tlingit*. Seattle: University of Washington Press.
1988a *From the Land of the Totem Poles: The Northwest Coast Indian Art Collection at the American Museum of Natural History*. Seattle and New York: University of Washington Press and American Museum of National History.
1988b "Women, Marriage, Mouths and Feasting: The Symbolism of the Tlingit Labret," in *Marks of Civilization: Artistic Transformations of the Human Body*, ed. A. Rubin, pp. 191–205. Los Angeles: University of California, Museum of Cultural History.
1991 "The Creation of an Exhibition," in *Chiefly Feasts: The Enduring Kwakiutl Potlatch*, ed. A. Jonaitis, pp. 20–62. Seattle and New York: University of Washington Press and American Museum of Natural History.
1992a "Franz Boas, John Swanton, and the New Haida Sculpture at the American Museum of Natural History," in *The Early Years of Native American Art History: The Politics of Scholarship and Collecting*, ed. J. Berlo, pp. 22–61. Seattle: University of Washington Press.
1992b "Chiefly Feasts: The Enduring Kwakiutl Potlatch—From Salvage Anthropology to a Big Apple Button Blanket," *Curator* 35:255–67.
1993 "Traders of Tradition: Haida Art from Argillite Masters to Robert Davidson," in *Robert Davidson: Eagle of the Dawn*, ed. I. Thom. Vancouver, B.C.: Vancouver Art Gallery.

Jonaitis, Aldona, and Richard Inglis
1992 "Power, History and Authenticity: The Mowachaht Whaler's Washing Shrine," *South Atlantic Quarterly* 91:193–214.

Jonaitis, Aldona, and Peter Macnair
1991 "Masks of the Ancestors," *Natural History* 10:42–46.

Jones, Joan M.
1968 "Northwest Coast Basketry and Culture Change," *Research Reports* 1, Thomas Burke Memorial Washington State Museum.

Karp, Ivan, and Steven D. Lavine, eds.
1991 *Exhibiting Cultures: The Poetics and Politics of Museum Display*. Washington, D.C.: Smithsonian Institution Press.

Karsten, Rafael
1926 *Civilization of South American Indians*. New York: Alfred A. Knopf.

Kasten, Erich
1992 "Masken, Mythen und Indianer: Franz Boas' Ethnographie und Museumsmethode," in *Franz Boas: Ethnologe–Anthropologe–Sprachwissenschaftler. Ein Wegbereiter der modernen Wissenschaft vom Menschen*, ed. M. Dürr, E. Kasten, and E. Renner. Berlin: Staatsbibliothek zu Berlin, Preussischer Kulturbesitz: 79–102.

Kaufmann, Carole
1976 "Functional Aspects of Haida Argillite Carvings," in *Ethnic and Tourist Arts: Cultural Expres-*

sions from the Fourth World, ed. N. Graburn, pp. 56–69. Berkeley: University of California Press.

Kew, Michael

1980 "Sculpture and Engraving of the Central Coast Salish Indians," *Museum of Anthropology Notes* 9. University of British Columbia.

1990 "History of Coastal British Columbia since 1849," in *Handbook of North American Indians*, vol. 7: *Northwest Coast*, W. Suttles, ed., pp. 159–68. Washington, D.C.: Smithsonian Institution Press.

Kluckhohn, Clyde

1936 "Some Reflections on the Method and Theory of the Kulturkreislehre," *American Anthropologist* 38:157–96.

Koch-Gruenberg, Theodor

1906 *Anfänge der Kunst im Urwald*. Berlin: E. Wasmuth.

Kopytoff, Igor

1986 "The Cultural Biography of Things: Commoditization as Process," in *The Social Life of Things: Commodities in Cultural Perspective*, ed. A. Appadurai, pp. 64–91. Cambridge: Cambridge University Press.

Krause, Aurel

1885 *Die Tlingit-Indianer: Ergebnisse einer Reise nach der Nordwestküste von Amerika . . . in den Jahren 1880–1881*. Jena: Hermann Costenoble.

Krickeberg, Walter

1925 "Malereien auf ledernen Zermonialkleidern der Nordwestamerikaner," *IPEK*, pp. 140–50.

Kroeber, A. L.

1900 "Symbolism of the Arapaho Indians," *Bulletin of the American Museum of Natural History* 13.

1901 "Decorative Symbolism of the Arapaho," *American Anthropologist* 3:308–36.

1923 "American Culture and the Northwest Coast," *American Anthropologist* 25:1–20.

Kroker, Arthur

1992 *The Possessed Individual: Technology and the French Postmodernism*. New York: St. Martin's Press.

Krupat, Arnold

1990 "Irony in Anthropology: The Work of Franz Boas," in *Modernist Anthropology: From Fieldwork to Text*, ed. M. Manganaro, pp. 133–45. Princeton: Princeton University Press.

1992 *Ethnocriticism: Ethnography, History, Literature*. Berkeley: University of California Press.

Kühn, Herbert

1923 *Die Kunst der Primitiven*. Munich: Delphin.

Kuper, Adam

1988 *The Invention of Primitive Society: Transformations of an Illusion*. London and New York: Routledge.

1991 *Conceptualizing Society*. New York: Routledge.

Laufer, Berthold

1902 "The Decorative Art of the Amur Tribes," *American Museum of Natural History Memoirs* 4.

Lee, Molly

1991 "Appropriating the Primitive: Turn-of-the-Century Collection and Display of Native Alaskan Art," *Arctic Anthropology* 28:6–15.

Lesser, Alexander

1981 "Franz Boas," in *Totems and Teachers*, ed. S. Silverman, pp. 1–34. New York: Columbia University Press.

Lévi-Strauss, Claude

1943 "Art of the Northwest Coast at the American Museum of Natural History," *Gazette des Beaux-Arts* 24:175–82.

1944/45 "Le Dédoublement de la représentation dans les arts de l'Asie et de l'Amérique," *Renaissance*

2–3:168–86. (Translated as "Split Representation in the Art of Asia and America," in *Structural Anthropology*, pp. 239–63: Garden City: Doubleday [1963].)

1982 *The Way of the Masks*. Trans. Sylvia Modelski. Seattle: University of Washington Press.

Lobb, Allan

1978 *Indian Baskets of the Northwest Coast*. Portland, OR: Graphic Arts Center.

Locher, Gottfried

1932 *The Serpent in Kwakiutl Religion*. Leiden: E. J. Brill.

Lowie, Robert

1937 *History of Ethnological Theory*. New York: Farrar and Rinehart.

Lumholtz, Carl

1904 "Decorative Art of the Huichol Indians," *American Museum of Natural History Memoirs* 3:279–327.

Lyotard, Jean Francois

1984 *The Postmodern Condition: A Report on Knowledge*, trans. B. Massumi. Minneapolis: University of Minnesota Press.

MacCannell, Dean

1986 *The Tourist: A New Theory of the Leisure Class*. New York: Schocken Books.

1992 *Empty Meeting Grounds: The Tourist Papers*. London and New York: Routledge.

McClaren, Carol Sheehan

1978 "Moment of Death, Gift of Life: A Reinterpretation of the Northwest Coast Image 'Hawk,'" *Anthropologica* 20:75–90.

MacDonald, George

1981 "Cosmic Equations in Northwest Coast Indian Art," in *The World Is as Sharp as a Knife*, ed. D. N. Abbott, pp. 225–38. Victoria: British Columbia Provincial Museum.

1983 "Prehistoric Art of the Northern Northwest Coast," in *Indian Art Traditions of the Northwest Coast*, ed. R. Carlson, pp. 99–120. Burnaby, B.C.: Archaeology Press.

1984 "Painted Houses and Woven Blankets: Symbols of Wealth in Tsimshian Art and Myth," in *The Tsimshian and Their Neighbors of the North Pacific Coast*, ed. J. Miller and C. M. Eastman, pp. 109–36. Seattle: University of Washington Press.

McGee, W J

1897 "The Science of Humanity," *American Anthropologist* (o.s.) 10:241–72.

1899 "The Trend of Human Progress," *American Anthropologist* 1:401–7.

1901 "Man's Place in Nature," *American Anthropologist* 3:1–13.

Mackenzie, Alexander

1891 "Descriptive Notes on Certain Implements, Weapons, etc. from Graham Island, Queen Charlotte Islands, British Columbia," *Transactions of the Royal Society of Canada* 2:45–59.

McMaster, Gerald, and Lee Ann Martin

1992 "Introduction," *Indigena: Contemporary Native Perspectives*, ed. G. McMaster and L. Martin, pp. 11–23. Vancouver: Douglas and McIntyre.

Macnair, Peter, and Alan Hoover

1984 *The Magic Leaves: A History of Argillite Carving*. Victoria: British Columbia Provincial Museum.

Macnair, Peter, Alan Hoover, and Kevin Neary

1980 *The Legacy: Continuing Traditions of Canadian Northwest Coast Indian Art*. Victoria: British Columbia Provincial Museum.

Malin, Edward, and Norman Feder

1968 *Indian Art of the Northwest Coast*. Denver: Denver Art Museum.

Manganaro, Marc, ed.

1990 *Modernist Anthropology: From Fieldwork to Text*. Princeton: Princeton University Press.

Maranhao, Tullio, ed.

1990 *The Interpretation of Dialogue*. Chicago: University of Chicago Press.

Marcus, George E., and Michael M. J. Fischer
1986 *Anthropology as Cultural Critique: An Experimental Moment in the Human Sciences*. Chicago: University of Chicago Press.
Mason, Otis T.
1884 "Basketwork of the North American Aborigines," *Report of the Smithsonian Institution for 1884* 2:291–306.
Mauss, Marcel
1967 *The Gift: Forms and Functions of Exchange in Archaic Societies*, trans. I. Cunnison. New York: Norton. (First published 1927.)
Mauzé, Marie
1992 "Premiers contacts entre les surrealistes et l'art de la côte Nord-Ouest," in *Destins croisés: Cinq siècles de rencontres avec les Amerindiens*, pp. 283–96. Paris: UNESCO/Albin Michel.
Mead, Charles W.
1906 "The Six-Unit Design on Ancient Peruvian Cloth," *Boas Anniverary Volume*, pp. 193–95. New York.
Miller, Daniel
1991 "Primitive Art and the Necessity of Primitivism to Art," in *The Myth of Primitivism: Perspectives on Art*, ed. S. Hiller, pp. 50–71. London and New York: Routledge.
Morgan, Lewis Henry
1877 *Ancient Society, or, Researches in the Lines of Human Progress from Savagery through Barbarism to Civilization*. New York: Holt.
Morphy, Frances
1977 "The Social Significance of Schematization in Northwest Coast American Indian Art," in *Form in Indigenous Art*, ed. P. Ucko, pp. 73–76. Atlantic Highlands, NJ: Humanities Press.
Munro, Thomas
1963 *Evolution in the Arts and Other Theories of Culture History*. Cleveland: Cleveland Museum of Art.
Muse
1988 *Museums and First Nations*. Special issue of *Muse*, Fall.
Neel, David
1992 "Artist's Statement" and "Life on the 18th Hole," in *In Celebration of Our Survival: The First Nations of B.C.*, ed. D. Jensen and C. Brooks, pp. 129–39. Vancouver: University of British Columbia Press.
Nelson, Cary, Paula Treichler, and Lawrence Grossberg
1992 "Cultural Studies: An Introduction," in *Cultural Studies*, ed. L. Grossberg, C. Nelson, and P. Treichler, pp. 1–16. New York and London: Routledge.
Nicks, Trudy
1982 *The Creative Tradition: Indian Handicrafts and Tourist Art*. Edmonton: Provincial Museum of Alberta.
Nordenskiöld, A. E.
1881 *The Voyage of the Vega round Asia and Europe*. London: Macmillan.
Nuytten, Phil
1982 *The Totem Carvers: Charlie James, Ellen Neel and Mungo Martin*. Vancouver, B.C.: Panorama Publications.
O'Neale, Lila
1932 "Yurok-Karok Basket Weavers," *University of California Publications in American Archaeology and Ethnology* 32:1–84.
Ostrowitz, Judith
1993 "Trail Blazers and Ancestral Heroes: Collaboration in the Representation of a Native Past," *Curator*.
Ostrowitz, Judith, and Aldona Jonaitis
1991 "Postscript: The Treasures of Siwidi," in *Chiefly Feasts: The Enduring Kwakiutl Potlatch*, ed. A.

Jonaitis, pp. 251–82. Seattle and New York: University of Washington Press and American Museum of Natural History.

Paalen, Wolfgang
1943 "Totem Art," *Dyn* 4–5, 7–39.

Paul, Lawrence
1992 "Lawrence Paul Xuxweluptun," in *Land Spirit Power: First Nations at the National Gallery of Canada*, ed. D. Nemiroff, R. Houle, and C. Townsend-Gault, pp. 220–26. Otttawa: National Gallery of Canada, 1992.

Penney, David
1981 "The Nootka 'Wild Man' Masquerade and the Forest Spirit Tradition of the Southern Northwest Coast," *Res* 1:95–109.

Phillips, Ruth B.
1989 "What is 'Huron Art'? Native American Art and the New Art History," *Canadian Journal of Native Studies* 9:167–91.
1991 "Glimpses of Eden: Iconographic Themes in Huron Pictorial Tourist Art," *European Review of Native American Studies* 5:19–28.
in press "Why Not Tourist Art?: Significant Silences in Native American Museum Representation," in *After Colonialism: Imperialism and the Colonial Aftermath*, ed. G. Prakash. Princeton: Princeton University Press.

Point, Susan
1988 "Susan Point," *Gallerie: Women's Art*. Vancouver, Gallerie Publications 1:108–10.

Powell, J. W.
1899 "Sociology, or, the Science of Institutions," *American Anthropologist* 1:695–745.

Pratt, Mary Louise
1992 *Imperial Eyes: Travel Writing and Transculturation*. London and New York: Routledge.

Preziosi, Donald
1989 *Rethinking Art History: Meditations on a Coy Science*. New Haven: Yale University Press.

Putnam, Frederic Ward
1886 "Conventionalism in Ancient American Art," *Bulletin of the Essex Institute* 18.

Putnam, Frederic Ward, and C. C. Willoughby
1896 "Symbolism in American Art," *Proceedings of the American Association for the Advancement of Science* 44:302–22.

Reichard, Gladys
1934 *Spider Woman: A Story of Navajo Weavers and Chanters*. New York: Macmillan.
1936 *Navajo Shepherd and Weaver*. New York: J. J. Augustin.
1939a *Dezba, Woman of the Desert*. New York: J. J. Augustin.
1939b *Navajo Medicine Man*. New York: J. J. Augustin.

Reid, Bill
1967 "The Art: An Appreciation," in *Arts of the Raven: Masterworks by Northwest Coast Indians*, ed. W. Duff. Vancouver, B.C.: Vancouver Art Gallery.

Reid, Martine
1987 "Silent Speakers: Arts of the Northwest Coast," in *The Spirit of Sings*, ed. J. Harrison, pp. 201–36. Toronto: McClelland and Stewart.

Ridington, Robin
1988 *Trail to Heaven: Knowledge and Narration in a Northern Native Community*. Iowa City: University of Iowa Press.

Riegl, Alois
1893 *Stilfragen: Grundlegungen zu einer Geschichte der Ornamentik*. Berlin: G. Siemens. (Second edition: 1923.)
1901 *Die spätromische Kunstindustrie*. Vienna: Osterreichische Staatsdruckerei.

Rohner, Ronald P., ed.
1969 *The Ethnography of Franz Boas*. Chicago: University of Chicago Press.

Roosevelt, Theodore
1889–96 *The Winning of the West*, 6 vols. New York: G. P. Putnam's Sons.
Rosaldo, Renato
1989 *Culture and Truth: The Remaking of Social Analysis*. Boston: Beacon Press.
Rushing, Jackson
1988 "The Impact of Nietzche and Northwest Coast Art on Newman's Idea of Redemption in the Abstract Sublime," *Art Journal* 47:187–95.
Rydell, Robert W.
1984 *All the World's a Fair: Visions of Empire at American International Expositions, 1876–1916*. Chicago: University of Chicago Press.
Said, Edward
1979 *Orientalism*. New York: Vintage Books.
1990 "In the Shadow of the West: Edward Said," by P. Mariani and J. Crary, in *Discourses: Conversations in Postmodern Art and Culture*, ed. R. Ferguson, W. Olander, M. Tucker, and K. Fiss, pp. 93–194. New York and Cambridge: New Museum of Contemporary Art and MIT Press.
Samuel, Cheryl
1982 *The Chilkat Dancing Blanket*. Seattle: Pacific Search Press.
1987 *The Raven's Tail*. Vancouver: University of British Columbia Press.
Sanjek, Roger
1990 *Fieldnotes: The Makings of Anthropology*. Ithaca: Cornell University Press.
Saussure, Ferdinand
1964 *Course in General Linguistics*. New York: McGraw Hill. (First published 1916)
Schurtz, Heinrich
1900 *Urgeschichte der Kultur*. Leipzig: Bibliographisches Institut.
Schuster, Carl
1951 "Joint Marks," Koninklijk Instituut voor de Tropen, Mededeling no. xciv, *Afdeling Culturele en Physische Anthropologie* 39. Amsterdam.
Seebohm, Henry
1882 *Siberia in Asia*. London: John Murray.
Semper, Gottfried
1861–63 *Der Stil in den technischen und tektonischen Künsten oder praktische Aesthetik*. Munich: Bruckmann.
Shadbolt, Doris
1986 *Bill Reid*. Seattle: University of Washington Press; Vancouver, B.C.: Douglas and McIntyre.
Sheehan, Carol
1981 *Pipes that Won't Smoke, Coal that Won't Burn: Haida Sculpture in Argillite*. Calgary: Glenbow Museum.
Silver, Harry R.
1979 "Ethnoart," *Annual Report of Anthropology* 8:267–307.
Smith, Harlan
1899 "Archaeology of Lytton, British Columbia," *American Museum of Natural History Memoirs* 2:129–61.
1900 "Archaeology of the Thompson River Region," *American Museum of Natural History Memoirs* 2:401–54.
1907 "Archaeology of the Gulf of Georgia and Puget Sound," *American Museum of Natural History Memoirs* 4:301–441.
Spencer, Herbert
1857 "Progress: Its Law and Cause," *The Westminster Review* 67:445–85. Reprinted in *Essays Scientific, Political, and Speculative*. New York: Appleton, 1892.
1896 *Principles of Sociology*. New York: Appleton. (First published 1876)

Spivak, Gayatri Chakravorty

1990 *The Post-Colonial Critic: Interviews, Strategies, Dialogues*, ed. S. Harasym. New York and London: Routledge

Stephan, Emil

1907 *Südseekunst*. Berlin: Dietrich Reimer.

Stewart, Hilary

1979a *Robert Davidson: Haida Printmaker*. Seattle: University of Washington Press; Vancouver, B.C.: Douglas and McIntyre.

1979b *Looking at Indian Art of the Northwest Coast*. Seattle: University of Washington Press.

1990 *Totem Poles*. Vancouver, B.C.: Douglas and McIntyre.

Stewart, Susan

1984 *On Longing: Narratives of the Miniature, the Gigantic, the Couvenir, the Collection*. Baltimore: Johns Hopkins University Press.

Stocking, George W., Jr.

1968 *Race, Culture and Evolution: Essays in the History of Anthropology*. Chicago: University of Chicago Press.

1974 *A Franz Boas Reader: The Shaping of American Anthropology, 1883–1911*. Chicago: University of Chicago Press.

1979 "Anthropology as Kulturkampf: Science and Politics in the Career of Franz Boas," in *The Uses of Anthropology*, ed. Walter Goldschmidt, pp. 33–50. Washington, D.C.: American Anthropologocial Association.

1985 "Philanthropoids and Vanishing Cultures: Rockefeller Funding and the End of the Museum Era in Ango-American Anthropology," in *Objects and Others: Essays on Museums and Material Culture. History of Anthropology* 3, ed. G. Stocking, Jr., pp. 112–45. Madison: University of Wisconsin Press.

1987 *Victorian Anthropology*. New York: Free Press.

1991 "Colonial Situations," in *Colonial Situations: Essays on the Contextualization of Ethnographic Knowledge. History of Anthropology* vol. 7, ed. G. W. Stocking, Jr., pp. 3–8. Madison: University of Wisconsin Press.

Stolpe, Hjalmar

1892 "Entwicklungserscheinungen in der Ornamentik der Naturvölker," *Mitteilungen der Anthropologischen Gesellschaft in Wien* 22:19–62.

Sturtevant, William

1991 "New National Museum of the American Indian Collections Policy Statement: A Critical Analysis," *Museum Anthropology* 15:29–30.

Suttles, Wayne

1982 "The Halkomelem Sxwayxwey," *American Indian Art Magazine* 8:56–65.

1983 "Productivity and Its Constraints: A Coast Salish Case," in *Indian Art Traditions of the Northwest Coast*, ed. R. Carlson, pp. 67–87. Burnaby, B.C.: Archaeology Press.

1987 *Coast Salish Essays*. Seattle: University of Washington Press.

1989 " 'Essentialism' in Northwest Coast Art." Paper presented at the Native American Art Studies Association Meeting, Vancouver, B.C.

1990 "Central Coast Salish," in *Handbook of North American Indians*, volume 7: *Northwest Coast*, W. Suttles, ed. pp. 453–75. Washington, D.C.: Smithsonian Institution Press.

1991 "Streams of Property, Armor of Wealth: The Traditional Kwakiutl Potlatch," in *Chiefly Feasts: The Enduring Kwakiutl Potlatch*, ed. A. Jonaitis, pp. 71–134. Seattle and New York: University of Washington Press and American Museum of Natural History.

Suttles, Wayne, and Aldona Jonaitis

1990 "History of Research in Ethnology," in *Handbook of North American Indians*, vol. 7: *Northwest Coast*, W. Suttles, ed., pp. 73–87. Washington, D.C.: Smithsonian Institution Press.

Swanton, John
1905 "Contributions to the Ethnology of the Haida," *American Museum of Natural History Memoirs* 8:1–300.
Tagg, John
1992 *Grounds of Dispute: Art History, Cultural Politics and the Discursive Field*. Minneapolis: University of Minnesota Press.
Tedlock, Dennis
1987 "Questions Concerning Dialogical Anthropology," *Journal of Anthropological Research* 43:325–37.
Teit, James
1900 "The Thompson Indians of British Columbia," *American Museum of Natural History Memoirs* 2:163–390.
1906 "The Lillooet Indians," *American Museum of Natural History Memoirs* 4:193–300.
Thomas, Nicholas
1991 *Entangled Objects: Exchange, Material Culture, and Colonialism in the Pacific*. Cambridge: Harvard University Press.
Thomas, Susan
1967 *The Life and Work of Charles Edenshaw: A Study of Innovation*. Master's thesis, University of British Columbia.
Thompson, Laurence C., and M. Dale Kinkade
1990 "Languages," in *Handbook of North American Indians*, vol. 7: *Northwest Coast*, W. Suttles, ed., pp. 30–51. Washington, D.C.: Smithsonian Institution Press.
Thoresen, Timothy
1977 "Art, Evolution and History: A Case Study of Paradigm Change in Anthropology," *Journal of the History of the Behavioral Sciences* 13:107–25.
Thurnwald, Richard
1926 *Handbuch der vergleichenden Psychologie der Volkerpsychologie*. Munich: Gustav Kafka.
Todd, Loretta
1992 "What More Do They Want?" in *Indigena: Contemporary Native Perspectives*, ed. G. McMaster and L. Martin, pp. 71–80. Vancouver, B.C.: Douglas and McIntyre.
Toren, Christina
1991 "Leonardo's 'Last Supper' in Fiji," in *The Myth of Primitivism: Perspectives on Art*, ed. S. Hiller, pp. 261–82. London and New York: Routledge.
Torgovnick, Marianna
1990 *Gone Primitive: Savage Intellects, Modern Lives*. Chicago: University of Chicago Press.
Townsend-Gault, Charlotte
1992 "Kinds of Knowing," in *Land Spirit Power: First Nations at the National Gallery of Canada*, ed. D. Nemiroff, R. Houle, and C. Townsend-Gault, pp. 75–101. Ottawa: National Gallery of Canada.
Tozzer, A. M.
1925 *Social Origins and Social Continuities*. New York
Trouillot, Michel-Rolph
1991 "Anthropology and the Savage Slot: The Poetics and Politics of Otherness," in *Recapturing Anthropology: Working in the Present*, ed. R. Fox, pp. 17–44. Santa Fe: School of American Research Press.
E. B. Tylor
1871 *Primitive Culture*. London: J. Murray.
1881 *Anthropology: An Introduction to the Study of Man and Civilization*. New York: Appleton.
Ulin, Robert C.
1984 *Understanding Cultures*. Austin: University of Texas Press.
Van Scheltema, F. Adama
1923 *Die Altnordische Kunst*. Berlin.

Vatter, Ernst

1926 *Religiose Plastik der Naturvölker*. Frankfurt am Main: Frankfurter–verlag.

Verworn, Max

1907 *Zur Psychologie der Primitiven*. Jena: G. Fischer.

1920 *Die Anfänge de Kunst*. Jena: J. Fischer.

Vierkandt, Alfred

1925 "Prinzipienfragen der ethnologischen Kunstforschung," *Zeitschrift für Aesthetick und allgemeine Kunstwissenschaft* 19:338.

Vincent, Joan

1991 "Engaging Historicism," in *Recapturing Anthropology: Working in the Present*, ed. R. Fox, pp. 45–58. Santa Fe: School of American Research Press.

von den Steinen, Karl

1894 *Unter den Naturvolkern Zentral-Braziliens*. Berlin: Dietrich Reimer.

1905 "Correspondenzblatt der deutchen anthropologischen Gesellschaft."

Von Sydow, Eckart

1926 *Kunst und Religion der Naturvölker*. Oldenburg: G. Stalling.

Wardwell, Allen

1978 *Objects of Bright Pride: Northwest Coast Indian Art from the American Museum of Natural History*. New York: Center for Inter-American Relations and the American Federation of Arts.

Waterman, T. T.

1923 "Some Conundrums in Northwest Coast Art," *American Anthropologist* 25:435–51.

Webster, Gloria Cranmer

1990 "Kwakiutl Since 1980," in *Handbook of North American Indians*, vol. 7: *Northwest Coast*, W. Suttles, ed. pp. 387–90. Washington, D.C.: Smithsonian Institution Press.

1991 "The Contemporary Potlach," in *Chiefly Feasts: The Enduring Kwakiutl Potlatch*, ed. A. Jonaitis, pp. 227–50. Seattle and New York: University of Washington Press and American Museum of Natural History.

1992 "From Colonization to Repatriation," in *Indigena: Contemporary Native Perspectives*, ed. G. McMaster and L. Martin, pp. 25–38. Vancouver: Douglas and McIntyre.

1992 "Chiefly Feasts," *Curator* 35:248–54.

West, Cornell

1989 "Black Culture and Postmodernism," in *Remaking History: Dia Art Foundation Discussions in Contemporary Culture* 4, ed. B. Kruger and P. Mariani, pp. 87–96. Seattle: Bay Press.

West, W. Richard, Jr.

1991 "The National Museum of the American Indian Repatriation Policy: Reply to William C. Sturtevant," *Museum Anthropology* 15:13–14.

White, Leslie

1963 *The Ethnography and Ethnology of Franz Boas*. Austin: Texas Memorial Museum.

1966 *The Social Organization of Ethnological Theory*. Houston: Rice University.

Wilson, Elizabeth

nd "*Das Ornament*." Ph.D. dissertation, University of Leipzig.

Wingert, Paul

1949 *American Indian Sculpture: A Study of the Northwest Coast*. New York: J. J. Augustin.

Winter, Amy

1992 "The Germanic Reception of Native American Art: Wolfgang Paalen as Collector, Scholar, and Artist," *European Review of Native American Studies* 6:17–26.

Wissler, Clark

1904 "Decorative Art of the Sioux Indians," *Bulletin of the American Museum of Natural History* 18:231–77.

Wolf, Eric

1982 *Europe and the People without History*. Berkeley: University of California Press.

Wright, Robin
1977 "Haida Argillite Ship Pipes," *American Indian Art Magazine* 5:40–47.
1980 "Haida Argillite Pipes: The Influence of Clay Pipes," *American Indian Art Magazine* 5:42–47, 88.
1982 "Haida Argillite: Made for Sale," *American Indian Art Magazine* 8:48–55.
1983 "Anonymous Attributions: A Tribute to a Mid-Nineteenth Century Haida Argillite Pipe Carver, the Master of the Long Fingers," in *The Box of Daylight*, ed. B. Holm, pp. 139–42. Seattle: Seattle Art Museum and University of Washington Press.
1985 *Nineteenth-Century Haida Argillite Pipe Carvers: Stylistic Attributions*. Ph.D. dissertation, University of Washington.
1987 "Haida Argillite Carving in the Sheldon Jackson Museum," in *Faces, Voices and Dreams: A Celebration of the Centennial of the Sheldon Jackson Museum*, ed. P. Corey, pp. 76–99. Sitka: Sheldon Jackson Museum.

Wundt, Wilhelm
1919 *Elemente der Völkerpsychologie: Der Kunst*, vol. 7. Leipzig: Alfred Kroner.

Wyatt, Victoria
1984 *Shapes of Their Thoughts: Reflections of Culture Contact in Northwest Coast Indian Art*. Norman: University of Oklahoma Press.

Young Man, Alfred
1992 "The Metaphysics of North American Indian Art," in *Indigena: Contemporary Native Perspectives*, ed. G. McMaster and L. Wilson, pp. 81–99. Vancouver, B.C.: Douglas and McIntyre.

Index

Pages in **boldface** refer to illustrations.